THE OXFORD HAND

THE ANCIEN RÉGIME

In *The Oxford Handbook of the Ancien Régime*, an international team of thirty contributors survey and present current thinking about the world of pre-revolutionary France and Europe.

The idea of the Ancien Régime was invented by the French revolutionaries to define what they hoped to destroy and replace. But it was not a precise definition, and although historians have found it conceptually useful, there is wide disagreement about what the Ancien Régime's main features were, how they worked, how old they were, how far they stretched, how dynamic or inert they were, and how far the revolutionaries succeeded in their ambitions to eradicate them.

In this wide-ranging and authoritative collection, old and newer areas of research into the Ancien Régime are presented and assessed, and there has been no attempt to impose any sort of consensus. The result shows what a lively field of historical enquiry the Ancien Régime remains, and points the way towards a range of promising new directions for thinking and writing about the intriguing complex of historical problems which it continues to pose.

William Doyle is Emeritus Professor of History and Senior Research Fellow at the University of Bristol. He is a Fellow of the British Academy.

THE OXFORD HANDBOOK OF
THE ANCIEN RÉGIME

Edited by
WILLIAM DOYLE

UNIVERSITY PRESS

Great Clarendon Street, Oxford, OX2 6DP,
United Kingdom

Oxford University Press is a department of the University of Oxford.
It furthers the University's objective of excellence in research, scholarship,
and education by publishing worldwide. Oxford is a registered trade mark of
Oxford University Press in the UK and in certain other countries

© Oxford University Press 2012

The moral rights of the author have been asserted

First Edition published in 2012
First published in paperback 2014

Impression: 1

All rights reserved. No part of this publication may be reproduced, stored in
a retrieval system, or transmitted, in any form or by any means, without the
prior permission in writing of Oxford University Press, or as expressly permitted
by law, by licence or under terms agreed with the appropriate reprographics
rights organization. Enquiries concerning reproduction outside the scope of the
above should be sent to the Rights Department, Oxford University Press, at the
address above

You must not circulate this work in any other form
and you must impose this same condition on any acquirer

Published in the United States of America by Oxford University Press
198 Madison Avenue, New York, NY 10016, United States of America

British Library Cataloguing in Publication Data

Data available

Library of Congress Control Number: 2011941288

ISBN 978-0-19-929120-5 (Hbk.)
ISBN 978-0-19-871361-6 (Pbk.)

Printed in Great Britain
on acid-free paper by
MPG Books Group, Bodmin and King's Lynn

Contents

List of Contributors   ix

1. Introduction   1
   WILLIAM DOYLE

PART I. GOVERNMENT

2. Absolute Monarchy   11
   PETER R. CAMPBELL

3. Diplomacy   39
   HAMISH SCOTT

4. Armed Forces   59
   DAVID PARROTT

5. Finances   75
   JOËL FÉLIX

6. Parlements and Provincial Estates   93
   JULIAN SWANN

PART II. SOCIETY

7. Nobility   111
   JOHN SHOVLIN

8. Bourgeoisie   127
   SARAH MAZA

9. Estates, Orders, and Corps   141
   GAIL BOSSENGA

10. Poverty   167
    ALAN FORREST

11. Gender — Julie Hardwick — 183

PART III. ECONOMY

12. Demography — Jack A. Goldstone — 201

13. Feudalism — Anthony Crubaugh — 219

14. Agriculture — Peter M. Jones — 236

15. Commerce — Silvia Marzagalli — 252

16. Slavery and Serfdom — William Doyle — 267

PART IV. RELIGION

17. The Established Church — Nigel Aston — 285

18. Popular Religion — Robin Briggs — 302

19. Jansenism — Thomas O'Connor — 318

20. Dissent and Toleration — Marisa Linton — 337

PART V. CULTURE

21. Education — Dorinda Outram — 357

22. Sociability — Pierre-Yves Beaurepaire — 374

23. Patronage MARK LEDBURY	388
24. The Public Sphere THOMAS E. KAISER	409

PART VI. SOLVENTS?

25. Enlightenment THOMAS MUNCK	431
26. Technological Change CHRISTINE MACLEOD AND ALESSANDRO NUVOLARI	448
27. Revolution MICHAEL RAPPORT	467

PART VII. TEST CASES

28. The Napoleonic Regimes MICHAEL BROERS	489
29. Reformed and Unreformed Britain, 1689–1801 JULIAN HOPPIT	506
30. Colonial America CHRISTOPHER CLARK	522
31. The Old Reich PETER H. WILSON	540
32. Conclusion WILLIAM DOYLE	556
Index	563

List of Contributors

Nigel Aston is Reader in History at the University of Leicester. His most recent book is *Art and Religion in Eighteenth Century Europe* (2009).

Pierre-Yves Beaurepaire is Professor of (Early) Modern History at the University of Nice Sophia-Antipolis, and a member of the Institut universitaire de France. In 2010 he published, with Silvia Marzagalli, the *Atlas de la Révolution française: Circulation des hommes et des idées 1770–1804* (Éditions Autrement); and edited, with Pierrick Pourchasse, *Les Circulations internationales en Europe, années 1680–années 1780* (Presses universitaires de Rennes).

Gail Bossenga, Scholar in Residence at Elizabethtown College in Elizabethtown, Pennsylvania, has written *The Politics of Privilege: Old Regime and Revolution in Lille* (Cambridge, 1991) as well as numerous articles dealing with politics, finances, and corporate institutions in the Ancien Régime. She is currently working on a book on institutional origins of the French Revolution.

Robin Briggs is Emeritus Senior Research Fellow, All Souls College, Oxford, and a Fellow of the British Academy. His books include *Early Modern France, 1560–1715* (1977, 2nd edn. 1989), *Communities of Belief* (1999), *Witches and Neighbours* (1996, 2nd edn. 2002), and *The Witches of Lorraine* (2007).

Michael Broers is Professor of Western European History at the University of Oxford, and Fellow and Tutor in History at Lady Margaret Hall. He is the author of six books, among them *The Napoleonic Empire in Italy* (Palgrave, 2004), which won the Grand Prix Napoléon in 2005. His latest book is *Napoleon's Other War: Bandits, Rebels, and their Pursuers in the Age of Revolution* (Peter Lang, 2010). He is currently writing a life of Napoleon for Faber & Faber.

Peter R. Campbell is since 2009 Professor of Early Modern History at the Institut d'Études Culturelles, Université de Versailles Saint-Quentin, and Elizabeth and J. Richardson Dilworth Member at the Institute for Advanced Study, Princeton (2010–11). He has published five books on the nature of the Ancien Régime and the Revolution, and several articles on ideology and politics. He is completing a major study of state failure and the origins of the French Revolution for Oxford University Press.

Christopher Clark is Professor of History at the University of Connecticut, Storrs, where he teaches early American history. His books include *The Roots of Rural Capitalism: Western Massachusetts, 1780–1860*; *The Communitarian Moment: The Radical Challenge of the Northampton Association*; and *Social Change in America: from the Revolution through the Civil War*.

Anthony Crubaugh received his BA from the University of Chicago and Ph.D. from Columbia University and is presently Associate Professor and Chairperson of the Department of History at Illinois State University. The author of *Balancing the Scales of Justices: Local Justice and Rural Society in Southwest France, 1750–1800* (2001), his current project focuses on representations of the peasantry in French revolutionary newspapers.

William Doyle is Emeritus Professor of History and Senior Research Fellow at the University of Bristol. A Fellow of the British Academy, he has written mainly about the Ancien Régime and the French Revolution. His most recent books are *Aristocracy and its Enemies in the Age of Revolution* (Oxford University Press, 2009) and *Aristocracy: A Very Short Introduction* (Oxford University Press, 2010)

Joël Félix is Professor of History at the University of Reading and the author of several works in French on the financial history of the Ancien Régime. The main purpose of his research is to renew the approach to political crisis by exploring the relevance of fiscal and financial issues in the European context of the struggle for great power status in the early modern period and the French Revolution.

Alan Forrest has been Professor of History at the University of York since 1989. He has written widely on the history of revolutionary and Napoleonic France, and the history of modern warfare. His most recent book is *The Legacy of the French Revolutionary Wars: The Nation-in-Arms in French Republican Memory* (Cambridge University Press, 2009).

Jack A. Goldstone, Ph.D. (Harvard) is the Virginia E. and John T. Hazel Jr. Professor of Public Policy at George Mason University. He was awarded the American Sociological Association's Distinguished Contribution to Scholarship Award for *Revolution and Rebellion in the Early Modern World* (1991) and the Historical Society's Arnaldo Momigliano Award for his essay 'Efflorescences in World History' in the *Journal of World History* (2002). His latest work is *Why Europe? The Rise of the West in World History, 1500–1800* (2008).

Julie Hardwick is Professor of History and Director of the Institute for Historical Studies at the University of Texas at Austin. Her publications include *The Practice of Patriarchy: Gender and the Politics of Household Authority in Early Modern France*

(1998) and *Family Business: Litigation and the Political Economies of Daily Life in Early Modern France* (2008).

Julian Hoppit joined University College London in 1987, where he is now Astor Professor of British History. He works on the economic and political history of Britain between 1660 and 1800. His published work includes *Risk and Failure in English Business 1700–1800* (1987) and *A Land of Liberty? England, 1689–1727* (2000). He is currently writing on *Britain's Political Economies, 1660–1800*, and is editor of the *Historical Journal*.

Peter M. Jones is Professor of History at the University of Birmingham. He has written extensively on the Ancien Régime and the French Revolution. In 2010 Pearson Education Ltd published a revised and expanded edition of his popular textbook *The French Revolution, 1787–1804*.

Thomas E. Kaiser is Professor of History at the University of Arkansas, Little Rock. The author of more than twenty-five articles on the political culture of the Old Regime and the French Revolution, he is also the co-author of *Europe, 1648–1815: From the Old Regime to the Age of Revolution* (2004), and co-editor of *Conspiracy in the French Revolution* (2007) and *From Deficit to Deluge: The Origins of the French Revolution* (2011). Currently he is working on a study of the interaction of French diplomacy and domestic politics, provisionally titled *Marie Antoinette and the Austrian Plot, 1748–1794*.

Mark Ledbury is Power Professor of the History of Art and Visual Culture and Director of the Power Institute at the University of Sydney. He has published widely on art–theatre relationships and on the artists of eighteenth-century France. Author of *Sedaine, Greuze and the Boundaries of Genre* (2000) and editor of *David after David* (2006), he is currently working on the history of history painting.

Dr Marisa Linton is Reader in History at Kingston University. She is the author of *The Politics of Virtue in Enlightenment France* (2001) and co-editor of *Conspiracy in the French Revolution* (2007). She has written a variety of articles and essays on the French Revolution and the political culture of eighteenth-century France.

Silvia Marzagalli is Professor of (early) Modern History at the University of Nice Sophia-Antipolis and Director of the Centre for the Modern and Contemporary Mediterranean. Specializing in the history of early modern seaborne commerce, in 1999 she published *Les Boulevards de la fraude: Le Négoce maritime et le blocus continental, 1806–1813*. Her most recent work (in collaboration with Pierre-Yves Beaurepaire) is *Atlas de la Révolution française: Circulation des hommes et des idées, 1770–1804* (2010).

Sarah Maza is Jane Long Professor in the Arts and Sciences and Professor of History at Northwestern University. She is the author of several books on the social and cultural history of France from the eighteenth to the twentieth century, including *The Myth of the French Bourgeoisie: An Essay in the Social Imaginary, 1750–1880* (Harvard University Press, 2003). Her most recent book, *Violette Nozière: A Story of Murder in 1930s Paris*, will be published in early 2011.

Christine MacLeod is Professor Emerita at the University of Bristol, and is the author of *Heroes of Invention: Technology, Liberalism, and British Identity, 1750–1914* (Cambridge University Press, 2007).

Thomas Munck is Professor of Early Modern European History at the University of Glasgow. In addition to his *Seventeenth Century Europe* (2nd edn. 2005) and *The Enlightenment* (2000) his research has focused on Scandinavian and north German history, including literacy, censorship, and print culture. He is currently working on a comparative study of print and political culture in northern Europe, 1650–1800.

Alessandro Nuvolari is Associate Professor of Economic and Social History at Sant'Anna School of Advanced Studies in Pisa, Italy. His research interests are mostly focused on the role of science and technology during the first industrial revolution. In particular, he has studied the origins and development of steam power technology and the impact of patent systems on the rate and direction of inventive activities.

Thomas O'Connor lectures in history at National University of Ireland, Maynooth, where he co-directs the Irish in Europe project and edits *Archivium Hibernicum*. He has published on early modern religion and Irish migration in Europe.

Dorinda Outram is the Gladys I. and Franklin W. Clark Professor of History at the University of Rochester, New York. She has written widely in the history of science and culture, including two surveys of the Enlightenment. She is currently preparing a book on the experience of religious conversion in the eighteenth century.

David Parrott is Fellow and Tutor in Modern History at New College, Oxford. He has published on aspects of seventeenth-century French military and administrative history, and diplomatic relations at the time of the Thirty Years War. He is the author of *Richelieu's Army: War, Government and Society in France, 1624–1642* (Cambridge, 2001)

Michael Rapport is Senior Lecturer in History at the University of Stirling. Since *Nationality and Citizenship in Revolutionary France. the Treatment of Foreigners, 1789–1799* (2000) he has published widely on the Age of Revolutions in Europe. His most recent book is *1848: Year of Revolution* (2008).

Hamish Scott is Professor Emeritus of History at the University of St Andrews, Honorary Senior Research Fellow at the University of Glasgow, and a Fellow of the British Academy. He has written several studies of early modern international relations, and edited volumes of essays on Enlightened absolutism and on European nobilities in the seventeenth and eighteenth centuries. He is currently completing a survey of the formation of Europe's aristocracy between the fourteenth and the eighteenth centuries.

John Shovlin teaches eighteenth-century French and European history at New York University. He is the author of *The Political Economy of Virtue: Luxury, Patriotism and the Origins of the French Revolution* (Cornell University Press, 2006), together with numerous articles and essays exploring French politics and culture in the Ancien Régime. He is currently preparing a study of the Franco-British international relationship in the eighteenth century.

Professor Julian Swann lectures at Birkbeck College, University of London, and is the author of *Politics and the Parlement of Paris under Louis XV, 1754–1774* and *Provincial Power and Absolute Monarchy: The Estates-General of Burgundy, 1661–1790*.

Peter H. Wilson is G. F. Grant Professor of History at the University of Hull, having worked previously at Sunderland and Newcastle universities. He has written or edited thirteen books on European history, including *Europe's Tragedy: A History of the Thirty Years' War* (2009).

CHAPTER 1

INTRODUCTION

WILLIAM DOYLE

We owe the idea of the Ancien Régime to the French Revolution.[1] As soon as it became clear, during the summer of 1788, that the structure and apparatus of authority in France was collapsing, people began to look forward to an era of change. Suddenly, it seemed, all their dreams of a better, juster, fairer, kinder, freer order of things might be made to come true. Nothing was exempt from these expectations, and they were only fanned in the spring of 1789 when all the King's subjects, prior to electing the Estates-General, which was expected to solve all the kingdom's problems, were invited to draw up lists of their grievances. These *cahiers de doléances* were carefully scrutinized by Alexis de Tocqueville in preparing the greatest of all analyses of *The Ancien Régime and the French Revolution* (1856). 'When I come to assemble together all these particular wishes', he concluded,[2] 'I perceive with a sort of terror that what is claimed is the simultaneous and systematic abolition of all the laws and all the customs obtaining throughout the kingdom.' A number of these *cahiers* described what they deplored as belonging to a former order of things: *l'ancien régime*. By the end of 1789 the term was in general use among legislators and journalists to describe French institutional life before that year. It meant what the Revolution had destroyed: the opposite of what it stood for.

But what the Revolution stood for changed and evolved. Although the deputies elected in 1789 commissioned a digest of the *cahiers* to guide them in reframing French institutions, their initial plans did not run to the wholesale destruction which so appalled Tocqueville. The original project was to turn an absolute monarchy into a constitutional one. The political Ancien Régime in these terms meant a state in which the sovereign ruled unconstrained by representative institutions, and was responsible for his actions only to God. No clear corpus of laws constrained him, and as late as November 1787 Louis XVI had declared that what was legal was what he wished. When the Estates-General transformed itself into the Constituent Assembly, it began by proclaiming that the Nation was sovereign, and dedicated itself to producing a written constitution which closely circumscribed the King's freedom of action and vested most power in an elected legislature. The Ancien Régime, by contrasting definition, had had no constitution. It governed itself by custom: a confused, overlapping, and often contradictory collection of precedents, habits, and special cases, a complex of countless vested interests. The revolutionaries were committed to a more ordered state, introducing rationality and uniformity to national life.

Written constitutions were a new idea. The only accessible models were the constitutions adopted by American states only a few years earlier when they threw off British rule. A number had been translated and published in French in 1783, and much discussed since. And everyone was aware that at the very moment of the Ancien Régime's final crisis the United States was elaborating a new federal constitution. All these American constitutions (even, eventually, the federal one) incorporated declarations of rights, and from an early stage admirers of the new transatlantic republic pressed for a similar declaration to be incorporated into the new French constitution. After some debate, the Declaration of the Rights of Man and the Citizen, destined to be the new constitution's preamble, was promulgated on 26 August 1789. It has been called the death certificate of the Ancien Régime,[3] in that it proclaimed the opposite of what had gone before. Sovereignty was now vested in the Nation; government was to be representative; state power was to be divided; the rule of law was to replace arbitrary authority. There was also to be civil equality, in other words no privileges or private law. All men were to be equal before the law, in the payment of taxes, and in access 'to all public dignities, offices and employments, according to their ability, and with no other distinction than that of their virtues and their talents' (article 6). Finally there was to be freedom: freedom from arbitrary arrest and imprisonment, freedom to do whatever was not harmful to others, freedom to believe or practise any religion, freedom to express opinions, and freedom to enjoy 'inviolable and sacred' property rights.

With its provisions for equality and freedom, the Declaration went beyond political structures to lay down ground rules for a new form of society, purged of what were increasingly called the 'abuses' of the Ancien Régime. In fact, some of the most extensive of these 'abuses' had already been consigned to destruction three weeks before the Declaration was passed. If the Declaration was the Ancien Régime's death certificate, the date of its death was 4 August, when, in the course of a confused and sometimes euphoric summer night, the National Assembly renounced or suppressed some of the most extensive and deeply rooted practices of French life. The session began as an attempt to defuse peasant unrest in the countryside by decreeing the end of the 'feudal regime'—a structure of dues and services inherited from the middle ages by which lords extracted surplus from vassals whose property fell within their private jurisdiction. The so-called 'feudal complex' defies clear or rational analysis, but for that majority of the French who were peasants, its demands and burdens were a central feature of their lives. They and their descendants, looking back, would simply call the former order of things the 'time of the lords'.

But much more than feudalism was abolished on the night of 4 August. All sorts of privileges and exemptions, mainly but far from exclusively benefiting the nobility, were suppressed by acclamation. So was the sale and heredity of public offices, the key to the recruitment of the judiciary and, insofar as many of these offices conferred noble status, the main avenue of entry into the nobility. Nobility itself, as a status, survived for the moment; but when its outward trappings were abolished in June 1790, in the eyes of many it only seemed the natural corollary of the wholesale abolition of its powers, prerogatives, and privileges ten months earlier.

Noble resistance to the last desperate reform plans of absolute monarchy had played a crucial part in precipitating its collapse. Resolving the crisis by convoking the Estates-General had then given the nobility unprecedented hopes of playing a regular role in future political life, since in the Estates, reflecting the medieval division of society into three functional orders (the clergy who prayed, the nobles who fought, and the third estate who worked) there was a separate chamber representing nobles. But the first great struggles of the Revolution, running from September 1788 to June 1789, had ended in the abandonment of the three separate chambers, and by implication the orders of society which they reflected. And the preceding frenzied attempts of nobles to preserve separate representation and powers had marked them out as the main enemies of national regeneration. The word 'aristocrat' became shorthand for anyone seeking a return to the Ancien Régime in any of its aspects. And, in case the successive suppression of all signs and relics of nobility had not been enough, the constitution when it was promulgated in September 1791 explicitly listed the main components of what was by then understood as the social Ancien Régime. The National Assembly, it declared

> abolishes irrevocably the institutions which were injurious to liberty and equality of rights.
>
> There is no longer either nobility, or peerage, or hereditary distinctions, or distinctions of orders, or a feudal regime, or inherited jurisdictions, or any of the titles, denominations or prerogatives deriving from them, or any order of chivalry, or any of the corporations or decorations for which proofs of nobility were required, or which presupposed distinctions of birth, or any other superiority other than that of public officials in the exercise of their functions.
>
> There is no longer either venality or heredity of any public office.
>
> There is no longer for any part of the nation or for any individual, any privilege or exception to the common law of all the French.

A further clause confirmed the suppression of guilds and corporations of the professions, arts, and crafts. This was one of the few mentions in the constitution of economic matters. Yet the *cahiers* had been full of complaints about economic abuses and injustices, and it soon became clear that the revolutionaries of 1789 believed that there was an economic Ancien Régime to eradicate as well as a political and social one. Disciples as most of them were of the liberalizing thought of the *économistes* or physiocrats of the pre-revolutionary years, they set about removing what they saw as unnatural and illegitimate constraints and burdens on the free exchange of goods and the production of wealth. Thus, economic ideology as much as social justice dictated the removal of the burdens which the 'feudal regime' placed on agriculture. Internal tolls and customs barriers, both public and private, were also abolished. Controls on the grain trade, an instrument of public order as much as of economic regulation, were abandoned. So were productive monopolies of all sorts, from the trade guilds of urban artisans, to professional associations such as the bar. The new regime was to be one in which the individual, rather than the order or corporation to which a person belonged, was to be the highest common factor in social and economic relations. Corporate bodies were perceived as profiting from privilege, that guiding principle of the former order that the revolutionaries were determined to uproot. Dedicated to the defence and promotion of their members' livelihoods, corporations were seen as more committed to their own sectional interests than to the common well-being of a nation of free and equal citizens. As one revolutionary, excluded from public life before 1789 because of his Protestantism, put it: 'every time one creates a corporate body with privileges one creates a public enemy, because a special interest is nothing other than this'.[4]

The greatest of all corporations, with the most extensive vested interests to promote, was the clergy. A separate order, largely run by nobles who filled its upper ranks, it monopolized public worship, controlled a sixth of the kingdom's land, exercised feudal rights over even more, and dominated the provision of education and charity. Sensing that the Church was increasingly under attack from freethinkers, the clergy initially saw the Revolution as an opportunity to restore its influence in national life. Clerical deputies were instrumental in breaking the deadlock which immobilized the first six weeks of the Estates-General. But subsequent months brought bitter disappointment. On 4 August the clergy lost extensive feudal rights along with all other lords. It also lost the tithe, the notional tenth of every parishioner's goods payable for the maintenance of parish priests. Less than three months later the entire property of the Church was confiscated to provide a fund of confidence to sustain the national finances. Monasteries and convents were effectively dissolved by the prohibition of binding vows. And, having committed the Nation in the Declaration of the Rights of Man and the Citizen to religious toleration and the free expression of opinion, the Constituent Assembly refused in April 1790 to recognize Roman Catholicism as the national religion. When, only weeks later, a new religious regime was established, the Pope was not consulted. The Civil Constitution of the Clergy denied him any jurisdiction within France; and, in its dying days, the National Assembly annexed the age-old enclaves of papal territory in Avignon and the Comtat Venaissin. The spiritual Ancien Régime, in many areas quite literally, had been reduced to ruins.

But the Catholic Church was an international body, and the revolutionary quarrel with its French branch began to internationalize the idea of the Ancien Régime. Another of Tocqueville's insights, overschematic perhaps but not essentially inaccurate, was that 'almost all Europe had exactly the same institutions' that had fallen into ruin everywhere (book 1, chapter 4). Insofar as the Ancien Régime was a world of absolute monarchs, a ruling order of privileged nobles, a monopolistic established church, and overlapping and conflicting customs and jurisdictions, all weighing heavily on economic activity, it or something like it could be found in most parts of Europe. The alarmed reaction of foreign kings, nobles, and clerics to the upheavals in France shows how clearly they understood that in the challenges to the Ancien Régime there was an implicit challenge to themselves. And when in 1792 the revolutionaries launched a war to protect what they had achieved, and the first casualty was the French monarchy itself, the new-minted republicans who invaded the Netherlands and western Germany saw themselves as carrying revolutionary values to the rest of Europe, proclaiming 'war on the castles', and inviting subject peoples everywhere to rise up against the old structure of authority. By 1799 the French had overthrown Anciens Régimes west of the Rhine, in Holland, Switzerland, and south of the Alps. Over the next decade Napoleon would continue this work throughout Germany and further east, and south of the Pyrenees. And the removal of the old Iberian authorities opened the way to the transformation of colonial Anciens Régimes throughout Latin America.

Much of the Ancien Régime as the revolutionaries defined it is still accepted by historians as a meaningful framework for study. Revolutionary destruction sliced like a guillotine through its fabric, and exposed for posterity a vivid cross-section or snapshot of how things were before the cataclysm struck. But in condemning the Ancien Régime to death so comprehensively, the revolutionaries tended to erase the memory of its previous life, bequeathing a static version of the world before their own emergence which denied it vitality. Part of the myth, indeed, which they elaborated to vindicate their own actions was to depict the old order as fossilized and unchanging, its rigidities stifling any hope of change or progress. Counter-revolutionaries developed a parallel perspective. In condemning the chaos and blind destruction which the Revolution had brought, they evoked a contrasting Ancien Régime arcadia of calm, harmony, and deference, where everybody knew their place under the rule of a paternalistic nobility, a clergy offering the consolations of true religion, and a benign monarchy. It was a caricature, but perhaps no more than the picture of tyranny and hopeless inertia and misery favoured by the revolutionaries. The challenge for historians is to investigate the vital functions of the Ancien Régime before it was cut off.

Not all contemporaries looked back on it as static and unchanging. Though vehemently condemning the destruction still going on in 1790 as he wrote his *Reflections on the Revolution in France*, Edmund Burke saw the old order as a living organism, the product of a long natural evolution on the soil of France, a rich and distinctive heritage which the French were now heedlessly throwing away in pursuit of rationalist illusions. It was still evolving, though at the slow pace of all natural things, when it was brutally killed off. Writing over half a century later, Tocqueville, too, saw the Ancien Régime as anything but static, although unlike Burke he thought its evolution was inexorably leading to a violent overthrow. Marxist perspectives, increasingly influential throughout the later nineteenth and early twentieth centuries, presented the Ancien Régime as the last phase of feudalism, an age of agrarian surplus extraction which came to a dramatic end on 4 August 1789. But the forces which brought about this conclusion—capitalism, and the bourgeoisie who were its products and beneficiaries—had been growing in scale and power below the feudal surface for centuries. In 1789 the Ancien Régime was merely a hollowed-out husk, easy for more dynamic elements to burst asunder.

By the mid-twentieth century a classic interpretation of the Revolution had emerged, a blend of myths inherited from the revolutionaries themselves and an overlay of Marxism, in which the Ancien Régime was depicted as both static *and* dynamic. In the eighteenth century a capitalist economy and a rising bourgeoisie demanding political rights commensurate with their economic importance confronted a despotic monarchy supported by reactionary privileged orders determined to maintain, if not to reinforce, their age-old hegemony. Later last century, however, the classic interpretation fell apart over several decades of cumulative criticism from so-called revisionist historians. Much of 'revisionism' focused on the origins rather than the course of the Revolution, and as a result historical perspectives on the Ancien Régime were transformed. The aim of this book is to present the pre-revolutionary order, and the template it offers for studying areas and periods beyond eighteenth-century France, as it appears in a new century when most of the dust of the revisionist challenge has settled.

No attempt has been made to forge a forced consensus. Contributors have been at liberty to interpret their themes in whatever way seems appropriate to them. The editorial role, apart from planning the overall shape of the volume and identifying contributors, has merely been to try to minimize overlaps. But the chapter plan, inevitably, reflects, as well as traditional categories, some topics and issues which have only come to prominence in scholarly debates since the 1950s. Most traditional, perhaps, is Part I, covering the state, its organization, and its resources. Even here, interpretation of how the various elements operated has been transformed. Part II, on social organization, while beginning with the groups which clashed in the terminal crisis of 1788–9, goes on to deal with wider aspects of social structuring, some of which, like gender, scarcely figured in earlier approaches. Comparably fresh topics appear in Part III, on the economy. Alongside well-established categories like feudalism, agriculture, and commerce there is discussion of the demographic old order, hardly recognized as distinctive before the mid-twentieth century, and of the slavery and serfdom which underpinned so much of the taste for luxuries which marked the old order's last century, and the social order of eastern Europe. The main novelties in Part IV on religion appear under well-established labels; but Part V reflects the now-predominant approach to the Revolution and its antecedents which sees it as a symptom of more profound long-term cultural changes which previously only attracted marginal interest.

It is now widely accepted that almost no aspect of the Ancien Régime came to an end as suddenly and decisively as the French revolutionaries had hoped when they gave it a name. Institutions might be summarily abolished, but the ideas and cultural practices which had moulded them changed at a different pace. With hindsight, the disappearance of some time-honoured ways appears to have been foreshadowed some time before revolution burst upon the scene. Others persisted far into the nineteenth century and perhaps beyond. Recognition of the untidy process by which the Ancien Régime disappeared is the rationale for Part VI, called *Solvents*, in which revolution ranks as only one of the factors which brought about the end of the old order. Part VII, finally, considers how far other countries beside France had recognizable Anciens Régimes. In its sheer heterogeneous variety, the Holy Roman Empire offers multiple areas for comparison. It has also been plausibly suggested that Great Britain in the 'long' eighteenth century, not to mention its North American colonies, had more in common with the French prototype than used to be thought credible. This section offers a critical exploration of these comparisons, concluding with a brief editorial overview.

No editor could hope for universal approval of a book's planned shape or the elements identified as important. I am only too conscious of certain obvious omissions. Some originally planned had to be abandoned: I had hoped, for instance, to include an essay on appearances, and one on pre-revolutionary Russia as an exemplary old regime. Nobody I approached was willing to take them on. A promised contribution on theatre was given up too late to find a substitute author. Too late, too, I realized how useful it might have been to include a piece on the Anciens Régimes of Latin America. But I thought slavery and serfdom too important to leave out in the absence of willing authors, so I rashly undertook to survey them myself. All this is less than satisfactory, and for that I accept full responsibility. On the other hand I am profoundly grateful to all the authors who have agreed to contribute, and for their patience in waiting for the final text to appear.

Notes

1. Although more specific uses of the two words were older. See Ch. 5, below, p. 75.
2. Book iii, ch. 1, tr. M. W. Patterson (Oxford, n.d.), 152–3.
3. Georges Lefebvre, *Quatre-Vingt Neuf* (Paris, 1939), 196–7.
4. Rabaut de Saint-Etienne, quoted in C. B. A. Behrens, *The Ancien Régime* (London, 1967), 179.

Bibliography

Baker, Keith Michael (ed.), *The French Revolution and the Creation of Modern Political Culture*, i. *The Political Culture of the Old Regime* (Oxford, 1987).
Behrens, C. B. A., *The Ancien Régime* (London, 1967).
Bély, Lucien (ed.), *Dictionnaire de l'Ancien Régime* (Paris, 1996).
Cabourdin, Guy, and Viard, Georges, *Lexique historique de la France d'Ancien Régime* (3rd edn., Paris, 2005).
Doyle, William, *The Ancien Regime* (2nd edn., Basingstoke, 2001).
Figeac, Michel (ed.), *L'Ancienne France au quotidien: Vie et choses de la vie sous l'Ancien Régime* (Paris, 2007).
Goubert, Pierre, and Roche, Daniel, *Les Français et l'Ancien Régime* (3rd edn., Paris, 2000).
Herr, Richard, *Tocqueville and the Old Regime* (Princeton, 1962).
Le Roy Ladurie, Emmanuel, *The Ancien Regime, 1610–1774* (Oxford, 1995).
Marion, Marcel, *Dictionnaire des institutions de la France aux xviie et xviiie siècles* (Paris, 1923).
Méthivier, Hubert, *L'Ancien Régime en France* (Paris, 1983).
Tocqueville, Alexis de, *The Ancien Regime and the French Revolution* (Paris, 1856; many edns. since).

PART I

GOVERNMENT

CHAPTER 2

ABSOLUTE MONARCHY

PETER R. CAMPBELL

INTRODUCTION

ABSOLUTE monarchy has long been considered the essential form of the early modern state. It is often regarded as an intermediate stage in a chain of development going from a feudal state based on patrimonialism, to a *Ständestaat* or 'state of estates' in which nobles and representative institutions have many powers, to absolute monarchy which eradicated these powers in order to rise pre-eminent, and finally to the constitutional and bureaucratic form of the state in the nineteenth and twentieth centuries.[1] This pattern is problematic because it is a drastic oversimplification and because it poses but does not answer the question of how the transition from absolute monarchy to the succeeding constitutional form was made. Was a liberal revolution necessary for some absolute monarchies to become constitutional, and did change come from outside influences, or from wide social and economic changes, or did absolute monarchy itself engender the next form within its own institutions and developments? What then were the ruptures and continuities between these forms? Where the latter scenario took place, as perhaps in France, then we must ask how did the idea of a constitutional monarchy emerge, and was the idea of representative government really excluded from the absolute monarchy? To what extent was there direct bureaucratic, administrative, and conceptual continuity between the institutions of the absolute monarchy and those of the modern state? Was the operation of power in the absolutist state already centralized and bureaucratic before the constitutional revolution, as the still influential Tocqueville believed, along with many historians before and since? If power was in fact not centralized but decentralized, shared, and negotiated, then surely the French Revolution must have been a much more creative rupture with the old regime state, and one that *may perhaps* have contributed more originally to the creation of a centralized state, than he was prepared to admit. The answers to these questions are not simple but they do suggest that the traditional views may need to be reconsidered. Perhaps the preoccupation with centralization should now be regarded as an anachronistic question whose very asking oversimplifies the complex processes of compromise and negotiation that took place in this period between elites and the state.[2]

In the light of such concerns, this chapter will argue that, in spite of absolute monarchy's success in seemingly rising above society, it developed claims and practices that ran counter to long-term representative tendencies contained within its own structures. It was never able to suppress these, nor did it intend to, because they remained enshrined in corporate society itself, on which it was based. Although the corporate society of the old regime was very hierarchical, its elites retained a large measure of autonomy in their own spheres. This sense of independence and the continued vitality of privilege provided fertile ground for a revival of conciliarist and later commonwealth arguments, and a historical belief in an ancient constitution. These arguments in favour of limited royal power eventually empowered an opposition that was able to take advantage of the excesses and contradictions that characterized some of the practices of absolute monarchy, whose power to enforce its central will was somewhat illusory.

As a form of state structure, absolute monarchy has its origins in both the late medieval and the renaissance monarchy. It is generally thought to have reached its apogee in France under Louis XIV. The French monarchy of the eighteenth century is supposed to have been unable to modernize sufficiently to survive the challenges of empire and the rise of other European powers. The collapse of the French absolute monarchy as a consequence of its own contradictions, inherent weaknesses, poor political management, and efforts at impossible reforms, opened the door to revolution. In the early modern period, however, 'absolute monarchy' existed both as a form of political organization, and as a theory of monarchical authority and its proper rights and limits. Absolute monarchies developed in Spain, the British Isles, Sweden, Denmark, Austria-Hungary, Brandenburg-Prussia, Russia, and Savoy-Piedmont, and formed the basis of the governance of several smaller states in Germany and Italy. It was a contemporary reality advocated by most as the best form of government. It could be described as a power that was absolved from the restraints of other powers, but in the sense of having the final word, rather than in the sense of having freed itself from all practical or legal restrictions. There was a difference between absolute power and absolute authority—for authority was never conceived as giving kings the right to exercise complete or unlimited power over their subjects. Absolute monarchies nevertheless had a tendency, common to most power, to try to further emancipate themselves from restraints on their action. In some states there was also a marked impulse towards ever greater regulation and control of the economy and local institutions. Theoretical justifications for royal authority were thus employed to enlarge the sphere of state power—but it must be stressed that much of this process owed more to the pressing needs of international warfare than to the independent influence of the theories in themselves.

This form of monarchy should never be confused with arbitrary authoritarianism, and for this reason the use of the term 'absolutism' to describe this government continues to sow considerable confusion. The word was invented at the end of the eighteenth century as a propagandist condemnation of authoritarian monarchies, deliberately associating them with 'despotism' or 'tyranny', so it reflects a very misguided idea of the more complex realities of the earlier period. All too often 'absolutism' is used lazily simply to mean 'royal policy' or, just as unhelpfully, to refer to a centralized bureaucratic form of government that existed only to a slight degree, and which was rarely the aim of royal policy. Centralization made little sense with slow communications, and strong regional cultures and elites, and different ways of getting things done were developed. The ethic of the rational bureaucracies of the nineteenth-century constitutional states so well analysed by Max Weber was very different from that of the earlier period, when officers had purchased their posts, which represented for them both a financial investment and social status.[3] The system of venal officeholding embodied concerns about social ascension and family strategies; clientage also played a role, for to acquire an office a family needed to be accepted by the corps and spoken for by a well-connected courtier or minister. Until very recently, too much focus on the origins of the modern state led historians to stress more the elements that seemed to be progressive and to lead to the next form in the nineteenth century, rather than on the specificity of the various elements that characterized 'absolute monarchy'. Rather than regard absolute monarchy as just a hybrid form of the earlier and later Weberian categories, we should recognize it as a specific form of state that is based upon the central importance of the royal court in its culture and governance.[4]

A NEW STATE FORMATION

For several generations of historians, from the nineteenth century right up to the 1970s, the dominant approaches to the state were the history of institutions and the history of legal doctrines, both usually based on administrative correspondence, legislation, and lawyers' explanations. In recent years there has been a change of perspective and we have learnt to take other important elements into account: the role of patronage and clientage; the function of the court; political management; and the persuasive significance of the representation of monarchy in image and ritual.[5] Biography and studies of government in practice have drawn these elements together in case studies that reveal structures and processes that were anything but simple—for they made up a very 'tumultuous reality'.[6] A much more complete understanding of absolute monarchy has become possible. Instead of interpreting absolute monarchies solely through the history of theory and institutions, we should try to understand the spirit or way of thinking that gave rise to them, and the ways in which early modern men operated within them. We need to set the state in the context of society and its ideas—thus decentring our vision. Viewing the state from the periphery rather than the centre helps to understand the limitations on the exercise of central authority. A major omission from the institutional vision of the state has only been remedied in recent years. Focusing on bureaucratic institutions led legal historians and sociologists to ignore the one institution that remained vital to this form of state throughout the period: the royal household or court. This neglect probably arose because it was hard to study an institution with so many different roles and therefore no single set of archival sources. The court was a political, social, and cultural space that brought together all the elements necessary for successful governance.

Paying due attention to the social, cultural, and political specifics of the period, we might therefore argue that the absolute monarchy was a specific form of the state that came into being in a recognizably coherent way towards the end of the sixteenth century, underwent rapid *ad hoc* development in the seventeenth century, and lasted until the Revolution. We can call this state formation a 'baroque state', not only in order to stress its key period of development associated with these artistic forms of representation, religious and monumental, but also to highlight its evident weaknesses. Such a term highlights the fact that its characteristic seventeenth-century style of governance, based on a range of techniques, perfected but not substantially changed, would prove inadequate a hundred years later in an age of Neo-Classicism.

Absolute monarchy was thus a form of government with deep historical roots. It was also a theory of legitimate royal authority widely subscribed to by early modern European monarchies, with significant variations.[7] To explore its nature the example of France will be used. In some important ways its key concepts existed before the modern word for the state itself was invented. In 1589 when the crown passed from the Valois to the Bourbons, the throne of France had been inherited by members of the same family since the first Capetian in AD 987, and it was to remain Bourbon to the Revolution. This provided unparalleled legitimacy in Europe, and since 800 an explicitly sacred dimension enhanced this. In that year Emperor Charlemagne was crowned by the Pope, and ever since then the link between church and monarchy had remained fundamental, and not just in France. It was symbolized in many ceremonies, among which were those of the coronation, the funeral, royal entries, the *lit de justice* in the parlement, and the rituals of the court, which paralleled those of the liturgy in regularity and analogous form; in a more popular vein, the royal touch or laying on of hands in a ceremony once a year, was believed to cure scrofula and reinforced the link with divine power in the mind of the people. Both the monarchy and the population were so Catholic that, in order to ensure that he kept the crown of France inherited in 1589, Henry IV, the first Bourbon monarch and a Protestant, felt it expedient to convert to Catholicism in 1593. In 1598 the Edict of Nantes granted limited toleration to Protestants—and this was for practical reasons, not those of principle. The French monarchy was thus confirmed as essentially and irrevocably Catholic.

Kings were also by definition warriors, protecting their dynastic interests with a bellicose foreign policy.[8] Foreign and civil war arose from both international challenges and internal religious tensions. The civil and religious wars of the second half of the sixteenth century tested the French monarchy and its embryonic state to the limits. Nevertheless, when Henry IV restored peace at the end of the sixteenth century, he was able to build upon some crucial developments in administration and governance of the later fifteenth and early sixteenth centuries that his immediate predecessors had taken further. In terms of territory, France was larger because a number of provinces had been attached to the monarchy by purchase, inheritance, or escheatment: Dauphiné in 1456, Burgundy in 1447, Provence in 1481, and Brittany, finally secured by marriage in 1532. The relationship of these provinces to the crown was contractual, which left them a fair measure of independence from French law, able to preserve their own legal structures and governing traditions. In 1472 a concordat with the Pope had confirmed the French crown's rights over appointments in the French church and thus given access to a vast source of patronage that could be exploited by the monarchy in its relations with the nobility. During the reign of Francis I (1515–47) venality of office was regularized as a system, such that the crown could profit from selling offices to raise war finance. In 1604 an annual tax on office known as the *Paulette* was imposed, which allowed officeholders to pass their charge to their heir if they died. Further important steps were taken towards a more efficient organization of royal business in the second half of the sixteenth century. Under Henry II (1547–59) four secretaries of state were created, each with a certain number of provinces to administer. Henry III (1574–89) reorganized the court more along Spanish lines. Henry IV re-established royal finances and compromised sufficiently with courtly and provincial elites to restore and extend royal authority.[9]

The power of the monarchy nevertheless remained very limited both in practice and theory. At this time the language used to discuss or describe the state was neither modern nor institutional. Authority was thought of in moral terms, for power itself carried with it, or was even defined as, a moral responsibility based on divine and natural law. It also reflected both the medieval and classical heritage. Relations between the King and his subjects were modelled in important ways on analogies between the Holy Roman Empire and the Papacy, which were in perpetual conflict over their temporal powers. Thus 'the king is emperor in his own kingdom', often cited by royal lawyers, was a maxim based upon the imperial victory in this contest, and it meant that just as the Holy Roman Emperor had won independence from Rome in temporal matters, so too had the kings of France emancipated themselves from the Holy Roman Emperor, recognizing no suzerain.[10] There was also a sense that the kings had the same temporal rights as the Emperor did in his domains.

The political entity that would later be called the state was also known in the renaissance as the 'république' or commonwealth, for the modern sense of 'the state' had not yet come into being and the word still meant something like 'the status' (of monarchy).[11] People thought in terms of a body politic, with harmonious relations between its various parts, just as in the human body, of which the King was the head, and they conceived of government as paternal. Although supreme power was thinkable, its legitimate exercise was regarded as being confined to certain spheres of activity and the notions of counsel by the *grands* and consent from the people were still important. Notions of consultation and representation were deeply embodied in village assemblies, in elections to town councils (even though they were effectively oligarchies), in provincial estates, in the corporate institutions of society, in the guilds therefore and in the occasional meetings of the Estates-General that brought together deputies from the three orders of the realm. At this time, the rather hazy notion of absolute monarchy therefore included elements of representation and consent. Even though the monarchy in the seventeenth century developed institutions and powers that made it very much more powerful, and a separate entity from society, the legacy of this more consensual or rights-based tradition continued to make itself felt. Conflict over legal rights was often quite marked both within and between corporate institutions, such as judicial bodies, trades corporations, and even religious orders. Indeed, notions of rights and representation would undergo a notable revival in the last decades of the regime.

From the sixteenth to the eighteenth century, the language of monarchy developed, always in the direction of pre-eminence over society and institutions. New words and concepts were invented, perhaps the most important being 'sovereignty', but the content of these concepts would also develop over time. There was a self-conscious royal politics of language. After the wars of religion, the monarchy insisted on a language of service to the King or to the state, rather than to the commonwealth. Although the change in language reflected new strengths as well as goals, it also masked notable continuities in the relationship between state and society. Many political beliefs remained remarkably constant over the centuries. One was that the right of the monarchy to interfere with private property by levying taxes without consent was limited. New taxes were always contested, unless it could be argued defending the public good made them necessary, as in wartime. Another fundamental belief was that it was the King's duty to dispense justice and therefore to himself respect the laws and contracts that bound together society and the state. If Bossuet could argue in *Politics taken from Holy Scripture* (1709) that subjects (and not citizens) should never challenge an unjust or arbitrary ruler, for God would punish him, he nevertheless also argued that the ruler should always behave justly and respect the traditional checks on his power. Bossuet's sense of the limitations on royal power did not differ very much from those put forward by Seyssel writing about the monarchy in 1517.[12] Over time some core political beliefs might be expressed in different language, or even with different justifications underpinning them, because the language had changed over time as ideologies developed. In the period coinciding with the rise of absolute monarchy, education for the social elites in the classics and theology became the norm. In a regime based on precedent, tradition, and contract, the French and classical past was always present and available for exploitation by all parties. It is important to appreciate that for the educated classes in the eighteenth century, the source of political ideas was by no means entirely 'the Enlightenment', which might seem dangerously radical. Theology, French history, and classical antiquity all remained powerful inspirations. Political writings and specific arguments also contained elements from the past that had been reappropriated, revisited, and were then expressed in association with more modern concepts. In eighteenth-century France new *bricolages* were put in place with cross-fertilization from other countries, most notably from England but also from European civic humanism.

Government and administration

Over the same two centuries, from about 1550 to 1750, many advances were made in terms of central and provincial administration. This was usually done by increasing the number of jurisdictions or adding a new layer to a pre-existing layer of officeholders.[13]

Yet it would be quite wrong to imagine an administrative geography that was coherent and rational. The various civil, ecclesiastical, and fiscal authorities generally had different and overlapping areas or jurisdiction, such that it was hard for even the central government to understand the local situation. Communications were slow and accurate maps were lacking. For most of the period, administrative developments were not prompted by an overall vision of a new kind of state or administration, but by needs and concerns that had to be addressed almost immediately. The two great impulses towards change were the fear of disorder and religious conflict, and the need for money to finance the foreign and civil wars. Military costs rose exponentially, around three-quarters of royal revenue was spent on war. Revenue needed to be increased and central authority enhanced in order to do so. There were challenges and resistances to this process. The development of central power and provincial obedience was not a story of progress on all fronts, for there were also periods of intense strain and even regression. We have noted the disorder of the civil and religious wars from the 1560s, and the long reign of Louis XIV (1643–1715) might more controversially (until recently) serve as another example of uneven development. This period has always been regarded as crucial in the development of absolute monarchy, largely because historians focus only on the first half of the reign. Even today there are very few studies of the period 1683–1715. For some historians the years from 1661 to 1683 witnessed the making of modern France, and a transformation in the very nature of the monarchy.[14] Wedded to an idea of institutional progress, they could not envisage that what they thought was made in twenty years was unmade in the next thirty. And yet the reign should not be regarded as a single period of progress, for although Colbert and Louvois brought about notable change, the extreme fiscal requirements of the later years may have witnessed the undoing of much of the administrative development. Many of the old expedients were revived out of desperation, including practices of Richelieu's time.[15]

The most positive argument that can be made is that the affirmation of administrative structures would later make it possible to extend the reach of the monarchy into and over society. Instead of accepting the idea of the making of the modern state, as Tocqueville did, most historians of the reign today stress the many weaknesses and contradictions that led Louis to create a working compromise with the elites, whose subjection owed more to the rewards on offer than it did to a policy of crushing noble power.[16] This compromise then became a permanent element in the structure, preventing subsequent reforms. Louis XIV was a master of political theatre and political management, able to create and manipulate an illusion of power without perhaps depriving other authorities and bodies of their powers as much as was thought. But behind the illusion lay nevertheless the extraordinarily costly achievement of fielding armies of 300,000–400,000 men for decades of almost constant warfare. It was not a modern state that developed this capacity, but a compromise state that resorted to a wide variety of *ad hoc* measures, bluff, negotiation, and intimidation to extract resources and of course it depended upon a huge system of royal debt. There was a price to pay: the monarchical state of the eighteenth century, while certainly more efficient and better ordered than its earlier incarnation, nevertheless suffered from the failures and compromises of the earlier period and found itself beset with contradictions and blockages, too weak to reform itself sufficiently to face even more expensive wars without severe strain. In the same period the Spanish monarchy failed to sustain itself, while in the British Isles a different kind of regime emerged with a more efficient system of public debt based on the confidence inspired by a representative regime.

Concepts

The concepts which gave structure to the monarchy also formed the basis of social organization. For this reason, absolute monarchy should not be seen as separate from society but as a socio-political system. In the middle ages royal power was based on seigneurialism, with the King as the seigneurial overlord, and to some extent this continued, until as a specific justification for royal authority it was largely superseded during the seventeenth century by other arguments. Other fundamentally important concepts that formed the basis of social organization were hierarchy, privilege, and corporatism, while notions of order, tradition, and precedent were crucial elements of the early modern psyche. Such notions were also deeply embedded in royal institutions, legislative practices, and assumptions, shared by everyone including the crown's servants. So royal power was paternal, traditionally limited, reasonable, and not arbitrary, and it could override its traditional limitations in time of need, for the safety of the people was the supreme law. To ensure continuity in the legal traditions, in a society that thought in terms of order, justice, and jurisdiction, the lawyers had even invented a fiction that the King never died: he had two bodies, one mortal and one immortal or symbolic. 'The King is dead, long live the King.' The kingdom's legislation remained in force, therefore, even when the actual person of the King died.[17]

It was agreed that authority to rule came from God, a notion we know as divine right. Royal authority was inextricably bound up with theological concepts and the monarchy is best described as theocratic from at least the time of Charlemagne. Many of the political ideas and debates that characterized the evolution of monarchical authority were rooted in the debates over the power of the Pope within the church in the middle ages, and the authority of the Pope over the Empire. Some argued that he was the supreme authority within the church, others that his power was limited by church councils—hence the word conciliarism. The same arguments and debates were transferred and applied to the secular rulers in the early modern period. Whatever the precise limits of church and state, the notion of divine right legitimized a patriarchal authority to command in matters pertaining to the state. Authority was limited by divine and natural law, and in 1519 Claude de Seyssel described the 'absolute power' of the kings of France as limited by three essential checks. These were religion, justice, and police. The first obliged the King to protect the Catholic religion and refrain from excesses, for 'selon la Loi et Religion chrétienne[il] ne peut faire choses tyranniques'—and if he did act despotically, clerics could remonstrate with him.[18] The second was justice, which meant that the King should respect all civil and criminal law and its procedures, just as his subjects should. The third is a particularly Ancien Régime notion, police, which combined both justice and administration, since in their eyes justice carried with it the duty of enforcement. It meant that the King should respect the institutions that adjudicated and administered the laws and ordinances, all the more so since power was regarded as needing to be exercised in a Christian and rational fashion.

These ideas remained powerful throughout the last centuries of the monarchy and characterized the debates of the eighteenth century between crown and parlement. The regime cultivated a sense of its own past through its ceremonies and rituals, the writings of its royal historiographers and of the men of letters it patronized. As we have seen, by 'absolute' power or authority, the men of the old regime meant an authority that was rather limited: this sovereign power was first of all confined to the proper sphere of the monarch and within that sphere was subject to these further limitations. The existing laws—which might be as much customary as written, and certainly included the contracts made between crown and various towns and provinces—implied limits to taxation without consent. Different legal systems existed, seigneurial, customary, and royal, making legal issues complex.[19]

We shall see below that there were also significant practical checks on the exercise of royal authority. However, the notion of the royal prerogative was a crucial advantage for the crown. It was of course a king's right to pardon the condemned criminal or judge specific cases himself, but that was of little significance compared with a much broader notion. Since the King had a duty to defend the commonwealth, it was acknowledged that he had wider powers when necessary. Just as God might dispense himself from following his own rational laws of nature on occasion, so too might the royal power be absolved from the usual limits when truly necessary. If such authority was exploited too frequently or for too long, as in England in the 1630s and France in the time of Richelieu and Mazarin, opponents and vested interests might argue that temporary expedients were becoming permanent and therefore unconstitutional. In an age of almost constant warfare and ever increasing fiscal necessities, the safety of the public good or later of the state meant levying heavy wartime taxes that were supposed to be rescinded when peace came. This was inevitably just when the royal debts were at their highest and when peacetime taxation was required to pay them off: so because such beliefs limited taxation, a fiscal crisis followed every major war.[20]

What was the proper sphere of the state and its king in which legislative and juridical authority should be exercised? Writing in 1610, Loyseau listed the regalian rights as the right to make laws, create offices, decide upon peace and war, to have the final decision in judicial matters, and mint money.[21] They certainly did not include the right to tax at will—which is thought by sociologists to be a crucial characteristic of a modern state, like a monopoly on taxation and military force. Even in terms of law the situation was not clear-cut. In theory royal legislation was paramount, but in practice, the local judicial-administrative rules drawn up by the sovereign law courts, the parlements, actually had the force of law in their areas of jurisdiction. Customary and provincial law was not necessarily subordinate to royal laws, and royal legislation was often modified by their existence. The King could indeed create offices, but the officeholders themselves decided who bought or inherited them, subject only to a small annual tax, and the royal administration was staffed by venal officeholders with mixed loyalties and conservative priorities.[22] Precisely because the crown's ability to impose long-term direct taxation was limited, the royal prerogative was exploited to the maximum, such that a whole second system of indirect taxation grew up alongside the traditional direct taxes, making for an extraordinarily complex fiscal system in which even accounting was difficult.

The evolution of the absolute monarchy was profoundly conditioned by these severe conceptual limitations, and its policies on government were constructed with the aim of circumventing them. To do this the crown took advantage of the haziness of the situation: there was no constitution, only a complex collection of practices, traditions and legislation. Edicts and innovations were endowed with propagandist preambles that justified them in terms of demand or traditional rights and duties. The great ordinances of the crown in the 1530s and 1660s were more of a codification than great innovations, although they did try to increase uniformity where possible.

The idea of a constitution did not exist for most of the period. When it did, by the 1770s, Turgot began an important *Memoir on the Municipalities* (by which he meant local institutions), by saying, 'Sire, the root of the problem comes from the fact that France has no constitution.' Some historians would disagree, arguing that France had, like England, a customary constitution, oscillating around a point, sometimes towards more power and sometimes towards less.[23] This English analogy misses the point because it implies that conflicts were essentially constitutional, when in fact they were mostly about the jurisdictional competence of various bodies, including the king's council *vis-à-vis* other institutions. Jurisdictional conflict was the stuff of life, taking place between council and church, clerical and secular judicial bodies (where the parlements had an advantage because a Gallican tradition gave them supreme jurisdiction here, if they dared to exercise it), and between corporate bodies in the towns. The old regime lived with ongoing confusions and contradictions that would be written out of any modern constitution worth the name. Legal historians have spilt much ink over the idea of fundamental laws in France. Yet, the only fundamental law that all sides agreed on was the Salic law, which prescribed inheritance of the throne in the male line and thus was an expression of paternalism. Even political theory had a jurisdictional tinge. Many of the 'political theorists' of the period were royal lawyers, or involved in state functions, and were therefore politically engaged. Discussion of royal policy or 'politics' was not encouraged, as these areas were mysteries of state that should remain veiled. With some notable exceptions, most authors were in the service of the King or his ministers. There were broadly speaking five types of writings that expressed ideas about monarchy. Royal legislation justified itself in terms of certain precepts that changed little over time, and these could be found in preambles to edicts as well as in speeches by the chancellors. There was a genre of advice to princes; another of royalist propaganda by loyal subjects or hired pens; the writings of critics of the monarchy, which were often prompted by religious persecution; and finally discussions of the nature of politics and authority by those we have come to regard as political theorists, from Hotman to Montesquieu and Mably.

A rather indefensible tradition in the history of ideas has tended to exclude lesser writers and particularly the Protestant and Jansenist opposition doctrines. These were in fact very influential even on the major theorists, as the references in Rousseau's works will confirm, and they served to change the image of the monarchy with the reading public much more effectively than the texts of those in the 'canon'. In the eighteenth century the French debate on the authority of the monarchy included, in addition to leading secular theorists, the influential works of canon lawyers such as Le Paige, Mey, and Maultrot, all Jansenists, and translations from British writers in particular. From the 1750s the English commonwealthmen were read, along with John Locke, and Shaftesbury on virtue, Bolingbroke on the notion of a patriot king.

In an essay devoted to showing how the many different elements of absolute monarchy fitted together, we can do no more than mention the importance of the key political theorists. Jean Bodin's notion of sovereignty helped crystallize the idea of a state as an entity with the crucial quality of sovereignty. Justus Lipsius's neo-Stoic insistence upon moderation and rationality in the use of power was perhaps even more influential, with the consequent development of the idea of rationality in the service of the state—*raison d'état*. Thomas Hobbes offered a defence of monarchy and the idea that the best form of legitimate power was a monarchy whose authority was based upon a contract that gave consent but which once given could not be revoked. In different ways, John Locke and Protestant opponents of the French persecution of the Huguenots after the revocation of the 1598 Edict of Nantes in 1685 stressed that government was based upon the consent of the people, in the form of a contract. Kings who behaved tyrannically broke the contract and forfeited their legitimate authority. The religious persecution by Louis XIV of both Protestants and Jansenists, to which could be added the devastation of the Palatinate, did indeed fuel an image of Louis as despotic or tyrannical. Fénelon and the circle of the duke of Burgundy, educating Louis's grandson, provided a well-informed critique of the monarchy in practice and called for a nobility of service. Fénelon's book *Télémaque* published in 1699 was a hugely popular text of the eighteenth century; he advocated a monarch who would be more virtuous in a new and secular sense, devoted to the interests of his people. But during the eighteenth century the ideological hegemony of the monarchy was further undermined by a revival of conciliarism and republicanism—the latter not in the sense of a desire for a republic without a king, but in the sense of a monarchy subordinate to the well-being of the people. Rousseau, Mably, and the Jansenists all challenged the notion of divine right monarchy with theories of legitimacy. The parlements expressed legal opposition to abuses of royal power, perhaps politicizing the public as much as the persecuted Jansenists themselves. The upshot was a decline in the sense of being ruled by a moderate and legitimate royal authority in favour of the idea that the French monarchy acted too frequently in a despotic fashion. Both the Jansenists and Rousseau regarded the source of sovereignty as popular, in the former case through a contentious interpretation of French history in terms of an ancient constitution going back to the Franks, and in the latter, on the basis of a theory of social contract. The remodelling of the parlements in 1771 by Chancellor Maupeou gave rise to a vehement patriotic critique of the monarchy in practice. The rise of a new concept of secular virtue undermined the social privileges of the nobility and legitimized a more egalitarian active citizenship.[24] The monarchy attempted to reconcile this with its own traditions somewhat unsuccessfully, by adopting the new rhetoric of a patriot king.[25] The tarnished image of Louis XV the (too) well-beloved gave way to Louis XVI as the philanthropist: *Louis le bienfaisant*. It failed to convince an educated public now steeped in a more participatory notion of citizenship.

INSTITUTIONS

What were the institutions of the absolute monarchy that enabled it to govern France? Beginning at the top, was the King in his council of state where policy was made. While kings could call whomever they liked to their council, in the middle ages and sixteenth century there was a presumption that great lords and princes of the blood would be called upon as 'ministers'—as members of the council of state were known. When Louis XIV desisted from this policy some years after the Fronde (civil wars, 1648–53), in which the princes played a part, it was because he both wanted to make clear his emancipation from this group, and could afford to do so. He found other ways of rewarding them with honours at court, in the army, and with provincial governorships. The secretaries of state were members of the council of state, but not all were called to the highest council, although they would all be members of at least one lesser council such as those of despatches, for internal affairs, the judicial council, or perhaps the council for finance. The religious council would contain the royal confessor, the archbishop of Paris, and perhaps another trusted cleric.

The central administration was in the hands of four secretaries of state: for foreign affairs; war; marine; Paris and the royal household combined; and at times a secretary for the Protestants; and in addition a superintendent of finances who was later, from Colbert's time, given the title of controller general; and a keeper of the seals and chancellor who were usually the same person. The chancellor had overall responsibility for the judiciary, the controller general for all aspects of financial administration, while the provinces were divided into four groups—one for each secretary of state, with the foreign affairs minister having the frontier provinces. The controller general did not have control over the ministerial budgets, so it was his duty to raise revenue, deal with the numerous commercial and economic issues that arose, as well as direct the intendants of finance. From the time of Louis XIV's minister Colbert, the financial bureaux were the most administratively developed in a bureaucratic sense. Sometimes the same minister held multiple offices, like Colbert, Louvois, or Pontchartrain.[26] Policy decisions were as far as we know genuinely conciliar, for although detailed records of the council have disappeared, it is known that even Louis XIV always sided with the majority (but of course ministers might seek to please him by taking his line). Numerous royal lawyers attended councils, drawn from a corporation of masters of requests, from whom commissioners might be drawn to serve as intendants in the provinces. The royal council as well as dealing with administration and policy, was the final court of appeal, for this long remained a judicial system of government more than an administrative one. A characteristic of the modern state was the development of different specialized councils. By the mid-eighteenth century many tasks had become a matter for routine administration, so some historians prefer to call the state at that point an 'administrative monarchy'. Given that so many aspects retained a juridical character and that informal techniques of power remained widespread, this remains a contentious assertion.[27]

The internal affairs of the kingdom can be considered as religious, judicial, or financial. The church formed a separate estate in this society and largely governed its own affairs, with its own courts and financial management. Its many clerical sees and offices offered considerable patronage to the monarchy, which used it chiefly to gratify the nobility in return for loyalty. The church prayed for society, so it offered a 'free gift' at its five-yearly assembly of clergy, which it collected through its own financial institutions. The alliance of throne and altar was close but not always easy, though it brought great advantages to the monarchy, as the church preached obedience to divinely-ordained power.

In terms of the development and reach of the state, the administration of justice was accepted by society. While disputes and differences took place between courts, their very existence was not unpopular. The royal courts were in a hierarchy. At the lower level were the *prévôtés*, then came the bailiwick or seneschal courts, and lastly the thirteen parlements. The latter were courts of appeal, with wide powers of 'police', making them extremely powerful institutions in their provinces, while the Paris parlement alone had jurisdiction over about two-fifths of France. Their *arrêts* or regulatory pronouncements had force of law, and royal legislation had to be registered by the parlements to ensure its conformity with previous legislation and provincial codes. They could and did remonstrate to the King if they felt that the law, the province, or their interests were being undermined. Conflicts between competing jurisdictions were the stuff of life in this regime, and early modern society was extremely litigious. By and large justice at this level was for the well-off, and concerned property cases. Nearly 100,000 seigneurial courts existed to deal with the affairs of the poorer rural population. Since there was until the eighteenth century no police force, only inefficient companies of archers in rural areas, criminal cases depended largely on local people or the *maréchaussée* first catching the offenders, which was relatively infrequent.

Financial administration

Royal lawyers exploited the concepts of the King as first magistrate of the kingdom, and the first seigneur, to erode independent jurisdictions, extending royal judicial authority as much as possible. The French monarchy was the richest and most populous of Europe, but the cost of war rose astronomically from the sixteenth century onwards. War was so constant from the 1630s that there were only brief periods of peace between then and 1713, while the eighteenth-century wars, lasting from three to seven years, were ever more costly. The strain on state finances was huge, always urgent, and it far outstripped the older-style credit system of the bankers. In the seventeenth century the crown needed to raise vastly greater revenues as well as develop different ways of raising loans. The great growth area of the state was therefore in the realm of fiscality and financial administration. A host of *traitants* and *financiers* came into being, as the credit system based on office and bankers in towns such as Lyon, gave way to a system based on office, estates, and above all, *la finance*—an extensive class of financiers tied to ministerial and noble clans.[28]

Two types of financial organization existed in regional France, those of the *pays d'élections*, and those of the *pays d'états*. The *élections* were areas of financial jurisdiction over direct taxation created in the fourteenth century, and extended over northern and central France; their tribunals, staffed by *élus*, numbered about 150 in the seventeenth century. The extension of larger *généralités* in the mid-sixteenth century, provided a further fiscal circumscription. Each *généralité* had a *bureau des finances* and a dozen or more treasurers general who oversaw its fiscal system. The peripheral provinces, most acquired by the crown later than the institution of the *élections*, had retained their provincial estates composed of representatives of the three orders of society, presided over by the royal governor or a loyal archbishop. The estates had their own financial organization and gave a free gift to the crown that was often agreed only after hard bargaining and royal confirmation of local privileges. Chancellor Marillac tried to extend the more productive system of *élections* to these provinces in the 1620s, but while he succeeded in Guyenne, he provoked revolt in Burgundy, Dauphiné, and Provence. These provincial estates subsequently bought off this attempt, and thus along with others retained a privileged position compared to the *pays d'élections*, as they paid far less—and therefore remained ripe for further fiscal pressure from the monarchy. Although the estates represented provincial particularism, the crown was not hostile in principle to the estates, for they were regarded as legitimate institutions providing a secure source of loans to the treasury on the basis of their relatively sound fiscal administration. Moreover, in a legitimate legal monarchy, there was no sense, until the later eighteenth century, that conformity should be introduced for its own sake.

The collection of taxes was of course an even more contentious aspect of the state. There was a strong belief that the King should live off his own revenues from his own lands or domain, from the taxes on commerce, the receipts from the sale of offices, and the receipts from the *taille*, a tax on persons and goods that had become permanent after the Hundred Years War. The parlements and estates would reject or undermine new peacetime taxes, and local hostility to fiscal agents was often vehement. In this time of perpetual fiscal crisis, the government therefore increasingly resorted to indirect taxation. It did indeed raise the *taille* as much as possible, but costs of collection were high, due to poor organization and corruption. A host of monopolies, tolls, entry taxes, urban sales taxes, known as *octrois* and *aides*, and the hated salt tax, the *gabelle*, were increased, invented, or extended. They were often collected by associations of tax farmers who paid in advance and kept the profits. Colbert united many of these indirect taxes into five great tax farms run by forty farmers general who bought the lease for five years with ready money up front. These men and many of the financial officials were also bankers of a sort, investing the state's receipts that they held temporarily for their own benefit. The farmers general built up a huge force of *commis* or employees who collected the taxes and were highly unpopular. This organization formed in parts of France what some might wish to interpret as a privatized modern administration.

Corruption was a matter of degree, but the whole system suffered from what we would regard as systemic inefficiency as well as more or less blatant corruption. The fact that the whole provincial and royal administration was run by people who had purchased their offices did not make for zeal and innovation. Venality of office was frequently extended, effectively raising loans from the rich who in return for the price of the office, and the office itself, would receive *gages* amounting to a rate of interest on their purchase price. Because the commissions paid to financiers to sell offices amounted to 25 per cent, and because the *gages* (which were interest payments not salaries) continued ever after, the sales provided a short-term gain and a long-term loss. The crown could never afford to abolish venality even though it was aware of the disadvantages.

In the face of its fiscal difficulties, the crown created a new level of administration, the intendants. They were invariably officeholders, often clients of governors or ministers, most often also masters of requests from the council, with special commissions that gave them wide powers of inspection to root out corruption and increase revenues. What made them different from many officials was the fact that their powers depended upon their royal commission. They were thus judicial officers specially appointed to a generality, to serve as the eyes and ears of the ministry with wide powers of intervention. Naturally, they often engaged in conflicts with existing authorities, most notably with the *élus* staffing the *élections,* whose task they almost supplanted. Their role developed over a long period. Officers with royal commissions had begun to be used under Henry II, they then became much more frequent in the 1630s, and were so extensively employed and so unpopular in 1648 that they had to be withdrawn upon the demand of the rebellious parlements. Cardinal Mazarin returned to them after the civil war, and then Colbert made them a mainstay of his administrative efforts in the provinces. He conferred a huge range of tasks upon them, requiring reports on all manner of matters, from the loyalty of local elites to fiscal corruption, commerce, and manufacturing. Too many local conflicts undermined their powers of action, and Colbert for example often had to remind them to respect established jurisdictions and work with powerful local allies. Naturally with so many tasks, they needed help, and gradually, in the eighteenth century, the intendant became an intendancy, with sub-delegates and clerks who were recruited locally. Tocqueville and later historians saw them as ruling provincial France and as the prime agents of administrative centralization. The picture today is more nuanced, for studies have shown that compromise with the local elites was often the way forward. Their functions became increasingly well organized as the century progressed.[29]

The great problem for the absolute monarchy was how to tax the rich. Most nobles and clerics were severely under-taxed in terms of their wealth, and even the richer urban bourgeois could manage to buy some minor office that would exempt them from the *taille*. Forced loans were levied on the corps and corporations, urban privileges were threatened and thus required to be bought off, and nobles might be subject to arbitrary levies (*taxes d'office*) by intendants and those who claimed exemptions had to produce their titles for royal inquiries. Failure to produce their written titles could of course push them down into the ranks of the bourgeois, as usurpers, and the inquiries were highly unpopular. Such an inquiry preceded the revolt in Brittany in 1675, where the local elite was more or less complicit with the rebels and notably failed to reimpose order. Nevertheless, such inquiries were successful in stamping out illegitimate exemptions through usurpation under Louis XIV—leaving the door open wider for the monarchy to sell titles of nobility to those who could live nobly and afford to buy ennobling offices.

Means and Techniques of Government

How did the absolute monarchy make use of the various means of government open to it, how did it operate in practice? The administration and judicial institutions of course provided a vital source of control over society. This was limited by the isolation of many areas of France, poor communications, a relative ignorance of provincial society and even geography by the central government, and by the serious limitations inherent in a venal system of office holding. Provincial parlements and estates may have been powerful, acting on behalf of the King, but they were often able to resist his demands by inefficiency, foot-dragging, and even open opposition. They were fiercely attached to their privileges and to their provinces, and were often dominated by conflicting factions. On the other hand, they tended to perform their functions relatively well given the prevailing standards, and were afraid of the King and his ministers. The fact that provincial society was dominated by powerful elites could be an advantage for the monarchy if it knew how to use them. These families either had ties to grand courtly families or had networks of friends and relations in many of the important local offices.[30] Far from such relations declining in the early modern period, they were co-opted into the service of the state over time, and perhaps the most efficient centralization that took place was the centralization of patronage and clientage in the hands of the King during the seventeenth century. As governors, the Condé dominated Burgundy from the 1630s right up to the Revolution, and controlled access to many local offices through their favour, and their regiments provided important opportunities for local nobles. Under Louis XIV the duc de Chaulnes was powerful in Brittany, the Villeroy for generations in the Lyonnais, the Noailles in Languedoc, the Harcourt in Normandy. Let us not accept the myth of the domestication of a nobility that was essentially in opposition to the monarchical power. The nobility as a whole had never been in opposition to the monarchy, only some families and interests, and the nobility had much to gain from the honour of service, and access to patronage and royal finance at court. The monarchy continued to rely on the informal techniques of political management that employed trusted members of the higher nobility right up to the 1780s.[31] Later in the eighteenth century it is possible that the noble or upper bourgeois elites, encouraged by their power sharing, yearned for fuller local control in the face of what they regarded as an inefficient, corrupt, and increasingly despotic monarchy. The urban elites were becoming citizens and wanted fuller rights.[32]

The price of advancement to lucrative and prestigious offices, in finances in particular, and social ascension, was loyalty to the crown and its ministers. While sixteenth-century France suffered from much weaker royal power in some regions, the ruthless policy of Richelieu and the astute political management of Louis XIV effected a transformation. A compromise emerged during the reign of Louis XIV between crown and local elites. Conflicts remained, for the differences of interest and perception were sometimes too great, but cooperation became a mutually beneficial system. The local elites, both urban and rural, worked for the monarchy, and for themselves. By means of their control of provincial estates, tax burdens were transferred to the peasants in *pays d'états*, and the elite profited from the attractive investment opportunities in royal finances. Nevertheless, such was the need for finance in the reign of Louis XIV, and so limited his means to raise direct taxes on the poor, that the nobility and officeholders came under huge fiscal pressure and it is clear they deeply resented it. Two direct taxes fell on them, a new departure: the *capitation* of 1695 and the *dixième* of 1710, both intended to do away with exemptions. These created precedents for the *cinquantième* of 1725 and the *dixième* of 1733 and the *vingtièmes* of 1749 and later.

In the last twenty-five years historians have come to understand the importance of patronage and clientage not only for social mobility but also for political control. Although official documentation was careful to avoid any suggestion of negotiation between crown and corps, the reality was different. Governors and intendants, loyal clients of royal ministers or of the King himself, would intervene behind the scenes to manage assembles and effect solutions. Ministers would try bluff, threats, often in parallel with covert intervention. Over generations these techniques created an impression of obedience and most of the time genuine obedience. Complex networks of patronage and clientage stretching out into the provinces, and back, came together at the royal court. Largely as a consequence of recognizing the importance of patronage, historians have re-evaluated the role of the court in the absolute monarchies. The court was a characteristic and defining institution in a monarchy, for every monarch had a household which reflected his *gloire*, his power, and influence. The court was a theatre of power, bringing together the principal actors in all spheres. Ceremonial and display were employed to exalt the monarchy, to impress foreign ambassadors and the nobility. Representation was an important facet of the government in all absolute monarchies. Courts brought together an impressive range of performance and image designed to enhance the *gloire* of the monarch and create a sense of the permanence and legitimacy of royal power and authority.[33] This cultural management emanated out into the provinces, challenging provincial cultural autonomy and creating a sense of unity.[34]

The style of the courts that so characterized these monarchies had its roots in the renaissance, and courts as social and cultural spaces represented the new codes of civility. This is a theme much stressed by the earliest sociologist of court society, Norbert Elias, whose work was taken up by historians in the 1970s. Elias made an invaluable point about rulers preserving equilibrium, because they could never entirely dominate their courts, and they therefore adopted a policy of maintaining a balance between rival factions. Elias saw court society as a coherent social figuration of key significance for the whole period and indeed for the subsequent spread of civility out into provincial and bourgeois society; more recent historians, while concurring, have extended the perspective into the political domain.[35] As English historians were the first to argue, the court was in fact the central institution of government in absolute monarchies. Ministers were courtiers, kept in place by factions, and their bureaux were often in close proximity to the court, if not actually in the same building (as in Versailles). To survive as bureaucrats, they had to operate within a realm dominated by the King and his courtiers, any of whom had posts giving them access to the royal ear. Such access carried influence, certainly for patronage, but also for policy in the case of aristocratic trusted advisers. The court was intimately connected to the royal finances, as the financiers in France at least were mostly nobles who were connected to ministerial clans and channelled the huge wealth of the rich seigneurs into royal financial contracts. Constant pressure was needed to make sure the crown did not renege on its deals, access was vital, and so the web of influences at court was crucial to the higher nobility. Many of these families had not only captured the important court offices under Louis XIV, to retain them for generations, but were also patrons of provincial networks of clientage and influence.[36] These were now put at the service of the King, as we have seen above. The court was thus the centre of power broking in an age when the administrative system with its embryonic bureaucracy was too corrupt, inefficient, and conflict-ridden to sort out a crisis. Thus the court was a vital institution for political management.

RESISTANCES

In spite of its lapses into force and exemplary punishments, the absolute monarchy was certainly not a dictatorial regime removing all rights and privileges from estates and corporations in society. On the contrary, it was acknowledged as the guarantor of justice, security, and religion. All groups in society needed this role to be played, and there was no credible alternative in France to monarchy. Not until the American constitution was agreed as late as 1789 was there a credible republican alternative for a large state. Monarchy was therefore not challenged and it provided what France wanted. Opposition came from the defence of interests within the regime and was not fundamentally opposed to it ideologically. Most nobles had remained loyal to the monarchy or their conception of it. The officeholders who sometimes resisted royal authority nevertheless had much to gain from loyalty to the regime, for their office was their investment. Nevertheless, although venality of office ensured a low-cost administration, it was hardly proactive and the beneficiaries could drag their feet to prevent innovation and change.

In the seventeenth century if serious local disorder threatened they would generally repress it if they could or dared, but they were not above secretly encouraging resistance to fiscal demands from the state that undermined their own position as well as that of their peasants—most officeholders owned rural property with seigneurial rights attached. In the sixteenth and seventeenth centuries popular revolts against fiscality were common, with some lasting some months, until harvest time, and involving villages, towns, and sometimes whole regions. Such were the *Croquants* of Périgord in 1594, the *Nu-Pieds* in Normandy in 1639, or the Breton revolts in the revolt of the stamped paper tax in 1675. Urban revolts were common, a typical one being in Aix-en-Provence in 1630. These revolts reveal intense hostility to the hated *gabeleurs*, as employees of the fisc were called, in the seventeenth century.[37] In the eighteenth century the hostility was redirected towards the seigneurs and seigneurial dues, probably owing in part to an increased acceptance of the legitimacy of state claims and institutions, and perhaps the population was more respectful because of transformation through the determined inculcation of Catholic reform, with internalized authority and respect for hierarchy.[38] And yet, the seigneurs were increasingly challenged…but by whom? Was it by richer peasants and even by other seigneurs, resentful of attempts to exploit even them, or was it by poorer peasants resentful of profit-oriented encroachments on common lands and much needed traditional rights of pasture and gleaning?[39] In 1789 the outpouring of hostility to the seigneurial system in the countryside showed how far hostility to seigneurialism had developed.

The monarchy had been able to cease calling a national representative institution after 1614. This gave it a huge advantage over England, with a parliament often reluctant to fund wars, while the Spanish monarchy in the seventeenth century made a sort of deal by which the nobility in the Cortes sold out the peasants to the monarchy.[40] In France the Estates-General remained alive in historical thought, but this victory left the monarchy pre-eminent. The only institutions that could cause serious disruption to royal policy were the provincial estates, which could be useful if well managed, and the parlements, and in particular the parlement of Paris. In the mid-seventeenth century a number of parlements resisted royal fiscal policies and administrative changes that accompanied them. They had little in common, for their own particularism prevailed, and even less in common with the princes who also joined in the Fronde, so the monarchy was able to put an end to the strife by 1653. The royal victory was less outright than subsequent propaganda suggested. In a policy not dissimilar to that of Henry IV after the Wars of Religion, Louis XIV and Mazarin offered concessions and honour at court in return for princely submission. Thus the *grands*, who had harboured ambitions of aristocratic liberty and a natural right to offer royal counsel, especially during a regency, began to appreciate the advantages of cooperation, at which point the era of the overmighty subject ended. During the personal rule of Louis XIV the courts were dealt with through a mixture of repression and intimidation combined with sensible political management that allowed them preserve most of their powers of jurisdiction and recruitment. They were after all necessary for the preservation of order and the governance of the regions. Late in the reign, in 1713, the crown's religious policy provoked several parlements to resistance, along with a number of bishops and many *curés* and ecclesiastical orders. The thorny issue of the relative powers of throne and altar, independence from Rome, and fiscal policy, fuelled a number of severe crises between crown and parlements. These have been variously interpreted as jurisdictional disputes, or as more constitutional conflicts. The probability is that jurisdictional conflict gave rise to constitutional rhetoric and claims. The result of decades of struggles, notably the 1730s, the 1750s, 1771–4, was to educate the public in those mysteries of state, and expose the constitutional issues that were best left under a veil.[41] In the 1760s there was significant conflict over fiscal reforms in which accusations of ministerial despotism were levelled by the courts at the ministry because fiscal measures were now regularly enacted without going through the royal council of state. The rhetoric of despotism was becoming increasingly familiar under the absolute monarchy.

The monarchy had, in spite of its fiscal pressure, remained largely respectful of intermediary institutions. It preserved its legitimacy by according respect to the parlements, except to those in areas that revolted. These were not of course representative institutions, but in the absence of the Estates-General after 1614, it was widely believed they defended the King's subjects against an excess of royal authority. To exile them, or worse to emasculate them as Chancellor Maupeou did in 1771, exposed the monarchy to accusations of 'despotism'. These had been rehearsed during the *parlementaire* crises, because the religious group appealing to the courts to defend themselves from persecution (the Jansenists) revived earlier constitutional arguments from the middle ages and the sixteenth century about despotism. Like the Protestants, who saw the 1685 revocation of the Edict of Nantes that had granted them freedom of worship as an illegitimate act and their persecution as tyrannical, the Jansenists believed persecution of their beliefs was equally tyrannical. The Jansenist quarrel dominated the politics of the period 1713 to 1771, providing a political education for the Parisian bourgeoisie and artisans. Thus, in 1771, the Maupeou coup destroyed the equilibrium in the state, and led to the association of monarchy with despotism. It set the stage for the revolution and for the idea of absolute monarchy that this essay has tried to counter.

The Baroque State in the Eighteenth Century

The eighteenth century witnessed important developments in the monarchy and equally some important failures. The absolute monarchy took on more tasks more efficiently and its administration became more routine. The intendancies became more like governing agencies, with sub-delegates and numerous *commis*, while their powers of interference were increased. In comparison with the sixteenth century France was more policed, more ordered, but we should still not imagine that the forces of order were able to face the challenges efficiently. New responsibilities assumed ranged from poor relief to road building for military purposes, to forestry management (for maritime construction). But in an age of ever increasing military and naval expenditure, the absolute monarchy struggled to play its role as the dominant European power. At the root of this was its most important failure: the monarchy was unable to reform and adapt the fiscal system sufficiently. Reforms were indeed undertaken, but resistance from the privileged and at court continued to undermine attempts by controllers general to include the wealthy more in the tax base. Administrative progress was made in gathering information on landed capital, making under-declarations more difficult, but the three major wars all resulted in fiscal crises. In spite of the spectacular growth in overseas trade, commercial wealth was never sufficiently taxed by a system that remained directed towards landed wealth. Alongside this went the inability to develop a system of state credit that could deliver loans in wartime at a low interest rate. The failure of John Law's system of paper money tied to a state bank in 1720 made it impossible to move away from the seventeenth-century credit mechanisms based on the farmers general, the sale of *rentes* (annuities) through provincial estates and municipalities, and loans registered through the Paris parlement. French credit was more expensive than British, based on the Bank of England and the assent of Parliament. Necker as finance minister favoured a more British model for French finances, but he overborrowed. The fiscal crisis that followed the American War prompted controller general Calonne, with the support of Louis XVI, to propose major reforms that fell short of conceding a share of power to the notables in society. At this point the resistance of the privileged and the parlements to what seemed to them to be an extension of despotism was crucial, and the final failure of the absolute monarchy was assured by incompetent political management. What could have been a fairly limited rescheduling of debts was turned into a huge crisis that snowballed.[42]

The court system of government dating from Louis XIV's time had developed serious weaknesses under his successors. Ministerial rivalries paralysed the system in the 1780s. The political culture of the regime required constant political management from the ruler, which was an art that Louis XIV excelled at, but Louis XVI was sadly lacking in this ability, while his Queen, Marie Antoinette, was a political disaster. Her Austrian origins and association with an unpopular alliance provided an excuse for vitriolic whispering and pamphleteering that originated at court from opposing factions and disappointed interests. The final crisis of the regime saw the political institutions of the monarchy in conflict with each other and a notable failure of management. The baroque state was not necessarily doomed to failure, but it had prolonged structures and practices that dated from its greatest period into an eighteenth century that underwent significant economic, social, cultural, and intellectual developments.

As we have suggested, the absolute monarchy survived and developed by rising above society, by taking an authoritarian direction shared by all states in this period, of necessity. With the benefit of hindsight, it could be argued that the absolute monarchy was in contradiction with the European heritage of representative ideas that, albeit weakened for generations, remained characteristic of many corporate institutions even in the monarchy. The eighteenth century witnessed the rise of a new language of virtue, citizenship, and patriotism, which found expression in a new public sphere in which the elites notably participated. The new ideas of the Enlightenment were widely diffused among the elites, and integrated into the monarchy itself, but the court and the nobility came to be seen as unvirtuous from the 1750s onwards. There was a cultural shift that made it hard for the mystery of monarchy to survive without major concessions or reforms in a more rational and sceptical age. Demystification of the monarchy was apparent in the relative failure of its own representation programmes. Neo-Classicism was inimical to monarchy, because of its classical republican imagery. A public sphere developed, with public participation increasingly taking place: in towns, public health measures, lighting embellishments, one senses a rise of citizenship in many small ways. This was legitimized by patriotic discourse and the concept of virtue. Virtue was no longer essentially Christian, it was no longer associated with warlike qualities befitting a noble or a king, but with *bienfaisance* and participation, with active citizenship.

Conclusions

From the later sixteenth century onwards the absolute monarchy developed into a state. This process owed most to *ad hoc* responses to internal disorder and external military requirements in an age of new military strategies, economic crisis, and fierce dynastic rivalry. The state was far from simply modern or bureaucratic, for it employed a range of techniques of government, from administration to patronage to representation. It was on the one hand increasingly above society, and on the other deeply embedded in it and dependent upon the social conceptions that structured it. In the end the absolute monarchy fell out of step with society and some of the strong European traditions of representation and liberty, and it had never been able to put an end to traditional forms of resistance. The pre-eminence of the monarchy, its incursions into everyday life, its corruption and inefficiency, its spectacular own goals such as imprisoning writers with *lettres de cachet*, or remodelling the parlements, as well as the far from majestic qualities of its later rulers—all these generated criticism. From the mid-eighteenth century everyone knew reform was necessary, but it was going to be conditional on granting more power to the nation. Thus the issue of who represented the nation became increasingly important. The royal claim was that the nation was embodied in the King himself. Critics saw the nation as separate, but who could speak for it? The parlements were not representative institutions, though they were able to block reform. Yet Maupeou proved that they could be silenced, while no one wanted an oligarchy of magistrates any more than they did an arbitrary government. The French remained royalist, but they wanted more participation, more citizenship, and less despotism from the monarchy.

In response to the reform proposals in 1787–8 society fractured along many different fault lines, some traditional, some new. This in turn led to a situation too complex and ideologically charged for the ministry to resolve successfully using the traditional techniques at its disposal. The credit crisis led to the calling of the long dormant Estates-General in 1789 just when an economic crisis hit hardest. The traditional form of the

Estates was widely criticized, and even before it met the tensions between the nobility and the Third Estate promised bitter conflict. Many were already arguing that what was needed was an assembly with wider powers truly representing the France of the day, not that of 1614. Such an assembly would be called not the Estates-General, but a National Assembly. Perhaps this road to a constitutional monarchy was inevitable, certainly it had an element of European typicality. Although the French conflicts of 1789 were significant, it is worth bearing in mind that from the sixteenth to the eighteenth century, whenever an absolute monarchy was forced to call upon its representative institution to ask for money, it usually had to trade power for money. The fiscal needs of monarchies at first led to more powerful states, and then in many cases tipped the balance in favour of representative institutions. This is what happened in 1789. A spectacular collapse spelt the end of the French absolute monarchy. What was new in 1789 was the desire of significant sections of society to participate in government not just to control money supply, but to play a role in governing themselves in a more liberal regime. The collapse of absolute monarchy created the space for the contentious construction of a representative regime. That process more than any other set the scene for the end of absolute monarchy in Europe during the following century.

Notes

1. Historians and historical sociologists have tended to look at state formation and the nature of the state differently, the former seeking patterns and the latter steeped in empirical research. For a textbook sociological survey see G Poggi, *The Development of the Modern State* (London, 1978). Looking very schematic and misleading today, such a view has been updated in sociology with works such as C. Tilly (ed.), *The Formation of National States in Western Europe* (Princeton, 1975). The view that bureaucratic centralization was a 'rational choice' in the face of war and economic development underlies much sociological thinking, which continues to draw heavily on the late and untypical Prussian case. More recently 'third wave' theories have appeared. See T. Ertman, *The Birth of Leviathan: Building States and Regimes in Medieval and Early Modern Europe* (Cambridge, 1997), esp. pp. 1–34; P. S. Gorski, 'Beyond Marx and Hintze? Third-Wave Theories of Early Modern State Formation', *Comparative Studies in Society and History*, 43/4 (Oct. 2001), 851–86; and J. Adams, *The Familial State: Ruling Families and Merchant Capitalism in Early Modern Europe* (Ithaca, NY, 2005); revisiting founding father Max Weber to rethink the role of the Protestant religion as an essential mental transformation facilitating the rise of the state, is P. S. Gorski, *The Disciplinary Revolution: Calvinism, Confessionalism and the Growth of State Power in Early Modern Europe* (Chicago, 2003). Two sociological survey essays that integrate recent historical research and include the imperial dimension until recently neglected by historians are K. A. Stanbridge, 'England, France and their North American Colonies: An Analysis of Absolutist State. Power in Europe and in the New World', *Journal of Historical Sociology*, 10/1 (Mar. 1997), 27–55; and J. C. A. Smith, 'Europe's Atlantic Empires: Early Modern State Formation Reconsidered', *Political Power and Social Theory*, 17 (2005), 100–50.
2. A. de Tocqueville, *The Old Regime and the Revolution*. For historical views since the 1960s, which often deal with the state in terms of 'the ancien régime', see classic collections of articles

by H. Lubasz (ed.), *The Development of the Modern State* (New York, 1964), and R. Hatton (ed.), *Louis XIV and Absolutism* (London, 1976). In the light of recent research, the French case, which has often been seen as paradigmatic, actually does not fit the sociological models very well, while historians have been reticent on broader questions of power. More dialogue between all these approaches is needed. See J. B. Collins, *The State in Early Modern France* (2nd edn., Cambridge, 2009) and for a highly pertinent monograph, D. Parrott, *Richelieu's Army: War Government and Society in France, 1624–1642* (Cambridge, 2001).

3. M. Weber, Guenther Roth, and Claus Wittich (eds.), *Economy and Society: An Outline of Interpretive Sociology*, i (Berkeley, Los Angeles, and London, 1978). On bureaucracy see Max Weber, 'The Presuppositions and Causes of Bureaucracy', in R. K. Merton, A. P. Gray, Barbara Hockey, and H. Selvin (eds.), *Reader in Bureaucracy* (Glencoe, Ill., 1952), 60–8, and on war, the influential essay by Otto Hintze, 'Military Organization and the Organization of the State', in F. Gilbert, *The Historical Essays of Otto Hintze* (New York, 1975), 178–215.

4. See P. R. Campbell and C. Grell, 'La Cour et les modèles du Pouvoir', in Marcello Fantoni (ed.), *Les Cours en Europe: Bilan historiographique* (Rome: Bulzoni collection 'Europa delle Corte', 2011).

5. B. Guénée, 'L'Histoire de l'État en France à la fin du moyen âge, vue par les Français depuis cent ans', *Revue historique*, 232 (1964), 331–60, and J. Vicens Vives, 'The Administrative Structure of the State in the Sixteenth and Seventeenth Centuries', in H. J. Cohn (ed.), *Government in Reformation Europe* (London, 1971), 58–87. The latter is a critique of R. Mousnier and F. Hartung, 'Quelques problèmes concernant la monarchie absolue', in *Comitato internazionale di Scienze storiche, X Congresso internazionale di Scienze storiche, Roma, 1955, Relazioni*, iv (Florence, 1955), 1–55—a seminal article that provoked considerable debate.

6. For this phrase, see Vicens Vives, 'Administrative Structure', 60. A new picture of this many-faceted 'tumultuous reality' has been emerging in e.g. A. Jouanna, *Le Devoir de révolte: La Noblesse française et la gestation de l'État moderne, 1559–1661* (Paris, 1989); D. Crouzet, *Les Guerriers de Dieu: La Violence au temps des troubles de religion, vers 1525–vers 1610* (Seyssel, 2005); M. Greengrass, *Governing Passions: Peace and Reform in the French Kingdom, 1576–1585* (Oxford, 2007); S. Carroll, *Martyrs and Murderers: The Guise Family and the Making of Europe* (Oxford, 2009); R. Mettam, *Power and Faction in Louis XIV's France* (Oxford, 1988).

7. See R. Mousnier, *La Monarchie absolue en Europe: Du ve siècle à nos jours* (Paris, 1982). For early 17th-cent. developments, see E. Thuau, *Raison d'État et pensée politique à l'époque de Richelieu* (Paris, 1966). Two more recent volumes trace the wider intellectual context: *The Cambridge History of Political Thought 1450–1700*, ed. J. H. Burns and M. Goldie (Cambridge 1995); and G. Burgess and H. Lloyd (eds.), *European Political Thought 1450–1700: Religion, Law and Philosophy* (New Haven, Conn., 2008), esp. chapters by J. H. Salmon and R. von Freidburg. On England in relation to absolute monarchy, see J. Sommerville, *Politics and Ideology in England, 1603–1640* (London, 1986); G. Burgess, *Absolute Monarchy and the Stuart Constitution* (New Haven, Conn., and London, 1996) both largely summarized in the preceding volumes. See the meticulous integration of new research on ideas by F. Cosandey and R. Descimon in *L'Absolutisme en France: Histoire et Historiographie* (Paris, 2002).

8. J. Cornette, *Le Roi de guerre: Essai sur la souveraineté dans la France du Grand Siècle* (Paris, 1993).

9. Nicolas Le Roux, *Un régicide au nom de Dieu: L'Assassinat d'Henri III* (Paris, 2006); J. Boucher *La Cour de Henri III* (Rennes, 1986); M. Greengrass, *France in the Age of Henri IV: The Struggle for Stability* (London, 1984).

10. On conceptions of authority in France, see H. A. Lloyd, *The State, France, and the Sixteenth Century* (London, 1983); Cosandey and Descimon, *L'Absolutisme en France*.
11. On the meaning of 'lo stato' in Machiavelli, see J. H. Hexter, *The Vision of Politics on the Eve of the Reformation: More, Machiavelli, and Seyssel* (London and New York, 1973), 150–78. The limited vision of authority that prevailed in society is stressed by J. Russell Major, 'The French Renaissance Monarchy as Seen through the Estates General', *Studies in the Renaissance*, 9 (1962), 113–25.
12. C. Seyssel, *The Monarchy of France*, ed. Donald R. Kelley, tr. J. H. Hexter, additional tr. by M. Sherman (1515, publ. 1519) (New Haven, Conn., 1981); J. B. Bossuet, *Politics Drawn from the Very Words of Holy Scripture*, ed. P. Riley (Cambridge, 1990).
13. A L. Moote, 'The French Crown Versus its Judicial and Financial Officers', *Journal of Modern History*, 34 (1962), 146–60; R. R. Harding, *Anatomy of a Power Elite: The Provincial Governors of Early Modern France* (New Haven, Conn., and London, 1978); for a contrasting view see R. J. Bonney, *Political Change in France under Richelieu and Mazarin, 1624–1661* (Oxford, 1976), which owes an interpretative debt to Pagès.
14. See G. Pagès, 'Essai sur l'évolution des institutions administratives en France du xvie siècle à la fin du xviie siècle', *Revue d'Histoire Moderne*, 12 (1932), and see his *La Monarchie d'ancien régime* (Paris, 1928). For the most recent French correctives, see O. Chaline, *La France de Louis XIV* (Paris, 2005); L. Bély, *La France au xviie siècle: Puissance de l'État, contrôle de la société* (Paris, 2009).
15. D. Dee, *Expansion and Crisis in Louis XIV's France: Franche-Comté and the Absolute Monarchy, 1674–1715* (Rochester, NY, 2009).
16. For studies, see n. 34, and for a comprehensive argument, W. Beik, 'Absolute Monarchy as Social Collaboration', *Past and Present*, 188/1 (2005), 195–224.
17. E. Kantorowicz, *The King's Two Bodies: A Study in Medieval Political Theology* (Princeton, 1981; originally 1957).
18. C. Seyssel, *La Grande Monarchie de France*, ed. Pujol (Paris, 1961), 116.
19. See R. Descimon in J. Le Goff (ed.), *La Longue Durée de l'État*, as well as Cosandey and Descimon, *L' Absolutisme*.
20. Philip Hoffman and Kathryn Norberg (eds.), *Fiscal Crises, Liberty, and Representative Government 1450–1789* (Stanford, Calif., 1994).
21. C. Loyseau, *Loyseau: Treatise of Orders and Plain Dignities*, ed. and tr. H. A. Lloyd (Cambridge, 1994).
22. On venality of office see K. W. Swart, *Sale of Offices in the Seventeenth Century* (Utrecht, 1980); R. Mousnier, *La Vénalité des offices sous Henri IV et Louis XIII* (Paris, 1971); D. D. Bien, 'Offices, Corps, and a System of State Credit: The Uses of Privilege under the Ancien Régime', in Keith Michael Baker (ed.), *The French Revolution and the Creation of Modern Political Culture*, i (Oxford, 1987), 89–114; W. Doyle, *Venality: The Sale of Offices in Eighteenth-Century France* (Oxford, 1996).
23. Antoine, *Conseil du roi*, 21.
24. See M. Linton, *The Politics of Virtue in Enlightenment France* (Basingstoke, 2001).
25. For patriotism, see D. A. Bell, *The Cult of the Nation in France: Inventing Nationalism, 1680–1800* (Cambridge, Mass., 2001); E. Dziembowski, *Un nouveau patriotisme français, 1750–1770: La France face à la puissance anglaise à l'époque de la guerre de Sept Ans*, SVEC 365 (Oxford, 1998); J. M. Smith, *Nobility Reimagined: The Patriotic Nation in Eighteenth-Century France* (Ithaca, NY, and London, 2005); P. R. Campbell, 'The Politics of Patriotism in France (1770–1788)', *French History*, 24 (2010), 550–75.

26. See 'Serviteurs du roi: Quelques aspects de la fonction publique au xviie siècle', special issue, *Dix-Septième Siècle*, 42–3 (1959); D. Richet, 'La Formation des grands serviteurs de l'État', *L'Arc*, 65 (1976), 54–61; more recently, J. Meyer, *Colbert* (Paris, 1984); C. Frostin, 'L'Organisation ministérielle sous Louis XIV: Cumul d'attributions et situations conflictuelles', *Revue d'histoire du Droit français et étranger*, 58 (1980), 201–26; an impressive survey of most aspects of the central government of France in the long reign of Louis XIV is now T. Sarmant and M. Stoll, *Régner et Gouverner : Louis XIV et ses ministres* (Paris, 2010).
27. R. Mousnier (ed.), *Le Conseil du roi de Louis XII à la Révolution* (Paris, 1970) and M. Antoine, *Le Conseil du roi sous le règne de Louis XV* (Geneva, 1970).
28. Recent work on state finance in practice has done much to revise the image of a powerful state by revealing its strategies: M. Wolfe, *The Fiscal System of Renaissance France* (New Haven, Conn., 1972); J. Dent, *Crisis in Finance: Crown, Financiers and Society in Seventeenth Century France* (New York, 1973); R. Bonney, *The King's Debts: Finance and Politics in France 1589–1661* (Oxford, 1981); F. Bayard, *Le Monde des financiers au xviie siècle* (Paris, 1988); D. Dessert, *Argent, pouvoir et société au grand siècle* (Paris, 1984); D. Hickey, *The Coming of French Absolutism: The Struggle for Tax Reform in the Province of Dauphiné, 1540–1640* (Toronto, 1986); J. B. Collins, *Fiscal Limits of Absolutism: Direct Taxation in Early Seventeenth-Century France* (Berkeley, Calif., 1988); J. Félix, *Finances et politique au siècle des Lumières: Le Ministère L' Averdy, 1763–1768* (Paris, 1999); M. Potter, *Corps and Clienteles: Public Finance and Political Change in France, 1688–1715* (Aldershot, 2004); and on the comparative weight of taxation, see R. Bonney (ed.), *The Rise of the Fiscal State in Europe, c. 1200–1815* (Oxford, 1999).
29. On intendants, see Harding, *Anatomy*; R. Bonney, *Fiscal State*; A. Smedley-Weill, *Les Intendants de Louis XIV* (Paris, 1995); F.-X. Emmanuelli, *Pouvoir royal et vie régionale en Provence au déclin de la monarchie* (2 vols. Lille, 1974); H. Fréville, *L'Intendance de Bretagne, 1689–1790* (3 vols. Paris, 1953); M. Bordes, *L' Administration provinciale et municipale en France au xviiie siècle* (Paris, 1972); and the classic J. Marchand, *Un intendant sous Louis XIV: L' administration de Lebret en Provence (1687–1704)* (Paris, 1889).
30. On patronage as government, see P. Lefebvre, 'Aspects de la fidélité en France au xviie siècle: Le cas des agents du prince de Condé', *Revue Historique*, 250 (1973), 59–106; Y. Durand, *Hommage à Roland Mousnier: Clientèles et fidélités en Europe à l'époque moderne* (Paris, 1981); S. Kettering, *Patrons, Brokers and Clients in Seventeenth-Century France* (New York, 1986); Mettam, *Power and Faction*; Campbell, *Power and Politics in Old Regime France* (London, 1996); K. Béguin, *Les Princes de Condé: Rebelles, courtisans et mécènes dans la France du Grand Siècle* (Seyssel, 1999).
31. The first study to stress compromise, management and negotiation under Louis XIV was A. N. Hamscher, *The Parlement of Paris after the Fronde: 1653–1673* (Pittsburgh, 1976) and almost all recent work on the parlements agrees. So too for other institutions: F.-X. Emmanuelli, *Un mythe de l' absolutisme bourbonien: L'Intendance, du milieu du xviie siecle la fin du xviiie siècle (France, Espagne, Amérique)* (Aix-en-Provence, 1981); M. Biard, *Les Lilliputiens de la centralisation: Des intendants aux préfets, les hésitations d'un modèle français* (Seyssel, 2007); M.-L. Legay, *Les États provinciaux dans la construction de l'État moderne aux xviie et xviiie siècles* (Geneva, 2001); J. Swann, *Provincial Power and Absolute Monarchy: The Estates General of Burgundy, 1661–1790* (Cambridge, 2003).
32. The implications of this independence are drawn out in e.g. Z. A. Schneider, *The King's Bench: Bailiwick Magistrates and Local Governance in Normandy, 1670–1740* (Rochester,

NY, 2008), and M.-L. Legay and R. Baury (eds.), *L'Invention de la décentralisation: Noblesse et Pouvoirs en France et en Europe xviie–xixe siècle* (Lille, 2009).

33. On the representation of royal power see Y. Bottineau, *Versailles: Miroir des princes* (Paris, 1989); J.-P., Néraudau, *L'Olympe du Roi-Soleil, ou comment la mythologie et l'Antiquité furent mises au service de l'idéologie monarchique sous Louis XIV* (Paris, 1986); Sabatier, G., 'Representare il principe, figurer l'État: Les Programmes iconographiques d'État en France et en Italie du xve au xviie siècle', in *Genèse de l'État moderne: Bilans et perspectives* (Paris, 1990), 247–58; P. Burke, *The Fabrication of Louis XIV* (London 1994); N. Hochner and Thomas W. Gaehtgens, *L'Image roi de François 1er à Louis XIV* (Paris, 2006).

34. C. Grell and A. Zysberg, *Histoire intellectuelle et culturelle de la France du Grand Siècle 1654–1715* (Paris, 2005). Cultural unity was challenged by local elites in a culture war: R. Mettam, 'Power, Station and Precedence: Rivalries among the Provincial Elites of Louis XIV's France', *Transactions of the Royal Historical Society*, 38 (1988), 43–62.

35. N. Elias, *The Court Society* (London, 1983); Campbell, *Power and Politics*; J. Duindam, *Myths of Power: Norbert Elias and the Early Modern European Court* (Amsterdam, 1996).

36. L. Horowski,' "Such a Great Advantage for My Son": Office-Holding and Career Mechanisms at the Court of France (1661 to 1789)', *The Court Historian*, 8 (2003), 125–75; idem, 'Der Preis des Erfolgs: Gunst, Kapital und Patrimonialisierung am Hof von Versailles (1661–1789)', *Zeitschrift für Historische Forschung*, 36 (2009), 71–91.

37. On the changing relationship of revolts to the demands of the state, see Y.-M. Bercé, *History of Peasant Revolts: The Social Origins of Rebellion in Early Modern France* (Ithaca, NY, 1990); Foisil, *La Révolte des nu-pieds et les révoltes normandes de 1639* (Paris, 1970); R. Pillorget, 'Genèse et typologie des mouvements insurrectionnels: La Provence de 1596–1715', *Francia*, 4 (1976), 365–90; W. Beik, *Urban Protest in Seventeenth-Century France: The Culture of Retribution* (Cambridge, 1997); J. Nicolas, *La Rébellion française: Mouvements populaires et conscience sociale, 1661–1789* (Paris, 2002); J. Markoff, *The Abolition of Feudalism* (University Park, Pa., 1996).

38. For social disciplining, see J. Delumeau, *Catholicism from Luther to Voltaire* (Westminster, 1977); N. Elias, *The Civilising Process* (2 vols. Oxford, 1969–82); R. Muchembled, *L'Invention de l'homme moderne: Culture et sensibilités en France du xve au xviiie siècle* (Paris, 1994); and P. Gorski, *Disciplinary Revolution*.

39. So much of the debate focuses just on Burgundy: the seminal work is P. de Saint Jacob, *Les Paysans de la Bourgogne du nord au dernier siècle de l'Ancien Régime* (Paris, 1960); the revisionist position of Hilton L. Root, *Peasants and King in Burgundy* (Berkeley, Calif., 1992), is based on untypical villages, as shown by the recent work of Jeremy Hayhoe, *Enlightened Feudalism: Seigneurial Justice and Village Society in Eighteenth-Century Northern Burgundy* (Rochester, NY, 2008); Robert Schwartz, 'The Noble Profession of Seigneur in Eighteenth-Century Burgundy', in Jay M. Smith (ed.), *The French Nobility in the Eighteenth Century: Reassessments and New Approaches* (University Park, Pa., 2006). On Artois, refreshingly, see J.-P. Jessenne, *Pouvoir au village et révolution: Artois 1760–1848* (Lille, 1987).

40. I. A. A. Thompson, 'Castile: Polity, Fiscality and Fiscal Crisis', in Hoffman and Norberg, *Fiscal Crisis*, 140–80. Resistance was strong, see R. McKay, *The Limits of Royal Authority: Resistance and Obedience in Seventeenth Century Castile* (Cambridge, 1999), 2–3: 'What has come to be known as Spanish absolutism did not conform to any of our available models, which leads me to suggest not that Spain was an exception but, rather, that the models are deficient. The seventeenth-century Spanish monarchy was a hybrid of elements—localism and centralization; representation and autocracy; traditional aristocracy

and modern state builders; order and improvisation...the form of rule in seventeenth-century Castile was not absolute in any sense.'

41. On the parlements, whose history is undergoing complete renewal of late, see W. Doyle, 'The Parlements', in Baker (ed.), *The French Revolution and the Creation of Modern Political Culture*, 157–67; P. R. Campbell, 'The Paris parlement in the 1780s', in P. R. Campbell (ed.), *The Origins of the French Revolution* (Basingstoke, 2006); and J. Swann 'Repenser les parlements au xviiie siècle: Du concept de l' "opposition parlementaire" à celui de "culture juridique des conflits politiques" ', in A. J. Lemaître, *Le Monde parlementaire au xviiie siècle: L'Invention d'un discours politique* (Rennes, 2010), 17–38.

42. For the crisis of the Ancien Régime see W. Doyle, *Origins of the French Revolution* (Oxford, 1980; 3rd edn., 1999); Campbell, *Origins of the French Revolution* (Basingstoke, 2006); and T. E. Kaiser and D. K. Van Kley (eds.), *From Deficit to Deluge: The Origins of the French Revolution* (Stanford, Calif., 2011).

Bibliography

Baker, K. M. (ed.), *The French Revolution and the Creation of Modern Political Culture*, i. *The Political Culture of the Old Regime* (Oxford, 1988).

Beik, W., *Absolutism and Society in Seventeenth-Century France* (Cambridge, 1985).

Campbell, P. R., *The Ancien Régime in France* (Oxford, 1988).

Chaline, O., *La France de Louis XIV* (Paris, 2005).

Collins, J. B., *The State in Early Modern France* (2nd edn., Cambridge, 2009).

Dessert, D., *Argent, pouvoir et société au grand Siècle* (Paris, 1984).

Hatton, R., *Louis XIV and Absolutism* (Basingstoke, 1976).

Henshall, N., *The Myth of Absolutism: Change and Continuity in Early Modern European Monarchy* (Basingstoke, 1992).

Jouanna, A., *Le Devoir de révolte: La Noblesse française et la gestation de l'Etat moderne, 1550–1661* (Paris, 1989).

Méchoulan, H., and E. Le Roy Ladurie (eds.), *L'État baroque: Regards sur la pensée politique de la France du premier xviie siècle* (Paris, 1985).

Mettam, R., *Power and Faction in Louis XIV's France* (Oxford, 1988).

Miller, J. (ed.), *Absolutism in Seventeenth-Century Europe* (Basingstoke, 1990).

Mousnier, R., *The Institutions of France under the Absolute Monarchy, 1598–1789* (2 vols. Chicago, 1979–84).

Parker, D., *The Making of French Absolutism* (London, 1983).

Swann, J., *Provincial Power and Absolute Monarchy: The Estates General of Burgundy, 1661–1790* (Cambridge, 2003).

Van Kley, D. K., *The Religious Origins of the French Revolution* (Princeton, 1996).

CHAPTER 3

DIPLOMACY

HAMISH SCOTT

I

KARL von Martens (1790–1863) was one of the best known diplomatic theorists of the nineteenth century.[1] Born into a celebrated family of Göttingen professors, he was the nephew of Georg Friedrich von Martens (1756–1821), who had compiled an influential series of handbooks of international law and diplomacy. Karl von Martens followed in the family tradition, publishing in 1822 a treatise with a title which made clear its exemplary nature: *Manuel diplomatique, ou précis des droits et des fonctions des agens diplomatiques; suivi d'un recueil d'actes et d'offices pour servir de guide aux personnes qui se destinent à la carrière politique.*[2] Two-thirds of this work consisted of samples of the kind of written communications—both formal and semi-formal—which a diplomat would regularly have to draft and send as part of his official duties. The remainder was dominated by the extensive protocol surrounding embassies, and outlined the changes institutionalized and, in some cases, introduced at the end of the wars of 1792–1815. Though Martens incorporated the important statements of practice made by the Congress of Vienna and by subsequent agreements, which systematized and, to an extent, developed eighteenth-century practice over matters such as rank and precedence, the first third of his handbook was dominated by the extensive and important continuities from the pre-revolutionary era.

Significantly, Martens did not devote very much space to the actual conduct of diplomatic negotiations, instead referring his readers to the established treatises which had appeared long before the great watershed of the French Revolution and which, he declared, remained the best guides. He particularly recommended those by Abraham van Wicquefort, *L' ambassadeur et ses fonctions* (1681), François de Callières, *De la manière de négocier avec les souverains* (1716), and Antoine Pecquet, *Discours sur l'art de négocier* (1737), three works which had collectively defined the craft of diplomacy during the Ancien Régime.[3] This highlighted the extensive and important continuities from the eighteenth-century political world. Yet Martens's own life also demonstrated the exact opposite: the profound disruption caused by the French Revolution and the new ideological tone it had imparted to international relations. Two years before the publication of the *Manuel diplomatique*, he had been appointed Prussian ambassador to Sardinia. But its strongly reactionary king refused to receive him, and his diplomatic *début* was over even before it had begun. The explanation was simple. Martens's wife was the daughter of a regicide: his father-in-law had voted for the execution of Louis XVI in January 1793 and this, even a generation after the event, remained an insuperable obstacle to a posting to Turin. In the end, he was able to follow a diplomatic career, serving Restoration France and becoming Baron Charles de Martens.

His writings and life encapsulate the central theme of this chapter: the crucial continuities from the world of Ancien Régime diplomacy which proved remarkably enduring, but came to be overlaid by important discontinuities which emerged during the revolutionary and Napoleonic era and principally by the new importance of ideology. Such an approach has not always been the scholarly orthodoxy. The first important Francophone study, by the great diplomatic historian Albert Sorel (1842–1906), devoted eight bulky volumes to the struggle between Europe and the French Revolution.[4] On the basis of extensive archival research, particularly in the volumes which deal with the period down to 1795, Sorel demonstrated the undoubted continuities between the conduct of diplomacy during the eighteenth century and the actions and ambitions of the revolutionaries, and even asserted that there was little or nothing which was novel about France's foreign policy during the 1790s. Finding the key—exactly like Georges-Jacques Danton—in the impact of geography, he asserted that at least since the sixteenth century, and perhaps since the twelfth, France had aimed to push forward to its natural boundaries. These 'ancient, natural frontiers [according to Lazare Carnot in February 1793] are the Rhine, the Alps and the Pyrenees'.[5]

Sorel's first proposition can be endorsed with only minor qualifications, but the second has aroused considerable controversy and would now be questioned if not rejected by most specialists. Later historians have insisted upon the ideological tone of diplomacy which originated in the struggle with the Revolution, together with the importance of a new concept of the balance of power, introduced by the Vienna settlement and based upon rational self-interest rather than simple fear.[6] Sorel's importance was and is to be found in his demonstration of the important continuities from the Ancien Régime into the 1790s and 1800s. There were, however, even more important continuities both from the eighteenth century and from the long years of fighting between 1792 and 1815 into the nineteenth century and beyond. The diplomatic Ancien Régime—exactly like its social, political, and economic counterparts—was to prove remarkably persistent and enduring, surviving until the early twentieth century.

One point about terminology must be clarified at the outset. The established modern definition of 'diplomacy' is that it is the continuous and peaceful management of international relations. The term describes the mechanisms through which relations between states and especially their political negotiations were and are managed. It describes, in other words, both the formal and semi-formal meetings during which these were transacted and the agents who handled such contacts: ambassadors, envoys, and the like. There is also a second and much broader definition of 'diplomacy', particularly when the term appears as an adjective. 'Diplomatic history' has been used by scholars to describe, and to some extent still signifies, the wider subject of relations between states, their alliances, wars and peace settlements, together with the underlying assumptions, attitudes, and prejudices which shaped policy: what in the past two decades has come to be labelled 'political culture'.

Sorel's approach was closer to the second, much broader definition. He argued for continuities in the actual content of policy and the persistence of established French territorial and strategic aims into the 1790s and even the 1800s, emphasizing the extent to which the revolutionaries were treading in the footsteps of the very Bourbon monarchy which they swept away in 1792–3. Though Sorel's first volume—*The Political Traditions of the Old Régime*—presented an unsurpassed account of the customs and practices of eighteenth-century international relations, his pages devote surprisingly little attention to the day-to-day conduct of diplomacy, the role of ambassadors, and the nature of negotiations. This present chapter embraces both the wider and narrower definitions, finding—exactly like Sorel—important continuities in each, but it also argues for the newly ideological nature of international relations from the early 1790s onwards.

The novel tone was created first by the radical upheavals within France itself, and then by the external policies pursued by successive revolutionary governments. In autumn 1792 the Bourbon monarchy was overthrown, and France became a republic. This dramatic change, and the violent way it was brought about in one of the leading European powers, created problems within the hierarchical and deeply monarchical world of later eighteenth-century diplomacy, in which republics were both few in number and politically negligible.[7] The existing republican polities were all states of the second rank at best: the Dutch Republic had declined both economically and politically from its seventeenth-century Golden Age, when it had been a leading European power, and was in any case periodically ruled by a quasi-monarchy in the shape of the House of Orange; Switzerland and Venice were now even less important; while the new American republic was struggling for international recognition after its successful rebellion against Britain little more than a decade earlier.[8]

The trial and execution of the King, Louis XVI (1774–93), and his wife Marie Antoinette further alienated monarchical and elite opinion throughout Europe. The only precedent had been the overthrow of Charles I's Stuart monarchy a century and a half earlier, with the execution of another king and the short-lived establishment of a republic headed by Oliver Cromwell. The problems of international recognition and acceptance which Cromwellian England had experienced indicated the problems which a deeply monarchical international community had in accepting and coping with a dramatic change of political system, involving the trial and execution of a king, and these were to be even more evident during the 1790s.

The increasing radical nature of political regimes in Paris, particularly before the establishment of the Directory in 1795, and the apparent determination of the revolutionaries to export political change, if necessary by armed force, raised the ideological temperature. The 'Fraternity and Assistance' decrees of November and December 1792 proclaimed support for any people who tried to imitate the French and overthrow their oppressors, while the substantial territorial gains made in 1792–3—Nice, Savoy, and the Austrian Netherlands were either annexed outright or 'incorporated'—highlighted France's aggressive and ambitious aims. By early 1793 the regicide and, before long, expansionist regime in Paris challenged monarchical Europe, and the threat increased during the next two decades. France's role in sponsoring a series of 'sister republics' increased anxieties, while the scale of its military successes and territorial gains, particularly under the dynamic leadership of Napoleon Bonaparte, overturned Europe's political geography and seemed to threaten the bases of monarchical authority everywhere. These developments transformed the political objectives of the rival powers. The older dynastic and territorial motives behind foreign policy remained significant throughout the wars of 1792–1815, but they were soon accompanied by the new ideological tone: on both sides the conflict quickly came to be seen as a struggle between competing views of society and politics. Underlying this was the French revolutionary doctrine that political legitimacy was rooted not in dynastic right—as had been assumed during the Ancien Régime—but in popular sovereignty, which in turn had its origins in the ideas of the Enlightenment and had been asserted, two decades earlier, in the successful American War of Independence (1775–83) against British rule.

Even within revolutionary France there were important sources of continuity from the diplomatic world of the Ancien Régime. One was the foreign ministry itself, at least until the end of the 1790s.[9] These years did see the evolution of a more powerful central secretariat, but with this exception the administrative mechanisms which existed before 1789, continued to operate even into the Napoleonic period. There was also surprising continuity in personnel: foreign ministers came and went with great rapidity, as the roulette wheel of revolutionary politics spun round and round, but many clerks and specialist advisers remained in post during the 1790s and even the 1800s. These figures were frequently not noblemen, unlike their superiors, and so benefited from the more meritocratic career structure which now prevailed. A second important source of continuity was France's geo-strategic position, at least until the series of major territorial gains which began with the Peace of Campo Formio in 1797. Sorel's emphasis on 'natural frontiers'—though exaggerated and in important respects questionable—correctly highlighted the persistence of certain fundamental strategic problems which had existed throughout the Ancien Régime. France believed herself open to invasion, and sought—as she had done since the seventeenth century—to extend her territory to the Rhine and to seal the vulnerable south-eastern boundary with the Italian peninsula: aims which were finally achieved under the Revolution, but had been pursued over many decades by the Bourbon monarchy.

A third source of continuity was the political culture of French diplomacy and revolutionary politics. The foreign policy of the Ancien Régime, and the debates which had surrounded it, provided a repertoire of arguments and propaganda which the revolutionaries in turn could employ.[10] The alliance with Austria which had existed since the celebrated 'Diplomatic Revolution' of 1756 had been subjected to severe criticism, both from the agents of Louis XV's private foreign policy, the *secret du roi*, and from military circles, who believed that France should ally with Prussia, a much more powerful military state at least until the 1780s. The links with Vienna were viewed as the fundamental cause of France's international decline, which the revolutionaries actively set out to reverse. Opposition to Austria and to the Habsburg Queen Marie Antoinette was a central theme in the early years of the Revolution, and this together with the presumed role of her brother the Emperor Leopold II (1790–2) in supporting the *émigrés* produced a significant deterioration in relations during the winter of 1791–2.[11] The war launched in the following spring was justified, to an important extent, by the use of established anti-Austrian arguments transformed to fit the new circumstances of the Revolution. Though these other continuities were significant, they soon became less important than the very new tone created by the political changes within France and their international repercussions.

II

The era of the French Revolution, and specifically the later 1780s and 1790s, saw the modern meanings first of 'diplomatic' and then 'diplomacy' become established in the political lexicon. A century before, when the Maurist monk Jean Mabillon wrote *De re diplomatica* (1681), his masterpiece devoted to the science of documents and the historical method, the term still retained its traditional meaning: relating to the study of diplomas or other documents. At this period the peaceful conduct of relations between states was known as 'negotiations' (*négociations*), a term which long continued to be employed. During the later eighteenth century, however, the terms 'diplomatic' and 'diplomacy' took on their present-day meaning both in French and in English. The Irish political journalist and British MP, Edmund Burke, did most to make the word familiar to Anglophone readers. In the *Annual Register* for 1787 he wrote of 'civil, diplomatique [sic] and military affairs', while a decade later, in one of his celebrated *Letters on a Regicide Peace*, he spoke of the French regime's 'double diplomacy'.[12] By shortly after 1800, the term was becoming established.

This linguistic shift occurred at the end of a century during which there had been fundamental and enduring changes in the way in which relations between states were conducted.[13] The origins of resident diplomacy went back to the renaissance, when rulers in western and southern Europe started to maintain permanent representatives in each other's capitals. These diplomats, however, primarily reported such news and intelligence as they could discover rather than conducting actual political discussions, and they were often of lower social status than later ambassadors and envoys were to be. Shorter-lived missions headed by great churchmen or aristocrats would be sent to transact any important negotiations, such as the conclusion of an alliance, peace treaty, or dynastic marriage. The long decades of warfare throughout Europe between the 1550s and the 1640s, together with the religious antagonisms which fuelled these conflicts, in the aftermath of the Protestant Reformation, had disrupted even the limited diplomatic network in existence by the earlier sixteenth century. Resident diplomacy had only been resumed after the peace settlements of 1648 and 1659–60, but it developed in several important ways during the next two generations.

The long personal rule of France's Louis XIV (1661–1715) and the large-scale struggle between the powerful and populous French state and its rivals in western and central Europe, near-continuous after 1672 when the Dutch War began, had promoted more extensive diplomatic contacts between the allies who sought to prevent what they believed was the threat of French hegemony. Resident embassies became more familiar and lasted longer, negotiations were conducted more frequently in order to conclude alliances and define military strategy, while the practice of holding congresses at the end of major wars—Nijmegen in 1678–79, Ryswick in 1697, Utrecht in 1712–13—fostered the development of diplomacy in important ways.[14] France too, as it sought allies against the various coalitions which opposed it, conducted more extensive and continuous diplomacy. The institutional structures which it developed to do this, and especially the much-enlarged foreign office, were soon being copied by its rivals. Simultaneously the existing network of embassies which had extended across western and southern Europe was enlarged to include courts in central, northern, and even eastern Europe. The first two decades of the eighteenth century saw the incorporation of Russia, then emerging as a major power under the dynamic leadership of Peter the Great (1689/94–1725), ending centuries of effective isolation from the European mainstream. There were important exceptions and exclusions, above all the Ottoman Empire, but a network of permanent ambassadors and residents now connected the continent's capitals to an extent that had not been the case half a century before. During the decades around 1800 even Constantinople began to send permanent embassies to Europe's other capitals, thus extending it still wider.

These decades were important in three further ways.[15] Diplomacy, its institutions and practices, did not merely come to be modelled on the French prototype; it came to be Francophone as well, as the language of negotiations and treaties across much of Europe increasingly became French. Wider developments contributed, with the final decline of Latin as an international language and France's immense prestige due to the political and cultural achievements of Louis XIV's reign. French was not yet and never became ubiquitous as the language of diplomacy. In a wide arc of southern and south-eastern Europe formerly under Ottoman sway a form of pidgin Italian was employed in commercial and political negotiations until the first half of the nineteenth century, while in the Holy Roman Empire and in northern and eastern Europe German long remained the dominant diplomatic language. But the trend towards the use of French in negotiations and formal treaties and, later in the eighteenth century, even in correspondence between diplomats and their superiors for whom it was not the native language, was undoubted.

The social composition of Europe's diplomatic corps simultaneously changed significantly, as ambassadors and envoys came to be drawn overwhelmingly from the nobility and, in major embassies, from the noble elite or aristocracy. Great nobles had always headed particularly important missions, but in the later seventeenth and earlier eighteenth century the high nobility and especially the leading families within it came to provide a significant proportion of resident diplomats for the first time. There were two important exceptions, countries whose social structures militated against any noble near-monopoly. Both the Dutch Republic and the emerging British state selected far less blue-blooded diplomats. Elsewhere the pattern was clear. It was exemplified by the social composition of the Austrian Habsburg diplomatic corps during the century after the Peace of Westphalia (1648). Over three-fifths (61 per cent) of all ambassadors and envoys were members of the high nobility (the so-called *Herrenstand* or 'Estate of Lords'), while almost a quarter (22 per cent) were either lesser nobles or had recently been ennobled. A mere 12 per cent had non-noble origins, where reliable information is available.[16] In Spain the grip of the leading families was even stronger, and actually increased during the eighteenth century. In the years from 1700 until 1759, no fewer than 76 per cent of all diplomats came from the traditional nobility, and the figure rose to 86 per cent for the reign of Charles III (1759–88).[17] By the second half of the eighteenth century there was even concern in Britain that the government was either unable or unwilling to appoint diplomats whose pedigree equalled that of their continental counterparts.

The aristocratic tone was linked to a third, equally important characteristic: the increasingly important role of monarchical courts in the lives of diplomats. These had become the natural habitat of the high nobility, particularly during the seventeenth century, and as aristocrats were sent as permanent envoys, often staying for several years at a time, they and their wives (if they accompanied them) naturally expected access to the entourage of the ruler to whom they were accredited. An important purpose of diplomacy had always been to represent your own monarch in another court, and it was now assumed that noblemen could do this far more successfully than their social inferiors, while the increasing formality of such embassies by the first half of the eighteenth century made aristocrats natural diplomats: there was a notable synergy between monarchical ritual and aristocratic lifestyle. Formally, diplomats were accredited not to states, but to their rulers and the courts they maintained, and this further strengthened the links between the social elite and the worlds of monarchy and diplomacy.

The result of these linked developments was that, by the second half of the eighteenth century, diplomats believed themselves to be part of a distinct 'independent society', bound together by a 'community of privileges': the phrase was first used and the notion initially articulated by the French foreign office functionary Antoine de Pecquet in his treatise published in the later 1730s. The experience of living and working together, as a distinct group at every court, fostered coherence and unity, and promoted a sense of loyalty not merely to their own monarch but to the other ambassadors, envoys, and ministers plenipotentiary who made up the elementary hierarchy of posts by that point. The entire diplomatic corps would take up the cause of any individual who was believed to have suffered an affront to his official status. This degree of integration in turn strengthened the concessive, negotiatory nature of diplomacy, which aimed to reach solutions through discussion and compromise during the decades before the French Revolution.

III

Developments during the preceding century ensured that Ancien Régime diplomacy became an immediate target for the revolutionaries.[18] Its monarchical and aristocratic nature clashed with the assumptions of the new French regime and soon created friction. The abolition of the status of nobility in June 1790 was a particular source of difficulties, since most diplomats accredited to Louis XVI's court were themselves noble, yet in theory they could now not use their titles, nor dress their servants in livery, nor display either their ruler's coats of arms or their own, on the portals of their embassy buildings or residences. Before long a revolutionary mob insulted the wives of diplomats from Madrid and Turin because of their servants' noble livery, while popular and official resentment was directed against the representatives of Ancien Régime states: throughout the 1790s there were a handful of incidents involving the remaining members of the diplomatic community in Paris, which was in any case being reduced in size with open hostilities after 1792–3 and with the widespread revulsion which followed the execution of Louis XVI and Marie Antoinette, leading some states to break off relations. As late as 1798 the papal and Portuguese ambassadors were both detained by over-zealous revolutionary officials, though they were soon released. All of these issues came to be points of friction, causing a series of minor disputes, but did not generate real international tension. The strongly legalistic culture of the French Revolution, together with a degree of political necessity, ensured that the persons and property of foreign diplomats in France were largely protected during the 1790s.

The actions of French diplomats in foreign courts produced rather more tension. During the 1790s successive French regimes maintained representatives in neutral and client states, but they ignored the established rules and conventions governing the conduct of diplomats. There were many points of friction, and these increased as the regime in Paris became more radical. The novel scale of interventions by French diplomats in the domestic politics of the countries to which they were accredited, together with the fact that they represented a regime which was feared and hated, very quickly isolated these individuals and cut them off from the society of other diplomats. What were, to agents of the new French Republic, simple and necessary actions, appeared provocative to their hosts. The planting of liberty trees in embassy courtyards and even more the decoration of official residences with the distinctive red, white, and blue flags of the Revolution were the kind of actions which highlighted the gulf separating the new order from the old and, at times, caused major clashes. When the first ambassador from the French Republic to the Habsburg court, General Bernadotte, displayed a four-foot-long tricolour outside his embassy on an Austrian national holiday, a crowd attacked the building and tore it down, leading to his temporary departure from Vienna. Envoys from France were murdered by mobs in Rome in 1793 and again in 1797, while—even more seriously—two French representatives at the conference at Rastadt were killed by Austrian hussars as the meeting broke up in spring 1799. These and similar episodes were in themselves relatively minor, but they caused bad feeling on both sides and, more importantly, highlighted the increasing gulf between republican France and monarchical Europe.

Distinctive dress and speech were one dimension of the established formality of Ancien Régime diplomacy, and here again the behaviour of revolutionary diplomats emphasized both the new political world which was being created in France and its potent challenge to the old order. Diplomats from the established monarchies all wore what had become standard garb by the second half of the eighteenth century: silk coats, ornate waistcoats, breeches and stockings, the clothing—of course—of an aristocrat. Their French counterparts shunned such finery and appeared in simple coats and trousers, the established dress of revolutionary politicians and citizens of the new republic. Old regime diplomats paced their steps in a choreographed manner, but the representatives of the new Republic strode purposefully into conferences, rejecting the established diplomatic *pas-de-deux*. Their notably blunt forms of speech and, before long, refusal to genuflect before the monarchs to whom they were accredited, as was customary at the start of an audience, or to utter words such as 'majesty' or even 'monsieur' (which designated a nobleman) further highlighted the chasm which had developed. Eventually, in August 1796, the term 'excellency' was prohibited by the Directory, and 'citoyen' was insisted upon as the only acceptable designation for a diplomat, whether French or foreign.

One important change was the disappearance of the social events which had been integral to eighteenth-century diplomacy, where political objectives could be pursued informally and valuable information gathered. Discussions were now confined entirely to formal conferences. But it was the negotiating style adopted by French representatives which did most to separate the old and new political worlds. Ancien Régime diplomacy had been characterized by give-and-take, by the reaching of agreements through discussion and compromise by ambassadors who believed themselves to be members of the same international society. The new French representatives by contrast were much blunter and far less flexible, seeing themselves as adversaries of the old order rather than participants in Europe's international society, while before long the scale of France's military victories enabled them to insist upon their demands in a way which would reach its peak under Napoleon Bonaparte's rule.[19] France's negotiators set out their terms and stuck to them, refusing the established forms of compromise and being quite prepared to shout and hector where needed: at the Rastadt conference the Directory's representative screamed and banged the table to underline his demands, actions which would have been quite unthinkable before 1789, but which were emblematic of the chasm which now existed between Paris and the other capitals. The future Austrian chancellor, Metternich—admittedly not an impartial witness—was outraged by this conduct, writing to his wife from the conference that he had never seen 'such ill-conditioned animals'.[20]

The changed social composition and political practices of French diplomacy contributed to this. Both the constitutional monarchy and the Republic which replaced it after August 1792 continued to maintain a network of embassies and consulates, though the military struggle inevitably reduced its size. Many noble *émigrés*, from the very beginning of the Revolution, had either been diplomats or were potential ambassadors and envoys, and each more radical lurch during the first half of the 1790s thinned the pool of available talent still further. The oath required to the 'Nation, Law and King' had always been a problem for noble diplomats, accustomed to serve the Bourbon monarch alone: loyalty to the ruler's person and an established sense of duty to serve the dynasty had been important foundations of the elite's willingness to become ambassadors, and this had been compromised. A number of aristocratic diplomats either resigned or were recalled in 1790–2. The fall of the Bourbon monarchy and, even more, the execution of the royal couple convinced many noblemen that their position had become untenable, and so helped to destabilize French diplomacy: here the diplomatic corps exactly mirrored developments in the royal army during these years, with its effectiveness being reduced by a significant haemorrhage of noblemen.

It was exacerbated by the actions of successive revolutionary governments. An initial cull of diplomats who had served the Ancien Régime monarchy was carried out during the spring and early summer of 1792 by the foreign minister, Charles-François Dumouriez (1739–1824), himself a former nobleman who had been an unofficial agent of Bourbon policy before the Revolution. His actions created a serious problem over replacements, with a shortage of experienced and appropriate candidates, and in many cases he was forced to reduce the level of representation to that of *chargé d'affaires*. Subsequent political events further weakened the experienced, professional, but noble, element in the diplomatic service, as a slow weeding out of suspected aristocrats was carried out by governments searching for ideological purity. It accelerated during the second half of the decade under the Directory. In the aftermath of the Fructidor coup (September 1797) anyone who had been born into the nobility or who had served the monarchy before 1789 was summarily dismissed. The impact of this concern with revolutionary orthodoxy and political reliability was evident by the next year, when no fewer than ten regicides were serving in important diplomatic posts.

One of these was none other than Emmanuel Joseph Sieyès, former abbé, celebrated revolutionary demagogue and notable political survivor, who was ambassador in Berlin. In July 1798, at the ceremony of homage (*Huldigungsfeier*) for the new Prussian King, Frederick William III (1797–1840), Sieyès provided a graphic illustration of the distance separating monarchical Europe and the republican regime. The standard diplomatic uniform of the French republic—intended to highlight the regime and not the individual—was now a Roman toga in the revolutionary colours of red, white, and blue. Sieyès's appearance at a deeply monarchical rite clad in republican dress startled onlookers and provided a dramatic visual *tableau* which encapsulated the struggle under way.[21]

IV

Ancien Régime diplomacy was the target of a more fundamental critique, which first surfaced in the debates of the Constituent Assembly in spring 1790, but had important roots in the mature Enlightenment.[22] The *philosophes* had emphasized internal reform rather than external ambition, reversing the established hierarchy in monarchical Europe, and had severely criticized the contemporary conduct of international relations and especially its frequent conflicts, in the aftermath of the destructive Seven Years War (1756–63). The *philosophes*' aversion to old-style dynastic warfare was most clearly set out in the *Encyclopédie*, which contained a notable article on 'Guerre'.[23] Denis Diderot's satirical *Political Principles of Rulers* continued the critique: 'Make alliances only in order to sow hatred. Incite wars between my neighbours and try to keep this going. Have no ambassadors in other countries, only spies.... To be neutral means to profit from the difficulties of others in order to improve one's own situation.' Continuing in this vein Jean-Jacques Rousseau declared that peace treaties were only 'temporary armistices', while the Abbé Raynal styled alliances mere 'preparations for treason'.[24] This extremely negative view was accompanied by strong censure of the secrecy which surrounded diplomacy, conducted entirely by kings and their leading ministers.

These criticisms of the eighteenth-century competitive states system and its wars contained an implicit and occasionally explicit programme for reform. This was rooted in the growing internationalism fostered by the Enlightenment, with its sense that all human beings belonged to a common European fatherland, rather than being subjects of rival nation-states. It also rested upon a rejection of the prevailing mercantilist assumption that there was a fixed volume of economic resources, competition for which was one important source of the recurring and destructive warfare. Instead the Enlightenment critique and especially the writings of the physiocrats, rejected such economic nationalism. It emphasized economic interdependence and contended that the expansion of international trade would benefit all countries equally, rather than strengthening one at the expense of its rivals as had hitherto been assumed. Wars would thus be rendered unnecessary, in an international order shaped by reason rather than the *raison d'état* which had previously guided monarchical policy.

Such ideas had an extremely limited practical impact before the outbreak of the Revolution, but became prominent during the debates in May 1790. The context was the collapse of French power in Europe, apparent by 1787 if not actually earlier and, more immediately, by urgent requests from Bourbon Spain, technically still an ally under the Third Family Compact (1761), for much-needed assistance in a confrontation with the dominant naval power of Britain over Nootka Sound, located off the distant north-west coast of America. The extensive discussions in the Constituent Assembly were dominated by the ideas of the *philosophes* and by a resulting rejection of war, conquest, and monarchical leadership—and the secrecy which accompanied and facilitated these—in the field of foreign policy.[25]

In these debates Maximilien Robespierre (the future revolutionary leader), Constantin François, Count de Volney, and Jean-François Reubell (later to be a Director) were the leading advocates of an enlightened approach. Rooted in the *philosophe* critique, it provides one of the clearest demonstrations of the Enlightenment's real influence upon revolutionary leaders. The extended discussions revealed an ambition to create a new political world of peaceful coexistence, mutually enriching trade, and an international legal system embodying the universal rights of man, which would replace the Ancien Régime's duplicitous diplomacy, destructive warfare, and positive international law. On 18 May 1790 Reubell loudly censured established practice, declaring that 'Alliance treaties lead only to the right of levying new taxes and of ruining the treasury... A great nation should have no other allies but providence, its [own] power and justice.'[26]

Such views were articulated by a radical minority, but permeated the whole debate. The Assembly determined that France would stand aloof from the struggles of the European great powers and adopt a neo-isolationist stance, hoping to avoid destructive conflicts in the future and instead to benefit from mutually enriching trade; in spring 1790 Spain was effectively refused aid; while the French King's powers to determine foreign policy—hitherto absolute—were subjected to constitutional limitation. He retained the right to appoint diplomats and conduct policy, but the Assembly now reviewed his actions and could block any decision for war. A commitment was instead made to an open and participatory conduct of foreign policy in the future. The Constituent Assembly's decree of 22 May 1790 renounced war and territorial conquests and proclaimed an era of international brotherhood, thus incorporating an enlightened approach and idealistically hoping to inaugurate an era of perpetual peace. In the following year it was incorporated into the Constitution, which declared that 'The French nation renounces the undertaking of any war with a view of making conquests, and it will never use its forces against the liberty of any people.'[27] Majority opinion in the Constituent Assembly probably had been far more moderate. It was best represented by Mirabeau's celebrated statement that, while 'undoubtedly the time will come when we shall have only friends and no allies, when there will be universal freedom of trade and when Europe will form one great family', for the moment prudence required that France did not 'trust to chance the influence which other powers exert on us and which we can exert upon other powers'.[28]

The arguments which were advanced during these debates resurfaced at later points in the Revolution, but their practical impact upon French policy was to be relatively limited. This was due to the fighting which began in 1792–3 and was to be far more influential in determining France's approach. The war's origins lay both in domestic French politics, where in the winter of 1791–2 a faction in the Legislative Assembly had begun to advocate conflict as a way of advancing its own political fortunes, and in the widespread and increasing hostility and revulsion which the established monarchies felt toward the regime in Paris, particularly after Louis XVI's execution (January 1793).[29] It inaugurated two decades of near continuous warfare during which successive French governments pursued very aggressive and traditional external policies, far removed from those which had been championed during the debates in spring 1790, and waged war and annexed territory on a scale undreamt of by the Bourbon monarchy.[30]

The enlightened critique did exert some influence, however. During the 1790s and especially the ascendancy of the Committee of Public Safety there was periodic opposition towards alliances with monarchical states, in keeping with the Assembly discussions, and it was formalized by a decree of 24 September 1793, which provided that as long as war and 'revolutionary government' continued, only low grade representation—at the level of *chargé d'affaires* and secretaries of legation—together with 'secret agents' could be sent to those monarchies at which France deemed it necessary to be represented. Only 'free peoples'—that it to say, fellow republics and, less certainly, a few non-aligned states of strategic significance—were to be entitled to receive French ambassadors or ministers. The consequence was that Paris's principal links were soon with the sister republics of Switzerland and the USA, together with a small number of neutrals: principally the Ottoman Empire, Sweden, and Denmark. The period of rule by the Committee of Public Safety saw the effective suspension of diplomatic activity of a traditional type: a member of the Convention subsequently likened its external policy to diplomacy by cannon shots. After Thermidor a return to a more traditional approach became evident, as France once again became prepared to negotiate with enemies and neutrals, but this in turn was overtaken by events.

Increasingly, the spectacular French military successes—which in their completeness were on a scale which would have been unimaginable to any Ancien Régime monarchy—had the effect of reducing the importance of, and scope for, diplomacy either by France or its opponents. The military revolution of the 1790s in France rendered negotiation unnecessary, at least temporarily. Eighteenth-century European diplomacy had evolved within a strategic world in which truly decisive victories, whether in single battles or entire wars, were impossible. The technological limitations upon seventeenth- and eighteenth-century warfare both on land and at sea had ensured that this was so. Governments and their commanders aimed only to secure tactical victories which diplomats could turn into territorial gains: this was why peace talks began informally almost as soon as fighting commenced and continued throughout any war, in an attempt to establish the likely terms of any settlement.

In the 1790s warfare became decisive, as campaigns and even single battles decided the outcome of entire conflicts in a way which was unprecedented in modern times. The forcible levying of conscript soldiers and material resources launched by the revolutionary regime in the emergency of late summer 1793 vastly expanded the size of the French army, which on paper may have risen to over one million men during subsequent campaigns. It also led to the adoption of a much more mobile, aggressive strategy, which was driven on by revolutionary fervour. Against enemies who long remained wedded to the conventions of Ancien Régime warfare and, crucially, were quite unable to increase the size of their own military establishments in the way France had done, the appearance of the 'nation in arms' brought a near-unbroken series of revolutionary victories during the wars of the First and Second Coalition, which had the effect of further narrowing the scope for diplomacy and, eventually, making it redundant. This trend was reflected in the growing prominence in the Directory's diplomatic corps of individuals who had served in the armed forces: six generals and one admiral acted as ambassadors or ministers during the second half of the decade.

The coming to power of Napoleon Bonaparte in 1799 accelerated this downgrading of traditional diplomacy for France. Notoriously impatient and increasingly imperious, the First Consul and, after 1804, Emperor had little or no time for the delays and compromises which were the essence of diplomatic negotiations, but increasingly he was able to ignore established conventions. His military genius for a decade fashioned overwhelming victories, and these rendered negotiations unnecessary and diplomacy impossible. France's enemies were routed, rather than merely suffering a temporary military reverse, after which they were expected to hand over a province as the price of a compromise peace, as had been the practice before 1789. By contrast, the scale of Prussia's shattering defeat in 1806 and Austria's three years later left no scope for negotiation. The vanquished state simply handed over the territory demanded and made whatever other concessions the French Emperor required.

Napoleon had an obvious contempt for the established conventions of diplomacy and international law, arresting diplomats and seizing their papers, detaining high-born tourists and ignoring territorial boundaries. The two most celebrated examples both came in 1804. In late March the Duke d'Enghien, a junior member of the Bourbon family, was abducted from the territory of the Holy Roman Empire, taken back to Paris and executed, outraging international opinion. In the following October the British envoy to Hamburg (which lay within the Prussian sphere of influence), Sir George Rumbold, together with all his diplomatic papers, was seized by Napoleon's soldiers and only released after vigorous protests by Frederick William III. Even then, Rumbold's papers were not returned to him. Actions such as these further increased the gulf between old Europe and the new French state, whose military victories were in any case destroying the assumption of political near-equality upon which the great power system had traditionally rested. France continued to maintain a network of diplomatic and consular posts throughout the Napoleonic era.[31] During the temporary restoration of peace in 1802–3, it had twenty-nine diplomats serving abroad: six ambassadors, one resident, four *chargés d'affaires*, and eighteen secretaries of legation. Crucially, these representatives did not conduct negotiations, which were monopolized by Napoleon himself. Instead French diplomats were expected to assemble information and particularly military intelligence, in a return to the pattern which had prevailed at the beginning of the early modern period. One significant long-term consequence was the development within embassies of the post of military *attaché*, which would become established during the nineteenth century.

The scale of revolutionary and, even more, Napoleonic military successes and the sweeping territorial changes to which these led, simultaneously strengthened cooperation between the other great powers, which could only resist by cooperating against the French Leviathan, and this revived diplomacy between the established monarchies, particularly from the early 1800s. Successive political reorganizations of Europe were especially frightening in one important respect: they involved territory being taken from leading states, rather than from minor countries. This was in sharp contrast to the eighteenth century when—with the exception of the extended transfer of the Duchy of Lorraine from the Habsburgs to French control and Prussia's seizure of Silesia from Austria—very little European territory had actually changed hands between the five great powers. Major territorial losses had been restricted to declining states such as Poland-Lithuania, partitioned out of existence between 1772 and 1795, and the Ottoman Empire, which lost provinces to its continental neighbours in the wars of 1683–1718 and 1768–92. A very different pattern prevailed during the revolutionary and Napoleonic struggle, when victorious France seized large tracts of land from the other great powers.

V

The final defeat of French military imperialism was brought about by several linked developments: France's own military and strategic overextension, especially under Napoleon's leadership; British financial and naval strength; Austrian resilience; Russian and finally Prussian military power. Diplomacy also played an important part, as successive coalitions saw an enhanced level of political and military coordination. These years saw the completion of the network of embassies and other missions which linked the belligerents and even some neutrals beyond the reach of French dominance, while the later phase of the wars saw intensive negotiations between the allies, culminating in extensive cooperation during the Final Coalition. The experience of fighting and defeating France brought the four allied powers much more closely together than hitherto: once again the real threat of a hegemonic power dominating Europe submerged established rivalries, at least temporarily. The importance of the prolonged military struggle for the relations of the great powers first became fully apparent in the Congress of Vienna (1814–15), which fashioned a general peace settlement for the continent.

The congress which met in the Austrian capital was consciously an eighteenth-century diplomatic occasion, with its glittering social round, extensive informal discussions, and intermittent formal conferences.[32] It was novel only in its scale and in the presence in Vienna of so many rulers and foreign ministers, as well as their ambassadors and other representatives. The Congress was a deliberate return to the monarchical, dynastic world which many of those present feared had been destroyed forever by the hated Bonaparte. The rulers and diplomats who assembled in Vienna, representatives of the established monarchies which had finally defeated French imperialism, embraced the traditional style of diplomacy which had prevailed during the Ancien Régime. It was slow-moving, achieved through extended formal and informal discussions and frequent compromises, and involved numerous and large-scale social events of the kind that French diplomats had disdained after the mid-1790s. Exactly as a century earlier the gathering at Utrecht had accelerated the development of a European diplomatic culture, the congress in Vienna fostered a restoration of that same culture, as part of wider efforts to restore the political and social world which had been lost, to the extent that this was compatible with the need for security against any future revival of French military imperialism. An important dimension of this was the Allied attempt to restore a framework of international law, which Napoleon had flagrantly ignored, but which was reasserted at Vienna and during the decades which followed.

One of the undervalued achievements of the 1815 Settlement, and the so-called 'Congress System' (1815–23) which followed, was a codification of diplomatic arrangements which perpetuated many of the characteristics of eighteenth-century diplomacy. Two established problems were definitively regulated, simplifying future practice. All diplomats were divided into three classes, later increased to four at the Congress of Aix-la-Chapelle (Aachen) in 1818. A rudimentary hierarchy of ranks had emerged during the hundred years before the French Revolution, and this was now formalized and made permanent. Diplomats were divided into four categories: ambassadors; envoys and ministers plenipotentiary; ministers resident; and *chargés d'affaires*. It was accompanied by a second agreement resolving an issue which had been a source of numerous and, at times, acrimonious disputes. The notoriously complex question of precedence between diplomats, which had previously been decided primarily by the hierarchy of a ruler's title (the representative of a King was outranked only by that of the Emperor), was definitively resolved by an agreement that, within each of these four classes, the date at which a representative had arrived in a particular capital would determine the precedence which he would enjoy on formal occasions. Together with a series of agreements on minor issues, these protocols simplified diplomacy in the future and also testified to its growing importance in international relations.

The Congress of Vienna looked forward as well as back. It saw the adoption of a new form of the traditional 'balance of power': that of political equilibrium rooted not in fear (as its eighteenth-century predecessor had been) but in enlightened self-interest. Forcefully advocated by the British foreign secretary, Viscount Castlereagh, its adoption was one crucially important element in the far more peaceful international system of the nineteenth century. There would be no war involving all the great powers before 1914 and no conflict between two or more great powers for four decades both at the beginning of the period (1815–53) and at its conclusion (1871–1914).[33] Exhaustion and a desire to concentrate upon domestic reconstruction, after two decades of extremely expensive, near-continuous and new-scale warfare, was a second factor which initially contributed to the long period of general peace.

Diplomacy provided a third significant source of international stability after the Vienna settlement. Eighteenth-century diplomacy had been overwhelmingly reactive, a matter of responding to problems as these arose. Its nineteenth-century counterpart by contrast was rather more constructive and proactive, seeking to identify problems and so defuse international crises before these arose: exemplified by the successful efforts of the 'Congress System' to maintain the peace so recently restored. One reason for this cooperation was a deeply ingrained fear of war and the dramatic political upheavals it had caused during the 1790s and 1800s. Another was the legacy of shared experience and political cooperation during the military struggle with France. The formal reincorporation of the restored French Bourbon monarchy into the international order at the congress of Aix-la-Chapelle (1818) was a final source of stability. France brought a very traditional type of diplomacy to her renewed membership of the great power system. The restored Bourbon monarchy was quickly reincorporated into the concert of Europe and reinforced its legitimist, dynastic, conservative, and religious approach to international relations. One purpose of the summit diplomacy conducted during the Congress System was to foster cooperation between the established powers against any revival of the revolutionary contagion—as it was seen—which had so nearly overthrown the European Ancien Régime after 1789. It involved a strident emphasis upon the dynastic basis of political legitimacy, against the challenge represented by the French Revolution's emphasis upon popular sovereignty.

The decades after 1815 did see some important changes. The adoption of the telegraph vastly speeded up communications and with it the pace of diplomacy, reducing the degree of personal initiative exercised by individual ambassadors; the network of embassies and consulates extended far beyond Europe; while economic and commercial issues were a more important part of a diplomat's duties. But these modified established practice, rather than overturning it completely and the extent of the continuities remained striking. At least down to the 1880s and 1890s, the diplomatic world remained essentially that of Ancien Régime Europe: concessive, negotiatory, francophone, monarchical, dynastic, focused on the court as much as the chancellery, dominated by nobles who were expected almost everywhere to possess a private income to supplement their meagre official salaries.[34] Between 1871 and 1914, 84 per cent of all German diplomats were noblemen, and for European capitals the figure was even higher; non-nobles were to be found primarily in overseas legations. No fewer than thirty-six out of thirty-eight heads of Austro-Hungarian missions were noblemen on the eve of the First World War. Indeed the British radical MP John Bright, speaking in 1858, characterized diplomacy as 'neither more nor less than a gigantic system of outdoor relief for the aristocracy'.[35] Family ties and the exercise of patronage remained the keys to appointment and advancement alike, while traditional attitudes were encouraged and perpetuated by the small size and restricted social composition of most foreign services.

Such obvious continuities were the principal reason why Karl von Martens's celebrated handbook, frequently reprinted but remaining deeply eighteenth-century in its contents and assumptions, remained the political lexicon of ambassadors, ministers, and envoys well into the second half of the nineteenth century. The reprints and new editions of the *Manuel diplomatique*, or the *Guide diplomatique* as it was renamed, underlined its immense practical utility for diplomats and the profound continuities within their world. The 'old diplomacy', as it came to be known in its twilight decades before 1914, had deep roots in the European past: roots which were social, institutional, and ideological in nature. Though the generation before the First World War did see some limited changes, the real end of the diplomatic Ancien Régime would not come until the peace conference at Versailles and the significant changes which it brought about in 1919.

Notes

1. I am very grateful to Thomas Munck and Brendan Simms, who commented helpfully on a draft of this article.
2. (Paris, 1822).
3. Wicquefort was published in 2 vols. in The Hague in 1681; Callières appeared in Paris in 1716, with an English tr. (London, 1716), a German version (Leipzig, 1717) and an Italian one (Parma, 1726). All three works were frequently republ. and re-edited during the 18th cent. and even subsequently.
4. *L'Europe et la Révolution française* (8 vols. Paris, 1885–1904); there is an English tr. of vol. i: Albert Sorel, *Europe and the French Revolution: The Political Traditions of the Old Régime*, tr. Alfred Cobban and J. W. Hunt (London, 1969).
5. Daniel Nordman, 'Des limites d'état aux frontières nationales', in Pierre Nora (ed.), *Les Lieux de mémoire*, ii. *La Nation* (3 vols. Paris, 1986), 27–55, quotation at pp. 50–1. On the whole issue of 'natural frontiers', see also Nordman's large-scale study, *Frontières de France: De l'espace au territoire xvie–xixe siècle* (Paris, 1996), and the penetrating article by Peter Sahlins, 'Natural Frontiers Revisited: France's Boundaries since the Seventeenth Century', *American Historical Review*, 95 (1990), 1423–51.
6. The classic statement of this is Paul W. Schroeder, *The Transformation of European Politics 1763–1848* (Oxford, 1994).
7. See the important article by Linda Frey and Marsha Frey, '"The Reign of the Charlatans is Over": The French Revolutionary Attack on Diplomatic Practice', *Journal of Modern History*, 65 (1993), 706–44, together with the overlapping account in Linda S. Frey and Marsha L. Frey, *The History of Diplomatic Immunity* (Columbus, Ohio, 1999), ch. 8.
8. An interesting perspective upon this is provided by Mlada Bukovansky, *Legitimacy and Power Politics: The American and French Revolutions in International Political Culture* (Princeton, 2002).
9. Frédéric Masson, *Le Département des Affaires étrangères pendant la Révolution 1787–1804* (Paris, 1877), remains an invaluable source of information; see also Jean Baillou (ed.), *Les Affaires étrangères et le corps diplomatique français* (2 vols. Paris, 1984).
10. This has recently been illuminated by the researches of Gary Savage: see 'Favier's Heirs: The French Revolution and the *secret du roi*', *Historical Journal*, 41 (1998), 225–58, and 'Foreign Policy and Political Culture in Later Eighteenth-Century France', in Hamish Scott and Brendan Simms (eds.), *Cultures of Power in Europe during the Long Eighteenth Century* (Cambridge, 2007), 304–25.
11. See two important articles by Thomas E. Kaiser, 'Who's Afraid of Marie Antoinette? Diplomacy, Austrophobia and the Queen', *French History*, 14/3 (2000), 241–71; idem, 'From the Austrian Committee to the Foreign Plot: Marie-Antoinette, Austrophobia and the Terror', *French Historical Studies*, 26 (2003), 579–617.
12. See *Abraham van Wicquefort: The Embassador [sic] and his Functions*, ed. Maurice Keens-Soper (Leicester, 1997), p. vii, n. 2, and *The Oxford English Dictionary* sub 'diplomacy'. Burke's sources here, as in so many of his writings, appear to be French: see *Encyclopédie méthodique: Économie politique et diplomatique* (Paris and Liège, 1784–8), iv. 814, 837, and Lucien Bély, 'L'Invention de la diplomatie', in Bély (ed.), *L'Invention de la diplomatie: Moyen âge, temps modernes* (Paris, 1998), 11 n. 1.

13. The best introductions are M. S. Anderson, *The Rise of Modern Diplomacy 1450–1919* (London, 1993), and Lucien Bély, *L' Art de la paix en Europe: Naissance de la diplomatie moderne xvie–xviiie siècle* (Paris, 2007).
14. See the pathbreaking study by Lucien Bély, *Espions et ambassadeurs au temps de Louis XIV* (Paris, 1990), which was the subject of a notable and extensive review article by John C. Rule, 'Gathering Intelligence in the Age of Louis XIV', *International History Review*, 14 (1992), 732–52.
15. For a fuller exposition of the argument which follows, see Hamish Scott, 'Diplomatic Culture in Old Regime Europe', in Scott and Simms (eds.), *Cultures of Power*, 58–85.
16. Klaus Maletkke, 'Les Diplomates de l'empereur: Une contribution à la recherché sur les élites politiques aux xviie et xviiie siècles', in Jean-Michel Boehler, Christine Lebeau, and Bernard Vogler (eds.), *Les Élites régionales (xviie–xxe siècle): Construction de soi-même et service de l'autre* (Strasbourg, 2002), 27.
17. See Didier Ozanam, *Les Diplomates espagnols du xviiie siècle: Introduction et répertoire biographique (1700–1808)* (Madrid and Bordeaux, 1998), the fullest national study which has yet appeared; figures from pp. 31–3, 35–7, 75, 123 (I have presented his totals in round numbers).
18. There is a lively account by Frey and Frey, 'Reign of Charlatans'.
19. The subject of a stimulating and provocative article by Paul W. Schroeder, 'Napoleon's Foreign Policy: A Criminal Enterprise', repr. in the same author's *Systems, Stability and Statecraft: Essays on the International History of Modern Europe* (New York, 2004), 223–41.
20. Quoted by Frey and Frey, 'Reign of Charlatans', 728.
21. Brendan Simms, *The Impact of Napoleon: Prussian High Politics, Foreign Policy and the Crisis of the Executive, 1797–1806* (Cambridge, 1997), 90.
22. See Marc Bélissa, *Fraternité universelle et intérêt national (1713–95): Les Cosmopolitiques du droit de gens* (Paris, 1998), esp. 179–97, and Felix Gilbert, 'The "New Diplomacy" of the Eighteenth Century', repr. in Gilbert's collected essays: *History: Choice and Commitment* (Cambridge, Mass., 1977), 323–50, esp. 345ff.
23. Denis Diderot and Jean Le Rond d'Alembert, *Encyclopédie, ou Dictionnaire raisonné* (20 vols. Paris, 1751–72), vii. 985–98.
24. All quoted by Gilbert, 'New Diplomacy', 328–9.
25. The debates are printed in *Archives Parlementaires de 1787 à 1860, première série (1787 à 1799)*, ed. M. J. Madival and M. E. Laurent (90 vols. Paris, 1867–), xv.
26. Quoted by Gilbert, 'New Diplomacy', 345.
27. Widely quoted, e.g. in J. H. Stewart (ed.), *A Documentary Survey of the French Revolution* (New York, 1951), 260.
28. Quoted by Gilbert, 'New Diplomacy', 346.
29. T. C. W. Blanning, *The Origins of the French Revolutionary Wars* (London, 1986), esp. chs. 3–4, which should be read in the light of the admiring critique by Thomas E. Kaiser, 'La Fin du Renversement des Alliances: La France, l'Autriche et la déclaration de guerre du 20 avril 1792', *Annales historiques de la Révolution française*, 351 (2008), 77–98.
30. See esp. the two studies by T. C. W. Blanning: *The French Revolution in Germany* (Oxford, 1983); *The French Revolutionary Wars 1787–1802* (London, 1996).

31. Edward A. Whitcomb, *Napoleon's Diplomatic Service* (Durham, NC, 1979).
32. There is a recent detailed account by Adam Zamoyski, *Rites of Peace: The Fall of Napoleon and the Congress of Vienna* (London, 2007). The wider significance of the settlement is made clear by Schroeder, *Transformation of European Politics*.
33. There are excellent brief surveys by Paul W. Schroeder: 'International Politics, Peace and War, 1815–1914', in T. C. W. Blanning (ed.), *The Nineteenth Century* (Oxford, 2000), 158–209, and 'The 19th Century System: Balance of Power or Political Equilibrium?', *Review of International Studies*, 15 (1989), 135–53; reprinted in Schroeder, *Systems, Stability and Statecraft*, 23–35.
34. There are some valuable essays in Markus Mösslang and Torsten Riotte (eds.), *The Diplomats' World: A Cultural History of Diplomacy 1815–1914* (Oxford, 2008).
35. Cf. T. G. Otte, '"Outdoor Relief for the Aristocracy"? European Nobility and Diplomacy', in Mösslang and Riotte (eds.), *Diplomats' World*, 23–59.

Bibliography

Anderson, M. S., *The Rise of Modern Diplomacy 1450–1919* (London, 1993).
Bély, Lucien, *Les Relations internationales en Europe, xviie–xviiie siècles* (Paris, 1992; 4th edn., 2007).
Blanning, T. C. W., 'Europe and the French Revolution', in Colin Lucas (ed.), *Rewriting the French Revolution* (Oxford, 1991), 183–206.
Bridge, F. R., and Bullen, Roger, *The Great Powers and the European States System 1815–1914* (2nd edn., Harlow, 2004).
Doyle, William, *The Oxford History of the French Revolution* (Oxford, 1989; 2nd edn., 2002).
Duchhardt, Heinz, *Balance of Power und Pentarchie: Internationale Beziehungen 1700–1785* (Paderborn, 1997).
Hamilton, Keith, and Langhorne, Richard, *The Practice of Diplomacy* (London, 1995).
Luard, Evan, *The Balance of Power: The System of International Relations 1648–1815* (Basingstoke, 1992).
Schroeder, Paul W., *The Transformation of European Politics, 1763–1848* (Oxford, 1994).
Scott, H. M., *The Birth of a Great Power System, 1740–1815* (Harlow, 2006).
Scott, Hamish, 'Diplomatic Culture in old regime Europe', in Hamish Scott and Brendan Simms (eds.), *Cultures of Power in Europe during the Long Eighteenth Century* (Cambridge, 2007), 58–85.
Sorel, Albert, *Europe and the French Revolution: The Political Traditions of the Old Régime* (1885; English tr. London, 1969).
Stone, Bailey, *The Genesis of the French Revolution: A Global-Historical Interpretation* (Cambridge, 1994).
——*Reinterpreting the French Revolution: A Global-Historical Perspective* (Cambridge, 2002).
Whiteman, Jeremy J., *Reform, Revolution and French Global Policy, 1787–1791* (Aldershot, 2003).

CHAPTER 4

ARMED FORCES

DAVID PARROTT

In early 1645 Field Marshal Lennard Torstensson led a Swedish army of 9,000 cavalry, 6,000 infantry, and 60 cannon against a Habsburg-Imperial army of 10,000 cavalry, 5,000 infantry, and 26 cannon commanded by Melchior von Hatzfeld. Both armies were composed of regiments commanded by international colonel-proprietors, who had used their funds or credit to raise and maintain military units. Many of the soldiers in both armies had been in service for ten years or more. The colonel-proprietors and generals in both armies regarded the recruitment of their experienced veterans as a long-term investment, and both were supported in their enterprises by an international network of private credit facilities, munitions manufacturers, food suppliers, and transport contractors. In both cases this elaborate structure was funded through control of the financial resources of entire territories, largely extracted and administered by the military high command. The armies clashed at Jankow in Bohemia, and the Imperial forces, though superior in cavalry, were held and eventually defeated by the Swedes, in part thanks to their artillery.

At the battle of Prague in May 1756, Frederick II of Prussia also faced an Austrian Habsburg army. In this case the Prussians fielded 65,000 troops and 214 cannon against Austrian forces of 62,000 and 177 cannon. While both armies contained mercenary units, the bulk of the forces were raised under the authority of the state. Prussia's rulers had adopted conscription early in the eighteenth century, as had the Austrian Habsburgs following the military disasters of the 1730s and 1740s. The state had assumed direct responsibility for the training, upkeep, and support of the armies, and in both the officers now served less as entrepreneurs, more as employees of the state. As at Jankow the result was a defeat for the Austrians, but the battle was extraordinarily costly, a pyrrhic victory for the Prussians, who suffered even heavier casualties than their opponents.

These two battles might be used as case studies to demonstrate the evolution of armed forces in the long century separating the end of the Thirty Years War from the Revolutionary Wars of the 1790s; they frame a style of warfare and of military force which may readily be identified with the dynastic states of the Ancien Régime. Yet while it is true that changes in scale, organization, technology, and tactics certainly took place both within land forces and at sea over this long century, it is important to avoid both oversimplifying the causes and exaggerating the extent of change. Above all, this period was not simply a story of the rise of modern forces controlled by the state overcoming a backward and ineffectual semi-private military system whose origins stretched back to the *condottieri* of renaissance Italy. The fierce and protracted fighting at Jankow provides a characteristic demonstration of the military qualities of privatized military forces, while the broader conduct of the 1645 campaign revealed operational skills of a high order. This effectiveness reflected the organizational and operational priorities of the military enterprisers themselves: small, high-quality, and extremely mobile campaigning armies—hence the very large proportions of cavalry—sustained on a broad base of territorial occupation and tax extraction, whose operations were carefully linked to an assessment of logistical and other support systems funded by these war taxes or 'contributions'. The same was true of navies, shaped by a combination of private and public initiatives in which a number of the largest warships were built and maintained by the ruler at direct charge to the state, but many more ships were built by subjects at their own cost and risk, commanded by captains whose main contribution to the war effort would be privateering activity, loosely integrated into collective naval operations. Such systems delivered impressive military results; they were also well-adapted to the needs and character of the early modern state. Military organization reflected a relationship between relatively weak central state power and the willingness of elites within and outside of particular societies to mobilize resources to provide military force on behalf of those states. It offered substantial incentives—financial, political, and social—to those members of the elites prepared to involve themselves in military activity, and who could mobilize resources considerably more effectively than rulers and their limited state administrations.

That said, the coming of peace at Münster and Osnabrück in 1648, then finally a settlement between France and Spain in 1659, did mark a turning point, and the emergence of a set of organizational and political compromises that defined the distinctive character of Ancien Régime armed forces. It was not, in general, that military enterprise was considered to have been a failure, but rulers nonetheless turned self-consciously back towards an ideal of direct control and maintenance of their armed forces. This was partly a matter of ideology: the ruler's self-projection as a *roi de guerre*, whose sovereignty was explicitly linked to personal control of his armed forces and the waging of war, made military enterprise appear an undermining of that sovereign authority. Moreover, while necessity in time of war could justify the collection of heavy taxes by the military itself, with the coming of peace it was less disruptive for the state and its agents to resume tax collection, especially as many rulers came out of the Thirty Years War with a clearer awareness of the taxable potential of their subjects. In France in the 1660s, despite the return of peace and a modest retrenchment of the main land tax, overall tax levels were kept at wartime levels.

Initially the objective of establishing military force under the direct control of the ruler, paid for from tax revenues collected and distributed by his administration, seemed attainable. The military reforms of Louis XIV's France in the decade after 1660 provide the paradigm for this reassertion of state control. More effective management of state finances and tax collection—considerably easier in a period of external peace and internal order—provided the basis on which a permanent army of around 55,000 troops could be created and funded, and allowed for the development of a virtually new navy and its support facilities. The army, in particular, was characterized by a much more intrusive administration under the aegis of the war ministers Michel Le Tellier and his son, the Marquis de Louvois. Codified regulations that were actually enforced, reasonable standards of discipline, especially with regard to civilian populations, and an insistence on external oversight of recruitment quality, equipment, and drill, all transformed the army into what was widely seen as an adjunct of royal authority and sovereignty. Such military initiatives were not merely the prerogative of the major powers: a similar bid to maintain and increase tax levels to sustain the army of Brandenburg-Prussia had created a peacetime army of 14,000 men under the direct control of the Elector by 1667.

This ideal of armies which were closely linked to the direct financial resources of the state, and of a manageable scale where central administration—a *Bureau de la guerre* or a *Kriegskommissariat*—could exercise a high degree of control and supervision over troop and officer recruitment, provisioning, discipline, and deployment, was a realistic target for the Ancien Régime state. Moreover, the forces that could be fielded through such direct systems of control and support were not necessarily limited to the comparatively small bodies assembled in the aftermath of the Thirty Years War; these were frequently envisaged as a nucleus of larger forces that would be raised in wartime, whether through recruitment at home or foreign mercenaries. The growth of state administration, both in numbers of personnel and the range of their activities and procedures, is an all-but universal phenomenon of the later seventeenth and eighteenth centuries. So, to some extent, is a steady increase in the burden of taxes that rulers could impose on their—usually unprivileged—subjects. Hemmed in by dependence on parliamentary grants for extraordinary tax revenues, even Charles II and James II of England were able to use their direct control over the growing and better-administered revenues from customs and excise to fund a standing army which grew from 15,000 in 1670 to something over 30,000 men in late 1688. So post-1650, rulers could in theory look to maintaining and controlling armies and navies that were compatible with their growing share of state resources and the developing range and sophistication of their administrations.

However, this was not how the armies of the Ancien Régime developed in practice. What occurred instead was a process in which the demands of armies and navies, and especially their costs, outstripped the capacity of the state to meet them. It was not, in most cases, a consciously-sought development, and its impact was largely counter-productive in terms of the effectiveness of armed forces. As so often in military history, the waging of war was driven forward by its own dynamic; once the self-regulatory and self-limiting style of entrepreneurial warfare had been abandoned, the road was opened to a type of armed force and style of combat which overwhelmed the resources of the state and led to military stagnation and a variety of political and social tensions through the later seventeenth and eighteenth centuries.

One factor in this transformation was military technology. The gradual introduction from the 1680s of muskets equipped with a cheap but reliable flintlock mechanism replaced the older weapons in which the charge in the musket's breech was ignited by applying a piece of lighted, slow-burning match. Virtually simultaneous with this was the development of the ring-bayonet, providing the musketeer with both an offensive and defensive weapon. The traditional infantry elite, the pikemen, whose solid presence had both served to protect reloading and vulnerable musketeers from the shock of cavalry or charging infantry, and had themselves proved a formidable offensive arm, were almost entirely phased out by the early eighteenth century. Although a standardized, flintlock- and bayonet-armed infantry may be thought to usher in an era of warfare dominated by the massed firepower of infantry, in fact musketry remained grossly ineffective: poor production qualities, limited range, and minimal accuracy were compounded by a rate of fire that by the standards of industrialized warfare remained cripplingly slow even in the best-drilled units. In fact, firepower did transform the battlefield, but it was developments in artillery which were the key. Though the basic technology of the muzzle-loaded field gun remained unchanged through this period, better casting, lighter barrels and carriages, more mobility, and standardization led to a huge increase in the numbers of artillery deployed on the battlefield: perhaps most significant, these improvements led to the proliferation of more mobile medium-weight guns, the nine- to twelve-pound field pieces which dominated the battlefields of Europe until the mid-nineteenth century. From the Thirty Years War with a couple of dozen guns on either side, though to an engagement like Malplaquet (1709) with 100 Allied guns against 60 French, to Torgau (1760) where 360 Austrian field guns were deployed against 320 Prussian, the role of the artillery was ever more central to the battlefield and the siege. Massive concentrations of artillery fire, equipped with a fearsome range of anti-personnel missiles, blasted infantry and cavalry formations alike.

These changes had some paradoxical consequences for tactics and deployment on the battlefield. The effectiveness of artillery led to a further increase in the numbers of gun crews and officers, but an obvious response to this greater lethality was an attempt to get larger forces, principally more infantry, onto the battlefield. Yet the infantry massed on the battlefield were not merely subject to slaughter by opposing artillery; the thinning out of the infantry line, which by the mid-eighteenth century was three rows deep and whose only defence after a handful of musket rounds was the bayonet, also made them much more vulnerable to cavalry. As many astute commanders recognized, the battle-winning arm, given that the artillery could not exploit the advantages that its firepower created, remained the cavalry. Yet cavalry as a proportion of armies declined steadily in the century from 1660 to 1760, from around one-third to around one-quarter of the total combatants. Military logic might have suggested a great increase in the proportions of cavalry, especially light forces of the sort that had been typical of eastern European warfare for centuries, but military budgets ensured that the cavalry remained underdeveloped.

The proliferation of artillery also had a drastic impact on siege warfare, seen since the late sixteenth century as the most typical form of combat, and another reason why the battlefield advantages brought by more cavalry could be downplayed. After decades in which artillery-resistant fortifications had proved an intractable challenge to besieging armies, the numbers of guns that could be assembled for a siege in the later wars of Louis XIV finally tipped the balance in favour of the offensive. Sieges of major fortified places in the sixteenth and earlier seventeenth century had been won through a haphazard, lengthy, and expensive process of blockade, the defeat of enemy relief forces and occasionally either mining or direct assault, rather than by artillery barrage and breach. This was superseded by methodical prescriptions for conducting a siege by parallel trenches dug progressively closer to the fortifications, and protected from the defenders' fire by zig-zag communication lines. Using these trenches to move artillery further forward, the fortifications and their defenders would be progressively ground into surrender. The only response was that pioneered by the French fortification-genius Marshal Vauban, whose *pré carré* provided a massive proliferation of state-of-the-art fortifications in a deep defensive barrier stretching along the French frontiers. Individual fortresses could be taken, but as the commanders of the Allied armies, Marlborough and Eugene of Savoy, were to discover in their campaigns after 1708, the time and cost required to take out a sufficient block of such fortified *places* reduced their invasion of France to a slow, attritional frontier struggle. On the defensive (down)side, the costs of building and then of garrisoning and maintaining such fortification systems was immense. Moreover, experiences such as Maurice de Saxe's campaign in the Austrian Netherlands in the 1740s cast doubt even on these massive fortress-systems as a means to ensure defensive security. The strongest fortifications were unlikely to hold out if it was clear to the fortress commanders that there was no supporting army in the field capable of driving off the besieging forces.

Artillery had the capacity to transform battlefields and sieges into more lethal spaces than hitherto, but one part of this capacity would reflect the rigorous training of artillery crews in manœuvring guns, and above all in loading, firing, and reloading them as rapidly as possible. This drew upon a much broader seam of organizational and, to an extent, social change: such effective fire would be best achieved, it was considered, by the imposition of a mechanical sequence of procedures on the gunners, learnt by rote and taught by rigorous practice and discipline. And to an even larger extent this would be the requirement for the infantry. If the musket/bayonet combination was to approach its (limited) maximum potential as a battlefield technology, then rates of fire needed to be optimized, as did the way in which firepower was deployed through a unit of soldiers, and the way that the unit was to manœuvre to defend itself or to exploit changing battlefield circumstances. The means to achieve this was through drill. Formal drill became the *raison d'être* of infantry training, imposed uniformly on cohesive groups of soldiers from the day of recruitment throughout their military careers. For drill to achieve mechanically disciplined, rapidly responsive, and cohesive infantry, more than a few weeks in a training camp were needed. The Marquis de Chamlay commented that whereas it was possible to have good cavalry troopers within a year of their enlistment, it took a minimum of five to six years to produce infantry who could deploy disciplined fire without losing cohesion.[1]

Three consequences stemmed from the development of drill. First, the time and expense involved was too great to allow the soldiers to go back into civilian life after a few years of service. Volunteers, as in France, Britain, and some of the German states, were contracted and compelled to stay in service sometimes for decades. Where conscription was introduced, adult male populations might benefit from relatively enlightened systems such as the Prussian, or the Swedish *Indelningsverk*, whereby after initial training the men were kept militarily effective by regular drill camps but otherwise allowed to pursue their civilian lives. Elsewhere they could be subject to more brutal demands, as in Peter the Great's Russia, where a proportion of the servants and tenants of the landowning class were simply conscripted for life. Conscription in its various forms became a characteristic of the Ancien Régime state; by the 1690s even France started to use the compulsory local service of provincial militias as a 'feeder-system' for the regular army. A second consequence was that the very long service required of conscripts and volunteers made soldiers more prone to desert. In consequence, military authorities sought to keep soldiers under close supervision. Typically, segregation from the civilian population was adopted as the most effective means to oversee enlisted soldiers, and when feasible this led to their confinement in purpose-built barracks. Both these factors contributed to a third: service as a common soldier lost any remaining social standing. While in the Thirty Years War veterans had seen themselves, and had been treated, as the equivalent of skilled workers, the Ancien Régime soldiers, often separated from the civil population and subordinated to a harsh military code, were relegated to the lowest status. A vicious circle developed in which low social esteem made recruitment more difficult, and encouraged the NCOs and officers to treat their men with even more brutal discipline and greater contempt.

Transformation in the organization and structure of navies under the Ancien Régime was no less evident. Here there was massive change from the 1650s, not because of rulers' concern about their sovereign status, but as a result of what has a proper claim to be regarded as a technological and tactical 'military revolution' at sea. The first Anglo-Dutch naval wars revealed a decisive shift in naval tactics towards sea battles waged through an outright reliance on firepower: line astern tactics permitted each warship to deploy the firepower of at least half its guns at close range against enemy vessels. There was no going back, and in a few decades naval tactics and naval technology were transformed. It required the creation of fleets of purpose-built warships, capable of carrying the maximum number of artillery pieces compatible with their size, and built so far as possible to protect them both from the strains of their own firepower and the impact of shot fired by enemy warships. The highest-rated ships were built on a scale and with an artillery provision which hugely increased the numbers of their crews and transformed the proportionate size (as well as expense) of the naval arm of most states' armed forces. Tactical developments brought a radical change to the mechanisms of assembling and maintaining fleets. The possibility of creating dual-purpose ships, able to carry an adequate armament to take part in naval engagements but also to perform as merchant vessels, and built to the standards and costings of the latter, disappeared after 1650 for ships from the first to the third rate—in the case of France, ships from 3,000 down to 800 tonnes displacement. Battle tactics placed a premium on large, heavily gunned warships and on their construction and maintenance through purpose-built dockyards. This had a direct consequence in terms of the numbers of sailors and marines now required—between 800 and 1,000 men each for the largest, first-rate ships—and placed the issue of recruitment at the forefront of the concerns of naval administrations and governments. A combination of official or unofficial conscription was characteristic: in Britain, reliance on the press-gang and other, formally speaking illegal, methods to seize sailors from merchant ships in ports and along the coasts; in France the Colbertian system of registration by 'classes'—lists of experienced sailors liable for naval service, usually for one year in three, who could not be hired to serve on merchant ships during the year when their 'class' was due for service. In contrast to military service on land, the skills possessed or acquired by sailors had considerable value in the civil economy, and though physical conditions on ships were generally appalling, a level of tolerance and forbearance in the treatment of sailors and in their relationships with their officers recognized this value.

Yet the transformation most evident in Ancien Régime armed forces was that of numbers and scale. Even the most exaggerated assertions about the size of armies raised in the century before 1650—most of which have no foundation in army rolls or muster details, and all of which ignore fluctuations between and within campaigns—are still dwarfed by the scale of the war effort sustained by armies and navies from the 1690s onwards.

To some extent the technological and consequent organizational change indicated above could account for an upward pressure on the scale of armed forces, and perhaps especially the size of forces concentrated on the battlefield. But it would not of itself have generated the growth in military establishments on the scale seen in the decades from the 1680s to the eighteenth century. The great increases in this period were not primarily driven by military factors and their implications, but were a consequence of the conduct of international politics. Louis XIV's inept and threatening diplomacy throughout the 1680s drew France inexorably towards a war against a coalition of every other major west–central European power. Holding her own against this alliance after 1688 required an unparalleled military effort. France's enemies responded with a scale of mobilization

Table 4.1. The strength of the armies (in 000s)

	1660	1675	1695	1710	1756	1780
France	55	250	340	255	290	136
England	16	15	65	75	47	39
Austria	30	60	95	120	210	314
Spain	77	70	51	50	56	85
Prussia	12	14	31	43	200	195
Dutch Republic	70	63	76	31	36	
Savoy-Piedmont	5.5	6	23	22	24	24
Russia		130	220	344	400	

Source: J. Luh, *Kriegskunst in Europa, 1650–1800* (Cologne, 2004), 17; J. Childs, *Armies and Warfare in Europe, 1648–1789* (Manchester, 1982).

Table 4.2. The strength of the navies (shipping tonnage in 000s)

	1660	1690	1700	1740	1760	1780	1790
Britain	88	124	196	195	375	372	473
France	20	141	195	91	156	271	324
Netherlands	62	68	113	65	62	70	123
Spain	(30)	(20)	91	137	196	253	
Russia (Baltic and Black Sea Fleets)	24	37	46	82	190		

Source: J. Glete, *Navies and Nations: Warships, Navies and State-Building in Europe and America, 1500–1860* (2 vols. Stockholm, 1993), i. 192, 241, 311.

which would collectively match and surpass the 340,000 soldiers and 150,000 tonnes of naval force that France managed to throw into the struggle. Military expansion moved eastwards in the mid-eighteenth century, where the triangular contest between Prussia, Austria, and Russia in the decades after 1740 had the same effect on army growth. Frederick II inherited an army of 80,000 in 1740, but the wars over Silesia pushed this up to 200,000. Austrian military expansion following the disasters of the 1740s was no less impressive, while exploitation of lifetime conscription ensured that Russia overtook all other European states in military manpower. The final driver of military—this time naval—expansion was European colonial and trade rivalry and warfare, and above all the determination of the British to maintain oceanic naval supremacy over any other European power. The Royal Navy, which reached a peak of 196,000 tonnes in 1700, underwent progressive increases through the 1750s when the total rose through 276,000 tonnes up to 473,000 tonnes by 1790. This increase in the size of British naval force was not surpassed by any other European power, but the attempt to build forces that were at least comparable stimulated naval growth throughout the eighteenth century. Whether this reflected the ambition of combined French and Spanish Bourbon fleets to challenge the British in the Atlantic, or concerned the exercise of naval power by Russia and the Scandinavian powers in the Baltic, the net effect was a steady growth in the size of naval forces, and for most states this naval growth moved in step with demands for massive land forces.

Yet European powers in the late seventeenth and early eighteenth centuries proved able to sustain these increases; states did not collapse under the burden of maintaining armed forces. It is not easy to explain this in terms of rising prosperity, demographic, or economic growth. For in west–central Europe the biggest military increases coincided with a long period of economic stagnation from 1650 to 1720/30. In this later seventeenth and early eighteenth century, Britain and the United Provinces were exceptional in achieving broad-based economic growth. France and the German or Italian states saw ever-more troops and revenues being extracted from peoples barely able to meet these demands. In contrast, it was certainly the case that from the 1730s European rulers began to benefit from economic and demographic growth. Economic progress fostered technological improvement and cheaper production of military goods such as reliable cast-iron cannon for both navies and land armies. A mid-century transformation of agriculture allowed more efficient land-use, which had effects on military operations through a steady growth in the populations which provided army and navy personnel. But the largest military expansion had occurred before these advantages came into play, in states whose economies remained depressed and limited.

Because the huge growth in military force achieved by rulers like Louis XIV, Charles XI of Sweden, Frederick-Wilhelm I of Prussia could not be attributed to expanding economic and demographic potential, a traditional and now easily-derided response was to shroud the process in a mysterious and frequently circular set of assertions about the personal power and capability of 'absolutist' monarchs. A slightly more plausible interpretation argued that this military growth was the result of growing bureaucratic and governmental effectiveness. Better-assessed taxes collected under the threat of military coercion allowed further tax increases, which in turn made possible further growth in the armed forces. Armed forces and central authority are assumed to grow in a single, internally-cohesive process. It is indisputable that the character of Ancien Régime armies would have been very different without the developing administrative competence and greater coercive power of the states concerned. The Austrian military reforms of the 1740s were the result of military experience working within an increasingly effective administration, while Frederick II's comments on the differences between Prussia and (unreformed) Austria stress the importance of administrative capacity: 'I have seen small states able to maintain themselves against the greatest monarchies, when these states possessed industry and great order in their affairs. I find that large empires, fertile in abuses, are full of confusion and only are sustained by their vast resources, and the intrinsic weight of the body.'[2]

Nevertheless, improvements in administration, better accountability, and more efficient collection and use of tax revenues would not alone have allowed Louis XIV in the early 1690s to support an army of 340,000 men and a navy of at least 30,000 sailors, any more than in 1740 would it have allowed Frederick William I of Prussia to maintain a standing army of 80,000 troops. Substantial elements of the costs of war were still met by extorting war taxes from occupied lands and from foreign subsidies such as those provided by Britain to Frederick William I. Both helped to maintain larger forces than could have been supported from native resources, but for the most part they were factors that operated only in wartime. And as the Swedes discovered to their cost in the aftermath of 1648, supporting troops at the cost of neighbouring states or through subsidies from powerful, self-interested paymasters, could involve a heavy political and military price.

An explanation for the sustainability of armed forces must recognize that Ancien Régime rulers and governments involved needed to draw upon the cooperation and interests of their economic and social elites, groups who did not necessarily share the priorities and culture of a central administration. The scale of warfare and of standing forces required far larger financial resources than were readily available to rulers who, despite the developments in their bureaucracies, still possessed limited fiscal leverage over the resources of their elites. Either the fiscal regime in practice conceded them virtual exemption from state taxation or, as in Britain and the United Provinces, accepted that taxes required negotiation via representative institutions composed of those elites. Raising and equipping unprecedented armed forces required turning to these under-taxed elites and finding ways of persuading them to commit resources to the ruler's war effort. Moreover, once in being, the day-to-day management and support of armies and navies might also require financial and administrative commitment from the senior and unit officers that went far beyond their strictly defined duties as military employees of the ruler. All of these were areas in which the active cooperation of elites were sought, and where the organization of military force was tempered by the compromises and recognition of interests that this required. One result was that during the eighteenth century military establishments became increasingly conservative, resisting attempts to change their organization or social structures.

These various points of intersection between the army as an instrument of the state and the army as a product of a continuing and evolving set of roles for the elites, make it plain that the world of military enterprise did not come to an abrupt end around 1650. The age of the great 'general contractors' of the Thirty Years War like Albrecht Wallenstein or Bernhard of Saxe-Weimar with direct control over the raising, operations, and support-systems of their armies was over; but for elites throughout this period, military command continued to hold a unique role in underpinning social status. They expected and wished to exercise roles in the army or navy, and in general demand for officerships, and especially for unit commands or senior positions, considerably exceeded supply. Most rulers were to some extent in a position to play off the military expectations of traditional nobles with high social status against wealthy, *arriviste* families, who would be prepared to pay heavily for the competitive privilege of holding prestigious military command. Moreover social competition once within the army or navy was a great incentive to competitive conspicuous consumption, which could be manipulated to support many of the costs of establishing and maintaining military units at the expense of the officers.

Emulation, magnificence, and status display would certainly persuade some officers to spend their resources in ways that would help to meet the financial burdens of the military establishment. Thus, while armies adopted military uniforms from the later seventeenth century, those uniforms were varied in design, detail, and expense to accommodate the whims of colonel-proprietors anxious to impose their own identity on their unit. Yet even very wealthy officers would for the most part exercise some prudence in the extent to which they would underwrite the expenses of their regiments or companies, whether to enhance their outward appearance through better uniforms or cavalry mounts, or to meet shortfalls in wages and rations for their soldiers. For the majority it was important to be assured not only that personal funds expended to enhance the unit would be socially visible and would enhance the prestige of the commander, but that some part of this investment could be recovered, or indeed enhanced by judicious spending. To tap these potentially larger and more sustained financial resources, most Ancien Régime states continued, modified, or introduced forms of proprietorship in their military establishments, in effect expanding their armed forces under what were public–private financial partnerships.

In France, and subsequently in the Bourbon Spanish empire, the system in the army did not take the form of outright regimental ownership, but was a series of established conventions by which commands of companies and regiments and of higher posts in the army would change hands on payment of a specified sum. In theory these sums would be fixed, but in practice they varied widely with the prestige of the unit and the state of its soldiers, equipment, and general effectiveness. Elsewhere, especially in the German territories, the traditional system of colonel-proprietors (*Obrist-Inhaber*) continued into the eighteenth century. In the Austrian army the regimental *Inhaber* would nominate an acting colonel, and could appoint directly all the officers up to the level of captain. During the first half of the eighteenth century the system of proprietorship continued at the company level, with the captain rather than the colonel as businessman-investor. The captain now kept his men clothed, their equipment in good order, and the company strength at the established level. This initial capital investment, much of it reclaimed from soldiers' wages and from judicious management of day-to-day expenses, provided some profit during the life of the unit, while rights of ownership ensured a realistic level of compensation when it changed hands. Profit and patronage on behalf of the state came together in the hands of landowner-captains who used their influence to raise recruits more cheaply and to reward local clients with junior officerships. Even in Russia, where military proprietorship as such did not exist, the government relied upon the interests of a 'servitor' class of officer-landowners who operated the conscription system in return for the power to appoint their clients as subalterns and NCOs, and to extract whatever financial gains they could without totally undermining the effectiveness of the troops.

In other spheres of military organization the relationship between state and entrepreneurial elites persisted, but with different emphasis. While uniforms, weapons, and regimental accessories were provided by the colonel or captain, the general supply of food and campaign munitions was contracted out to entrepreneurial consortia or individual suppliers. The convenience of drawing on the organizational efficiencies of private suppliers and their networks remained an incentive, even to more efficient administrations. Both in providing for the logistical needs of the armies, and in the case of navies providing much of the capital and materials required to push forward massive construction programmes, the Ancien Régime state drew on the availability of immediate financial resources from its elites, and made contracts with private suppliers for the provision of equipment and services. Rulers accepted the greater costs of the latter in cumulative interest payments and debt servicing but, as ever, prioritized rapid access to resources and the organizational expertise and professional contacts of the financial and mercantile elites. Despite administrative systems of revenue-collection which were more efficient and reached deeper into the resources of the unprivileged majority in these societies, many of the absolute monarchies continued to fund warfare through systems of revenue anticipation which were clumsy, informal, and hugely expensive and wasteful in terms of interest payments and repayment of short-term borrowing. The obvious beneficiaries of these clumsy and essentially corrupt systems of war finance were those elite groups whose capital could be deployed through financier consortia and privileged, informal agreements to provide high-interest loans to the state. Contemporaries were well aware of the implications of these links between government and elite interests. For example, large elements of the construction, maintenance, and supply of the navy created by Colbert from the 1660s drew as a matter of policy on the financial and organizational resources of networks of private contractors and financiers. It was this which paved the way for one of the most dramatic reversions from public back to private military administration in this period, the decision by the hard-pressed French crown in 1693–4 to eliminate the French battle fleet, to lay up and abandon the major warships, and to encourage the captains of fourth- and fifth-rate vessels to take on personal financial responsibility for these as privateers, serving under letters of marque issued by the government.

By the mid-eighteenth century, and in some cases earlier, there was a widening recognition that the 'partnership' which rulers had accepted with their elites to sustain the organizational and financial burdens of their armies was something of a Faustian bargain. It entrenched a series of vested interests—social, economic, and political—within the armed forces, via an officer corps whose stranglehold became increasingly apparent as the need to rethink the structuring, professionalization, and recruitment of armed forces became a priority. Although wealthy commoners and those with noble status which did not reflect extensive lineage or appropriate quarterings were a small and shrinking proportion of the officer corps of the major armies, the predominance of traditional nobles in these Ancien Régime officer corps was not in itself the problem. If Frederick II was explicit about the need to purge the 'commoner riff-raff' from his officer corps after the Seven Years War, and the non-noble component of the French officer corps in the eighteenth-century amounted to no more than 20–25 per cent, such exclusivity was justified by assertions about noble aptitude for war: they were born to command and possessed a developed sense of honour and devotion to duty. Yet there were persistent antagonisms among the nobles themselves which offset this presumed homogeneity in service. Appointment and promotion mechanisms created a deep fissure between the minority of high/court nobility, possessing large financial resources, and the majority of ordinary provincial nobles with good lineage but little or no wealth that could be used to advance their positions within a structure of purchased military office. In the French, Austrian, and British armies a minority of great noble families virtually monopolized both unit commands and the high command, not through any proven military accomplishments, but because they could provide the financial wherewithal for their rulers to raise and maintain large forces. Lesser nobles found themselves blocked for promotion, despite the long service or display of other criteria for high rank. Even in Prussia, where the contrast between wealthy and poor nobles was less marked, professionalism and proven merit counted for less than influence and access in filling the highest ranks of the army.

Social tensions within the armed forces could have erupted elsewhere, but in France the particular sharpness of the contrast between the opportunities offered to rich and poor nobles, combined with spectacular military failure in the Seven Years War—most notoriously at the battle of Rossbach in 1757—caused a reaction which brought together an alliance of dissatisfied noble career officers and a series of reformist war ministers, notably Choiseul, Saint Germain, and Brienne. The main point of agreement was that reform of army and navy must start with the officers, and that, while remaining the preserve of the nobility, the officer corps should be opened to meritocratic promotion. In 1776 the greatest blockage to promotion for long-serving subalterns, venality of captaincies and colonelcies, began to be phased out. The huge surplus of senior officers who were merely on the lists and the pay-rolls of the French army was to be cut back, while the lack of professionalism amongst those who did offer active military service was the other target. These initiatives provoked massive opposition from vested interests, and at times in the decades after 1760 the alliance of reformist ministers with dissatisfied subalterns threatened both the careers of ministers and the survival of the administration. Yet the French war ministers and their counterparts in other states were greatly assisted by a broader, open debate about the future character and methods of waging war, and by the resulting acknowledgement that changes to the structure, organization, and deployment of military forces were unavoidable.

The key areas of this debate from the mid-eighteenth century were about military organization and resources. On land, tactical theory and practice dictated a military system which had demanded much more than raw recruits hastily pushed into the ranks. The unprecedented forces placed in the field required equally unprecedented levels of training via the drill manual and the barrack square. This could easily create a situation in which years, sometimes decades, of drill and training aimed at maximizing firepower and inculcating forbearance under that fire was deployed on the battlefield or the siege in an attritional combat that would ensure heavy casualties on both sides. A war of battles on the scale of the Seven Years War was exceedingly costly in the lives of trained soldiers. The combination of massed artillery, infantry that were resilient in defence but lacked the weight and momentum to carry through an offensive, and cavalry in too small numbers to exploit a potentially decisive role, all ensured that battles were murderous slaughters in which winning an outright victory was as much a matter of chance as of any kind of genius in command or tactical progress.

The alternative model, contributing to the ongoing debate, was based on the theory and practice of a war of manœuvre, the possibility of denying an enemy army opportunities to advance, threatening its communication and supply lines in order to prevent any operational gains, and with luck, ensuring that it was driven into territory where inadequate supply potential would decimate the soldiers through hunger and desertion. It was war as a direct extension of diplomacy: a means to increase pressure on another power, not by confronting them with the prospect of annihilating military defeat and invasion, but by bringing incremental military advantages that would shape protracted negotiations over issues of territorial rights and succession. This is often, mistakenly, seen as the characteristic form of eighteenth-century warfare: in contrast to the bloodiness of the seventeenth century and the still greater blood-letting of the Revolutionary and Napoleonic Wars, military operations and combat are presented as convention-bound, modest in aspiration, and sparing in casualties. Many rulers of states might actually have preferred war to have been fought under these forms and conventions, but actual eighteenth-century combat reveals a different picture in which large-scale battles and equally hard-fought sieges were as characteristic of military operations as in any other period, and from the 1690s to 1760s as bloody and attritional as anything fought before.

For there were two practical problems which undermined this theory of a virtually bloodless war. The first was that military supply systems with all their physical and man-made limitations presented logistical problems which had become exponentially worse now that an army campaigning in a single theatre could reach a strength of 50,000–60,000, and on occasions as many as 100,000 men. The military orthodoxy of supply lines and magazines had been well-established by the later seventeenth century. It was assumed—correctly in the 1690s, but with less justification as the agrarian and demographic transformation of the decades from the 1730s made itself felt—that a substantial field army could not sustain military operations by local requisitioning of supplies. Moreover, given the conditions under which soldiers served, it was considered that detaching them from the army to act as foraging or fodder parties, except under the most stringent and counter-productive surveillance, was a recipe for mass desertion. As a result armies were tied to the traditional logistical system of magazines, and to the supply convoys and mobile ovens which could ensure provision of bread to the troops. In such circumstances it was the very exceptional commander who could move a large army with speed and operational purpose in a genuinely effective campaign of manœuvre. This explains the predominance of siege warfare; it was not just the widely shared conviction that no significant fortified place could be left in the rear of an advancing army without posing an unacceptable threat to supply and communication lines, but the fact that a set-piece siege, just over the frontiers into enemy territory, was the optimum objective for the cumbersome and elaborate logistical systems that dominated military thinking. The second problem with a war of manœuvre was that it was only possible if both sides were prepared to work within the same conventions; when military commanders like Marlborough, Eugene of Savoy, Charles XII, Frederick II, were prepared to envisage and pursue battle as an operational objective, any opponent not prepared to adopt the same aggressive *modus operandi* would face a shattering defeat, ruling out any prospect of a relatively bloodless outcome and subsequent piecemeal negotiation. The Austrian military crisis of the 1740s illustrates this initial failure to adjust to an enemy who was playing to very different operational rules.

By the middle third of the eighteenth century the sense that a military impasse had been reached was strong and pervasive. Even naval warfare was not immune from the growing awareness that it was impossible to build on success to establish any kind of unassailable advantage. If the Seven Years War had been an apparently comprehensive triumph for the ships and sailors of the Royal Navy, the American War of Independence had demonstrated British vulnerability in the face of a determined and powerful naval alliance of her enemies. The extraordinary French naval build-up of these years had emphasized just how much effort would be required in future to safeguard a position of naval superiority, one which remained vulnerable despite investment in technical improvements and maintenance of warships, high levels of discipline and training amongst the sailors, and an officer corps far more professionally minded than their landed counterparts.

Some theorists, especially those who appreciated the changing agrarian/demographic environment in which future wars would be fought, began to refine ideas of *kleine Krieg*. If a war of manœuvre was unsustainable with typical large campaign armies, a return to numbers of smaller, independent forces, which could sustain themselves by living off the land in fast-moving, hard-hitting campaigns, would offer a plausible solution—one in fact that had been demonstrated by the enterpriser-commanders of army corps in the last decade of the Thirty Years War. Coordinating these smaller forces in a larger operational strategy would be a challenge, but there is evidence that this was being achieved both by Frederick II in the Seven Years War, and by the Russian armies in the Russo-Turkish War of 1768–74.

But it was not clear how such a new military system would work against an enemy who continued to concentrate massive forces and pursued strategies of confrontation and annihilation. Given the likely realities of land warfare, the optimum military solution to the problems that had opened up in the later eighteenth century would involve raising armies of sufficient size that high casualties would be less important to final outcome, and finding means by which they could attain acceptable levels of military competence and effectiveness without years—decades—of intensive drill and training. While the Prussian model of precision-trained infantry was admired, above all after the Seven Years War, it was widely acknowledged that this was an unsustainably extravagant system—Prussia's own reserves of drill-perfected troops were being ground down to nothing by 1761. To others, moreover, it could seem that insistence on such mechanically learnt drill would deprive nations with a different martial ethos of their own best fighting qualities. It was in this atmosphere that the ideas of Count Jacques de Guibert, most notably, could find echo in the reforming aspirations of ministers. The first objective was to professionalize the officer corps, the 'soul' of the army, and to imbue them with a sense of duty and commitment that a system based on proprietorship and interest could never manage to achieve. It was also important to revolutionize the recruitment and subsequent training and treatment of ordinary soldiers. Guibert's *Essai Général de Tactique* of 1772, with its idealization of the Roman citizen militia, might seem to look backwards to Machiavelli rather than forward to the *levée en masse* of 1793. But in its recognition of the potential force of national sentiment, and its conviction that the military future lay in involvement of the people, that quantity and *élan* might overwhelm the finite resource of disciplined, highly drilled troops, it offered a radical but not unattainable solution to the problems of late eighteenth-century warfare. The huge expansion of armed forces seen from the 1790s as a result of ever-more ruthless and extensive conscription; the rhetoric of the 'nation in arms' and of the exigencies of national defence, so easily exported from France to other European states, with all of its implications for raising revenues and establishing ever vaster military support systems; the professionalization and nationalization of officer corps: all of these were prefigured in the debates about the character of warfare and the changing demands that this placed on armed forces. As in so many other areas of politics and society, the traditional assumption that the Ancien Régime was immobile and incapable of change without violent upheaval needs sceptical reassessment.

Notes

1. Cited in H. Drévillon, *L'Impôt du sang: Le Métier des armes sous Louis XIV* (Paris, 2005), 365.
2. Quoted in T. C. W. Blanning, *The French Revolutionary Wars, 1787–1802* (London, 1996), 6.

Bibliography

Bien, D., 'The Army in the French Enlightenment: Reform, Reaction and Revolution', *Past and Present*, 83 (1979), 68–98.

Black, J., *European Warfare, 1660–1815* (London, 1994).

Blanning, T. C. W., *The French Revolutionary Wars, 1787–1802* (London, 1996).

Büsch, O., *Military System and Social Life in Old Regime Prussia, 1713–1807*, tr. J. Gagliardo (Leiden, 1997).

Childs, J., *Armies and Warfare in Europe, 1648–1789* (Manchester, 1982).

Cornette, J., *Le Roi de Guerre: Essai sur la souveraineté dans la France du Grand Siècle* (Paris, 1993).

Dessert, D., *La Royale: Vaisseaux et marins du Roi-Soleil* (Paris, 1996).

Drévillon, H., *L'Impôt du sang: Le Métier des armes sous Louis XIV* (Paris, 2005).

Duffy, C., *The Fortress in the Age of Vauban and Frederick the Great, 1660–1789* (London, 1985).

—— *The Military Experience in the Age of Reason* (London, 1987).

Glete, J., *Navies and Nations: Warships, Navies and State-Building in Europe and America, 1500–1860* (2 vols. Stockholm, 1993).

Keep, J. H., *Soldiers of the Tsar: Army and Society in Russia, 1462–1874* (Oxford, 1985).

Lund, E., *War for the Every Day: Generals, Knowledge, and Warfare in Early Modern Europe, 1680–1740* (Westport, Conn., and London, 1999).

Paret, P., 'Conscription and the End of the Ancien Régime in France and Prussia', in Paret, *Understanding War: Essays on Clausewitz and the History of Military Power* (Princeton, 1992), 53–74.

Pritchard, J., *Louis XV's Navy, 1748–1762: A Study of Organization and Administration* (Montreal, 1987).

Redlich, F., *The German Military Enterpriser and his Work Force, 14th to 18th Centuries. Vierteljahrschrift für Sozial- und Wirtschaftsgeschichte*, 47–8 (2 vols. Wiesbaden, 1964).

Rodger, N. A. M., *The Wooden World. An Anatomy of the Georgian Navy* (London, 1986).

Rowlands, G., *The Dynastic State and the Army under Louis XIV: Royal Service and Private Interest, 1661–1701* (Cambridge, 2002).

CHAPTER 5

FINANCES

JOËL FÉLIX

REFERENCES to an Ancien Régime probably first began to appear about a quarter of a century before the outbreak of the French Revolution. The expression emerged within the buoyant mid-eighteenth-century economic literature which sought to promote the modernization of the structures of the Bourbon monarchy and became, in the immediate aftermath of the Seven Years War (1756–63), the main driving force behind the reforming agenda implemented by the crown in order to pay off war debts, in particular, and restore the dynasty's prestige in general. Crop failures, however, forced economic reformers to react against the possibility of a return to what they then named the a*ncien régime*, in other words the 'mercantile' legislation which they regarded as the cause of all the evils. In a pamphlet entitled *Instructions aux magistrats* (1769), Abbé Roubaud used the words *ancien régime* three times to warn against the repealing of the liberal corn laws introduced in 1763–4 which, according to their opponents, far from boosting economic growth, were fostering a sharp rise in the price of bread and generating popular riots.[1]

It is quite possible that the new vocabulary, which briefly reappeared in a few writings published during the time of Turgot's economic ministry (1774–6), remained limited to the diminishing pool of diehard supporters of the physiocrat movement. Yet the terminology was already available in circulation and would reach a wider audience when manuscript news sheets, subscribed in France and Europe, once again used the words *ancien régime*, this time to comment upon the resignation of Jacques Necker, the famous Swiss-born minister of Louis XVI's finances, in 1781: 'it seems that the old regime of finances will be restored: one cannot say the old system, as it is not certain that one has been adopted'.[2] Although the words Ancien Régime do not figure in the volumes of the *Encyclopédie méthodique* devoted to *Finances* (1784/7), Rousselot de Surgy, its editor, also called for 'a new system of finances' to replace the old and inefficient existing rules, so as to further the well-being of generations to come.[3]

The term *Ancien Régime* was thus a main product of the discussions generated by the reflections of the French economists who, as Adam Smith rightly put it, 'treat not only of what is properly called Political Economy, or of the nature and causes of wealth of nations, but of every other branch of the system of government'.[4] For in their analysis of the production and distribution of wealth, physiocrats participated in the wider agenda of the Enlightenment: they aimed to discover a set of basic and simple universal rules, like Newton's laws of gravitation, that would allow governments to administer national resources for the well-being of society rather than abandon this task to *financiers* whose selfish interests underlay the arcane system of taxes, the hardships of the population, the shortfalls in state revenue, and, not least, inter-state wars. This economic analysis was of course integrated into new political systems (notably because change seemed to require a new political order capable of freeing government from the influence of the *financiers* and entrenched interests). Among the most influential was Abbé Sieyès's revolutionary formulation, in January 1789, of the principle of the sovereignty of the Third Estate on the grounds of their economic usefulness, which by the same token excluded from the Nation all *privilégiés* for being non-productive and, even worse, parasites on the wealth of the nation. It appears, therefore, that in the three decades prior to 1789, economic reforms, or public discussion of reforms, either successful or short-lived, accustomed the French—and many European states equally engaged with fiscal issues and the economic ideas of the Enlightenment—to the existence of two different and opposite worlds, that of the Ancien Régime and a new and better one which had still to be given a name but that historians would later label and define as the Modern World.

The ideas of reformers about the most efficient economic and fiscal system should not, however, prevent the historian from studying the characteristics of state finances prior to the Revolution as they actually functioned, not only in France (considered as the epitome of the old order) but in Europe in general. In effect, historians have taught us to treat with caution the reflections of contemporaries about pre-1789 fiscal systems, as the latter were complex ensembles combining a mixture of archaic features and more modern developments. Furthermore, when dealing with the issue of state revenue and expenditure in the Ancien Régime, historians have to take on board other valid notions such as *financial revolution, tax state* or *fiscal state*, and *fiscal-military state*. The concept of a *financial revolution* was first coined by Peter Dickson to characterize the financial and political changes brought about in England after the accession of William III (1688). Although the words 'financial' and 'revolution' were apparently not mentioned together in eighteenth-century literature, evidence shows that many commentators believed that something special had happened in Britain which explained the ability of what was a small country, in comparison with the main continental powers, successfully to challenge both the Bourbon monarchy and revolutionary France, and to establish Britain's military and economic supremacy in the nineteenth century. Building upon Dickson's financial analysis of the origins of cheap long-term credit, Patrick O'Brien and John Brewer have emphasized Britain's skills in developing an original system of taxation, which made it possible to service an ever-growing debt and set in motion self-sustained growth.

The principles of sound fiscal systems were certainly not known only to British administrators. In 1733, for instance, Angran de Fonpertuis, a high-ranking French government official in the Conseil Royal du Commerce, devised for the attention of Louis

XV's ministers twelve rules which, he believed, could serve as a yardstick against which to measure the efficiency of fiscal administration and to decide on the need for reform policy:

1. Revenues must provide for expenses.
2. Taxes must be proportional to the wealth of everyone.
3. Taxes levied must not harm commerce, agriculture, and consumption of basic foodstuff.
4. Taxes levied should, as far as possible, go into the royal coffers in their entirety.
5. Tax administration fees should not absorb too large a portion of revenue.
6. Taxes should be of a nature to allow them to be increased according to the needs of the state and lowered when these needs stop, therefore avoiding the introduction of new taxes which needlessly create additional collection costs.
7. Peasants, craftsmen, and manufacturers should be protected from taxes.
8. Taxes should not be injurious to trade and consumption.
9. Taxes should be exempt from fraud, as fraud ruins both those who perpetrate it and those employed to prevent it.
10. The sovereign must uphold public faith and honour his predecessors' engagements.
11. Taxes must be general; exemptions and privileges are abuses contrary to the well-being of the state, and even to the interest of *privilégiés*.
12. Taxes must be simple, levied at a low cost and by the minimum number of officials possible, as they are a drain on the purse of both king and people, and subjects engaged in tax collection are unavailable to engage in trade, manufacture, and agriculture.[5]

These twelve rules describe the principles of modern fiscal systems and, by contrast, the evils of the Ancien Régime structures that reformers never ceased to denounce: the inequality of taxation and the absence of progressiveness resulting from fiscal privileges and the differences in status; the inadequacy of control of fiscal administration leading to excessive spending and the risk of default by the sovereign; the multiplicity and complexity of ill-designed and relatively inflexible taxes harming consumption and economic growth, and fostering fraud and smuggling; the high costs of collection resulting from the lack of tax uniformity and reliance on privatization of tax farming instead of direct collection and state centralization of revenue and expenses.

In the Ancien Régime, no European state fully complied with Angran's rules, although the British fiscal 'constitution' was obviously the closest match to such a virtuous system. This was especially true in the aftermath of the American War, when Parliament decided to support 'economical reform' and started cutting costs by abolishing sinecures and further enforcing centralization in the Exchequer of outstanding balances in cash kept by receivers and treasurers. Yet, reviewing compliance by governments to Angran's laws would in any case be pointless. In the 1770s a policy of savings was also introduced in France by Necker and its merits hotly debated. Overall, the sustainability of fiscal systems depended upon the interplay of their various components and the possibility of overcoming limitations placed upon governments. Only fiscal crises following long-term evolutions were able to bring about financial revolutions. The transition described by J. Schumpeter, from the *domain state*, where the sovereign had to live off his personal revenue, to the *tax state* capable of extracting additional and regular taxation to fund standing armies, is one of the most enduring legacies of medieval warfare. Recent historical studies show that the financial revolutions which took place in the seventeenth-century Dutch Republic and Britain resulted from long-term economic change and financial innovation, but their full potential was unleashed, as in the case of the French Revolution, by a fiscal crisis.

In the early modern age, warfare was the driving force of fiscal novelty. Charles Davenant gave an apt summary of the root of the problem when, towards the end of the Nine Years War (1688–97), he warned that 'whenever this war ceases, it will not be for want of mutual hatred in the opposite parties, not for want of men to fight the quarrel, but that side must first give out where money is first failing', because 'nowadays that Prince who can best find money to feed, cloath, and pay his Army, not he that has the most Valiant Troops, is surest of Success and Conquest'.[6] While old regime conflicts were not as bloody as those of the twentieth century, they were virtually ubiquitous. Even if the eighteenth century experienced two periods of lasting peace, the major old regime powers were, on average, at war every other year. The recurrent experience of long years of conflict without significant periods of respite always had a profound, if varied, impact on all belligerents. Wars largely impinged on periods of peace: in addition to economic disruption during conflict, servicing and paying off debts made it incumbent upon government to maintain high levels of taxation in peacetime, a situation which potentially threatened political stability, especially if harvests failed or economic crisis suddenly struck. The significant impact of war on society and the polity generated considerable anxiety. In the eighteenth century, the merits of the British fiscal-military model were not obvious to everyone. Many observers, like David Hume (who wondered, in his famous *Essay on Money* (1752), if the state would destroy the national debt or the debt destroy the state), were prone to pessimism concerning the future of British power, economic growth, and the overall impact of war on the political constitution of their country. A similar pessimism was experienced publicly in France towards the end of Louis XIV's reign: some of the elite developed a new agenda in favour of a more peaceful relationship between European states, based on a more liberal approach to international trade. If not durable, the ambition became at least official policy when the Constituent Assembly, in 1790, declared that France would from now on decline aggressive wars.

The structural role of war on Ancien Régime finances can be seen in the overwhelming burden military and military-related expenses placed upon them. To be sure, this phenomenon would last well beyond the storming of the Bastille: the cost of funding revolutionary wars would leave a deep scar on European peacetime budgets well into the nineteenth century. Only in the aftermath of the revolutions of 1848 would the old expenditure structure start evolving from the typical fiscal-military state, spending between 70 and 80 per cent of its expenses on the armed forces, to a modern social state where civil investment would grow steadily. The financial impact of war is also reflected in many attempts to assess the relative military capabilities of European states. In the late seventeenth century, Gregory King pioneered such a comparison between England's resources and those of France. Although connected to the development of economic information and the marketing of government bonds, the development of national statistics was above all meant to assist domestic policy. In the 1740s major surveys, including population censuses, were commissioned by controller-general of the finances Orry, and their results were regularly updated. One of his successors, L'Averdy, required in the 1760s that French diplomats send to Versailles detailed reports about the systems of taxation in their places of residence, so as to help the work of a commission established to discuss fiscal reform in France.

Previously locked in the cabinets of sovereigns and foreign ministers, fiscal data were now available to the public and constantly refined by state officers and professional 'statisticians'. Jacques Necker's *De l'Administration des finances de France*, translated into several languages, was the most famous among the many publications available to E. Zimmerman, author of *A Political Survey of the Present State of Europe in sixteen tables* (1787), devoted to that 'new branch of political knowledge, which has for its object the actual and relative power of the several modern states, the power arising from their natural advantages, the industry and civilization of their inhabitants, and the wisdom of their governments'. Quantitative information also circulated in newspapers, such as the Florentine *Notizie del Mondo* published in 1783, which collected information from the works of Templeman and Büsching to provide their readers with 'an empirical state of the population, revenue, and military force of Europe'.[7] Yet the most elaborate, perhaps, of all those attempts to describe European states according to their resources, was probably presented in October 1789 to the French deputies to the Estates-General who, further to the abolition in August of feudalism and privileges, had the amazing opportunity of building a brand-new fiscal system from scratch.

Table 5.1 reproduces the economic, fiscal, and military statistical information communicated to the French deputies. These data, which relate to twenty-three European states, provide statistics about their surface, population, annual revenue from taxation, expenditure, military expenses, size of the army and the navy, and the value of colonial imports. Of course, this table should not be regarded as containing absolute data but rather guidelines. Various control procedures to test the accuracy of this information, which is not easily accessible to historians, have confirmed that it is generally reliable. More importantly, the figures tend to freeze the dynamic of European state finances, which was real both in the long term and over shorter periods. 'For instance, the net fiscal revenue of Great Britain, which stands at 312 million in the table, corresponds to the financial situation in 1783, so before Pitt's reforms successfully increased annual taxation up to 425 million and balanced the shortfall to pay for annual expenditure. Also, between 1783 and 1789 the net revenue of Austria varied between 168 and 239 million *livres tournois* (lt) (±30 per cent).[8] In 1778 army mobilization by Prussia to oppose Austria's move in the Bavarian succession cost 17 million *taler*, more than one year of net revenue.

In his *Political Survey*, Zimmerman chose to divide the states of Europe into three groups. This classification tweaked the revenue-size ranking order adopted in the table to take into account a state's 'intrinsic power and influence abroad'. In the first class, Zimmerman placed Britain, France, Austria, Prussia, and Russia, countries which had both the biggest revenues and the largest standing armies (or navy in the British case).

Table 5.1. Economic and fiscal strengths of the European states at the end of the Ancien Régime

	Land area (000 km²)	Population (mn inhab.)	Annual revenue from taxation (mns)	Annual expenses (mns)	Military expenses (mns)	Army	Navy (warships/other)	Revenue from colonies (mns)
France	417	24.8	486	614	155	230 000	72/189	240.6
England	253	10.8	312	408	90	60 000	108/380	239.5
Ottoman Empire	1975	50.0	250	200	60	220 000	20/52	
Austria	529	19.5	215	208	79	300 000		
Russia	2430	23.8	160	130	86	300 000	60/190	6
Spain	461	8.4	140	180	(50)	90 000	48/90	178.8
Prussia	196	6.2	96	88	55	200 000		
Portugal	76	2.5	72	58	20	25 000	20/42	72.9
Dutch Republic	26	2.4	68	87	42	35 000	25/90	125.7
Two Sicilies	77	5.8	40	33	16	28 000	6/30	
Denmark	257	2.5	33	28	17	50 000	20/55	14.5
Sweden	540	2.4	29	31	18	47 500	12/101	5
Sardinia	112	3.2	28	19	9	24 000	0/18	
Saxony	24	1.7	28	21	6	21 000		
Venice	26	2.8	27	25	12	14 000	8/30	
Bavaria	24	1.6	23	20	6	22 000		
Rome	33	2.0	20	28	7	6 000	0/10	
Milan	18	1.7	16	12	3	6 000	0/14	
Hanover	14	0.8	15	10	5	15 000		
Genoa	7	1.2	15	12	4	5000	0/20	
Poland	544	9.0	10	15	9	18 000		
Württemberg	11	0.6	6.5	8	2	4 600		
Hessen-Kassel	10	0.54	6.0	3.8	4	12 000		

Source: British Library. Additional MSS 74100, Aperçu de la Balance du Commerce de la France. Année 1789. Ensemble le Relevé de la Population des Finances et Forces Militaires des Principales Puissances de l'Europe. (In 1789, £1 = c.25 livres tournois.)

Turkey, however, with revenues and an army that should have put the Ottoman Empire in the category of the major powers, was downgraded by Zimmerman to the second class—with Spain, Holland, Denmark, Sweden, and Sardinia—on the ground of its inferior and ill-disciplined troops. All the second-class states were naval powers, with the exception of the Kingdom of Sardinia, whose mainland territories in Piedmont, nonetheless, occupied a strategic position. Although the standing armies in these states were not of a size to challenge the major powers, their military forces were nevertheless two to three times larger than the remaining states ranked in the third class. None of these latter states were able to afford a navy or, in the case of Venice, capable of making a difference in a general European conflict.

With few exceptions, Zimmerman's classification corroborates the data presented to the French deputies in 1789. The latter were given additional information that allows statistical calculations to better understand the structures of European states' finances at the end of the Ancien Régime (see Table 5.2). Data in Tables 5.1 and 5.2 indicate that the main fiscal powers can be defined as those states which, in 1789, were extracting a net annual revenue equivalent to 200 million lt, or £8,000,000. They were only four in number—France, Great Britain, the Ottoman Empire, and Austria—and they were the most heavily populated. In a mercantilist framework, which dominated European economic thought well into the 1750s, the strengths of a state came above all from the size of its population. Since they enabled self-sufficiency and national independence, an abundance of human beings was seen as the key to economic development and to playing a political role in the international balance of power. The medieval city-states were not able to withstand the development of the modern state. One key element to Dutch economic decline after 1670 is to be found in the size of its population, which not only stopped growing but was too small for the Dutch Republic to remain independent in a much more competitive environment, whatever the form of its political system.

The foremost European fiscal powers also had the largest land area. Prussia's growth in the eighteenth century exemplifies the fiscal advantages of getting bigger: between 1740 and 1786, thanks to the conquest of Austria's wealthier province, Silesia, and the first partition of Poland, Frederick II almost doubled Prussia's territory (119,000 to 195,000 km^2) and population (2.2 to 5.4 million), while rational exploitation of resources tripled Prussia's annual net revenue (7.4 to 19–20 million *taler*). Yet, in fact, size alone was not enough: the largest European states—Russia, Turkey, and Poland—were also those which extracted the smallest per capita revenue of all European countries. In addition to population and land area, access to international markets and the degree of internal organization were essential components in both creating and taxing wealth. The Holy Roman Empire offers a striking example of disparity between size and political power due to its inability to raise taxes. Italian states, so successful in the late Middle Ages, had long lost out to the major reorientation of international trade on the Atlantic Ocean and the rise of nation-states. Yet the land area to revenue ratio of Venice, Tuscany, and Genoa, which ranked high in comparison to less economically developed states, reminds us of their past fortunes and their ability to resist total decline. Genoa, for instance, which had long been involved in lending money to Spanish kings, benefited

Table 5.2. Finances in European states at the end of the Ancien Régime

	Density	Revenue per capita (l.t.)	Expenses per capita (l.t.)	Deficit %	Colonies per capita (l.t.)	Revenue:land area ratio (l.t.)	Soldier:citizen ratio (l.t. per km²)	Military as % of annual expenses	Military expenses per capita (l.t.)
France	59	19.6	24.8	−26	9.7	1.2	0.9	32	6.3
England	43	28.9	37.8	−31	22.2	1.2	0.6	29	8.3
Ottoman Empire	25	5	4	20		0.1	0.4	24	1.2
Austria	37	11	10.7	3		0.4	1.5	37	4.1
Russia	10	6.7	5.5	19	0.3	0.1	1.3	54	3.6
Spain	18	16.7	21.4	−29	21.3	0.3	1.1	36	6
Prussia	32	15.5	14.2	8		0.5	3.2	57	8.9
Portugal	33	28.8	23.2	19	28.8	0.9	1	28	8
Dutch Republic	91	28.3	36.3	−28	52.4	2.6	1.5	62	17.5
Two Sicilies	75	6.9	5.7	18		0.5	0.5	40	2.8
Denmark	10	13.2	11.2	15	5.8	0.1	2	52	6.8
Sweden	4	12.1	12.9	−7	2.1	0.1	2	62	7.5
Sardinia	28	8.8	5.9	32		0.2	0.8	32	2.8
Saxony	72	16.5	12.4	25		1.2	1.2	21	3.5
Venice	108	9.6	8.9	7		1	0.5	44	4.3
Bavaria	66	14.4	12.5	13		0.9	1.4	26	3.8
Rome	60	10	14	−40		0.6	0.3	35	3.5
Milan	93	9.4	7.1	25		0.9	0.4	19	1.8
Hanover	58	18.8	12.5	33		1.1	1.9	33	6.3
Genoa	156	12.5	10	20		2	0.4	27	3.3
Poland	17	1.1	1.7	−50		0	0.2	90	1
Württemberg	55	10.8	13.3	−23		0.6	0.8	31	3.3
Hessen-Kassel	52	11.1	7	37		0.6	2.2	67	7.4

from the expertise of its bank, the Casa of San Giorgio, and continued to offer valuable financial services to more powerful states which, in the eighteenth century, relied on foreign investors to fund their deficit.

Among the four wealthier European states, France and Britain were clearly well ahead, with annual expenses standing at 614 and 408 million respectively, or two to four times that of their immediate followers (Austria, Spain, Prussia, the Dutch Republic, Russia). In addition, France and Britain—like Spain and the Dutch Republic—spent far more money than they actually collected from taxation. Their net budgetary deficit—between a quarter and a third of their annual revenue—was of course the consequence of previous military conflicts, but even more so of their overall economic potential. In effect, the states which ran a substantial deficit in 1789 were all colonial powers. Their expenditure per head, which ranged from 21 lt in Spain to 37 lt in Britain, was far higher than other European states. For example, Prussia, which ranked top of continental powers, only spent 14 lt per head in 1789 compared to 24 lt in the case of France and 36 lt in the Dutch Republic. Colonial powers derived significant fiscal and monetary advantages from provisioning their captive colonial markets with home-produced goods and commodities, and even more by importing and re-exporting colonial products to European states which had no access to colonies. Although Portugal was a second-rank state, its revenue per capita was the highest in Europe with England and the Dutch Republic. The fiscal impact of colonial assets is particularly visible in the case of the Spanish peninsula: in Portugal and Spain the per capita revenue, compared to continental states, was much bigger than the land area to revenue ratio. For these colonial powers, revenue did not derive solely from taxation of their domestic wealth—which was limited—but from their valuable colonial empire, in particular the profits from gold and silver mines in Brazil and Mexico.

The importance of trade between colonies, the mother country, and European consumers accounts for some fiscal specificities in the Atlantic states. In England, Portugal, and Spain, customs duties on the movement of goods made up to a quarter of total taxation. There was, however, a downside to financing a budget by collecting duties on the import of consumer goods, like sugar, tea, coffee, etc. which became increasingly part of daily diets. In the society of the Ancien Régime, fraud was a very tempting and rewarding activity. Smugglers benefited in particular from prohibitive systems put in place between colonies and the mother country which artificially raised the price of basic foodstuffs and commodities. For instance, financial loss to Spain's transatlantic system between 1747 and 1761 was estimated at just over half the annual output of colonial mines and agriculture. Tariffs, which were systematically increased in wartime to provide additional resource but rarely reviewed when peacetime conditions resumed, were so complex that merchants had to rely on fiscal officers to calculate the tax. The dire state of British finances after the American War amply explains Pitt the Younger's determination in fighting tea smuggling and successfully increasing customs revenue by about £1 million per annum, or about 8 per cent of annual net revenue.

Overall, data on per capita revenue and expenditure outline a specific fiscal-political geography. While Atlantic powers are ranked at the top of fiscal-military states, governments on the eastern borders of Europe (Poland, Turkey, and Russia), which were also the poorest, were the least successful in extracting taxes from their population. The remaining European countries can be divided into two groups: the Italian states, which levied between 5 and 10 lt per capita and usually spent less; and the central and north European states with revenue per head at between 11 and 18 lt per annum. Montesquieu, in *The Spirit of Laws* (1748), had already stressed the link between the ability of states to levy taxes and political freedom. Patrick O'Brien's study of the British system of taxation and Douglass North's institutional analysis of economic performance confirm a phenomenon that Montesquieu believed to be 'a rule from nature that never varies: we find it in all parts, in England, in Holland and in every state where liberty gradually declines till we come to Turkey'.[9]

This geo-fiscal distribution of major European states is also reinforced by statistics concerning military density and expenditure. Being German, Zimmerman could not fail to notice a striking difference in the military density of Europe. While on average one in seventy European inhabitants was a soldier (1.5 per cent), the ratios for the German and Italian states were respectively one in fifty-two (20 per cent) and one in 133 (0.75 per cent). This difference between the German and Italian states regarding the military is also visible in the per capita expenditure on troops (1 to 3 lt) which ranked Italy the bottom. The federal structure of the Holy Roman Empire, Franco-Austrian rivalry, British support for Hanover, and Prussian aspirations converged in maintaining a strong military presence in most German states. The relative size of these states was less important than the strategic position of the German territory. Whereas history usually situates military conflicts within the boundaries of national states, wars, like economies, did not strictly coincide with national borders. Wars pitted against each other diplomatic systems rooted in economic and political interests. In the absence of a diplomatic system of alliances (defensive or offensive), it was impossible for any major power to win a major conflict, as shown by France's difficulties in the War of the Spanish Succession (1701–14) or Britain's isolation in the American War (1776–83). Conversely, victorious coalitions brought newcomers, such as Prussia, Savoy, and Russia, to the forefront while once powerful or successful fiscal-military states, like Spain and Sweden, saw their international standing damaged and threatened by these rising powers.

The fiscal structures of several German territories were heavily dependent on the European diplomatic system. Subsidies explain why Hessen-Cassel, the smallest and one of the poorest of all the third-class states, could be the most heavily militarized of all Europe. In addition to its 12,000-man field army, 12,000 militia men served in garrisons. In Hessen-Cassel the ratio of soldiers to citizens was 1:15, twice Prussia's 1:30. As a mercenary state, Hessen-Cassel was able to derive considerable fiscal advantages through the negotiation of subsidy treaties. It is estimated that between 1702 and 1763, Hessen-Cassel might have gained 25 million *taler* in subsidies, enough to meet half of the government's needs over that period. In the American War, Britain once again bought Hessen-Cassel's troops for a total of 21 million *taler* (c.50 million lt), subsidies which Landgrave Frederick II wisely invested in British bonds and other loans. Towards the end of his reign, the annual interest on his investments totalled 30 per cent of the country's ordinary revenue, therefore allowing for a lowering of domestic taxation which fell from 3 *taler* per capita to a low of 2.2 *taler*. This was significantly below the level of taxation not only in Prussia (4.1 *taler*) but also in Bavaria (3.8 *taler*) and Baden-Württemberg (3.8 *taler*) where the army presence was then among the lowest in the Holy Roman Empire. In Württemberg too, troops were a goldmine. In 1752 Duke Carl-Eugen of Württemberg was able to conclude a treaty with Louis XV whereby France would pay an annual subsidy of 387,000 florins (peace) to 479,000 florins (war) for a five-year period, sums equivalent to 20 per cent of annual revenue. Although mercenary states were often too small to play an independent role in international politics, Prussia's rise to the status of first-class power was based on wise use of foreign subsidies, cost savings, and militarization which, taken together, allowed for victories on the battlefield and strategic growth through exploitation of military conquests. Apart from military prowess, the international standing of the House of Savoy owed a lot to the possibility of borrowing on the British market against subsidy payment.

Notwithstanding impressive martial presence in several German states, maximum military spending per capita remained confined to the wealthy colonial powers, with the Netherlands at the top of the league. To protect themselves against potential external threats the Dutch spent twice as much per capita as any other country, including Prussia, Britain, and France. Spain also invested heavily in its defence: expenditure on the navy and the army totalled about 60 per cent of annual expense, a proportion that matches the German military states, but also the northern powers, such as Denmark and Sweden, who maintained high military expenditure in response to threats from Prussia and Russia. In 1789 only France spent relatively little in proportion to its European status as a major European power. This was partly the result of its sheer size, which made it fairly easy, in comparison to smaller states, to fund a substantial peacetime army of 200,000 men, and also due to cuts imposed by the fiscal crisis of 1787–8. More importantly, the two main fiscal-military powers had found ways of fighting war on credit, in other words of spreading their military expenses over peacetime years. France and Britain, who had recently been at war in America and India, were struggling to service a huge debt which cost them, respectively, about half and two-thirds of annual expenses. Since loans were deferred taxation, the dynamics of fiscal systems were essential to absorb debts and avoid the disastrous effects of snowballing deficits.

Despite a considerable variety in their local names, early modern taxes were of a similar nature in most European countries. They were levied on wealth (direct) and consumption (indirect) and usually paid in cash. Only a few states, like Sweden, collected a portion of their revenue in kind, essentially to check inflation. In addition, most continental rulers required forced labour from the peasantry, at least until reformers pleaded in favour of substituting more efficient cash for reluctant manpower. In France, however, the case of the *corvée*, which was extended by Orry, shows that the evolution of taxes was not linear but a reaction to specific national problems: paid in kind, forced labour could not be diverted to balance deficits or fund less useful expenditure than the development of an efficient road network linking Paris and the main provincial towns. The most relevant difference between fiscal systems lies in the relative balance of their main sources of revenue. In this respect, part of German territories conformed to a singular financial structure: the demesne, which was fiscally insignificant in most European countries, remained a vital resource to the rulers of several states in the Holy Roman Empire. In the 1760s, for instance, revenue from demesne (including mines) and regalian rights contributed respectively 26, 30, and 48 per cent of the net intake of Prussia, Bavaria, and Hanover. Everywhere else, the bulk of annual revenue came from a mixture of direct and indirect taxes, its ratio varying according to the nature of national wealth to be taxed. In Austria and France, for instance, direct and indirect revenue split more or less equally, whereas customs and excises made up to three-quarters of the British revenue. The balance of taxes also mirrored economic trends: in the late seventeenth century, parts of the Electorate of Hanover switched to indirect taxes to fight an agricultural downturn while, in the eighteenth century, the development of trade tended to raise the proportional intake of indirect taxes. Even in agricultural monarchies, like the Kingdom of Naples, revenue from direct taxation progressively gave way to indirect taxes as consumption rose.

Fiscal policy was potentially a powerful instrument for overcoming fiscal discrepancies which were a key element of early modern finances. For instance, in France, tax per capita at the end of the American war was calculated at 23 lt. At the provincial level, however, it varied from a minimum of 12 lt per head in the *géneralités* of Nancy and Rennes, to 30 lt in the *généralités* of Lyon and Rouen, and to a maximum 64 lt in the *généralité* of Paris. Wealth, of course, accounted for such differences. So did unequal geographic distribution of the fiscal burden. For most Ancien Régime sovereigns ruled over composite states of differing fiscal and legal status. This might seem obvious in the case of monarchies whose territories were not geographically contiguous. In the territories of the Habsburg monarchy, the Hungarians, the Belgians, and the Italians were traditionally less taxed than the Austrian homeland. But even states like Spain or France, with a homogeneous geography, or even the Dutch Republic, were essentially composite when it came to taxation. The absolute king in France ruled over a country which was made up of an old medieval centre or core, around Paris and the Loire, and a periphery of provinces which had been progressively added—either by marriage, inheritance, or conquest—and which had managed over the centuries to preserve not only their immunities but even the names of their old taxes. In addition France, like all other European states, had no unified system of weights and measures (not to mention language), and no unified fiscal, administrative, and legal system.

The Dutch Republic combined some strikingly modern economic features, in particular the introduction of a progressive tax system, with more typical Ancien Régime ones. In 1789 the fiscal contribution of the Dutch provinces was still determined by a quota system set up in the sixteenth century, at the time of the revolt against Spain. With such glorious origins and in a political system based on the principle of decentralization, fiscal adjustment to economic evolution was an unlikely event. In the absence of reform, the taxpayer was more heavily taxed in the province of Holland, where growth in the eighteenth century was stagnating, while in the agrarian province of Overijssel, rising prices and population increase saw tax per capita reduced, between 1720 and 1790, from

9.8 to 6.5 guilders. Such regional inconsistencies were characteristic of most European countries. They were only too well known to governments which unremittingly tried to reduce disparities in the distribution of taxes. All French ministers aimed at putting taxes in the *pays d'états*, where local estates were able to act as a buffer against state demands, on a par with other provinces. In 1749, Machault d'Arnouvillle was able to establish a universal tax, the *vingtième* or 5 per cent levy on all net revenue. Yet the greater part of the church succeeded in gaining an exemption from it and provincial estates were granted the right to negotiate their annual contribution.

However 'absolute', early modern states were obliged constantly to renegotiate fiscal agreements with institutions and social groups which absorbed a large share of the national wealth, and they were not at liberty to tax at will. In this exhausting and costly bargain, war played a vital role in fostering change. Aragon lost its traditional immunities in the War of the Spanish Succession for supporting the wrong candidate to the throne of Spain, while nobles in Silesia were stripped of their exemptions after the Prussian conquest and, worse, taxed at a higher rate than the clergy and commoners. Such dramatic transformations remained exceptional. For early modern states could not and would not easily suppress privileges. Certainly bureaucrats seriously considered schemes for abolishing exemptions or replacing all taxes by a single contribution. Yet, despite the volume of literature devoted to the improvement of fiscal administration, governments were often pragmatic and conservative in their attitudes: their duty to maintain order serves to explain their belief that the passing of time would help heal the wounds caused by wars. Ministers were usually happy to find ways of funding expenditure on an *ad hoc* basis and without provoking too much discontent. Justified in time of national emergency, extraordinary taxes were usually abolished or their incidence reduced after the war. The recurrence of conflicts, however, made it possible for governments to re-employ the same successful measures, so that, in the end, extraordinary levies could eventually be made permanent. Conversely, peacetime taxes which targeted fiscal loopholes were likely to be greeted with staunch resistance. In Britain, Lord Bute's cider excise (1763), aimed at bringing southern counties on a fiscal par with northern beer drinkers, had to be repealed in the face of well-organized opposition, not to mention George Grenville's new taxes on the American colonies.

In many respects, military conflicts simultaneously attacked and reinforced fiscal immunities. Forced loans, the sale of offices, poll taxes, customs tariffs, new excise duties, land taxes, were among the methods all governments used at some stage to tap the money of the wealthy who often happened to be *privilégiés*. This resulted in highly intricate fiscal systems. In most European countries, there were as many types of fiscal status as taxes. Over the years, more and more *privilégiés* were becoming taxpayers: yet they simply did not pay the same amount of tax, let alone the same taxes. Figuring out how much less tax they paid in comparison to non-immune groups is a daunting task. The case of the church is complex because its revenue contributed to the salaries of its members and financed institutions which provided services to the community, not only spiritual but also administrative, educational, medical, and charitable. Yet the land register which the Marquès of La Ensenada ordered to be drawn up showed that in the province of Castile the income of the property of the church represented 19 per cent of the total income from real property, but the *subsidio* it paid annually to the crown represented only 3.6 per cent of the *rentas provinciales* collected from the rest of the population. Like the land tax in Britain, the yield of the French *vingtième* varied according to the accuracy of fiscal declarations produced by landowners. Strong support for the government explained why Whig taxpayers in England were willing to contribute a fair share of their revenue income. When it came to financial matters, however, citizenship usually took second place to personal interest, as the verification of *vingtièmes* assessments were to prove. The major campaign undertaken between 1771 and 1782 in the *pays d'élections* raised the overall revenue of the tax by one-quarter.

The relative success of early modern states in progressively eroding entrenched immunities makes it difficult to fully appreciate the way privileges prevented the development of self-sustaining fiscal systems. The French Revolution and the ensuing revolutionary wars were at least to prove that the Ancien Régime structures of continental states could not resist the unleashed power of republican France. While most of those states were reaping the benefits of peace and growth after 1763, France was walking a tightrope. Unlike Britain, where a centralized and fairly uniform fiscal system supported the development of an internal economic market, the provinces of France, like the many states of the Holy Roman Empire, were separated by internal customs barriers. Trade was also curtailed by private tolls. A commission established under Louis XV to investigate private tolls on roads and rivers found that one-third of their owners had no legal claims to tax trade. Despite their suppression, 2.000 private tolls were still active in 1789 and raised about £1.7 million annually on the movement of goods. These checks on internal trade limited opportunities for growth through regional specialization and possibilities for governments to raise the yield of indirect taxes by adjusting duties on more profitable goods.

Internal customs and excise barriers at the entry of towns meant that the presence of the *ferme générale* was at a maximum: in the 1740s it employed 5,800 officers to control the movement of goods in Paris and in main towns, and an additional 10,600 *commis* were deployed in the countryside to crack down on fraud. On the other side of the Channel, the growth of custom duties was also accompanied by resentment against more complex laws and the intrusive powers of excise officers who, like the French *commis des fermes*, enjoyed extraordinary powers to visit houses at any time of the day or the night. In England, however, the method of levying taxes on producers was conducted in a particularly efficient manner of 'keeping up the deceit', to quote Montesquieu's phrase, because the tax was included in the retail price. To be sure, rising duties generated anger everywhere and rebellions in some places. Yet direct collection by officers appointed by the state considerably reduced social discontent in England in comparison to countries where taxes were levied by private syndicates of tax farmers: in 1748, for instance, tax riots in Holland forced the abandonment of the farm system, which was replaced by direct collection, a trend which was followed in most European countries, even in France, where several duties were taken out of the hands of the general farms and given to *régisseurs* to collect. The hatred of the *fermiers généraux* did not recede, nor did their role as the main providers of fiscal revenue and credit facilities. Given these problems, the flexibility of the French fiscal system depended on the ability to reduce the inequality of direct taxation, a long, difficult, and costly task since it required mapping the plots owned or cultivated by more than 20 million peasants. In the Savoyard monarchy, the inquiry into land values in Piedmont known as *perequazione* was initiated in 1697, completed by 1711, but its execution only decreed in 1731.

Paradoxically, France moved from one fiscal crisis to another because it was, in absolute terms, the most powerful European country and had potential for growth. This situation gave the government sufficient leeway to adopt a credible, if not sustainable, deficit policy. For not all French kings were as unsuccessful as Louis XVI in their attempt at extracting additional revenues to match increased expenditure. When Montesquieu was reflecting on the political foundations of taxation, he had in mind Britain in contrast to France where the tax per capita was then at the lowest point but was to grow as a result of the War of the Austrian Succession (1740–8) and the Seven Years War (1756–63). The creation of the *vingtième* certainly further eroded fiscal privilege but the efficiency of the financial system, although it produced more, was neither significantly altered nor more cost-effective. Unlike Britain, where the Treasury had to be consulted before any financial decision was made, and revenue voted by Parliament, in most European countries control of spending was weak and resources wasted. In France, extraordinary expenditures were often decided in personal meetings between the King and each of his ministers, who enjoyed dangerous financial autonomy. This could potentially destroy the fiscal strategy of the *contrôleur général*, not to mention his personal reputation among money lenders. Of course, the financial system of a large country like France was far from a total shambles and most of the problems there existed in other states, even in Britain to some extent, because war emergencies allowed accounting rules to be by-passed while financial management loopholes offered possibilities for personal enrichment. Financial control procedures had the potential of improving use of resources in countries where uniformity and centralization were poor. After the War of the Austrian Succession, the major reforms in the Habsburg dominions initiated by Haugwitz included the development of an efficient accounting system to better manage the disparate components of this composite monarchy. In the absence of solid representative institutions, state finances in the Ancien Régime remained highly secretive and fiscal management the territory of a small group of technicians who expected to have their services properly rewarded, which constituted a cause of further anger against financiers and gave rise to demands for more transparency.

The gap between potential tax revenue and immediate expenditure, especially in times of war, was met by a mixture of economic, fiscal, and monetary expedients, including recoinage and circulation of short-term bills issued by tax-collectors or by banks, such as, for instance, the exchequer bills of the Bank of England, the *bancozettel* of the Vienna City Bank, or the *vales reales* of the Bank of Saint-George. The scale of these expedients varied according to needs, places, and times but also to the structures and evolution of the financial institutions and markets in Europe. After the Mississippi Bubble, France stopped changing the value of coins, unlike Piedmont and Prussia whose limited fiscal and economic resources called for the manipulation of currency in the 1740s and 1760s. In the eighteenth century, credit traditionally provided by bankers, corporate bodies of venal officers, or fiscal agencies was progressively replaced in Europe by borrowing money directly from the public, mostly at home but also on the international market. Prussia was the only power which tried to avoid the creation of a debt through the accumulation of a large war treasury capable of funding several campaigns. For borrowing was neither easy nor always successful: cheap credit required sophisticated institutions, in particular a transparent secondary market, and an economy capable of generating savings. External loans were usually connected to the fundamental problem of international payments and monetary exchanges. In time of war, smaller states, like Hessen-Cassel, could borrow on the English security market against their subsidies. Similarly foreign policy allowed Austria to capitalize on the trade of its quicksilver mines to access the Dutch money market, a resource which was lost after Prussia's conquest of Silesia. In the Savoyard monarchy, external trade, which was heavily dependent on silk worms, restricted the pool of foreign capital to her immediate neighbours, Genoa and Geneva. In many German territories, the multiplicity of fiscal agencies—federal, princely, and provincial—entailed high administrative costs and fragmented both resources and liability, therefore postponing the creation of national public debts until 1815.

Among continental European states, France was the largest borrower and also the country which had to offer the highest return to home and foreign lenders. French bonds were usually sold at a premium in comparison to Holland or Britain, where interest rates were half those offered in France, in both wartime and peacetime. This additional cost is usually deemed to represent the price the King had to pay to his creditors against default in the absence of a national guarantee that the debt would be regularly serviced. It seems more likely that returns on loans depended on market mechanisms, which were partially neutralized when the King borrowed money through financiers or corporate institutions, like towns or provincial estates. The development of financial capitalism based on an efficient secondary market was further delayed in France in the aftermath of the Mississippi Bubble (1720). French debts were paid through a massive emission of perpetual annuities which were difficult and costly to trade because of their legal status as real estate. In the 1740s, France had started to recover and chose to issue bearer bonds which carried a low interest (3–5 per cent). They nevertheless remained expensive as the capital had to be fully repaid over a period of ten to fifteen years, and repayment prevented a policy of debt conversion like Pelham's successful reduction of the British consol to 3 per cent. After Terray's bankruptcy (1771), the suspension of short-term bills, the depreciation of new perpetual annuities issued to convert war debts, and the suppression of the Sinking Fund again raised the real interest rate. It forced the government to issue more life annuities, which were costly (7–12 per cent), to pay for the war effort. In 1787 the combination of high interest rates, heavy capital repayments, and the suppression or war taxes generated a massive deficit, almost the size of Spain's annual revenue, which directly called into question the sustainability of Ancien Régime structures as a whole. In contrast to Britain, where a policy of incremental reforms were implemented over the years to build a more efficient financial system, the Bourbon monarchy failed to execute the many reforms designed by its bureaucrats which might have helped in balancing revenue and expenses, limiting the cost of international conflicts, and therefore making it easier to find ways out of fiscal crisis.

Ultimately, Ancien Régime financial systems were all put to the test after long periods of war, when states faced the daunting task of servicing and paying off debts. Many Frenchmen believed that in their rich country fiscal crisis would always be overcome by a talented minister—like Sully, Colbert, or Desmaretz—supported by a strong king who would persuade the wealthy to contribute a fairer share. In the Age of the Enlightenment, the methods for achieving such results were not obvious as fiscal crisis called into question the government's policy and prompted authoritarian responses to maintain a social and political system which was at the root of most problems. Given its strategic importance in Europe, the fiscal crisis of the French monarchy and the ensuing revolutionary wars would inevitably pave the way for the collapse of Ancien Régime finances which had long been abolished in the minds of many.

Notes

1. Abbé Morellet and Jacques Necker also use the words a*ncien régime* in their pamphlets published in 1769 about the status of the Compagnie des Indes.
2. *Correspondance secrète inédite sur Louis XVI, Marie-Antoinette, la cour et la ville de 1777 à 1792*, published by...M. de Lescure (2 vols. Paris, 1866), i. 402–3, 5 June 1781.
3. Vol. i, *Discours préliminaire*.
4. Adam Smith, *An Inquiry into the Nature and Causes of the Wealth of Nations* (3 vols. Dublin, 1776), iii. 28.
5. Senate House Library, University of London, MS 97, 'L'utilité du crédit public démontrée en quatre parties avec un avant-propos'.
6. *An Essay upon Ways and Means of Supplying the War* (London, 1701). 28–9.
7. This document is reproduced in F. Venturi, *The End of the Old Regime in Europe* (2 vols. Princeton, 1989–91), ii. 949.
8. *European State Finance Data Base*. Or 64–87 million florins. For the same period expenses varied between 71 and 120 million florins.
9. *The Spirit of Laws*, bk. xiii, ch. 12.

Bibliography

Ashworth, W. J., *Customs and Excise: Trade, Production and Consumption, 1640–1845* (Oxford, 2003).
Bonney, R., *The Rise of the Fiscal State in Europe c.1200–1815* (Cambridge, 1999).
Bosher, J. F., *The Single Duty Project: A Study of the Movement for a French Customs Union in the Eighteenth Century* (London, 1969).
—— *French Finances 1770–1795: From Business to Bureaucracy* (Cambridge, 1970).
Brewer, J., *The Sinews of Power: War, Money and the English State, 1688–1783* (Cambridge Mass., 1989).

Dickson, P. G. M., *The Financial Revolution in England: A Study in the Development of Public Credit, 1688–1756* (Oxford, 1967).
—— *Finance and Government under Maria Theresia, 1740–1780* (2 vols. Oxford, 1987).
Félix, J., 'The Financial Origins of the French Revolution', in P. Campbell (ed.), *Origins of the French Revolution* (Basingstoke, 2006), 35–62.
Glete, J., *War and the State in Early-Modern Europe: Spain, the Dutch Republic and Sweden as Fiscal-Military States, 1500–1660* (London, 2002).
Harling, P., *The Waning of 'Old Corruption': The Politics of Economical Reform in Britain, 1779–1846* (Oxford, 1996).
Ingrao, C., *The Hessian Mercenary State: Ideas, Institutions, and Reform under Frederick II, 1760–1785* (Cambridge, 1987).
Kwass, M., *Privilege and the Politics of Taxation in Eighteenth-Century France* (Cambridge, 2000).
North, D., *Institutions, Institutional Change and Economic Performance* (Cambridge, 1990).
O'Brien, P. K., 'The Political Economy of British Taxation, 1660–1815', *Economic History Review*, 41 (1988), 1–32.
Reitan, E., *Politics, Finance, and the People: Economical Reform in England in the Age of the American Revolution, 1770–92* (New York, 2008).
Riley, J. C., *The Seven Years War and the Old Regime in France: The Economic and Financial Toll* (Princeton, 1986).
Schremmer, D. E., 'Taxation and Public Finance: Britain, France, and Germany', *The Cambridge Economic History of Europe*, viii (Cambridge, 1989).
Storrs, C. (ed.), *The Fiscal-Military State in Eighteenth-Century Europe: Essays in Honour of P. G. M. Dickson* (Aldershot, 2009).
t'Hart, M., Jonker, J., and Van Zanden, J.-L., *A Financial History of the Netherlands* (Cambridge, 1997).
Uhlmann, H. P., 'The Emergence of Modern Public Debts in Bavaria and Baden between 1780 and 1820', in P.-C. Witt (ed.), *Wealth and Taxation in Central Europe: The History and Sociology of Public Finance* (Leamington Spa, 1987), 63–79.
Wilson, H., *War, State and Society in Württemberg, 1677–1793* (Cambridge, 1995).

CHAPTER 6

PARLEMENTS AND PROVINCIAL ESTATES

JULIAN SWANN

After the King and his councils, the French parlements and provincial estates stood out as two of the most prestigious political, legal, and administrative institutions in the kingdom. By the eighteenth century, there were no fewer than thirteen parlements, proudly dominating the social, cultural, and even economic lives of cities such as Aix-en-Provence, Besançon, Rennes, and Toulouse.[1] It was, however, the Parlement of Paris that was generally recognized as the senior court, with a jurisdiction covering approximately one-third of France, including provinces such as Auvergne, Champagne, and Poitou as well as the major cities of Orléans and Lyon.[2] The Paris Parlement and its many ardent apologists frequently claimed that it 'was as old as the monarchy' and a direct descendant of the Frankish assemblies that had once met on the Champs de Mars. It was an argument that placed the Parlement above the Estates-General as the French national representative body, but it was, in reality, little more than antiquarian wishful thinking and the Parlement was of more recent vintage, having been founded during the fourteenth century. The various provincial parlements had been established later, often when formerly independent provinces had been absorbed into France.

Identifying the origins and even the number of provincial estates is a much more complicated task. During the sixteenth century, the majority of the kingdom belonged to what were termed *pays d'états*, but the number declined rapidly in the first half of the seventeenth century and the Estates of Auvergne, Dauphiné, Gascony, and Normandy, to name just a few, fell into abeyance.[3] Of those that remained, the Estates of Artois, Brittany, Burgundy, and Languedoc were amongst the most significant, while those of Provence existed in an intermediate stage with administrative responsibility exercised by the Assemblée générale des Communautés and the *procureurs du pays* despite the fact that the estates themselves were not assembled. If these were the most prominent examples, there were many smaller bodies whose history is less well known. If we take the example of Burgundy, the local estates were termed the Estates-General because they included deputies from the smaller *états particuliers* of Charolles and Mâcon, each of which had their own organization and assemblies.[4] Like the Parlement of Paris, the larger estates could boast of an ancient pedigree as most predated the union of their respective provinces to the French crown, and local antiquarians were quick to claim that their particular estates were part of a provincial constitutional history. According to president Bouhier in Burgundy or Robien in Brittany, their provincial estates were older than those of France, with a genealogy that could be traced back to Roman times.[5] Similarly those who pined for the restoration of the Estates of Normandy or Dauphiné frequently maintained that these institutions were the descendants of the Norman exchequer or *Conseil Delphinal* and were therefore an integral part of the provincial constitution.[6] Even if some of the historical evidence was a little tenuous, it is clear that these were institutions with immense status and authority, something that was reinforced by their membership, which was drawn from amongst a broad section of the French social elites.

The Parlement of Paris had perhaps the most distinguished membership of all as it was also the court of peers. As a result, on great ceremonial occasions such as a major state trial or a *lit de justice*, the King, together with the princes of the royal blood, the peerage, and the great officers of the crown, attended the Parlement, where they joined the judges who were its permanent members. Such gatherings were rare and usually of short duration and in normal times the parlements were the preserve of the *noblesse de robe*, so-called because of the legal attire of the magistrates. Like so many other positions of authority in early modern France, judicial offices in the parlements had become part of the venal system and had been purchased by wealthy members of the upper classes and, especially, by aspiring members of the Third Estate. After 1604 the levy of an annual tax, known as the *Paulette*, had ensured that the owners could pass their office on to their descendants as part of their patrimony, thus consolidating the emergence of the robe nobility which by the seventeenth century had acquired a distinct cultural and professional ethos. In Paris, generations of the d'Aguesseau, Potier de Novion, Molé, d'Ormesson, and Talon clans provided the leadership for a robe culture that prized the virtues of duty, austerity, and personal rectitude as part of the comportment needed to uphold the law.[7] Similar patterns are detectable in the provincial parlements, and the names of Ripert de Montclar in Aix, Boisot in Besançon, Legouz in Dijon, or Godart de Belbeuf in Rouen symbolized a robe culture that dominated their respective cities. Even today, anyone taking a stroll through the streets of Besançon, Rennes, or Toulouse cannot help but be struck by the imposing *hôtels* or town houses that once housed the *parlementaires*. As many were substantial landowners in the surrounding countryside their wealth, and the commerce and trade associated with the lawyers and litigants who attended upon the courts, meant that the robe nobility was central to the local economy. The *parlementaires* were also to the fore in the cultural sphere, playing a formative role in the establishment of, for example, municipal libraries, provincial academies, theatres, masonic lodges, and salons. If we should not forget that the *parlementaires* were part of a privileged elite, it remains true that for much of the early modern period they enjoyed a certain popularity and were lauded as the 'pères de la patrie' (fathers of their country).

The membership of the provincial estates was more varied and fluid than that of the parlements, and their diverse origins were reflected in their organization and entrance requirements.[8] However, with due respect to individual nuance, it is possible to identify a number of common features. It was the King who convoked an assembly of the estates and although there were established conventions that they met annually in Languedoc, biennially in Brittany, or triennially in Burgundy, they could not gather without his prior approval. All of the estates were composed of separate chambers, representing the clergy, nobility, and Third Estate. The episcopate dominated the clerical chambers and the archbishop of Narbonne and the bishop of Autun presided over the assemblies of Languedoc and Burgundy respectively, while the honour rotated around the dioceses of Brittany. The other clerical deputies were a mixture of *abbés*, deans, and deputies of religious houses and cathedral chapters, although the numbers involved varied from one province to the next. Regional diversity was also a feature of noble representation in the provincial estates. In Brittany the right to attend the estates was enjoyed by all those able to prove their noble status, although those nobles sitting in the Parlement or another of the great law courts were excluded. Many would choose to exercise their privilege and there are reports of hundreds attending the assemblies, where they expected to be wined and dined at the government's expense. The Estates of Languedoc, on the other hand, restricted noble membership to a handful of barons, while those in Burgundy welcomed holders of all, or part of, a fief, on condition that they could prove at least one hundred years of unbroken nobility and they were not sitting in the Parlement. Finally, the deputies of the Third Estate were, in theory, to represent the principal towns of the province, and it was the mayor or another prominent local officeholder who was expected to fulfil the role. It is noteworthy that the peasantry, which formed the overwhelming majority of the population, did not have direct representation. Its interests were supposedly safeguarded by their lords, an ideal that would look increasingly threadbare by the eighteenth century.

As the supreme courts within their respective jurisdictions, the parlements were primarily concerned with legal matters, hearing a wide variety of civil and criminal cases. Given the gravity of their profession, it has frequently been noted that, on account of the venal system, many *parlementaires* were appointed when still in their teens or early twenties, and therefore lacked the maturity or even the necessary qualifications to decide on matters of life or death. The image of the judiciary was further tarnished by very real miscarriages of justice such as the notorious Jean Calas affair of 1762, when an innocent Protestant father was sentenced to be broken on the wheel by the Catholic Parlement of Toulouse for the alleged murder of his son.[9] Voltaire famously campaigned for the posthumous rehabilitation of Calas, and he was to the fore in censuring the supposedly reactionary and incompetent *parlementaires* whose other heinous crimes included sentencing his, and other, enlightened publications to be lacerated and burnt by the public executioner. For their critics what made matters worse was the slow and expensive nature of litigation.[10] In addition to having to trek to Paris or to an often distant provincial capital to seek justice, litigants were also expected to pay for the privilege. In return for hearing cases, judges received payments known as *épices*, and it is easy to imagine how this practice could lead to accusations of corruption.

Of course, as with almost any legal system, it is possible to find examples of injudicious behaviour, but any indictments against the *parlementaires* need to be balanced by an awareness of the heavy weight of expectation imposed by family and peer group pressure. As members of the robe elites, most had received an excellent classical and legal education as well as having had the opportunity to learn their profession while sitting alongside their fathers or other close relatives. France was split between regions of customary and Roman law and each Parlement had its own jurisprudence that the *parlementaires* were assiduous in collecting and codifying. The robe was also deeply imbued by the ethos of the French Catholic Reformation, a movement that it had helped shape, and had in turn been formed by, and in theory the office of judge was akin to a religious vocation, even if few ever genuinely lived up to such lofty ideals. However, the key point to remember is that the parlements were filled by many educated and conscientious judges, whose largely conservative intellectual tastes were underpinned by a strong sense of pride and commitment to their profession.

With such qualifications it might seem surprising to learn that the parlements played a major political role and that they were, at times, in serious conflict with the King. In the midst of one acrimonious quarrel with the Parlement of Paris in January 1632, an angry Louis XIII had informed its members that their task was 'to judge between *maître* Pierre and *maître* Jean', adding menacingly that if they failed to heed the warning he would cut their nails to the quick. While the King was perfectly correct to suggest that the principal responsibility of the parlements was to act as a law courts, his attempt to portray them as limited to purely legal matters was a little disingenuous. In addition to hearing cases, the parlements were also responsible for a broad range of issues affecting public order and administration, overseeing fairs and markets, prices of bread and firewood, rents and leases, weights and measures, and much else besides. When riots broke out, it was frequently the judges, dressed only in their magisterial robes, who braved the crowds, imposing order through the force of their own personal authority and that of the institutions they represented. Should such measures fail, they always had the option of hanging suspected ringleaders as a last resort. However, what annoyed Louis XIII, and monarchs before and after him, was the ability of the parlements to intervene in the process of lawmaking through their rights of registration and remonstrance.[11]

By the sixteenth century, it had become a convention that whenever the King issued or amended legislation he sent the necessary law to the relevant Parlement for registration. The judges were expected to scrutinize the text and to verify that it did not contain errors or conflict with existing jurisprudence before adding it to their registers. If they found something objectionable, or simply felt that modifications were required, the judges could vote to petition the King, using a variety of formal and informal mechanisms, including entering into correspondence with ministers, sending deputations to court, or by making remonstrances. Although the nature of these various strategies differed, what they had in common was an ability to delay the legislative process. As these tactics could be varied and remonstrances repeated, the parlements had the potential to obstruct the government indefinitely, unless it was prepared to use measures such as a *lit de justice* to impose the disputed law in the King's presence. If we consider that even fiscal legislation could be opposed in this fashion, Louis XIII's frustration becomes comprehensible because new taxes would have to be registered by all of the parlements in turn. Louis XIV, with typical firmness, dealt with the problem by changing the constitutional rules in February 1673, forcing the parlements to register laws before permitting them to remonstrate.[12] That decision was reversed after his death by the incoming regency government, and historians have argued almost ever since about whether or not the parlements' remonstrances paved the way for the revolution of 1789.

It is true that by the early eighteenth century, the *parlementaires* had become solidly entrenched amongst the upper reaches of the French nobility. Many families had sons serving as officers in the army and had daughters married into the old aristocratic houses of the court or the provincial sword nobility. As a result, the political activities of the parlements were long described as being part of an aristocratic reaction against the modernizing fiscal policies of the monarchy.[13] It is an interpretation that continues to find favour amongst a small number of scholars in France, but it does not stand up to close scrutiny. Although numbers tended to decline during the eighteenth century, there were still more than 200 members of the Parlement of Paris in 1750, and between sixty and one hundred in the provincial courts. To imagine that 200 educated and wealthy men would all share the same outlook or be prepared to voice privileged interests (if they could agree what they were) is scarcely convincing.

Instead, the parlements contained an immensely rich range of talents and opinions. A few examples taken from those holding office in the Parlement of Paris in 1750 help to illustrate just how diverse their ideas and ambitions were. Sitting alongside each other were Clément L'Averdy, abbé Joseph Marie Terray, and Claude-Guillaume Lambert, all of whom would later serve as the King's controller-general of finance, as well as René-Nicolas de Maupeou, the last chancellor of France, and Lamoignon de Basville, Louis XVI's *garde des sceaux*. L'Averdy would prove to be the force behind a number of liberalizing measures, including the freeing the grain trade and reintroducing elections into local government, while Terray and Maupeou were associated with the royal revolution of 1771 that not only reversed these measures, but also destroyed the Parlement and exiled its members.[14] As for Lamoignon, he would be a steadfast opponent of Maupeou before, in turn, attempting a thorough remodelling of the judicial system in 1788 that brought an abrupt end to his own career and contributed to the summoning of an Estates-General.

These conflicting political trajectories reflected deeper divisions within the Parlement. During the first half of the eighteenth century, politics was largely defined by the rather unlikely issue of the papal bull *Unigenitus*.[15] Louis XIV had all but commanded the bull from a reluctant Pope in order to destroy what he believed was the pernicious heresy of Jansenism. Condemning what many saw as a perfectly orthodox strand of Augustinianism within the Catholic Church was a risky strategy at the best of times, but *Unigenitus* was an almost comical document that succeeded in anathematizing texts that contained almost direct quotations from Holy Scripture. Many perfectly respectable Catholics, from the archbishop of Paris downwards, were horrified, and the Parlement was drawn into the quarrel because it was expected to register the bull. Many *parlementaires* had doubts about the wisdom of such a policy, but their resistance was redoubled on account of the King's unwillingness to follow the legal forms and first secure the agreement of the French bishops. By trying to impose the bull by royal command, the King flounted the so-called Gallican liberties of the French Church, which were intended to protect his own rights relative to the papacy, and were cherished by the *parlementaires* who were traditionally charged with upholding them. *Unigenitus* would subsequently provoke a near schism in the French church, caused quills to be sharpened for a polemical campaign unmatched since the Fronde, and provided the raw materials for almost interminable legal and theological wrangling. Finally, it would revive long dormant debates about the constitutional role of the parlements.

During the civil wars of the sixteenth century, political theorists had debated the origins of French government and institutions, with François Hotman famously imagining the primitive constitution of *FrancoGallia*. According to his interpretation, France had once had annual national assemblies convoked to advise the King. These Frankish assemblies were presented as the direct precursors of the contemporary Estates-General, offering a defiant alternative to the emerging theories of absolute royal sovereignty. During the Fronde similar arguments resurfaced, and this time polemicists such as Louis Machon claimed that it was the Parlement of Paris rather than the Estates-General that was the true heir to the ancient assemblies. Constitutional speculation was driven underground during the personal rule of Louis XIV, but it had not gone away. The crisis over *Unigenitus* revived these debates and the Jansenists in particular contributed to their development as they looked to the Parlement to protect them from persecution. It was almost certainly one of their adherents who published the *Judicium Francorum* in 1732, setting out the claims of the Parlement to the Frankish inheritance, and these ideas were given a new gloss by the influential Jansenist lawyer Louis-Adrien Le Paige in his *Lettres Historiques* of 1753.[16] His ideas and those of a circle of sympathetic lawyers and magistrates had by mid-century found their way into both the Parlement's debates and its remonstrances and had also been widely disseminated through pamphlets and other polemical literature. Put simply, the constitutionalists argued that the Parlement was as old as the monarchy, and that no law was binding unless it had been freely verified in the court. The theory was even extended to include the ceremony of a *lit de justice*, something which threatened the King's ability to impose his will in the last resort. As for the provincial parlements, they too were integrated into the picture as what were termed 'classes', or extensions, of the one and indivisible Parlement of France.[17] Provincial reaction was mixed, the Parlement of Rouen embraced the theory with alacrity, while others were more lukewarm, but the theory was certainly seen as pernicious by the government which regularly condemned it.

Yet it is always necessary to be wary when looking at these constitutional arguments because *parlementaire* opinion was rarely unanimous. Within every Parlement it is possible to find a group of magistrates whose support for the absolute authority of the monarchy was unequivocal. When forced to choose between obedience to the King or supporting the pretensions of their colleagues they were prepared to opt for the former, often exposing themselves to intense hostility in the process.[18] In reality, the majority of *parlementaires* were not zealots of any particular cause, and when they adopted bold constitutional arguments it was frequently to defend the privileges and jurisdiction of the Parlement or to reinforce its position in disputes over religion, taxation, or the conduct of the royal administration. Yet, if the parlementaires were not driven solely by ideology or self-interest, they did have a strong sense of their duty to uphold the law and, when necessary, to present their remonstrances to the feet of the throne.

The parlements were, therefore, an important part of the political system and although French monarchs would occasionally seek to curb their influence most were aware that they were an indispensable part of the monarchical government. It was an opinion underlined by various political aphorisms, most famously perhaps that coined by Louis XVI's mentor, the count de Maurepas, who declared: 'pas de Parlement, pas de monarchie' (no Parlement, no monarchy).[19] Maurepas was no doubt influenced both by his own practical experience as a minister and the persuasive intellectual arguments of Montesquieu. According to the great constitutional theorist, France was a monarchy and not an oriental despotism or Russian-style autocracy, a distinction he attributed to the existence of intermediary powers such as the parlements or nobility which could temper the effects of unbridled royal sovereignty. These ideas were widely shared by the elites and the literate public, and it was faith in the ability of the parlements to act as a check on government that was largely responsible for the ability of successive monarchs to rule for 175 years without summoning an Estates-General. Of course it might be objected that the parlements were not representative institutions to be compared to the British Parliament, the Swedish Riksdag, or the Polish Sejm. The *parlementaires* were venal officeholders not elected deputies, and they enjoyed no popular mandate to justify their interventions on the public stage. As a result, generations of historians have denounced the *parlementaires* as the self-serving defenders of privileged noble interests. They were certainly willing to act in their own interests, but that should not obscure a genuine sense of responsibility to speak out against perceived injustice or maladministration.

It is also important to avoid thinking about the parlements in purely oppositional terms, and many of the delaying tactics employed by the magistrates were deliberately targeted signals to the government. The decision to make representations, to send a deputation, or even to take more drastic action such as threatening a judicial strike was all part of a finely calibrated system for exerting pressure on the ministry.[20] Similarly the crown had an impressive repertoire of options to choose from when replying to a *parlementaire* gambit, from offering conciliatory words to imprisoning those it felt were responsible for opposing royal commands. Both sides were constantly alert to the actions of the other and went to considerable lengths to decipher the significance of a particular gesture, and there was tacit agreement about what represented legitimate behaviour in any given situation. Although much of this political manœuvring took place behind closed doors, whether at Versailles or in the Palais de justice, the public was nevertheless an important part of the political equation. On issues such as taxation or the religious disputes arising from *Unigenitus*, the *parlementaires* knew that the public expected them to speak out and would judge them harshly if they failed to do so. As for the King, he could not respond too peremptorily, otherwise he risked being accused of failing to listen to legitimate grievances. The dialogue between monarch and the parlements was therefore conducted with a constant eye on public opinion and, in some ways, these rules governing judicial politics are reminiscent of an unwritten constitution, albeit one that was subject to periodic bouts of instability. In 1673, Louis XIV had weakened the power of the parlements considerably by refusing to receive remonstrances before a law had been registered and Louis XV attempted something similar in 1771. Yet when looked at across the 175 years that separated the meeting of the Estates-General in 1614 from that of 1789, it is clear that absolute monarchy was both limited and yet paradoxically strengthened by the existence of the parlements.

In theory at least, the provincial estates did represent a broader cross-section of society than the parlements, and they liked to think of themselves as the upholders of provincial rights and liberties. Great emphasis was placed upon the various 'treaties' accorded by the French kings when adding previously independent territories to their realm, and these texts were subsequently cherished as the founding charters of the *Artésien, Béarnais,* or Breton constitutions.[21] By far the most valuable of these constitutional liberties was the right of consent to taxation. The assemblies of the estates almost invariably opened amidst great pomp with the King's representatives, who usually included the governor, local military commandant, and intendant, presenting the King's demand for a *don gratuit* and after the introduction of universal taxation in 1695 for the capitation, *dixième, vingtième,* and other levies. In order to secure approval for the King's demands, the royal officials were expected to employ every available tactic. In an effort to create a favourable atmosphere, the governor would entertain on a lavish scale, inviting the deputies of the three orders to banquets, while trying to influence public opinion through balls and entertainments for distinguished local citizens and by supplying fireworks, music, and copious quantities of drink for the ordinary people.[22]

Such hospitality was not to be spurned, but it was rarely enough on its own to open provincial purses and the crown was also obliged to spend money, offering 'gifts' to influential deputies, distributing promises of patronage, and calling in favours from those it had aided in the past. The ability to draw upon a group of loyal clients was a great advantage, and it was not a coincidence that the Estates of Burgundy, where the governor was a member of the House of Bourbon-Condé for most of the seventeenth and eighteenth centuries, were renowned for the efficient conduct of government business.[23] It is true that the Burgundian governors did not have to face hundreds of truculent nobles, as was frequently the case in Brittany, where even the most skilful political managers could run into difficulty. One of the problems was the increasingly distant role of the governor of Brittany, who was replaced by the military commandant of the province and the intendant. As they were directly implicated in daily administrative activities, they almost invariably attracted criticism and were often obliged to leave the province under a cloud.[24] In Burgundy, on the other hand, commandants and intendants came and went, but the authority of the governor remained largely unchallenged to the extent that he was regularly described as acting like a viceroy in the province.

If taxation was usually the most contentious subject for discussion at meetings of the estates, there were also plenty of other issues to address. These would include matters such as the raising of the militia, the garrisoning of royal troops, the state of roads and waterways, and the distribution of pensions, all of which had the potential to be contentious because they ultimately cost money.[25] The estates would also deal with more parochial matters, hearing the petitions submitted by individuals, towns, villages, or other institutions, requesting their aid. Much of this tended to boil down to pleas for financial assistance, although it was also possible for broader commercial or agricultural interests to find expression. During the eighteenth century, for example, requests for the estates to campaign for the right to partition common lands or to protect local glass, cotton, or woollen industries were regularly made. Finally, the estates would deliberate about their own internal affairs, deciding the regulations governing entrance requirements, policing the conduct of their own officials, and settling disputes about precedence and ceremony.

The assemblies of the different provincial estates followed a similar general pattern, but there was one key distinction. Those that assembled annually like Languedoc or were in the habit of remaining assembled for long periods, which was the case in Brittany, tended to concentrate power in the assembly itself. Languedoc was a model in this regard, and the local estates were regularly praised for their diligence and effectiveness. In Burgundy, where the estates met for only a few weeks every three years, the situation was very different. Since at least the sixteenth century, the estates had vested power in a permanent commission, known as the chamber of *élus*, which contained representatives of the three orders, the mayor of Dijon, and two officers of the local Chambre des Comptes that acted in its name between assemblies.[26] There were real advantages to having a permanent body to protect the interests of the estates, even if the growing power of the *élus* caused unease in the eighteenth century, and a similar commission was established in Brittany during the early years of Louis XV's reign.

Whichever model the estates followed they were, like the parlements, an essential part of the governing process in the *pays d'états*, and the fundamental principle of the right of consent offers an alternative to the classic view of the absolute monarchy being defined by unfettered royal sovereignty. It was long assumed that, with the possible exceptions of Brittany and Languedoc, the estates had become empty shells with pomp and ceremony replacing any real provincial autonomy.[27] It was an interpretation that dovetailed neatly with prevailing assumptions about the rise of absolutism, a process that was assumed to be a Europe-wide phenomenon that had led to the demise of the provincial estates which were supposedly superseded by the more modern bureaucratic forms of administration associated with the intendants. It is an argument that is no longer tenable, and where they survived estates proved to be adaptable and effective institutions that in the Habsburg Empire would continue to meet until the mid-nineteenth century. In France too, the estates would demonstrate that there was nothing incompatible about powerful provincial institutions and absolute monarchy.

The cornerstones of that relationship were taxation and credit. For much of the early modern period, the crown struggled to raise loans cheaply, something that would have serious implications from the middle of the seventeenth century when France was engaged in a series of European and colonial wars against the Dutch Republic and Great

Britain. There was no French equivalent to the Bank of England, and to the consternation of successive finance ministers their smaller and theoretically poorer island neighbour continued to raise loans at a fraction of the cost of those available to them. Part of the explanation lay in the absence of a national French Parliament to vote taxes, to underwrite loans, and to scrutinize the activities of an absolute monarchy that preferred to hide its activities behind a veil of secrecy. As bankruptcy was also a real threat, investors were understandably wary and demanded high interest rates as insurance against possible default.

In such a climate, the provincial estates offered the crown a very useful alternative source of credit.[28] Although not representative bodies in any modern democratic sense, they nevertheless contained a broad cross-section of the local elites or were connected to them through kinship, professional, or patronage ties. No less importantly, the estates had retained considerable autonomy in terms of the levy of taxation. When the King asked for a *don gratuit* or later universal taxes such as the capitation, *dixième*, or *vingtième*, he rarely collected the taxes himself. Instead he was happy to leave that crucial responsibility to the estates. Even more importantly, the monarchy discovered that it could ask the estates to advance the proceeds of taxation almost immediately by allowing them to borrow against future tax revenues. This system had emerged during the seventeenth century, when Louis XIV in particular had imposed unwanted offices or new indirect taxes on the *pays d'états*, knowing full well that they would try to buy him off. There was clearly a limit to what could be gained from these expedients, but the King helped the estates with these 'buy outs' by alienating indirect taxes on commodities such as salt or wine in order to allow the estates to borrow, which they did far more cheaply than he could have done on his own account.

Once universal taxes were introduced in 1695, the government was keen to extend this system, known as *abonnements*, entering into negotiations with the estates or their representatives for advances against the capitation or *dixième*. As we might expect, the result was an elaborate process of bargaining with the King asking for more than he expected to receive and the estates offering less than they intended to pay, pleading poverty and citing every conceivable form of man-made or natural disaster in mitigation. The result was usually a compromise acceptable to both sides. It was a mutually rewarding system in the sense that the monarch had access to a quick and effective form of credit which was always a bonus, especially in times of war, while the estates preserved their own autonomy and were able to keep the administration of provincial finances out of the acquisitive hands of the intendants.

Over the course of the century that preceded the Revolution, this system became entrenched throughout the *pays d'états*, reaching its apogee during the ministry of Jacques Necker, the Genevan banker who oversaw French finances at the outset of the American War for Independence. By then, the direct tax system was dominated by *abonnements* as the crown accepted cash payments raised as loans by the estates and alienated the proceeds of taxation to cover the interest payments and the reimbursement of the capital. During the seventeenth century the loans had been on a comparatively modest scale and had been provided by networks of local elites, including members of the estates, provincial parlements, and influential courtiers. However, as the system expanded, the number of investors multiplied dramatically, drawing in men and women from almost every social station and, at the same time, attracting funds from international investors in the Dutch Republic, Switzerland, and Italy.

By providing much needed credit, the provincial estates performed a valuable service for the monarchy and this, combined with their control of tax collection, had a profound impact on their institutional development. First, the estates were obliged to develop their own systems to cope with universal taxation and to recruit and police the officials charged with implementing their orders. Secondly, their control over the taxation system inspired confidence amongst investors that loans would be secure because ultimately the estates could, if they chose, raise more revenue than was actually required and could either reduce the size of the provincial debt or use these additional funds for their own purposes. In Burgundy and Languedoc the results were frequently impressive and the estates actively pursued a wide range of administrative tasks such as building roads, constructing canals, and encouraging agricultural improvement. As their administrative remit expanded, both bodies were obliged to develop teams of officials to oversee taxation, public works, and the immense amount of paperwork generated by these and other tasks, and it is not an exaggeration to claim that by the reign of Louis XVI they had taken on some of the features of modern bureaucracy.[29] The officials and their clerks were working fixed hours to predictable patterns and were rewarded with regular salaries and retirement pensions. It is true that most of these officials were recruited through traditional kinship and patronage networks, but they were certainly not holders of sinecures and the incompetent or workshy were liable to be disciplined and even, on occasions, dismissed.

The Estates of Artois, Flanders, and Brittany were, it has to be said, less active than those of Burgundy and Languedoc in the administrative sphere, possibly because they were late to develop a permanent commission and therefore had to compete with the intendant. However, even with these reservations in mind, it is still possible to state that between the reign of Louis XIV and the French Revolution the provincial estates had reinvented themselves as powerful instruments of local government, developing in parallel with the intendants, who were once thought to have replaced them. Many would-be reformers, including Fénelon, Montesquieu, and the elder Mirabeau, supported the idea of establishing provincial estates throughout the kingdom, and the Parlements of Dauphiné and Normandy in particular campaigned for the restoration of their assemblies. In some ways, these demands might seem rather surprising because there were obvious rivalries between the parlements and the provincial estates. In Dijon the Palais des états physically dominated the local landscape, standing proudly in the centre of the city and dwarfing the Palais de justice inhabited by the *parlementaires*. Such obvious rivalries were avoided in Languedoc, where the estates were based in Montpellier and the Parlement in Toulouse or in Brittany, where the Parlement dominated the provincial capital of Rennes, while the estates rotated around the provincial sees.

These issues of authority and precedence often masked deeper rivalries about respective histories, rights, and privileges and would occasionally cause conflict, especially if one institution trod on the jurisdiction or professional competence of the other. The Parlement of Dijon, for example, flew into a rage in 1760 when the chamber of *élus* signed an *abonnement* before the relevant fiscal edict had been registered.[30] This issue brought to a head a number of other disputes and resulted in a public quarrel that continued for more than three years, involving remonstrances, pamphlets, deputations to Versailles, the confinement of the *parlementaires* to the city of Dijon, and much else besides. These sensitivities about jurisdiction and administrative competence ensured that there was always a certain distance between provincial parlements and estates, even if many of their familial and financial interests overlapped. Not that we should exaggerate the degree of friction because both sides would try to avoid conflict where possible, and they were frequently adept at petitioning the crown when it came to protecting provincial interests.

Given the success of the provincial estates of Languedoc and of Burgundy, it is surprising that the crown was reluctant to experiment by heeding calls for their restoration in other major provinces such as Normandy. It is possible that its hesitancy was the result of the precarious state of royal finances, which made any alteration to a regular income stream problematic. Whatever the cause of its pusillanimity, the government rejected such a bold gesture and instead chose to tinker with the idea by, for example, re-establishing estates in the Boulonnais in 1766 or by creating new provincial administrations in Berry and Haute-Guyenne in 1778.[31] While interesting and potentially significant innovations, neither policy was likely to have the impact of re-establishing estates in a large province, and it was not until 1787–8 that the monarchy finally decided to take the plunge. First, it proposed the establishment of new provincial assemblies throughout the *pays d'élections*, which was one of the more impressive and successful of the measures put before a specially convoked and ultimately truculent Assembly of Notables. The provincial assemblies have received guarded approval from those who have investigated their activities in detail, but as France was almost simultaneously engulfed by the political and financial crisis that culminated in the revolution of 1789 it is difficult to predict what their impact might have been in less dramatic circumstances.[32] The same is true of the situation in provinces like Franche-Comté and Provence which succeeded in persuading the government to allow the assembly of long dormant provincial estates. It is, however, noteworthy that the provincial Estates of Dauphiné were to the fore in proposing the model of doubled representation for the Third Estate and voting by head that would become the rallying cry of the Third Estate and the catalyst for revolution in the spring and early summer of 1789.

As for the existing *pays d'états*, there is compelling evidence to suggest that by the second half of the eighteenth century, the estates were the targets of mounting criticism.[33] As they had accumulated power and responsibilities, they had effectively filled the role of the intendants in the *pays d'élections*. That would not have mattered if they had been seen as genuinely representative of local interests, but this was clearly not the case. Only in Brittany was the nobility as a whole eligible to sit in the estates, elsewhere access was confined to a much narrower elite within an elite. The same could be said of the clergy, where the episcopate dominated and the voices of the ordinary parish priests were rarely, if ever, heard. Finally, the Third Estate had few genuine spokesmen, as most deputies were the mayors of towns, an office that had ceased to be elective since the introduction of municipal venality at the end of the seventeenth century. As for the inhabitants of the countryside, they were almost totally excluded. The lack of proper representation combined with the many inequalities in the fiscal and administrative system account for the hostility directed at the provincial estates in the *cahiers de doléances* and it left them vulnerable to the great administrative upheaval that followed the night of 4 August 1789.

On that great revolutionary occasion, deputies from the various social orders, provinces, towns, corporate bodies, and other institutions had literally queued up to renounce their own privileges. One of the results was the demise of the provincial 'constitutions' and with them the estates that would be swept away as part of the local government reorganization that would divide France into *départements*. Few would mourn the passing of the provincial estates, and perhaps more surprisingly the same was true of parlements. Despite the many laurels won during the great battles against ministerial despotism in 1771–4 or 1787–8, the *parlementaires* were, by 1789, seen as part of the nation's problems rather than their solution. Firmly associated with the defence of the society of orders and its 'ancient constitution', the parlements were seen as a threat to a revolution that preached the virtues of civic equality and they were abolished in 1790.

Notes

1. The provincial parlements have inspired a truly monumental amount of scholarship, but for an introduction see Frédéric Bidouze, *Les Remontrances du Parlement de Navarre au xviiie siècle : Essai sur une culture politique en province au siècle des Lumières* (Biarritz, 2000); Olivier Chaline, *Godart de Belbeuf: Le Parlement, le roi et les Normands* (Luneray, 1996); Clarisse Coulomb, *Les Pères de la patrie: La Société parlementaire en Dauphiné au temps des Lumières* (Grenoble, 2006); Monique Cubells, *La Provence des Lumières: Les Parlementaires d'Aix au xviiie siècle* (Paris, 1984); William Doyle, *The Parlement of Bordeaux and the End of the Old Regime, 1771–1790* (London, 1974); Jean Egret, *Louis XV et l'opposition parlementaire* (Paris, 1970); and Maurice Gresset, *Gens de justice à Besançon: De la conquête par Louis XIV à la Révolution française, 1674–1789* (2 vols. Paris, 1978).
2. For an introduction to the history of the Paris Parlement, see Peter R. Campbell, *Power and Politics in Old Regime France: 1720–1745* (London, 1996); Albert N. Hamscher, *The Parlement of Paris After the Fronde, 1653–1673* (Pittsburgh, 1976); J. M. J. Rogister, *Louis XV and the Parlement of Paris, 1737–1755* (Cambridge, 1995); J. H. Shennan, *The Parlement of Paris* (2nd edn., Stroud, 1998); Bailey Stone, *The Parlement of Paris, 1774–1789* (Chapel Hill, NC, 1981); and Julian Swann, *Politics and the Parlement of Paris under Louis XV, 1754–1774* (Cambridge, 1995).
3. The works of J. Russell Major, *Representative Government in Early Modern France* (New Haven, Conn., 1980), and *From Renaissance Monarchy to Absolute Monarchy: French Kings, Nobles and Estates* (Baltimore, Md., 1994), are particularly relevant for the period before 1660.
4. Julian Swann, *Provincial Power and Absolute Monarchy: The Estates General of Burgundy, 1661–1790* (Cambridge, 2003), 41–90.

5. Gauthier Aubert, *Le Président de Robien: Gentilhomme et savant dans la Bretagne des Lumières* (Rennes, 2001), and Michael P. Breen, *Law, City and King: Legal Culture, Municipal Politics, and State Formation in Early Modern Dijon* (Rochester, NY, 2007), 180–206.
6. Coulomb, *Les Pères de la patrie*, 430–3.
7. François Bluche, *Les Magistrats du parlement de Paris au xviiie siècle* (Paris, 1960).
8. For an introduction, see Marie-Laure Legay, *Les États provinciaux dans la construction de l'état moderne* (Geneva, 2001); Armand Rebillon, *Les États de Bretagne de 1661 à 1789: Leur organisation, l'évolution de leurs pouvoirs leur administration financière* (Paris, 1932); and Swann, *Provincial Power and Absolute Monarchy*.
9. David D. Bien, *The Calas Affair: Persecution, Toleration, and Heresy in Eighteenth Century Toulouse* (Princeton, 1960).
10. Shennan, *Parlement of Paris*, 9–85.
11. In addition to the works cited above, see John J. Hurt, *Louis XIV and the Parlements: The Assertion of Royal Authority* (Manchester, 2002), and Lloyd Moote, *The Revolt of the Judges: The Parlement of Paris and the Fronde 1643–1652* (Princeton, 1971).
12. Hurt, *Louis XIV and the Parlements*, 38–66.
13. The classic exposition of this was Franklin L. Ford, *Robe and Sword: The Regrouping of the French Aristocracy after Louis XIV* (Cambridge, Mass., 1953).
14. Joël Félix, *Finances et politique au siècle des Lumières: Le Ministère L'Averdy, 1763–1768* (Paris, 1999), and Swann, *Politics and the Parlement*, 284–351.
15. For an introduction to the Jansenist imbroglio, see B. R. Kreiser, *Miracles, Convulsions, and Ecclesiastical Politics in Early Eighteenth-Century Paris* (Princeton, 1978).
16. Le Paige and the development of Jansenist constitutional and theological thought have been analysed from different perspectives by Catherine Maire, *De la cause de Dieu à la cause de la Nation: Le Jansénisme au xviiie siècle* (Paris, 1998), and Dale Van Kley, *The Religious Origins of the French Revolution: From Calvin to the Civil Constitution, 1560–1791* (New Haven, Conn., 1996).
17. Julian Swann, 'Robe, Sword and Aristocratic Reaction Revisited: The French Nobility and Political Crisis, 1748–1789', in R. G. Asch (ed.), *Der europäische Adel im Ancien Régime: Von der Krise der standischen Monarchien bis zur Revolution, 1600–1789* (Cologne, 2001), 151–78.
18. See Olivier Chaline, 'Les Infortunes de la fidélité: Les Partisans du pouvoir royal dans les parlements au xviiie siècle', *Histoire Économie et Société: Époques moderne et contemporaine*, 3 (2006), 335–54; Clarisse Coulomb, 'L'Échec d'un serviteur du roi: Vidaud de la Tour, premier president du Parlement de Maupeou à Grenoble', *Histoire Economie et Société: Époques moderne et contemporaine*, 3 (2006), 371–84; and Julian Swann, 'Silence, Respect, Obedience: Political Culture in Louis XV's France', in Hamish Scott and Brendan Simms (eds.), *Cultures of Power in Europe during the Long Eighteenth Century* (Cambridge, 2007), 225–48.
19. Maurepas was presumably inspired by Montesquieu, and is quoted by John Hardman, *Louis XVI* (London, 1993), 30.
20. An argument developed by William Doyle, 'The Parlements', in Keith Michael Baker (ed.), *The French Revolution and the Creation of Modern Political Culture*, i. *The Political Culture of the Old Regime* (Oxford, 1987). The concept of judicial politics is discussed further in Julian Swann, 'Repenser les parlements au xviiie siècle: Du concept de l'"opposition parlementaire" à celui de "culture juridique des conflits politiques"', in Alain J. Lemaître (ed.),

Le Monde parlementaire au xviiie siècle: L'Invention d'un discours politique (Rennes, 2010), 17–38.
21. William Doyle, 'The Union in a European Context', Transactions of the Royal Historical Society, 6th ser. 10 (2000), 167–80, and Julian Swann, '"Le Roi demande, les états consente": Royal Council, Provincial Estates and Parlement in Eighteenth-Century Burgundy', in David Hayton and James Kelly (eds.), Lawmaking in Periphery and Centre: Constitutional Relations in Composite States, 1690–1800 (Basingstoke, 2010), 190–210.
22. F. Dumont, Une session des états de Bourgogne: La tenue de 1718 (Dijon, 1935), provides a good insight into the organization of these assemblies.
23. Swann, Provincial Power and Absolute Monarchy, 41–90, 230–61.
24. The most famous example being that of the duc d'Aiguillon in 1768: Barthélemy Pocquet, Le pouvoir absolu et l'esprit provincial: Le Duc d'Aiguillon et La Chalotais (3 vols. Paris, 1900–1).
25. Legay, Les États provinciaux, 239–324.
26. Swann, Provincial Power and Absolute Monarchy, 91–125.
27. The misguided view popularized by Tocqueville, Ancien Régime, supplementary chapter.
28. The financial relationship between the provincial estates and the crown has been analysed by Legay, Les États provinciaux, 177–238; Mark Potter and Jean-Laurent Rosenthal, 'Politics and Public Finance in France: The Estates of Burgundy, 1660–1790', Journal of Interdisciplinary History, 27 (1997), 577–612; and Swann, Provincial Power and Absolute Monarchy, 154–93, 295–329.
29. The situation varied amongst the different pays d'états, and the provinces of Burgundy and Languedoc were noticeably more active than those of Artois or Brittany.
30. Julian Swann, 'Power and Provincial Politics in Eighteenth-Century France: The Varenne Affair, 1757–1763', French Historical Studies, 21 (1998), 441–74, and Stéphane Pannekoucke, 'L'Affaire Varenne (1760–1763): Jeux de clientèle et enjeux de pouvoir entre Versailles, Paris et Dijon', Annales de Bourgogne, 78 (2006), 33–67.
31. Félix, Finances et politique au siècle des Lumières; Marie-Laure Legay, 'Un projet méconnu de «décentralisation» au temps de Laverdy (1763–1768): Les Grands États d'Aquitaine', Revue Historique, 631 (2004), 533–54.
32. Peter M. Jones, Reform and Revolution in France: The Politics of Transition, 1774–1791 (Cambridge, 1995), 139–66.
33. Legay, Les États provinciaux, 468–514, and Swann, Provincial Power and Absolute Monarchy, 365–99.

Bibliography

Bordes, M., L'Administration provinciale et municipale au xviiie siècle (Paris, 1972).
Carcassonne, Elie, Montesquieu et le problème de la constitution française au xviiie siècle (Paris, 1927).
Doyle, William, 'The Parlements' in Keith Michael Baker (ed.), The French Revolution and the Creation of Modern Political Culture, i. The Political Culture of the Old Regime (Oxford, 1987).
Egret, Jean, Louis XV et l'opposition parlementaire (Paris, 1970).
Hurt, John, Louis XIV and the Parlements: The Assertion of Royal Authority (Manchester, 2002).

Legay, Marie-Laure, *Les États provinciaux dans la construction de l'État moderne aux xviie et xviiie siècles* (Geneva, 2001).
Lemaître, Alain J. (ed.), *Le Monde parlementaire au xviiie siècle. L'invention d'un discours politique* (Rennes, 2009).
Le Mao, Caroline, *Parlement et parlementaires: Bordeaux au Grand Siècle* (Seyssel, 2007).
Shennan, J. H., *The Parlement of Paris* (London, 1968).
Stone, Bailey, *The French Parlements and the Crisis of the Old Regime* (Chapel Hill, NC, 1986).
Swann, Julian, *Provincial Power and Absolute Monarchy: The Estates-General of Burgundy, 1661–1790* (Cambridge, 2003).

PART II
SOCIETY

CHAPTER 7

NOBILITY

JOHN SHOVLIN

Historians of the Ancien Régime long viewed the nobility as a holdover from a feudal age, an antiquated breed condemned to a slow, and ultimately terminal, decline. Nobles were regarded as the casualties of secular political and social transformations: the rise of the absolutist state, which stripped them of political power; and economic transformations, which increased the relative wealth of non-nobles, and empowered them to challenge the nobility's supremacy. Since the 1960s, however, revisionist scholarship has almost entirely jettisoned this view. The nobility is now widely seen as a social group that participated massively in the processes of modernization that transformed seventeenth- and eighteenth-century Europe. Through its economic role and values, its service to the monarchical state, its openness to new recruits, and its engagement in the public sphere, the nobility moved with the times. Revisionists also challenged the idea that the French Revolution represented the culmination of deep-seated social conflicts between the nobility and other social groups. The antipathy to nobles that burst forth in 1789, they argued, could as readily be viewed as the product of immediate political struggles unleashed by the calling of the Estates-General, as of long-simmering social resentments.[1]

Recent scholarship confirms and deepens many of the principal conclusions of the revisionist perspective, but also challenges certain aspects of this new consensus. Considered as a whole, the nobility consolidated, and may even have increased, its power, wealth, and cultural influence in the century before 1789. Economic conditions brought prosperity for many noble families in the eighteenth century, and newcomers joined the Second Estate in droves, bringing with them their ambition, their skills, and their money. But what was good for the nobility as a social group was not beneficial for all nobles. Recent research has shown that poorer nobles faced a crisis of social reproduction; they struggled simply to preserve their status and their lineages, and many failed. On the question of revolutionary hostility to nobles, some historians have come to question the idea that such sentiments sprang mainly from the political circumstances of the pre-revolutionary crisis. They point to rich veins of anti-noble feeling in the old regime, and suggest that these must be taken into account if the anti-aristocratic character of the French Revolution is to be properly understood. One factor of particular importance in generating antagonism to nobles, and to nobility as an institution, was conflict over honour. Non-noble elites increasingly demanded that their honour be recognized, and resented noble claims to distinction and superiority. The revolutionary attack on nobility emerged, in part, out of a long-brewing status crisis with its roots deep in the social transformations that remade the French elite over the course of the eighteenth century.

Scholarship on nobles since the 1960s demonstrates that the commercialization of social relations was not inimical to the interests of the nobility as a social group. This was especially the case for the wealthiest nobles who were often well-placed to reap the benefits of the long economic expansion that marked the decades between the 1720s and the 1760s. Rich nobles made use of their economically privileged position to invest in some of the most dynamic, profitable (and often risky) sectors of the French economy. Noble investors were particularly prominent in mining and metallurgy, and in industries dependent on government contracts, such as cannon founding and munitions. Noble capital also played a role in international trade and, to some extent, in colonial production.[2] While such opportunities were closed to less affluent nobles, who lacked the capital and access to credit that such investments required, many nobles of modest fortune made a successful transition to a world in which their primary social function was as collectors of agricultural rents (and to a lesser extent as agricultural entrepreneurs). Nationally, the nobility owned 25–30 per cent of all French land on the eve of the Revolution and, locally, their position could be even more dominant. In the diocese of Toulouse in 1750, a noble cadre representing 1 per cent of the population owned 44 per cent of the land. As major landholders, the nobility benefited from the steady rise in prices for grain and wood in the eighteenth century, and also from the more fluctuating profits of the wine trade. The wages paid to agricultural labourers did not grow nearly as fast as agricultural commodity prices. Lucrative seigneurial rights could be exploited or leased out to supplement income from rents, and many nobles capitalized on this resource by reviving forgotten or dormant claims. But the long-term trend was for rents to replace seigneurial exactions as the most significant source of noble landed income.[3]

Provincial noble families, in some regions at least, enjoyed rising mean incomes in the second half of the eighteenth century. A sample of noble magistrates from the Parlement of Aix suggests that, in most cases, their revenues increased over the course of the century, sometimes quite spectacularly. At the beginning of the century in Upper Normandy, 40 per cent of rural noble households had incomes of less than 1,000 livres; by the 1750s this proportion had fallen to 16 per cent in the *élection* of Rouen and 11 per cent in the *élection* of Gisors. In the latter district, median noble income increased by nearly 200 per cent between 1703 and 1788. The trend appears to have continued even in the difficult years after 1770. In the lower Norman *élection* of Alençon in 1766, only 25 per cent of noble families earned more than 3,000 livres annually. Twenty years later, this proportion had increased to 40 per cent. In the town of Abbeville in Picardy, between 1770 and 1784 the proportion of nobles earning more than 10,000 livres increased from 15 per cent to 25 per cent, while the proportion earning less than 3,000 fell by one-third.[4]

One factor skewing average noble wealth upward was the ennoblement of wealthy commoners. According to William Doyle, perhaps 10,000 men were ennobled over the course of the eighteenth century, the vast majority through venal office. Every officer who joined the nobility brought his family with him, so 10,000 ennoblements might have entailed 50,000 new nobles. This was a significant influx of new blood, and combined with high rates of ennoblement in the sixteenth and seventeenth centuries, it meant that relatively few nobles in 1789 descended from families with immemorial nobility. In Franche-Comté, only 21 per cent of noble families in 1789 had been noble for at least four generations. Two-thirds of the Angevin nobility in 1789 had been ennobled since 1667. In the *bailliage* of Beauvais, among the fifty-eight nobles who met in 1789 to elect a deputy to the Estates-General, almost half came from families ennobled since 1700. Rates of ennoblement were probably not unusually high in the eighteenth century, but access to the nobility had become more firmly tied to money. The most prolific ennobling office—that of *secrétaire du roi*—could cost as much as 120,000 livres by the 1780s. There were 800 such offices, and they brought nearly 4,000 officeholders into the nobility between 1700 and 1789. All of these new recruits were necessarily wealthy men, and in aggregate they must have significantly raised the total income of the Second Estate.[5]

Rising median incomes also derived, in some measure, from a shrinking nobility. While the French population as a whole rose from 21 or 22 million to over 28 million between 1700 and 1789, over the same period the number of nobles, by the best recent estimate, fell from around 230,000 to about 140,000.[6] This global fall in numbers masks significant regional differences. The *généralité* of Bordeaux maintained its share of nobles, while noble density in the Lyonnais actually increased. The noble population of Languedoc was also growing.[7] But in most regions the demographic trend was downward. In Brittany between 1667 and 1789, the percentage of nobles in the population decreased from 1.08 per cent to 0.60 per cent; in the Orléanais during the same period, they fell from 1.22 per cent of the population to 0.39 per cent; in Berry there was a 43 per cent decrease in the proportion of nobles in the population, while the fall was over 50 per cent in Lower Normandy.[8] The number of noble families living in the countryside near Rouen fell by 60 per cent between the early eighteenth century and 1789, while the number of noble households in the town itself declined from 272 to 176—a fall of 35 per cent.[9] Regional changes in density can be accounted for in part by the migration of wealthier nobles towards the cities. While the noble populations of small Breton towns fell in the eighteenth century, for example, those of Nantes and Saint-Malo grew. However, to account for the global fall in the number of nobles, we must look elsewhere.[10]

Many nobles may have slipped, over time, into the ranks of the Third Estate, forced to take up derogating occupations to make ends meet. Such impoverishment appears to have been a significant drain on the nobility, at least in some French regions, during preceding centuries.[11] However, though the evidence here is mixed, the most plausible explanation of the fall in the number of nobles is limitation of reproduction. A significant proportion of all nobles in the eighteenth century remained unmarried, and noble couples were having fewer children. The trend is clearest in the uppermost reaches of the order, among the dukes and peers. Between marriages contracted in the second half of the seventeenth century and those contracted a century later the proportion of childless couples increased from 9 per cent to 35 per cent, while among women who bore at least one child the proportion bearing no more than two rose from 13 per cent to 46 per cent.[12] Natality in French noble families as a whole appears to have fallen rapidly from the second half of the seventeenth century, a trend in line with several other European nobilities.[13]

One way to interpret such dramatic shifts in reproductive behaviour is in terms of a decision to conserve family wealth by limiting the number of children who had to be provided for. If nobles were better off generally in the eighteenth century, the economic burden of merely preserving status was increasing. This was so for several reasons. In earlier times it had been possible for petty gentlemen to sustain a noble identity by serving in the households of greater nobles. This option had almost disappeared by the beginning of the eighteenth century.[14] As education and refinement became increasingly important to the identity of nobility, the costs of raising children and presenting an appropriate face to the world increased. Finally, the consumer revolution of the eighteenth century placed noble households under new pressures. Many nobles expressed regret at having to spend so much in order to keep up appearances. Other noble households acquired a taste for comforts and luxuries they could ill afford. Such circumstances pushed noble families further into debt, which exposed them to ruin.[15]

The overall shrinkage of the Second Estate and its simultaneous absorption of tens of thousands of wealthy newcomers must certainly be viewed as beneficial to the relative position of the nobility, viewed in aggregate. By the 1780s, nobles on average were wealthier, better educated, and probably more influential culturally than they had been a century earlier. But the same trends invigorating the group spelled desuetude for thousands of noble families who either failed to reproduce, or slipped into the Third Estate. To the latter we should certainly add those thousands of impoverished nobles who were unable to enjoy a lifestyle commensurate with noble status and who therefore suffered social eclipse even if they managed to retain their privileged legal status.[16] These problems of social reproduction gave rise to a bitter chorus of recrimination. Lesser nobles complained that the social order had been undermined by money, that virtue and merit were no longer recognized, and that the polity was corrupted by luxury—a perspective that resonated with significant sections of the order, not just with ruined provincial squires.

Nobles were long regarded as the losers in a competition for power with the monarchy in early modern France. In the last thirty years, however, a new understanding of the absolutist monarchy has developed which views it as a form of government based less on the suppression of aristocratic power than on compromise and cooperation between the crown and social elites.[17] Nowhere is the historiographical shift more evident than in scholarship on the court. Versailles was long parodied as an arena where the aristocracy came to be domesticated, where independent magnates were transformed into simpering courtiers grovelling for imaginary rewards. In recent scholarship, by contrast, the court emerges as the principal national political institution, the site where the multiple networks of patronage which tied the polity together converged, and where their competing claims were managed. Aristocrats came to Versailles because it was the nerve centre for the distribution of power, position, and prestige. The court was the key source of information about opportunities, and the focal point for lobbying efforts. The administration was embedded in the life of the court, and any minister who could not manage court factions did not stay in office for long. Factions exerted influence even in such royal preserves as foreign policy. A clique around the Duke de Belle-Isle helped push France into war in the 1740s, while another, linked to Mme de Pompadour, engineered France's new alliance with Austria in 1756.[18]

One of the most striking developments of Louis XV's reign was the presence of *grands seigneurs* in the ministries.[19] From the 1750s, until the King's death in 1774, the ministries of foreign affairs, the army, and the navy were dominated by nobles of ancient extraction. Under Louis XVI, most of the ministers of war and the navy continued to be sword nobles, though foreign affairs was presided over by Charles Gravier de Vergennes, who emanated from a robe family. The distinction between ministerial and courtly power was further eroded as the ministry became a springboard to the highest reaches of aristocratic society. One of the daughters of Germain-Louis Chauvelin, a career magistrate who became Keeper of the Seals, married a La Rochefoucauld and another wed the Count de l'Aigle. One son of Chancellor René-Charles de Maupeou followed in his father's footsteps, another rose to the rank of general in the army, while a daughter married the Marquis de Calvisson. Vergennes's son married the adoptive daughter of the Marshal Duke de Mouchy.[20]

Royal government, the new perspective holds, depended on a partnership with the nobility; nobles were less the victims of the monarchy than its agents. Aristocratic governors, their lieutenants-general, bishops, and magnates played an informal role in the government of provinces functioning as key channels of influence, patronage, and communication between the monarchy and its provincial subjects. They could induce locals to execute the will of the centre, and they could also advance the interests and perspectives of the periphery in its dealings with the crown. The role of nobles in the *pays d'états* was even more vital because here the king had to negotiate with provincial estates dominated by nobles and their clienteles.[21] Nobles served the monarchy in the courts, in the administration, and especially in the army. Many embraced an ideal of service as a defining feature of their political identity. Military service was such an important component of noble honour that noble officers were willing to take on considerable personal expense in order to serve. In the eighteenth century, nobles were drawn to the rhetoric of patriotism that became such a central aspect of public discourse, claiming *esprit public* as a defining virtue of the Second Estate, and representing their order as an institution essential to the well-being of the *patrie*.[22]

Yet as recent scholarship has recognized, the older view that the rise of the monarchical state came at the expense of noble power also captures a part of the truth. Louis XIV broke the power of noble magnates in the late seventeenth century, at least to the extent that open rebellion became largely a thing of the past. Noble authority and independence decreased in other ways also: proprietary regiments in the army gave way to more centralized control; nobles could no longer sustain large numbers of retainers once they were ensconced at Versailles, and this reduced their influence; the state undermined the power of nobles as seigneurs, especially by weakening lordly justice; and many aristocrats became heavily dependent on the monarchy to supplement their incomes, which reduced their autonomy.[23] Michael Kwass has suggested that the implicit bargain that tied ordinary nobles to the absolutist monarchy was fraying by the second half of the eighteenth century. The terms of this bargain held that nobles should be exempt from direct taxation, indeed that part of the taxes levied on the peasantry be channelled to the nobility in the form of pensions, salaries, *gages*, and interest payments. The monarchy disrupted this redistributive arrangement by introducing universal taxes such as the *capitation* and the *vingtième*—taxes specifically designed to tap the wealth of the privileged. Antipathy to universal taxation was a key source of noble restiveness in the eighteenth century, and a particularly important factor driving the resistance of noble-dominated parlements to the monarchy. Noble magistrates even resorted to a rhetoric accusing the King of behaving despotically. From the 1750s there were calls for the reintroduction of provincial estates which, it was hoped, would restore to the nobility some control over fiscal exactions. The desire for political agency, combined with the diminishing profits of cooperation, may help to explain why so many nobles looked forward with enthusiasm to the reform of the kingdom in 1789.[24]

Nobles were well-placed to benefit from the greatest cultural transformation of the age—the rise of the public sphere. The emergence of a public, claiming a kind of cultural authority, grounded in new and renovated institutions of sociability, and mediated by the periodical press, would naturally advantage the more educated elements in the population.[25] Having evolved from an order defined principally by military values in the sixteenth century to one marked by education, consumption, and refinement in the eighteenth, the Second Estate was well-placed to play a leading role in public debate. Nobles were both major producers and significant consumers of the intellectual production of the eighteenth-century public sphere. They composed over 40 per cent of the membership of provincial academies—learned societies that dominated intellectual life outside Paris. They were disproportionately represented among readers of Enlightenment literature. In the city of Besançon, for example, nearly 40 per cent of the subscribers to one edition of the *Encyclopédie* were nobles. Among the hundreds of authors who published works on economic subjects between the 1750s and the 1780s, a third or more were noble. In the salons of the capital, men of letters validated the norms of aristocratic *mondanité* and were, in turn, admitted to aristocratic patronage networks. And, of course, many of the *philosophes* themselves were nobles: Buffon, Condillac, Condorcet, Grimm, Holbach, Jaucourt, Mably, Montesquieu, Saint-Lambert, and Turgot, to name only the most prominent.[26]

However, the public sphere also served as a forum, and echo-chamber, for a great deal of anti-noble invective. One set of critics harped on the uselessness and idleness of nobles, representing the Second Estate as a drag on the French economy. In his *Lettres philosophiques* (1734), Voltaire praised the English nobility which, he claimed, was less snobbish about entering trade than its French counterpart. This theme was developed in political economic works published in the 1750s, such as the *Remarques sur les avantages et les désavantages de la France et de la Grande Bretagne,* by Louis-Joseph Plumard de Dangeul, which argued that the nobility was a source of depopulation and that aristocratic conceptions of honour were a hindrance to the development of commerce. The full implications of this perspective were spelt out in Gabriel-François Coyer's *La Noblesse commerçante* (1756), which argued that the culture and corporate identity of the nobility was an obstacle to the development of national wealth and that the nobility ought to merge itself into the body of the nation by taking up commerce. Coyer was also an exponent of a closely related criticism—that nobles were bearers of baneful feudal attitudes that had no place in an enlightened polity. He excoriated the domineering spirit of country squires which, he claimed, made them quarrelsome and abusive.[27]

Ironically, attacks on 'aristocracy' in the old regime sometimes channelled the social resentment of less privileged nobles. In 1788, the nobility of Blois blamed the 'degradation of their order' on the 'fatal influence of the *grands*, the principal and almost unique source of the misfortunes which afflict the kingdom'.[28] In 1770, Jean-Baptiste Cotton des Houssayes, a Norman cleric from a poor noble family, rejoiced that 'every shadow of aristocracy' had been rooted out of the Academy of Rouen, and a regime of equality established there among men of learning.[29] Some military nobles denounced the army reforms of 1787–8 as the work of 'aristocrats' because they adopted a two-track system of promotion in which middling nobles were channelled into functionally important, but less prestigious, posts in regiments while the plum positions were reserved for courtiers. Such complaints drew on long-standing petty noble resentment that men lacking in 'merit'—often the sons of courtiers or wealthy ennobled commoners—enjoyed better promotion prospects than poorer nobles from families with established military traditions.[30] There were also sharp divisions within the nobility over the apportionment of the tax burden. The wealthiest and most powerful nobles were able to use their influence to limit their tax assessments under the *vingtième* and the *capitation*. Middling nobles found it harder to do so.[31]

The most virulent eighteenth-century critics of the nobility directed their ire against court nobles. Pamphlets and *libelles* routinely represented courtiers and *grands seigneurs* as corrupt, degenerate, and venal. Attacks on court women were especially venomous and ubiquitous. At Versailles, aristocratic women lived a public life; they were fully involved in the management of client networks, and in the struggle for rewards, that was the stuff of aristocratic politics.[32] In their supposed venality, selfishness, and luxury, court women were held to exemplify the dissoluteness of their class. It should be noted, however, that rather than representing the hostility of other social groups to the nobility, many of these attacks emanated from within Versailles itself. In the course of political struggles for power and the spoils of office, courtiers hired hack writers to publish scurrilous attacks on their rivals. Other sources of such rhetoric were the published judicial briefs, authored by lawyers, which were intended to influence court rulings in favour of clients who were suing aristocratic defendants.[33] Regardless of the source or motivation of such attacks, however, the vigorous print culture of the old regime allowed these tales of corruption to circulate widely, and to shape perceptions of the nobility.

Another criticism levelled against court nobles was that they were corrupted by luxury—that venality rather than virtue had become their defining ethos. Such criticisms were plausible because of the fantastic wealth of many court nobles and the spectacular fashion in which they spent it. Over the course of the century, expenditure on clothing by Paris nobles more than tripled. It was not uncommon for court families to spend 10,000 livres or more a year on dress. Charges of luxury also referenced the notorious fact that court nobles had financial stakes in the tax farms and marriage alliances to financiers (the quintessentially luxurious class). In the words of the moralist Charles Pinot Duclos, 'people of condition have already lost the right to despise finance, since there are few who are not allied to it by blood'.[34] But it was not just courtiers who were vulnerable to the charge of venality. Over the course of the eighteenth century the nobility as a whole became more obviously defined by wealth. High levels of ennoblement, in William Doyle's words, transformed the nobility into 'a sort of open plutocracy'. As capitalists became nobles and nobles became capitalists there was little to distinguish members of the Second Estate from other landowners and entrepreneurs. The consumption practices of provincial nobles were different from those of the court aristocracy; in the words of Robert Forster, 'sobriety, not profligacy, was the dominant note in the provincial noble family'. But luxury is in the eye of the beholder, and even the more modest spending habits of ordinary nobles might have appeared extravagant to their less affluent neighbours. The rising average wealth of nobles, combined with the gradual disappearance of poorer nobles, may have contributed to a sense that money had become the defining feature of the order.[35]

The increasingly plutocratic cast of the nobility was a liability because it conflicted with what was perhaps the most compelling rationale for noble privilege in an eighteenth-century context. Nobility remained an attractive ideal in the eighteenth century in part because it represented a kind of antidote to the acquisitiveness and pettiness of an increasingly commercial society. Commerce in the last decades of the old regime elicited a double cultural response, both positive and negative. The benefits of trade to national power, and its links to processes of refinement and civilization, were recognized and celebrated. Simultaneously, the profit motive on which commerce depended aroused suspicion as a disposition that might be incompatible with patriotic virtue and cultural achievement. Social and cultural critics valorized disinterestedness, the reverse of mercantile acquisitiveness. Nobles were supposed to exemplify a disinterested attitude, to serve as a reservoir of the kind of qualities a commercial society needed to preserve its virtue and its vitality. A nobility infected with the virus of venality could not reasonably be viewed in such a light. Nobility remained a powerful ideal in the eighteenth century, but one to which actual nobles had difficulty measuring up.[36]

What was the significance of the anti-noble feeling that historians have identified in the last decades of the old regime? The representation of the 'aristocrat' that took shape during the French Revolution was a compound of all these anti-noble elements—the proud idler, the degenerate intriguer, and, perhaps most of all, the man of luxury. But did such old regime critiques actually bring about the revolutionary attack on nobility? The prevalence of overt hostility to nobles in the last decades of the old regime is surely important, but may have diverted our attention from less obvious, and ultimately more important, long-term social and cultural developments which played a role in producing the great anti-aristocratic convulsion of the 1790s. I have in mind a slow-building conflict over status and honour created by the social and cultural transformation of the early modern elite.

In one of the most important revisionist works of the 1970s, Colin Lucas argued that the revolt of the Third Estate in 1789 derived in part from a status crisis sparked by the calling of the Estates-General in the traditional forms of 1614—that is, in three separately voting chambers. The differences between nobles and non-noble elites had been disappearing over the course of the eighteenth century, Lucas pointed out. With the calling of the Estates, however, 'the frontier between noble and non-noble, which had been of diminishing importance, was suddenly and artificially reimposed'. The upheaval that ensued was 'a revolt against a loss of status by the central and lower sections of the elite'. They bridled at their symbolic exclusion from society's superior ranks—at being thrust into the same social category as peasants and manual labourers.[37] Lucas's argument remains a powerful one, but his claim that the distinction between noble and non-noble had been diminishing in importance is only partially true. What had been diminishing constantly were many of the objective differences—economic, political, professional, educational, and legal—between nobles and elite non-nobles. However, as these differences lessened, the symbolic weight attached to formal noble status seems to have endured, if not increased. The high and rising price of rapidly ennobling venal offices testifies to this.

So does the conception of noble identity that appealed to many members of the order in the late eighteenth century. Despite the fact that the nobility had been totally transformed by ennoblement—or perhaps because it had been—many nobles adopted an archaized vision of their order. A number of historians have recently noted the renewed appeal of chivalric ideas and images in France from the 1760s.[38] This resort to the past exalted noble heroes and noble values, and was avidly consumed by the latter-day knights of the Second Estate. Timothy Tackett notes of the noble deputies elected to the Estates-General that 'the majority was strongly penetrated with a military, even feudal sense of honour and duty. There were frequent references in their writings and speeches to models of noble courage and chivalry from the past.' One clerical deputy complained of 'a conversation with a noble delegate from his *bailliage* who "spoke of serfs and vassals like a baron of the fourteenth century."' Nor were such expressions meant only for public consumption. According to Tackett, 'the chivalric vocabulary of defending one's honour and proving one's loyalty to the king permeated the Nobles' letters and diary entries, and increasingly dominated over all other motives in the Nobles' appraisal of their situation'.[39]

This noble investment in chivalry and feudalism might be regarded as a kind of invented tradition, a set of symbols that established a largely fictive continuity with a suitable historical past—one that emphasized the distinctive character of the group in the present.⁴⁰ Far from being a sign of the traditionalism of the nobility, such a construction of identity bore witness to its modernity. The way a self-conscious 'traditionalism' could appeal to very 'modern' nobles is exemplified by the Duke de Croÿ. An aristocratic magnate, Croÿ was obsessed with his family history and genealogy. During sojourns on his estates in Picardy he spent much of his time travelling to sites linked with the bygone glory of his family. He engaged in extensive genealogical research in an effort to prove his descent from medieval kings of Hungary. Yet for all his apparent obsession with the past, Croÿ was a founding shareholder of the Anzin mining company, one of the largest industrial concerns in Europe.⁴¹

If the narrowing of objective differences between nobles and elite commoners prompted the former to identify with a chivalric past, on the part of non-nobles the same convergence generated a demand for collegial treatment, an increased sensitivity concerning their own honour. This desire for parity of esteem—or at least for a modicum of respect—was manifested in a wide variety of ways. For many non-nobles, patriotism was an ethos that promised to override distinctions of estate and to give non-nobles a place of honour beside nobles in the shared title of Frenchman. (Nobles, by contrast, tended to see patriotism as another realm of noble distinction.⁴²) An aspiration for an egalitarian ethos that would override social distinctions was also expressed in Freemasonry, which enjoyed tremendous success in France, and which drew large numbers of non-noble elites to its lodges and its rites. It became increasingly common in the decades before 1789 for economic writers to demand that the monarchy confer honours on quotidian activities such as trade or farming in order to reward and encourage them. Such arguments acknowledged the sentiments of honour possessed by farmers and merchants, and implicitly faulted a social order that failed to give them the honour that was their due.⁴³ Non-nobles criticized privileges they perceived to be dishonouring. 'That, for example, a noble guilty of a certain crime should have his head cut off, while a non-noble guilty of the same crime should die hanging from a gibbet', complained one *cahier* in 1789, 'indicates that there are base executions and others that are not, that the noble belongs to a privileged class, and that the commoner belongs to the despised class of citizens, the class disfavoured by the laws, and whose honour is totally degraded by the laws.'⁴⁴ According to Tackett, in the pre-revolutionary writings of numerous Third Estate deputies there was 'indignation over questions of status'.⁴⁵

It was not simply the non-noble elite who rejected the nobility's right to special treatment on the grounds of its innate superiority. In the villages of France, peasants increasingly contested lordly rights, and feudal jurisdiction, in the royal courts. Such legal contestation had been going on for centuries, but it intensified in the eighteenth century as lords sought to revive forgotten seigneurial claims or to exploit existing rights more efficiently. Briefs produced in these courtroom battles sometimes went so far as to contest the very foundation of such lordly privilege, implicitly questioning the special status of the *seigneur*. The counterpart of these legal struggles was a spate of violent incidents— over 300 between 1760 and 1789—in which crowds or small groups challenged the rights or the symbols of lordship. While it would be inaccurate to see these acts as assaults on nobility *per se*, they certainly help to explain the explosion of popular attacks on seigneurialism in the summer of 1789.[46]

The social vision of nobles and non-nobles came into direct conflict with the calling of the Estates-General and the subsequent struggle over whether the assembly should debate and vote as one body. Nobles perceived the call for voting by head—that is, the merging of the social orders into one body—as a symbolic attack on their social distinction and special status. A majority of nobles were willing to give up their tax privileges, whittled away in any case by the *vingtième*, the *capitation*, and the increasing weight of indirect taxation. What they could not imagine losing, and what drove many into opposition to the Revolution, was their symbolic status. The same tension was manifest in noble attitudes to seigneurial rights. While noble *cahiers* expressed a willingness to give up lucrative rights in return for indemnification, most wished to retain honorific rights. Moreover, there was a close correlation between the desire to protect honorific seigneurial privileges and the desire to keep the three orders separate in the Estates-General.[47] In Tackett's words, 'It was on the question of symbols and honorific rights, those symbols "which most recall the feudal system and the spirit of chivalry", that the nobility would draw the line against cooperation with the Revolutionary regime.'[48]

Explaining why the French Revolution took on such a markedly anti-aristocratic cast was one of the abiding puzzles generated by revisionist scholarship on the nobility in the 1960s and 1970s. Why did such bitter conflict erupt between nobles and elite non-nobles if the two groups had come to form a functionally unified ruling class? That antagonism between the two groups was brought to a head by the power struggle of 1788–9 must surely be a key component of any explanation. The other critical factor, this one structural rather than conjunctural, was the divergent effects on noble and non-noble identity produced by the objective narrowing of social differences between the Second Estate and the upper part of the Third. If nobles and notables were united in their possession of property, wealth, education, legal privilege, and a common culture, nobles nevertheless continued to insist on their distinctiveness and superiority. Simultaneously, non-noble elites yearned for fraternal relations with nobles and increasingly felt that such was their due. The conflict this tension produced might never have given rise to a wholesale assault on aristocracy without the catalyst of political events that directly raised the question of noble distinctiveness, but there is little doubt that, in substance, the struggle between nobles and non-nobles in 1789 had roots deep in the social fabric of the old regime.

Notes

1. For the traditional view of the nobility, see Jonathan Dewald, 'French Nobles and the Historians, 1820–1960', in Jay M. Smith (ed.), *The French Nobility in the Eighteenth Century: Reassessments and New Approaches* (University Park, Pa., 2006). For the revisionist view, see esp., Guy Chaussinand-Nogaret, *La Noblesse au xviiie siècle: De la féodalité aux Lumières* (Paris, 1976); William Doyle, 'Was there an Aristocratic Reaction in Pre-Revolutionary France?', *Past and Present*, 57 (1972), 97–122; Robert Forster, *The Nobility of Toulouse in the*

Eighteenth Century (Baltimore, Md., 1960); Colin Lucas, 'Nobles, Bourgeois and the Origins of the French Revolution', *Past and Present*, 60 (1973), 84–126; Guy Richard, *Noblesse d'affaires au xviiie siècle* (Paris, 1974); George V. Taylor, 'Noncapitalist Wealth and the Origins of the French Revolution', *American Historical Review*, 72 (1967), 469–96.

2. Mathieu Marraud, *La Noblesse de Paris au xviiie siècle* (Paris, 2000), 309–18; Richard, *Noblesse d'affaires, passim*.
3. Michel Figeac, *L'Automne des gentilshommes: Noblesse d'Aquitaine, noblesse française au siècle des Lumières* (Paris, 2002), 135–82; Forster, *Nobility of Toulouse*, 36; Jonathan Dewald, *The European Nobility, 1400–1800* (Cambridge, 1996), 70–1. On nobles as agricultural entrepreneurs, see also Michel Combet, 'Agronomes, physiocrates, les nobles et le progrès dans les campagnes françaises dans la seconde moitié du xviiie siècle', in Jarosław Dumanowski and Michel Figeac (eds.), *Noblesse française et noblesse polonaise: Mémoire, identité, culture, xvie–xxe siècles* (Pessac, 2006); and Monique Cubells, 'Un agronome aixois au xviiie siècle: Le Président de la Tour d'Aigues, féodal de combat et homme des Lumières', in Cubells, *La Noblesse provençale: Du milieu du xviie siècle à la Révolution* (Aix-en-Provence, 2002).
4. Monique Cubells, *La Provence des Lumières: Les Parlementaires d'Aix au xviiie siècle* (Paris, 1984), 124–6; Jonathan Dewald, *Pont-St-Pierre 1398–1789: Lordship, Community, and Capitalism in Early Modern France* (Berkeley, Calif., 1987), 114–15; François-Joseph Ruggiu, *Les Élites et les villes moyennes en France et en Angleterre (xviie–xviiie siècles)* (Paris, 1997), 179–82.
5. William Doyle, *Venality: The Sale of Offices in Eighteenth-Century France* (Oxford, 1996), 165; Claude Brelot, *La Noblesse en Franche Comté de 1789 à 1808* (Paris, 1972), 22–3; Laurent Bourquin, 'Les Mutations du peuplement nobiliaire angevin à l'époque moderne', *Histoire, Économie et Société*, 17 (1998), 241–59; Pierre Goubert, *The Ancien Régime: French Society 1600–1750*, tr. Steve Cox (New York, 1973), 189; David Bien, 'Manufacturing Nobles: The Chancelleries in France to 1789', *Journal of Modern History*, 61/3 (1989), 445–86.
6. Michel Nassiet, 'Un chantier en cours: Les Effectifs de la noblesse en France et leur évolution du xvie au xviiie siècle', in Dumanowski and Figeac (eds.), *Noblesse française et noblesse polonaise*.
7. Michel Nassiet, 'Le Problème des effectifs de la noblesse dans la France du xviiie siècle', *Traditions et innovations dans la société française du xviiie siècle: Actes du colloque de 1993* (Paris, 1995); Didier Porcer, 'La Noblesse languedocienne en 1789: Définition d'un groupe social, esquisse numérique', *Bulletin de l'Histoire de la Révolution française* (1984–5), 47–55.
8. Nassiet, 'Problème des effectifs'.
9. Dewald, *Pont-St-Pierre*, 114.
10. Noble lineages in all European countries had a tendency to die out at a steady rate over time because of failure to produce surviving male heirs. Only constant new ennoblement could sustain a constant, or rising, number of noble families. See M. L. Bush, *Rich Noble, Poor Noble* (Manchester, 1988), 97–100. In 18th-cent. France, however, it was not a question of the extinction of noble lineages only but of a significant decrease in the size of the whole social group.
11. Michel Nassiet, 'Histoire sociale et méthode lignagère: L'Exemple de la petite noblesse de Haute-Bretagne', *Histoire, Économie et Société* 9 (1990), 545–54. See also Figeac, *L'Automne des gentilshommes*, 113–21.
12. Claude Lévy and Louis Henry, 'Ducs et pairs sous l'Ancien Régime: Caractéristiques démographiques d'une caste', *Population*, 5 (1960), 807–30. The figures refer to women who entered marriage by the age of 20, a majority in all periods.

13. Stéphane Minvielle, 'Les Comportements démographiques de la noblesse française de la fin du xviie siècle à la Révolution française: Une tentative de synthèse', in Dumanowski and Figeac (eds.), *Noblesse française et noblesse polonaise*, 327–56; Bush, *Rich Noble, Poor Noble*, 98.
14. Sharon Kettering, *Patrons, Brokers, and Clients in Seventeenth-Century France* (Oxford, 1986), 213–23.
15. Dewald, *Pont-St-Pierre*, 210–11; Ruggiu, *Les Élites et les villes moyennes*, 210; Yves Castan, *Honnêteté et relations sociales en Languedoc (1715–1780)* (Paris, 1974), 351–2; Philippe Béchu, 'Noblesse d'épée et tradition militaire au xviiie siècle', *Histoire, Économie et Société*, 2/4 (1983), 507–48; Valérie Piétri, '"Sage mesnage" ou dissipation: Consommation nobiliaire et crédit d'après les livres de raison dracénois au xviiie siècle', *Provence Historique*, 52 (2002), 87–104.
16. Michel Figeac, *La Douceur des Lumières: Noblesse et art de vivre en Guyenne au xviiie siècle* (Bordeaux, 2001), 258–66.
17. This literature is surveyed in William Beik, 'The Absolutism of Louis XIV as Social Collaboration', *Past and Present*, 188 (2005), 195–224.
18. Peter R. Campbell, *Power and Politics in Old Regime France 1720–1745* (London, 1996); Bernard Hours, *Louis XV et sa cour: Le Roi, l'étiquette et le courtisan* (Paris, 2002); Emmanuel Le Roy Ladurie and Jean-François Fitou, *Saint-Simon, and the Court of Louis XIV*, tr. Arthur Goldhammer (Chicago, 2001); Munro Price, *Preserving the Monarchy: The Comte de Vergennes, 1774–1787* (Cambridge, 1995).
19. Julian Swann, *Politics and the Parlement of Paris under Louis XV, 1754–1774* (Cambridge, 1995), 49–50.
20. Arnaud de Maurepas and Antoine Boulant, *Les Ministres et les ministères du siècle des Lumières (1715–1789): Étude et dictionnaire* (Paris, 2000), 134, 101; Price, *Preserving the Monarchy*, 72.
21. Kettering, *Patrons, Brokers, and Clients*; Roger Mettam, *Power and Faction in Louis XIV's France* (Oxford, 1988).
22. On service and noble identity, see Rafe Blaufarb, *The French Army, 1750–1820: Careers, Talent, Merit* (New York, 2002); Jay M. Smith, *Culture of Merit: Nobility, Royal Service, and the Making of Absolute Monarchy in France, 1600–1789* (Ann Arbor, 1996). On expenses incurred by army officers, see John A. Lynn, *Giant of the Grand Siècle: The French Army, 1610–1715* (Cambridge, 1997), 251–4; Guy Rowlands, *The Dynastic State and the Army under Louis XIV: Royal Service and Private Interest, 1661–1701* (Cambridge, 2002). On nobles and patriotism, see Jay M. Smith, *Nobility Reimagined: The Patriotic Nation in Eighteenth-Century France* (Ithaca, NY, 2005).
23. Lynn, *Giant of the Grand Siècle*, 284–87; Kettering, *Patrons, Brokers, and Clients*, 213–23; Dewald, *Pont-St-Pierre*, 211–12; Marraud, *La Noblesse de Paris*, 308.
24. Michael Kwass, *Privilege and the Politics of Taxation in Eighteenth-Century France: Liberté, Egalité, Fiscalité* (Cambridge, 2000); Wolfgang Mager, 'De la noblesse à la notabilité: La Formation des notables sous l'Ancien Régime et la crise de la monarchie absolue', *Histoire, Économie et Société*, 12/4 (1993), 487–506.
25. T. C. W. Blanning, *The Culture of Power and the Power of Culture: Old Regime Europe 1660–1789* (Oxford, 2002).
26. Daniel Roche, *Le Siècle des Lumières en province: Académies et académiciens provinciaux, 1680–1789* (2 vols. Paris, 1978), ii. 387; Robert Darnton, *The Business of Enlightenment: A Publishing History of the Encyclopédie, 1775–1800* (Cambridge, Mass.,

1979), 291; Jean-Claude Perrot, *Une histoire intellectuelle de l'économie politique xviie–xviiie siècle* (Paris, 1992), 78; Antoine Lilti, *Le Monde des salons: Sociabilité et mondanité à Paris au xviiie siècle* (Paris, 2005).

27. Voltaire, *Philosophical Letters*, tr. Ernest Dilworth (Indianapolis, 1961), 39–40; Louis-Joseph Plumard de Dangeul, *Remarques sur les avantages et les désavantages de la France et de la Grande Bretagne, par rapport au commerce, & aux autres sources de la puissance des Etats* (Leiden, 1754), 16–17, 31; Gabriel-François Coyer, *La Noblesse commerçante* (London, 1756).

28. Rafe Blaufarb, 'Nobles, Aristocrats, and the Origins of the French Revolution', in Robert M. Schwartz and Robert A. Schneider (eds.), *Tocqueville and Beyond: Essays on the Old Regime in Honor of David D. Bien* (Newark, Del., 2003). See also Olivier Royon, 'La Noblesse de province face à la noblesse de la Cour, entre admiration et rejet, de l'imitation à l'élaboration d'un contre-modèle social dans la dernière moitié du xviiie siècle', in Josette Pontet, Michel Figeac, and Marie Boisson (eds.), *La Noblesse, de la fin du xvie au debut du xxe siècle: Un modèle social?* (Anglet, 2002).

29. Dewald, *Pont-St-Pierre*, 121.

30. David Bien, 'The Army in the French Enlightenment: Reform, Reaction and Revolution', *Past and Present*, 85 (1979), 68–98; Blaufarb, *The French Army, 1750–1820*, 42–4.

31. Mager, 'De la noblesse', 498–9.

32. Robert Darnton, *The Literary Underground of the Old Regime* (Cambridge, Mass., 1982), 30; Jeffrey Merrick, 'Sexual Politics and Public Order in Late Eighteenth-Century France: The *Mémoires secrets* and the *Correspondance secrète*', *Journal of the History of Sexuality*, 1 (1990), 68–84; Sara Chapman, 'Patronage as Family Economy: The Role of Women in the Patron–Client Network of the Phélypeaux de Pontchartrain Family, 1670–1715', *French Historical Studies*, 24 (2001), 11–35.

33. Jeremy Popkin, 'Pamphlet Journalism at the End of the Old Regime', *Eighteenth-Century Studies*, 22 (1989), 351–67; Sarah Maza, *Private Lives and Public Affairs: The Causes Célèbres of Prerevolutionary France* (Berkeley, Calif., 1993).

34. Daniel Roche, 'Between a "Moral Economy" and a "Consumer Economy": Clothes and their Function in the 17th and 18th Centuries', in Robert Fox and Anthony Turner (eds.), *Luxury Trades and Consumerism in Ancien Régime Paris* (Aldershot, 1998); Natacha Coquery, *L'Hôtel aristocratique: Le Marché du luxe à Paris au xviiie siècle* (Paris, 1998), 130; Charles Pinot-Duclos, *Considérations sur les mœurs de ce siècle*, ed. F. C. Green (Cambridge, 1939), 125.

35. Doyle, *Venality*, 319; Robert Forster, 'The Provincial Noble: A Reappraisal', *American Historical Review*, 68 (1963), 681–91.

36. John Shovlin, *The Political Economy of Virtue: Luxury, Patriotism, and the Origins of the French Revolution* (Ithaca, NY, 2006), 175–81. The idea of the noble would go on to enjoy an immense popularity in the century after the French Revolution where it was viewed as a corrective to what was perceived to be the increasingly materialist orientation of French society. See Harry Liebersohn, *Aristocratic Encounters: European Travelers and North American Indians* (Cambridge, 1998); Robert A. Nye, *Masculinity and Male Codes of Honor in Modern France* (Oxford, 1993).

37. Lucas, 'Nobles, Bourgeois and the Origins of the French Revolution'.

38. Smith, *Nobility Reimagined*, 156–66; David A. Bell, *The Cult of the Nation in France: Inventing Nationalism, 1680–1800* (Cambridge, Mass., 2001), 81, 110–19. See also Pierre-Yves Beaurepaire, *Nobles jeux de l'arc et loges maçonniques dans la France des Lumières:*

Enquête sur une sociabilité en mutation (Groslay, Val d'Oise, 2002). Earlier explorations of this theme include Lionel Gossman, *Medievalism and the Ideologies of the Enlightenment: The World and Work of La Curne de Sainte-Palaye* (Baltimore, Md., 1968); René Lanson, *Le Goût du moyen âge en France au xviiie siècle* (Paris, 1926).

39. Timothy Tackett, *Becoming a Revolutionary: The Deputies of the French National Assembly and the Emergence of a Revolutionary Culture (1789–1790)* (Princeton, 1996), 136–7.
40. Eric Hobsbawm and Terence Ranger (eds.), *The Invention of Tradition* (Cambridge, 1983).
41. Marie-Pierre Dion, *Emmanuel de Croÿ (1718–1784): Itinéraire intellectuel et réussite nobiliaire au siècle des Lumières* (Brussels, 1987), 89–91, 95.
42. Smith, *Nobility Reimagined*, 182–221.
43. John Shovlin, 'Towards a Reinterpretation of Revolutionary Anti-Nobilism: The Political Economy of Honor in the Old Regime', *Journal of Modern History*, 72/1 (2000), 35–66.
44. Quoted in George Armstrong Kelley, 'Dueling in Eighteenth-Century France: Archaeology, Rationale, Implication', *The Eighteenth Century*, 21 (1980), 236–54.
45. Tackett, *Becoming a Revolutionary*, 107–10.
46. Hilton L. Root, 'Challenging the Seigneurie: Community and Contention on the Eve of the French Revolution', *Journal of Modern History*, 57 (1985), 652–81; Jean Nicolas, *La Rébellion française: Mouvements populaires et conscience sociale, 1661–1789* (Paris, 2002), 216.
47. John Markoff, *The Abolition of Feudalism: Peasants, Lords, and Legislators in the French Revolution* (University Park, Pa., 1996), 190, 197.
48. Tackett, *Becoming a Revolutionary*, 294–5.

Bibliography

Bien, David, 'The Army in the French Enlightenment: Reform, Reaction and Revolution', *Past and Present*, 85 (1979), 68–98.
Chaussinand-Nogaret, Guy, *La noblesse au xviiie siècle: De la féodalité aux Lumières* (Paris, 1976).
Dewald, Jonathan, *Pont-St-Pierre 1398–1789: Lordship, Community, and Capitalism in Early-Modern France* (Berkeley, Calif., 1987).
Doyle, William, *Venality: The Sale of Offices in Eighteenth-Century France* (Oxford, 1996).
—— *Aristocracy and its Enemies in the Age of Revolution* (Oxford, 2009).
Dumanowski, Jarosław, and Figeac, Michel (eds.), *Noblesse française et noblesse polonaise: Mémoire, identité, culture, xvie–xxe siècles* (Pessac, 2006).
Figeac, Michel, *L'Automne des gentilshommes: Noblesse d'Aquitaine, noblesse française au siècle des Lumières* (Paris, 2002).
Forster, Robert, *The Nobility of Toulouse in the Eighteenth Century* (Baltimore, Md., 1960).
Lucas, Colin, 'Nobles, Bourgeois and the Origins of the French Revolution', *Past and Present*, 60 (1973), 84–126.
Marraud, Mathieu, *La Noblesse de Paris au xviiie siècle* (Paris, 2000).
Pontet, Josette, Figeac, Michel, and Boisson, Marie (eds.), *La Noblesse, de la fin du xvie au début du xxe siècle: Un modèle social?* (2 vols. Anglet, 2002).
Richard, Guy, *Noblesse d'affaires au xviiie siècle* (Paris, 1974).

Smith, Jay M., *The Culture of Merit: Nobility, Royal Service, and the Making of Absolute Monarchy in France, 1600–1789* (Ann Arbor, 1996).
—— *Nobility Reimagined: The Patriotic Nation in Eighteenth-Century France* (Ithaca, NY, 2005).
—— (ed.), *The French Nobility in the Eighteenth Century: Reassessments and New Approaches* (University Park, Pa., 2006).

CHAPTER 8

BOURGEOISIE

SARAH MAZA

The concept of a group called 'the bourgeoisie' is unusual in being both central to early modern and modern European history, and at the same time highly controversial. In old regime France, people frequently used the words 'bourgeois' or 'bourgeoisie' but what they meant by them was very different from the meaning historians later assigned to those terms. In the nineteenth century the idea of a 'bourgeoisie' became closely associated with Marxian historical narratives of capitalist ascendancy. When this kind of historical account began to fall on hard times in the later twentieth century, historians no longer knew quite what to do with the bourgeoisie. Does it still make sense to speak of a 'bourgeoisie', and if so what do we mean?[1]

This chapter attempts to lay out and clarify the terms of the problem by posing a series of questions about this aspect of the social history of Ancien Régime France, with a brief look across the Channel for comparison. We will consider first the problem of definition: what was and is meant by 'the bourgeoisie' in the context of early modern French history? Second, what is the link between eighteenth-century economic change (capitalism, commerce, consumerism) and the existence and nature of such a group, and can we still connect the origins of the French Revolution to the 'rise' of a bourgeoisie? And finally, can the history of perceptions and representations of a bourgeoisie or middle class help us to understand why the concept has been so problematic in the longer run of French history?

Most general histories of Ancien Régime France recognize the vagueness and fluidity of the category 'bourgeoisie' and rely on common-sense, if imprecise, definitions of the group. The bourgeoisie is usually understood to include a wide swath of people who were not members of the nobility or the clergy, but who were of a higher status than manual workers.[2] So loose a definition obviously leaves room for plenty of disagreement about who should or should not belong in the category: is it appropriate to include master artisans, some of them wealthy employers, but who were close to the working classes culturally and usually engaged in manual labour themselves? What about shopkeepers, most of whom were also artisans? Why exclude the lower clergy, educated lower middle-class professionals? And does it make sense to speak, as some have done, of a 'rural bourgeoisie' of wealthier peasants?

Furthermore, one may legitimately ask whether it makes any sense even to conceive of a group made up of such disparate elements. The bourgeoisie is usually assumed to include on the one end the richest non-nobles, some of whom, bankers and tax-collectors like Antoine Crozat and Joseph Pâris-Duverney, had more wealth and power than most aristocrats, and on the other artisan-shopkeepers who were barely removed from the working classes. Bona-fide capitalists such as merchants, bankers, and industrialists are always included in the category, but so are royal administrators, legal and medical professionals, and intellectuals ranging from the most established to the most marginal. While it is true that no social group ever was, or is, homogeneous, the material and cultural range of 'the bourgeoisie' stretches the group's definition perilously thin. Few, if any, scholars nowadays adhere to a strictly Marxist definition of the group as owners of the (industrial) means of production. Most historians of Ancien Régime France currently adopt a loose common-sense definition of the bourgeoisie as comprising comfortably off, mostly urban, commoners.

Matters of definition are further confused by the fact that under the old regime, 'bourgeois' and 'bourgeoisie' were very specific juridical terms with distinct social connotations. As every textbook on old regime France explains, the status of bourgeois was given to a group of legally privileged, non-noble urban residents, whose status varied from town to town: to be a bourgeois of Paris, Lyon, or Chartres entailed a generally similar but in each case slightly different set of rights and duties.[3] On the one hand, such bourgeois enjoyed their own set of fiscal exemptions and honorific advantages, on the other they were expected to serve in the town militia or contribute to the upkeep of the city walls. Most significant was a *de jure* or *de facto* requirement that one live off one's income without engaging in obvious work, a parallel to the aristocracy's duty of non-*dérogeance*. To live *bourgeoisement* was to live without working, a cultural assumption which flies in the face of modern definitions of the bourgeois as a being quintessentially engaged in productive activity.

The term *bourgeoisie* also had a specific political meaning, since it harked back to medieval understandings of burghers as urban citizens. This definition is the one that comes first in Ancien Régime dictionaries. The dictionary of the Académie française begins its definition of *bourgeois*: 'Citizen, inhabitant of a town... In the definite mode one says "the Bourgeois" in reference to the whole body of a town's inhabitants.'[4] In sum, contemporary definitions of the bourgeoisie further complicate the matter because they are so radically at odds with modern ones. While modern historians of the Ancien Régime have typically viewed the bourgeoisie, however defined, as the group of the future, contemporary definitions anchor it firmly in the traditional world of privilege, particularism, and status-bound inactivity. In the old regime the 'bourgeoisie' were a sort of shadow aristocracy who enjoyed a lesser version of the rights and duties of nobles, and of course sought to emulate their titled betters. Furthermore, the group was strongly associated with urban 'freedoms' and 'privileges' which the Revolution and succeeding regimes were wholly to repudiate. As a 1791 dictionary put it: '[T]he French were not citizens before the Revolution returned them to their natural rights...*Citoyens* and *bourgeois* were synonymous for them; the latter title, like that of noble, referred only to the privileges enjoyed by the inhabitants of a few towns.'[5]

If modern definitions of the bourgeoisie are too capacious, and contemporary ones too restrictive, is there any way of defining a reasonably cohesive middling to upper class non-titled group in Ancien Régime France? It is sometimes suggested that culture and manners might provide the key to such a group, and that analyses inspired by the sociologist Pierre Bourdieu's concept of 'habitus' could offer the elements of a definition. Did the bourgeois of the old regime recognize one another implicitly, on the basis of manners, habits, and taste? A recent study by Christine Adams, for instance, chronicles in close detail the life of the Lamothe family in mid-eighteenth-century Bordeaux.[6] Thanks to a large trove of family letters, she is able to reconstruct the beliefs and behaviour of the family of Daniel de Lamothe, a provincial barrister, his wife, and their children (three lawyers, a doctor, a priest, and two unmarried daughters). The Lamothes maintained strong family ties, and frequently expressed affection for each other; they were generally pious, and engaged in civic and charitable identities. The men in the family identified strongly with, and were proud of, their professional identities. Such traits were probably quite representative of provincial professional families like the Lamothes. Were they also typical of other members of a wider bourgeoisie, of the capital as well as the provinces, of commercial or rentier, as well as professional, families? We still do not have enough such detailed studies even to begin to generalize.

While the bourgeoisie remains elusive and ill-defined, historians are still intent on pinning down such a group because of its central role in the standard narratives of the origins of the French Revolution, and more generally the transition to political and social modernity. It is widely assumed that the bourgeoisie became the hegemonic social group in the nineteenth century and beyond, hence it has always seemed important to locate its origins in Ancien Régime society. The classic debate about capitalism, the bourgeoisie, and the origins of the French Revolution continues therefore to recur in new iterations.

Was the bourgeoisie 'rising' in the eighteenth century? The answer is yes if by rising one means simply increasing in numbers. Counting the 'class' as such sends one right back to those pesky questions of definition; more reliable is the incontrovertible fact that France's urban population grew dramatically over the course of the eighteenth century. The best recent estimates suggest that the number of French men and women living in towns of over 2,000 inhabitants grew from about four million in the first quarter of the century to five to six million around 1790: a growth of about 15 to 20 per cent.[7] While much of the increase was due to a general expansion of the population that pushed the poorer elements of the peasantry onto the roads to seek survival in towns, it is also the case that a booming urban sector with its increasing need for goods and services is unthinkable without the concurrent growth of an urban middle class.

No historian would argue with the proposition that France's middle class grew steadily in both absolute and relative terms over the course of the Ancien Régime, most markedly in the eighteenth century. A host of matters, however, still cause sharp disagreements:

does it make sense to speak of any sort of unified middle class under the old regime, and should that group be called a bourgeoisie? How important was capitalism to the period's social change? And what is the connection, if any, between social change and the outbreak of the 1789 Revolution?

Even scholars outside of the field of French history know of the shift. It has been likened to a Kuhnian 'scientific revolution' which took place in the study of the French Revolution in the 1960s and 1970s.[8] Prior to that time, a broad consensus had reigned since the nineteenth century around the assumption that the French Revolution was caused, at the deepest level, by the rise of a bourgeois class which, buoyed by nascent capitalism, challenged and eventually toppled the 'feudal' complex of monarchy and aristocracy, to emerge triumphant in the wake of the revolutionary chaos. The 'normal' explanation of the origins of the French Revolution, which non-Marxists as well as Marxists accepted, neatly connected an array of different phenomena. France's booming Atlantic trade and eighteenth-century economic and demographic growth were signs of burgeoning capitalism; the Enlightenment, with its meritocratic ideals and denunciations of 'feudalism', was a quintessentially bourgeois ideology; the aristocracy stepped obligingly into its role as reactionary blackguard by closing ranks against the intrusion of talented commoners and noisily resisting any attempt to curtail its fiscal and social privileges.

The British scholar Alfred Cobban was the first to question this comfortably entrenched consensus, in the 1950s and early 1960s.[9] Soon many distinguished British and American scholars, and eventually some French ones, followed him into the breach. Once the established paradigm was rattled it became obvious, as in the Kuhnian model, that a lot of familiar information simply did not fit it. Such capitalism as existed in France was marginal to the country's overwhelmingly agrarian economy, and this was to remain true long after the Revolution; the Enlightenment was heavily patronized and consumed and partly produced by nobles, while the more capitalist segments of the bourgeoisie showed no interest in the new ideas; nobles may have resisted the curtailing of their privileges, but so did everyone else including artisanal corporations and, yes, the bourgeoisie; right up to 1789 political opposition to the monarchy came overwhelmingly from aristocratic institutions such as the parlements; successful bourgeois even of a progressive bent did not think twice about acquiring land and mansions and calling themselves 'de Voltaire', 'de Beaumarchais', or 'd'Anton'. On the other hand, the rebellion of the Third Estate in 1789 turned out to have been largely organized and led by liberal nobles. If the French economy was not capitalist, the Enlightenment was not bourgeois, most bourgeois were conservative, and many nobles enamoured of the new ideas, what was left of the idea of a 'bourgeois revolution'? By the 1980s scepticism about the concept of an eighteenth-century 'bourgeois revolution' had become, under the general label of 'revisionism', the new orthodoxy.

For a while historians left the question of the social origins of the Revolution in abeyance to focus, following scholars like François Furet and Lynn Hunt, on questions of culture, gender, and politics in order to explain how and in what form democracy became imaginable in one of Europe's oldest monarchies.[10] While some proposed alternative, more general, scenarios to explain the social origins of the Revolution, such as demographic pressure and blocked upward mobility,[11] scholars more commonly turned their energies to exploring such matters as political symbols and practices, festive and print culture, or patterns of language and rhetoric both before and during the French Revolution. Only in the early 1990s were there signs of a return to the debate about the revolutionary bourgeoisie. Fuel for the 'revision of revisionism' came from new research on the consumer revolution in eighteenth-century French towns.

Following the bleak economic conditions of the seventeenth century, the French economy experienced an upswing in the decades after 1720. The consensus among economic historians nowadays is that French growth in the eighteenth century, while it did not hew to the English model, was on its own terms remarkable. France saw a sevenfold increase in its industrial output over the course of the century, its volume of foreign trade quintupled, and its share of European markets grew faster than England's. A combination of agricultural improvements and better climatic conditions led to the abatement of famines, with the result that the realm's population increased from 21 to over 28 million. The population of the largest towns rose on average by 48 per cent. Regardless of how much can be ascribed to 'capitalism', there is no question that, in the century before the Revolution, France was getting significantly richer, more populated, and more urban.[12]

For contemporaries, the most striking manifestation of change was the influx and ever-wider accessibility of consumer goods. Even a southern provincial town like Montpellier was awash in the spoils of commerce, according to a 1768 chronicler. The rich flaunted obscenely wealthy clothes and accessories, 'plumes, earrings, rings, glittering buckles, gold watches on clasps with dangling charms, gold snuff-boxes, and gold-encased perfume bottles, muffs and fans'. They breakfasted on new colonial delicacies like chocolate and coffee, served out of precious silver pots and jugs. But they were not the only ones to revel in 'luxury', this observer reported. All manner of people changed their cuffs and linen every day, working girls wore white silk stockings and took snuff, and labouring families ate out of new matching sets of brightly coloured earthenware. All this was unprecedented, and, to the chronicler, alarming.[13]

Montpellier after mid-century was not at all atypical. The last two decades' worth of work by historians of material culture has revealed that in France, as in contemporary Britain, the daily lives of eighteenth-century urban dwellers were transformed by the accessibility of new consumer goods.[14] Most conspicuously, town dwellers from the rich to even the working poor had more and better clothing than before, prompting many an anxious moralist to exclaim, with some exaggeration, that it was impossible to tell who was who anymore. The average value of wardrobes tripled or quadrupled, and persons of modest standing adopted clothing more similar to those of their 'betters' (working women, for instance, were more likely to wear dresses instead of skirts and bodices.) The eighteenth century saw the beginning of a long evolution whereby commercially driven 'fashion' replaced status as the organizing principle of costume. Commercial goods invaded the private sphere as well, with comfort edging out display or mere functionality in the conception of furniture. For the wealthy this meant upholstered sofas and armchairs, but modest households too now owned chests of drawers instead of all-purpose trunks, and middling interiors as well as rich ones were better heated, lit, and decorated. Even people of modest standing bought mirrors, clocks, prints, fans, snuff-boxes, watches, books, cards, and games. The new consumerist search for 'comfort' extended to bodily well-being, as witnessed by the advertisements in eighteenth-century provincial newspapers, which hawked an array of health-related goods and services, including pills, elixirs, and assorted medical implements.

This literature of what has been called the eighteenth-century consumer revolution is new in the field, and it throws open once again the matter of the relationship between eighteenth-century social change and the outbreak of the Revolution in 1789. If more people than ever before had access to consumer goods, does this mean that a bourgeoisie, defined not by capitalism but by the profits and spoils of commerce, was rising after all? Colin Jones made a spirited case for this argument in a notable piece, published in 1991, 'Bourgeois Revolution Revivified: 1789 and Social Change'.[15] After a thorough review of France's economic and demographic growth, increasing market orientation, and burgeoning consumer revolution, Jones boldly concluded that pre-revolutionary France was 'a society characterized as much by circulation, mobility, and innovation as by the traditionalism, subsistence farming and cultural stagnation of the New Revisionist Orthodoxy'. Egalitarian, secular, and commercialized attitudes affected everything from sex (*coitus interruptus*) to the sale of offices to the creation of socially mixed voluntary associations such as masonic lodges and learned societies. 'Given the development of commercial capitalism in eighteenth-century France,' he concludes, 'the spread of a consumer society, the development of professionalization within the service sector of the economy...the appearance of associated forms of civic sociability, it no longer looks realistic to disparage the vitality, nor indeed the ideological autonomy, of the Old Regime bourgeoisie.'[16]

Colin Jones thus proposes to resurrect the bourgeoisie's centrality on the basis of the newest research in social and economic history. The bourgeoisie has also made something of a comeback, if a quieter one, in the context of the history of the Enlightenment. This trend goes back to the 1960s when a younger generation of historians of France broke with the tradition of focusing solely on canonical texts and began to redefine the Enlightenment as not just a set of texts but a form of communication: the medium, they proposed, deserved as much attention as the message. Critical ideas were of great consequence, of course, but so was the fact that books, newspapers, and pamphlets were increasingly plentiful on both the legal and the booming clandestine market. Robert Darnton's was the pioneering work in this vein, and it is significant that his landmark study of the diffusion of Diderot and d'Alembert's *Encyclopedie* bears the defiantly paradoxical title *The Business of Enlightenment*.[17] If one were looking for a proto-bourgeois hero, one could hardly do better than Darnton's Balzacian protagonist, the ruthlessly entrepreneurial publisher of Enlightenment texts Charles-Joseph Pancoucke. Certainly print was a major item in France's emerging commercial culture: the production of books tripled between 1701 and 1770, the newspaper press went from three titles to several hundred, and the volume of pamphlet literature grew by leaps and bounds after mid-century. If France's increasing commercial orientation is symptomatic of bourgeois assertion, then the Enlightenment could be called bourgeois.

Those are not the only arguments for reclaiming the adjective 'bourgeois' for Enlightenment culture in France and elsewhere. Since the 1980s, scholars have increasingly drawn on the ideas that Jürgen Habermas articulated in his influential *The Structural Transformation of the Public Sphere*.[18] Writing in the middle decades of the twentieth century, Habermas took a Marxian framework for granted, locating the origins of eighteenth-century critical thinking in the growing tensions between the developing commercial classes on the one hand, and a predatory absolutist state on the other. But where others of his generation saw the Enlightenment as simply the ideological programme of the rising bourgeoisie, Habermas proposed that it was 'bourgeois' in a different sense. Habermas approached the Enlightenment not as a set of ideas but as a system of practices and a network of communication; its essence lay less in oppositional ideas, though those were important, than in the development of institutions like salons, coffeehouses, literary academies, and masonic lodges. It was also manifest in the flowering of print culture and the networks of collaborators and correspondents who made up the 'republic of letters'.

In Habermas's view, what was historically significant about the Enlightenment was its instantiation as what he called a 'public sphere': a public realm which served as an alternative to the monarchy and its servants, and which existed in critical opposition to the latter. The public sphere of enlightened Europeans thus constituted a virtual blueprint for the democratic political institutions which came into their own, in the shorter or longer terms, after 1789. Habermas systematically labels the new public sphere 'bourgeois', though his late twentieth-century followers have tended to downplay this aspect of his model. What Habermas means by 'bourgeois public sphere' is a space distinct from, and opposed to, the public realm of the monarchy, court, and aristocracy, made up of private subjects and increasingly configured as a legitimate alternative to the established powers.

For Habermas the Enlightenment is 'bourgeois' in being rooted in both private experience and critical reasoning; it is defined relationally in opposition to the state and aristocracy, and historically as the nucleus of the public realm of the future. The German philosopher's extremely influential model has reinvigorated the question of the relationship between the Enlightenment and 'bourgeoisie'. While few if any historians nowadays would argue that the Enlightenment was 'bourgeois' because it reflected individualistic or capitalistic values, some would still hold that its attacks on noble privilege were instrumental in promoting the interests of the middle classes; and many others hold that the Enlightenment was 'bourgeois' in the sense of *bürgerlich*: that its very forms (salons, academies, and expansive print culture) represented the triumph of a rational and secular civil society over the religious and monarchical states of the Ancien Régime.

In short, there is little consensus today about the nature of the Ancien Régime bourgeoisie, or about the relationship of such a group to the upheaval that began in 1789. Some would agree with Colin Jones that commerce, mobility, and the new world of goods must herald the advent of a bourgeoisie. Others, following Habermas, discern such a group in the birth of new forms and spaces of critical thought and debate. Are a family of provincial professionals or an entrepreneurial publisher representative bourgeois? Can the bourgeoisie be found in the political thought and programme of the Abbé Sieyès? In the identities and beliefs of the Third Estate deputies who came to Versailles in 1789? In the heavily intermarried networks of local notables who ran the city of Paris?[19] While historians have productively investigated all of these matters, no agreement has taken shape. The bourgeoisie, an ill defined group if there ever was one, remains very much in the eye of the beholder.

The beholder in early modern France, however, was rarely well-disposed towards something called 'the bourgeoisie', when he or she perceived it at all. The problems historians have experienced in recent years locating and describing such a group are closely linked to the fact that generally speaking 'the bourgeoisie' was not positively valued by Ancien Régime contemporaries, and that people did not normally identify themselves as such: in the seventeenth and eighteenth centuries, as is still largely the case in France today, *bourgeois* was almost always what someone else was.

The category 'bourgeoisie' rarely appears in contemporary enumerations of social categories. Officially, of course, the realm's population was made up of the three ancient groups who duly appeared in their traditionally distinct costumes at the convening Estates-General in May 1789: nobility, clergy, and third estate. Much of the pamphlet warfare of 1788–9 arose because to most people outside a conservative elite, the division of the realm into two small elite groups and one massive category of 'everyone else' had stopped making sense.[20] In traditional interpretations of the French Revolution, it was simply assumed that the third estate, in whose name the early weeks of the revolution were fought, was the embodiment of the rising bourgeoisie. The third estate *deputies* who came to Versailles in May 1789 can plausibly be described as bourgeois, since they were practically to a man upper-middle-class professionals, primarily lawyers, doctors, engineers, and writers and some rentiers, soon to be joined by liberal priests and noblemen. As has long been noted, however, they included almost no industrialists or merchants, and therefore the group was hardly representative of a modern bourgeoisie.[21]

Furthermore, the abundant pamphlet literature of 1788–9 which took up the cudgels in defence of the interests and rights of the third estate never described the group as an elite or a middle class. Jean-Paul Marat, in a 1789 pamphlet, described the third estate as '[t]he class of servants, laborers, workers; of artisans, merchants, businessmen, traders, cultivators, landed proprietors, and non-titled rentiers; of teachers, surgeons, doctors, men of letters and science, men of law … ministers of religion, of the army on both land and sea'.[22] Or, as the Abbé Sieyès put it with memorable concision: 'What is the third estate? *Everything*.' He elaborated on the point in his opening chapter, 'The Third Estate is a Complete Nation'.[23] The abundant print imagery which accompanied the pro-third propaganda campaign represented the third estate as a hard-working, often miserable, peasant or worker, not as a middle-class figure. The third estate, then, was equated with the working poor for purposes of propaganda, and for analytic purposes, with the productive nation as a whole.

Neither in 1789 nor before did the category Third Estate habitually designate a middle class. But even when social commentators offered more specific enumerations of social groups, there was no consensus on the existence or location of a bourgeoisie.[24] Sometimes it did appear, as in a description of society in six groups offered by the Chevalier d'Arcq: higher and lower clergy, higher and lower nobility, and a *peuple* divided into bourgeois and popular groups. Other writers offered a fourfold division of society as more accurate than the traditional tripartite model, although no consensus emerged as to which four groups these might be. The economist Mirabeau listed the realm's estates as clergy, nobles, magistrates, and a 'municipal order' which included the middle and artisanal classes, while a later writer listed the four groups as clergy, nobles, magistrates, and 'the people'. Enumerations of France's main social groups sometimes gave the nobility two categories, either did or did not include the working poor, and variously offered a separate category to clergymen, magistrates, merchants, cultivators, or some form of 'bourgeoisie'. In short, in the century before the Revolution even when social observers identified a 'bourgeoisie' as such, they invested no special importance in such a group.

More frequently, the bourgeoisie was identified only inasmuch as it was disparaged. Since the middle ages, an abundant satirical literature in France had used the bourgeois as a target, branding him crude in manners, vain, avaricious, and ambitious. Molière's *Le Bourgeois Gentilhomme* is only the best known of a large corpus of novels and especially plays on similar themes.[25] For all their familiarity, the themes of anti-bourgeois literature are revealing of the problems posed by a group thus defined. In cultural terms, the bourgeois was described by what he did not have. The standard dictionary articles quoted above do not merely depict the bourgeois as an urban citizen; they also describe him, as does Molière, as a failed nobleman: '[a] man who is not of the court', 'not polite enough, too familiar, not respectful enough', 'in contrast to a courtier, a man with little gallantry or wit'.[26] Within the legal world of the old regime, the bourgeoisie was a shadow aristocracy: a wealthy, privileged, idle group, which wielded a local power analogous to the nobility's national power without displaying the martial or cultural prowess associated with an idealized aristocracy.

The bourgeoisie, in short, was a liminal group, a transitional area in which one parked one's family for a few generations on the way to noble status. In the rigidly ordered society of the old regime, a group so closely associated with social mobility was perceived as dangerous and often singled out as a scapegoat. This is a major reason why individuals did not generally identify themselves as bourgeois except in the most technical sense ('bourgeois de Paris'), and why, long before the advent of capitalism, social commentators never singled out a bourgeoisie for praise or emulation. 'Bourgeoisie' was a problematic concept in old regime France, linked to privilege and a threatening social slipperiness. Contemporaries did not think, much less desire, to see in such a group a harbinger of the future.

In eighteenth-century France, indeed, debates about social ills and prescriptions for the nation's future focused on groups other than the bourgeoisie. At mid-century, for instance, the most resounding debate about social change occurred because of the publication of a pamphlet by the Abbé Coyer, *La Noblesse commerçante* (*The Trading*

Nobility), which argued that for the good of the nation and of their own future as a class, nobles should be freed of the ancient threat of *dérogeance* if they engaged in trade.[27] Coyer's proposal touched off a blizzard of irate responses with titles like *La Noblesse militaire*, from writers who protested that if the nobility engaged in monetary pursuits they would jeopardize not only their own identity as a class, but that of the nation as a whole. Did the French really want to become like the English, the slaves of material interests? Did they want to jettison the honour and glory which, as incarnated in nobles, defined the realm as a whole?

Interestingly, the bourgeoisie went pretty much unmentioned throughout this whole debate. Nor did it figure in the century's historical controversies, which centred on the respective roles of the nobility and the monarchy. Champions of the aristocracy, like the Count de Boulainvilliers, maintained that the monarchy were originally mere military commanders who answered to their peers among a primal Germanic nobility. Monarchist writers such as the Abbés Dubos and Mably argued, on the contrary, that the monarchs were from the start all-powerful rulers appointed by the Roman emperors, and through the centuries had saved the nation from the depredations of a potentially lawless aristocracy.[28] The bourgeoisie was as largely absent from the historical debate as it was from the controversy about nobility and trade. Nor, finally, does the bourgeoisie occupy any significant role in the polemical writings of the *philosophes*. Among the writers of the Enlightenment, the nobility had influential champions, such as Montesquieu, and famous detractors like Voltaire, who mocked their idleness and arrogance, and Beaumarchais, who successfully propagated the legend of the *droit de seigneur*. While many *philosophes* came from middle-class backgrounds, none was remotely interested in promoting 'bourgeois' ideals.

When Ancien Régime writers commented on the striking changes wrought by commerce and consumption, the bourgeoisie was featured neither as hero nor as villain of the story. In the second half of the eighteenth century especially, literally hundreds of texts lamented the scourge called 'luxury'.[29] Writers ranging from Christian moralists to followers of Rousseau complained that rural folk were leaving the land to seek wealth in towns, abandoning the realm's most precious source of wealth. Once city-based, they opted for 'sterile' occupations like domestic service, failed to marry or produce many children, and engaged in a destructive pursuit of goods and clothing above their station. They engaged in the pursuit of Mammon in imitation of their betters from the aristocracy on down who, corrupted by an influx of money and goods, taught others by example to pursue only trivial and selfish pleasures. The villain, in this tirelessly reiterated scenario, was not one group or another but everyone—all town dwellers, that is—and an abstract moral entity labelled 'le luxe'.

Once again, the bourgeoisie is not especially conspicuous in this voluminous literature about luxury; being merely featured sometimes as one link in the destructive cascade of imitation whereby each group mimicked the one above, with devastating effects for the social order. Neither is it singled out as a villain in a massive corpus lamenting the destructive effects of wealth and materialism. One social group was promoted, however, as a counterpoint to the alleged moral dissolution of the eighteenth-century social order:

the land-dwelling peasantry. A central feature of eighteenth-century social discourse was the relentless idealization of rural life. All manner of writers from economists to playwrights—not to mention painters and musicians—produced rhapsodic visions of the countryside as a place where a sense of community still flourished and closeness to nature made for fertility as well as moral and physical health.[30]

In sum, eighteenth-century French depictions of and debates about society singled out the nobleman, who was construed either as a hero or as a villain, or the peasant, who was relentlessly idealized. The striking absence of any substantial contemporary discourse about the bourgeoisie, or of any claims made by self-identified bourgeois, no doubt explains why later historians have found it so difficult to write about such a group. Except when the legal category of bourgeois is being discussed, the bourgeoisie has always been defined retrospectively. 'The bourgeoisie' became prominent as a historical agent starting in the early nineteenth century, first in the 1820s when the Restoration liberals—historians and politicians like Mignet, Guizot, Royer-Collard, and Thiers— lionized the French bourgeoisie as an ideological weapon against the reactionary Ultras; and even more when Karl Marx made it into the protagonist of his narrative of historical development.[31] Even in nineteenth-century France, however, bourgeoisie or social middlingness were never successful rallying points for politicians. The July Monarchy's attempt to promote an ideal of *juste milieu* stood no chance against those, on the left and right, who invoked the glories of Empire, Republic, or Monarchy.[32]

The peculiarity of the absence of a bourgeoisie or middle class in old regime French normative or descriptive texts comes out most clearly in comparison to the English counter-example. Social taxonomies in eighteenth-century England always featured middle classes or middling sorts. The 'Middle Ranks' take pride of place in the famous estimates of income distribution in England and Wales drawn up by Gregory King in 1688 and Patrick Colquhoun in 1803. Both surveys had the 'middle ranks' adding up to a third of all families, and 60 per cent of the national income. Regardless of the accuracy of these estimates, King's and Colquhoun's surveys testify abundantly to the conceptual importance of social middlingness, as do all manner of eighteenth-century English texts praising the virtues of the 'middle sort'. Decades before Charles Dickens made it the organizing principle of his *Tale of Two Cities*, English contemporaries of the French Revolution chalked up the causes of that event to the regrettable fact that in France 'there was no yeomanry, no middle class of people, all were either Princes or beggars, Lords or Vassals'.[33] Aside from the indubitable fact that eighteenth-century England was far more urbanized than France, it would be difficult to assess the differences in the actual size of the middle classes in either context. The moral and cultural importance vested in the equivalent of a bourgeoisie in England (inasmuch as one can establish such a parallel) is undoubtedly linked to such deep-seated aspects of English society as the existence of a gentry and 'country ideology' and the rallying force of dissenting religion.[34]

Central aspects of the history and political culture of France made the coalescence of a middle-class identity around a concept of 'bourgeoisie' difficult. The weight of Catholic tradition vested power, as Bernard Groethuysen, observed, only in greatness, modelled on God, or poverty as embodied in Christ.[35] The sort of transcendent polity embodied by the absolute monarchs, on the one hand, and the republican or imperial state on the other, was not easily associated with a class defined by mere numbers (the middle), or materialistic pursuits (the bourgeoisie). Under the old regime, the official ordering of society into multiple 'privileged' groups, including the legally defined bourgeoisie, stood in the way of any concept of a unitary bourgeoisie or middle class, while after the Revolution social distinctions of any sort were repudiated as smacking of the old regime. The revolutionary *peuple* or the republican nation was inhospitable to concepts such as that of bourgeoisie that harked back to the days of state-sanctioned privilege: freedom thrived on unity, while tyranny was represented as a many-headed hydra.

A cultural approach which highlights contempt of or resistance to the idea of bourgeoisie before—and indeed even during and after—the French Revolution helps to explain why historians have found it so difficult to agree on the existence or definition of such a group in the Ancien Régime. While almost no historians cling to a classic Marxian view of the eighteenth-century bourgeoisie as a rising capitalist group, most are still committed to the notion that it existed, although there is no general agreement about what it was and what its existence signifies within a larger historical picture. While some have called for an approach to the bourgeoisie based on social practices—how one dressed, ate, moved, spoke—no wide-ranging or systematic study of the question exists to date. In the end, the thorny question of the bourgeoisie remains engrossing because in its very complexity it raises questions that remain at the centre of historical thinking, about the relationship between 'objective' and 'subjective' approaches to social history, and the very definition of social classes.

Notes

1. For a fuller discussion of the issues I raise here, see Sarah Maza, *The Myth of the French Bourgeoisie: An Essay on the Social Imaginary, 1750–1850* (Cambridge, Mass., 2003).
2. See e.g. Elinor G. Barber, *The Bourgeoisie in Eighteenth Century France* (Princeton, 1955); Régine Pernoud, *Histoire de la Bourgeoisie en France* (2 vols. Paris, 1960–2); Pierre Goubert, *The Ancien Regime: French Society 1600–1750*, tr. Steve Cox (New York, 1973), 239–52; Adeline Daumard, *Les Bourgeois et la bourgeoisie en France* (Paris, 1987).
3. Michel Vovelle and Daniel Roche, 'Bourgeois, rentiers, propriétaires: Éléments pour la définition d'une catégorie sociale à la fin du xviiie siècle', *Actes du 77e congrès des sociétés savantes*, 84 (1959), 419–52; Pernoud, *Histoire de la bourgeoisie*, i, chs. 2–3; Joseph di Corcia, '*Bourg, Bourgeois, Bourgeois de Paris* from the Eleventh to the Eighteenth Century', *Journal of Modern History*, 50 (1978), 207–331.
4. These words can be found in all 18th-cent. edns. of the Dictionary of the *Académie française*; for similar definitions see the 18th-cent. edns. of the dictionaries published by Antoine Furetière and Pierre Richelet. See Maza, *Myth of the French Bourgeoisie*, 21–4.
5. Sonia Branca-Rosoff, 'Les Mots du parti-pris: *Citoyen, Aristocrate*, et *Insurrection* dans quelques dictionnaires, 1762–1798', in *Dictionnaire des usages socio-politiques, 1770–1798* (Paris, 1988), 71.

6. Christine Adams, *A Taste for Comfort and Status: A Bourgeois Family in Eighteenth-Century France* (University Park, Pa., 2000).
7. Georges Duby et al., *Histoire de la France urbaine* (4 vols. Paris, 1981), iii. 295–8; Daniel Roche, *La France des Lumières* (Paris, 1993), 160–3, and *Histoire des choses banales: Naissance de la consommation, xviie–xviiie siècles* (Paris, 1997), 45–8.
8. The best account of this shift, with bibliographic details on the main contributions to 'first-wave' revisionism in the field, remains William Doyle, *Origins of the French Revolution* (3rd edn., Oxford, 1999), 5–34. The comparison is to the model of cognitive shift laid out in Thomas Kuhn's classic *The Stucture of Scientific Revolutions* (3rd edn., Chicago, 1996).
9. Alfred Cobban, *The Social Interpretation of the French Revolution* (Cambridge, 1964).
10. François Furet, *Penser la Révolution française* (Paris, 1978); Lynn Hunt, *Politics, Culture and Class in the French Revolution* (Berkeley, Calif., 1984).
11. Colin Lucas, 'Nobles, Bourgeois, and the Origins of the French Revolution', *Past and Present*, 60 (1973), 84–126.
12. Patrick O'Brien and Caglar Keydar, *Economic Growth in Britain and France, 1780–1914: Two Paths to the Twentieth Century* (London, 1978); Richard Roehl, 'French Industrialization: A Reconsideration', *Explorations in Economic History*, 13 (1978), 233–81; Robert Aldrich, 'Late Comer or Early Starter? New Views on French Economic History', *Journal of European Economic History*, 16 (1987), 89–100.
13. Joseph Berthélé (ed.), *Montpellier en 1768 et 1836, d'après deux documents inédits* (Montpellier, 1909). The text by the anonymous 1768 chronicler of the city has been analysed by Robert Darnton in *The Great Cat-Massacre and Other Episodes in French Cultural History* (New York, 1984), ch. 4.
14. The following summary is based on: Daniel Roche, *The People of Paris: An Essay on Popular Culture in the Eighteenth Century*, tr. Marie Evans and Gwynne Lewis (Berkeley, Calif., 1987); *Histoire des choses banales*, and *The Culture of Clothing: Dress and Fashion in the Ancien Régime*, tr. Jean Birrell (Cambridge, 1994); Annick Pardailhé-Galabrun, *La Naissance de l'intime: 3000 foyers parisiens, xviie–xviiie siècles* (Paris, 1988); Colin Jones, 'The Great Chain of Buying: Medical Advertisement, the Bourgeois Public Sphere, and the Origins of the French Revolution', *American Historical Review*, 101 (1996), 13–40.
15. Colin Jones, 'Bourgeois Revolution Revivified: 1789 and Social Change', in Colin Lucas (ed.), *Rewriting the French Revolution* (Oxford, 1991), 69–118.
16. Ibid. 114.
17. Robert Darnton's focus on the production and dissemination of books and pamphlets was evident from his earliest articles, which have been collected as *The Literary Underground of the Old Regime* (Cambridge, Mass., 1982); his most systematic work on the artisanal and commercial side of the book trade is *The Business of Enlightenment: A Publishing History of the Encyclopédie, 1775–1800* (Cambridge, Mass., 1979).
18. Jürgen Habermas, *The Structural Transformation of the Public Sphere*, tr. Thomas Burger (Cambridge, Mass., 1989).
19. William H. Sewell, Jr., *A Rhetoric of Bourgeois Revolution: The Abbé Sieyès and What is the Third Estate?* (Durham, NC, 1994); Timothy Tackett, *Becoming a Revolutionary: The Deputies of the French National Assembly and the Emergence of a Revolutionary Culture, 1789–1790* (Princeton, 1996); David Garrioch, *The Formation of the Parisian Bourgeoisie, 1690–1830* (Cambridge, Mass., 1996).
20. Kenneth Margerison, *Pamphlets and Public Opinion: The Campaign for a Union of Orders in the Early French Revolution* (West Lafayette, Ind., 1998).

21. Tackett, *Becoming a Revolutionary*.
22. Jean-Paul Marat, *Offrande à la patrie ou discours au tiers-état de France* (Paris, 1789), 14.
23. Emmanuel Sieyès, *Qu'est-ce que le Tiers-état?*, ed. Roberto Zapperi (Geneva, 1970), 119–22.
24. For a fuller version of this account of 18th-cent. social taxonomies, see Maza, *Myth of the French Bourgeoisie*, 15–21.
25. Jean Alter, *Les Origines de la satire antibourgeoise en France* (2 vols. Geneva, 1970).
26. See the article *bourgeois* in the *Dictionnaire de l'Académie française* of 1694 and 1798, the *Dictionnaire universel* of 1704, and those of Richelet (1680) and Furetière (1690).
27. Élie Carcassonne, *Montesquieu et le problème de la constitution française au xviiie siècle* (Paris, 1927), 223–32; J. Q. C. Mackrell, *The Attack on 'Feudalism' in Eighteenth-Century France* (London, 1973), ch. 4; Jay Smith, 'Social Categories, the Language of Patriotism, and the Origins of the French Revolution: The Debate over *Noblesse commerçante*', *Journal of Modern History*, 72 (2000), 339–74.
28. Mackrell, *Attack on 'Feudalism'*, ch. 2; Carcassonne, *Montesquieu*, ch. 4; Jean-Marie Goulemot, *Le Règne de l'histoire: Discours historiques et révolutions, xviie–xviiie siècles* (Paris, 1996), chs. 9 and 10.
29. Ellen Ross, 'The Debate on Luxury in Eighteenth-Century France: A Study in the Language of Opposition to Change', Ph.D. diss., University of Chicago, 1975; Renato Galliani, *Rousseau, le luxe, et l'idéologie nobiliaire* (SVEC 268; Oxford, 1989); John Shovlin, *The Political Economy of Virtue: Luxury, Patriotism and the Origins of the French Revolution* (Ithaca, NY, 2006).
30. See for instance Sarah Maza, *Private Lives and Public Affairs: The Causes Célèbres of Prerevolutionary France* (Berkeley, Calif., 1993), ch. 2.
31. Stanley Mellon, *The Political Uses of History: A Study of Historians in the French Restoration* (Stanford, Calif., 1958); Pierre Rosanvallon, *Le Moment Guizot* (Paris, 1985).
32. Vincent Starzinger, *Middlingness: Juste-Milieu Political Theory in France and England, 1815–1848* (Charlottesville, Va., 1965).
33. Dror Wahrman, *Imagining the Middle Class: The Political Representation of Class in Britain, c.1780–1840* (Cambridge, 1995), 26.
34. Ibid., and Harold Perkin, *The Origins of Modern English Society* (2nd edn., London, 2002).
35. Bernard Groethuysen, *Origines de l'esprit bourgeois en France* (Paris, 1927), 167–77.

Bibliography

Adams, Christine, *A Taste for Comfort and Status: A Bourgeois Family in Eighteenth-Century France* (University Park, Pa., 2000).

Barber, Elinor, *The Bourgeoisie in Eighteenth-Century France* (Princeton, 1955).

Daumard, Adeline, *Les Bourgeois et la bourgeoisie en France* (Paris, 1987).

Garrioch, David, *The Formation of the Parisian Bourgeoisie, 1690–1830* (Cambridge, Mass., 1996).

Maza, Sarah, *The Myth of the French Bourgeoisie: An Essay on the Social Imaginary, 1750–1850* (Cambridge, Mass., 2003).

Sewell, William H., Jr. *A Rhetoric of Bourgeois Revolution: The Abbé Sieyès and 'What is the Third Estate?'* (Durham, NC, 1994).

Wahrman, Dror, *Imagining the Middle Class: The Political Representation of Class in Britain c.1780–1940* (Cambridge, 1995)

CHAPTER 9

ESTATES, ORDERS AND CORPS

GAIL BOSSENGA

Estates, orders, and corps provided one of the most important means of conceptualizing and organizing society in the old regime. According to a long-standing, and not infrequently contested ideal, European society was composed of a series of hierarchically arranged social groups (estates, orders, and corps), each with a prescribed function and corresponding degree of honour and privileges. In its simplest form, society consisted of three basic groups: the First Estate, the clergy, who prayed; the Second Estate, the nobility, who fought; and the Third Estate, the common people, who worked. This hierarchy of superiority and inferiority was, according to some theorists of the period, inscribed in the order of the universe, so that the terrestrial human hierarchy participated in a greater, divinely sanctioned celestial hierarchy. Smaller, subhierarchies existed within the larger divisions, allowing all members of society to be classified in their proper place and thereby ensuring social harmony under divine guidance. Following the clergy and noble warriors in terms of dignity were magistrates, doctors, men of letters, financiers, court officials, merchants, farmers, and artisans. Even though the particulars of this grand schema might differ slightly in their expression—sometimes a 'fourth estate' of lawyers, urban bourgeois, or other professional groups was inserted—the concept of a tripartite, stratified society of estates reinforced critical social distinctions between the noble and non-noble, and between the clerical and lay persons. The destruction of the hierarchical society of orders during the French Revolution, which abolished the clergy and nobility as legal estates, is one of the main reasons why historians have applied the term Ancien Régime to the period before 1789.[1]

One of the central problems in evaluating the society of estates is that this term refers both to an ideal prescribing how society was supposed to be structured and to the actual institutional organization, which, of course, was far more complex. Historians have sometimes argued that it was only in the eighteenth century, with the fast-paced growth of commercial capitalism, that the basis of the tripartite society of orders came to be called into question. Yet there had always been a great deal of diversity within the society of orders and repeated attacks on its ideal representation. As Georges Duby has shown, the idea of the three orders took root in medieval France during a period of social turmoil. The idea that there were three estates or orders, each with their own functions, privileges, and fixed duties, was strongly associated with a reform programme of the monarch who in alliance with his bishops and knights, it was hoped, might restore order to society by guaranteeing the rightful duties and prerogatives of each group. The ideal of the three harmonious orders was also aimed at cutting off competing representations of the social hierarchy, notably the egalitarian oath of the urban commune and heresies that espoused religious freedom while denying the necessity of priestly rituals for salvation.[2]

The latter alternatives to the hierarchical vision of the society of orders—religious egalitarianism and communal fraternity—surfaced again and again in periods of social strife across Europe. During the tumultuous upheaval of the Reformation, Protestant 'heretics' in areas such as England and Germany succeeded in disestablishing the clergy as a separate order in the state and seizing the church's wealth for the benefit of the state. The Italian urban communes were fertile environments for the renaissance civic humanism, while *Frondeurs* in Bordeaux attempted to revive the fraternal ideal of the commune in 1648, as did Parisian rebels in 1789.[3] Significantly, unlike members of the three orders with their assigned tasks, another new category of the medieval period, *bourgeois,* had no functional connotation: these were men described by a place, a *bourg,* a space for new kinds of urban liberties and wealth.

The existence of rival views of ideal social organization suggests that the perpetuation of any of these views over time was not simply the result of habitual, internalized beliefs, but also of the exercise of power, that is, which social groups were dominant and able to persuade others to accept their rendition of a legitimate social order, whether peaceably or by force. Furthermore, it appears that some of the key words in the cultural vocabulary used to attack and eventually destroy the society of orders went back deep into European history and were not simply a product of 'modern' forces.

One of the great problems that the society of orders has continually posed for scholars is how to relate the ideal conceptualization of social organization to the actual exercise of power. Can a study of the operation of power justify calling early modern society a 'society of orders'? The debate on this subject has fallen broadly into two camps, the first exploring the role of wealth and social status in the society of orders, and the second analysing the power of political authorities and the definition of liberty.

The French historian Roland Mousnier was particularly important in launching a debate over whether early modern society was a society of 'orders' or one of 'classes', a debate that was part of a wider historiographical discussion over the utility and relevance of Marxist categories to historical social analysis. According to Mousnier, a society of orders

> consists of a hierarchy of degrees... arranged not according to the wealth of their members and the latter's capacity to consume, and not according to their role in the production of material goods, but according to the esteem, honour and

dignity attached by society to social functions that can have no relationship with the production of material goods.[4]

A society of orders, then, was a society in which groups were ranked by degrees of honour independently of any links to their wealth as generated through agriculture, trade, and manufacture. Thus by dint of their innate honour, for example, impoverished nobles still enjoyed a rank superior to wealthy merchants, whose association with the profit motive made them unworthy of social esteem. To illustrate and justify his argument, Mousnier drew extensively on the *Treatise of Orders* (1610) by Charles Loyseau, a seventeenth-century jurist who presented an elaborate description of the titles, marks, and privileges accorded to the various orders constituting society. The members of the ecclesiastical order wore long robes and the tonsure; to bishops were reserved the mitre, crozier, gloves, and ring. Nobles had crested coats of arms, while doctors of universities had different kinds of hoods corresponding to their different faculties.

This organization of society did not last. By the mid-eighteenth century, according to Mousnier, the society of orders was being replaced by a society of 'classes' in which a person's place in the social hierarchy was derived from wealth and ownership of property. Although the principles of this new society were freedom and equality before the law, it was the rise of the bourgeoisie—wealthy financiers, merchants, bankers, and the like—whose boundless productivity was making possible the vigorous growth of the emerging class-based society. Mousnier, who started out presenting the society of orders as an alternative, non-Marxist way of conceptualizing early modern society, paradoxically ended up agreeing with the Marxists that the French Revolution, which destroyed the society of orders, was essentially a 'bourgeois' revolution set in motion by the rise of capitalism that confirmed the role of a new dominant class. Where Mousnier differed from the Marxists, and it was a critical difference, was in his claim that class was not a universal concept and could not be used fruitfully to analyse society before the mid-eighteenth century.

By bringing the concept of a society of orders to the fore, Mousnier raised an important issue of how the early modern social hierarchy might best be analysed. Mousnier's presentation of the problem and his underlying assumptions, as well as the general parameters of historiography at the time, however, led to a debate bereft of fruitful conclusions. One problem was Mousnier's tendency to set up the problem as a stark choice between two opposed types of social organization: either early modern society was a society of orders, or it was one of classes. Society in this period, apparently, could not simultaneously have both forms of organization, except in the transitional phase from one to the other. If that were so, then where did classes come from? Mousnier's presentation of the problem implied that the categories of the society of orders—honour, rank, and status—had nothing to do with wealth. He left historians with no viable strategy for studying the intersection between wealth and status and the emergence of classes. Implicitly, Mousnier set up a historical narrative in which categories of honour and status were relatively stable, unchanging, and traditional, while classes, which were rooted in economic processes, were the motors of historical change. Since 'orders' were supplanted in the end by 'classes', Mousnier's interpretation seemed, at the end of the day, to validate a study of classes over orders, and economic production over status. Mousnier could not offer a viable alternative to the Marxist thesis of history. He had no theory of historical change, except through economic development, which was supposedly irrelevant to the society of orders.

In contrast to Mousnier, early revisionist scholars wanted to remove consideration of class completely from studies of the origins of the Revolution. Marxist scholarship implied that the organization of estates and orders connoting different levels of honour was actually an outgrowth of underlying class relations. The conflict between the Second and Third Estates in 1789, therefore, represented a class conflict between the feudal nobility and capitalist bourgeoisie. One of the first tasks of revisionist social historians was to attack the idea that the nobility was an economic class at all and that class conflict produced the French Revolution. George Taylor, in an oft-cited article, for example, showed that nobles and wealthy non-nobles owned the same kind of property and invested in the same kinds of enterprises. Membership in the Second and Third Estates, therefore, could not be correlated directly to membership in noble and bourgeois classes.[5] As mounting evidence showed how difficult it was to view the nobility, or other members of orders and estates, as 'classes', one historian, William Reddy, advocated abandoning the idea of class altogether, at least for the analysis of the French Revolution.[6]

Although revisionists dismantled the idea of class, they did not put in place a new vocabulary for social analysis of the old regime, and they certainly did not seek to replace the idea of class with that of estates and orders. The definition of estates and orders remained amorphous, unrelated to social and economic processes. It was pointed out that many members of society, particularly those at the very bottom, did not belong to any estate or order at all, except in the broadest sense of belonging to the catch-all Third Estate. The privileges attached to orders and estates often seemed to be of limited practical value, valuable more for show than substance. Monopolies, such as those enjoyed by the guilds, were frequently circumvented. Although juridical texts depicted estates and orders as static groupings, social mobility was common in early modern society. The role of wealth always presented a problem. As Alfred Cobban wrote:

> the society of the *ancien régime* was never the simple stratification by classes [i.e. orders] that has so often been described and denounced. Privileged classes and *tiers état* were little more than juridical categories, a formal legal framework that did not correspond to the actual complexity of social life. Acquired riches, which cut across and conflicted with these categories had become a great force in French society even in the age of the *roi soleil*.[7]

Faced with complex social organizations that either evaded or spilled out of the boundaries described by jurists, many social historians tended to agree with Pierre Goubert that the literate elites in the old regime who talked about orders and estates were 'incapable of looking social reality in the face'.[8] It seemed, as William Doyle observed, that the debate over social orders and social classes had been 'an expensive diversion yielding dividends of limited value'.[9]

The concept of a society of orders has not generated much scholarly attention since the end of the debate stimulated by Mousnier. However, the problem that Mousnier raised—what exactly were estates, orders, and corps?—deserves to be re-examined, in part because a central goal of the French revolutionaries was to destroy the estates, orders, and corps of the old regime in France. If it were true that individuals in the old regime were unable to look social reality in the face, then a critical part of the Revolution must be seen as a big mistake, something made by misguided people who were somehow under the erroneous impression that abolishing estates, orders, and corps was essential to creating a new socio-political order. Obviously that was not the case. The battle over the fate of the hierarchical, corporate organization of society was, in fact, a defining feature of the Revolution. But how can this elusive concept of social organization be a help to historians, a guide to the comparative understanding of social organization in the old regime and the origins of the Revolution, rather than a historiographical albatross of uncertain worth?

A more multi-faceted view of the society of orders is called for, one which can encompass the central question of honour and status at the heart of this society, but go beyond a static conception of social hierarchy in order to relate status to questions of social power, economic development, and the state. The society of orders rested on a complex institutionalization of the power of status that drew sustenance from multiple levels of socio-cultural organization. The benefit of this complexity was the flexibility of the overall organization and the multiple purposes that it fulfilled. Yet its very complexity was also susceptible of generating internal tensions. The collapse of this type of society was not the result of dynamic outside forces bearing down on its archaic, outmoded organization. Rather, in France the society of orders had been called upon to accomplish too much, frequently at the behest of the royal government. In the end this type of social organization fell along with absolute monarchy. With the coming of the Revolution, the society of orders was not transformed into an entirely different kind of power—that of socio-economic class. Rather, the society of orders was instrumental in giving birth to modern citizenship, its seeming egalitarian antithesis. Both corporate organization and citizenship gave individuals membership in a political community, legally assigned those individuals functions and rights, and established basic criteria of social worth, but they did so in radically different ways, one through legalized hierarchy, the other through equality before the law.

The central type of power operating within the society of estates was status. Indeed, the words estate, *état*, and *Stand* all come from the Latin word for status. Status has often been seen as a byproduct of economic circumstance, but, as Max Weber observed, it is a distinct type of power with a logic of its own. Two definitions of status are important for understanding the society of estates, one emphasizing the importance of honour in creating a social hierarchy; the second emphasizing the legal nature of status positions. According to Weber, status involved life opportunities for individuals that are 'determined by a specific, positive or negative, social estimation of *honor*'.[10] Honour was a complex concept, but its central thrust was captured by the German jurist Pufendorf (1632–94) who stated that honour was 'the indication of our judgment of another's superiority'.

Honour thus created hierarchical relationships based on notions of superiority and inferiority. These relations, as Pufendorf further observed, gave rise to 'a right strictly so called to require honour from others as one's due'.[11] Groups of individuals enjoying a similar degree of honour as determined by a common lifestyle, sense of prestige, or other shared characteristics such as a profession, might come together to form a ranked series of 'status groups'. Status could be considered a type of power because it opened up or closed off opportunities for social advance. In a status-oriented society such as the old regime, opportunities for education, marriage, entrance into professions, and state service were all strongly conditioned by one's status.

A second definition of a society of estates and orders by T. H. Marshall (1893–1981) drew attention to its legal dimension. In a society of estates, wrote Marshall, 'people have a position (status) to which is attached a bundle of rights, privileges, obligations and legal capacities enforced by the public authority'.[12] In this case, the emphasis is not on status as a system of superiority and inferiority (although that always existed), but on status as type of stable condition endowed with 'legal capacities' and specific duties. Often when referring to an active and participatory view of legally constituted status groups, scholars use the German word *Ständestaat* rather than the more passive term 'society of orders'. As Gianfranco Poggi has emphasized, in a *Ständestaat* estates not only enjoyed rights and privileges, but also took on public roles and played a part in governing, whether by cooperating with rulers or contesting their power. Estates thus helped to define what was 'public' and opposed rulers who tried excessively to narrow the scope of public affairs.[13] Usually in the old regime, the two branches of status—honourable and legal—were joined together. The higher a group's social status, the greater the rights, privileges, and legal entitlements that accrued to that position. It is important to note, however, that there was not always a perfect correspondence between legal and social status. Many groups throughout the social hierarchy were accorded privileges, and although these groups were accorded far less power and esteem than those at the top, their rights still had to be respected.

The penetration of legal rights far down the social hierarchy is best illustrated by the diversity of corporate bodies (*corps*) that existed in the old regime. Technically, a corporate group was a legally constituted body that was considered to be a *personne morale*, that is, an institution that had the ability to act in an ongoing fashion independent from the individuals who composed it. This legal status allowed a corporate body to be perpetuated over time—'a corporation never dies'—which, in turn, allowed it to accumulate and pass down resources over the generations. Corporate groups also had the right to have *doyens* to represent their interests, were able to bring cases to court, and could make formal representations to the government to defend their interests.[14] These powers were critical to the eventual formation of representative government. Owing to the plurality of authorities in the medieval period, there were a variety of governing institutions which claimed the right to grant corporate status to social groups including popes, kings, town councils, and seigneurial authorities. Increasingly in France, the King claimed the sole power to incorporate groups as a mark of his sovereignty.

There was a multitude of corporate bodies at all levels of the social hierarchy in the old regime, ranging from some types of peasant assemblies up to sovereign judicial courts. Guilds, universities, cities, provincial estates, professional groups of various sorts, magistracies in judicial courts, cathedral chapters, chambers of commerce, rural communes, and the like were often constituted as corporate bodies. Because the corporate group was treated as an individual, it was given its own rank commensurate with the dignity of its functions. The internal social composition of a corporate group might be homogeneous—exclusively noble or artisanal, for example—or it could be heterogeneous: nobles and bourgeois sat together on some town councils, and some councillors in the Parlement of Paris were clerics. It was possible for an individual in the society of the old regime to belong to more than one corporate body and thus to have more than one rank. During his social ascent, the merchant of modest means, Jean-Joseph Laborde, who eventually became the enormously wealthy court banker to Louis XV, simultaneously acquired letters of bourgeoisie in the city of Bayonne and an ennobling office of the king's secretary in the chancellery of the Parlement of Paris. Both were necessary because each kind of corporate membership provided access to different kinds of privileges: commercial rights highly useful for trade and a title of nobility appropriate to the court at Versailles.[15] All corporate groups were granted privileges, that is, entitlements or rights enjoyed by a particular group to the exclusion of subjects as a whole. Even corporate groups ranked far down the social ladder were usually granted some degree of exemption from onerous duties, some recognition, however slight, of their distinctive place in the social hierarchy. The Company of the Farmers General, a corporate body that collected indirect taxes for the royal government, for example, was granted the right to pay the *capitation* at a special rate, to enjoy exemption from lodging military troops and from serving on the watch, and to carry a sword.[16]

The society of orders was not an enclosed, hermetically sealed, coherent system of ranks. It was a system of power which was institutionalized on many levels and which offered a way of organizing society, legitimating the power of elites, governing localities, and generating and distributing resources to various social groups. Three levels of institutionalization are important for understanding how the society of estates, orders, and corps functioned. First, symbols and stories formed cultural systems of meaning that legitimated the idea of hierarchy and made it appear 'natural'. The work of social theorists recently has called attention to the importance of cultural symbols in establishing the meaning of social activities, and thus in helping to construct those activities themselves. The importance of honour was continually being articulated and demonstrated through symbols at all levels of the social hierarchy. These symbols were important not only because they shaped identity, but also because they oriented human action, which helped to reproduce certain patterns of behaviour over time. The social division between nobility and commoner remained essential, hence the continued importance of the myth of the three orders, in which the nobility's superiority was legitimated by its origins in the deeds of illustrious ancestors, its purity of blood, and its innate generous temperament and chivalric spirit.[17] Even when it seemed obvious, at least to a historian today, that many French nobles owed their nobility to the purchase of an office, had blood like anyone else, and were petty-minded, one still finds this legitimation of noble superiority being invoked right down to the Revolution. In 1788 the chronicler of noble privilege, Louis Nicolas Henri Chérin, defended the legitimacy of noble privileges by observing that these preferments were the nobility's 'patrimony, the price of its services and its blood'. He did add, however, that some people of his day claimed that such prerogatives were founded only on 'ancient prejudices'.[18]

Status carried moral connotations, which had become encoded linguistically. Many words once used specifically to describe nobility or superior social status gradually became part of a wider word-stock of ethical concepts applicable to anyone engaging in reputable conduct.[19] Frank (*franc*) was originally someone of the Germanic tribe from which the nobility reputedly was descended. Gentle (*gentil*), linked to gentleman (*gentilhomme*), came from the old French for 'high born', and generous (*généreux*) was derived from the Latin word meaning superior stock or nobility. Status was also marked by public displays of deference, in which individuals actively perpetuated the system of superiority and inferiority through their own actions, by deferring to those above them or by receiving acts of homage from those below them. Those of lesser status, for example, were obliged to remove their hats in the presence of their superiors, while honorific privileges, such as hunting, were reserved to nobles. Ongoing rituals and symbols such as these were designed to make status seem to be an innate natural condition, part of one's identity, something beyond human contrivance that could not be questioned. Although these rituals at times may have seemed petty, they were ways of signifying relations of power that reached far down into the daily lives of individuals.

Second, status was institutionalized through normative interpretations—the writings of jurists, religious authorities, officials, philosophers, and the like—that attempted to reinforce certain readings of the meaning of status and to close off alternatives. A good example is the work of the jurist Loyseau, who almost completely excised the legal dimension of corporate groups from his oft-cited *Treatises of Orders*. According to Loyseau, *orders* had no authority or public administration of their own; they were species of dignities. However, Loyseau continued, some orders did have 'corporations and colleges, which sometimes possess the right to make regulations and elect higher officers who have power over the whole body', such as craft guilds. Nowhere did Loyseau explore the regulatory and legal nature of corporate bodies— their right to sue in court, elect representatives, exercise some degree of self-governance—powers that were essential to the independence of these groups and gave them at least a limited ability to check the monarch's arbitrary power. Instead, by constructing his text as a description of the orders as a hierarchy of dignity, he depicted the society of orders and corps as depoliticized bodies under the King's sovereign authority.

By contrast, at nearly the same time as Loyseau's work, the *Politics* (1603) of the German Calvinist Johannes Althusius (1563–1638), a syndic in the town of Emden near the Dutch border, provided an astonishingly radical view of the state as formed by concentric levels of corporate bodies. These corporate groups were created by the members' 'common consent', and the state as a whole was rooted in popular sovereignty. According to Antony Black, Althusius 'surely ranks as one of the few great theorists of corporatism', because he saw these groups 'not—as we tend to—as mere instruments of convenience, but as essential components of human society'. Carl Friedrich described Althusius as the theorist of 'the developed Germanic city states' and, more broadly, of 'the corporatist state', while Pierre Mesnard called him a theorist of 'corporative democracy'.[20]

Althusius's vision of corporate society was grounded in the highly decentralized world of the Holy Roman Empire and also in Calvinism. During the Wars of Religion, the most radical strands of Calvinist political theory championed the people as a whole as a corporation vested with sovereign authority. Drawing on medieval scholasticism and Roman law, the French *monarchomach* Duplessis Mornay (1549–1623), for example, characterized the people as a timeless corporate body perpetually able to elect and depose kings: 'If you should charge that kings have been established by the people who were living perhaps five hundred years ago, not by those who live today, I, on the other hand, say that, although kings die, a people, like any other corporation, in the meantime never dies.'[21] It is hardly surprising that royalist French jurists like Loyseau sought to obliterate theories that legitimated the independent, self-authorizing nature of corporate bodies and preferred to depict orders as groups vested with dignities protected by royal authority.

Third, the possession of resources was critical to perpetuating the power of status groups. Legal privileges, that is, entitlements or rights enjoyed by a particular group to the exclusion of subjects as a whole, were one of the most important resources of status groups in the old regime. There was a continual dialogue between the codes of status and corresponding privileges that turned cultural expectations of superiority or inferiority into claims enforceable by the state. As Montesquieu stated, 'in governments where there are necessary distinctions of persons, there must likewise be privileges'.[22] Norms of status created expectations for behaviour and lifestyle that had to be met. They demanded that honourable groups and individuals be given special marks demarcating their distinctive place, that they be recruited to eminent positions of authority and released from servile obligations, like paying taxes or performing demeaning labour services, and that they be given freedom to act and not be constrained by arbitrary power. Cultural codes of status thus shaped social opportunities, closing off access to resources to those deemed unworthy and opening up avenues to those holding the right credentials. Through this constant winnowing process which sorted individuals and groups into those deserving of social opportunities and those undeserving of them, status operated as a significant source of power.

Widely internalized through symbols and rituals, the claims of status were continually reinforced by the legal system, by rights and privileges enumerated in customs, historic charters, letters of incorporation, oaths, titles, writs of sale, and the like. Privileges gave a more fixed and permanent quality to status distinctions than cultural scripts alone provided. The existence of privileges, such as tax exemptions or professional monopolies, helped to turn the honour inhering in status into material gain. The right to self-recruitment of members allowed corporate groups to exclude individuals who were deemed unworthy of membership in the group for whatever reason—family pedigree, marital status, prior unacceptable occupations, residence, and the like. Status demanded that nobles be distinguished from commoners and thus be granted the privilege of having their own separate chamber for doing business in representative institutions like provincial estates or the Estates-General. Because the claims of status were constituted as privilege, as part of the juridical system, status was insinuated formally and visibly into the political order itself. For this reason, the society of estates, orders, and corps could only be ended when the standing of these groups in law was formally abolished and new laws were put in its place.

Privilege and the resources associated with it were not only justified by reference to social honour. Because corporate groups were established to perform services necessary to society as a whole, privileges also helped to provide the means by which corporate groups fulfilled their duties, and served as a reward for a job well done. As one magistrate stated, 'Of all the professions that contribute the most to the public good, that of the military seems to merit one of the first ranks...; this is why men of this profession have at all times deserved to be honored by many distinguished privileges...'[23] Corporate groups were granted monopolies over their assigned functions and given specific regulatory powers to enforce them. Some corporate bodies were virtual extensions of the government itself. In addition to its extensive trading privileges, a seal, and flag, the East India Company, for example, had regalian rights: it could maintain armed forces, declare war, make peace, and sign treaties. To repress smuggling, the General Farm had the privilege of arming its employees, equipping vessels, and inspecting soldiers' baggage.[24] Corporate privileges protected the professional identity of the group and helped it to rebuff attempts by the government or others to exercise arbitrary power over them. The Assembly of the Clergy had the right to tax its own members and provide a 'free gift' to the royal government in lieu of paying ordinary taxes. All corporate groups had the right to discipline their members for violating their statutes by imposing fines, expelling them from the group, seizing defective products, and the like. Before the Estates-General of 1789, corporate groups served as primary electoral units and drafted lists of their grievances (*cahiers de doléances*).

It has sometimes been said that historians should not speak of a society of orders because large segments of the population at the bottom of society were not included in these status groups and their privileges. Status, however, represented both the positive and negative expressions of honour in the old regime. When peasants were forced to do arduous labour services known as *corvée*, when a person was excluded from entrance into a *collège* because his father worked with his hands, when a commoner was denied entrance into the army officer corps because his grandfather was not a noble, or when women were usually prohibited from membership in corporate groups, the logic of status underpinning the society of orders was responsible. Its cultural codes and privileges sifted and sorted individuals into gradations of social worth and opened or closed off opportunities in society in accordance with the corresponding level and type of status. The exclusion of groups from distinction was necessary for distinction to operate.

It has also been argued that the growth of the market and strong patterns of social mobility in the old regime renders the concept of a society of estates of little value for social analysis. This is true only if one sees status as a static concept with no effect on economic decision-making. That is certainly not true. Status exerted an important influence on the economy by coding what economic activities were of particular worth, what professions could be filled by persons at different levels of the status system, and what kind of economic investments should be made. In the old regime, money and status existed in a relationship that was simultaneously productive and tension filled. On the one hand, cultural codes of status were designed to rebuff the pull of the market. The paradigmatic traits of nobility—illustrious ancestry, chivalric actions on the battlefield, blood, generosity, and a nonchalant attitude towards debt—were all attributes far removed from the supposedly crass, self-interested sentiments associated with the market. On the other hand, the performance of status demanded a lifestyle commensurate with elevated rank, which called for copious amounts of conspicuous consumption. Throughout the old regime, various laws tried to prevent commoners from acquiring goods on the market that connoted distinction. Sumptuary laws prohibited commoners from wearing clothing and jewels associated with nobility, often to little effect. Of more practical worth, primogeniture laws were designed to prevent noble estates from being divided up equally among all heirs. Although this custom was not practised in all French provinces, in those where it did exist, it helped to keep aristocratic dynastic lines intact, until the French revolutionaries deliberately abolished the practice in order to stop the perpetuation of noble dynasties.[25]

Two trends illustrate the complexity of evaluating the influence of the market on the society of orders. The first is venality, that is, the sale of offices and titles by European governments, the second the so-called 'consumer revolution'. As Koenraad Swart once observed, the widespread practice of selling offices only developed in areas of Europe where commercial capitalism was taking root; the practice scarcely existed in eastern Europe.[26] Through venality, the widespread desire for rank and privileges characterizing the society of orders was grafted onto the financial capitalism sponsored by early modern governments. Venality reached its highest point of development in France, where the monarchy sold large numbers of offices in the royal judicial courts, town councils, guilds, and financial administration—all of them endowed with privileges and functions—as a way of raising funds for war.[27] One result was to give corporate groups at many levels a reputation for being bloated and inefficient, a situation that has sometimes been blamed on the 'medieval' or 'feudal' quality of corporate groups, but owes much more to the monarchy's own blatant multiplication of corps for financial gain.

A central motive for individuals who purchased offices, particularly in the judiciary, was enhancement of their rank and reputation. To a large extent, venality was a market in status. Technically the initial purchase of an office represented a loan to the royal government. Instead of a salary, the government paid the officeholder *gages*, or interest, on the funds advanced to the crown. Periodically, the government held officeholders hostage and subjected them to forced loans: they could either advance more money to the crown or risk losing their office.[28] The return on offices was quite modest, and, far from enriching a noble, some offices 'could even drain family wealth because revenue from them was insufficient to maintain the style of life expected of the official'.[29] At the Parlement of Bordeaux, *gages*, *épices*, and other payments did not return more than 5 per cent of the capital laid out for the office.[30] Although the monetary return on venal offices in the judiciary was modest, they secured the rank of the officeholder, provided a dignified profession, and allowed him to enjoy other privileges attesting to his status. They were, as George Taylor observed, an 'investment in standing'.[31] This was particularly true of the offices of the king's secretaries in the chancelleries of the parlements. These costly offices had few real duties, but they held a choice prize: the officeholder and his posterity were ennobled after twenty years or death in office.[32]

As estimates on the sums invested in venal offices shows, status was an important factor in shaping the economy, and was not a mere derivative of other economic processes. On the eve of the Revolution, Frenchmen had invested approximately 450 million *livres* in venal offices in the royal judiciary, another 52 million in the royal households, and 35 million for commissions purchased in the military.[33] It has been calculated that in the period 1774 to 1789 a total of 2,477 men were ennobled. Roughly 350 of them received letters of ennoblement from the King, the rest had purchased offices.[34] All in all, perhaps one-third of all the nobles in France before the Revolution were from families ennobled during the eighteenth century. If one adds to this total the number of families ennobled through purchase of office in the seventeenth century, it can be concluded that the majority of nobles in France on the eve of the Revolution were products of the market in status and public functions set up by the monarchy.

While a jurist like Loyseau was describing how ranks and orders fit into a divinely ordained celestial hierarchy, then, French monarchs were busy finding ways to develop and exploit a market in status. This was feasible, in part, because the legal system allowed the monarchy to constitute privileges as marketable commodities, as 'things' that could be transferred, possessed, owned, and sold.[35] The commodification of privilege made it possible to abstract and to divorce the legal possession of status and privilege from its original sociocultural setting. The ranks and privileges of the society of orders could no longer be presumed to express an innate natural condition or an ancestor's exceptional deeds. Increasingly, they could be traced back to commercialized entitlements backed by the state.

Gradually the definition of noble status became more legal in emphasis. The old nobility might still claim that nobility was a product of blood. 'Kings make *anoblis* [new nobles],' sniffed the Duke de Saint-Simon at the time of Louis XIV, 'but not nobles.'[36] True nobility (*noblesse de race*), it was claimed, required purification over time, a natural process over which the monarch had no control. Eighteenth-century jurists, however, were prone to stress the role of the sovereign in creating nobility: 'nobility is defined as a *quality that the sovereign power imprints upon private persons*, so as to raise them and their descendants above the other citizens'.[37] Nobility properly so-called, stated the article on nobility in Diderot's *Encyclopédie* under the article nobility, 'is a civil status (*état civil*) that one can only acquire by certain routes admitted by law'.

On the eve of the Revolution, the nobility as an order *per se* was not under attack, but there was fairly strong sentiment that ennoblement through venal office should be ended. In his analysis of 492 *cahiers*, William Doyle found that 7.3 per cent of the clergy, 51.6 per cent of the nobility, and 24.3 per cent of the Third Estate attacked ennoblement by venal office.[38] The cahiers denouncing venal ennoblement were not opposed to the legitimacy of the Second Estate *per se*; rather they wanted nobility to be solely a reward for public service. In a sample of 95 cahiers that denounced venal ennoblement in the *Archives parlementaires*, over two-thirds (66) stipulated that nobility should be given as a reward for things such as 'patriotic virtues and devotion to public affairs', and 'real, publicly important services'. Although most cahiers simply demanded an end to ennoblement by venal charge or purchase, some denounced the practice more explicitly. The parish of Saint-Mexme-les-Champs in the province of Touraine, for example, observed that it was humiliating for members of the Third Estate and harmful to the public welfare to see men leave their estate as soon as they obtained a small fortune, take on noble airs, and cease being useful to their country. In Franche-Comté a pamphleteer in 1789 wrote that with the advent of 'venal nobility', merit 'was nothing more than a base piece of parchment; everything was put up for auction.... it was truly a nobility to the highest bidder.'[39]

The desire to make nobility a reward for public service was part of a broader cultural shift during the old regime away from ascribed status to achieved status as the legitimate basis for social distinction. The corporate groups of the old regime were becoming more professionalized and, although the concept of utility had always been integral to the justification of corporate privileges, there was more insistence on this principle as the basis for entitlement. The process of professionalizing corporate groups was not without ambiguities. Colin Jones has suggested that there were two kinds of professionalization, a corporate professionalization, in which 'expertise, internal discipline and segregation from the wider society was the key', and a civic professionalization, which was more egalitarian and open to accepting members from the wider society.[40] The breadth of corporate professionalism before the Revolution, and the reintroduction of corporate controls to ensure standards of competence in certain professions after the Revolution, suggest that corporate groups were hardly moribund entities.

Professionalization of corporate groups occurred at all levels of the social hierarchy. By 1789, according to one study of Catholic reform movements, 'well-trained bureaucrats were in charge of the French church'.[41] The clergy may have lacked fervour, but they made up for it in the standardization of ecclesiastical practices, efficient management of parish affairs, and uniform educational standards. The lower rungs of the General Farms evolved towards a semi-bureaucratic form of organization, including a hierarchically organized system of grades, salaried employees who did not own their offices, and, after 1780, evaluation of personnel according to efficiency reports and related data. The General Farms also instituted one of the first formal retirement and pension systems, with scheduled contributions according to rank and grade.[42] In professions that had traditionally been considered inferior, the introduction of scientific and mathematical training helped to raise the status of members by creating a new impersonal marker of merit. The corporation of surgeons, traditionally regarded as one of the lowly 'mechanical arts', was able to found a school (1724) and a royal academy (1731) in order to define higher educational standards for their practitioners. In the artillery corps, the army corps of engineers began to require students to take exams in mathematics and by 1780 the graduating class was ranked numerically, a situation designed both to legitimate the officers' authority and to undercut the influence of connections at court.[43]

The rise of corporate professionalism, however, did not mean that older practices and assumptions were discarded. The parish clergy was better educated than ever before, but priests still had no representation at the Assembly of the Clergy which set ecclesiastical policy. Only bishops were deemed worthy of that honour. The General Farms had a bureaucratic component, but the financiers who ran the organization owed their positions to influential ties at court. The artillery was modernizing, but it had always been viewed as a lesser branch of the army, best suited to *anoblis* or poor provincial nobles. Wealth, distinguished birth, and connections at court, rather than actual experience on the battlefield, were still necessary to experience rapid promotion in the military. The emergence of more impersonal, quantifiable, achievement-oriented markers of merit, therefore, could help to increase resentment towards the all-too-common disjuncture between status and function and the remunerative titles without duties that permeated the society of orders.

The 'consumer revolution' of the eighteenth century also had ambiguous effects on the society of orders.[44] By unleashing an unprecedented amount of consumer goods onto the market—watches, umbrellas, fans, snuff-boxes, mirrors, wigs, ornate clothing, and the like—the consumer revolution allowed individuals at the middling and lower levels of the social hierarchy to purchase goods previously reserved to the elite. The signs of distinction that accompanied the traditional rankings, it was said, were thrown into confusion, and traditionalists bemoaned the mixing up of ranks. The massive marketing of consumer goods revealed once again that acquiring status was an extraordinarily powerful motor of human behaviour in the eighteenth century. The consumer revolution pushed individuals to engage in more lavish conspicuous consumption than ever before in European history. Because distinction demanded rarity, an unrivalled display of possessions, the pressure on nobles at the top of the social hierarchy to maintain the *éclat* of their rank was enormous. In 1788, for example, 20,000 *livres*, one-third of the Duke de Saulx-Tavanes's total annual expenditures, went to purchase clothing and accessories.[45] The growth of the market in consumer goods undoubtedly created tension in the society of orders by allowing so many individuals to flaunt the trappings of a lifestyle seemingly beyond their rank. Nonetheless, the scramble to purchase the visible accoutrements of status would hardly seem responsible for the legal abolition of the society of orders in 1789. Individuals who purchased goods wanted to enhance their standing in society, not destroy rank and its sense of entitlement.

The debate between Mousnier and his critics was concerned with the problem of social mobility and hierarchy. Another debate, however, has looked at the relationship between 'centralization' and the society of estates. The debate owes much to Tocqueville, who contended that administrative centralization in the old regime had gradually stripped corporate groups of their privileges and functions and turned over control of provincial affairs to royal agents, the intendants. By abolishing the vestiges of the corporate regime, the French Revolution consolidated a strong, centralized state and put an end to the remaining bits of liberty that corporate bodies had defended.[46]

Historians today are far more likely to question whether the rise of the state was antithetical to the existence of corporate bodies, and even whether the state itself was characterized by a process of 'centralization'. The French state had grown early on by enlisting the aid of aristocratic brokers—the patron–client networks beholden to ministers like Richelieu, Mazarin, and Colbert—and by creating corporate groups—like the parlements and company of Farmers-General—to help it with its work. The rise of the French state thus occurred in tandem with an expansion of corporate groups. The goal of the royal government was not to eliminate corporate groups, but to direct their resources towards monarchical goals through a policy of cooptation. Sometimes this tactic was successful, but the nature of corporate groups made them Janus-faced: their sense of honour and royal charters of incorporation could lead them to serve the royal government as loyal servants, but if a royal command was considered arbitrary, they were just as apt to resist it in the name of customary rights or the public welfare.

One reason for the growing number of corporate groups during the old regime was financial. Prevented from taxing the privileged elites to pay for wars, the crown, as noted earlier, took to selling the privileges and public functions attached to corporate bodies instead. Offices in the judicial courts, town councils, guilds, and royal treasury were all put on the market. Historians have drawn attention to the importance of trust and confidence as preconditions for the expansion of capital markets. Owing to their legal status, corporate groups were able to provide collective accountability to creditors that 'absolute' monarchs, whose will was law, could not. In England, the so-called 'financial revolution' following the Glorious Revolution of 1688 utilized several corporate institutions to make low-cost loans available to the government. The Bank of England of 1694 advanced the government funds, and the English Parliament guaranteed that there would be no default.[47]

In France, by contrast, the royal government relied on a whole series of intermediate corporate bodies to extend credit to the monarchy, without which it could not survive. The Assembly of the Clergy, the municipality of Paris, corps of venal officeholders in the judiciary and treasury, provincial estates, and the Company of Farmers-General were all called on to aid the royal government. During Louis XIV's reign, borrowing through corporate groups was solidified. The royal government ceased its earlier policy of dismantling provincial estates and turned to the remaining ones for loans instead. For the first time, venal officeholders began borrowing money on behalf of the King collectively as corporate groups, rather than as individual officeholders. The royal government stopped threatening rights of property in office, because without firm property rights, offices could not be used as collateral for loans. Finally, new corporate bodies were created, like Colbert's company of General Farmers, with the extension of credit in mind.[48]

The use of corporate groups for financial aid had repercussions that permeated the entire socio-political organization of France. Corporately based financial aid solidified a degree of localism and particularism: loans from provincial estates, for example, were serviced by taxes specifically assigned to the province in question and administered by provincial authorities themselves, rather than royal agents. The sale of offices spawned the growth of privilege and reinforced the demand of venal officeholders that the crown respect their tax exemptions, which were contractually part of their rights of property in office. The latter policy also accelerated legal social mobility, because large numbers of elite venal offices were ennobling. The crown thereby became the most important agent of legal social mobility in the old regime. Finally, the use of corporate financial intermediaries created an entrenched network of groups with a vested interest in perpetuating their privileges. If the resistance of privileged corporate groups to royal programmes of reform was responsible for bringing France to the brink of revolution, then the monarchy itself was partly to blame, because it had helped to multiply these groups during its rise to power.

Tocqueville lamented the abolition of corporate groups because, for him, these bodies defended 'liberty'. The debate over the relationship of estates and corporate groups to political liberty, the rule of law, and constitutionalism is a long-standing one. Montesquieu famously argued that the prerogatives of 'intermediate bodies' were necessary to prevent a monarchy from exercising uncontrolled, arbitrary power and degenerating into despotism. His stance is common to the tradition of the 'ancient constitution', whereby a set of unwritten, customary procedures and acquired rights were critical to limiting irresponsible central authority. The royal minister Turgot, by contrast, told the King that the problems facing France stemmed

> from the fact that your nation has no constitution. It is a society composed of different orders badly united, and of a people among whose members there are but very few social ties. In consequence each individual is occupied only with his own particular, exclusive interest.... The rights of men gathered together in society are not founded on their history, but on their nature. There can be no grounds for perpetuating institutions created without reason.[49]

Turgot looked forward to a kind of modern constitutionalism where law was derived from abstract, universal, first principles, such as natural law or reason, that could bound all subjects simultaneously and equally. From this perspective, corporatism lacked constitutionality, because its sense of law still was embedded in idiosyncratic and personalized elements of status and inheritance.

The lack of a theory to guide enquiry into the relationship of corporate groups to constitutionalism has obscured their role. The natural law tradition of jurisprudence, the most important theoretical justification for modern citizenship, excludes corporate groups from theoretical consideration. The abstract, individualistic, and contractual terms underpinning this discourse leave no place for corporate groups as constituent parts of civil society. For Rousseau, any kind of 'sectional association' was anathema because it would prevent the sovereign general will from operating.[50]

The tendency to write corporate groups out of existence can also be seen in the theoretical work of Jürgen Habermas, who posed the important problem of how a modern 'public sphere' developed. A public sphere, according to Habermas, was an arena independent of the government in which individuals came together to debate matters of public concern and put pressure on the government through the force of public opinion. Habermas traced the rise of this sphere primarily to new communication networks, all of which were extra-corporate in nature: the growth of print journalism, the development of the market, a more bureaucratic state which treated subjects as a 'public', and horizontal patterns of sociability in coffee shops, literary clubs, reading rooms, and the like.[51] Overall, the basis for the public sphere was individualistic and voluntaristic in nature. Corporate groups, with their peculiar mixture of public functions and private advantages, inherited rights, and differential status, did not fit into the scheme.

Empirical research, however, has shown that corporate groups did play a critical role in the development of the rule of law and public opinion. In particular, the parlements—which published large runs of remonstrances criticizing royal actions and claimed to be 'tribunes of the people'—were one of the institutions in the old regime that did the most to foster the growth of public opinion.[52] This should not be surprising. As royally chartered sovereign law courts, members of parlement could make claims on the government through channels unavailable to ordinary subjects. Whereas the right of freedom of speech was denied to individuals, for example, the parlements enjoyed protected speech in the form of remonstrances and legal briefs. The ability of the parlements to play such an important role in the development of public opinion stemmed, in part, from the fact that they were already part of the state: they were supreme courts. Their role as public bodies was critical not only to the development of public opinion, but to the rule of law. The rule of law means that a government agrees to put its own actions under legal scrutiny and accountability. Because the parlements were authorized to be, as Montesquieu termed it, 'depositories' (*dépôts*) of the law, there was an institutional mechanism for demanding legal accountability built into the early modern state itself. Eventually when the Maupeou coup and subsequent events demonstrated that the parlements' corporate powers were too weak to resist the monarchy, the parlements used their voice to demand the Estates-General instead.

It can be said, of course, that the parlements were protesting arbitrary government merely to protect their own privileges. If 'liberalism' is defined as a system of government designed to protect the rights of subjects and limit arbitrary power, then the corporate regime was predominantly a kind of 'aristocratic liberalism'.[53] Rights existed, but they were not the universal rights of citizens: they were part of one's station and locality. And, as Turgot observed, they did not naturally lead towards the creation of a national interest. The dilemma of hierarchical, corporately organized rights was that politics could be liberal, that is, groups could block arbitrary power by dint of their privileges, but it could not be egalitarian. To destroy privilege and embrace equality would be to strip society of its legal defences.

The elitist and exclusive nature of corporate rights and liberties cannot be discounted. Nonetheless, corporate rights cannot simply be equated with aristocratic ones; in the society of orders, social status and legal status were not completely commensurate. Villagers sued lords for failure to observe traditional rights or to challenge impositions, and journeymen took cases to court to defend their wages and working conditions. Women were generally excluded from membership in corporate bodies, but in cases where they were allowed to enter guilds, such as the seamstress guild, 'their corporations enjoyed privileges that were entirely comparable to those possessed by the masters of other corporations'.[54] The privileges of such female guilds were also important for allowing the mistresses to escape the constraints of patriarchal control exercised by their husbands. The legal identity and collective resources of corporate groups were an important reason why the old regime became such a litigious society. According to Jonathan Dewald and Liana Vardi, in the eighteenth century litigation, rather than rebellion, 'became villagers' preferred means for dealing with oppression'. Michael Sonenscher has contended that in the trades during the same period, the lawsuit, rather than the food riot, was 'the typical form of protest'.[55]

As micro-sites of civic awareness, political participation, worthy status, and legal rights, corporate groups had obvious affinities to citizenship, and some scholars have argued that they were forerunners of modern citizenship. Peter Riesenberg contended, for example, that the corporate, legal language of protest against arbitrary power was stronger than the classical tradition of virtue in shaping the rhetoric of citizenship. Citizenship survived because individuals continued to act as citizens 'in little oligarchies and bureaucracies in historic regions where estates function even if they did not flourish and even in kingdoms—England, for example, where citizens voted for Parliament'.[56] Citizenship was possible, stated Michael Bush, because nobles retained a sense of dignity and preserved rights that later could be extended to a wider population: 'Democracy was born of noble privilege, not simply by destroying it, but converting it into the rights of citizens.'[57] Likewise, David Bien suggests that 'with the Declaration of the Rights of Man and of the Citizen ideas and habits coming from inside the regime of privileges and corps entered the fully public sphere, where they went on conditioning the terms of discourse and conflict'.[58]

According to these scholars, then, corporate groups provided an institutional site where political rights and participation in the government could be preserved. At the same time, those rights and participatory habits were particularistic, restricted to members of the corps themselves. The transition to citizenship required the democratization of corporate privileges into a wider national setting. The extension of corporate rights and status to a wider national setting was, in large part, a consequence of the interaction of, and at times clash between, the absolute monarch and corporate groups. The French monarchy had multiple, and at times, contradictory policies towards privilege and corporate groups. The monarchy had, as noted, put privilege up for sale and thereby enlarged the legal scope of privilege at the local level. It had also, in contrary fashion, created a network of bureaucratic agents, the intendants, on top of pre-existing corporate groups. The intendants sometimes took over the tasks of corporate groups, but more often tried to coordinate the resources of localities, including those of corporate groups, and use them for the benefit of the monarchy. Finally, by the mid-eighteenth century, the monarchy had begun to attack the concept of privilege itself, but in a rather haphazard manner, because so much of the monarchical tradition and administrative structure was still rooted in privilege. At stake in the attack on privilege was the concept of fiscal immunity, that some groups, owing to their status, were exempt from the obligation to pay taxes to the state for the general services that the crown provided, notably defence. New direct taxes, notably the *dixième* and the *vingtième*, which the crown attempted to levy on all subjects, including privileged ones, set the stage for this debate.[59]

During the clash over taxation, the monarchy challenged a central tenet of the corporate regime, that privilege represented exemption from a common law and that corporate status allowed members to be free from civic duties that were necessary for the survival of the state. When it came to the defence of the state, all subjects had to be put on a common footing. Everyone had to be regarded as equal in the pursuit of that particular aim. In 1751 the pro-royalist Abbé Chauvelin, for example, denounced tax privileges of the clergy by appealing to citizenship: 'he is not a citizen who is not obligated to contribute of his goods to the interior good order of the State and to its defense against outside enemies'. Three decades later, the physiocrat LeTrosne similarly declared that tax exemptions tended to put the clergy 'outside the class of citizens and to strip them of all right to civil protection'.[60] The requirements of the absolute monarchy for efficiency and success in war thus played a central role in creating a top-down notion of citizenship as 'a general abstract status, characterized by equality of citizens before the law'.[61]

The monarchical concept of citizenship of equality before the law, however, was passive; it did not include the participation of the governed in the state. The latter component came from corporate groups, but only after the exclusive nature of corporate groups, which connected a particular status with specific rights, was reconfigured so that corporate rights could be made available to the citizenry as a whole. The thesis of a democratization of corporate rights is difficult to demonstrate because citizenship was created through the abolition of privilege. The intellectual justification of citizenship came to be rooted largely in theories of natural right that regarded corporate entities as unnatural and anti-civic, and national citizenship only came into existence during the French Revolution through the legal abolition of privilege. Citizenship thus was seemingly constituted in opposition to privilege. Yet historians have shown some ways in which democratization of corporate rights was laying a foundation for citizenship. One aspect was a change in the underlying cultural classification system that coded status as honourable or base. During the eighteenth century, the qualities of honour and virtue, which had been viewed primarily as descriptors of nobility and monarchy, started to be used to qualify the *patrie* and all who served it.[62] After decrying the 'honours' without work and dignities without functions of the old regime, for example, the article *honneur* in the *Encyclopédie* entreated the government to revive and purify honour so that 'honor will soon be in each citizen, the conscience of his love for his duties'.[63] The word *citizen* began to replace noble as the standard of social excellence. Simply by placing the word citizen in front of a social group conferred a sense of dignity and civic-mindedness of that group: one began referring to citizen-nobles, citizen-*philosophes*, citizen-soldiers, even citizen-kings.[64] In his work *The Citizen Soldier* (*Le Soldat Citoyen*) of 1780, Servan de Gerbey advocated raising the status of the common soldier by looking back to the Roman Republic and recasting aristocratic honour as patriotic service regardless of estate: 'honor, that divinity of our ancient knights' was merely 'another name for the ancients' love of their country (*patrie*)'.[65]

A similar transformation was occurring in the municipal meaning of citizenship. Originally in Europe citizenship was a municipal corporate identity. Citizens were full members of an incorporated city who shared in urban privileges: they were the *bourgeoisie*. In France under absolute monarchy, municipal citizenship had lost its lustre, and Loyseau scarcely considered it on his *Treatise on Orders*. In the mid-eighteenth century, however, citizenship shook off its municipal associations and started to convey membership in society as a whole. A citizen, stated Diderot in the *Encyclopédie*, was 'a person who is a member of a free society' and 'who partakes of the rights of that society'. The word citizen, he continued, 'is appropriate neither to those who live in servitude, nor to those who live in isolation'.[66] Diderot's discussion was framed by considerations of both republican Rome and Hobbes, but the corporate, republican tradition of the Swiss cantons was equally present. Despite the grandeur of the citizens of Rome, wrote Diderot, 'it seems to me that the government of the Roman Republic was so composite that a less precise idea of citizenship prevailed there than in the canton of Zurich'. Likewise, Rousseau made the Swiss city-state of Geneva a touchstone for his discussion of citizenship, which brought together the traditions of natural jurisprudence and classical republicanism with that of the corporate republicanism of the city-state.[67]

Above all, political conflict played a central role in transforming the perception of corporate rights and extending their reach. The parlements, staunch defenders of noble privilege, were important actors in the process. In 1776 when Turgot proposed subjecting nobles to a tax compounding for the *corvée* from which they had been exempt, the Parlement of Paris vigorously defended the legal rights of status: 'the first rule of justice is to preserve for every man what belongs to him'. This included not only rights of property but also 'rights attached to the person and those which derive from the prerogatives of birth and Estate'.[68] Yet the parlements also claimed for themselves the defence of the rights of the 'Nation', which rhetorically became a virtual co-sovereign of the King. The so-called Nation, in the eyes of the parlements, was not internally egalitarian; it was an amalgam of the three traditional estates and subsidiary corps which constituted France, with claims for pre-eminence of the nobility, even if 'citizens' were ultimately represented.[69] That is why the Parlement of Paris could defend the Nation with increasing vigour and simultaneously recommend voting by order and argue against doubling the Third Estate in 1788 once the Estates-General had finally been called.

The society of estates, orders, and corporate groups in France did not wither away; it was legally abolished after a revolutionary transfer of sovereignty in 1789. In the end, political representation was the specific issue that led to its overthrow. The Third Estate refused to agree to allow the nobility and clergy to vote in separate chambers, which would have continued vesting the latter's status with special political prerogatives and hence undue power. Instead, the Third Estate claimed the right to speak for the Nation, to consent to taxes, and to guarantee the national debt. (The new national debt, it might be noted, absorbed the immense debts generated through corporate intermediaries that the crown earlier had used to finance the state.) On the night of 4 August, pressure from the peasantry, including violence, led to dismantling the special prerogatives that had been attached to birth, locality, offices, and other forms of status in the old regime. In one sense legal privileges had been abolished; in another sense, it can be argued, rights were reconstituted as the property of citizens.

It is perhaps not surprising that the society of estates, orders, and corps was abolished in France. Elsewhere on the continent, the organization of this type of society did not seem to have generated the heated controversy that wracked France. This was not because France had a higher level of capitalist organization than the rest of Europe. Parts of the Netherlands, the Austrian Low Countries, the Italian city-states, and north-western German territories boasted breakthroughs in techniques of finance and commercial capitalism, yet these regions also retained strong corporate traditions. The society of orders was overturned in France because the French monarchy had made it unworkable. It had expanded the numbers of privileged corporate groups; accelerated social mobility and created inter-elite tensions; relied on corporate groups for tasks, like financing, that were not often part of their original mission; tried to circumvent corporate groups with a fledgling bureaucracy when corporate groups remained too independent; and eventually tried, unsuccessfully, to uproot corporate groups that it had originally created.

On the eve of the Revolution the society of orders was beset with contradictions. There were too many Frenchmen, not just among the lower classes, but also within the elite, who no longer had a strong vested interest in perpetuating corporate privileges, yet some of the remaining corporate bodies were powerful and deeply rooted. Corporate groups posed roadblocks to greater efficiency necessary to the survival of the state, but the monarchy could not remove them, in part owing to its own previous policies. Thus, the society of orders did not fade quietly away. It exploded in a battle over citizenship, which rewrote the basic rules about how to channel social resources, constitute political membership, and ascribe social worth, and it did so in the name of liberty, equality and national sovereignty.

Notes

1. For conceptual overviews see Emile Lousse, *La Société d'ancien régime: Organisation et représentation corporatives* (Louvain, 1943); François Olivier-Martin, *L'Organisation corporative de la France d'Ancien Régime* (Paris, 1938); Emile Coornaert, *Les Corporations en France avant 1789* (Paris, 1941); Roland Mousnier, *The Institutions of France under the Absolute Monarchy* (2 vols. Chicago, 1980–3). Recent case studies include William H. Sewell, Jr., *Work and Revolution in France: The Language of Labor from the Old Regime to 1848* (Cambridge, 1980); Gail Bossenga, *The Politics of Privilege: Old Regime and Revolution in Lille* (Cambridge, 1991); and Simona Cerutti, *La Ville et les métiers: Naissance d'un langage corporatif (Turin xviie–xviiie siècles)* (Paris, 1990).
2. Georges Duby, *The Three Orders: Feudal Society Imagined*, tr. Arthur Goldhammer (Chicago, 1980).
3. On the republican tendencies of the *Ormée* of Bordeaux see William Beik, *Urban Protest in Seventeenth-Century France* (Cambridge, 1997), 219–49; for Paris see Charles L. Chassin (ed.), *Les Élections et les cahiers de Paris en 1789* (4 vols. Paris, 1880; repr. New York, 1974), i. 163.
4. Roland Mousnier, *Social Hierarchies, 1450 to the Present,* tr. Peter Evans (New York, 1973), 19.
5. George V. Taylor, 'Noncapitalist Wealth and the Origins of the French Revolution', *American Historical Review*, 72 (Jan. 1967), 469–96.

6. William Reddy, 'The Concept of Class', in Michael L. Bush (ed.), *Social Orders and Social Classes in Europe since 1500: Studies in Social Stratification* (London, 1992), 25.
7. Alfred Cobban, *A History of Modern France*, i. *1715–1799* (Harmondsworth, 1957), 37.
8. Pierre Goubert, *The Ancien Régime: French Society, 1600–1750*, tr. Steve Cox (New York, 1969), 216.
9. William Doyle, 'Myths of Order and Ordering Myths', in Bush (ed.), *Social Orders and Social Classes in Europe*, 224. See also the collection *Ordres et Classes*, Deuxième Colloque d'Histoire Sociale, Saint Cloud, France, 1967 (Paris, 1973).
10. Max Weber, *Economy and Society* (2 vols., ed. Guenther Roth and Claus Wittich, tr. Ephraim Fischoff *et al.* (Berkeley, Calif., 1978), 305. A helpful explication is Anthony Giddens, *Capitalism and Modern Social Theory: An Analysis of the Writings of Marx, Durkheim and Max Weber* (Cambridge, 1971).
11. Samuel Pufendorf, *On the Duty of Man and Citizen*, ed. James Tully, tr. Michael Silverthorne (Cambridge, 1991), 164.
12. T. H. Marshall, *Class, Citizenship and Social Development, Essays* (Garden City, NY, 1974), 176.
13. Gianfranco Poggi, *The Development of the Modern State* (Stanford, Calif., 1978), ch. 3. See also Jacques Revel, 'Les Corps et commuautés', in Keith M. Baker (ed.), *The Political Culture of the Old Regime* (Oxford, 1987), 226–7.
14. For works on corporate organization see n. 1. On the concept of *personne morale* see Pierre Michaud-Quantin, *Universitas: Expressions du mouvement communautaire dans le Moyen-Age Latin* (Paris, 1970), 204.
15. François d'Ormesson and Jean-Pierre Thomas, *Jean-Joseph de Laborde: Banquier de Louis XV, mécène des Lumières* (Paris, 1992), 46–8, 50.
16. Yves Durand, *Les Fermiers généraux au xviiie siècle* (Paris, 1971), 49.
17. Arlette Jouanna, *Ordre social: Mythes et hiérarchies dans la France du xvie siècle* (Paris, 1977); Ellery Schalk, *From Valor to Pedigree: Ideas of Nobility in France in the Sixteenth and Seventeenth Centuries* (Princeton, 1986); Jay M. Smith, *The Culture of Merit: Nobility, Royal Service, and the Making of Absolute Monarchy in France, 1600–1789* (Ann Arbor, 1996).
18. *La noblesse considerée sous ses divers rapports dans les Assemblées générales et particulières de la Nation* (Paris, 1788), 16.
19. On the socio-ethical content of status words see Clive S. Lewis, *Studies in Words* (Cambridge, 1967), 21–3.
20. All of these quotations are cited by Antony Black, *Guilds and Civil Society in European Political Thought from the Twelfth Century to the Present* (Ithaca, NY, 1984), 141, 142.
21. Cited by Richard Jackson, *Vive le Roi! A History of the French Coronation from Charles V to Charles X* (Chapel Hill, NC, 1984), 119–20.
22. Montesquieu, *Esprit des Lois*, 6. 1.
23. Lebret, officer of the *cour des aides* of Rouen in the 1590s, cited by Michael Kwass, *Privilege and the Politics of Taxation in Eighteenth-Century France* (Cambridge, 2000), 27.
24. Henri Weber, *La Compagnie française des Indes, 1605–1875* (Paris, 1904), 210–13; Durand, *Fermiers généraux*, 49.
25. See Montesquieu's comment in *Esprit des Lois*, 6. 1, on how difference in rank and birth 'is frequently attended with distinctions in the nature of property', including primogeniture. 'Each sort of goods is subject to particular rules, which must be complied with in the disposal of them.' Rules governing status, in other words, impinged on the working of the market. On primogeniture see Michael L. Bush, *Noble Privilege* (New York, 1983), 140–2.

26. Koenraad W. Swart, *Sale of Offices in the Seventeenth Century* (The Hague, 1949).
27. Roland Mousnier, *La Vénalité des offices sous Henri VI et Louis XIII* (Paris, 1971); William Doyle, *Venality: The Sale of Offices in Eighteenth-Century France* (Oxford, 1996).
28. David D. Bien, 'Officers, Corps and a System of State Credit', in Baker (ed.), *Political Culture of the Old Regime*, 87–114.
29. Ralph E. Giesey, 'Rules of Inheritance and Strategies of Mobility in Prerevolutionary France', *American Historical Review*, 82 (1977), 284.
30. William Doyle, *The Parlement of Bordeaux and the End of the Old Regime, 1771–1790* (New York, 1974), 42.
31. Taylor, 'Noncapitalist Wealth', 478.
32. David D. Bien, 'Les Sécretaires du Roi: Absolutism, Corps and Privilege under the Ancien Régime', in Ernst Hinrichs, Eberhard Schmitt, and Rudolf Vierhaus (eds.), *Vom Ancien Regime zur Französischen Revolution: Forschungen und Perspektiven* (Göttingen, 1978), 153–86.
33. John F. Bosher, *French Finances, 1770–1795: From Business to Bureaucracy* (Cambridge, 1970).
34. David Bien, 'La Réaction aristocratique avant 1789', 514; See also Michael Fitzsimmons, 'New Light on the Aristocratic Reaction in France', *French History*, 10 (1996), 425, 427.
35. J. G. A. Pocock makes interesting observations on the possessive nature of Roman jurisprudence in 'The Idea of Citizenship since Classical Times', in Gershon Shafir (ed.), *The Citizenship Debates: A Reader* (Minneapolis, 1998), 31–41.
36. Cited by Marcel Reinhard, 'Elite et noblesse dans la seconde moitié du xviiie siècle', *Revue d'Histoire Moderne et Contemporaine*, 3 (1956), 29.
37. Mousnier, quoting either Louis-Nicolas-Henri Chérin (1784) or P. J. J. G. Guyot (1788) in *The Institutions of France under the Absolute Monarchy*, i. 121.
38. Doyle, *Venality*, 269.
39. *Archives parlementaires, première* série (Librairie Administrative de P. Dupont, 1787–99), ii. 12, art. 12; iii. 677; vi. 57, art. 17; and *Réflexions d'un citoyen de Franche-Comté sur les privilèges et immunités de la noblesse* (n.pl., 1789). See also Gail Bossenga, 'Monarchy, Status, *Corps*: Roots of Modern Citizenship in the Old Regime', in Robert Schwarz and Robert Schneider (eds.), *Tocqueville and Beyond: Essays on the Old Regime in Honor of David Bien* (Delaware, 2003), 127–54.
40. Colin Jones, 'Bourgeois Revolution Revivified: 1789 and Social Change', in Colin Lucas (ed.), *Rewriting the French Revolution* (Oxford, 1991), 96.
41. J. Michael Hayden and Malcolm R. Greenshields, *Six Hundred Years of Reform: Bishops and the French Church, 1190–1789* (Montreal, 2005), 171.
42. George T. Matthews, *The Royal General Farms in Eighteenth-Century France* (New York, 1958), 216.
43. Toby Gelfand, 'A "Monarchical Profession" in the Old Regime: Surgeons, Ordinary Practitioners, and Medical Professionalization in Eighteenth-Century France', in Gerald Geison (ed.), *Professions and the French State, 1700–1900* (Philadelphia, 1984), 162; Ken Alder, *Engineering the Revolution: Arms and Enlightenment in France, 1763–1815* (Princeton, 1997), 65–75.
44. Some works on the consumer revolution include Annick Pardailhé-Galabrun, *The Birth of Intimacy: Privacy and Domestic Life in Early Modern Paris*, tr. Jocelyn Phelps (Philadelphia, 1991); Daniel Roche, *The People of Paris: An Essay on Popular Culture in the Eighteenth Century*, tr. Marie Evans and Gwynne Lewis (Berkeley, Calif., 1987); Daniel

Roche, *Histoire des chose banales: Naissance de la consommation, xviie–xviiie siècles* (Paris, 1988); Cissie Fairchilds, 'The Production and Marketing of Populuxe Goods in Eighteenth-Century Paris', in John Brewer and Roy Porter (eds.), *Consumption and the World of Goods* (London, 1993), 228–48; Jones, 'Bourgeois Revolution Revivified'; Jan de Vries, 'The Industrial Revolution and the Industrious Revolution', *Journal of Economic History*, 54 (June 1994), 249–70; and Neil McKendrick, John Brewer, and J. H. Plumb, *The Birth of a Consumer Society: The Commercialization of Eighteenth-Century England* (Bloomington, Ind., 1982).

45. Robert Forster, *The House of Saulx-Tavanes: Versailles and Burgundy, 1700–1830* (Baltimore, Md., 1971), 126.
46. Tocqueville, *The Old Regime and the Revolution*, bk. ii, ch. 5.
47. Douglass C. North and Barry R. Weingast, 'Constitutions and Commitment: The Evolution of Institutions Governing Public Choice in Seventeenth-Century England', *Journal of Economic History*, 49 (1989), 803–32; Barry Weingast, 'The Political Foundations of Limited Government: Parliament and Sovereign Debt in 17th and 18th Century England', in John Drobak and John Nye (eds.), *Frontiers of the New Institutional Economics* (London: Harcourt Brace, 1997); David Stasavage, *Public Debt and the Birth of the Democratic State: France and Great Britain, 1688–1789* (Cambridge, 2003).
48. On the growth of provincial credit see William Beik, *Absolutism and Society in Seventeenth-Century France* (Cambridge, 1985), 273–5; James Collins, *Classes, Estates and Order in Early Modern Brittany* (Cambridge, 1994); Julian Swann, *Provincial Power and Absolute Monarchy: The Estates General of Burgundy, 1661–1790* (Cambridge, 2003), 176–88; Jean-Laurent Rosenthal and Mark Potter, 'Politics and Public Finance in France: The Estates of Burgundy, 1660–1790', *Journal of Interdisciplinary History*, 27 (1997), 577–612; Marie-Laure Legay, 'Le Crédit des provinces au secours de l'État: Les Emprunts des états provinciaux pour le compte du roi (France xviiie siècle)', in *Pourvoir les finances en province sous l'Ancien Régime, Actes de la journeée d'études du 9 décembre 1999* (Paris, 2001). On solidification of corporate borrowing and property rights of officeholders see Bien, 'Officers, Corps and a System of State Credit'; Mark Potter, 'Good Offices: Intermediation by Corporate Bodies in Early Modern French Public Finance', *Journal of Economic History*, 60 (Sept. 2000), 606–7, and his *Corps and Clienteles: Public Finance and Political Change in France, 1688–1715* (Burlington, Vt., 2003).
49. Cited in Baker, *Readings in Western Civilization*, 98.
50. *Social Contract*, bk. ii, ch. 1.
51. Jürgen Habermas, *The Structural Transformation of the Public Sphere: An Inquiry into a Category of Bourgeois Society*, tr. Thomas Burger and Frederick Lawrence (Cambridge, Mass., 1989).
52. Sarah Maza, *Private Lives and Public Affairs: The Causes Célèbres of Prerevolutionary France* (Berkeley, Calif., 1993), 19–67; David Bell, 'The "Public Sphere", the State and the World of Law in Eighteenth-Century France', *French Historical Studies*, 17 (1992), 912–34.
53. Denis Richet, *La France moderne: L'Esprit des institutions* (Paris, 1973), 144–6, 148–50.
54. Michael Sonenscher, *Work and Wages: Natural Law, Politics, and the Eighteenth-Century French Trades* (Cambridge, 1989), 44, quoted by Clare Haru Crowston, *Fabricating Women: The Seamstresses of Old Regime France, 1675–1791* (Durham, NC, 2001), 224. On women and guilds see also Daryl Hafter, *Women at Work in Preindustrial France* (University Park, Pa., 2007) and her edited collection, *European Women and Preindustrial Craft* (Bloomington, Ind., 1995); Carol Loats, 'Gender, Guilds and Work Identity:

Perspectives from Sixteenth-Century Paris', *French Historical Studies*, 20 (1997), 15–30; Judith G. Coffin, 'Gender and the Guild Order: The Garment Trades in Eighteenth-Century Paris', *Journal of Economic History*, 54 (1994), 768–93; and the essays in 'Métiers, Corporations, Syndicalismes', a special issue of *Clio, Histoire, Femmes et Sociétés*, 3 (1996).

55. Jonathan Dewald and Liana Vardi, 'The Peasantries of France, 1400–1789', in Tom Scott (ed.), *The Peasantries of Europe From the Fourteenth to the Eighteenth Centuries* (New York, 1998), 43; Michael Sonenscher, 'Journeymen, the Courts and the French Trades, 1781–90', *Past and Present*, 114 (1987), 90.
56. Peter Riesenberg, *Citizenship in the Western Tradition: Plato to Rousseau* (Chapel Hill, NC, 1992), 242.
57. *Noble Privilege*, 210.
58. David D. Bien, 'Old Regime Origins of Democratic Liberty', in Dale Van Kley (ed.), *The French Idea of Freedom: the Old Regime and the Declaration of Rights of 1789* (Stanford, Calif., 1994), 71.
59. For the debate on universal taxation see Michael Kwass, *Privilege and the Politics of Taxation in Eighteenth-Century France* (Cambridge, 2000).
60. Chauvelin, *Examen impartial des immunités ecclésiastiques contenant les maximes du droit public et les faits historiques qui y ont rapport* (London, 1751), 16; Guillaume François Le Trosne, *De l'administration provinciale* (Basle, 1779), 501.
61. Williams Rogers Brubaker, 'The French Revolution and the Invention of Citizenship', *French Politics and Society*, 7 (Summer 1989), 39. Brubaker states that the clash between the anti-corporate centralizing state and 'archaic privilege-based' participatory municipal citizenship was critical to the formation of modern citizenship. In emphasizing municipal citizenship, however, he ignores the importance of other corporate bodies with participatory features.
62. Marissa Linton, *The Politics of Virtue in Enlightenment France* (New York, 2001). On the extension of honour to simple privates see André Corvisier, 'La Mort du soldat depuis la fin du moyen âge', *Revue Historique*, 254 (1975), 21; on the nationalization of honour within the nobility see Jay Smith, *Nobility Reimagined: The Patriotic Nation in Eighteenth-Century France* (Ithaca, NY, 2005), esp. chs. 5 and 6.
63. Saint-Lambert, cited by John Pappas, 'La Campagne des philosophes contre l'honneur', *Studies on Voltaire and the Eighteenth Century*, 205 (1982), 43.
64. Pierre Rétat, 'The Evolution of the Citizen from the Ancien Régime to the Revolution', in R. Waldinger, P. Dawson, and I. Woloch (eds.), *The French Revolution and the Meaning of Citizenship* (Westport, Conn., 1993), 13.
65. Smith, *Nobility Reimagined*, 201.
66. ARTFL *Encyclopédie*, http://artfl.uchicago.edu, 'Citoyen', iii. 489.
67. Brubaker, 'Invention of Citizenship', 38. See also Olivier Krafft, 'Les Classes sociales à Genève et la notion de citoyen', in *Jean-Jacques Rousseau et son œuvre: Problèmes et recherches* (Paris, 1963), 219–27. In a footnote to bk i, ch. 6, of the *Contract Social* Rousseau criticizes the French first for equating the term *citoyen* with that of *bourgeoisie* and then for making them both 'designate social status and not legal right'. On the traditions of natural law and civic humanism in Rousseau see Keith Michael Baker, 'Transformations of Classical Republicanism in Eighteenth-Century France', *Journal of Modern History*, 73 (Mar. 2001), 32–53. On urban, corporate contexts of citizenship see also Marc Boon and Maarten Prak (eds.), *Statuts individuels, statuts corporatifs et statuts judiciaires dans les*

ville europèenes (moyen âge et temps modernes): Individual, corporate and judicial status in European Cities. Proceedings of the Colloquium Ghent, October 12th–14th 1995 (Leuven and Apeldoorn, 1995).

68. Cited in Keith Michael Baker (ed.), *The Old Regime and the French Revolution*, vol. vii of *University of Chicago Readings in Western Civilization* (Chicago, 1987), 119.
69. In its well-known remonstrance against suppressing the guilds, 12 Mar. 1776, the Parlement of Paris said that the 'body of the nation' was composed of 'as many different bodies (*corps*) as there are different Estates in the kingdom...which can be regarded as links in a great chain, the first link of which is in the hands of Your Majesty'. Ibid. 122–3.

Bibliography

Bien, David D., 'Officers, Corps and a System of State Credit', in Keith Michael Baker (ed.), *The French Revolution and the Creation of Modern Political Culture*, i. *The Political Culture of the Old Regime* (Oxford, 1987), 89–114.

Black, Antony, *Guilds and Civil Society in European Political Thought from the Twelfth Century to the Present* (Ithaca, NY, 1984).

Bossenga, Gail, *The Politics of Privilege: Old Regime and Revolution in Lille* (Cambridge, 1991).

Bush, Michael L. (ed.), *Social Orders and Social Classes in Europe since 1500: Studies in Social Stratification* (London, 1992).

Cerutti, Simona, *La Ville et les métiers: Naissance d'un langage corporatif (Turin xviie–xviiie siècles)* (Paris, 1990).

Coornaert, Emile, *Les Corporations en France avant 1789* (Paris, 1941).

Doyle, William, *Venality: The Sale of Offices in Eighteenth-Century France* (Oxford, 1995).

Jouanna, Arlette, *Ordre social: Mythes et hiérarchies dans la France du xvie siècle* (Paris, 1977).

Jones, Colin, 'Bourgeois Revolution Revivified: 1789 and Social Change', in Colin Lucas (ed.), *Rewriting the French Revolution* (Oxford, 1991), 69–118.

Labrousse, Ernest, and Roche, Daniel (eds.), *Ordres et classes: Colloque d'histoire sociale, Saint Cloud, 24–25 mai 1967* (Paris, 1973).

Lousse, Emile, *La Société d'ancien régime: Organisation et représentation corporatives* (Louvain, 1943).

Mousnier, Roland, *Social Hierarchies, 1450 to the Present*, tr. Peter Evans (New York, 1973).

Olivier-Martin, François, *L'Organisation corporative de la France d'Ancien Régime* (Paris, 1938).

Revel, Jacques, 'Les Corps et communautés', in Keith Michael Baker (ed.), *The French Revolution and the Creation of Modern Political Culture*, i. *The Political Culture of the Old Regime* (Oxford, 1987), 225–42.

Sewell, William H., Jr., *Work and Revolution in France: The Language of Labor from the Old Regime to 1848* (Cambridge, 1980).

CHAPTER 10

POVERTY

ALAN FORREST

POVERTY was an endemic condition across Europe from the later middle ages until the end of the eighteenth century. It was the most intractable of the social problems which beset Europeans and offered a constant rebuke to monarchs and church leaders alike, proving almost as difficult to define as it was impossible to cure. This was an age before social science or social medicine, when there were still no agreed definitions of what constituted poverty, no clear sense of who was and was not poor; and there was little understanding of basic levels of subsistence in terms of protein or diet. Nor were there serious attempts before the eighteenth century to count the poor, or to assess the extent and pervasiveness of poverty. This is partly a question of social and religious attitudes. Poor relief was seen as a matter for the church and for clerical charity. The assumption that poverty was a problem for governments to legislate on still lay in the future, while the almost obsessive concern with statistics which characterizes modern government began only during the French revolutionary and Napoleonic period.[1] Before then, governments had little interest in trying to enumerate the poor, and where lists do survive, they are mostly limited to a single town or parish. The exceptions are few and, like Gregory King's overview of poverty in England in 1688, notoriously unreliable.[2]

IDENTIFYING THE POOR

The poor in early modern Europe were not a firmly defined category of people, clearly delineated from the rest of society. A minority, it is true, fell into the category of the 'structurally poor', those incapable of earning a living because of poor health, old age, or physical handicap; but most poverty was contingent, a condition that engulfed peasant and labouring families when harvests failed, when taxes fell due, illness and disease struck, or breadwinners were left without work; it was a condition that would blight the lives of a majority of the working population at one time or another. Most villages had a hard core of structurally poor—largely widows and the old, and those men who were sick, injured, or physically unable to do hard agricultural work.[3] Towns, too, were home to sizeable numbers of the structurally poor, artisans and day-labourers in the main, and here the problem was intensified by the lack of a sense of local community or the family support system that so often protected the weakest members of rural society. Those who worked in the less skilled trades or earned their livelihood through physical labour were always most at risk. In Lyon, for instance, those in receipt of charity on the eve of the French Revolution were predominantly textile workers, tradesmen, carters, and domestic servants.[4]

In many parts of Europe life was a constant struggle to get by, to feed an extra arrival in the family, to survive until the new harvest came in, or to find casual labour until the next sowing season. The death of a wage-earner and the incorporation of a son in the army were circumstances that could reduce whole families to destitution. Even normal times were hard. The living conditions of working families were often miserable, with millions condemned to survive in dank, humid, overcrowded conditions where the air was fetid and disease took hold easily. Poverty, whether in towns or in the countryside, bred ill-health, which left the poor vulnerable to the ravages of infection and plague. Between the Black Death in 1348 and the beginning of the eighteenth century, it is estimated that there were visitations of plague in some of the larger European towns every ten or fifteen years, with the most deadly outbreaks carrying off as many as half the population, the toll always disproportionately heavy in the most populous quarters.[5] Poor diet and inadequate nourishment over a protracted period were responsible for such heavy death tolls during major epidemics; it is noticeable, indeed, that in places where people ate more fats and animal proteins—as in the stock-farming and fishery areas of the Dutch coastline—even the Black Death could be held in check.[6] Poverty and disease, as all Europe knew, were intimate bedfellows.

The sufferings resulting from poverty may have been constant in early modern Europe, but its causes changed according to economic circumstances. The Black Death in 1348, and the agrarian depression that followed, had decimated the population of many parts of Europe, a demographic disaster from which it took more than a century to recover. This recovery was hindered by cyclical famines and regular visitations of plague and typhus. A further threat was posed by war, especially such devastating conflicts as the Wars of Religion in France and the Thirty Years War across much of German central Europe. War caused the untimely deaths of young men, of course, distorting the balance of the population and leaving women to work the farms and children without fathers. But the effects were not restricted to young men. Whole communities were impoverished by continued levies and requisitions, while disease was spread to civilians by passing armies. The Thirty Years War provides dramatic instances of such losses. During the 1630s, for example, Bavaria is reckoned to have lost between 30 and 50 per cent of its population; Pomerania around 40 per cent; Lorraine 60 per cent; and Württemberg 75 per cent, both as a result of the war itself and of the outbreak of plague that followed.[7] The armies also devastated the lands they passed through, stripping the fields of grain and making it impossible for new crops to be planted. In absolute terms the population of Germany fell from over 15 million in 1620 to only 10 million in 1650, and the age and geographical distribution of that population were dramatically altered.[8] Those communities that were caught in the cross-fire of war recovered only slowly.

But most did recover, and from the sixteenth century most parts of Europe experienced a sustained period of demographic growth. Yet this too had damaging side-effects. The increased numbers of consumers put severe pressure on food supplies and other essential resources, resulting in inflated prices and further misery for the most vulnerable groups in society. Nor did the rise in population bring a commensurate increase in the agricultural labour force, or in grain production. These were years of rapid social and economic development throughout much of Europe, especially in the more temperate north. Towns and commerce expanded, regional markets developed, and more communities became integrated into the market economy. There was a significant change, too, in the balance between rural and urban populations, with more and more country people, especially the young, migrating to the towns in search of work and what they hoped would be greater prosperity. At the same time the settlement of overseas territories and the genesis of European empires offered new economic prospects, but also posed new dangers for the living standards of the poor. In some regions substantial opportunities were offered by new industrial developments, though these, too, often led to recession and to the threat of impoverishment elsewhere. A period of rapid economic change produced losers as well as winners.

Poverty and the Economy

Economic prosperity was cyclical, with periods of economic growth giving way to recession and further poverty. During the early modern period, for instance, there were devastating famines and mortality crises at regular intervals, most notably in the 1520s, 1590s, 1630s, 1640s, 1650s, 1690s, 1710s, 1720s, and again in 1764–6; and at such moments peasant families would flee the countryside to seek charity elsewhere.[9] The years from around 1630 to 1750 were particularly marked by economic uncertainty and recurrent periods of depression, which hit the poor especially hard because they were also years of significant economic restructuring. Destructive wars in the late seventeenth and early eighteenth centuries played a part here; but there were more structural causes, too. The drift to the towns had caused rural depopulation and reduced levels of agricultural production in many parts of Europe, while the new merchant elites paid low wages which failed to keep up with basic food prices. Industrial workers often had little recourse against summary dismissal, and in the growing urban centres their ability to eat and to find shelter was dependent on their capacity to earn a basic wage. The loss of their job risked condemning them to poverty, begging, and petty crime. In Britain, France, and the northern German states much spinning and weaving was outsourced to the countryside, causing unemployment among journeymen and placing further strains on agrarian production. It was not until the second half of the eighteenth century, with the expansion of overseas trade, wealth flowing in from the colonies, and the beginnings of an agrarian revolution in parts of northern Europe, that years of relative prosperity could return.[10] In Britain especially, changes in farming methods produced high-yielding fodder crops on a substantial scale, resulting in a reduction in land left fallow and a real intensification of agricultural production.[11]

But that prosperity was unevenly distributed, and it did not necessarily bring benefits to the poorest in society. With industrial development came new working methods and a workforce of day labourers who enjoyed little or no security. In England, while economic changes provided opportunities for members of the professions and offered upward mobility for many of the 'middling sort', many rural husbandmen were transformed into day labourers, and journeymen-artisans in the towns became depressed into the ranks of wage labour. This in turn produced poverty of a new kind that caused dismay among contemporaries, and contributed to the creation of what Keith Wrightson describes as 'a permanent proletariat'.[12] The change was not restricted to England alone, or to the most advanced industrial economies. In Antwerp, Catharina Lis links commercial resurgence in the second half of the eighteenth century with new levels of impoverishment, as capital investment at an accelerated pace brought with it 'the proletarianization of the majority of craftsmen and the disintegration of the guild system'. Old skills were rendered valueless, and labour became increasingly casual, to be hired and fired at will. For the fortunate few these were years of unparalleled prosperity and opportunity, but for the poor of the city they spelt economic disruption and an accompanying insecurity.[13]

Where the economy remained primarily agricultural, as it did in Russia and much of eastern and central Europe, the age-old problems of peasant society remained, with a denial of personal freedom, few rights in law, and an oppressive regime of seigneurial privileges and serfdom. In much of continental Europe social rank was still determined by privilege, with society divided into legal estates or orders. The First and Second Estates, the clergy and the nobility, were distinguished by the privileges they enjoyed, the privileges to which the functions of praying or fighting on behalf of the people gave them entitlement. The Third Estate, on the other hand, enjoyed no corporate rights, no freedoms or liberties, no tax remission. They formed the vast majority of the population, and their role was to till the soil and provide for the material needs of others. The degree of misery they endured was shown by the large number of beggars, vagabonds, and runaways that were a feature of all the servile lands, and their numbers were only inflated by the severe demographic pressures created during the seventeenth and eighteenth centuries.[14]

In most of western Europe the rigid division into estates became more blurred as the power of commerce increased and states resorted to a new fiscal realism. Status became increasingly linked to material wealth, leaving those without money as the least powerful and least regarded members of society. Throughout Europe peasants struggled to produce enough to feed their families, or to create the modest surpluses they needed if they were to benefit from the opportunities of the market. They did not share in the new prosperity any more than did manual workers and the unskilled. In most of Germany, for instance, much of the period between the Peace of Westphalia in 1648 and the revolutionary and Napoleonic Wars was a desperate struggle to re-establish the agricultural conditions and production levels that had been seen before the Thirty Years War. The area of land under cultivation was reduced, peasant holdings operating at a marginal profit in good years, and accumulating debt in bad. To make things worse, legal restrictions made it well-nigh impossible to leave the land, and credit was often unobtainable.[15] Wealth became concentrated in the hands of the few, and the gulf between rich and poor became more extreme. Thus while landowners, merchants, bankers, and industrialists might reap huge rewards from the opportunities that were on offer, the mass of the population was denied any chance to share in the riches. European society became more polarized, more sharply stratified, and more people faced the threat of insecurity and the degradation occasioned by poverty.[16]

By the second half of the eighteenth century European states showed greater willingness to intervene in periods of dearth and famine through the purchase and distribution of grain supplies, but these were exceptional measures, to be taken only in the most critical circumstances or when officials were faced with the threat of riot. More commonly the poor—even in more advanced commercial societies like Britain and France—were left to their own devices. How did they survive? Many, it is clear, struggled to do so, their poor diet and chronic undernourishment destroying their health and condemning them to a premature grave. This is reflected in the persistently high mortality figures amongst the relatively young. Death rates only began to fall after around 1740, while infant mortality among the poorest members of society remained stubbornly high until late in the century: Sweden before 1750 was recording rates of 20–22 per cent during the first year of life.[17] In the Sologne in France, an area marked by widespread rural poverty, the corresponding figure was around one-third, while deaths in later childhood and adolescence culled each succeeding generation before the age of majority. Moreover, these figures were getting worse across the eighteenth century. Whereas in 1680 53 per cent of the inhabitants of Sennely-en-Sologne survived beyond the age of 20, by 1779 the percentage of the townspeople reaching adulthood had fallen to 38 per cent.[18]

Robert Schwartz has used the unusually full hospital registers of Bayeux and Caen to construct what he terms a 'life cycle of impoverishment' in the eighteenth century and to identify those age-groups who were most in need of assistance. Unsurprisingly the very young figure prominently, babies and infants who were vulnerable to disease and whom their parents often could not afford to nourish. Poverty is an important factor in the rise of child abandonment in the later eighteenth century: during the 1770s in France alone some 40,000 babies were left every year on the steps of churches or hospitals, or were left for others to find and for the authorities to care for.[19] Children under the age of 14 formed nearly 50 per cent of those hospitalized in Lower Normandy in the late 1720s, with a strikingly higher proportion of boys than girls figuring on the rolls. French society held different attitudes towards boys and girls, and boys experienced hardship at an earlier age, perhaps because they were sent out to work earlier and were less protected in childhood than girls. On the other hand, among adults women strongly outnumber men in the registers, reflecting their greater life expectancy, but also the lower level of women's wages, and the vulnerability of mothers after childbirth, when many had no job to return to. Few men between 20 and 50 were interned. The other major group among the country's poor were the old of both sexes, often left without any means of support once they were no longer able to perform hard manual labour.[20]

People seldom died of malnutrition alone, but poor diet so weakened their constitutions that they became vulnerable to every disease that threatened; their cramped and filthy houses bred germs, while the damp and fetid conditions in which they worked took a dreadful toll on their health and strength. Smallpox and pleurisy were major killers in the countryside.[21] In years when harvests failed the numbers of deaths grew inexorably, with the old and the very young the most at risk. It was only in the later years of the eighteenth and across the nineteenth centuries that diet and sanitation started to improve, and with them these very high death rates began to decline. The substantial population growth that characterized most of Europe in the nineteenth century was due more to this fall in the death rate than to any rise in the birth rate, and hence to an improvement in the nutrition and public health of the poor.

An Economy of Makeshifts

In seventeenth- and eighteenth-century Europe survival was not simply a matter of luck. It demanded cunning and resourcefulness, and resort to an 'economy of makeshifts', the often desperate measures that sustained the poorest classes of society.[22] For the poor cannot be dismissed as helpless victims: they had to take conscious decisions and adopt survival strategies. In times of shortage many rural communities could not find the bread and other staples needed if they were to feed their inhabitants through the lean months until the new harvest was brought in. Prices soared as bread became scarce, leaving the poor, those without a surplus or without money to spend, facing the spectre of starvation. A new baby, an extra mouth to feed, could spell disaster for the family economy; while those too old or too sick to work might pose a threat to the sustainability of the whole family unit. Some found succour with relatives or threw themselves on the mercy of the parish priest, who would control what limited funds were available for poor relief. Others delayed marriage or practised birth control as ways of keeping down consumption and avoiding costs that would drive them into pauperism.[23] Others again looked to the local hospice or hospital, which in many country areas was more concerned to keep the frail and elderly alive than to offer cures for illness. In Aix-en-Provence, Cissie Fairchilds has shown that around 20 per cent of the population were in receipt of some form of charity in the seventeenth and eighteenth centuries.[24] But in times of dearth or extreme cold there was rarely enough provision: hospitals became overcrowded, food and firewood were scarce, and whole villages were incapable of sustaining their inhabitants. Some had to leave so that the remainder could share the limited resources available.

Temporary or seasonal migration was seen as a necessity in many parts of rural Europe, especially in mountainous areas where the soil was poor and where survival depended on having a trade outside agriculture, a trade that could be plied elsewhere until the new harvest. There was a long tradition of migration in many parts of Europe, notably from communities in the Alps, the Apennines, and the Pyrenees. In the Auvergne, for example, there were many villages where all the young and able-bodied workers left home during the winter months to find work and income in more prosperous regions. Some drifted south to the Midi to harvest grapes or chestnuts or olives, each additional crop serving to extend their agricultural year by a few precious weeks. Others left their villages each year for the towns of the east and the north, finding work as sawyers and builders' labourers, masons and flax-combers, pedlars and secondhand-clothes dealers. At the end of the season they might return home with a little money; but just as importantly, they had not been there when the village's food stocks were at their lowest and the price of staples at its peak. It was crucial that they did, as their absence meant that their wives and children could find enough to eat and the community survive for a further year.[25] The money they brought back to the village also allowed them to maintain a degree of respectability and avoid the social stigma attached to those who were reduced to begging or vagrancy.

Some, of course, found much to attract them in the towns they wintered in, not least the chance to earn some money of their own, to enjoy some independence, to experience a limited amount of leisure time. Increasing numbers chose to migrate permanently, and became first-generation townsmen in their own right. And with the colonial expansion of the eighteenth century some left their home country altogether. France sent settlers to Quebec and the Caribbean in the eighteenth century, and Spain and Portugal to Latin America. From northern Europe large numbers of English, Scots, Irish, Germans, and Scandinavians chose to exchange poverty in Europe for a new life in North America.[26]

Perceptions of the Poor

The stigma attached to poverty was a constant threat, since many of the expedients open to the poor were viewed with alarm and hostility by sections of the public. Attitudes to begging varied widely according to the perception of the beggar. The very old and the very young elicited most sympathy, and they were always more likely to be rewarded with alms or a donation from the poor box at the parish church. Their cries were piteous, and their need evident; besides, they came close to the Christian image of the suffering children of Jesus to whom one had a duty of care. Not all, however, were so fortunate, and in times of general shortage not all could hope even for a few coins or a hunk of bread. Women begging on street corners or outside church doors had long understood that a brood of ragged children were a useful accompaniment, their presence likely to encourage the charitable impulse of passers-by; where they had none of their own, it was common practice to borrow or hire the children of others to create greater visual impact and augment the spectacle of suffering. The fit and able-bodied, those who found it hardest to soften the hearts of strangers, were often forced to turn to more desperate ploys in order to survive. Some dressed in their most ragged clothes to exaggerate the depths of their poverty. Others, true to centuries-old traditions across Europe, invented sores and injuries to inspire sympathy or arouse fear of infection. Deceit in its many forms became part of the beggar's armoury, a necessary expedient if he was to win the sympathy needed for survival.

Others did more than elicit sympathy. As shortages became more pressing, many gave in to the temptations of crime to keep themselves alive, using threats of physical violence to extract food and money from unwilling householders, grouping themselves into bands, descending on lonely farms after sunset, and threatening to destroy crops, maim animals, or burn down barns if alms were denied them. Hayricks were destroyed, and in some regions of Europe—like Picardy in northern France—gangs attacked horses in the fields, hacking at their legs with axes to render them useless for ploughing. In coastal regions men joined bands of smugglers to earn a little money, and when thefts were reported beggars and vagrants were always among the prime suspects. Among women a high percentage turned to prostitution, which often led them to associate with criminals of other kinds. Hence when times got desperate there was little to distinguish beggars from bandits in the minds of many country people.[27] This had unavoidable consequences for the ways in which the poor were perceived. Poverty was seen by many as a moral failing, rather than as the consequence of economic misfortune. In some Protestant cultures, where material well-being was equated with divine grace and taken as evidence of personal virtue, it was only too easy to associate poverty and godlessness. In 1524 the Nuremberg artist Barthel Behaim identified twelve different sorts of beggars and ascribed reasons for their descent into poverty. Eleven of them were depicted as deviants whose fall from grace resulted from their own actions, their fecklessness and moral failings.[28]

The principal change in Europeans' perception of the poor came during the eighteenth century, with the development of a more harsh and repressive culture. The old remedy of handing out alms to beggars on the street corner became less prevalent in a society where poverty was increasingly equated with violence and deviance, and where misery and crime were identified in many people's minds. Handing over money indiscriminately might only increase drunkenness and disorder, and encourage the recipient to expect alms and lose any desire to work. The development of state institutions during the seventeenth century was accompanied by a desire to regulate and control the poor, to increase the policing of fairs and markets, to insist that those travelling between towns must carry papers or passports, and to impose restrictions on those in receipt of charity. This was the intention of the English Act of Settlement of 1662, for instance, which forced migrant workers to carry personal papers at all times and refused them any official aid unless they returned to their parish of origin. Prussia adopted very similar measures in the years up to 1700.[29]

The imperative to control and regulate was spreading across Europe; but much of that regulation remained in the hands of local authorities. What was still largely lacking until the following century were the administrative and policing structures that would make it possible to regulate the poor on a national scale.

Religion and the Care of the Poor

The poor were visible, of course, whether trudging along country roads during their seasonal migration or congregating at markets or outside churches, begging for alms or for food for their children. Yet in most European societies governments had adopted a minimalist role, except when dearth threatened whole regions or when the presence of large numbers of beggars posed a threat to public health. In such circumstances kings and princes might make some finance available to staunch the crisis or avert the risk to public order. In Prussia Frederick William I and Frederick II would remit taxes or distribute free seed from government warehouses to needy peasants when there was a serious risk of agricultural failure.[30] In France summer snows and hail, flash floods, and other freak weather conditions often triggered a response from Versailles; indeed, it is striking how often the limited sums voted for poor relief by central government were channelled to areas hit by exceptional storms or flooding.[31] But in normal times the poor were largely left to the conscience of the public, especially in Catholic Europe, where decrees and laws frequently linked the public interest to charitable instinct and Christian duty. In the words of the Great Council of Venice in 1545, piety and improvement were inalienably linked. 'Finding a means to relieve beggars and the shamefaced poor in this city in their calamities is not only laudable, pious and pleasing to our Lord God, but also honourable and healthy for our State because of the diseases which on many occasions have resulted.'[32] The relief of poverty, in other words, was dependent on the perception and the ideology of the giver, of the rich, of respectable society; and it is through their eyes, not those of the poor themselves, that poverty was generally viewed and need assessed. Besides, the aim underlying most schemes for poor relief was the preservation of the existing social and political order, together with the maintenance of a moral society that would help to ensure the salvation of the greatest number of souls.[33] And that in turn implied greater emphasis on control and punishment.

New ideas originating in the Protestant Reformation, the Catholic Counter-Reformation, and the Enlightenment would in different ways affect men's perceptions of poverty and of the poor. This explains why descriptions of poverty and remedies for begging and vagrancy changed markedly between the early sixteenth and the eighteenth century, a change that was as evident in Protestant northern Europe, more open to humanist ideas and more given to legislate for the poor, as it was in the Catholic south.[34] These changes stemmed mainly from the growth of commercial markets, and the growing appreciation that poverty had its roots in the workings of the economy. Prayer and Christian notions of charity came to be seen as less and less adequate to resolve a problem that originated in economic failure, so that by the fifteenth century even the charity provided by the church was appreciated more for its social utility than for its role in absolving sin. In testaments and in the targets of charitable giving there was a greater insistence on the public good, and gifts were showered on hospitals, hospices, civic almshouses, and confraternities, all of which rationed and directed charity towards those seen as most needy. New religious orders were founded which ministered directly to the poor—most notably, perhaps, the Capuchins—and hospitals were opened to care for the sick and aged. In France Saint Vincent-de-Paul founded the Daughters of Charity, a community of nursing sisters who, during the seventeenth and eighteenth centuries, provided care to the sick and dying in hospitals across the country and offered succour to the poor. They also, as Colin Jones has shown, had a significant role as proponents of medical care in institutions which had often limited their role to easing pain and suffering.[35]

These developments suggest a new desire on the part of the authorities to control and regulate the poor, to assess the degree of need, and to ration alms. Like the state, the Catholic Church hesitated to encourage almsgiving to the non-domiciled poor, whose conduct was unregulated, and who were now deemed to constitute a menace to society. In France, Italy, Spain, and throughout the Catholic Mediterranean the same tendency is to be observed. In the words of a recent study of Portugal, 'the Counter-Reformation accompanied aid with a preoccupation with suppressing deviant behaviour, combining charity to the poor with a desire to save their souls'.[36] There was an increased desire to categorize the poor, to distinguish between the 'deserving poor', who were the rightful recipients of charity, and the 'undeserving', those who could work but chose not to do so, those who were a burden on society and had no claim on public sympathy.

But how far, one may legitimately ask, did such changes have their roots in religion? If Counter-Reformation ideologies were developed to combat supposedly more rational and modern ideas that had emerged in Protestant countries, can it really be shown that things were better managed or explained in northern Europe, or that the changes in charitable provision were fundamentally religious in inspiration? There is certainly evidence of rapid implantation of charities and relief agencies throughout northern Germany, Holland, and Scandinavia, a concern to assuage poverty and cure sickness which some are wont to link to Protestant rationalism. Ole Peter Grell puts the case concisely. Unlike Catholics, Protestants traditionally spent little on the dead and their place in the afterlife. Hence, he suggests, 'because Protestant charity became solely a Christian obligation towards the Christian Commonwealth, it is focused on the living and on the present as opposed to the hereafter'.[37] He sees religion as lying at the heart of more rational approaches to charity and to the poor.

But should we insist so uncompromisingly on differences between Protestant and Catholic, or seek to ascribe the changes which affected Europe in the early modern period solely to Christian ideologies? Both Catholics and Protestants accepted the need for greater investment in poor relief, and states and civic authorities acted in remarkably similar ways, whether north or south of the religious divide. Because of the mercantile revolution of the age it is true that the charitable activity may seem more dynamic in Protestant countries, not least in Holland. But Brian Pullan is surely justified in seeing the genesis of this charitable impulse more in necessity, in economic and demographic crises, than in any difference of religious principle.[38] What was different in the Catholic south from the Protestant north, he suggests, was not the extent of charitable provision, but its organization. The place of charity was just as critical to the survival of the population, but poor relief remained largely decentralized, left to myriad different bodies. These continued to adapt in the early modern period, till by around 1700 there were four distinctive layers of charity, giving money to the poor or providing material assistance: the parish, hospitals, *monti di pietà*, and confraternities.[39]

THE ENLIGHTENMENT AND THE POOR

The growing focus on humanity and the needs of the suffering became even more salient during the eighteenth century, under the influence of the Enlightenment. Again this is a change that can be discerned alike in both Catholic and Protestant countries. Enlightened authors wrote of indigence and begging as a source of humiliation, the sight of suffering and misery as unacceptable in any civilized nation. They saw it as the duty of the state to alleviate the suffering of the poor, a social obligation that should not be left to individual acts of charity or to what many saw as the failing institution of the church. Mankind was perfectible and must be saved from poverty and marginality. Helvétius argued that social inequalities were not hereditary but were the results of environment; d'Holbach wrote that morality would improve if men's physical environment was more supportive; and Rousseau looked to education to root out misery, prostitution, and crime.

In France, an increasingly enlightened generation questioned the adequacy of voluntarism and the Catholic teaching of Saint Vincent-de-Paul, arguing that the root of the problem lay in the management of the economy and in the fiscal structure: the state must commit itself to eradicate poverty if progress was to be achieved. The clergy might be motivated by charitable impulses, but institutionally the church was ill-prepared to administer poor relief, given the random distribution of legacies and the inadequacy of money for almsgiving in many regions of Europe. In the poorest regions, indeed, it was almost axiomatic that there was a shortage of wealthy donors and hence a paucity of funding. Poor relief had always depended heavily on the outlook of the rich and on the willingness of local elites to make generous donations to the disinherited. In Grenoble across the seventeenth century the proportion of local people making charitable donations for the poor had increased substantially, rising from 32 per cent in the 1620s to 45 per cent in the 1690s.[40] Charity had traditionally depended heavily on local initiative: in 1766 when the olive crop failed disastrously in the Midi, it was the Estates of Provence that came to the rescue of the poor, not central government. This approach was changing, however, in the later eighteenth century, and in 1784 Necker could conclude, both as an economic theorist and a former Controller-General of Finances, that 'it is for the government, as the interpreter and depositary of social harmony, to do everything for this numerous and disinherited class that order and justice make possible'. The poor, and the eradication of poverty, must be at the heart of the enlightened agenda.[41]

But who was to be helped, and how? The eighteenth-century state had more means at its disposal to aid poverty, but it had priorities to establish and approaches to define. The state did not have the resources to help everyone, and the hardening of public opinion towards vagabonds and criminals meant that few saw them as people to be helped out of their plight. Assistance was therefore focused on the 'deserving poor', those who had not the strength to work or who through harvest failure or family misfortune had fallen upon hard times. State aid was not seen as an automatic right: the poor were expected to help themselves wherever possible, and to turn to their families and friends for care and assistance; only when these networks failed were they deemed worthy of receiving public funds. But for those who for reasons of age or infirmity could not cope independently—the terminally ill, orphans and abandoned children, and those old people without families to sustain them—alms from the parish poor box or admission into a local hospital would provide a minimum of nutrition and care. The indiscriminate distribution of alms, on the other hand, was increasingly frowned upon, since it was seen as encouraging the workshy and allowing the able-bodied to carry on a dissolute and unregulated lifestyle at the expense of the public purse. Throughout Europe there was greater unwillingness to offer money to the poor that would allow them to make ends meet in their own homes, and eighteenth-century governments preferred to commit them to institutions where they could oversee their behaviour and impose firm discipline. In England it was the route that led from the Speenhamland system of graduated relief to the New Poor Law, and in most European states we see a version of that journey during the Age of Enlightenment. For vagrants and vagabonds, those without fixed abode for whose probity local people could offer no assurances, the last decades of the Old Regime were years of increased surveillance and repression.

Whereas hospitals took in the deserving poor, those perceived as vagrants were more likely to be imprisoned or committed to workhouses, where their freedoms were severely curtailed and they were forced to do manual labour in return for their food and lodging. The Bridewell in London was probably the first modern workhouse, dating from 1550, and workhouses were established in the course of the seventeenth century in Holland, north Germany, and throughout much of central Europe. By the eighteenth century many Catholic countries had followed, and inculcating work discipline was seen as a necessary response to indigence. Louis XV's France is a good example of this new emphasis on work and social control. The Royal Declaration of 1724 launched a huge programme of internment, which aimed to bring begging under control throughout the country, using hospitals as places of confinement for the armies of the poor. Hospital archers and royal constables were charged with making arrests, as the government sought to turn the idle poor into a workforce of labourers on public works projects and in the economy at large.[42] But few cities had either the resources or the will to carry out the scheme, and when beggars were brought before the courts it was more common to punish them with branding, whipping, or banishment from the province. A further attempt was made by the commission headed by L'Averdy in 1764, which proposed harsher penalties for able-bodied *vagabonds*—the first offence being punished by three years in the galleys—and advised the establishment of workhouses (*dépôts de mendicité*) in all parts of the country. They were not hospitals but houses of correction, on the model of the Dutch *Tuchthuis*, and from 1767 they were the cornerstone of French government policy against vagrancy. Conditions were harsh, and fevers and disease rampant. Of the

71,000 beggars and vagabonds arrested in the first six years, nearly 14,000 died in the course of a short sentence.[43] The *dépôts* were intended to deter rather than to care for their inmates.

The Role of Philanthropy

The state did not act alone. Private philanthropy played a vital role in charity during the Enlightenment, reflecting many of the humanitarian concerns of the age and focusing on particular groups of the poor who could be idealized and were judged to be most in need of protection. Many municipal authorities directed benefactions to young children and unmarried girls, showing the same concern for female honour as had predominated in the clerical charities of the sixteenth century.[44] In particular, institutions were established to care for the large numbers of poor and illegitimate children abandoned by their mothers at birth, often exposed on the steps of the parish church or the local hospital. They were clearly worthy of compassion, tiny innocents left to face the world alone because of the misery or the dissolute lifestyle of their parents. But their chances of survival were poor. Diseases and fevers spread quickly, and those families who voluntarily placed infants in the local children's hospital or handed them over to the care of wet-nurses were only too often sentencing them to death. The institutions did the best they could in the light of available medical knowledge, but their care was often woefully inadequate. The children were aided by Protestant charities and Catholic confraternities alike, since it was widely agreed that they had the most urgent call on charitable funds. Besides, they were little given to revolt; they were not a threat to the balance of the social order. In this sense the social attitudes that had been inculcated over past centuries continued to inform the choices made by the state in judging the claims of the poor and apportioning assistance. Charity and deference still went hand-in-hand, with assistance directed towards those who posed no threat to society and its existing hierarchies.

Enlightenment philanthropy took different forms, but it generally emphasized the secular and advocated changes in social structure and social organization as the means to cure the ills of society. Elite groups saw it as their duty to help the poor, and by doing so they established their right to be counted among the elite, to take their place within the broader culture of Enlightenment sociability. Provincial academies, salons, and masonic lodges all sought to do good for their fellow men, and one result was an outpouring of benefactions to charitable and educational endowments. Indeed, philanthropy became a major source of social status within communities in a world which recognized the value of good works; philanthropists were hailed as heroes for improving the human condition and honoured for their acts of munificence. A good example is that of the Duke de La Rochefoucauld-Liancourt, who would go on to preside over the *Comité de mendicité* under the Constituent Assembly. During the Ancien Régime he had been an agricultural improver on his estates in the Clermontois, where he opened a school on his farm to educate the sons of invalids and orphans of soldiers in his regiment. The boys were given military instruction as well as training in agriculture and manual trades that could set them up for life; so successful was it that in 1786 the school was authorized by the King to educate the sons of soldiers from other regiments, and by the eve of the Revolution it had 160 pupils.[45] There was a particular role, too, for philanthropic women in eighteenth-century public life, with court ladies and the wives of financiers and lawyers finding in philanthropy a public function that would otherwise have been denied them. Women's philanthropic action focused especially on the needs of poor women and orphaned children. Their favoured causes lay in stereotypically female areas such as nursing and education, or, more generally, issues of public morality. The Société de Charité maternelle, founded in Paris in 1788, declared that it aimed to 'recall to nature hapless mothers, degraded by poverty, who abandon their infants', as part of a crusade to 'restore the morals of the people'.[46]

Always there was the idea of improvement, of engendering a work ethic or destroying the climate of immorality in which poverty was seen to flourish. Both the state and private philanthropists sought to cleanse society of its ills, idleness and prostitution, depravity and corruption. The poor were increasingly seen as standing apart from respectable society, a people to be educated and converted. Many saw themselves that way: there was a degree of solidarity among the poor that stemmed from a sense of rejection, of being outcast from civilized society. If Europe in the eighteenth century began to speak of the poor as people to whom they felt some social obligation, this was not entirely a philanthropic attitude. It contained a significant measure of self-defence, offering an insurance policy against violence and insurrection. And underlying it was fear, fear of the populace, fear of those with no stake in society, or—as was demonstrated in the Great Fear on the eve of the French Revolution—an unspecified general fear of the unknown.[47]

Notes

1. Jean-Claude Perrot and Stuart Woolf, *State and Statistics in France, 1789–1815* (Chur, 1984).
2. Robert Jütte, *Poverty and Deviance in Early Modern Europe* (Cambridge, 1994), 45.
3. Stuart Woolf, *The Poor in Western Europe in the Eighteenth and Nineteenth Centuries* (London, 1986), 6–7.
4. Jean-Pierre Gutton, *La Société et les pauvres: L'Exemple de la généralité de Lyon, 1534–1789* (Paris, 1971), 42–5.
5. Ibid. 22.
6. B. H. Slicher van Bath, *The Agrarian History of Western Europe, AD 500–1850* (London, 1963), 89–90.
7. Peter H. Wilson, *Europe's Tragedy: A History of the Thirty Years War* (London, 2009), 786–9.
8. Rudolf Vierhaus, *Germany in the Age of Absolutism* (Cambridge, 1988), 3.
9. Woolf, *The Poor in Western Europe*, 8.
10. Jütte, *Poverty and Deviance*, 27–36.
11. Mark Overton, *Agricultural Revolution in England: The Transformation of the Agrarian Economy, 1500–1850* (Cambridge, 1996), 197.

12. Keith Wrightson, *English Society, 1580–1680* (London, 1982), 140–1.
13. Catharina Lis, *Social Change and the Labouring Poor: Antwerp, 1770–1860* (New Haven, Conn., 1986), 164.
14. Jerome Blum, *The End of the Old Order in Rural Europe* (Princeton, 1978), 189.
15. John G. Gagliardo, *From Pariah to Patriot: The Changing Image of the German Peasant, 1770–1840* (Lexington, Ky., 1969), 4–5.
16. Peter H. Wilson, 'Poverty', in Peter H. Wilson (ed.), *A Companion to Eighteenth-Century Europe* (Oxford, 2008), 111–12.
17. Slicher van Bath, *Agrarian History of Western Europe*, 92.
18. Gérard Bouchard, *Le Village immobile: Sennely-en-Sologne au dix-huitième siècle* (Paris, 1972), 75–6.
19. Olwen Hufton, *The Poor of Eighteenth-Century France, 1750–89* (Oxford, 1974), 318.
20. Robert M. Schwartz, *Policing the Poor in Eighteenth-Century France* (Chapel Hill, NC, 1988), 101–5.
21. Hufton, *The Poor*, 109–14.
22. Ibid. 69.
23. Lis, *Social Change*, 149.
24. Cissie Fairchilds, *Poverty and Charity in Aix-en-Provence, 1640–1789* (Baltimore, Md., 1976), 75.
25. Abel Poitrineau, 'Aspects de l'émigration temporaire et saisonnière en Auvergne à la fin du dix-huitième et au début du dix-neuvième siècle', *Revue d'Histoire Moderne et Contemporaine*, 9 (1962), 15.
26. C. A. Bayly, *The Birth of the Modern World, 1780–1914* (Oxford, 2004), 132–4.
27. Alan Forrest, *The French Revolution and the Poor* (Oxford, 1981), 9–10.
28. Jütte, *Poverty and Deviance*. 147–8.
29. Wilson, 'Poverty', 117.
30. Gagliardo, *From Pariah to Patriot*, 5.
31. S. T. McCloy, *Government Assistance in Eighteenth-Century France* (Durham, NC, 1946), 23–9.
32. Richard Palmer, 'Ad una sancta perfettione: Health Care and Poor Relief in the Republic of Venice in the Era of the Counter-Reformation', in Ole Peter Grell, Andrew Cunningham, and Jon Arrizabalaga (eds.), *Health Care and Poor Relief in Counter-Reformation Europe* (London, 1999), 87.
33. Brian Pullan, *Rich and Poor in Renaissance Venice: The Social Institutions of a Catholic State, to 1620* (Oxford, 1971), 641.
34. Andrew Cunningham, 'Some Opening and Closing Remarks', in Ole Peter Grell, Andrew Cunningham, and Bernd Roeck (eds.), *Health Care and Poor Relief in Eighteenth and Nineteenth Century Southern Europe* (Aldershot, 2005), 3.
35. Colin Jones, *The Charitable Imperative: Hospitals and Nursing in Ancien Regime and Revolutionary France* (London, 1989), 6–7.
36. Isabel Mendes Drumond Braga, 'Poor Relief in Counter-Reformation Portugal: The Case of the Misericórdias', in Grell et al., *Health Care in Counter-Reformation Europe*, 210.
37. Ole Peter Grell, 'The Protestant Imperative of Christian Care and Neighbourly Love', in Ole Peter Grell and Andrew Cunningham (eds.), *Health Care and Poor Relief in Protestant Europe, 1500–1700* (London, 1997), 51.
38. Pullan, *Rich and Poor in Renaissance Venice*, 223–4.
39. Jütte, *Poverty and Deviance*, 125.
40. Kathryn Norberg, *Rich and Poor in Grenoble, 1600–1814* (Berkeley, Calif., 1985), 117.

41. Jacques Necker, *De l'administration des finances de la France* (Paris, 1784), iii. 160–1.
42. Schwartz, *Policing the Poor*, 34.
43. Hufton, *The Poor*, 230–2.
44. Woolf, *The Poor in Western Europe*, 24.
45. Catherine Duprat, *Le Temps des philanthropes*, i. *La Philanthropie parisienne des Lumières à la monarchie de Juillet* (Paris, 1993), 24–5.
46. David Garrioch, 'Making a Better World: Enlightenment and Philanthropy', in Martin Fitzpatrick, Peter Jones, Christa Knellwolf, and Iain McCalman (eds.), *The Enlightenment World* (London, 2004), 496.
47. Georges Lefebvre, *La Grande Peur* (Paris, 1932), *passim*.

Bibliography

Blum, Jerome, *The End of the Old Order in Rural Europe* (Princeton, 1978).
Grell, Ole Peter, Cunningham, Andrew, and Arrizabalaga, Jon (eds.), *Health Care and Poor Relief in Counter-Reformation Europe* (London, 1999).
Hufton, Olwen, *The Poor of Eighteenth-Century France, 1750–89* (Oxford, 1974).
Jütte, Robert, *Poverty and Deviance in Early Modern Europe* (Cambridge, 1994).
Overton, Mark, *Agricultural Revolution in England: The Transformation of the Agrarian Economy, 1500–1850* (Cambridge, 1996).
Pullan, Brian, *Rich and Poor in Renaissance Venice: The Social Institutions of a Catholic State, to 1620* (Oxford, 1971).
Schwartz, Robert M., *Policing the Poor in Eighteenth-Century France* (Chapel Hill, NC, 1988).
Slicher van Bath, B. H., *The Agrarian History of Western Europe, AD 500–1850* (London, 1963).
Wilson, Peter H., *Europe's Tragedy: A History of the Thirty Years War* (London, 2009).
Woolf, Stuart, *The Poor in Western Europe in the Eighteenth and Nineteenth Centuries* (London, 1986).

CHAPTER 11

GENDER

JULIE HARDWICK

When I was an undergraduate in the early 1980s, there was no gender in the old regime. Very few women existed in the pre-modern France of my college education. Now gender is one of the central pivots for any exploration of the dynamics of old regime France. Twenty-five years or more of pioneering work has positioned gender not only as a critical variant in life course, in many aspects of daily life, in social rank, in spirituality, and in work experience, but as a crucial signifier in the debates and decisions that transformed political culture in the hundred years or so before the Revolution. While the early obliviousness to gender is a characteristic of old regime historiography shared with the historiographies of many other times and regions, perhaps nowhere has gender become so central as in work that seeks to explain the events of the decades that led up to the Revolution.[1]

In the emergence of gender, that is of the ways in which differences between men and women are socially and culturally constructed in ways that were integral to political, religious, economic, and cultural developments as well as individual lived experiences, historians of old regime France have explored to great effect both gender as a key part of the lives of many groups of women and the rhetorical deployment of gender as a powerful form of political critique. We know much less, however, about masculinity as a gender construct, a void that contrasts with the rich literature British historians of the same period have produced.[2] Likewise, from Lake Ponchartrain to Port au Prince to Pondicherry, across the vast expanse of the French colonial world, gender remains far less explored as an imperial category than in the parallel British, Spanish, or Portuguese domains. This chapter, therefore, reflects that unevenness while aiming to highlight some of the areas for possible future projects.

The historiography of gender in the Ancien Régime (which I will take here to mean approximately the mid-seventeenth century to 1789) has explored two sets of inter-related issues. One is the question of the changing nature of men's and women's experiences and the ways in which they related to each other. Another is the way in which gender had an integral role in shifting cultural, political, and—explored to a much lesser extent this far—economic patterns. In both cases, historians have debated whether gender hierarchy intensified and women's opportunities became more constrained, whether changing patterns reformulated gendered expectations but not in a way that a 'better or worse' paradigm is appropriate, or whether new forms of gender relations created new opportunities.

In the Ancien Régime, gender made a difference: for all social ranks whether peasants, artisans, or nobles, for economic matters as market practices intensified and a consumer revolution ushered in new fashions for Parisians and peasants alike, for cultural processes as traditional categories were problematized and new possibilities were debated, and for political debates as novel forms of politics as well as innovative ideas about sovereignty and authority emerged. Gender freighted sexual difference with meanings that shaped religious lives and legal ones, aristocracy as well as poverty, micropolitics and national movements.

SOCIAL

The historians associated with Fernand Braudel and the journal *Annales* who provided an extraordinary foundation for the social history of working people in pre-modern France from the early 1960s were famously—or infamously—blind to gender. Women rarely appeared in early *Annaliste* work and there was no attention to questions of differential power within families or extra-familial roles. Yet the ground-breaking work they did provided information and raised new topics as subjects of legitimate historical enquiry that were crucial to the development of modern understandings about gender in the Ancien Régime: about family, sexuality, demography, deviance, popular culture, and rank.[3] Our questions and answers may be different today but the pioneering efforts of *Annaliste* historians made possible our current understanding of the social world of the old order, and the role of gender in it.

Even today, our grasp of old regime society remains uneven. We know far more about men than women—although surprisingly little about masculinity as a construct in that historians of France who work on gender have primarily focused on its implications for women. Elite women have received more attention than working women, and urban women's lives have been more closely scrutinized than those of rural women. Robert Forster's ground-breaking work on the eighteenth-century French nobility in the 1960s, heavily influenced by the *Annalistes*, spearheaded the emergence of family history as a discipline and the roles of women and marriage as foundations of rank and status. The Toulousain noble widows who efficiently ran their estates and the issues about access to the national 'marriage market' centred at Versailles—or lack thereof—that determined the fortunes of Burgundian elites opened up a raft of subsequent work on the French noble families of various different ranks and in different parts of France. Elite women were central to the creation of kinship networks and the patronage circles which often built on them, on the dowries they brought as defining elements of family patrimonies and fortunes, and in the conspicuous consumption patterns that ever more forcefully divided great aristocrats from petty nobles who were hardly distinguishable from their non-noble peers.[4]

Urban working people began to come to the forefront of historiography perhaps a generation later, starting with the skilled workers who were guild members. We learnt much about the work, sociability, and marriage patterns of bakers and hatters in Paris, for instance, and rather less about the parallel experiences of their sisters, daughters, and wives. Recently, however, books by Claire Crowston on Parisian seamstresses, Daryl Hafter on women guild workers in Rouen and Lyon, and Janine Lanza on guild widows in Paris have remade the picture of gender and guild work. Crowston and Lanza persuasively demonstrate in eighteenth-century Paris how lively one important women's guild was and how widows' rights to be masters in the wake of their husbands deaths were actively protected in almost all guilds through the eighteenth century. Hafter shows how important female workers were in one of the major industries of the old regime, Lyon silk production, in a city dominated by the huge silkworkers' guild called the *fabrique*.[5]

However, the fact remains that most female urban workers, like many workers of all stripes, were not members of guilds, and it remains to be seen if the generally optimistic representation of female work and status laid out by Crowston, Hafter, and Lanza extended more broadly to the vast majority of women whose working lives were spent outside the privileges of the guild framework. Women worked in many occupations in urban areas, some perhaps surprising, such as the involvement of women in the construction trades in Brittany traced by Elizabeth Musgrave. She demonstrates how women worked as plumbers and glazers, and served as contractors, albeit at a participation rate and wage level lower than their male contemporaries.[6] Women also dominated second-hand selling (a pivotal sector of old regime commercial life), petty marketing of other kinds, and provisioning trades. Young women and widows worked as servants. That is they, like men who were outside of guilds, were central cogs in urban economies even if their activities are less obvious and more difficult to recover. These non-guild occupations offered their own opportunities as well as perils, but without the legal standing guild work provided, the vast majority of working women certainly did the best they could—but with a not very attractive set of options.[7] It is important to note in this regard that we still know very little about men who did manual work coded as 'unskilled', that is non-guild, in French towns and cities—perhaps even less than about 'unskilled' women at this point. They too lacked access to guild privileges, legal standing, confraternities, and the networks of sociability and assistance these provided. When we know more about them, we may think gender was less significant as a variable than access to these resources, although Arlette Farge's empathetic and lively description of the domestic and working lives of eighteenth-century Parisian men and women, many non-guild, emphasizes both the centrality of female labour in working communities and how distinctively gendered men's and women's experiences were.[8]

While the demographics of peasant households have been much studied, we still know surprisingly little about the dynamics of gender among rural working families. Many of the issues raised about gender in village communities by Natalie Davis in *The Return of Martin Guerre* with its microhistorical explanation of the implications of the *ménage-à-trois* of Bertrande de Rol, Martin Guerre, and Arnaud du Tihl in the late sixteenth century may still have pertained in the eighteenth century. Marital status and inheritance practices continued to be important definers of status, experience, and opportunity. Yet the eighteenth-century peasantry was coming under new pressures that may have affected men and women differently and in which we see gender roles being altered. Cynthia Bouton's work on the Flour War in the regions around Paris in the 1770s, for example, has observed that in food riots, long a female preserve in early modern Europe, men became increasingly active. She argues that men who were small rural producers experienced a particularly sharp dislocation as production and supply networks shifted to feed the ever growing needs of Paris. The resulting loss of status marked a kind of *de facto* feminization that explains their new level of participation in the popular politics of revolt around subsistence issues.[9]

Indeed demography and law provided powerful common gender axes across region, whether province to province or rural to urban, and even across rank to a degree. Elite men and women often married young as teenagers in marriages that were part of noble families' patrimonial strategies to preserve and enhance all their forms of capital, financial, social, and political. Yet younger brothers and sisters often did not marry in aristocratic or urban elite families where primogeniture privileged the prospects of the oldest son, leaving the others to careers in army, church, or domestic support for their families.[10] Working men and women, rural and urban, married later in their mid to late twenties in the now classic west European marriage pattern. While working parents clearly had the right to veto children's marriages following the new marriage formation legislation of the late sixteenth and early seventeenth centuries, these marriages were never arranged and it remains unclear how often working parents ever invoked their legal ability to object. In non-elite families, strict and widely observed rules about partible inheritance meant that daughters as well as sons received shares of parental estates, however small, and perhaps because of the costs of entering convents or even minor officers' posts in the army, working people may have been less likely to remain single than elites.

For women of all social ranks, age of marriage was the primary effective means to control fertility, despite ample evidence that female desire to control fertility was powerful. Thus repeated pregnancies and high rates of infant and childhood mortality shaped the lives of every woman in the old regime. Managing those pressures was challenging, especially for working women whose families had few resources and whose labour was essential to household survival. In elite families, wet nurses were recruited who came to live in with their charges. The differing options and pressures women faced led them to make a range of choices, as the widespread practice of putting infants out to paid wet nurses illustrates. For urban working women, sending their newborns to wet nurses allowed them to resume the challenge of making a living more quickly. For rural women seeking to supplement their households' resources, taking in infants for pay, however low paid and unreliable, seemed like an option only attractive in the context of very limited possibilities. The human costs, to mothers who sent their newborns away, to the foster mothers who received them, and to the psychological development of the babies reared in this way (if they survived—mortality rates among wet-nursed children were notoriously high, perhaps as high as 80 per cent) have yet to be explored, not least because of very scanty evidence of any kind beyond the demographic. The occasional surviving archival glimpse illuminates the harshness of the choices for all involved. Parents sent layettes with their babies to wet nurses, indicating a desire to provide, but regular payments, much less visits, did not always follow. The wet nurse who wrote (or likely had someone write for her) to the parents of her charge to report both that he at the age of twenty months was just starting to walk and was so charming and funny that he would make his parents laugh if they saw him, also noted that she had not been paid for three months and would have to put him out of her house if she did not receive money immediately, revealing how the practice allowed for complicated equations of interest and emotion on every side.[11]

The Ancien Régime did see some striking shifts in patterns of marriage and motherhood. By the second half of the eighteenth century, if not before, new ideas about matrimony were taking hold, at least among elites and urban families. The pragmatic partnerships based on property and mutual interest in a sustainable household that were typical of early modern marriages were increasingly replaced, at least rhetorically, by new emphases on romantic love and personal choice of soulmates as the appropriate bases for choice of spouses. The much discussed 'rise of companionate marriage' reframed domestic expectations between men and women, and—as we have seen—was inextricably linked to political debates too. This shift was accompanied in France, although tantalizingly inexplicably not in other western countries where modern marriage ideals emerged at the same time, by the first noticeable shift in fertility patterns. Marital fertility did begin to drop in France, even in rural parts of Normandy, for example, from the mid-eighteenth century and did not do so until much later in other western countries. How can we explain this? Is there a correlation between the shift in fertility and the rise of companionate marriage or are they coincidentally parallel developments? The explanations continue to elude demographers and historians. No new contraceptive technology became available, which suggests spousal practices must have changed. Jean-Jacques Rousseau, the master articulator of new marriage, railed against wet nursing and advocated maternal breastfeeding as a key to domestic and political change. Certainly, in pre-modern diets that were low in fats and many nutrients, breast feeding had a contraceptive effect. But Rousseau's *Emile*, the most popular representation of a different model of marriage, was not published until the 1760s when shifts in marital fertility had already started to occur and, for all its popularity, it is difficult to find this link broadly persuasive. Effective contraception, especially without new technology, has often been seen as requiring spousal cooperation, which perhaps hints at a correlation to companionate marriage, but leaves aside the question of why new expectations about marriage would quickly contribute to declining marital fertility in France but not elsewhere. We still it seems have not advanced past the kind of observation typified by David Kertzer in his 2001 *History of the European Family*: 'Fertility began to drop, provoked by the decision of a growing number of families to limit the number of children they produced.'[12] The how, why, and who of this decision remain elusive.

Whether new expectations led to greater happiness is difficult to assess, even for contemporaries, much less by modern indications like high divorce rates. Dena Goodman's recent analysis of the marital expectations and experiences of two Ancien Régime couples is based no doubt on a tiny and unrepresentative sample, but the spousal letters provide an unusually rich and suggestive window into the gap between promise and reality. The marriage of a couple whose choice had been based on traditional pragmatism about property and family seemed more successful than that of a couple swept into matrimony on the currents of romantic love.[13] Domestic violence persisted and may have become less visible, separations became harder to get, property remained very important even as discussion about it became more coded.[14] Even today marriage may seem to be all about romantic love at weddings, but divorces make clear how large property continues to loom in conjugal affairs, as do pre-nuptial contracts.

Moreover other changes, like the exploding rate of child abandonment through the eighteenth century, highlight the ambiguous consequences of shifts in gendered expectations about relationships. Although premarital conception rates were high in the sixteenth and seventeenth centuries (30 per cent or more in some areas), illegitimacy rates were very low at 3 per cent or less. Throughout the eighteenth century, illegitimacy rates increased dramatically as did the frequency of babies being abandoned. The reasons for this strikingly new pattern were undoubtedly complex and have yet to be fully elucidated, and paralleled other shifts in sexuality that remain shadowy, such as the emergence of homosexual subcultures in eighteenth-century Paris and the spectrum of sex for pay practices evident in many varieties of forms of prostitution. Yet the apparently increased vulnerability of single women who found themselves pregnant, not to mention the cost to their infants, suggests again that the new emphasis on personal choice of partners based on love and romance—or simply desire—did not easily translate into improved circumstances or more harmonious gender relations.[15]

Economy

Gender was integrally linked with all aspects of the Ancien Régime economy, from household budgeting to important shifts in production and consumption patterns that we characterize today (albeit with oversimplification) with terms like the consumer revolution, the industrious revolution, or the transition to capitalism. Household production remained the mainstay of manufacturing, and even the largest enterprises like the production of silk in Lyon dispersed production among numerous household sites, but gender structured the organization of work and the changes in that organization. Consumption patterns were transformed in the century or so before the Revolution, and gender was at the centre of those shifts too.

Olwen Hufton's brilliant 1975 insight about the centrality of women and family economies for survival in the old regime has framed subsequent debates about gender in households.[16] Hufton's thesis that survival depended on the pooled contributions of all household members, women as well as men, imagined Ancien Régime households in what became a classic family economy model where husbands worked at an identity-defining occupation, and wives assisted their husbands as best they could, either directly or when times were pressing through a range of 'makeshifts' (any work that would produce income) or 'expedients' (begging or even theft). It has become clear that family economies were more varied than Hufton anticipated, as many married women followed their own occupations in what we might now call two-income households (especially when or even when their husbands were not guild masters), while single women who lived together comprised another version of family economy (a phenomenon Hufton noticed and termed 'spinster clustering', although the reality of single women who chose to live together rather than marry has been elucidated by Crowston among others).[17]

Some regions of France did participate in proto-industrial production in the eighteenth century, and the expansion of manufacturing through rural households in this way depended on the reallocation and specialization of the labour of women and children. Pierre Deyon's work on northern France and Jan De Vries's broader overview that includes parts of France as well as many other western European regions in the shifts that he characterized as an 'industrious revolution' (to explain and encapsulate how a dramatic expansion of manufacturing took place before industrialization) emphasize not only the way in which a gendered specialization of labour underlay economic growth, but argue that the shift increased the spending power of families and lowered the age of marriage in ways that bettered the lot of rural households and strengthened wives' position by enhancing their importance as cash producers and consumers. There remains room for scepticism about this reading of a changing gender power dynamic rooted in spouses' evolving relationship to rural manufacturing. Gay Gullickson's work on proto-industrial families in the nineteenth century, for example, argued that such shifts in wage earning increased domestic violence. Rural households bought many items on credit, even from pedlars as Laurence Fontaine has shown, so cash was not essential for their entry into the world of expanded consumption and in fact other needs rather than wants, especially tax bills, may have had a primary claim on any increased cash income.[18]

Moreover, if the ways in which gender shaped and was impacted by such shifts in production remain an open question, the centrality of gender in every aspect of changes in attitudes and practices surrounding consumption have been elaborately and persuasively framed out. Historians disagree about when the consumer revolution 'happened' in France and about issues such as whether it preceded or succeeded the contemporaneous remaking of consumption patterns in England, but concur that gender was pivotal to the new central place consumption has assumed by the later eighteenth century as profession, pastime, performance of identity, and political football.[19]

Women shaped the emergence of consumer culture in the old regime and consumption as an economic and political project was profoundly gendered. The new Parisian female shopkeepers, the *marchandes de mode*, and the young female retail specialists who worked for them became the arbiters of style joined in a newly democratized world of dress where their peers took up window shopping, and fashion became a pastime and means of self-expression for all French women, and not only the prerogative of elites.

The volume of men's clothes doubled in the eighteenth century, but the quantity of dresses women owned increased exponentially. In vogue dress shapes, colours, and fabrics began to evolve quickly as consumption became gendered specifically as female. As women became devoted wives and mothers or seamstresses by nature, so they too became natural shoppers.[20]

Consumption became as heavily coded a signifier of economic productivity as companionate marriage or political corruption and financial turbulence: as such, the task of consuming became a perilous project for women who might either skilfully demonstrate their wifely skills and husband-pleasing success in Rousseauian terms or inappropriately imperil the very stability of the economy and perhaps even the nation as well as risk the ruin of their families. Eighteenth-century authors could find the new consumption as the key to economic progress or the proof of looming economic disaster. The archetype of the dangerous consumer became the French Queen, Marie Antoinette, whose extravagant spending and expensive obsession with the latest fashions were pilloried in the popular press of the 1780s, especially in terms of her relationship with the reigning Parisian *marchande de mode*, Rose Bertin. Clare Crowston has demonstrated how the entangled connections between the monarch and her 'minister of fashion' conflated conspicuous consumption and political liability—with inappropriate female weakness as well as wantonness as the linking pivot.[21]

Religion

The history of Ancien Régime religion has become a perhaps unlikely site of intense work in terms of gender, whether in terms of the significance of women's experiences (much less on men's) or of developments in political culture. Elizabeth Rapley and Mita Choudhury, among other historians, have transformed our knowledge about and understandings of the lives of female religious in the seventeenth and eighteenth centuries.[22] Alas we know much less about male religious *per se*, and even less about the gendered or political significations of their experiences.

A striking aspect of the religious life of France in the Ancien Régime is the large increase in the number of nuns. The emphasis on enclosure associated with the Council of Trent reforms of Catholic practice encouraged a modern tendency to presuppose that women would have been less attracted to religious life post-Trent than earlier. Yet in France, a veritable 'conventual invasion' began in the early seventeenth century at a time when traditional female religious communities were at a very low ebb in terms of property and population.[23] A plethora of new foundations, contemplative and teaching, mushroomed up across France. While the number of men entering monasteries also increased, both contemporaries and historians have been especially struck by the proportionally larger number of new female foundations and of nuns. While overall numbers are difficult to estimate, certainly tens of thousands of women lived as nuns in France by the eighteenth century.

The women associated with these foundations not only experienced a particularly potent form of spiritual life, but as historians have increasingly argued, they actively imprinted the religious culture of the Ancien Régime. Despite the emphasis of the leaders of the Catholic Reformation on female enclosure, and certainly many women who lived as nuns observed enclosure and devoted their lives to contemplation, in seventeenth-century France new active orders of nuns appeared that became part of the fabric of French society. In particular the Ursulines, a teaching order originally founded in Italy that established itself in France early in the seventeenth century, and the Daughters of Charity, a native French project of nuns devoted to poor relief that was founded in the 1630s, offered many female religious the possibility of active lives within the church, and the services they provided became integral to the pedagogical and philanthropic endeavours of the nation. For these women at least, the religious foundations of the Ancien Régime provided expanded opportunities, even if—as Susan Dinan notes—their acceptance despite the neglect of strict enclosure was due in large part not only to the value of the services they provided but to the fact that in their modesty, deferential speech, and service to others nobody perceived them as a threat to the larger political or gender order.[24]

Yet female religious and their actions also became vehicles for intense political debates about the nature of authority and the future of France. Abbesses in particular were the subject of close scrutiny and sometimes vitriolic attacks in print where they were portrayed as the worst examples of abusive female and aristocratic power conflated. Mita Choudury's work has interrogated the role of nuns as key figures in eighteenth-century political culture who, for critics from the 1730s onwards, exemplified 'tyranny and social disorder' in ways that broader critiques of aristocratic women, above all Queen Marie Antoinette, were to do later in the century.[25] These representations of gendered behaviour conveyed meanings far beyond the practices of female religious.

Political Culture

The ways in which the language of gender and family and ideas about 'the right kind' of gender roles and family life were integrally linked to 'the right' political order provided a fertile site for political debate throughout the old regime. If women had no official role in the institutional politics of bureaucracies and judiciary, they were important actors in legal processes that were highly politicized and gender issues were at the centre of evolutions in political culture. In the seventeenth century, broad agreement existed about the local and national benefits of patriarchal households writ small and large from the individual to the household of the nation. Over the course of the subsequent decades, as Choudury, Sarah Maza, and others have shown, reworkings of family order were integral to possible reworkings of political order.

By the last decades of the seventeenth century, the monarchical government and local communities invested in strong families that provided foundations for cultural morality, economic productivity, and political stability. Jean-Baptiste Colbert, Louis XIV's chief minister, promoted an explicitly pronatal policy in instituting the 1666 edict that offered tax exemptions to the fathers of ten living children, and the Paris Foundling hospital was established in which unwanted babies were positioned as the 'children of the state'.[26] Political rhetoric was filled with familial references: families, to take only three examples, were 'the seminaries of the state', 'the fecund sources from which the strength and greatness of the state derives', and 'the natural reverence of children' for parents linked 'the legitimate obedience of subjects towards their sovereign'.[27]

As new ideas about gender, families, and politics began to emerge in the later seventeenth century, the Parisian salons that became an important site of Enlightenment debate and patronage quickly established women in prominent roles as hostesses, formulators of new gender expectations, and as social arbitrators. Carolyn Lougee explored how early *salonnières* articulated new bases for spousal relationships in which love replaced interest. However, these new marriages would be part of larger social changes and in particular they also provided new vehicles for social mobility through marriages between newcomers and the hereditary nobility. Salons offered a site for the creation of a new elite that assimilated suitably talented aristocrats and on the rise families on the basis of manners and money, then a novel way of defining merit.[28]

As the influence of salons reached its peak in the 1760s and 1770s, when the men who were the lions of the Enlightenment frequently attended the salons that various elite women hosted daily in Paris, a similar dynamic prevailed. *Salonnières* governed the salons, controlling invitations, managing conversations, and often providing financial support for writers. Joan Landes strikingly highlighted Jean-Jacques Rousseau as the primary source of the eighteenth-century emergence of a highly gendered new public sphere from which women were excluded as democratic imperatives challenged absolute monarchy. Yet work on salon culture more broadly, notably Dena Goodman's *The Republic of Letters*, has argued that many other leading *philosophes* participated in the drawing rooms where the High Enlightenment took shape. Rousseau did not dominate these gatherings or the polite conversations that framed intellectual debate, supervised by female patrons like Suzanne Necker and Madame Geoffrin, and others. From this perspective, the intellectual sociability of the salons had an ethos of gender equality absent from Rousseau.[29]

Nor were these family politics debates only top down. Individual households and local communities likewise invested in stable family life, and not merely in emulation of elite imperatives. In the seventeenth century, family litigation over marriage, borrowing, and violence demonstrated the intense energy devoted to associating order of all kinds with particular gender roles and hierarchies at grassroots too. Occasionally, explicit political language could be mobilized, as when wives described themselves as slaves and their husbands as tyrants. Wives as well as husbands and their neighbours constantly mobilized the spectre of familial disorder—whether caused by spouses who squandered their families' resources instead of working to increase them, husbands whose violence towards their wives disrupted households they were supposed to discipline, or creditors whose threats to seize goods to cover unpaid debts put families on the street or made them charges on their communities. In resorting to local courts to authorize and legitimize opinion about the right and wrong kind of family, wives and husbands made politics personal and the personal political.[30] On local streets as well as in ministerial offices at Versailles and Parisian salons, the right kind of gendered family was essential to the right ordering of polity, economy, and society.

Evolving ideas about gender difference also had roots beyond Enlightenment reasoning and debates about the political shortcomings of the monarchy and elites. Claire Crowston has emphasized the ways in which working women—and men—developed new ideas about gender difference from the late seventeenth century and that these popular notions had as much to do with changing perceptions as those of elites. She argues that seamstresses in Paris who sought to justify privileges and monopolies for their guild drove the emerging sense of biological difference naturally suiting men and women to different tasks. While the contemporary appeal of Rousseau and of the version of family life he rhapsodized in *Emile*—with wives devoted to developing charms that pleased husbands—can seem elusive to modern observers for whom the limitations of remaking of old gender roles into new but equally hierarchical forms seem paramount, the resonance of his new familial vision to middling French men and women at the time is clear. Dena Goodman has recently explored the 1780s marriage of an army officer, Bernard de Bonnard, and his wife, the all too aptly named, Sophie Silvestre. Their letters to each other represent them as the model new conjugal spouses, enamoured with each other and the task of childrearing. Bonnard's diary recorded that he and his Sophie spent every evening reading *Emile* (where the idealized wife was also named Sophie), and took to heart the advice Rousseau gave about maternal breastfeeding while awaiting the birth of their first child.[31] We may be too quick to read such evidence as indicating the influence of Rousseau rather than framing it in terms of his ability to resonate with patterns that were already emerging.

Likewise, debates about appropriate family life and gender roles also became a primary vehicle across many forums far beyond the traditional Enlightenment in the eighteenth century for proponents of political reform: Rousseau's *Emile*, lawyers who made *causes célèbres* out of domestic disputes, or Grub Street writers who made salacious attacks on the alleged improprieties, sexual and otherwise, of leading nobles, royal mistresses, and above all Marie Antoinette, wife of Louis XVI and queen of France as his consort from 1774. The gender politics of these sites seem more clearly antagonistic, and fixed on remaking gendered dynamics in different but still clearly hierarchical forms rather than in the egalitarian impulse of the salons.

Some unlikely heroes of new family and new politics emerged in these varied genres, especially in the new sites of public opinion and scurrilous mass media. Rousseau himself, a father who abandoned the five children born to his long out-of-wedlock relationship with a former servant, Thérèse Levasseur, became in *Emile* (published in 1762) the chief immensely popular and popularizing articulator of new marriages on which new republics could be built. In this version of family politics, spouses married for love, complemented each other's natural aptitudes, and wives devoted themselves to raising sons to be citizens and daughters to be domestic paragons. The Count de Sanois, a crabby, financially maladroit noble who abandoned his wife, children, and France to flee to Switzerland to escape the chaos of his finances and family was artfully represented by his politically ambitious lawyer, Pierre-Louis de Lacretelle, in the courtroom and in widely circulated published legal briefs about his case as a maligned father whose vulnerability in the face of a shrewish, social-climbing wife foisted on him through arranged marriage symbolized the inappropriate feminized noble privilege of the old regime. Marie Antoinette was an easy target as villain but the virulence of the highly sexualized attacks on her as the epitome of a bad wife (adulterer), a bad mother (committer of incest), and aristocratic impotence and sterility (lesbian affairs) breathtakingly and poisonously conflated the wrong kind of wife with political corruption.[32] Who could argue against regime change in the face of such potent emblems of women who undermined the state instead of making it stronger? If a patriarchal family was integral to a monarchical state, companionate marriage based on conjugal mutuality could provide the essential basis for a reformed political order.

Conclusion

Almost twenty-five years ago, Joan Scott, in a famous call to arms for a new paradigm to end the marginalization represented in such stereotypical framings as 'My understanding of the French Revolution is not changed by knowing that women participated in it', lamented the tendency to segment feminist history into a separate subgenre where work on women did little to impact larger historiographical debates or historians' metanarratives. Scott advocated a focus on how gender was a primary but historically specific signifier of power.[33] In the intervening years, historians have demonstrated how gender was a centre of all aspects of the Ancien Régime in ways that have transformed our disciplinary understanding of the characteristics and changes of the decades before the Revolution. Whether as symbol, discourse, shaper of economic patterns, or lived experience, gender has become essential to understandings of eighteenth-century France, as in fact it was to contemporary experiences and culture, both popular and elite.

Notes

1. In this sense, I have some reservations about my own assignment here, i.e. to write about 'gender' as a separate category rather than as an issue integral to the topics covered in the other essays in this collection.
2. For only one example, see the essays and bibliography in Tim Hitchcock (ed.), *English Masculinities, 1660–1800* (London, 1999). A rare but interesting and suggestive exception is

Gary Kates's work on a notorious 18th-cent. cross-dresser, Monsieur D'Eon. See Gary Kates, *Monsieur D'Eon is a Woman: A Tale of Political Intrigue and Sexual Masquerade* (New York, 1995).
3. Much of this work first became widely available and visible to Anglophone audiences in multiple volumes edited by Robert Forster and Orest Ranum. See e.g. the articles in Forster and Ranum (eds.), *Family and Society: Selections from the Annales Économies, Sociétés, Civilisations*, tr. E. Forster and P. M. Ranum (Baltimore, Md., 1976). For the shortcomings of the historical work associated with the *Annales* in terms of gender, see Susan Mosher Stuard, 'The *Annales* School and Feminist History: Opening Dialogue with the American Stepchild', *Signs*, 7 (1981).
4. Robert Forster, *The Nobility of Toulouse in the Eighteenth Century: A Social and Economic Study* (Baltimore, Md., 1960) and *The House of Saulx-Tavanes: Versailles and Burgundy, 1730–1810* (Baltimore, Md., 1971). See also Jonathan Dewald, *Pont-St-Pierre, 1398–1789: Lordship, Community, and Capitalism in Early Modern France* (Berkeley, Calif., 1987) and *The European Nobility, 1400–1800* (Cambridge, 1996).
5. Claire Crowston, *Fabricating Women: The Seamstresses of Old Regime France, 1675–1791* (Durham, 2001); Daryl Hafter, *Women at Work in PreIndustrial France* (University Park, Pa., 2007); Janine Lanza, *From Wives to Widows in Early Modern Paris: Gender, Economy, and Law* (London, 2007).
6. Elizabeth C. Musgrave, 'Women in the Male World of Work: The Building Industries of Eighteenth-Century Brittany', *French History*, 7 (1993), 30–52.
7. On the need for caution about highlighting one kind of work or shift in opportunities for women too optimistically, see the work of Judith Bennett who concludes that the majority of such situations—although they might constitute 'a good job for a woman'—shared low pay, low status, and the perception of low skill. Judith Bennett, *Ale, Beer and Brewsters: Women's Work in a Changing World, 1400–1600* (New York, 1996), and *History Matters: Patriarchy and the Challenge of Feminism* (Philadelphia, 2006).
8. Arlette Farge, *Fragile Lives: Violence, Power and Solidarity in Eighteenth-Century Paris* (Cambridge, Mass., 1993).
9. Natalie Zemon Davis, *The Return of Martin Guerre* (Cambridge, Mass., 1984); Cynthia Bouton, *The Flour War: Gender, Class, and Community in Late Ancien Regime French Society* (University Park, Pa., 1993).
10. For unusually careful attention to the roles of siblings, see Christine Adams, *A Taste for Comfort and Status: A Bourgeois Family in Eighteenth-Century France* (University Park, Pa., 1999).
11. Archives Départementales du Rhone 8B724, 8 May 1742.
12. David Kertzer and Marcio Barbagli, *The History of the European Family in Early Modern Times, 1500–1789* (New Haven, Conn., 2001), 174.
13. Goodman, 'Marriage Choice and Marital Success', in Suzanne Desan and Jeffrey D. Merrick (eds.), *Family and State in Early Modern France* (University Park, Pa., 2009), 26–61.
14. Hardwick, *Family Business*.
15. Matthew Gerber's forthcoming book, *The End of Bastardy: Politics, Family and Law in Early Modern France*, ch.4, for the 18th-cent. abandonment crisis as illegitimacy rates increased. However the focus of this book is on illegitimacy as a political and legal problem rather than its social or gender aspects. Older explanations, reviewed in Gerber, seem clearly partial or outright misplaced, as in Edward Shorter's famous assertion that the rise in illegitimacy was tied to the liberation of women's libido that resulted from their shift to

industrial work. For the emergence of a homosexual subculture in 18th-cent. Paris, see Bryant T. Ragan, 'The Enlightenment Confronts Homosexuality', in Jeffrey Merrick and Bryant T. Ragan, *Homosexuality in Modern France* (Oxford, 1996). For 18th-cent. prostitution, see Nina Kushner, 'Unkept Women: Elite Prostitution in Eighteenth-Century Paris, 1747–1771' (Ph.D. dissertation, Columbia University, 2005).

16. Olwen Hufton, 'Women and the Family Economy in Eighteenth-Century France', *French Historical Studies*, 9 (1975), 1–22.
17. For the varieties of family economy now evident, see e.g. James R. Farr, *Artisans in Europe, 1400–1900* (Cambridge, 2000), and Crowston, *Fabricating Women*.
18. Pierre Deyon, 'Protoindustrialization in France', in Sheilagh Levine and Markus Cerman (eds.), *European Proto-Industrialization* (Cambridge, 1996); Jan De Vries, *The Industrious Revolution: Consumer Behavior and the Household* (Cambridge, 2008); Gay Gullickson, *The Spinners and Weavers of Auffay: Rural Industry and the Sexual Division of Labor in a French Village* (Cambridge, 1986); Laurence Fontaine, *History of Peddlers in Europe* (Durham, 1996).
19. Daniel Roche pioneered work on consumption patterns in 18th-cent. France with subsequent work by Cissie Fairchilds, Clare Haru Crowston, and Jennifer Jones among others redefining our understanding of the 18th–cent. economy and of relationship of women and gender to those shifts. See Daniel Roche, *The People of Paris: An Essay in Popular Culture in the Eighteenth Century* (Berkeley, Calif., 1987), *The Culture of Clothing: Dress and Fashion in the Ancien Regime* (Cambridge, 1994), and *History of Everyday Things: The Birth of Consumption in France* (Cambridge, 2000); Cissie Fairchilds, 'The Production and Marketing of Populuxe Goods in Eighteenth-Century Paris', in John Brewer and Roy Porter (eds.), *Consumption and the World of Goods* (London, 1993); Crowston, *Fabricating Women*; Jennifer Jones, *Sexing La Mode: Gender, Fashion and Commercial Culture in Old Regime France* (Oxford and New York, 2004).
20. One of the ways in which masculinity remains under-explored in the Old Regime pertains to consumption. While women became arch consumers of fashion and other 'new' household goods like crockery, men certainly became specialized consumers too e.g. as collectors, and we know much less about the forms of consumption coded as masculine.
21. Clare Haru Crowston, 'The Queen and her "Minister of Fashion": Gender, Credit and Politics in Pre–Revolutionary France', *Gender and History*, 14 (2002), 92–116.
22. See e.g. Mita Choudhury, *Convents and Nuns in Eighteenth-Century French Politics and Culture* (Ithaca, NY, 2004) and Elizabeth Rapley, *A Social History of the Cloister: Daily Life in the Teaching Monasteries of the Old Regime* (Toronto, 2001). Barbra Diefendorf's *From Penitence to Charity: Pious Women and the Catholic Reformation in Paris* (New York and Oxford, 2004) deals with an earlier period than this essay but makes a critically important argument about the role of women in shaping the Catholic Reformation in France.
23. The phrase 'conventual invasion' is J. P. Bardet's, quoted in Rapley, *Social History*, 16.
24. Susan Dinan, *Women and Poor Relief in Seventeenth-Century France* (Aldershot, 2006), 4–5.
25. Mita Choudhury, 'Women. Gender, and the Image of the Eighteenth-Century Aristocracy', in Jay. M. Smith (ed.), *The French Nobility in the Eighteenth Century: Reassessments and New Approaches* (University Park, Pa., 2006) and *Convents and Nuns*.
26. For the establishment of the Edict of 1666 and the subsequent history of pronatalist rhetoric and policy, see Leslie Tuttle, *Conceiving the Old Regime: Pronatalism and the Politics of Reproduction in Early Modern France* (Oxford, 2010); for the Foundling Hospital,

see Matthew Gerber's forthcoming book, *The End of Bastardy: Politics, Family and Law in Early Modern France*. I thank Professors Tuttle and Gerber for permission to cite their forthcoming work.
27. Julie Hardwick, *Family Business: Litigation and the Political Economies of Daily Life in Early Modern France* (Oxford, 2009), 6–7.
28. Carolyn Lougee, *Le paradis des femmes: Women, Salons, and Social Stratification in Seventeenth-Century France* (Princeton, 1986).
29. Joan B. Landes, *Women and the Public Sphere in the Age of the French Revolution* (Ithaca, NY, 1988); Dena Goodman, *The Republic of Letters: A Cultural History of the French Enlightenment* (Ithaca, NY, 1994).
30. Hardwick, *Family Business*.
31. Clare Crowston, *Fabricating Women: The Seamstresses of Old Regime France, 1675–1791* (Durham, 2001), 11 and *passim*; Dena Goodman, 'Marriage Choice and Marital Success: Reasoning about Marriage, Love, and Happiness', in Suzanne Desan and Jeffrey Merrick (eds.), *Family, Gender and Law in Early Modern France* (University Park, Pa., 2009).
32. For the Count de Sanois and other *causes célèbres*, see Sarah Maza, *Private Lives and Public Affairs: The Cause Celebres of Pre-Revolutionary France* (Berkeley, Calif., 1993); ibid., for the Grub Street attacks on Marie Antoinette, and Lynn Hunt, *The Family Romance of the French Revolution* (Berkeley, Calif., 1992).
33. Joan Scott, 'Gender: A Useful Category of Historical Analysis', *American Historical Review*, 91 (Dec. 1986), 1053–75.

Bibliography

Adams, Christine, *A Taste for Comfort and Status: A Bourgeois Family in Eighteenth Century France* (University Park, Pa., 1999).
Desan, Suzanne, and Merrick, Jeffrey (eds.) *Family, Gender, and Law in Early Modern France* (University Park, Pa., 2009).
Hardwick, Julie, *The Practice of Patriarchy: Gender and the Politics of Household Authority in Early Modern France* (University Park, Pa., 1998).
—— *Family Business: Litigation and the Political Economics of Daily Life in Early Modern France* (Oxford, 2009).
Hufton, Olwen, *The Prospect Before Her: A History of Women in Western Europe*, i. *1500–1800* (London, 1995).
Ketzer, David, and Barbagli, Marcio, *The History of the European Family in Early Modern Times, 1500–1800* (New Haven, Conn., 2001).
Landes, Joan B., *Women and the Public Sphere in the Age of the French Revolution* (Ithaca, NY, 1988).
Scott, Joan, 'Gender: A Useful Category of Historical Analysis', *American Historical Review* (1986).
Spencer, Samia I. (ed.), *French Women and the Age of Enlightenment* (Bloomington, Ind., 1984).

PART III
ECONOMY

CHAPTER 12

DEMOGRAPHY

JACK A. GOLDSTONE

I. The Demographic Ancien Régime

The Ancien Régime in France was part of a global, centuries-long period of very slow population growth, characterized by high rates of mortality and long cycles in which population would grow for a century or more and then enter a long decline. Between the Black Death of the fourteenth century and the modern industrial era that began in the latter half of the nineteenth century, leading civilizations around the world enjoyed advanced agrarian economies that participated in extensive long-distance trade, supported substantial urban and rural elites, and grew a diversity of crops for local consumption and for market sale. However, lacking artificial fertilizers, the output of crops was always limited by the fertility of the soil, the beneficence of the climate, and the toil that could be drawn from human and animal labour. Since throughout this period roughly 80 per cent of the population drew its living directly from working the land, the output of crops was the chief limit on how many people the land could support.

Yet the match between food supplies and population was not easy or automatic. During the Ancien Régime people had little control over the aggregate size of a country's population. Rather, people's family size was determined by their health and when they married. The population of the Ancien Régime did not practise birth control prior to the late eighteenth century. An exception was the nobility, who began to use a combination of behavioural and barrier methods to avoid conception in the early eighteenth century; but they comprised less than 1 per cent of the population and so had negligible impact on overall fertility.[1] Thus, once they married, couples had as many children as the wife could bear. What determined whether the population would grow or decline was how many of those children survived. If more than two children per couple survived to adulthood, on average, then population would increase. If only two or fewer children survived to adulthood then the population would be stable or even decline.

Ordinary people did have some recourse to control overall population growth—when times were good, more people were able to save the money needed to marry and start a new household, thus increasing the proportion of women who were able to bear children (in Ancien Régime Europe, births out of wedlock were roundly condemned by the church and visited disaster on ordinary people—only nobles got away with such departures from normal moral constraints). But when times were bad, fewer people could marry and start new households, and people would delay marriage or put it off altogether, reducing the number of births. Unlike in Asia, where infanticide was an accepted practice that allowed families to control directly how many of their children survived, European families reacted more indirectly to changing fortunes through changes in the timing and incidence of marriage.

Still, once children were born, factors such as climate or the incidence of disease epidemics determined whether they survived. Since married couples typically had five to six live births in the course of their marriage, fluctuations in the rate of child mortality—that is, whether it was two or three out of their five or six children who managed to survive to adulthood—were generally more important in shaping overall population growth rates in the Ancien Régime than fluctuations in the rate of marriage. Youth mortality was extremely high—half or even fewer of all children survived to see their sixteenth birthday.[2] The typical pattern of populations in Europe was for them to grow during times of better weather and better health as more children survived, while populations were stagnant or declining during periods of colder weather or greater incidence of disease (where the former could well have contributed to the latter), when more children died.

However, the *rate* at which population grew or declined would be moderated by families' reactions, as an extended period of population growth would usually lead to falling real wages and less land being available to start new families, so that marriage rates would decline. Conversely, a long period of population stagnation would usually lead to rising wages or more land becoming available to start new families, so that marriage rates and birth rates would climb. In contrast to modern societies, the very high rates of child mortality meant that even in favourable times, with slightly more births and fewer deaths than normal, population growth was still rather slow—almost always under 1 per cent per year.

The vital rates of populations in the Ancien Régime have been subject to extensive historical reconstruction. However, there is so much variation across communities and regions that national averages can be misleading. For most of the period from 1400 to 1750, one can say that birth rates and death rates ranged around 3 per cent per year (as against less than 1 per cent in modern industrial societies). In some periods birth rates were slightly higher than death rates, in other periods this reversed, but both generally remained in the range of 2.5–3.5 per cent per year throughout this period. Life expectancies were quite low. As we noted, roughly half the population died before reaching the age of 16; those who survived were usually dead by age 50. Thus overall life expectancy was in the range of 30 years.[3]

Histoire immobile?

During the Ancien Régime, the upper limits of population size appear to have remained unchanged for many centuries. Thus the peak population within the modern borders of France at the beginning of the fourteenth century, before the Black Death, was probably 18–20 million people.[4] For the mid-seventeenth century, we can say with somewhat more confidence that the population of France was about 20.3 million, a change of probably not more than 5 per cent across 350 years.[5] Some historians of France have therefore suggested that, while population had its ups and downs, the same basic economic and demographic limits persisted across the Ancien Régime—an *histoire immobile*.[6]

It is certainly true that the same basic conditions of peasant landholding, family formation, mortality-determined population growth, and a society whose output was limited by the basic inputs of land and human and animal labour persisted across, indeed defined, the demography of the Ancien Régime. Yet to the people who lived through this period, conditions were far from constant; indeed they usually seemed to be rapidly changing.

In the short term—from year to year and decade to decade—the harvest was subject to violent fluctuations. Two or three bad years in a row, caused by untimely floods or frosts or drought, could deplete food stocks, send prices skyrocketing, and lead to local food shortages and malnutrition, followed by a marked rise in disease and death. With so much of the population directly dependent on the produce of the land, and with storage difficult and rapidly depleted by rodent and insect pests or spoilt by fungus or rot, people lived in constant anxiety over whether the harvest would succeed. Failure in one year followed by a good year was alright; some storage of grains allowed people to smooth out year-to-year fluctuations in output. But a series of bad years quickly exhausted supplies and led to a sharp spike in mortality.

Such demographic crises occurred in France in 1628–32, 1649–54, 1693–4, and 1709–20. These crises reflected not only local harvest failures, but the difficulties of moving grain from surplus to shortage areas at a time of poor roads, limited carrying capacities, and high internal tariffs. Indeed, localities often considered locally grown grain as 'their own', and preferred to store surpluses locally against the risk of a future shortfall than to have their grain shipped to distant, if needier, communities. State officials and merchants, both of whom sought to alleviate or profit from local shortages by moving grain from surplus to shortage areas, often encountered food riots in communities that resisted movement of their precious grain. After 1720, however, great improvements in internal trade and transport capacity, and the development of an increasingly national market for grain, alleviated this situation, and even when local harvests fell short and prices rose, these conditions no longer resulted in sharp spikes in deaths.

Nonetheless, even when such crises arose—and they occurred every few decades during the Ancien Régime—they did not have a major impact on long-term trends of population growth. This is because while the death rate might increase by 50–100 per cent during such a short-term harvest crisis, those who died were usually the very young and the very old—those who would likely have died in the next few years regardless of the harvest. Such crises thus accelerated deaths, but did not necessarily increase them. Indeed, when older people died in larger numbers, their property passed to their heirs, who were then better placed to start or increase their own families. Thus the short-term increase in deaths was usually followed by a decline in deaths (as the most vulnerable members of the population were no longer there) and an increase in marriages and then births. The net result was that, while death rates, marriage rates, and birth rates could move up and down rapidly with such crises, the net change in overall population across the decades was slight.[7]

While the year-to-year fluctuations of harvests and the demographic responses were always present throughout the Ancien Régime, they were imposed on much longer-term cycles of population growth and decline. For people living during a long up-cycle, or a long down-cycle, although the year-to-year changes were gradual, the cumulative effect of a century or more of population growth, or an equally long period of stagnation or decline, were quite evident.

The long demographic cycles

After a period of substantial growth in the middle ages, population growth slowed down or halted all across Europe around the turn of the fourteenth century. Then at mid-century, the Black Death arrived, and recurrent attacks of the plague brought population declines of roughly 30 to 50 per cent to most European societies by the early fifteenth century. The population of France likely declined from 18–20 million before the Black Death to 12–14 million by 1450. Thus for people living in these years, there would have been no doubt they were living in a period of demographic decline. Villages were abandoned, cities emptied, and land grew increasingly plentiful while labour to work the land became scarce.

For people living in the following century and a half, however, things looked very different. From 1450 onwards, the plague ceased its recurrent visits, and the population began to recover. Mortality continued to decline all the way into the seventeenth century. Earlier losses were made good and then some during the next century and a half, with population reaching 19.5 million by 1550 and 20.6 million by 1660.[8] The population likely peaked in the late 1630s or early 1640s at 23–24 million people. Thus people living in the years from 1450 to 1640 saw themselves as living in a period of slow but steady population growth, with numbers roughly doubling over six generations.

This pattern then repeated, in slightly shorter intervals. Sometime between 1630 and 1660, population growth in France ceased and then reversed, as plague and other diseases returned to boost mortality. By 1700 the population had likely fallen 10 per cent from its mid-seventeenth-century peak, and probably had been even lower in the last decades of the seventeenth century. Thus the generations living from 1640 to 1700 endured another period of population decline. This was followed by a resumption of growth. This time, an expansion of foreign trade bringing Baltic grain to French cities, and the expanded cultivation of maize in the south, boosted output and population

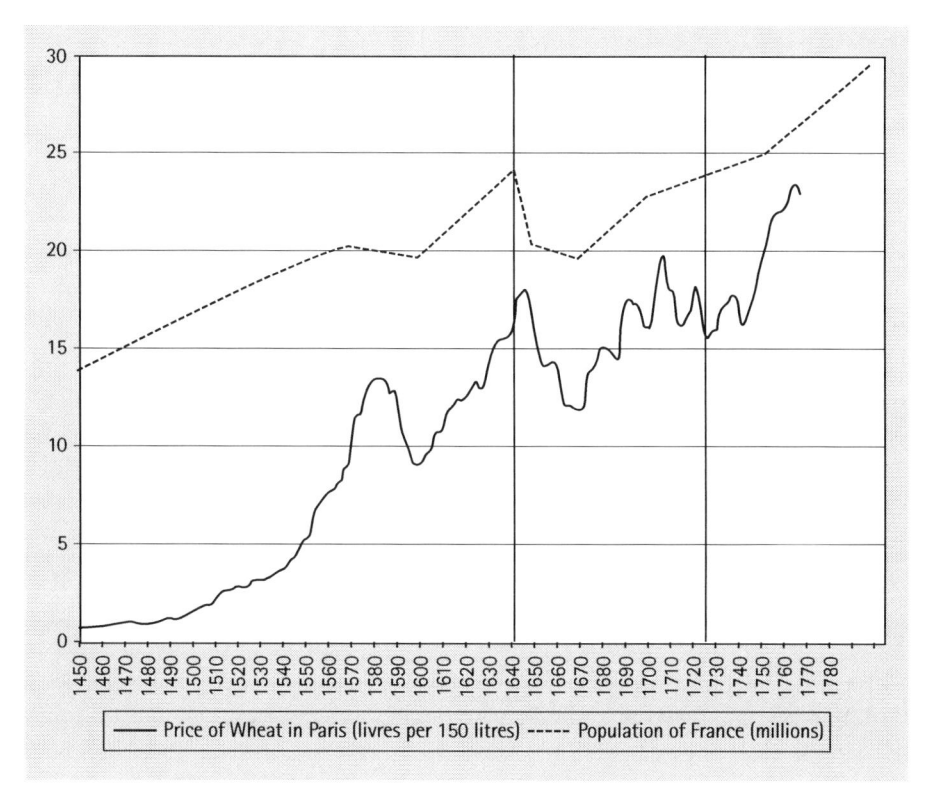

FIGURE 12.1. Population and grain prices during the *Ancien Régime*

beyond its former limits. Population increased from roughly 22.6 million in 1700 to 24.5 million by mid-century and 29.3 million by 1800.[9]

This trajectory of population growth in France is shown in Figure 12.1. This shows a clear alternation between long periods of growth, decline/stagnation, and growth again. From 1450 to 1640, every generation—excepting those in the 1590s—was larger than earlier ones. Then from 1640 to 1725, France's population declined sharply and only slowly recovered, so that population during these seventy-five years remained below the earlier peak. Then after 1725 growth accelerated again and population rose faster in the eighteenth century than it had done any time in the prior three centuries.

II. Demography and Society

The demography of the old regime involved much more than just the rate of population growth or decline, or the size of the population. Demographic ups and downs also shaped the size of cities and towns, the level of prices and wages, the age-structure of the population, patterns of social mobility, and rates of long-distance and local migration. In short, much of the broad structure of society reflected underlying demographic trends.

Cities and villages

Old regime France was predominantly a society of villages—substantial cities were few. As late as 1750, in the midst of a major urban expansion, France still had only fifty-four cities with a population over 10,000. Paris, the capital, towered over all of them. It was the largest city in Europe until 1800, with roughly 700,000 inhabitants at that date. Lyon, the second largest city in France and a centre of silk manufacturing and finance, was but a fraction of that size, reaching perhaps 150,000 by 1800. Other large cities—Nantes, Bordeaux, and Marseille—flourished with the growth of trade in the eighteenth century, but had been much smaller through most of the Ancien Régime.[10]

Both cities and villages grew disproportionately during periods of overall population growth. Peasant families who had multiple surviving children often divided their assets or their lands among their children; but as the parcels grew too small to support a family, the children would sell their inheritance and head for the towns and cities to find work. Growth in provincial towns and cities enabled ambitious men to save and move to larger cities to seek to further improve their fortunes. Opportunities in trade and construction drew people from the countryside to the towns and cities.

This migration from the countryside was essential for urban growth, as the crowding and lack of sanitation made the cities hotbeds of disease and early death. Indeed, rates of natural increase (the margin of births over deaths) remained negative for most cities until 1800. It was only when there were substantial migration flows that cities would grow; without them urban populations would decline.

However, all these processes went into reverse when overall population growth ceased. When rural villagers had only one surviving male child, their children stayed and took over the farm. When rural population stagnated, so too did the markets for urban production, and employment opportunities in the towns were reduced. With less migration and reduced employment, construction work in cities diminished as well. A pattern of urban stagnation or decline set in, until overall population growth resumed. Thus 'the fortunes of European cities as a whole were to a large extent cyclical between 1300 and 1800, periods of stagnation or contraction balancing those of expansion'.[11]

The urban system saw two main periods of expansion during the Ancien Régime: from 1500 to 1640 sustained population growth leading to land shortages in the countryside provided waves of migrants to provincial towns and the major cities. This trend reversed from 1640 to 1700, as all towns excepting only Paris stagnated or shrank in size. But then in the eighteenth century growth returned and urban populations boomed. Dupâquier estimates[12] that from the 1740s to the 1780s smaller towns increased in size by 24 per cent, middling towns by 20 per cent, and the larger cities by 38 per cent, while the rural population increase was only 8.3 per cent. This rapid urban growth was driven in part, again, by rural overcrowding, but also and perhaps even more by the economic development of France in the eighteenth century. Large increases in overseas trade created jobs in ports on the Atlantic, the North Sea, and the Mediterranean, while improvements in internal roads and domestic trade led to the expansion of towns at the junctures of major trade routes. Administrative and judicial capitals flourished with the growth of the professional classes, who expanded the market for luxury crafts and imports. The last decades of the Ancien Régime were thus marked by rapid urban expansion as towns and cities grew significantly more rapidly than the population as a whole.

Price and wages

As population and urbanization expanded and contracted in cycles throughout the Ancien Régime, so too did prices and wages. In the primarily agricultural economy of early modern France, while short-term price movements were highly sensitive to the vagaries of the harvest, the longer-term movements of prices and wages responded strongly to patterns of population growth.

As shown in Figure 12.1, France's population grew rapidly from 1450 to 1640, excepting for a slight halt from 1570 to 1600. While food output initially responded well to this population stimulus, recovering fields that had been abandoned in the aftermath of the Black Death and intensifying and commercializing production, by the second quarter of the sixteenth century prices began to rise. The rise in prices accelerated rapidly in the sixteenth century (driven also in part by imports of silver from the New World), reversed briefly in the late sixteenth century when population fell, then resumed growing with increasing population up to its seventeenth-century peak.

France then experienced roughly eighty years, from 1640 to 1720, during which population fell then returned to earlier levels. During that period, prices too fell and then recovered but generally did not exceed their earlier peak. This period, roughly coincident with the reign of Louis XIV, was thus an extended period of net stability in population and prices. But for the rest of the eighteenth century, population advanced beyond its earlier levels, breaking out of the traditional ceiling of 20–22 millions, and prices rapidly escalated as well.

Real wages also moved in long waves, in virtually the mirror-image of prices. The level of nominal wages—the number of *sous* per day paid to artisans and labourers—tended to be fixed by custom and was only altered rarely and under great duress. Workers would violently protest any reduction in their daily rate of pay, so those rates tended to stay fixed even when prices were falling. But those were also times in which workers had some real bargaining power, since falling prices usually reflected a decline or stagnation in population and a decline in migration, so that urban labour was becoming scarce. Thus during times of population stagnation or decline, the real wages—that is, the actual buying power—of worker's earnings tended to increase. The highest and steadiest real wages were thus enjoyed by rural and urban wage workers during the era of Louis XIV.

By contrast, the periods before and afterwards were times in which real wages fell. Over the eighteenth century, real wages fell by about one-third, with conditions being especially harsh in the 1770s, which was marked by numerous bread riots. Periods of sustained population increase were also periods in which surpluses of labour made jobs harder to come by; thus added to the pressures of lower real wages was a scarcity of work. People were lucky to find jobs that lasted throughout the year. The rapidly growing cities of the eighteenth century may have been prosperous places for the professionals and bourgeoisie, whose trade and work were growing. But they were often desperate places for the working poor, who found work harder to come by, wages stagnant or falling, and the prices of housing, food, and other necessities rising year-by-year.

Age structures and migration

Demographers characterize a society's population by many measures. In addition to the size of the population, its urbanization, and how fast it is growing (or declining), demographers note changes in society's age structure—that is, what proportion of the population is in various age groups, e.g. 0–15, 15–25, 25–35, 35 and older.

In modern industrial societies, the age structure is fairly uniform. The number of people born each year is very close to the number who die. Most of the latter are the elderly, as the death rate of children is quite low. The age structure of such populations is fairly uniform: the proportion of the population under 35 and the proportion over 35 is roughly equal.

In poor developing societies, however, as in the society of the Ancien Régime, child mortality is very high. Large numbers of children are born, but roughly half of them die before reaching their fifteenth year. The result is that the age structure of the society is very heavy tilted towards the very young, as at any time there are large numbers of children who were recently born, but a much smaller number of surviving adults. The percentage of the population under 15 years old may be 40 or 50 per cent.

The most crucial age group, or cohort, for employment and political rebellion is the population aged 15–25. This is the group that has just entered, or recently entered, the labour force, and so is most sensitive to recent changes in employment levels and wages. This is also the age group that has usually not yet formed a large family, and thus is free to take risks. This is also the most mobile group, making up the majority of people who are moving from countryside to city, or from city to city, to seek work.[13]

A striking thing happens to this particular cohort in response to the cycles of population increase and decline. Because population increase is driven mainly by more children surviving their early years, during periods of population growth the age group from 15 to 25 greatly swells relative to the rest of the population. As the greater numbers of surviving children enter this age group, they greatly exceed the numbers in the older cohorts who had faced much lower survival rates in youth. The ratio of youth aged 15–25 to adults 25 and older can suddenly tilt in the course of a few decades.

In the Ancien Régime, the periods 1600–40 and 1740–90 were marked by exceptionally youthful populations. In these periods the numbers of youth aged 15–25 were likely larger than the adult population aged 25–40. This fuelled surges in migration.

Young men and women moved from poorer areas, where the land gave out first (the Massif central, the Alpine regions) to areas with richer fields that could employ their labour. People also moved from the country to the towns in search of work, and the ambitious and energetic moved from smaller towns to larger ones, and from the larger towns to the major cities. These streams of migrants also made the city populations—where migrant youths were concentrated—overflowing with young.

Again, all these patterns reversed when population growth slowed. When the numbers of surviving children virtually matched the numbers of their parents, it was simple for inheritance to preserve the existing social order. Titles and lands could be inherited without being broken up and shared, or younger sons being turned out on their own; peasant farms would be handed down to sons or sons-in-law who would simply take over the existing lands. Migration was reduced to a trickle, with only the very largest towns, which continued to attract the most talented and ambitious, still able to attract adventurous souls. This had significant consequences for social mobility.

Social mobility

Social mobility is the movement of people up and down across the status divisions of society. When more people are moving up from being workers to becoming professionals, from being small farmers to becoming commercial landowners, or are moving down from well-off to poorer status, we say that social mobility is high. By contrast, when most people remain in the same social category where they and their parents were, social mobility is low.

The long cycles of population movements in the Ancien Régime also had powerful impacts on social mobility. We might think of Ancien Régime France as a society in which social mobility was low almost by definition. After all, only about 1 per cent of the population was noble, many with hereditary nobility that automatically fell to their children, while most people were commoners, and the great majority of them rural villagers and peasants. Yet that is an oversimplified view.

Commoners could enter the nobility in many ways. Valour on the battlefield was one route, but more common by the seventeenth and eighteenth centuries was government service, as many state offices awarded their holder noble rank. Moreover, as the government was often eager for ready cash, most offices were available for sale to those who could afford them. Since periods of population expansion were usually periods of expanding trade and commercial opportunities for merchants and professionals, and rising prices offered exceptional profits to farmers and urban landlords who managed their property well, such periods produced large numbers of people with the resources to bid for office.

At the same time, larger numbers of surviving children meant a division and decline in landholdings per family for those—including nobles—who divided their estates among their heirs (as was the custom in many parts of France). Two or three generations of good luck with surviving children, but no such good luck in managing one's property or increasing one's assets, meant downward mobility for middling and even wealthy families. The capitation rolls of the late eighteenth century show that many noble families dropped out of the order or requested exemptions due to poverty. The surging number of youth aged 15–25 meant both risks and opportunities; those who were able to profit from expanding markets and purchase offices could move up rapidly in the world. By contrast, the fact that the number of youth greatly exceeded the number of adults in the existing elite positions meant that many aspirations were bound to be frustrated. Even while the enrolments at law schools and schools of medicine and theology surged and apprentices in trade and manufacturing multiplied, the number of positions as state officials, provincial lawyers and notaries, and master craftsmen could not keep pace. Downward mobility and upward mobility were thus both more common during periods of population expansion.

Periods of population stagnation, by contrast, offered a tableau of low social mobility. When the number of children was virtually the same as the number of their parents, inheritance acted to 'lock in' the existing social order. During such periods, lands could be inherited without being broken up and shared, and titles could passed down without younger sons being denied. Peasant farmers could know that their children would have the same amount of land and tools and animals that they had enjoyed. The ranks of the elite could easily absorb the few exceptionally able and advancing youth who sought to move up even in such periods of stability. Thus while times of population growth presented a field of increased competition and relatively rapid upward and downward social mobility, periods of population stagnation or decline appeared to foster a stable and certain social order, with migration and social mobility both relatively low.

The patchwork quilt: local and regional variations

The preceding paragraphs have focused on broad overall trends in French society in response to patterns of demographic growth and stagnation. Yet during the Ancien Régime, France was not a well-integrated society. Communications and transportation, though improving, remained slow and unreliable. France did not even have a common language, with Brittany, Languedoc, Roussillon, and other regions preserving their own medieval tongues. Demographic trends similarly varied greatly across the landscape.

In the sixteenth and seventeenth centuries, population growth was likely greatest in the Mediterranean regions and the south-west. The introduction of American crops and favourable weather made for substantially increased population in the sixteenth century, a population increase that continued, after a slight pause at the end of the century, into the first half of the seventeenth. Yet in the eighteenth century, the north-east appears to have grown most rapidly—population gains may have reached 100 per cent in the far north and Alsace.[14] The economic consequences of population growth varied regionally as well. In areas well suited to viticulture, very small plots of land could sustain a family. By contrast, in the large open plains of the north-east, population pressures led to smaller farms being sold and consolidated, so that population growth produced a polarization of larger landowners and landless or smallholding peasants. The uplands and poorer soil regions produced streams of out-migrants, while the fertile river valleys and coastal regions absorbed those migrants and concentrated youth and newcomers.

The Ancien Régime was thus a patchwork of varying local trends and responses. The overall cycles of demographic increase and stagnation/decline washed over the entire society, but broke with different strength, and with different results, in different regions. These differences were most evident in the responses to the final crisis of the old order.

III. Demography and the French Revolution

The end of the Ancien Régime was marked by many changes in French society—changes in public discussion, in views of royal authority, and in attitudes toward the church and the nobility. But these changes had substantial links to changes in the underlying demography of the eighteenth century, when France's population mounted upward to previously unseen heights.

We should be absolutely clear that an analysis of the role of demography in the end of the Ancien Régime and the origins of the French Revolution has nothing to do with simple Malthusian notions of crowding or overpopulation or even poverty. France at the end of the Ancien Régime was not only more populous, it was also richer, more urbanized, and had a more diversified economy than ever before. However, not all Frenchmen and women benefited equally from these changes, and the economic gains and losses of various groups, in conjunction with some of the above-noted effects of demographic changes on age, migration, and social mobility, undermined the arrangements that had supported the monarchy in the days of Louis XIV. These changes provided a potential for new social arrangements and incentives for social and political change.

The political strategy of the Sun King

When Louis XIV took power in 1661, France looked back at decades of turmoil, from the Wars of Religion in the late sixteenth century to the peasant uprisings of the 1630s and 1640s and the urban conflicts and civil wars of the Frondes in the 1650s. In this, France was not alone. Britain too had suffered from civil wars, and Germany had been torn asunder in the Thirty Years War. All across Europe, rulers sought ways to gain firmer control of their countries, and of the fractious nobilities whose religious and factional fights had produced so much disorder.

In the latter half of the seventeenth century, the royal houses of Europe developed diverse strategies for coping with their powerful nobilities. In Britain the crown learnt it had to work with the gentry who controlled Parliament as partners in rule, accepting a joint sovereignty and limited—if not yet constitutional—monarchy. In Prussia and

Russia the traditional nobility was turned into a service nobility, largely stripped of any independent political or financial role.

In France the monarchy strode something of a middling path, neither giving up claims to royal absolutism, nor fully subordinating noble power to royal administration. Instead, the French monarch acted as the fulcrum in a critical balancing act, allowing the nobility to play a key role at court and in the royal household and in the military, and to maintain many of their local privileges and even their administrative and financial roles in certain provincial estates and as governors of the provinces and major cities. However, the nobility's power was diluted by two countervailing factors. First, with land rents stagnant in the late seventeenth and early eighteenth centuries, as a result of falling population, the high nobility became increasingly dependent on the largesse of the royal court and the favour of the King to achieve exceptional wealth and status among their peers. Second, the monarchy greatly expanded the number and functions of administrative elites, granting many of them noble status and privileges, and allowing their power in provincial administration, judiciary, finance, and the ministries to parallel or even exceed that of the traditional nobility. With the crown maintaining its claims to absolute authority, it claimed to stand above the older military nobility and the new administrative nobility, funding and directing this vast machinery to maintain the glory and prosperity of France. Yet keeping this balancing act going successfully depended on the crown enjoying the vast revenues of the largest and richest kingdom in Europe, and on persuading the various groups of the nobility, as well as urban professionals, to work together in their parallel and sometimes criss-crossing roles.

In the late seventeenth century, demographic trends were favourable to supporting these arrangements. The sharp decline and then slow recovery of population allowed food output to move ahead of demand, leading to lower prices for most goods. This meant that the tax revenues of the crown, which grew moderately in nominal terms, grew even faster in terms of purchasing power. Since at the same time the rents and land values of the nobility fell as the population decline reduced the demand for land, the financial leverage of the crown over the nobility greatly increased.

The demographic slowdown also curbed the growth of towns and limited the income gains of merchants and professionals, while also reducing the number of excess youths from noble families. These trends reduced the competition for noble ranks and places at court. The crown could thus satisfy the great majority of aspirants for elite positions, and relations between different sectors of the nobility and professional groups were not inflamed by a shortage of places or anxieties about downward mobility.

Finally, the peasantry enjoyed stable family sizes and low rents for land, while urban workers benefited from scarcities of labour and higher real wages. The latter half of the seventeenth century was thus marked by far fewer and smaller peasant uprisings and urban riots, unlike the tumultuous period from the end of the sixteenth century to the middle of the seventeenth.

Over the course of the eighteenth century, however, with the return of rapid population increase, these conditions for stability gradually broke down.

The convergence of demographic, social, and political factors in the eighteenth century

With the unprecedented population growth of the eighteenth century came a number of diverse social and political trends. First, population growth joined with expanding overseas and domestic trade to create a more diversified and commercial economy. Although even as late as 1789 agriculture provided over two-thirds of France's GDP, trade and industry had become the more dynamic sector, its value growing almost three times as fast in real terms as the output of agriculture. Over the course of the eighteenth century, the growth in the real value of trade and industry provided almost half of the total increase in French output.[15] The wealth of the urban/commercial sector thus had to be tapped if the crown was going to secure access to France's growing wealth.

However, France remained more dependent on taxes on agriculture than its British rival. In fact, from 1700 to 1789 the rate of direct taxes on agriculture rose more than the rate of indirect taxation on trade and industry, even though the output of the latter sectors rose much faster. As the government struggled to keep pace with rising expenses the per capita taxes on the relatively stagnant agricultural sector doubled during the eighteenth century.[16]

The crown thus faced a growing financial struggle. Rising prices for labour and materials and food—and especially for military supplies—meant that the crown's need for funds was steadily rising. Yet the tax system, failing to capture as much as it might of the gains to trade and industry, failed to produce the revenues necessary to sustain the crown's military and administrative activities.

From the perspective of the taxpayers—both noble and commoner—this was an outrageous situation. The crown constantly complained of lack of funds and the need to raise taxes. Yet in the agricultural sector, which comprised most of the population and two-thirds of output, the growth of population was pressing on available land and supplies. The output of grains and animal products barely kept pace with the growth in population; indeed overall it seems likely that real output per capita in the agricultural sector was flat or even suffered a slight decline.[17] Thus the increase in taxes on agriculture was deeply felt and widely resented.

This was even more the case as landowners, in the last decades of the eighteenth century, took advantage of the land hunger of a growing peasantry to impose a variety of fees and to sharply escalate land rents. In years of poor harvests, as the 1770s and in 1788, poorer peasants could scarcely hang on to enough output to feed their families, and acted vigorously in crises to block the movement of grain outside their areas, or to defend their own supplies against perceived threats from the growing number of landless, jobless vagrants migrating across the countryside in search of work. Conflicts were particularly harsh in the north-east, where large tracts of grain-producing land were becoming ever more valuable and peasants faced some of the greatest encroachments from grasping landlords, and in the south and central regions, where population growth imposed some of the gravest burdens on lighter soils and dryer climes.

At the same time, the rise in land rents and the growth of the commercial economy provided great opportunities for upward social mobility for professionals and merchants, many of whom invested their professional earnings in land outside the towns. Yet the crown, which had sold increasing numbers of ennobling offices and others with various privileges and status benefits in the seventeenth century, reduced the creation of new offices by the early eighteenth century, preferring to meet its financial needs by borrowing rather than by conferring the permanent tax-exemptions that sales of privileged offices generally provided. As a result, the larger and richer array of merchants, bankers, and urban professionals could only bid for ennoblement by seeking to purchase existing offices when they became vacant or came on the market.

This meant that by the last decades of the eighteenth century the most desirable offices—like the most desirable lands—were bid up in price beyond the reach of most aspirants. The crown also stepped up tax collection from officeholders, increased taxes on noble landlords, and imposed additional fees and renewals on many royal offices. The urban professionals, administrative nobility, and landholders all opposed these efforts to curtail or undermine their privileges and the value of their positions, decrying such efforts as 'tyranny' that threatened the 'liberties' embodied in their control of their offices and traditional tax exemptions.

In addition, as noble privileges seemed to become more valuable in light of the crown's efforts to raise taxes and of commoners' efforts to buy their way into noble ranks, older noble families sought to conserve their status by reducing the numbers of their children, to avoid burdening their estates and subdividing assets. As the nobility moved in large numbers to the cities in the eighteenth century, they also adopted methods of contraception. Compared to the 1660s, noble families had only two-thirds as many children per family in the fifty years prior to the Revolution. Since the number of surviving children was never large, this meant the number of adult surviving male heirs dropped from an average closer to two to an average closer to one, essentially ensuring that properties passed intact to the next generation.

The lack of surviving younger siblings also meant that there was little establishment of new cadet lines to counterbalance the substantial number of poorer nobility who were, in effect, dropping from the roles of recognized nobility due to poverty. Nassiet[18] observes an overall decline in the number of nobles on the *capitation* rolls of almost 40 per cent over the course of the eighteenth century. The lack of cadet lines and younger siblings surviving to adulthood also meant fewer opportunities for wealthy commoners to marry their children into the nobility. Just as with the crown's decision to reduce the sale of privileged offices, and their escalation in price, the reduction of marriage opportunities restricted the avenues for access to noble status at precisely the time that urban and commercial expansion was increasing the demand for that status.

While the crown fretted over its finances, peasants anguished over their livelihoods, and the growing numbers of urban and professional elites fought with the traditional nobility over access to offices and ranks, the swelling numbers of workers and artisans in France's growing cities faced their own difficulties.

As we noted, the eighteenth century was a period of major urban expansion; Paris likely grew from 500,000 to 700,000, and smaller cities grew even faster, increasing by half or even doubling in size. Yet this influx of young urban migrants increasingly overloaded urban job markets, while the ability of the countryside to afford urban products stagnated as the price of land and basic foods climbed. By the 1770s, real wages in Paris had fallen by roughly one-third compared to the 1720s; the decline in wages was even more marked in some provincial cities. Wages recovered somewhat in the 1780s with better harvests, but urban wages collapsed after the terrible harvest of 1788–9. These hardships fell upon cities bursting with youth, who would provide ready recruits for urban uprisings.

All of these trends set the stage for the political and social struggles that would bring an end to the Ancien Régime. When the crown, unable to resolve its financial problems without seeking major concessions from French elites, consented to call the Estates-General for the first time in 175 years, the assemblies of peasants, nobles, and urban groups gave rise to choruses of complaints. Peasants railed against taxes and the revival of feudal impositions and fees and raids on their common lands by grasping landlords. Nobles complained that their ancient privileges and esteemed status was being eroded by the numbers of recently enriched merchants and professionals or their sons who were buying up positions in the court and military and administration. Professional elites complained of the fiscal irresponsibility of the crown, of the privileges still reserved for those with noble rank, and the venality of the church. All complained of the corruption and mismanagement of the King's ministers, who had let such disorder arise.

When the Estates-General finally met, it is unsurprising that the hereditary nobles and the recently enriched professional elites would not agree over who should hold a leading role in designing and approving any reforms. It is understandable that the crowds of Paris, expecting that the Estates would bring them some relief from their deteriorating economic straits, would rise to protect the Estates when the King, dismayed at their internal wrangling, seemed on the point of dismissing them. And when these disorders paralysed the capital, the peasantry can hardly be blamed for seeking to reverse the recent encroachments by landlords, declaring invalid recent increases in fees and changes in land tenure and burning the charters that held those terms. In short, the demographic changes of the eighteenth century, and their social and economic consequences, laid the foundations for the conflicts and struggles that closed the eighteenth century.

IV. The End of the Demographic Old Regime

The French Revolution ushered in a new age of reason and equality in politics and society. It also ushered in a new era in French demography.

At the end of the Ancien Régime, France had the largest population of any state in western Europe, and its families—with an average of five births per woman—were as fertile as any. But after the Revolution fertility went into a sharp decline, as France became the first country in Europe to begin the 'demographic transition' to lower fertility and mortality and slower population growth. The number of children per woman fell from 5.0 to 3.5 from 1790 to 1855.[19] Though industrialization greatly increased the availability of food in France, as railways brought fertilizers to fields and delivered crops from distant markets, and mortality sharply declined—changes that sharply increased population growth everywhere else in Europe—the rate of population growth in nineteenth-century France was no greater than it had been in the eighteenth century. France thus moved swiftly, and relatively early, from an Ancien Régime demographic pattern of high fertility and high mortality to a more modern pattern of lower fertility and lower mortality.[20]

The reasons for France's early fertility decline are not well understood. It appears that it involved voluntary efforts to reduce conception within marriage and increase the spacing of births by traditional methods, as well as by some early adoption of contraceptive methods. It also appears that the fertility decline began early in the eighteenth century among the nobility and highest income classes, but then spread relatively rapidly throughout the population. It is still speculation, but it may be that the new ideals of social equality that arrived with the end of the Ancien Régime also extended to equality in demographic behaviour, with all French men and women imitating the smaller family size and lower fertility that began to appear in the upper classes at the end of the eighteenth century.

By 1850, the demographic characteristics of the Ancien Régime were becoming a thing of the past. With much lower mortality, even with lower fertility, population grew steadily, instead of the old pattern of long cycles of growth and decline. Urban population, fuelled by industrialization and overall population increase, rocketed to levels previously unknown, so that by the twentieth century over half the population was urban. The Ancien Régime demography of rural agricultural society, long cycles, slow growth, high fertility, and high mortality did not long outlast the Ancien Régime itself.

Notes

1. Michel Nassiet, 'Un chantier en cours: Les Effectifs de la noblesse en France et leur évolution du xvie au xviiie siècle', in Jarosław Dumanowski and Michel Figeac (eds.), *Noblesse française et noblesse polonaise: Mémoire, identité, culture. xvie–xxe siècles* (Bordeaux, 2006); S. C. Watkins, *From Provinces into Nations: The Demographic Intergration of Western Europe, 1870–1960* (Princeton, 1991).
2. M. Livi-Bacci, *The Population of Europe: A History* (Oxford, 2000), 113.
3. Ibid. 134–5.
4. J. Kelly, *The Great Mortality* (New York, 2005), 46.

5. Jacques Dupâquier in Dupâquier (ed.), *Histoire de la population française*, ii. *De la Renaissance à 1789* (Paris, 1988), 68–81.
6. Emmanuel Le Roy Ladurie, *The Peasants of Languedoc*, tr. John Day (Urbana, Ill., 1974).
7. F. Lebrun, 'Les Crises démographiques en France aux xviie et xviiie siècles', *Annales ESC*, 35 (1980); S. C. Watkins and J. Mencken, 'Famines in Historical Perspective', *Population and Development Review*, 11 (1985), 647–75.
8. Dupâquier, *Histoire de la population française*, 64–5.
9. Livi-Bacci, *Population of Europe*, 8.
10. Jack A. Goldstone, *Revolution and Rebellion in the Early Modern World* (Berkeley, Calif., 1991), 180.
11. P. M. Hohenburg and M. H. Lees, *The Making of Urban Europe, 1000–1950* (Cambridge, Mass., 1985), 106.
12. *Histoire de la population française*, 245.
13. John R. Gillis, *Youth and History* (New York, 1974).
14. Goldstone, *Revolution and Rebellion*, 178–9.
15. Ibid. 204.
16. Ibid. 204–5.
17. Philip T. Hoffman, *Growth in a Traditional Society: The French Countryside, 1450–1815* (Princeton, 1996).
18. 'Un chantier en cours'.
19. E. A. Acampo, 'The Gendered Nature of Contraception in France: Neo-Malthusianism, 1900–1920', *Journal of Interdisciplinary History*, 34 (2003), 235–62.
20. A. J. Coale and S. C. Watkins (eds.), *The Decline of Fertility in Europe* (Princeton, 1986).

Bibliography

Acampo, E. A., 'The Gendered Nature of Contraception in France: Neo-Malthusianism, 1900–1920', *Journal of Interdisciplinary History*, 34 (2003), 235–62.
Coale, A. J., and Watkins, S. C. (eds.), *The Decline of Fertility in Europe* (Princeton, 1986).
Dupâquier, J., and Lepetit, B., 'La Peuplade', in J. Dupâquier (ed.), *Histoire de la population française*, ii. *De la renaissance à 1789* (Paris, 1988).
Gillis, J., *Youth and History* (New York, 1974).
Goldstone, J. A., *Revolution and Rebellion in the Early Modern World* (Berkeley, Calif., 1991).
—— 'The Social Origins of the French Revolution Revisited', in Thomas Kaiser and Dale Van Kley (eds.), *From Deficit to Deluge: The Origins of the French Revolution* (Stanford, Calif., 2011), 67–103.
Hoffman, P. T., *Growth in a Traditional Society: The French Countryside, 1450–1815* (Princeton, 1996).
Hohenberg, P. M., and Lees, L. H., *The Making of Urban Europe 1000–1950* (Cambridge, Mass., 1985).
Kelly, J., *The Great Mortality* (New York, 2005).
Lebrun, F., 'Les Crises dèmographiques en France aux xviie et xviiie siècles', *Annales, ESC*, 35 (1980), 205–34.
Le Roy Ladurie, E., *The Peasants of Languedoc*, tr. John Day (Urbana, Ill., 1974).
Livi-Bacci, M., *The Population of Europe: A History* (Oxford, 2000).

Nassiet, Michel, 'Un chantier en cours: Les Effectifs de la noblesse en France et leur évolution du xvie au xviiie siècle', in Jarosław Dumanowski and Michel Figeac (eds.), *Noblesse française et Noblesse polonaise: Mémoire, identité, culture. xvie–xxe siécles* (Bordeaux, 2006), 19–43.

Watkins, S. C., *From Provinces into Nations: The Demographic Integration of Western Europe, 1870–1960* (Princeton, 1991).

—— and Mencken, J., 'Famines in Historical Perspective', *Population and Development Review*, 11 (1985), 647–75.

CHAPTER 13

FEUDALISM

ANTHONY CRUBAUGH

> *It is a universally recognized maxim that seigneurial rights are imprescriptible, even after 200 years of cessation of payment.*[1]

THE term 'feudalism' did not exist during the medieval period it purportedly explains. Like 'absolutism', feudalism lacks an agreed upon definition, provokes scholarly debate about the concept's validity as well as complaints about its over-application, and constitutes a central feature of the 'old regime' abolished by French revolutionaries.

The revolutionary summer of 1789 in France witnessed widespread peasant attacks on châteaux and the burning of *chartriers* containing records of feudal obligations. In response to this rural upheaval, representatives in Versailles promulgated the famous 4 August decree that 'the National Assembly destroys the feudal regime in its entirety'. The opening article abolished serfdom immediately and without indemnity while stipulating that other feudal rights would be redeemable according to a future formula issued by the legislature. Subsequent clauses put an end to the vexatious right of lords to have dovecotes and their monopoly on hunting rights as well as to seigneurial courts. Article 5 stated that 'tithes of every condition … are abolished, on condition, however, that some other method be devised for the expense of public worship'—a fateful decision that played out tragically in the Revolution. Representatives next proclaimed that perpetual ground rents were also redeemable. In a shift of focus from issues that mainly impacted the countryside, later clauses abolished venality of office, tax privileges, and all particular privileges so that all provinces and cities could be 'absorbed into the law common to all Frenchmen'. The eleventh clause announced the eligibility of all citizens regardless of birth to any military, ecclesiastical, or civil office or dignity.

This brief summary of the 4 August decree raises several critical points that inform this chapter. First, the document contains a 'fatal ambiguity'[2] insofar as it loftily broadcast the destruction of feudalism while simultaneously communicating the preservation of substantial elements of it in the guise of redeemable dues. The premature obituary of feudalism had major ramifications for the course of the Revolution and impacts the historian's assessment of the significance of the 'abolition of feudalism' on the night of 4 August. Second, the decree highlights the confusing nature of 'feudalism'. Students encountering a supposedly world-historical document wonder why pigeons and dovecotes merit such prominent mention; the inclusion of the tithe puzzles readers who understand the origins and function of that charge on agricultural productivity; and the conflation of venality of offices or provincial pecuniary privileges with feudalism is likewise perplexing. The confusion is not merely a problem of moderns failing to understand a prior historical context, for revolutionaries themselves, after first destroying the thing, had to unpack the meaning of the *complexum feodale* and assigned the difficult task to the Feudal Committee of the National Assembly. Third, and closely related, while the term frequently causes confusion, the concept's capaciousness and elasticity are important aspects of 'feudalism' as it pertains to eighteenth-century France. For by 1789 the limited sense of feudalism as a compendium of rights and form of surplus extraction had merged with the broader understanding of a 'feudal regime' as an entire political and social system rooted in violence, based on aristocratic privilege and inequality, and antithetical to the regeneration of the French nation on the foundations of individual rights and civil equality.

Feudalism generally refers to a medieval system of political, social, and economic organization based on vassalage and the granting of a *foedum* (fief) that developed in western Europe with the collapse of authority following Germanic invasions. Medieval feudal contracts involved the establishment of a hierarchical but mutually supportive relationship among private individuals, cemented by a ceremony in which a vassal paid homage and promised material and military support to a lord in return for the lord's protection and the investiture of a fief. Although feudal contracts governed the reciprocal obligations among the noble military elite, the landed estates that served as the basis of the warrior class's economic power required the labour of peasants. In need of protection, free peasants supposedly delivered their persons and lands to the authority of a lord, who returned land to peasants (now serfs) in perpetual tenancies but exacted from them various dues, services, and obligations. The authority of overlords and obligations of peasants towards them together constitute the concept of 'seigneurialism' or 'manorialism', which stems from the basic physical unit—the *seigneurie*—into which nearly all of rural France was parcelled.

Obviously, feudalism and seigneurialism are inextricably linked, for, as Guy Lemarchand notes, 'the seigneurie [was the] instititution *par excellence* of medieval feudalism'.[3] As a result, some historians of the eighteenth century use the terms interchangeably even if they recognize that state-building and the growing strength of the monarchy created political and military conditions vastly different from the medieval period. (For example, Louis XIV last invoked the *ban* and *arrière-ban*, or the obligation of vassals to assist a lord in war, in 1694.) Other historians employ 'seigneurialism' to emphasize that they are essentially describing a socio-economic system based on the seigneurie as a system of land tenure and jurisdiction of rights. Still others insist on the validity of 'feudalism' to describe the legal status of property in old regime France.

David Parker, for one, argues that jurists focused on feudal law during the reign of Louis XIV and throughout the eighteenth century because the fundamental attributes of a feudal hierarchy—acts of fealty and homage, hereditary seigneurial justice, *dénombrements* (descriptions of the land, dues, and obligations of a fief that a new vassal owed to a lord), and monarchical claims of honorific and financial benefits stemming from lordship (*domaine directe*)—remained central to the conception and the regulation of property.[4] Or, as Sydney Herbert pronounced: 'Political feudalism, then, was dead; economic feudalism was living and vigorous ...'[5]

Contemporaries cited neither 'féodalisme' nor 'seigneurialism', but 'fief' and its adjectival form (feudal) as well as the notion of a 'feudal complex' were commonplace legal terms governing the litany of rights exercised by lords within the seigneurie, as evidenced in treatises such as Renauldon's *Dictionnaire des fiefs et des droits seigneuriaux*. Furthermore, the idea of a 'feudal system' (*féodalité*) had existed since the sixteenth century and attained prominence in political discourse in the eighteenth century.[6] Although Boucher d'Argis's entry on *féodalité* in the *Encyclopédie* of Diderot and d'Alembert concentrated on the legal aspects of the fief contract, the term had already gained broader currency in historical writing. Montesquieu's *L'Esprit des lois* exerted special influence over the discussion that focused on the 'feudal system' as a type of government that linked the destinies of the King and France's nobility after Germanic conquests of Gaul. Whereas Montesquieu celebrated the liberty-preserving development of a French monarchy that, although sovereign, experienced limitations on its authority because of feudalism's legacy, other thinkers employed the idea of the 'feudal system' as an organizing tool of French history to pursue different political agendas. Boulainvilliers traced the feudal system to conquests at the origins of French history and therefore considered monarchical power a distortion of the original constitution and a usurpation of the prerogatives of nobility. Physiocrats such as Le Trosne in *Dissertation sur la féodalité* traced the disintegration of royal sovereignty to hereditary fiefs and the concomitant independence of lords, while absolutist apologists such as Linguet simply denounced the 'feudal system' as anarchy based on violence and celebrated the centuries-long rise of royal power. Thus, the perception of the feudal system as the critical villain of French history—so central to the Revolution—owed much to the proponents of absolutist and rational monarchy in the eighteenth century. In a significant innovation, Mably's *Observations sur l'histoire de France* in 1765 saw both feudalism and absolutism (now 'despotism') as destructive of the egalitarian citizenship and primitive democracy in the fields putatively practised in France's early history. Mably's denunciation of the feudal system and absolutism and his call for a restoration of the nation's rights reverberated in numerous writings during the political crisis beginning in 1787. According to François Furet, the explosion of pamphlets prior to 1789 treating the feudal system as originating in violence and antithetical to law indicates that 'a revolution had taken place in people's minds prior to the Revolution'.[7]

Although locales in such provinces as Languedoc acknowledged the maxim 'no lord without title', thereby ensuring vast allodial lands free of seigneurial exactions, most of France adhered to the concept of 'no land without lord'. Thus, most of the countryside fell under the institution of the seigneurie, consisting of the land owned directly by a lord (*réserve* or desmesne/domain) and that granted hereditarily to others (*mouvance*) and all of which was subject to the lord's judicial power. The Roman law notion of a single owner in complete enjoyment of property (*jus utendi, jus fruendi, jus abutendi*) as well as the modern idea of property rights (limited by the state's taxation, eminent domain, criminal statutes, and inheritance laws) were foreign to the seigneurie as exemplified by the distinction between *domaine utile* and *domaine directe*. Persons within the *mouvance* in possession of *domaine utile* enjoyed the right to sell, rent, exploit, or bequeath their land and in this respect seemingly resembled modern proprietors. But because land tenures were considered to be held in perpetuity from a seigneurial concession, a lord retained the *domaine directe* or ultimate jurisdiction entitling him not only to recognition as lord in the form of acts of fealty and homage (for supposedly noble land, or fiefs) or payment of *cens* for common land (*censives*) but also to a plethora of honorific and material rights. As John Markoff writes, 'The web of property relations, then, was conceived as intertwined with a web of personal relations among unequals.'[8]

Of what, then, did feudalism consist in eighteenth-century France? In theory, jurists differentiated feudal from seigneurial rights, as explained by Jean Gallet:

> Seigneurial rights are distinguished from feudal rights properly speaking; the latter *cens, lods et ventes, quints*, etc. weigh only on vassals, censitaires, and other tenants holding *propriété [domaine] utile* and because of this property; conversely, seigneurial rights concern all those who, whether proprietors or not, inhabit the seigneurie.[9]

In practice, however, the difference between feudal obligations stemming from land tenures and seigneurial obligations falling on everyone within a lord's jurisdiction meant little, especially to rural denizens. Recognizing contemporaries' proclivity to view various rights interchangeably, a composite sketch of the institution can be drawn according to the following outline. First, feudalism entailed obligations of tenants or 'vassals' that functioned simultaneously to establish their relationship of dependence upon lords and to assist the latter in the economic management of seigneurial property. Thus, upon the transmission of a fief, feudal law required a vassal's performance of faith and homage within forty days. Renauldon's ten-page entry covering eighteen clauses emphasizes the importance of this ritual to a society steeped in status distinctions. Faith and homage, he reports, included 'the promise to serve the seigneur against all' and in most areas required genuflecting 'hatless, beltless, and swordless' at the principal manor of the seigneur.[10] Archives abound to demonstrate that in some places faith and homage followed these solemn rules while in others it had become a mere formality in which representatives for both parties conducted the performance; the difference probably depended on the extent to which lords emphasized the prestige value as opposed to merely the economic value of a seigneurie.

In addition to performing faith and homage, new vassals provided an *aveu et dénombrement* to a lord within forty days of taking possession of a fief. These detailed listings of the composition and dues of a fief allowed lords and their fiscal agents to survey property and enforce obligations. A *déclaration en censive* or *reconnaissance* functioned similarly insofar as it enumerated the holdings and dues of possessors of *censives*. A *saisie féodale* or authorization for a lord to take possession of a property might ensue in the event of a failure to produce the requisite declaration. As a sign of the importance of the *aveu et dénombrement* and *reconnaissance* to the supervision and exploitation of a lord's property, it is instructive to note that 58 per cent of the hearings in the seigneurial court of the Marquisat d'Archaic in Saintonge from 1759 to 1765 involved these itemized lists of holdings and obligations.[11]

A second category of 'feudal' rights in old regime France stemmed from the idea of the inalienability of the *domaine directe*, which brought lords windfall profits and opportunities to reconstitute the domain whenever feudal tenancies or usufructuaries (owners of the *domaine utile*) changed hands. Foremost among these *droits de mutations* were the seigneur's right to one year's revenue in the event of a fief's transfer by succession or donation (*rachat* or *relief*) and the *quints*, a 20 per cent tax occasioned by the sale of a fief. A lucrative, corresponding right named *lods et ventes* entitled seigneurs to demand indemnification for the sale of *censives*; the *lods et ventes* normally brought in one-sixth or one-eighth of the sale price but was assessed at one-twelfth in such regions as the Toulousain. Ultimately, someone might forego the *quints* after the sale of a fief, opting instead to invoke the right of *retrait féodal* or *prélation* that authorized seigneurs to reimburse purchasers the price of the sale and integrate that 'alienated' land into the lord's domain. Surveying the land market to snap up good property at bargain prices thanks to their rights of lordship, the Depont family had recourse to *retrait féodal* five times at Aigrefeuille from 1730 to 1778.[12]

If faith and homage harkened back to medieval times, then various forms of servitude linked to property or persons also reminded eighteenth-century French people of the feudal relics in their midst. Although serfdom had for all intents and purposes disappeared from France, a bevy of practices including marriage restrictions, residence requirements, seigneurial *tailles*, unpaid labour services (*corvées*), and mortmain still gave off a whiff of servility in the old regime. Importantly, the entire gamut of French courts ranging from seigneurial tribunals to the parlements upheld these practices whose legitimacy rested on customary law. Most servile practices existed in small pockets scattered throughout the kingdom, with the exception of a swath of France running from Hainault in the north through eastern and southern Champagne and into parts of Lorraine around Nancy and then covering Burgundy—a 'living museum of archaic seigneurial institutions'[13]—and especially Franche-Comté. Mortmain was the most widespread form of servitude and thus most exercised reformers.[14] Its continued existence prompted even apologists of lordship such as Renauldon to comment:[15]

> The serf is not a slave, because there are none in France; but he isn't free enough to prevent us from seeing with pain in our midst, in a kingdom that is the center of liberty, so many unfortunate men who make us feel sadness by continually reminding us of the slavery and the irons carried by our forefathers.

In the middle ages peasants performed compulsory labour on the lord's manor as the principal requirement of a feudal holding. As with most feudal customs, these *corvées* continued to exist in the eighteenth century, though in lighter form amounting to several days of harvesting or carting per year and more ubiquitous in such regions as Auvergne and Alsace. Still, centuries of peasant emancipation and the growth of a money economy meant that most labour services had been commuted into fixed quitrents known as *cens*. As an annual tribute, the *cens* impinged relatively lightly on tenants, whose payments ranged from a small measure of produce to several fowl and perhaps some coins whose value had diminished due to inflation. Two seigneurial court cases from Saint-Seurin d'Uzet in 1787 revolved around the failure of vassals to pay the *cens* valued at several bushels of grain and three chickens plus fifty-two *sols* (small change), respectively. The quitrents acquired greater significance when lords let slip the annual tribute only to sue later for the payment of arrears as stipulated by most customs for up to twenty-nine years. Under these circumstances, arrears could be the avenue for increasing rural indebtedness, and the failure to pay them allowed lords to reintegrate foreclosed territories into the domain or reap *lods et ventes* from land sold to pay arrears.

Far more important to seigneurial and peasant revenue was the obligation of tenants in many regions of France to pay lords a percentage of the harvest. Unlike *cens* paid in cash or fixed in amount, these rents in kind, known as *terrage*, *champarts*, or *agrières* depending upon the locality and the crop, proved immune to inflation and skimmed considerable produce from tenants. Again, rates varied throughout France and provinces and even within seigneuries; on 306 tenures at Aigrefeuille outside La Rochelle, the assessed percentage of the *terrage* on vines ranged from zero to one-sixth of the harvest, with half of the land surface subject to a rate of one-tenth. Regionally heaviest in the South-West and Massif central, 'harvest dues constituted the most burdensome aspect of seigneurialism'.[16] Not surprisingly, then, lords jealously guarded their prerogatives by exercising the judicial authority to proclaim and enforce the harvest dates for various tenures and then sending agents to collect the produce on the spot (a *quérable* due as opposed to *portable* dues).

Technically unrelated to feudal tenures, in parts of France the tithe nevertheless became indistinguishable from seigneurial harvest dues, in some instances because the lord was a religious institution or personage and in others because of the granting of tithes to—or usurpation by—laypersons, a process known as infeudation. Alphonse Aulard insisted, and John Markoff's research supports the assertion, that tithes formed part of the *complexum feodale* for both French peasants and revolutionary legislators.[17] After all, who besides jurists understood or cared about the difference between a monastery, in its capacity as lord, collecting the *champart* and a lay seigneur collecting an impropriated or infeudated tithe?

If 'feudal' rights pertained to relationships with holders of specific tenures, then the lord's possession of justice brought other seigneurial rights and thus impinged upon everyone in the seigneurie. Some rights were purely honorific and others economic (*utile*), but many combined both aspects. Seigneurs could place a weather-vane on their barns, a not-so-trivial symbol of power that peasants attacked frequently in 1789. Lords of 'high' justice might erect gallows, striking in its symbolism even if criminal cases whose penalties might require the gallows were automatically appealed to royal courts. They also enjoyed numerous honours in the local church, including a privileged bench, mention by name in the priest's prayers, and so on. The sole right to bear arms and hunt on the seigneurie, treated as an important honorific right in noble *cahiers de doléance*, irritated agriculturalists whose land lords trampled over in pursuit of aristocratic pleasures. Closely related, seigneurial rights to maintain rabbit warrens and dovecotes angered peasants who not only witnessed animals destroying their seeds and crops but who could not kill the game for food. The lord's sole right to fish on the seigneurie likewise deprived inhabitants of the means to supplement their incomes and diets but agitated peasants less than hunting because it did not entail a similar destruction of crops.

Numerous economic monopolies and advantages accompanied lordship in old regime France. Despite mercantilist attacks from the time of Colbert and subsequent denunciations by physiocrats, seigneurial tolls (*droit de péage*) still existed in pockets throughout the kingdom, with the *pontonnage* levied at bridges, *pulverage* taxing heads of cattle passing through a seigneurie, and various other taxes falling on the sale of merchandise at markets. Lords in the Bordelais collected 361 tolls on roads and waterways. Rights such as the *banvins* afforded lords the opportunity to sell their wine before others by a day or two in places and up to a month in others. Most importantly, lords possessed monopolies on certain economic activities that enriched seigneurial coffers while attracting inhabitants' ire. These *banalités* compelled inhabitants to grind grain at the seigneurial mill, to bake bread in the seigneurial oven, or to crush grapes or produce oils at the seigneurial presses. The Feudal Committee of the French Revolution acknowledged the ubiquity of these monopolies throughout France, which peasants hated for material reasons and notables for honorific ones and were therefore all the more enforced by seigneurial agents as remunerative and prestigious. Alfred Cobban justly described *banalités* as a 'commercial racket',[18] and countless lawsuits over them clogged court dockets.

A general outline of 'feudalism' in old regime France necessarily ends with seigneurial justice, 'the soul of the fief' and 'its last safeguard'.[19] A seigneurie entailed rights of high, middle, or low justice, which then determined the civil and criminal competencies of the courts, the types of fines and punishments imposed, and the nature of the prerogatives enjoyed. Lords with rights of justice also had significant 'police' responsibilities. They enforced the King's ordinances and regulated public health, roads, weights and measures, and the price of basic foodstuffs. Additionally, they had the power to impose fines, confiscate unclaimed or abandoned property, and take possession of livestock that destroyed crops. Although some recent studies claim seigneurial courts discharged their civil and criminal functions satisfactorily, few question the central role lords' courts played in buttressing the seigneurial regime. Justice served a dual function within the seigneurie: it first allowed lords to supervise the *mouvance* in their territories by extracting from 'vassals' declarations of the extent and obligations of their property, and it then allowed lords to enforce exactions and the recognition of their rights. In other words, the seigneurie as a system of land tenure and jurisdiction of rights was coterminous with a legal system that policed tenures and guaranteed rights. Thus, any claim by a lord to a certain right received an immediate sanction in a court of law under the auspices of the lord's official advocate (*procureur fiscal*) acting as the 'public' party and a judge appointed and salaried by and responsible to the lord.

A composite sketch such as the preceding one risks creating the impression that feudalism was a uniform institution in old regime France. Nothing could be further from the truth, as the practices, obligations, and ultimately weight of feudalism varied from region to region, custom to custom, seigneurie to seigneurie, and even plot to plot. On the Marquisat of Montendre in Saintonge, for example, the renewal of the terrier (the 'constitution' of a manor, mapping and listing all rights, properties, and tenant obligations) in 1782 provides a clear picture of feudalism on this seigneurie. The Marquis claimed the following rights: high, middle, and low justice; hunting and fishing; *cens*; harvest dues; *lods et ventes*; *retrait féodal*; *marché/foire* (right to hold markets and tax goods sold); *mesurage d'huile* (right to measure oil and levy a tax); *banalité du four* (monopoly on baking bread); seigneurial toll; *guet et garde* (which forced tenants to contribute to the maintenance of the château); and the *corvée*.[20] Every seigneurie in France would have its corresponding terrier emphasizing different rights as allowed by customary or written law and sanctioned by historical practice, while feudalism took on various inflections depending on the province. In Franche-Comté feudalism largely meant mortmain, while in the Massif central and provinces south and west of Paris—Poitou, Aunis, Saintonge, Périgord—heavy harvest dues predominated. Conversely, Burgundian seigneurialism was noted for its widespread nature and the energy with which lords pursued their rights rather than its unremarkable harvest due rate. In Guyenne and Gascony, hunting and heavy tithes exercised the local populace, and in Brittany the proliferation of seigneurial courts and a quasi-feudal form of tenure known as *domaine congéable* served as defining characteristics.

Attempts to assess the economic impact of feudalism encounter difficulties because of the institution's lack of uniformity and especially because of the challenges of reconstituting peasant accounts. Nevertheless, detailed local studies suggest that lords skimmed approximately 10 per cent of peasant wealth in Auvergne, where seigneurialism weighed heavily on the countryside, only 1–2 per cent in the Norman Pays de Caux, and an average of 6–7 per cent in the region of Bordeaux. Jonathan Dewald's masterly study of one seigneurie, Pont-Saint-Pierre from 1398 to 1789, argues that by the eighteenth century inflation rendered previously onerous seigneurial dues largely insignificant. The most up-to-date survey on the subject concludes: 'The general consensus would be that the peasants' seigneurial payments were mildly burdensome in the earlier centuries and much less so by the eighteenth', but then qualifies the summary by recognizing that the figures do not include the tithe, an 8–12 per cent expropriation 'which was largely seigneurial in form', and that a payment of even 1 to 5 per cent constituted a serious burden for those peasants on the edge of subsistence.[21] Figures for the seigneurial share of lords' revenue are easier to come by but again vary according to the institution's regional weight and the nature and economic strategy of each seigneurie, as some lords enforced dues on the *mouvance* while others expanded and cultivated or leased the *réserve* in reaction to market opportunities. As a reflection of those different strategies, around Toulouse Jean Bastier found that the seigneurial share of revenue in forty-eight lordships was 19 per cent, while Robert Forster arrived at 5 per cent for sixty-eight *parlementaire* families with extensive holdings and diversified economic interests. In Auvergne traditional revenues amounted to 33 per cent of lords' wealth, while in parts of Normandy the rate fluctuated between 20 and 50 per cent. William Beik settles on a 'conservative' figure of 10 per cent but acknowledges that it could be much higher, especially for small seigneuries; Jean-Noël Luc states that it reached 87 per cent at Beauvais-sur-Matha and 73 per cent at Migré.[22]

As highlighted in the example of Pont-Saint-Pierre, where seigneurial revenue as a percentage of total revenue went from 92 in 1399 to 11 in 1780, for many lords the seigneurie had become just one—albeit important—form of economic activity that included rental or exploitation of the domain, industrial activities such as mining, and investment in government offices and annuities or colonial commerce. Again, Beik merits citation: 'In the course of three centuries, the seigneurie had evolved from a personally ruled mini-state to an investment portfolio, although the personal element remained important.'[23] To manage their investments, lords engaged a stable of agents who operated within the structural and legal advantages afforded by seigneurialism to maximize the power, profit, and honour of lordship. Lords leased the collection or enjoyment of seigneurial rights to energetic *fermiers* or millers (*banalité du moulin*). They employed activist *procureurs fiscaux* to enforce the payment of dues in their courts and keep abreast of property transfers that led to lucrative *quints, lods et ventes,* or *retrait féodal*. They hired *feudistes*, experts in feudal law, archives, and paleography, as well as surveyors to renew terriers with the hope of finding dues and rights that had fallen into desuetude. In some places, seigneurial lawyers invoked a royal ordinance from 1669 to press the lord's *droit de triage* that granted the seigneur a right to claim one-third of any division of the common land.

In a different historiographical universe, Marxist scholars considered the renewal of terriers and heightened seigneurial activities, including attempts to reconstitute the domain and squeeze more dues from peasants, as evidence of a 'feudal reaction' in the eighteenth century. In other words, the feudal reaction was the last gasp effort of an agrarian-based nobility to preserve its power and wealth at a time when the future, which actually arrived in 1789, belonged to a commercial bourgeoisie. Revisionist historians of the French Revolution led by Alfred Cobban, William Doyle, and François Furet obliterated the Marxist interpretation of the Revolution as the triumph of a capitalist and class-conscious bourgeoisie that inevitably followed a structural shift in France's economy from agrarian feudalism to commercial and industrial capitalism. While acknowledging that revisionists won the war, perhaps historians might reinterpret several of the battles, for Cobban went too far in his assertion that 'feudalism' was a reification invented to support claims that the Revolution was bourgeois. The seigneurial system was indeed widespread and far from moribund on the eve of the Revolution. Similarly, Doyle's suggestion in a seminal 1972 article that the supposed feudal reaction in the late eighteenth century was part of a long tradition of maintaining seigneurial rights can be nuanced by many new studies showing an increased attention to and efficiency in collecting revenues linked to lordship.

Nevertheless, the vocabulary of 'reaction' misleadingly associated the activities of seigneurial agents solely with retrograde practices that in the Marxist interpretation hindered the development of agrarian capitalism and stood as the antithesis of physiocratic modernization exemplified by enclosure, the partition of commons, and liberalizing of the grain trade. (The idea of a feudal reaction stems from the physiocratic-inspired pamphlet by Boncerf in 1776, *Les inconvéniens des droits féodaux*.) A better concept, one employed by Pierre de Saint-Jacob for the Burgundian context, is 'seigneurial offensive' since it allows for the existence of prior waves of heightened seigneurial activity. The notion of an 'offensive' also implies that the exploitation of lords' rights could occur either in the context of traditional seigneurialism as seems the case in the South-West or in the context of entrepreneurial estate management or as part of the 'noble profession of seigneur', as was likely in Burgundy, provinces of eastern France, and grain-growing areas around Toulouse. Ultimately, the seigneurie constituted an advantageous form of property that could be exploited to produce revenue. Some lords pursued rights to revenue in response to market forces and the increase in grain prices and so demonstrated that feudalism might reinforce agrarian capitalism. Other lords pursued seigneurial revenue as a traditional and lucrative (because inflation-proof and low-cost) form of surplus extraction in a 'feudal rentier economy' rather than an environment of modernizing capitalism.[24]

Although the fief may have appeared headed for an English destiny in commercialized pockets of the Ile-de-France and on the estates of improving lords such as the Marquis de Turbilly in Anjou, seigneurialism remained deeply woven into the social and economic fabric of old regime France. That does not mean, however, that the institution remained uncontested. A smattering of Enlightenment thinkers contributed to the charge on humanitarian grounds, but physiocrats led the elite opposition, with Boncerf seeing in lordship a form of 'co-proprietorship that diminishes the work of the possessor as well as the benefits that he derives from it'. Encouraged by Turgot and inspired by Charles Emmanuel III's 1772 decree in Savoy that emancipated peasants while indemnifying lords, Boncerf's 1776 pamphlet railed against feudalism as 'a continually reborn hydra' and insisted that 'the conservation of feudal institutions is not useful to public order, the king, the state, or individuals'.[25] In 1779 the attack on mortmain for economic and social justice reasons persuaded Louis XVI to issue an edit liquidating that institution on the royal domain and the *droit de suite* everywhere (a right allowing lords to confiscate the estate of a *mainmortable* who died without a direct heir, even if the deceased lived, and the estate existed, outside the seigneurie). If Boncerf's pamphlet announced a section of elite opinion's hostility to seigneurialism, then the Parlement of Paris's order that it be burnt as a 'type of frenzy...injurious to the laws and customs of the realm, the sacred and inalienable rights of the crown, and the individual's right of property' signalled that other powerful elites stood in defence of the institution. Another such signal emerges from the fact that practically no lords emulated the King's enfranchisement of *mainmortables*; the Parlement of Besançon in Franche-Comté refused to register the edict. Elite 'attacks' on seigneurialism in pre-revolutionary France, then, failed to alter fundamentally rural realities. Certainly the crown, despite its undeniable assault on the military and political powers that lords enjoyed around 1600 and attempts to circumscribe seigneurial justice in criminal matters, did not undermine the seigneurie. Thus, Jean Gallet's Tocquevillian argument that the Revolution inevitably completed a long process of state centralization—'the elimination of lords [in 1793] marked the end of the struggle between the monarchy and the feudal system'[26]—overstates the royal challenge to seigneurialism before 1789, especially by the King's jurists. True, in order to expand the base of taxable resources the crown did side with peasant communities against lords and their seigneurial claims in several high-profile court cases in the 1770s and 1780s in Burgundy, Languedoc, Provence, and Normandy. But no noticeable string of legal victories heralded a royal onslaught against seigneurialism, and elsewhere royal jurists reinforced feudal law by insisting on the King's and lords' seigneurial rights.[27]

Popular anti-seigneurial activity increased in the eighteenth century, and here royal policies did play a role. The experiments in grain trade liberalization exacerbated social tensions by throwing vulnerable lower classes onto the market in a century of growing population and rising prices, and the 1669 ordinance granting lords protection of forests and the right of *triage* engendered both outright conflict and innumerable lawsuits. In fact, most communities in parts of Champagne, many in Burgundy, and approximately one half in Provence were engaged in litigation over commons on the eve of the Revolution.[28] Jean Nicolas's study of French popular rebellion reveals importantly that in the second half of the eighteenth century collective revolts shifted away from traditional tax issues and targeted seigneurialism. Hovering around twenty to thirty per decade between the 1660s and 1750s, the 1760s witnessed fifty-four anti-seigneurial rebellions, the 1770s had seventy, and the 1780s 122. The defence of collective rights or the commons motivated the most rebellions—158 out of 512 from 1661 to 1789, or 30.9 per cent. In Burgundy, an insurgency at Molesmes in 1777 saw the burning of 40 *arpents* of forest belonging to the Abbey, one at Spoy involved the destruction of enclosures and the cutting of lords' trees, and in many other places insurgents vandalized symbols of seigneurial authority such as family coats of arms, gallows, and dovecotes.[29] The second greatest source of anti-seigneurial rebellion was the payment of seigneurial dues, which caused eighty-eight uprisings (17.2 per cent). Another forty-one movements, half of which included over fifty participants, originated in opposition to the renewal of terriers. The Marquis de Lafare in Velay warned that his region abounded with faithless and lawless peasants who 'carry themselves even to the excess of killing the persons I employ to serve as guides for my *feudistes* who are at this moment renewing my terrier'.[30]

In vain would a haruspex sift through the entrails of anti-seigneurial violence prior to 1789 to divine signs of a revolutionary ideology, but it would be equally misguided to contend that the attack on and abolition of feudalism in 1789 materialized out of thin air. Rather, the context of 1788–9 is critical for understanding the liquidation of the institution, as the seed of undeniable popular hostility to seigneurialism found fertile soil when a socio-economic crisis occasioned by freakish weather intersected with unprecedented opportunities for peasants to participate in political life through the drafting of *cahiers de doléances* and the election of deputies to the Estates-General. Under these circumstances, peasant opposition to seigneurialism—three-quarters of village *cahiers* criticized lords' rights (though the largest number focused on taxation)—possessed explosive potential because calls for the reform or abolition of the material rights that burdened the countryside got incorporated into the expansive definition of 'feudalism' constructed during the revolutionary process. In other words, as explained by John Markoff, 'revolutionary legislators and revolutionary peasants confronted one another, posed problems for one another, and implicitly negotiated with one another'.[31]

Elections and the formulation of grievances produced an expectation among anxious and sometimes hungry peasants of a tremendous diminution of their burdens. In certain regions rural inhabitants stopped paying taxes, tithes, and seigneurial dues as part of a larger struggle against privilege being waged simultaneously by the Third Estate in the Estates-General. Some *cahiers*, such as the one from Sagy north of Paris, already foreshadowed the fateful amalgamation of burdens toward the state, church, and lord, as villagers wished 'to pay taxes in proportion to their capacity, with the clergy and nobility, and to enjoy in freedom the cultivation of their land without being troubled by any form of servitude'. News of Louis XVI's acquiescence in the defeat of the privileged orders after 14 July 1789 heightened expectations of change while instilling fear that aristocrats plotted to undermine the popular cause by starving the people and unleashing brigands to terrorize the countryside. The indescribable combination of excitement and foreboding fuelled the Great Fear that gripped vast swathes of France, leading communities to arm themselves, form popular militias, and mobilize against perceived enemies: Jews in parts of Alsace, monasteries in Flanders, and above all lords in nearly all of France. The Duke de Montmorency's steward recounted one incident among thousands in this rural uprising:[32]

> Brigands and pillage are practised everywhere. The populace, attributing to lords of the kingdom the high price of grain, is fiercely against all that belongs to them... The vassals are so outraged they are prepared to commit the greatest excesses... Vassals of Mme the Marquise de Longaunay have stolen the titles of rents and allowances of the seigneurie, and demolished her dovecotes: they then gave her a receipt for the theft signed *The Nation*.

If insurrection was implicit negotiation, then the legislation of 4–11 August announced the response of the peasantry's negotiating partner, the political elite in the National Assembly. Horrified by reports of pillage, arson, and the forced renunciation of seigneurial rights, representatives at first seemed paralysed over how to protect property. But more radical deputies forming the 'Breton Club' argued that only a spectacular act such as the renunciation of feudalism could pacify the countryside, while insisting the *cahiers* pointed in this direction anyway. Thus, the Club hatched a plan in which a liberal noble, the Duke d'Aiguillon, would propose the abolition of feudal rights, presumably with compensation. But in a chaotic environment on the night of 4 August, successive deputies mounted the rostrum to denounce or renounce a dizzying number of rights and privileges ranging from hunting to private tolls, from tithes to venality. This 'moment of patriotic intoxication' produced what one prominent historian describes as 'the most sweeping and radical legislative session of the whole French Revolution', for the clauses of the 4–11 August decrees—summarized at the beginning of this chapter—added up to nothing less than the destruction of the foundation of French society: privilege.[33]

The decree at least created the perception of calm in the countryside, but overall the process of negotiation between legislators and rural inhabitants continued. For its part, the Assembly clearly stipulated that dues not expressly abolished by the 4 August decree—and harvest dues and tithes would fall into this category—should be collected until indemnification occurred. Also, much remained in limbo until the Assembly's Feudal Committee translated the slapdash decrees of August 1789 into practical legislation. That committee, headed by prominent feudal lawyers such as Merlin de Douai and Goupil de Préfelne, 'invented a myth of the origins of seigneurial overlordship'[34] by distinguishing between 'personal rights' and 'real rights'. Personal rights (such as justice), the committee contended, may have been legitimate in the middle ages when lords offered security and work for peasants but by 1789—with lordship becoming 'an inert and injurious organism'—only reflected the violence and usurpation of public authority of that earlier epoch. 'Real rights', in the committee's estimation, stemmed from an original concession of land and hence as legitimate property could be ended only through contractual means. As Merlin de Douai explained:[35]

> In destroying the feudal regime you did not mean to despoil the legitimate proprietors of fiefs of their possession, but you changed the nature of these properties. Freed henceforth from the laws of feudalism, they remain subject to those of landed estate; in a word, they have ceased to be fiefs and have become true *alleux* (freeholds).

The upshot of this interpretation meant that the monetary dues most hated by peasants and highly advantageous to seigneurs—especially harvest dues but also *cens*—were redeemable at a rate of twenty or twenty-five times the value of the annual due, depending on whether it was paid in cash or in kind.

For their part, peasants in many areas simply ceased payments of seigneurial dues, tithes, and taxes, seeing the 4 August legislation as substantiation of their grievances. On the seigneurie of Beaupuis in relatively peaceful Saintonge, 75 per cent of the vassals who had paid seigneurial dues in 1788 refused to pay them in 1789. Peasants also ignored rights of *banalité* even though the legislation made no mention of them. The dual strategy of non-payment and continued agitation convinced the Assembly in March 1790 to abolish the right without compensation. Most importantly, notwithstanding a brief lull after 4 August, attacks on châteaux resumed at a high rate, with scores occurring in Périgord in late 1789 and over 100 taking place in a triangle from Rodez to Montauban to Périgueux in early 1790. Continued peasant pressure on the national government to live up to the promise of the 4 August decrees finally paid huge dividends in the changed political climate of summer 1792, when the Legislative Assembly passed on its deathbed a series of laws that announced seigneurialism would soon follow the Assembly to the grave. Most importantly, the law of 25 August 1792 undermined the entire notion of 'no land without lord' by presuming all property to be free of feudal dues except where lords could prove that a due originated in a concession of land upheld by law. Whereas before peasants had to produce titles showing they did not have to pay dues, the burden of legal proof now shifted to lords, few of whom had such titles. In effect, by outlawing harvest dues the Legislative Assembly cut out the economic heart of seigneurialism, and so 25 August 1792 rather than 4 August 1789 might more accurately represent the date for the abolition of feudalism in its economic sense. Whatever the case, on 17 July 1793 the National Convention definitively ordered both the abolition of all seigneurial dues without compensation and the burning of all feudal records, in part because it sought the political loyalty of rural dwellers under the dangerous circumstances of foreign war and popular counter-revolution in the West.

Jean-Pierre Jessenne asserts that for peasants the fundamental triumphs of the Revolution included freedom of one's person, abolition of the seigneurial system, and consecration of the full ownership of land.[36] Taken together, the last two gains highlight that, although all segments of peasant society and a significant portion of the middle classes exhibited hostility to seigneurialism in 1789, the abolition of feudalism largely benefited peasant proprietors whose earlier *domaine utile* now constituted property unencumbered by feudal accretions. The abolition proved especially beneficial to proprietors formerly subject to heavy harvest dues. Still, all peasants regardless of their status as proprietors, tenants, or landless labourers, reaped economic rewards linked to the liquidation of monopolies, tolls, exclusive hunting rights, and the like. In fact, the 4 August decrees immediately set off a veritable explosion of shooting and fishing, as Arthur Young noted to his annoyance. Summarizing the impact of seigneurialism's abolition on people of the countryside, John Markoff writes:[37]

> [It] seems clear that the principal beneficiaries were peasant proprietors who had owed the lord period payments and mutation fees; but tenants and laborers would seem to have benefited along with peasant owners from the ending of tolls, compulsory labor, monopolies, pigeon- and rabbit-raising and hunting rights not to mention the innumerable affronts to dignity. We may dismiss the charge that the Revolution's accomplishments, on the whole, were in this area nonexistent or downright perverse...

This last idea about dignity serves as a reminder that an assessment of the non-economic impact of the termination of lordship also points to significant peasant gains. Not only did the termination of seigneurial justice and its replacement with a system of elected *juges de paix* render adjudication faster, cheaper, and presumably fairer, but the undermining of seigneurial authority paved the way for community self-governance that peasants defended fiercely.[38] And a whole culture of deference and system of social dependence ended with the abolition of the economic aspects of feudalism and the destruction of private persons' possession of the right to exercise the public power of justice.

Despite its relevance as a desideratum of the peasantry, the abolition of feudalism was neither a panacea for rural dwellers nor an act that immediately and fundamentally restructured France's agrarian economy. In two studies, Donald Sutherland argues first that the Revolution's legislation allowing proprietors to add the value of former tithes to their leases deprived tenants in upper Brittany of any tangible advantages from the supposed abolition of tithes and, second, that the ultimate beneficiary of the abolition of feudalism was the state, whose increased tax revenues substituted for the expropriation of agricultural surplus once exacted by lords and the church.[39] Such arguments serve as valuable reminders that the Revolution's impact on the peasantry, a stratified group united in opposition to seigneurialism but little else, was complex and even contradictory, especially after taking into account divisive issues such as the land settlement and the division of the commons. As for the failure of the abolition of feudalism to restructure France's rural economy, this should come as no surprise given the fact that market agriculture already occurred prior to 1789 in some regions within the institution of seigneurialism. In addition, revolutionaries' unwillingness to sanctify agrarian individualism (against their better judgement) by authorizing the complete privatization of common land meant that, in the words of Georges Lefebvre, 'they destroyed the feudal regime but consolidated the agrarian structure of France'.[40] The abolition of feudalism, then, may not have marked the historical turning point at which capitalism triumphed. But it did alter the rules of the game of maximizing revenue by undermining the 'feudal rentier economy' and by shifting structural, legal, and institutional advantages in the pursuit of wealth from seigneurs, who no longer enjoyed seigneurial obligations as property rights, to proprietors.

French peasants and revolutionaries were not the first groups in Europe to embark upon an anti-seigneurial programme with the goal of emancipating rural inhabitants and the land from real and perceived shackles of feudalism. As seen, the Duke of Savoy's plan to free serfs in 1772 inspired the French monarch's attempt to do the same on the royal domain in 1779, and Baden and Denmark also initiated emancipation plans in the 1780s. Other emancipation plans emerged as pre-emptive strikes against rural rebellion on the French model, such as those in some western German territories as early as 1789. Prussia's path dates from 1807 reforms aimed at mobilizing peasants from their torpor into a patriotic defence against the superior arms and fighting spirit of the French Empire. In the latter cases as well as in Belgium, the Helvetic Republic, and the Duchy of Warsaw, the impulse towards emancipation stemmed from fear or emulation of France or was imposed by French arms. Nearly everywhere in Europe, as Jerome Blum's comparative study shows, emancipation arrived very slowly—the revolutionary wave of 1848 completed the process in many countries with the notable exception of Russia—and not always on terms favourable to the peasantry, which paid indemnities, traded land for freedom, or, in the case of Denmark, became renters instead of proprietors.[41] Thus, it is likely that the swift (1789–93) destruction on advantageous terms of a centuries-old social and economic system in the French countryside depended upon the frightening violence of a popular uprising in the unique circumstances of the Revolution. For rural dwellers, a system born in violence was destined to die in it.

Notes

1. Anonymous, 'Traité sur les fiefs: conforme à la jurisprudence du Parlement de Provence' (manuscript, c.1750; Newberry Library, Vault Folio Case MS 5211), 18.

2. Sydney Herbert, *The Fall of Feudalism in France* (London, 1921), 118.
3. Guy Lemarchand, *La Fin du féodalisme dans le pays de Caux: Conjoncture économique et démographique et structure sociale dans une région de grande culture de la crise du xviie siècle à la stabilisation de la Révolution (1640–1795)* (Paris, 1975), 17.
4. David Parker, 'Absolutism, Feudalism, and Property Rights in the France of Louis XIV', *Past and Present*, 179 (May 2003), 60–96.
5. Herbert, *Fall of Feudalism*, p. xviii.
6. This discussion follows François Furet, 'Feudal System', in François Furet and Mona Ozouf (eds.), *A Critical Dictionary of the French Revolution*, tr. Arthur Goldhammer (Cambridge, Mass., 1989), 684–93.
7. Furet, 'Feudal System', 690.
8. John Markoff, *The Abolition of Feudalism: Peasants, Lords, and Legislators in the French Revolution* (University Park, Pa., 1996), 44.
9. Jean Gallet, *Seigneurs et paysans en France, 1600–1793* (Rennes, 1999), 127.
10. Renauldon, *Dictionnaire des fiefs et des droits seigneuriaux, utiles et honorifiques* (Paris, 1765), 308.
11. Archives départementales de Charente-Maritime (hereafter ADCM), B 2524 (registre des affaires particuliers au marquisat, 1759–65).
12. Robert Forster, *Merchants, Landlords, Magistrates: The Depont Family in Eighteenth-Century France* (Baltimore, Md., 1980), 88.
13. James Lowth Goldsmith, *Lordship in France, 1500–1789* (New York, 2005), 29.
14. See William Doyle's Ch. 16 on 'Slavery and Serfdom'.
15. Renauldon, *Dictionnaire*, 237.
16. Peter Jones, *The Peasantry in the French Revolution* (Cambridge, 1988), 45. The figures for Aigrefeuille are from Claudy Laveau, *Le Monde rochelais des Bourbons à Bonaparte* (La Rochelle, 1988), 323.
17. Alphonse Aulard, *La Révolution française et le régime féodal* (Paris, 1919), 158; Markoff, *Abolition of Feudalism*, 157.
18. Cobban, *The Social Interpretation of the French Revolution* (Cambridge, 1964), 51.
19. Pierre de Saint Jacob, *Les Paysans de la Bourgogne du nord au dernier siècle de l'ancien régime* (Paris, 1960), 407.
20. Archives départementales, Charente maritime B 2403 (lettre de terrier), Marquisat de Montendre.
21. Figures and quotation from William Beik, *A Social and Cultural History of Early Modern France* (Cambridge, 2009), 36.
22. Ibid. 36; Jean-Noël Luc, *Paysans et droits féodaux en Charente-Inférieure pendant la Révolution française* (Paris, 1984), 65–6.
23. Beik, *Social and Cultural History*, 40.
24. Parker, 'Absolutism, Feudalism, and Property Rights', 72.
25. Pierre-François Boncerf, *Les inconvéniens des droits féodaux* (Paris, 1776), 59.
26. Gallet, *Paysans et seigneurs en France*, 263.
27. Stephen Miller, 'The Absolutist State of Eighteenth-Century France: Modern Bureaucracy or Feudal Bricolage?', *Socialist History*, 33 (2008), 36.
28. Serge Bianchi, 'Contestations et révoltes paysans', in Serge Bianchi, Michael Biard, and Alan Forrest, *La Terre et les paysans en France et en Grande-Bretagne du début du xviie siècle à la fin du xviiie siècle* (Paris, 1999), 222.
29. Jean Bart, *La Révolution française en Bourgogne* (Clermont-Ferrand, 1996), 54.

30. Quoted in Jean Nicolas, *La Rébellion française: Mouvements populaires et conscience sociale 1661–1789* (Paris, 2002), 185. The figures are from pp. 217 and 154.
31. Markoff, *Abolition of Feudalism*, 5.
32. From Peter McPhee, *Living the French Revolution, 1789–99* (New York, 2006), 44–5.
33. William Doyle, *The Oxford History of the French Revolution* (Oxford, 2002), 116.
34. Jones, *Peasantry*, 88.
35. Quoted in Aulard, *La Révolution française et le régime féodal*, 109.
36. Jean-Pierre Jessenne, *Les Campagnes françaises entre mythe et histoire (xviiie–xxie siècle)* (Paris, 2006), 70.
37. Markoff, *Abolition of Feudalism*, 590.
38. Anthony Crubaugh, *Balancing the Scales of Justice: Local Courts and Rural Society in Southwest France, 1750–1800* (University Park, Pa., 2001).
39. D. M. G. Sutherland, *The Chouans: The Social Origins of Popular Counter-Revolution in Upper Brittany, 1770–1796* (Oxford, 1982); 'Peasants, Lords, and Leviathan: Winners and Losers from the Abolition of French Feudalism, 1780–1820', *Journal of Economic History*, 62 (Mar. 2002), 1–24.
40. Georges Lefebvre, 'La Révolution française et les paysans', in his *Études sur la Révolution française* (Paris, 1963), 257.
41. Jerome Blum, *The End of the Old Order in Rural Europe* (Princeton, 1978), 398–9.

Bibliography

Aubin, Gérard, *La Seigneurie dans le Bordelais au xviiie siècle* (Rouen, 1989).
Aulard, Alphonse, *La Révolution française et le régime féodal* (Paris, 1919).
Blum, Jerome, *The End of the Old Order in Rural Europe* (Princeton, 1978).
Gallet, Jean, *Seigneurs et paysans en France, 1600–1793* (Rennes, 1999).
Godechot, J. (ed.), *L'Abolition de la 'féodalité' dans le monde occidental; Toulouse 12–16 novembre 1968* (2 vols. Paris, 1971).
Herbert, Sydney, *The Fall of Feudalism in France* (London, 1921).
Jones, Peter, *The Peasantry in the French Revolution* (Cambridge, 1988).
Lefebvre, Georges, *Les Paysans du Nord pendant la Révolution française* (Paris, 1924).
Markoff, John, *The Abolition of Feudalism: Peasants, Lords, and Legislators in the French Revolution* (University Park, Pa., 1996).
Nicolas, Jean, *La Rébellion française: Mouvements populaires et conscience sociale 1661–1789* (Paris, 2002).
Parker, David, 'Absolutism, Feudalism, and Property Rights in the France of Louis XIV', *Past and Present*, 179 (May 2003), 60–96.
Soboul, Albert, *Problèmes paysans de la Révolution* (Paris, 1956).

CHAPTER 14

AGRICULTURE

PETER M. JONES

INTRODUCTION

THE agricultural history of the Ancien Régime is inseparable from the socio-economic history of France between 1660 and 1789 if only for the reason that husbandry remained the principal wealth-generating activity and by far the largest sector of the economy. Even after 1789 this situation would not alter radically. Notwithstanding the collapse of Bourbon absolutism, the broad thrust of change in the countryside proceeded without major interruption. The agrarian history of western Europe in the early modern period provides scant evidence of climactic moments, and researchers are in general agreement that its rhythms can only be discerned over a time span of many decades. In France specifically there were no agricultural breakthroughs in the eighteenth century—whether in land-use, tenurial practice, agronomic technique, or institutional reform. Instead, rural historians have to content themselves with the task of identifying and making sense of modulations in a constantly evolving pattern of organic development.

Yet this context of steady and undramatic change still leaves plenty of room for scholarly debate. In the absence of fundamental disagreement about the trajectory of the agricultural economy, specialists juxtapose instead rival models for understanding stasis and movement in the countryside. Ever since the time of Marc Bloch,[1] historians of the *Annales* school have been fleshing out an interpretation of the Ancien Régime economy with strong socio-cultural, even anthropological underpinnings. They envision largely sedentary communities consisting of peasant cultivators whose main objective was to diminish the risk of starvation by practising, wherever possible, subsistence-oriented polyculture. Whilst few historians embracing this approach would pretend that more than a small minority of cultivators could hope to achieve the target of self-sufficiency, they would certainly play down the role of the market. Country dwellers participated in the market—according to this scenario—as a necessary evil: in order to raise capital with which to meet state tax obligations and seigneurial dues, and as a means of turning seasonal underemployment to good account as a source of supplementary income.

Whether peasant cultivators really did aim for household self-sufficiency is more a plausible than a provable hypothesis, although there does exist some family and ethnographic evidence which points in this direction. Nevertheless, the proposition enables many researchers to insist on the cultural unity of the rural community, the collective—indeed cooperative—nature of decision-taking in the agricultural domain, and the risk-minimizing behaviour of its members. This approach is often labelled 'stagnationist' and commanded the assent of the vast majority of agrarian historians until the 1980s. It was summed up memorably by Emmanuel Le Roy Ladurie, one of the last of the mature generation of *Annales* historians, in a 1973 lecture on 'L'histoire immobile' (history that stands still).[2]

Critics of the 'immobile history' model have stretched the concept for rhetorical purposes far beyond what its author originally intended. It is now commonly suggested that the Malthusian relationship between population and agricultural resources which lies at the heart of Le Roy Ladurie's conceptualization applies to the eighteenth century as well as earlier periods. The phrase has also come to be understood more generally as the contention that country dwellers remained imprisoned in a world of routine and narrow horizons which was as much physical as mental. Nevertheless, there can be no disputing that an alternative interpretation of the Ancien Régime rural economy has taken shape in more recent decades which challenges the Annalist vision at almost every turn. For students of the French countryside whose views were not fashioned during the heroic age of 'la vie rurale' thesis production (1930–70), the peasant 'community' is not a given, and nor for that matter are the agrarian 'civilisations' espied by the Vidal de la Blache school of human geographers.[3]

It follows, therefore, that village cultivators and artisans are now viewed as individuals who were as likely to be engaged in strident competitive as consensual activity. They did not shun the market and nor is there any reason to suppose, a priori, that they adhered to a subsistence ethic. Where once historians assessed the rural economy in terms of stasis, stagnation, and the avoidance of risk they now measure it in terms of mobility, dynamism, and entrepreneurial endeavour. Nearly all peasants, we are reminded, were caught up in the market nexus, whether for the purchase or sale of foodstuffs, land, labour, or credit. Some indulged in speculative forms of husbandry, particularly those farming within easy reach of towns, and all moved around a great deal more than has previously been allowed.

Overlaps and even common ground between the two interpretations of France's agricultural history are evident as researchers address the key question of the slow and piecemeal character of Ancien Régime economic growth, but the fundamental divergence regarding the nature of the rural community ensures that different conclusions are drawn from similar bodies of evidence. For instance, both models allow room for the shaping impact of institutional factors. Yet, where the *Annales* historians stress the braking effect of a burdensome seigneurial regime, the protagonists of the dynamic rural economy model point rather to the etiolating consequences of heavy state taxation, military expenditure, inadequate infrastructure, and unclear property rights.

This shift in our understanding of the countryside and the manifold activities practised at village level has been driven by economic historians in the main. The Annalists' depiction of the rural economy was hugely reinforced by the early researches of Ernest Labrousse.[4] For Labrousse made the performance of agriculture the bellwether for the entire Ancien Régime economy. His quantitative analysis of prices, wages, and rents yielded two main conclusions which satisfied researchers for a generation and more. In an economy dominated by the primary sector, agricultural production would always have a determining influence on industrial output. As the intendant of Rouen put it in a report of 1768, 'the price of bread is the compass of the workshops; they become sluggish when bread is too dear'.[5] Labrousse's corollary finding placed this conclusion in a structured setting, for his data appeared to show a long-term decline in the standard of living of the labouring classes across the eighteenth century. Over five decades (1726–41 to 1785–9) the purchasing power of wage earners was eroded by a quarter. This adverse conjuncture became particularly acute in the 1780s, and it provided the hard quantitative underpinning for a crisis of the rural economy which many historians believe accompanied the descent into political revolution of 1787–9. Not surprisingly, therefore, it is among the social and political historians of eighteenth-century France that Labrousse's researches continue to command the most respect.

All attempts to model statistically the performance of the Ancien Régime economy are built on fragile foundations as we shall see. As for Labrousse, there can be little doubt that his vision owed much to the preconceptions of the *Annales* historians. It is rooted in an undynamic, even static, assessment of the day-to-day lives of country dwellers: one in which their relationship to food resources and therefore their material well-being is expressed in terms of simple, ineluctable equations. His price-driven approach depicts consumers as perpetual victims with little freedom of manœuvre when faced with an unfavourable harvest cycle. When purchasing power is depressed it would be reasonable to suppose that consumers sought out additional opportunities for gainful employment, yet Labrousse's approach makes small allowance for this possibility. Some economic historians therefore question his key finding of a long-term decline in living standards among the poor of both town and country. It is more likely, they argue, that real wages remained broadly stable after mid-century. One may legitimately question, too, whether even those industries located in the countryside responded solely to the rhythms of the agricultural economy. Ernest Labrousse was reluctant to grant any autonomy to the world of commerce and industry. He even maintained that the surging prosperity of France's overseas trade was peripheral and of little importance when formulating conclusions about growth in the primary sector. From this angle too, therefore, his researches served to buttress the *Annales* historians' insistence on the profound insularity of a peasant-based rural economy.

The fragility of Labrousse's quantitative edifice in the eyes of modern economic historians will not explain the divergent approaches taken towards the chief source of wealth and employment in Ancien Régime France, however. As we have noted, both visions are fuelled from broadly similar datasets: the difference lies more in the area of method, interpretation, and judgements about balance. In a country the size of France, there are few common denominators which would enable us to depict its agricultural history in bold brush strokes. Ernest Labrousse's laboriously compiled statistics on prices, wages, and rents should be seen as an early attempt to overcome the piecemeal nature of the evidence relating to the agricultural economy. The attempt of J.-C. Toutain[6] to construct an agricultural production series across two and a half centuries (1700–1958) is another; and Philip Hoffman's[7] sophisticated effort to evaluate growth in the French countryside over an even longer time span using a 'total factor productivity' index a third. What all of these efforts to overcome the recalcitrance of the sources demonstrate is that the results tend to validate the assumptions underpinning the inquiry in the first place. As such, each falls victim in turn to the next exercise in quantitative 'objectivity'. Labrousse, modern economic historians insist, has given us only a part of the picture, whereas Toutain's calculation of a 60 per cent increase in agricultural production across the eighteenth century appears to many specialists to be wildly optimistic. It remains to be seen what final judgement the scholarly community will pass on Hoffman's data. But since 'total factor productivity' raises considerable methodological questions and can only be calculated for the most dynamic segment of the rural economy (stable farm holdings let on cash rentals), it seems likely that once again we will find ourselves with, at best, an oblique perspective on the evolution of the rural economy.[8]

The very unreliability of contemporary numerical data relating to agriculture cautions against the quantifying approach. Ancien Régime intendants and subdelegates routinely falsified their returns in order to deflect the attentions of a state hungry for revenue; during the Revolution mayors systematically inflated population figures in a bid to secure institutions of local government; and the statistical compilations of the Napoleonic period are probably best described as monumental propaganda exercises. The 'before' and 'after' (the Revolution) agricultural data they contain are impressionistic at best and fraudulent at worst. Even the incomplete Agricultural Enquiry of 1814 is scarcely exempt from reproach as a source. Inevitably, therefore, historians wishing to focus their attention on the agricultural component of the Ancien Régime rural economy are forced to rely on piecemeal and qualitative evidence which can never be made to provide a view of the whole. No doubt this is why the rare synthetic accounts left by travellers are so highly prized. The English agricultural commentator Arthur Young travelled the length and breadth of France between 1787 and 1790, and published his observations in a journal format some three years later. For the historian of landscape, land-use, husbandry, agrarian custom, and government policy at a time when the first round of government-inspired agricultural reform initiatives had run into the sand, it is an invaluable source.

To be sure, Young's insistence that his depiction of the state of French agriculture on the eve of the Revolution was the work of a 'mind free from prejudice, particularly national prejudice'[9] cannot be taken at face value. Modern economic historians variously accuse him of comparing French agriculture with an 'ideal type' husbandry which owed more to wishful thinking than to actual practice across the Channel. They point out that he misunderstood the role played by viticulture in the rural economy of southern France, and completely failed to grasp that commons and wastes in Brittany and the South-West were far from being unproductive surfaces. The distinction between uncultivated waste and long fallows in the *bocage* regions of the West was often lost on contemporaries as well. It is true that Young regarded eradication of the fallow via enclosure as the royal route to agricultural progress, but the fact that this judgement now appears rather suspect stems more from recent research in English agrarian history than from unreasoning prejudice at the time he was writing.[10]

Other criticisms levelled at Arthur Young's travelogue seem less justified. He could be an acute observer of local custom and practice as, for instance, when he recorded that the omnipresence of common rights in Lorraine deterred landowners from planting fodder crops. Despite some recent evidence that sharecropping could be combined with market-oriented stock-raising, his generally negative appreciation of this mode of tenure does not seem misplaced either. In any event, he was certainly aware of the significance of the fat-stock industry in Normandy and the Limousin. The commonplace criticism that Young supposed that only large farms could facilitate good husbandry and generate high yields is in need of considerable qualification, too. In Flanders, Alsace, and the valley of the Garonne, he would acknowledge, even small farms could achieve spectacular results on fertile soils. Notwithstanding the strictures of modern-day historians, contemporaries clearly found Young's *Travels* a useful overview of Ancien Régime agriculture. Upon its first English printing the journal was rushed out in a pirated French-language edition, and towards the end of 1793 the revolutionary government commissioned a fresh translation of the first four chapters of the work with the intention that it be distributed as required reading throughout the Republic.

Fundamentals

Demography, most researchers would agree, provides the key to an understanding of the changes taking place within the agricultural sector of the economy. In the course of the eighteenth century (1715–1801) the population of France grew by around 34 per cent (from 19.2 to 29.3 million) and since urbanization was sluggish at best (a peak of 20.1 per cent achieved in the 1780s), most of the expansion took place in the countryside. However, this growth was neither steady nor even. After a net population loss during the initial decade and a half of the century, momentum began to build—albeit hesitantly—in the 1730s and 1740s to produce an increase approaching 20 per cent over the second half of the century. There were regional discrepancies, too, with population growth fairly galloping ahead in those eastern provinces (Lorraine, Alsace, Franche-Comté) which had been prostrated by the military calamities of the seventeenth century, whereas in the West (Brittany, Anjou, Maine, etc.) the profile of growth was curtailed in the 1770s and 1780s by epidemic disease to yield only a small net increase across the century. Simple subtraction will produce a figure of about 23 million country dwellers by the end of the Ancien Régime. But further calculation is required if we are to determine the number of households residing in non-urban centres (fewer than 2,000 inhabitants) who were actively engaged in agricultural pursuits. If no distinction is made between cultivators and rural artisans, it seems likely that they numbered at least 18 million (64 per cent of the total population) as the Ancien Régime drew to a close.

Most visitors to France arrived from the north, more often than not on one of the Calais packets that plied the Channel and the North Sea. They commented first and foremost on the agrarian landscapes that greeted them—an unending vista of cereal plains. The Revd John Symonds, a Cambridge history professor, passed through Calais on his way to Lorraine towards the end of the summer of 1785, and like most English tourists he was staggered to see not 'a single acre of *inclosed* arable land'[11] throughout his entire journey from the coast to Châlons-sur-Marne. This was the openfield region of northern and north-eastern France which Arthur Young accurately mapped as an irregular quadrilateral. It stretched from the estuary of the Seine and the granary of the Beauce in the west, to follow the banks of the Loire as far as Orléans, before snaking away east and south-eastwards across the Nivernais and the Gâtinais to touch the Saône river and embrace the plain at the foot of the Côte de Beaune. The dominant traits of this undulating plateau landscape were, as Symonds noted, a strip-based cereal agriculture, a lack of hedgerows, a near-total absence of wasteland, and plentiful evidence of successful cultivation of the fallow. Only fodder crops (clover, sainfoin, luzerne) appeared to be protected by enclosures.

Here we have depicted the 'pays de grande culture' beloved of mid-century agrarian reformers: a region of large, highly capitalized farms; substantial nucleated villages containing a ready supply of wage labourers; a favourable natural endowment; and a well-tuned commercial husbandry geared closely to the needs of urban markets. Moving beyond the Norman plateau, the Beauce, the middle valley of the Loire, and the frontier zones of the Berry and the Nivernais the traveller entered a visually congested landscape in which the horizon, whether for reasons of relief or afforestation, always seemed close to hand. It would be wrong to imply that this vast area (two-thirds of the country) possessed an ecological coherence, for it comprised upland and mountain eco-systems as well as regions of viticulture and a littoral agro-pastoral economy along the Mediterranean shoreline. The South was not without pockets of openfield, too (the Grandes Causses, the Limagne, the valley of the Garonne, etc.). But contemporaries knew what they were talking about when juxtaposing *bocage* with openfield; 'grande culture' with 'petite culture'. Small, irregularly shaped fields surrounded by hedges or dry stone walls, which in turn were surrounded by heath or forest denoted *bocage* country. Voyagers journeying from the south to the north, or north-east were no less struck by the contrast. On emerging from the Sologne and crossing the Loire at Orléans an eighteenth-century traveller would not have caught sight of an enclosed cornfield again until he neared the town of Valenciennes, not far short of the border with the Austrian Netherlands.

Land-use statistics, or rather estimates, exist for the eighteenth century but they do not reveal a great deal unless employed for the purpose of international comparison. With nearly three-quarters of its agricultural territory used for grain production by the end of the eighteenth century, France massively outstripped England (30 per cent) in this regard—even when due allowance is made for the difference in physical size of the two countries. On the other hand, natural and planted meadows were far more extensive in England, where they covered about 57 per cent of the agricultural territory compared with just 14 per cent in France.[12] Vines, it is true, came to occupy an increasing amount of agricultural territory in southern France as the century progressed (around 6 per cent according to Young[13]), whereas in England they were virtually non-existent.

In truth, however, the best comparisons that can be made require us to partition France along the river Loire. For it is evident that the 'pays de grande culture' described above had more in common with the high-yield and intensive husbandry of southern and eastern England than with the extensive, subsistence-oriented cultivation of bread grains in the western *bocage* provinces, and the 'pays de petite culture' of the deep south. Commercial wheat and fodder production by means of a sophisticated three-year crop rotation was the chief objective of farmers working the rich loams around Paris (the capital's stables contained 16,500 horses in 1789). Up to three-quarters of the surface was regularly ploughed; traditional fallow had disappeared almost completely (in common with regions such as Flanders and the Artois); and grain yields were, by the 1780s, approaching the highest performances noted by Arthur Young during his English tours of the 1760s and 1770s.

By contrast, the characteristic landscapes of the 'pays de petite culture' not only looked different but catered for different human needs. Rye grain for domestic consumption was nearly everywhere the staple. It was cultivated in a biennial rotation, although this is to schematize a husbandry that might more closely resemble 'slash and burn' agriculture as arable plots were hacked from the heath more or less at will. Oxen rather than horses were chiefly used for ploughing, and the majority of cultivators organized their farming mainly to minimize the risks inherent in tilling poor or otherwise unsuitable soils, rather than to take advantage of decidedly distant urban markets. Back-ups designed to mitigate the effects of harvest shortfall were always to hand, whether bread-grain substitutes (buckwheat, chestnuts, oats), stock-raising, rural crafts, or even seasonal migration to more favourable environments.

In such conditions it was rare for farms to be compact or, indeed, balanced. A Burgundian correspondent advised the Agriculture Committee of the Legislative Assembly in 1792 that in his district a 'holding' might consist of two or three hundred dispersed parcels of land. The planting of artificial fodder crops was not to be contemplated in these conditions for they could scarcely be defended from the common herd. In any case farm animals usually found sufficient nourishment on the extensive wastes and commons. 'Petite culture' on thin acidic soils that were often fundamentally ill-adapted to cereal husbandry could not be expected to generate regular surpluses either. In the West and in the Massif central yields barely reached half of those routinely being achieved by the end of the Ancien Régime on the northern plains.

Who owned the land on the eve of the Revolution? As Lucien Febvre once famously remarked: 'France can call itself diversity',[14] which is another way of saying that computations of an average or typical situation are apt to mislead. Nevertheless, historians now conclude that it is most likely that peasant cultivators owned perhaps 40 per cent of the soil surface, rather than one-third—the estimate usually given in older works of reference. On the whole, the peasantry retained freehold title to the soil which they tilled in those regions where there was least competition from noble, ecclesiastical, bourgeois, or institutional landlords. As might be expected, therefore, in upland areas of 'petite culture' on stony, unyielding soils (Limousin, Béarn, Haute-Guyenne, Auvergne, Haute-Provence, Dauphiné, etc.) peasant tenures reigned supreme. By contrast, ownership among the agricultural workforce of the cereal plains around Paris amounted to little more than scattered plots. Here the dominant force was the commercial tenant farmer as we have already noted. These *grands fermiers* leased the best arable surfaces from the church and the aristocracy. Their economic role and style of living made them more akin to a rural bourgeoisie than a peasant cultivator class. The incidence of ecclesiastical landholding varied enormously at the end of the Ancien Régime: from under 1 per cent of the soil surface on the unproductive *landes* of the South-West to 20 per cent around Paris, and perhaps as high as 40 per cent in the Cambrésis. However, an averaging of data for the kingdom as a whole produces a figure of not more than 6 per cent. Noble and bourgeois owners seem to have possessed around 22 and 25 per cent respectively, and the surfaces remaining were either considered to be common land or else waste. As demographic pressure intensified from the 1760s, considerable tracts of marginal land were cleared (for arable purposes or viticulture), to produce an extension approaching 2 per cent of the agricultural surface of the kingdom. But the clearance movement does not seem to have altered fundamentally the balance of ownership between social groups.

Our knowledge of the different modes of land tenure practised tends to highlight the *pays de grande culture*—an unfortunate consequence of the lop-sided nature of research into the agrarian history of Ancien Régime France. On the strength of his tours and related enquiries, Arthur Young[15] ventured the opinion that seven-eighths of the farmland of the kingdom was held on a share-crop basis. Subsequent research (Loutchisky,[16] Lefebvre[17]) would suggest that this estimate is likely to be too high. The terms *métairie* and *métayer* which appear to indicate a share-crop relationship have to be interpreted with care. Even so, it seems safe to conclude that roughly two-thirds of non-freehold land must have been leased out on share-crop contracts, whether written or verbal. Ernest Labrousse,[18] for his part, reckoned on a ratio of seven sharecroppers for every tenant farmer. It would be wrong, however, to present sharecropping and cash renting as monolithic alternatives for there existed many hybrid forms of land tenure as well (*domaine congéable* in Lower Brittany; perpetual leases in the South-West; emphyteotic tenancy in Provence and Languedoc, etc.). Peasant cultivators might very well own land, rent land in return for an annual cash payment, and practise animal husbandry on a share-crop basis (*bail à cheptel simple*) at one and the same time.

Nevertheless, contemporaries such as Turgot, the intendant of Limoges and future Controller-General of the Finances, would draw a broad distinction between *pays de fermage* and *pays de métayage*. It was a distinction which in many ways mirrored that between the *pays de grande culture* and the *pays de petite culture* discussed earlier. For cash tenancy was an unmistakable characteristic of the high-yield, and market-oriented, openfield zone of the North and East. In these provinces, together with Lorraine and Alsace, sharecropping had all but died out by the end of the Ancien Régime. South of the river Loire, however, sharecropping formed an omnipresent feature of the tenurial landscape. Indeed, it was the dominant mode of tenure, whether for land or for livestock, in the Bas-Maine and Anjou, Poitou, the Limousin, the Périgord, much of Guyenne, and in the Berry and the Bourbonnais towards the east. Arthur Young's[19] estimate that just one-sixth or one-seventh of the territory of the kingdom was held on the basis of money rents, like Robert Forster's[20] equivalent computation of one-quarter of all leased land, gives pause for thought, therefore. Unless it can be argued that peasant polyculture under share-crop tenancy contained an unsuspected capacity for dynamism, the traditional picture of the Ancien Régime rural economy still has a lot to recommend it.

Trends

Rather than crudely juxtaposing 'mobile' and 'immobile' peasantries, we would do better, perhaps, to envisage a rural economy which was layered according to economic function. In the Roannais and the Brionnais, for instance, share-crop farms marginally outnumbered cash tenancies and they appear to have exhibited most of the regressive tendencies which prompted Young[21] to declare that not a single argument could be mustered in favour of this mode of husbandry. The croppers practised a fail-safe polyculture; they employed stock for ploughing and dung-making but little else; they shied away from innovative practices; and they auto-consumed nearly everything grown on the farm once the owner had carted off his share. The tenant farmers of the region, by contrast, were firmly linked to the monetary economy for they took their produce to the local market where owners of the *métairies* (mainly urban professionals, merchants, and nobles) would also hasten in order to dispose of their crop and cattle shares.

Yet it is hard to reconcile this classic image of the sharecropper with the stock-raising cropper-entrepreneur brought to light by Annie Antoine and other researchers in the Bas-Maine and mid-Poitou. Here we find evidence from quite early in the eighteenth century of a joint initiative by seigneurs and their croppers to exploit and adapt the extensive heaths for the purpose of commercialized cattle-raising. Although there remains some ambiguity attached to the appellation *métairie*, Antoine is in no doubt that the share-cropped landholding constituted 'the most high-yielding and efficient branch of agriculture in the region'.[22] Plainly there existed 'subsistence' and 'speculative' versions of stock-raising, and even districts embedded deep in the *pays de petite culture* could be linked, relay fashion, to distant urban markets. Beef cattle raised in the Maine or Limousin were sent to Normandy for fattening; mules raised in Poitou were sold on to markets in regions of difficult access to wheeled transport such as the Massif central and Spain; and the well-to-do peasant cultivators of the Haut-Léon in Lower Brittany bred horses for export.

Nevertheless we must be cautious about construing the trend towards agricultural specialization, for much of the evidence relates more properly to the first half of the nineteenth century. Despite the substantial recovery of the rural economy in the 1750s, 1760s, and early 1770s, urban growth, and therefore urban demand, registered in a sluggish fashion at best, and after 1789 both would slacken measurably for a decade and more. Markets for foodstuffs remained short-range and poorly connected for the most part. If we may judge by the persisting disparities in regional cereal prices, it seems unlikely that France possessed a fully integrated grain market before the middle of the nineteenth century. Even in 1852, researchers have discovered, approximately seven-eighths of the harvest (seed corn deducted) tended to remain in its immediate zone of production. At this date, around 70 per cent of net production was taken to a nearby market and perhaps 30 per cent was auto-consumed.[23] We can detect here the braking effects of inadequate infrastructure on the development of the rural economy. In the absence of canals and turn-piked roads, bulky or heavy and relatively low-value goods could only be moved overland for short distances. Marshal Vauban had acknowledged in 1699 the crucial role played by waterborne transportation, for when a navigable river was not within easy reach, 'the regular market for farm products disappears; one grows only for subsistence or, at best, for local demand'.[24] Even a century later, this situation had not fundamentally altered.

Only cultivators situated within the attractive forcefield of urban markets were likely to respond to the opportunities they enshrined, then. The case of the *grands fermiers* of the Paris grain belt explored by Gilles Postel-Vinay[25] and Jean-Marc Moriceau,[26] and others has already been mentioned. Yet even here, the basic pattern of agrarian development had been apparent long before the start of the eighteenth century. The steady advance of fodder crops (*prairies artificielles*) apart, there were no major changes in land-use or significant productivity increases as the Ancien Régime proceeded to its climax. All sizeable towns were surrounded by a zone in which agriculture had been replaced by horticulture, of course, and in the case of the capital this zone extended to a considerable radius and was highly specialized. Only in Lower Normandy, however, is there indisputable evidence that whole landscapes were caught up in the process of transition. An expanding fat-stock industry geared to the Paris meat market had resulted in soil surfaces being removed from cereal production and put under grass in the Pays d'Auge, whilst the Pays de Bray was pursuing simultaneously a vocation for dairy production. But neither trend would have occurred if the Norman population had not had ready access to bread-grains grown on the nearby cereal plain.

Royal bureaucrats and the influential body of *économistes* or physiocrats who surrounded them during the third quarter of the eighteenth century imagined that agricultural growth could be kickstarted from on high. In common with the rest of Europe, educated observers in France subscribed to the complacent Enlightenment belief that what the rural economy needed most urgently was a remodelling of its formative 'institutions'. If so-called wasteland could be eradicated, if crop-bearing surfaces could be regrouped into more productive units, if customary rights over private property could be curtailed, then the phenomenon of the market-driven farmer with substantial security of tenure could be generalized. Converted into an immense *pays de grande culture*, the countryside would routinely generate grain surpluses over and above the needs of domestic consumption. Landlords would chiefly benefit, but so would the royal treasury as the tax-bearing capacity of the soil expanded in proportion.

However, what proponents of the 'new husbandry' failed to grasp—with a few exceptions—was the interlocking character of the Ancien Régime rural economy. No single component had evolved in isolation. Grain production presupposed plentiful supplies of animal manure which presupposed stock, whose upkeep presupposed, in turn, the retention of waste, common, and fallow surfaces devoid of crops; indeed the preservation in many localities of customary grazing rights over unenclosed private land holdings. Between 1766 and 1771 government ministers sponsored a series of measures to clear wasteland, partition and enclose commons, and restrict free grazing, but the tangible results of this policy to instil a spirit of 'agrarian individualism' were scarcely encouraging. Quite the contrary, for in 1789 the intendant of Champagne would complain that the edict of enclosure applied to his province twenty years earlier had done more harm than good.[27] The restrictions placed on *vaine pâture* (collective grazing) in hay meadows had caused the total number of stock to contract. The fodder crisis consequent upon the drought of 1785 seems a more likely explanation for this decline. Nevertheless, it is hard to point to concrete instances where the government's initiatives of the 1760s and 1770s achieved an ameliorative effect.

Nowadays most researchers discount the idea that physiocrat-inspired reforms or the encouragements offered by agricultural societies had much bearing on the long-term trajectory of the rural economy. Progress in agriculture, when it happened, was largely a matter of incremental changes driven by on-the-spot experimentation with crops and rotations, and buttressed by verbal dissemination of good practice between farmers at the level of the marketplace. It is in this context that discussion of the putative 'agricultural revolution' of the eighteenth century tends to occur. Specialists generally agree that agricultural production kept pace with demographic growth across the eighteenth century. Indeed, it was probably outstripping the rate of population increase from the second half of the eighteenth century—albeit not on the scale discerned by Toutain. There is much less agreement on the question of the productivity of land surfaces under cereals, however. Persuasive evidence exists for surging cereal yields in the Cambrésis from mid-century, and Jean-Michel Chevet[28] points to the planting of fodder crops as the main factor in securing productivity improvements in the Ile-de-France. Yet in the absence of significant advances in plough technology or of new additives to improve soil fertility, it seems likely that the grain lands around Paris had reached a productivity ceiling well before the demise of the Ancien Régime. As for the other openfield landscapes, Lorraine for instance, the incremental growth registered across the century seems not to warrant the use of the term 'revolution' either. In the rest of the country, where share-crop agriculture was widely practised, we may question whether even sustained incremental progress occurred. All in all, Gérard Béaur's judgement on the eighteenth-century growth debate seems apt: 'neither an explosion in yields, nor a stagnation.'[29]

IMPACTS

The revolutionaries of 1789 inherited the wisdom of the Ancien Régime in matters relating to the reform of agriculture. After a hiatus in the late 1770s and early 1780s, the terrible stock loss and harvest shortfall triggered by the spring drought of 1785 rekindled interest in 'institutional' remedies for the frailties of the rural economy. Antoine Lavoisier, whose model estate at Freschines had been brought to the brink of collapse by the defaulting of two tenant farmers, pressed for the establishment within the Contrôle-Général of a Committee of Agriculture. For two years (1785–7) this body debated the direction which agricultural reform should take, and its recommendations were rapidly incorporated into the thinking of ministers and legislators following the change of regime in 1789. Meanwhile, executive responsibility in the agricultural sphere was transferred from Finances to the Ministry of the Interior. Early in 1793 a Bureau Central d'Agriculture came into being and it was entrusted with the task of maintaining a channel of communication with the departments. However, the main source of energy in the area of public policy formulation during these years were the members of the Agriculture Committees of each succeeding legislature. It is thanks to the parliamentary activities of these men, and the huge quantities of correspondence on agrarian issues arriving daily in the bureaux of the Ministry of the Interior, that we are able to take stock of the impact of the Revolution on the rural economy.

The cardinal point to note is that the Revolution did not bring in its train a radical transformation of the countryside. Indeed, many specialists would still subscribe to the view enunciated by Georges Lefebvre[30] in 1933 that by and large the political and social upheavals of the 1790s served principally to consolidate the existing agrarian structures. The growth curve may have been flattened for the best part of a generation, but it was not dislocated. Contemporary observers often supposed that the land of France had been sold off to the highest bidder, however the most recent quantitative research makes it clear that this was not the case. Over the revolutionary decade nationalization of church and *émigré* noble estates affected perhaps 10 per cent of the soil surface, and the steady liquidation of these assets probably doubled the size of the land market for the duration of the sales (1791–1812). Peasant cultivators certainly benefited from these transactions, even if they conspicuously failed to buy at auction. Overall their share of the land seems to have risen from around 40 to 44 or 45 per cent.[31] It is true, of course, that such averages conceal huge discrepancies. In the north-east of the country the normal land market was completely submerged when ecclesiastical and noble property amounting to 25 per cent of soil surfaces was put up for auction, whilst in Lower Alsace the Revolution released for sale between 45,000 and 72,000 hectares (15–24 per cent of village agricultural territory).[32]

In 1791 the revolutionaries promulgated a general law on agriculture which began with the ringing declaration: 'the entire territory of France is as free as the persons who inhabit it'.[33] This was a piece of political casuistry as they knew full well. Far from liberating the soil, the so-called Rural Code left much of the edifice of collective rights intact. Whilst proprietors were legally empowered to enclose their land and thereby to remove it from the sway of compulsory crop rotation, the customary practices of common grazing and gleaning were not condemned and therefore survived more or less intact. Indeed, the political empowerment of the rural masses ushered in by the Revolution seems to have made the securing of the reforms advocated by the physiocrats rather less likely than more so. Arthur Young conceded as much in the postscript reflections accompanying the 1793 edition of his *Travels*, observing: 'I know of no country where the people are not against inclosures.'[34] Somewhat paradoxically, therefore, the revolutionaries found themselves presiding over a retreat from enclosure and a reaffirmation of customary practices. Not only were farmers deterred from exercising the right to enclose, they were sometimes intimidated into reinstating cereal husbandry on land they had previously switched to fodder crops or else to viticulture. In short, the revolutionary and Napoleonic law codes would succeed in clarifying property rights in nearly every sphere except that of the rural economy.

Yet in other areas the turbulent final decade of the eighteenth century left a more palpable imprint. The abolition of the tithe and of seigneurial dues, whether paid in cash or in kind, removed a burden which weighed down agriculture and sapped the enterprise of country dwellers. No doubt the material benefits accruing from abolition were distributed rather unevenly, for in 1790 a law was passed which entitled landlords to add the value of the tithe to existing leases. Over time, however, it is likely that even those who actually tilled the soil received a share of the proceeds. In any case, direct and indirect taxes dwindled dramatically after 1788 to produce a real, if unintended, windfall from which nearly everybody involved in the rural economy was able to benefit. Tax collection resumed with a vengeance from 1797—and at a time when agricultural commodity prices were plunging. Many smallholders found themselves in real difficulty as a result, although it seems unlikely that the arrears from the early 1790s were ever called in. By this date the inflationary spiral triggered by the revolutionaries' decision to issue a paper currency had left a durable mark on agriculture as well. Cultivators discovered that they could extinguish farming debts with a handful of banknotes. Even sharecroppers contrived to benefit from the conjuncture by redeeming cattle leases using depreciated paper, and then selling off their share of the stock at a profit. Since most of the debt in the countryside belonged to landowners, researchers now recognize that inflation accomplished one of the most important, if stealthy, wealth transfers of the revolutionary period.

Historians have long debated whether the turmoil of the 1790s and early 1800s served to strengthen or to weaken the subsistence sector of the rural economy; whether indeed the persistent image of the insular and self-sufficient peasant does not belong more properly to the nineteenth than to the eighteenth century. There can be little doubt that market 'pull' pressures eased on the morrow of the Revolution. The big cities lost population, their hinterlands deindustrialized, and peasant cultivators seem to have set about consuming surpluses which they were no longer constrained to market. On the other hand, the Revolution may well have facilitated a further extension of high-performance 'petite culture' in those regions where it was already well established. Furthermore, specialists have pointed to instances where the reinvigoration of the land market enabled a new class of small-scale producers to emerge whose cropping choices (horticulture, fruit growing, vines, etc.) unmistakably oriented them to the market. The fundamental characteristics of France's agrarian landscapes emerged from the episode of the Revolution little altered, however. In 1801 William Russell, a Birmingham wholesale merchant, went to live on a former monastic estate he had purchased which was located outside Caen on the Norman cereal plain. 'The land', he reported, 'is all in one connected body, uncommonly rich in quality and produces as fine wheat as any land I ever saw in England.' As for husbandry, he had nothing but admiration for the agricultural labourers: 'their work in plowing, mowing, reaping etc is all very good and in some parts of France is quite equal to the best I have ever seen in England'.[35] British tourists who returned to the Continent in shoals once peace had been restored in 1814–15 were also pretty sanguine about the health of French agriculture in the zone to the north of the river Loire: not 'an acre of waste all the way from Paris to Lyons', reported James Weston in 1819.[36]

Notes

1. M. Bloch, *Les Caractères originaux de l'histoire rurale française* (Oslo, 1931).
2. Reproduced in E. Le Roy Ladurie, *Le Territoire de l'historien* (2 vols. Paris, 1973–8), ii. 18–29, and tr. as 'history that stands still' in *The Mind and Method of the Historian* (Brighton, 1981), 1–27.
3. See P. Claval, 'The Historical Dimension of French Geography', *Journal of Historical Geography*, 10 (1984), 229–45.
4. C. E. Labrousse, *Esquisse du mouvement des prix et des revenus en France au xviiie siècle* (2 vols. Paris, 1933); Labrousse, *La Crise de l'économie française à la fin de l'Ancien Régime et au début de la Révolution* (Paris, 1944).
5. See *Études et documents*, ii (Paris, 1990), 37.
6. J.-C. Toutain, 'Le Produit de l'agriculture française de 1700 à 1958: ii, La Croissance', *Cahiers de l'Institut de Science Économique Appliquée*, suppl. to 115 (1961), 1–287.
7. P. T. Hoffman, *Growth in a Traditional Society: The French Countryside, 1450–1815* (Princeton, 1996).
8. See M. Overton, *Agricultural Revolution in England: The Transformation of the Agrarian Economy, 1500–1800* (Cambridge, 1996), 84, and K. G. Persson, *An Economic History of Europe: Knowledge, Institutions and Growth, 600 to the Present* (Cambridge, 2010), 62–4.
9. Arthur Young, *Travels during the Years 1787, 1788 and 1789 undertaken more particularly with a View of ascertaining the Cultivation, Wealth, Resources and National Prosperity of the Kingdom of France* (2 vols. Dublin, 1793), i, p. vii.
10. For a re-examination of Young's writings as a source of information on English agriculture, see L. Brunt 'Rehabilitating Arthur Young', *Economic History Review*, 56 (2003), 265–99.
11. British Library, London Additional MS 35126, J. Symonds to A. Young, Liancourt, 3 Oct. 1785.

12. J.-M. Chevet, *La Terre et les paysans en France et en Grande-Bretagne du début du xviie siècle à la fin du xviiie siècle* (2 vols. Paris, 1998), i. 15.
13. Young, *Travels*, ii. 364.
14. Lucien Febvre, 'Que la France se nomme diversité: A propos de quelques études jurassiennes', *Annales: ESC*, 3 (1946), 271–4.
15. Young, *Travels*, ii. 237.
16. J. Loutchisky, 'Les Classes paysannes en France au xviiie siècle', *Revue d'Histoire Moderne et Contemporaine*, 15 (1911), 297–323; 16 (1911), 5–26.
17. Georges Lefebvre, *Questions agraires au temps de la Terreur* (La Roche-sur-Yon, 2nd edn., 1954), 91.
18. Cited in Robert Forster, 'Obstacles to Agricultural Growth in Eighteenth-Century France', *American Historical Review*, 75 (1970), 1605 n. 30.
19. Young, *Travels*, ii. 233.
20. Forster, 'Obstacles to Agricultural Growth', 1605.
21. Young, *Travels*, ii. 241.
22. See A. Antoine, *Fiefs et villages du Bas-Maine au xviiie siècle: Étude de la seigneurie et de la vie rurale* (Mayenne, 1994), 246.
23. G. Postel-Vinay and J. M. Robin, 'Eating, Working and Saving in an Unstable World: Consumers in Nineteenth-Century France', *Economic History Review*, 45 (1992), 496–7 and tables.
24. Cited in Hoffman, *Growth*, 180.
25. G. Postel-Vinay, *La Rente foncière dans le capitalisme agricole: Analyse de la voie 'classique' du développement du capitalisme dans l'agriculture à partir de l'exemple du Soissonnais* (Paris, 1977).
26. J.-M. Moriceau, *Les Fermiers de l'Ile-de-France, xve–xviiie siècles: L'Ascension d'un patronat agricole* (Paris, 1994); J.-M. Moriceau and G. Postel-Vinay, *Ferme, entreprise, famille: Grande Exploitation et changements agricoles, xviie–xixe siècles* (Paris, 1992).
27. A.-J. Bourde, *Agronomie et agronomes en France au xviiie siècle* (3 vols. Paris, 1967), iii. 1407.
28. Chevet, *La Terre et les paysans*, ii. 83–103.
29. G. Béaur, 'Les Chartier et le mystère de la révolution agricole', *Histoire et Mesure*, 11 (1996), 371.
30. Georges Lefebvre, 'La Révolution française et les paysans', repr. in F. Gauthier and C. Wolikow, *Les Caractères originaux de l'histoire rurale de la Révolution française: Recueil d'articles publiées dans les Annales historiques de la Révolution française de 1924 à 1998* (Paris, 1999), 113.
31. G. Postel-Vinay, 'A la recherche de la Révolution économique dans les campagnes, 1789–1815', *Revue Économique*, 6 (1989), 1039.
32. R. Marx, *La Révolution et les classes sociales en Basse-Alsace: Structures agraires et vente des biens nationaux* (Paris, 1974), 50–1.
33. *Loi relative à l'agriculture. Donné à Paris le 12 juin 1791. Décret du 5 juin 1791* in *Lois et actes du gouvernement* (Paris, 1834), iii.
34. Young, *Travels*, ii. 231, 529.
35. Archives and Heritage, Birmingham Central Library MS 660351–3, Papers of Thomas Pougher Russell.
36. Archives and Heritage, Birmingham Central Library, MS 3219/6/70, J. Weston to J. Watt, jun., 28 Aug. 1819.

Bibliography

Bloch, M., *French Rural History: An Essay on its Basic Characteristics* (London, 1978).
Broad, J. (ed.), *A Common Agricultural Heritage? Revising French and British Rural Divergence. Agricultural History Review*, supplement ser. 5 (2009).
Cleary, M. C., 'French Agrarian History after 1750: A Review and Bibliography', *Agricultural History Review*, 37/1 (1989), 64–74.
Forster, R., and Ranum, O. (eds.), *Rural Society in France: Selections from the 'Annales, économies, sociétés, civilisations'* (Baltimore, Md., and London, 1977).
Hoffman, P. T., *Growth in a Traditional Society: The French Countryside, 1450–1815* (Princeton, 1996).
Jones, P. M., 'Agricultural Modernization and the French Revolution', *Journal of Historical Geography*, 16/1 (1990), 38–50.
Jones, P. M., 'Recent Work on French Rural History', *Historical Journal*, 46 (2003), 953–61.
Poussou, J.-P., *La Terre et les paysans en France et en Grande-Bretagne au xviie et xviiie siècles* (Paris, 1999).
Price, R., *The Economic Modernization of France: 1730–1880* (London, 1975).

CHAPTER 15

COMMERCE

SILVIA MARZAGALLI

INTRODUCTION

In the course of the fifteenth century, Iberian navigators transformed Europe's knowledge of the world and opened new maritime trade routes. From the beginning of the sixteenth century, the mental and commercial horizons of Europeans successively opened up to the coasts of Africa, trading posts in India and Asia, and the unknown lands to be called henceforth the New World. The colonists and states who claimed them slowly began to exploit them and their products, and to build commercial networks around them, to the point where, by the eighteenth century, transatlantic trade became an integral feature of the economies and societies of countries with Atlantic coastlines. Whilst the trade of the Mediterranean and the Baltic did not disappear, and indeed did well out of international demand and supply, they now appeared subordinate to the fortunes of Atlantic commerce.[1]

Over the three centuries between the European 'discovery' of the Americas, and the French and Haitian revolutions, not to say the independence of all the Americas, the Atlantic became a pivotal area, linking three continents together and also enabling Europeans to reach directly by sea the wealth of the Asiatic world. This 'protoglobalization', as François Crouzet has called it,[2] affected the lives of a substantial number of those inhabiting these continents and led states to formulate new commercial and colonial policies. There is lively disagreement about the scale of this steady integration of markets,[3] but it is beyond doubt that the process boosted European trade, as well as certain sectors of agriculture and industry. The most extensive trade of the Ancien Régime was seaborne, and took place around the Atlantic.

Though better and better known, tamed, and controlled, nevertheless Asian and American lands remained remote both in space and time from the Europeans who took most of the economic and commercial decisions affecting trade with them. The character of international commerce under the old order was formed by a series of constraints linked to the relationship of time and distance which Fernand Braudel thought so fundamental.[4] Once they were overcome by the technological advances of the nineteenth century, it would spell the end of a commercial world in which information often travelled only at the speed of sailing ships, and open the way to new forms of organization and exchange.

Yet the widening of horizons, and the growth of the volume and nature of goods exchanged, which the opening of transatlantic trade routes made possible, did not supplant the realities of traditional trade, the age-old rhythms of daily exchange on the European continent or along its coasts, the everyday trade of internally produced goods. Wine, salt, wood, and cereals still formed the bulk, in volume, of goods transported within Europe. In societies whose staple food was cereals, the grain trade was a constant preoccupation of state and municipal governments, which over the centuries had put together a formidable apparatus of regulation to guarantee the provisioning of towns and, beyond that, public order.

Accordingly, constraints on internal and external traffic in goods and money were the other fundamental characteristic of European trade under the Ancien Régime. Although in the course of the eighteenth century there emerged in several European countries a desire to set the economy and trade free, in the French case it took the Revolution to sweep away a whole range of restrictions which weighed upon the circulation of goods. Even so, the gradual ending of the commercial system which had underpinned the prosperity of European ports under the Ancien Régime was also, in fact primarily, the consequence of structural changes in the European economy and in the apparatus of colonial domination in America.

This chapter does not offer a complete picture of trade under the Ancien Régime, but rather attempts to bring out the distinctive characteristics which would disappear between the end of the eighteenth century and the middle of the nineteenth with the arrival of more modern systems of exchange.

The Structural Features of Trade under the Ancien Régime

Ancien Régime trade was powerfully conditioned by the structural characteristics of European societies and economies, and above all by the priority given to the production of grain. Diets were based on massive consumption of cereals either as bread or as soup: 1.5 to 2 kg per person per day when supplies were plentiful. Low agricultural productivity meant that three out of four Europeans were obliged to cultivate the soil to produce the surplus necessary to feed the other quarter of the population. Accordingly, society was organized around the land and its products: various forms of income from land and agriculture, such as dues levied by the church and lords, or rents, were the basis of most wealth, while relationship to the land and the unequal distribution of its yield formed the basis of social hierarchies and determined economic inequalities. Only a few parts of the Dutch Republic and of England proved able, over early modern times, through productivity gains and regular grain imports from the Baltic, to lower the relative weight of agriculture in their economies and to free themselves somewhat from these constraints. Even the possibility of bringing cereals from abroad was confined to areas close to navigable routes (seas, rivers, and canals), since the cost of transporting heavy goods overland was prohibitive. Thus most Europeans under the Ancien Régime had to produce the food they needed locally.

This priority given to cereals had a profound influence on the nature and character of trade, in the sense that it affected the supply and demand of other goods: other products could only emerge after a basic local supply of foodstuffs was assured, and demand for anything else, agricultural or industrial, was subordinated to the prior supply of whatever grain was needed. Subsistence crises, most often brought on by poor weather or by the devastation of passing armies, often had knock-on effects on the industrial sector, in the sense that most wage-earners had then to spend the bulk of their income on buying dearer foodstuffs, thus reducing their demand for manufactures. It was the same for peasants unable to profit from selling a market surplus of grain.[5]

The vital question of subsistence had equally produced over the centuries a series of collective limitations on the exploitation of the land and the selling of grain, as well as the establishment of state and municipal policies to ensure the provisioning of towns and provinces. In France grain exports were forbidden not only abroad, but also between provinces of the kingdom. Experiments during the 1760s and 1770s to challenge these practices by allowing the free circulation of cereals were a spectacular failure. For lifting controls on the sale of agricultural products, although profitable for large-scale farmers who could thereby take advantage of price differentials within the national market, was of enormous concern to peasants and wage-earners who saw part of local production disappearing elsewhere and feared the rise in prices which this would inevitably bring locally.

Not only cereals were affected by restrictions. In order to keep money, that tangible sign of wealth, within the frontiers, early modern sovereigns attempted to limit the import of finished luxury goods and to encourage industrial production in their lands by prohibiting or discouraging the export of raw materials. Tariff policies designed to achieve these ends could give rise to conflicts in Europe, as with Louis XIV's wars against the Dutch. Similarly, rulers tried to confine the advantages of navigation to their own subjects, excluding foreigners from certain sectors of national and international carrying. Here, too, navigation policies had to be imposed by force, as in the three Anglo-Dutch Wars (1652–74). These procedures of international regulation were also pursued by diplomatic means, notably by ever-proliferating bilateral commercial treaties. The result could be to boost certain areas of exchange, but to limit others: the Anglo-Portuguese Methuen Treaty of 1703, for example, cut back the export of French table wines to England through import duties which prevented them from competing with the wines of Portugal.

Thus commercial policies and international agreements held back the process of integrating markets which comes about when price differentials between provinces and markets converge. Integration was uneven, not only at the European level, but also within the realm of a single ruler, where other factors could also apply. Accordingly in France as in most other European countries, trade was subject to countless tolls and taxes levied by lords, local authorities, or the state when goods passed through; dues were levied not only at external frontiers, but also when internal barriers were passed. France had to wait until 1789 for the suppression of the *traites*—internal customs duties.

Finally, Ancien Régime commerce was weighed down by the ultimate constraint on the integration of markets: the cost of transport. Before the coming of railways, long-distance overland transport was confined to non-bulky goods of high value. Wherever navigable rivers were available, they were preferred: in the eighteenth century, it cost six times more to send goods between Orléans and Lorient by land than by river. Accordingly, provinces far from a navigable route were deprived not only of a whole range of products, but also of the possibility of developing goods for distant markets. One of the decisive factors in the economic advance of Holland and England in the eighteenth century was their development of internal navigable routes.[6]

Ways of securing products also varied widely. Commerce was characterized by the interlocking of different levels of exchange widely inherited from the middle ages, linking territories unevenly. A village or nearby small town market brought local buyers and producers into direct contact in exchanging agricultural and animal products. In towns, the products of urban monopoly corporations were sold directly by master craftsmen in their shops. Then there were often weekly markets, more or less specialized according to the size of the place, allowing inhabitants to buy their food and locally made everyday objects under the watchful eye of authorities checking on quality but also on the weights and measures used. Finally there were fairs, held in important towns once or several times a year. They allowed consumers but also all sorts of intermediaries access to a much wider range of goods and products without the burden of dues. Depending on their importance, they attracted merchants from some distance: the most important, such as Beaucaire, Leipzig, or Frankfurt, were internationally important. Consumers, finally, were served by itinerant pedlars carrying a varying range of products throughout the countryside.[7]

Alongside all these ways largely inherited from the past of linking producers and consumers there were new ways of making contact more regular between markets, avoiding fairs and inventing disparate patterns of production which bypassed urban corporations and allowed a considerable widening of exchanges. Thus almost everywhere in western Europe networks were established to bring the products of rural manufacture to distant consumers. This was not the same thing as the ordinary handicrafts of peasant families, things made during dead seasons in the agrarian calendar and intended for local markets. Rather it was a matter of massive production of spun or woven goods, or small hardware destined for very distant markets, sometimes across the Atlantic. Raw materials were provided or sold by merchants organizing these networks, who also handled the final product. The producer was quite unable to exercise any control over what he or she was paid, and had no alternatives if demand fell. The expansion of this proto-industrial activity also fed into the colonial trade, as in the case of Breton or Silesian textiles made for Spanish America and exported in large quantities from Cadiz.[8]

More generally, the expansion of trade beyond Europe stimulated the activity of Atlantic ports, which expanded their entrepôt and redistribution roles. Whereas formerly trade in exotic products had taken place through fairs, merchants involved in Atlantic trade went beyond these limitations and organized independent networks of sale and resale, although subject to restrictions and norms fixed by states seeking to control them.

The intervention of the state was all the more significant when the widening of European horizons and interest towards other continents had multiplied the circulation of wealth and expanded what was at stake. The search for a sea route to Asia by the Spanish and Portuguese had led on the one hand to a greater flow of Asiatic spices onto European markets (notably at Lisbon and Antwerp) and on the other to the takeover of territories in America. On the way to Asia, the Portuguese became involved in the African trade in slaves, which initially they brought as much to the Iberian peninsula, where they served as domestic servants, as to islands off the African coast—notably São Tomé—where they established the first sugar plantations.[9] Towards the middle of the sixteenth century, two major events increased the importance of the Americas: first, the discovery of silver mines in Mexico and at Potosí in the 1540s considerably increased the availability of coinage for European economies and confirmed the importance of the discovery of the 'new' world, which until then had only been of value to Europeans in the context of an economy of predation. It also aroused, in France and England, renewed efforts to establish sovereignty in America, which came to fruition in the seventeenth century. Secondly, the Portuguese established the cultivation of sugar cane in Brazil, which began to supply ever more significant quantities of sugar. It required a large labour force, which the Portuguese brought from the coasts of Africa. In the north Atlantic, intensive fisheries fed into financial and exchange activity, while the first encounters with North American Indians set up a profitable trade in furs.[10]

Little by little, networks of transatlantic trade grew up, along with inter-European networks for provisioning the ports from which ships sailed across the Atlantic, and which on their return provided for the redistribution of American and Asiatic products among European consumers. From the seventeenth century, the colonization of North America and the Caribbean by the English and French added to sugar other products like tobacco, indigo, and other dyestuffs necessary in textile production, and then coffee. The number of African captives taken to the Americas went from some 270,000 in the sixteenth century to more than 1.7 million in the seventeenth, reaching 6.5 million in the eighteenth.[11]

On the eve of the French Revolution, some 1,300–1,400 vessels of all flags crossed the ocean each year from east to west carrying slaves, manufactured goods, wines, and, in the case of the French West Indies without nearby continental colonies to supply them, flour. Some 1,500 ships went each year to fish off Newfoundland, which supplied impressive quantities of cod both to Catholic Europe and to the slaves in American plantations. They gave employment to tens of thousands of sailors.

In its turn, this activity of ships, men, and cargoes fostered various circuits of production and distribution which gave work to thousands who, while never setting foot aboard ship, lived through navigation and trade as dockers, carters, customs officers and port workers, shipbuilders, or coopers. These exchanges also enriched the merchants of the Atlantic seaboard and of the ports which took part, directly or indirectly, in the growth of these trades, as well as the industrial sectors, textiles above all, which now sent their goods all over the world.

The flow and the geography of these trades remained strongly dictated by the restrictions imposed by states. From the beginnings of colonization, the main European powers were determined to confine the monopoly of trade with colonies they claimed to their own subjects. In the Spanish case, the importance of the silver shipments which enabled the Spanish monarchy to pursue European hegemony over more than a century brought the establishment of a special department for the close supervision of departing ships, their cargoes, and their passengers. To ensure better protection and control, ships were obliged to leave in groups from a designated port (Seville, then Cadiz) and their route was strictly determined under the Carrera de Indias. Other countries, like France or Portugal, did not establish group sailings (although France established a monopoly in Lorient for all shipping to Asia) but demanded that all trade going to or arriving from their colonies should be conducted exclusively with ports in the home country. England, on the other hand, designated a series of products which could only be traded through the home country, allowing colonists relative freedom to sell non-enumerated products directly to certain foreign markets. Beyond the different forms they took, all these European policies shared a common desire to maximize the benefits which the home country could derive from its transatlantic possessions.

Within these constraints commercial circuits took shape. This was why sugar produced in Saint-Domingue (present-day Haiti), which emerged from the 1730s as the world's main producer of sugar and soon enough of coffee, could only be sent to French ports, although its consumers were found very widely across northern Europe and to a lesser extent in the Levant. Similarly, tobacco was distributed almost exclusively through British ports because it was one of the 'enumerated' products, even if most of its consumers lived beyond the English Channel.

The demand of early modern European consumers for American goods grew astonishingly.[12] In 1800, western Europe absorbed almost 120 million pounds of tobacco, now coming almost exclusively from the Chesapeake (Virginia and Maryland). Consumption of tobacco soon became almost universal and socially 'egalitarian', affecting the whole of society from the elites—women included—down to the lowest town-dwellers. As with tea, coffee, and chocolate, tobacco consumption followed precise rituals, culturally and socially determined, marking off usage in taverns from that of drawing rooms: pipes and cigars, chewing tobacco, or snuff, all had their addicts.[13]

Sugar consumption boomed just as spectacularly: from 10,000 metric tonnes in 1670, it went to some 280,000 metric tonnes (equivalent in unrefined sugar) in 1789. If sugar was the dominant commodity, it was because the taste for exotic drinks—tea, coffee, chocolate—boosted its use. English consumption of tea grew ninefold over the second half of the eighteenth century, to become already a national habit.

The production of West Indian goods and of tobacco depended on the labour of slaves, and so in its turn sustained the networks which supplied the main slaving ports with goods of European or Asian manufacture used in the slave trade.

Further on, products flowing into Europe from America sustained not only inter-European re-export networks, but also Asian ones. European countries—Portugal in the sixteenth century, Holland, England and France from the seventeenth—got their spices, tea, and Asian textiles like cottons and silks essentially by paying for them with silver from American mines. In return, the tea trade benefited that in sugar, just as Indian manufactures were used in the slave trade.

By all their different connections, these exchanges thus linked up the ports and hinterlands of four continents and affected the lives of their inhabitants more or less profoundly: types of consumption, migrations forced or free, markets for work and productive sectors, all were permanently affected by the steady expansion of Europe's commercial horizons and by the direct links which she established with the worlds beyond.

This trade was equally marked by the establishment of specific management practices, whose shape was determined by constraints inherent in Ancien Régime commerce, notably the time required for ships and information to circulate. These problems would only be overcome by the technological advances of the nineteenth century.

Space and Time in Ancien Régime Trade: A Fundamental Constraint

Long-distance trade depends on merchants' knowledge of demand in different markets, and on their ability to organize the transfer of products from one place to another while making a profit. Much of demand and supply is structural and recurs year upon year: it is the bedrock of trade. However, accidental variations constantly disrupt plans: famines, epidemics, wars, weather, all have short-term effects on the productive capacity and the needs of a region. To handle these unforeseeable phenomena, merchants need up-to-date information.[14]

Yet men and women under the Ancien Régime lived when information circulated at rates far different from our own day, where news travels in real time. Before the electric telegraph,[15] the telephone, fax, and the internet, covering any distance took time. This limitation entailed the establishment of specific ways of reducing lags which at the same time conditioned and moulded economic activity.

Time and distance weighed heavily in particular on relations with remote lands, American colonies, Asia, and the Levant, in other words those regions which sustained European economic growth from the sixteenth to the eighteenth centuries, facilitating unprecedented enrichment and accumulation of capital, and supplying at the same time a notable part of the resources of states, whether in the form of the *quinto real* levied by the crown of Spain on the product of American silver mines, or as customs duties.

In order for goods or information about distant lands, enabling economic actors to take their decisions, to reach their destinations, several factors came into play. Geographical distance, availability of ships to go, weather conditions on the voyage, all heavily influenced how long it took. Still in the mid-eighteenth century, it took on average five weeks for news from Constantinople to reach Venice, two and a half months to link the Levant with Spain.[16] But averages are meaningless unless they reflect actual situations: thus a crossing from New York to Bordeaux took an average of forty-five days in the period 1790–1815, but it could be as little as twenty-seven days or as long as seventy-nine. In the other direction, where currents or winds were less favourable, two extra weeks were needed for ships, men, and correspondence to come into port: the average passage from Bordeaux to New York took sixty-one days, with extreme cases between thirty and 189 days.[17]

This relative slowness in the transfer of information strongly limited the possibility of reacting promptly to circumstances affecting exchanges, of whatever sort (shortages, declarations of war, changes in customs policies, etc.). Imagine a merchant who, on receipt of news from the east or across the Atlantic, decides to organize an expedition to exploit the market conditions he has heard about: this expedition, even under the most favourable circumstances, with a ship and adequate cargo to hand, is unlikely to reach its destination until five or six months after the information on which it was based was sent. In many cases there would be little prospect of profit. To this spatial constraint is added that of availability of ships ready to leave, without which merchants, commercial agents, and consuls must either wait, or send their response by roundabout routes which extended the time yet further it took for news to arrive.

Braudel's 'enemy number one', the time it took to transmit information, profoundly affected the processes of exchange under the Ancien Régime. Before technological innovation allowed information to travel in real time, economic and political life had to find ways of reducing these disadvantages as much as possible.

These problems, though recognized by contemporaries as normal, had a profound influence on behaviour.[18] It was because he had to operate on necessarily out-of-date information that an Ancien Régime merchant was forced to delegate a fundamental number of decisions to others. Correspondents, captains, and supercargoes were told to buy and sell cargoes, to handle the ship as they thought best, and more generally to take all the decisions where it was impossible because of distance and time to consult owners directly involved. This gave them wide room for manœuvre.

The indirect way in which all exchanges operated under the Ancien Régime followed directly from the constraints of time on the circulation of economic information. Since business decisions which profoundly affected the profit margins of an operation were entrusted to others, everything depended on trust between principals and their agents. Merchants did business with agents they trusted rather than people unknown to them, even if the latter offered better prices: without the bond of confidence which ensured that the operation could take place in good conditions, the price in itself counted for little.

Confidence was bred in many ways:[19] family or religious ties lent opportunities for redress if trust was breached; geographical origins underpinned local knowledge and a common language. Information conveyed by reliable contacts might recommend third parties: the circulation of information facilitated exchanges at the same time as it allowed internal monitoring and control of networks. But at the root of these indirect ways of management which governed the expansion of European trade in early modern times was the central problem of the time it all took, which brought a systematic unevenness of information.[20]

As well as affecting management, the limitations on the circulation and transmission of information also helped to remodel the pattern of early modern economic activity. The effect was that, as the scope of European economic activity widened, it concentrated its energies around a handful of great ports offering multiple functions: entrepôts, redistribution, financial services, insurance. Whether favoured by their geographical position linked to rich and varied hinterlands (London, Bordeaux, Nantes, Hamburg, etc.), or enjoying specific privileges granted by the state (Lorient, Marseilles, Seville, and then Cadiz), the greater ports which emerged over early modern times were also information hubs which gave them a comparative advantage which every day increased their predominance over ports of the second rank. Aware several days or weeks in advance of what was happening on the other side of the Atlantic or the Mediterranean thanks to the more frequent arrival of ships, merchants in these leading ports were in a position to react more promptly to opportunities, and the availability of ships and products to put together a cargo was also greater than in a port engaged almost exclusively in regional trade.

The End of the Commercial Ancien Régime: The French Case

Observing things from one of the great ports which had done best out of the productive growth of the New World, and its needs in products and labour, such as Bordeaux or Nantes, a merchant in the late 1780s would scarcely have foreseen the upheaval about to affect his business, which would change forever the opportunities available to his town. The suddenness of the change has led several historians to attribute the end of the commercial world which had made the fortune of the French Atlantic seaboard in the eighteenth century to the Revolution.[21] However, if the slave revolt of Saint-Domingue of 1791, and the loss of the colony in 1804 was a huge blow to the French Atlantic ports, the effects of the revolutionary period can be better understood by setting it in a wider context in which technological changes, new ways of thinking, and productive structures came together to put an end to the old commercial order and open up the modern world. This process embraced not only France, but the whole of European trade.

A more subtle analysis of the revolutionary and imperial period, led by some of the historians who have studied French ports in the eighteenth century, has allowed us to refine the chronology of overseas trade and to attribute its disruption more to the war at sea which began in 1793 than to the Revolution.[22] War was a recurrent phenomenon in early modern times, and French merchants had learnt how to deal with its disruptions during numerous conflicts over the eighteenth century, in order to avoid the final collapse of their business. It is true that the price *maximum* in France under the Terror, and later the continental blockade, confronted all those involved in trade with unprecedented situations, but the essence of how to get round the difficulties of navigation in wartime was well known and mastered by merchants: putting ships and cargoes under neutral flags, roundabout routes through non-belligerent ports, privateering, reinvestment in land until the war was over. There is no doubt that the collapse of sugar production in Saint-Domingue as a result of the slave revolt of 1791, and then the same thing in all the French colonies after the first abolition of slavery in 1794, had a much more serious effect on French commercial interests.

But in seeking short-term causes for the end of the trading system that France had known in the eighteenth century, we can lose sight of its own elements of fragility. The idea put forward by some that, in the long run, these weaknesses could only bring about the disappearance of the system which had made the fortune of French seaborne trade under the last Bourbons diminishes the importance of the break made by the Revolution or the Empire. French trade was enormously dependent on the colonial sector, and more and more narrowly on the production of Saint-Domingue. Less diversified than that of other empires, that of France was accordingly more vulnerable. And the Saint-Domingue revolt cannot simply be viewed as a result of the French Revolution: it was much more the product of choosing to cultivate with slaves, the foundation of the whole Caribbean system of production, which made colonial prosperity entirely dependent on keeping up an expensive slave trade, given that the cost of reproducing a slave population was greater than that of importing and exploiting them in bulk.

A second weakness came from the fundamental contradiction between a trading system confined to one nation and international demand:[23] this contradiction was a source of permanent conflict between colonists and the home country, certainly not something specifically French but common to all European countries with American colonies. The desire to be free of the shackles of the *Exclusif*—the metropolitan trading monopoly—fuelled a vigorous smuggling trade which damaged the profit margins of home merchants, which were already tending downwards over the last third of the eighteenth century through wider participation and the general rise in the volume of trade. Colonial indebtedness, often pinpointed as the main cause of difficulty for home merchants, was also the result of the colonists' prioritizing payment for goods outside the legal framework imposed from Europe: they paid foreigners before their own merchants, knowing that in the end the latter were captive suppliers.

Finally, the weight of the colonies in the French trading structure was a real weakness, as Louis Meignen, Pierre Léon, and Michel Morineau have pointed out.[24] While it is true that demand from African and colonial markets was a stimulus to certain inland industries and crops,[25] and that some of the sugar imported was refined in France, the fact remains that colonial imports only gave a modest stimulus to the French economy as a whole, in contrast to the British economy, characterized by the importance of exporting manufactures. The growth of French overseas trade, with its strong colonial component, did not on the whole benefit the rest of the French economy, and was only a sort of 'bubble' depending on special conditions laid down for a time by the French state.[26] In this perspective, the remodelling of patterns of trade after the revolutionary and Napoleonic wars and the shrinkage of colonial business lose the dramatic impact they have if we believe that a growth dynamic very profitable to the French economy as a whole was suddenly brought to an end by political events.[27]

Conclusion

On the eve of the French Revolution, a merchant from the end of the fifteenth century would not have known where he was. Admittedly ways of paying for transactions through credit, relations of trust, networks of correspondents in various markets would have still been familiar, but what acceleration and generalization in the circulation of correspondence and information there had been! Similarly, if the design and capacity of ships had progressed, the hazards of seaborne transport were still there, even if insurance was now general. But how many new products, and above all how many new lands were now part of the world of commerce! And how much more regular were all these links! With the widening of geographical horizons and the quantity of goods traded, wealth was no longer confined to a few great trading houses, but enriched some major ports which had succeeded in distinguishing themselves from a host of lesser ones. Trade was also far better controlled by the authorities than before, with systems of health supervision, registration of entrances and clearances, logging of crews, levying of duties: all these were now well organized, although this did not prevent widespread fraud. Rhythms of exchange had also changed, for to the regular rhythm of international fairs had been added a torrent of daily arrivals of boats and ships which carried goods for sale locally, regionally and internationally. The system of routes was unrecognizable, and in several parts of Europe internal navigation was highly developed.

From the European discovery of the route to Asia and the opening up of the Americas, the range of products traded and above all the volume of goods available to consumers, or at least for those of them able to afford goods beyond basic necessities, had widened. This increased circulation of products sustained for centuries Europe's agricultural and industrial production, enriched states, formed a world of production in the Americas, established new relationships of power and domination but also new forms of collaboration among those involved at the four corners of the world.

These patterns were however subject to the technological constraints of the age and to state action to regulate traffic. Certain choices made at the outset of American colonization and notably in sealing off colonies from foreign trade, and, even more dramatically, recourse to a labour force of slaves and the transportation of captives from Africa—were beginning to show their limits as the stakes rose and tensions increased. On the eve of the French Revolution, these limits had already opened up the first cracks in the system: with hindsight, the independence of the thirteen colonies proved only the beginning of a process which within a few decades would envelop the whole of the Americas. The slave revolt in Saint-Domingue, the American territory with the greatest concentration of slaves, would soon bring to light the problems of massive reliance on slavery, and ultimately accelerate abolition.

By the 1780s the European economy and the Atlantic economy had begun to undergo structural modifications which would change forever the framework to which French maritime business had grown accustomed,[28] removing all hope of any return to the trading structure which the last century of the Ancien Régime had known, and progressively modifying the conditions under which that trade operated. As the economic heart of western Europe shifted from the coastline towards the Rhine, to the disadvantage of the French Atlantic ports, European colonial dominance in America came under challenge, opening up a time when the ability to conquer markets through competitiveness supplanted the pattern of exclusive colonies. New forms of imperialism emerged, even as the structure of international demand moved towards trade in manufactures to the detriment of growth based on exporting agricultural goods and re-exporting colonial goods within a framework of a system of mandatory metropolitan monopoly such as that which prevailed in France. These modifications happened alongside a progressive diversification of the functions which still characterized the world of seaborne trade at the end of the eighteenth century, leading ultimately to the separation of the functions of handling trade from those of shipping it, insuring it, and bankrolling it.[29] The transport revolution, with the coming of steam, and the communications revolution, with the invention of the telegraph, brought the commercial Ancien Régime to an end in the course of the nineteenth century.

Notes

1. For a reassessment of the relative position of the Mediterranean and the Atlantic, see the issue 'La Méditerranée dans les circulations atlantiques', *Revue d'Histoire Maritime*, 13 (2011).
2. 'De la mondialisation', *Historiens et Géographes*, 378 (2002), 231–41. See also K. H. O'Rourke and J. G. Williamson, *Globalisation and History* (Cambridge, Mass., 2005).
3. P. Emmer even disputes the existence of an 'Atlantic Economy': see 'In Search of a System: The Atlantic Economy, 1500–1800', in Horst Pietschmann (ed.), *Atlantic History: History of the Atlantic System* (Göttingen, 2002), 169–78.
4. *The Mediterranean and the Mediterranean World in the Age of Philip II* (2 vols. 1966; tr. London, 1972), part ii, ch. 1, 'Distance, the First Enemy'.
5. The link between subsistence crises and industrial crises is demonstrated by Ernest Labrousse, 'Les Ruptures périodiques de la prospérité: les crises économiques', in Fernand

Braudel and Ernest Labrousse (eds.), *Histoire économique et sociale de la France*, ii. *1660–1789* (2nd edn., Paris, 1993), 529–63.

6. Gerald Crompton (ed.), *Canals and Internal Navigation* (Aldershot, 1996); Andreas Kunz and John Armstrong (eds.), *Modern Europe: Inland Navigation and Economic Development in Nineteenth Century Europe* (Mainz, 1995).
7. On these interlocking markets of differing scale, see Fernand Braudel, *Civilization and Capitalism, 15th–18th Century*, ii. *The Wheels of Commerce* (London, 1983), part ii.
8. Since the pioneering article by Franklin F. Mendels, 'Proto-Industrialization: The First Phase of the Industrialization Process', *Journal of Economic History*, 32 (1972), 241–61, the idea has been developed by Peter Kriedte, Hans Medick, and Jürgen Schlumbohm, *Industrialisation before Industrialisation: Rural Industry in the Genesis of Capitalism* (Cambridge, 1981). For overall introductions, see Sheilagh Ogilvie and Markus Cerman, *European Protoindustrialization* (Cambridge, 1996), and René Laboutte (ed.), *Proto-industrialisation: Recherches récentes et nouvelles perspectives. Mélanges en souvenir de Franklin Mendels* (Geneva, 1996).
9. For a synthesis on the slave trade, see Hugh Thomas, *The Slave Trade: The History of the Atlantic Slave Trade, 1440–1870* (London, 1997).
10. A masterly study of the commercial networks and financing of fishing is André Lespagnol, *Messieurs de Saint-Malo: Une élite négociante au temps de Louis XIV* (Rennes, 1997); for the establishment of networks for exporting furs to France, see Bernard Allaire, *Pelleteries, manchons et chapeaux de castor: Les Fourrures nord-américaines à Paris (1500–1632)* (Paris and Quebec, 1999).
11. Figures from www.slavevoyages.org.
12. Paul Butel, *The Atlantic* (London, 1999).
13. On the consumption patterns and rituals of Madeira wine, see David Hancock, *Oceans of Wine: Madeira and the Emergence of American Trade and Taste* (New Haven, Conn., and London, 2009).
14. Pierre Jeannin maintains that merchants tended to rely more on their own information and knowledge, following familiar routes and ways, rather than constantly trying to adapt their activities to the whirlwind of incoming news. See P. Jeannin, 'La Diffusion de l'information', in Simonetta Cavaciocchi (ed.), *Fiere e mercati nella integazione delle economie europee: Secoli XIII–XVIII* (Florence, 2001), 231–75.
15. Freeing the use of the telegraph, originally invented for military purposes, happened slowly in France from the middle of the nineteenth century, whereas in England at this time there were already over 6,500 km of lines to which the public had had access for a decade. The first transatlantic cable was laid in 1866. See Armand Mattelart, *L'Invention de la communication* (Paris, 1994), 64–5, 188–9. In a general way at the same time railways and steamships considerably increased postal rapidity through regular schedules. For all these reasons, the economic and commercial old regime can be said to have come to an end in the mid-19th cent.
16. Braudel, *Mediterranean*, i, 357.
17. Silvia Marzagalli, 'Bordeaux et les États-Unis, 1776–1815: Politiques et stratégies négociantes dans la genèse d'un réseau commercial' (thèse d'habilitation, Université de Paris I/Sorbonne, 2004; publication forthcoming from Droz, Geneva), ch. 6. The calculation takes no account of the fortunes of war: all ships captured or held by the British are excluded.
18. In his analysis of the circulation of information within the British Empire, Ian K. Steele concludes that contemporaries thought it normal to exchange news once a month: *The*

English Atlantic, 1675–1740: An Exploration of Communication and Community (New York, 1986), 50. For circulation within the French Empire, see Kenneth Banks, *Chasing Empire across the Sea: Communications and the State in the French Atlantic, 1713-1763* (Montreal, 2002).

19. Catherine Carté-Engel has studied the almost exemplary case of the confessional networks established by the Moravian brothers in Saxony, in the West Indies, and on the North and South American continents: *Religion and Profit. Moravians in Early America* (Philadelphia, 2009). For an illuminating presentation of different ways of thinking about how networks functioned and the possibilities for opportunism, see Francesca Trivellato, 'Juifs de Livourne, Italiens de Lisbonne, Hindous de Goa: Réseaux marchands et échanges interculturels à l'époque moderne', *Annales: Histoire, Sciences sociales*, 58 (2003), 581–603. For a critical approach to the operation of networks, see David W. Hancock, 'The Trouble with Networks: Managing the Scots' Early Modern Madeira Trade', *Business History Review*, 75 (2009), 464–91.

20. On the application of concepts deriving from the new institutional economy to the realities encountered by the historians Mark Casson and Mary B. Rose, see the introduction to the special number of *Business History*, 39 (1997), 'Institutions and the Evolution of Modern Business', p. 3.

21. The verdict applies to the whole of the French economy. See Pierre Chaunu's preface to François Crouzet, *De la supériorité de l'Angleterre sur la France: L'Économie et l'imaginaire, xviiie–xxe siècles* (Paris, 1985), p. iii: 'At the end of the Ancien Régime…it was by no means impossible to think…that France might end up ahead.…in the eight years from 1792 to 1800, everything was thrown away.' In the Atlantic trade, J. P. Poussou asserts even more clearly: 'The Revolution…in eliminating…the West Indies trade and maritime activity…certainly brought on a catastrophe': 'Le Dynamisme de l'économie française sous Louis XVI', *Revue Économique*, 40 (1989), 982.

22. See Paul Butel, 'Les Difficultés du commerce maritime bordelais sous le Directoire: Exemple de l'adaptation à la conjoncture de guerre maritime', *Congrès National des Sociétés Savantes*, 94/2 (1969), 332–44, and 'Crise et mutation de l'activité économique à Bordeaux sous le Consulat et l'Empire', *Revue d'Histoire moderne et contemporaine*, 17 (1970), 540–58. Charles Carrière, *Négociants marseillais au xviiie siecle* (2 vols. Marseilles, 1973), i, 152, notes that the real turning point was 1793.

23. This point has been made by André Lespagnol, 'Mondialisation des trafics interocéaniques et structures commerciales nationales au xviiie siècle: Contradictions et compromis', *Bulletin de la Société d'Histoire moderne et contemporaine*, 1–2 (1997), 89–91.

24. Michel Morineau, 'La Vraie Nature des choses et leur enchainement entre la France, les Antilles et l'Europe (xviie–xviiie siècles)', *Revue Française d'Histoire d'Outre-Mer* (1997), 3–24; Louis Meignen, 'Le Commerce extérieur de la France à la fin de l'Ancien Régime', *Revue Historique du Droit français et etranger* (1973), 583–614; Pierre Léon, 'Structure du commerce extérieur et évolution industrielle de la France a la fin du xviiie siècle', in F. Braudel (ed.), *Conjoncture économique: Structure social. Hommage à Ernest Labrousse* (Paris, 1974), 407–32.

25. On the importance of the West Indian market for the products of Aquitaine, see Paul Butel, 'Succès et déclin du commerce colonial français, de la Révolution à la Restauration', *Revue économique*, 40 (1989), 1079–96.

26. The clear conclusion of Meignan, 'Commerce extérieur'.

27. For a survey of historiographical debates in France, see Silvia Marzagalli, 'Le Négoce maritime et la rupture révolutionnaire: Un ancien debat revisité', *Annales historiques de la Révolution française*, 352 (2008), 183–207.
28. These transformations had already attracted the attention of Francois Crouzet forty years ago in his 'Wars, Blockade, and Economic Change in Europe, 1792–1815', *Journal of Economic History*, 24 (1964), 567–88.
29. See the remarks of Louis Bergeron, 'Le Négoce international de la France a la fin du xviiie siècle: Quelques remarques en guise de conclusion', in François Crouzet (ed.), *Le Négoce international, xiie–xxe siècles* (Paris, 1989), 199–203.

Bibliography

Banks, Kenneth, *Chasing Empire across the Sea: Communications and the State in the French Atlantic 1713–1763* (Montreal, 2002).

Braudel, Fernand, *Civilisation and Capitalism, 15th–18th Century* (3 vols. London, 1981–3).

—— *The Mediterranean and the Mediterranean World in the Age of Philip II* (2 vols., 1966; tr. London 1972).

Buti, Gilbert, *Les Chemins de la mer. Un petit port méditerranéan: Saint Tropez (xvii–xviiie siècles)* (Rennes, 2010).

Canny, Nicholas, and Morgan, Philip (eds.), *The Oxford Handbook of the Atlantic World c.1450–c.1850* (Oxford, 2011).

Carrière, Charles, *Négociants marseillais au xviiie siècle: Contribution à l'étude des économies maritimes* (2 vols. Marseilles, 1973).

Cheney, Paul, *Revolutionary Commerce: Globalization and the French Monarchy* (Cambridge, Mass., 2010).

Clark, John G., *La Rochelle and the Atlantic Economy during the Eighteenth Century* (Baltimore, Md., 1981).

Crouzet, François, 'Wars, Blockade and Economic Change in Europe, 1792–1815', *Journal of Economic History*, 24 (1964), 567–88.

—— *De la supériorité de l'Angleterre sur la France: L'Économie et l'imaginaire, xviiie–xxe siècles* (Paris, 1985).

Davis, Ralph, *The Rise of the Atlantic Economies* (London, 1973).

Jeannin, Pierre, *Marchands du Nord. Espaces et trafics à l'époque moderne* (Paris, 1966).

Panzac, Daniel, *La caravane maritime: marins européens et marchands ottomans en Méditerranée* (Paris, 2004).

Pritchard, James, *In Search of Empire: The French in the Americas, 1670–1730* (Cambridge, 2004).

Revue d'histoire maritime, 8 (2007), 'Histoire du cabotage européen'.

CHAPTER 16

SLAVERY AND SERFDOM

WILLIAM DOYLE

When the English traveller and agronome Arthur Young criss-crossed France on horseback to examine economic conditions between 1787 and 1790, he was amazed by its emptiness and disgusted by its agriculture. But when he reached Bordeaux in August 1787 his astonishment knew no bounds. 'Much as I had read and heard of the commerce, wealth, and magnificence of this city,' he wrote,[1] 'they greatly surpassed my expectations. Paris did not answer at all, for it is not to be compared to London; but we must not name Liverpool in competition with Bordeaux.' The luxurious lifestyle of its merchants, the magnificence of the theatre, new buildings going up everywhere, all 'mark, too clearly to be misunderstood, the prosperity of the place'; and the number of large ships moored in the Garonne 'makes it, I suppose, the *richest* water view that France has to boast'. Visiting Nantes a year later, he was again impressed by a grand new theatre, the finest hotel he had ever stayed in, and building sites everywhere.[2] And at Le Havre, the harbour was 'full of ships, to the number of some hundreds, and the quays all around are thronged with business; all hurry, bustle and animation.'[3] If Young had gone along the smartest street in Nantes, where slave traders lived in luxury, he might have looked up at the anthropomorphic keystones over handsome window embrasures: not the usual faces of gods and satyrs, but negroes. And did he notice in Bordeaux, like his aristocratic compatriot the Duchess of Northumberland, thirteen years before him, the 'vast quantity of Blacks of both Sexes' parading along the quayside?[4] If he did, he would have seen some of the few visible hints of whose labours sustained the extraordinary activity and prosperity of these Atlantic ports. Thousands of miles away to the west and the south, almost 700,000 slaves, all black, passed short lives of unremitting toil in producing luxuries for which Europeans had developed an insatiable taste. These ports prospered by bringing the products of tropical islands to France, and then re-exporting them to the rest of Europe. They also ensured that the demographically fragile workforce of slaves was kept up, and expanded as demand burgeoned, by buying slaves in Africa and transporting them across the Atlantic to sell. Only the end products of this intercontinental economy were visible in Europe, and accordingly the slavery at its productive heart has tended to receive relatively little attention in general historical writing about the Ancien Régime. Yet that regime, whether in France or in Europe at large, is unimaginable without the tastes and habits (sugar, chocolate, coffee, coffee houses, smoking, snuff, mahogany furniture) ultimately sustained by slave labour; without the industrial and agricultural stimulus which the demand of slave colonies gave to the production of textiles, hardware, and staple foodstuffs; or without the wealth which colonial trade and possessions pumped into the pockets of social elites and the surroundings they constructed.

There was no slavery in France itself. A long legal tradition going back at least to the sixteenth century supported the principle that any slave setting foot on French soil automatically became free.[5] It remained largely notional until in the late seventeenth century prosperous white colonists began to bring domestic slaves with them when they visited France. Did they then risk losing them when they landed? Laws promulgated in 1716 and 1738 allowed them to retain ownership if they declared their slaves, but these measures remained unregistered by the Parlement of Paris and thus technically inoperative in a large part of the kingdom. Accordingly, slaves brought to France remained able to claim their freedom, and over the eighteenth century increasing numbers had their emancipation upheld in the courts. All told, almost 250 won their freedom in this way between 1730 and the Revolution.[6] By then, there were between 4,000 and 5,000 blacks in the kingdom[7] but the authorities were becoming increasingly worried about racial intermixing, and even more about the discontent and insubordination that freed slaves might spread if they returned to the colonies. In 1777 it was decided to prohibit further black immigration. Black people already in France were to be 'policed', which meant registering with the courts and carrying identity cards. New arrivals were to be interned rather than accompany their owners, and sent back within two years. Until the end of the Ancien Régime, residence in France and slavery remained legally incompatible; but the law of 1777 carefully spoke of 'blacks' irrespective of their status. Its clear aim was to prevent France from being further contaminated by reminders of overseas exploitation now deemed essential to the kingdom's prosperity.[8]

France was a latecomer in the acquisition of colonies worked by slave labour. By the time colonists sent out by the 'Company of the Islands of America' settled in Guadeloupe and Martinique in the 1630s, the Portuguese and the Spaniards had been importing slaves from Africa into their mainland American colonies for over half a century, and the British were beginning to use them to produce tobacco in Barbados. But by the time Louis XIV formally acquired Saint-Domingue, the western part of the island of Hispaniola, in 1697, there were so many slaves in the other French islands that a special set of laws, the Code Noir, had been promulgated to regulate their management (1687). As in the British islands, early cultivation through indentured European labour was in steep decline as tobacco cultivation gave way to the far more lucrative sugar. Since its introduction into Brazil during the previous century, large-scale sugar production had employed captives brought from Africa. The process was intensive, and demanded a large and sturdy labour force which could be supplied neither by indentured labourers from Europe nor from the increasingly sparse Amerindian population. So sugar meant black slaves, and the pattern was not questioned when its production spread to the islands of the Caribbean. Thus by 1687 there were already 27,000 slaves in the French islands, outnumbering whites by 8,000. And this imbalance grew at an ever-accelerating rate over the subsequent century as demand for sugar boomed, supplemented from the 1730s by coffee. When these crops were established in Saint-Domingue, a far larger territory than all the other islands put together, the slave population mushroomed. By the 1780s Guadeloupe had 90,000 slaves, Martinique 83,000, and Saint-Domingue 465,000; not to mention around 50,000 in the Indian Ocean islands of Ile de France (now Réunion) and Ile Bourbon (Mauritius). Everywhere slave populations dwarfed those of whites, and in between there was a growing group of mixed-race coloureds, mostly free, but with a real sense of separate identity. On Saint-Domingue they were almost as numerous as the 30,000 whites, and many were themselves slave owners.

The black population of most tropical islands never reproduced itself. Lives were short, work debilitating, there were too few women, and infant mortality was very high in appalling sanitary conditions. Yet the demand for labour in the booming colonial economy was insatiable. All this sustained *la traite*, the slave trade. Beginning in the later seventeenth century with chartered companies mainly dealing in the monopoly of shipping slaves to the Spanish colonies (*asiento*), French slaving was gradually opened over the early decades of the next century to free competition between metropolitan ports. By mid-century the lion's share had fallen to Nantes, which fitted out just under half of all French eighteenth-century slaving expeditions. In the notorious 'triangular trade', goods of European or Asian manufacture—textiles above all, but also spirits, hardware, weapons, tobacco—were traded on the coasts of Africa for slaves. In the 'middle passage' these captives were shipped to the islands and there sold. The third side of the triangle, carrying the precious luxuries back to Europe, was normally in other hands plying directly between the islands and the home ports, although luckier slave ships might sometimes return with holds full of more than ballast to boost their profits. Nevertheless, despite high risks, the potential rewards of slaving were so great that the volume of trade never ceased to grow. Between 1700 and 1745, 910 French ships delivered 255,000 slaves; but between 1780 and 1792 no fewer than 1,143 ships brought 370,000 to the islands.[9] Over the century the French shipped more than 1,100,000 Africans to their colonies. This was less than half the number shipped by the British, and half a million fewer than the Portuguese, but on the eve of the Revolution the French were carrying more than any other slaving power. Some 55,000 were landed in the West Indies in 1789–90 alone. But even this did not sate the colonies' appetite for manpower, and many slaves were bought in the French islands from British or American shippers.

The number of merchants directly involved in full-time slaving was never great, even in Nantes. Many expeditions formed only part of much more widely spread mercantile portfolios, even if other elements were mostly colonial too. But all slaving depended heavily on credit from Parisian bankers and financiers, who in turn raised capital from the highest levels of metropolitan and court society. So the hidden tentacles of the slave trade reached to the very heart of the Ancien Régime. And the wider links of high society to the colonial economy based on slavery were not even hidden. The wealth of 'the isles' was so proverbial that few with spare capital to invest felt able to resist it. Colonial heiresses were among the most coveted prizes in the marriage market. The best known, though far from the wealthiest example, is Rose Tascher de la Pagerie from Martinique, who was sent to France at 16 in 1779 to marry Viscount Alexandre de Beauharnais. Twenty-three years later, widowed in the Terror and now married to First Consul Napoleon Bonaparte and known as Josephine, she lobbied her husband for the reintroduction of slavery. Through marriage or outright purchase, many of the greatest families in the kingdom came to possess plantations in the islands. When inventoried, they were invariably valued complete with their stock of cattle, horses, mules—and slaves. Colonial property, seldom if ever visited and managed on the spot by often unscrupulous Creole stewards, subject to violent tropical weather, earthquakes, volcanoes, oceanic uncertainties, and periodic wars, was by no means a guaranteed source of riches. If anything the only thing it guaranteed was escalating debt. But in good years the rewards were more spectacular than anything that domestic agriculture could match; and in Bordeaux, for example, some of the most lavish new mansions thrown up during the frenetic building boom of the 1780s were those of colonial proprietors.

Bordeaux was only a secondary slaving port. The bulk of its trade with the slave colonies was *en directe*, two-way, not triangular. The economy of slave-produced luxuries was so concentrated and all-pervasive that the islands had little room to provide their own basic necessities—whether hardware, textiles, consumer goods, and even foodstuffs like flour, salt fish, and wine. All these had to be imported, and legally that meant from France. Under the principle known as the *exclusif*, only French ports and French ships might trade with French colonies. The idea, going back to Colbert and beyond, was that France alone should receive all the benefits of her own colonies. Colbert's instinct, long shared by his successors, was to create monopoly trading companies; but sooner or later most of these failed, and gradually the merchants of most French ports were allowed to trade freely with the colonies. This was still a form of monopoly, however, and there was increasing resentment among the colonists that they were prohibited from supplying themselves from cheaper, non-French sources. Smuggling flourished, especially during wartime when links with France were disrupted. By mid-century, the mainland British colonies of North America could supply almost everything the islands needed more cheaply, even though the British vainly tried to redirect this trade to the exclusive benefit of their own islands. To howls of metropolitan outrage, in 1767 two small *entrepôts* for the import of foreign goods were created at opposite ends of the French Caribbean. Seventeen years later, with formerly British North America now an independent state and seeking support from its only ally, France widened this *exclusif mitigé* by opening at least one port to foreign traders in each French island. American ships flooded in, bringing every sort of commodity, including slaves. Yet the expansion of France's Atlantic ports was scarcely dented by this competition. Higher quality French-produced sugar captured every European market except Great Britain. By then, coffee and cotton were expanding spectacularly, too. Seemingly there was enough trade in the French Atlantic economy for everyone. On the eve of the Revolution, it accounted for a third of the kingdom's trade, with a further third coming from mainly colonial re-exports. And Saint-Domingue alone, by then the most valuable territory on earth, dominated every sector.

As in so many other areas, the Ancien Régime of the colonies was never more brilliant and apparently dynamic than on the very eve of its downfall.

It had benefited throughout its evolution from the support of the state. French ministers never doubted the value of tropical colonies, and over the eighteenth century they devoted ever-increasing proportions of the King's resources to their protection. On the seas, great mid-century wars between 1744 and 1763 against Great Britain were a contest between rival slave-based empires to secure the lion's share of colonial riches. They brought serious disruption to all branches of French maritime trade, as superior British seapower largely cut off the islands from France. Guadeloupe and Martinique fell to the enemy in the 1750s, and British slavers took over the entire supply of new captives. But when peace negotiations were opened the French were determined to get the lost islands back, and in 1763 they cheerfully gave up the whole of Canada for the return of Guadeloupe. By a massive and expensive effort, the French rebuilt a navy, which helped to rob Great Britain of thirteen mainland colonies in the American War of Independence. This time none of the precious Caribbean islands was lost.[10] But once again the *exclusif* proved unenforceable in wartime and it could not be restored after the peace of 1783. Instead, the government taxed all slaves landed on French islands from foreign ships, and passed the proceeds to French slavers. They, in turn, were offered substantial bounties on slaves landed from their own ships.[11] These advantages underpinned the last surge in French slaving before 1790. But by then the Ancien Régime back in France had collapsed, overwhelmed by the cumulative costs of international competition, with investment in the navy representing an ever-increasing share.

It is not, therefore, a complete exaggeration to suggest that the costs of upholding a colonial system that could only work through slavery were what ultimately brought down the Ancien Régime in France. But nobody thought in those terms before it happened. Most European anxiety about slavery revolved around fears that one day a slave uprising might destroy colonial prosperity. All educated men knew about Spartacus, whose servile rebellion had nearly destroyed the Roman Republic. Many people knew that life in the colonies was dogged by the resistance of maroons, escaped slaves— although these were more active in the British than in the French colonies. And if, in the earlier part of the eighteenth century, doubts began to be voiced about whether colonies in general were worth the trouble of their establishment and retention, the issue of slavery was never in the forefront of the argument. Among the great mid-century thinkers, only Montesquieu condemned it unequivocally—and even he thought it might be unavoidable in hot climates.[12] By the 1760s, however, economic writers were beginning to speculate that slavery impeded rather than encouraged the most efficient production. This tendency peaked in 1776 with Adam Smith's declaration, in the *Wealth of Nations*,[13] that unfree labour could only be economic in an unfree market. Smith was soon easily available in French, but the first widely diffused denunciation of slavery in the language appeared in 1772.[14] Guillaume Thomas Raynal's multi-volume *Philosophical History of the Two Indies* was in fact a compendium by various hands, and issued in successive revised editions until the end of the century. It recounted the history of European overseas expansion since the 1490s as a long record of greed, exploitation, and cruelty.

Among its most vicious achievements was the installation and expansion of slavery in the new world. Raynal predicted that sooner or later the massive imbalance in colonial populations would lead to an irresistible uprising of the oppressed blacks. The work was a best-seller, but it had few immediate practical results. It was not until 1788 that a prominent and influential group of Parisian intellectuals came together to form the Amis des Noirs (Friends of the Blacks). Their inspiration was the Society for Effecting the Abolition of the Slave Trade established in London in 1787, and their initial aim was the same: to stir up public demand for the abolition of the trade, in the long-term belief that, without it, slave owners would behave more humanely, reform the ways they exploited their workforce, and ultimately perhaps turn their minds to abandoning slavery itself. But like their London counterparts, they recognized that, for better or worse, slaves were property, and that if slavery were abolished compensation would have to be found. Nobody could realistically imagine how. And, however influential the illustrious members of the Amis—men like Condorcet, Lafayette, Lavoisier, Mirabeau, several dukes—momentous events nearer home were absorbing most educated opinion in 1788. Their attempts the next spring to make condemnation of slavery and the trade a priority among the demands of the *cahiers* brought only a tepid and diffuse response.[15] In August 1789 a proposal to free slaves on the night of the 4th was drowned out in the tumultuous shower of other renunciations and abolitions, and on 26 August slavery went unmentioned in the Declaration of the Rights of Man and the Citizen.

Yet there was an obvious problem for a nation which proclaimed its commitment to the natural equality of all men, but which operated the world's most prosperous and successful slave-based economy. No sooner had the Amis des Noirs launched their efforts than planter and mercantile interests began to organize against them. In that same month of August 1789 a group of rich absentee plantation owners set up what became known as the Club Massiac to lobby the National Assembly on colonial issues.[16] It soon had affiliates in most of the western seaports. And when deputies elected by the whites of Saint-Domingue arrived unbidden and demanded seats in the Assembly, they were admitted. Pressure from these groups ensured that neither the principle of slavery nor even the slave trade were ever openly debated either in the Constituent Assembly or its Legislative successor. Discussion of colonial issues was largely confined to whether free coloureds (almost as numerous as the whites in Saint-Domingue) should be given political representation; and while politicians in Paris wavered uncertainly, coloured unrest was brutally suppressed by colonial whites now beyond metropolitan control. Relentless faction-fighting among the colonial elites in Saint-Domingue eventually opened the way, in August 1791, to what everybody had dreaded for half a century—a massive slave uprising.

It would prove to be the greatest slave rebellion in history. It overthrew the Ancien Régime in Saint-Domingue with far more violence than was seen in France, and it marked the beginning of the end for the Atlantic slave empire which had been so integral to the last century and a half of the old order. Its fate was finally sealed after war with Great Britain once more broke out in 1793, and British seapower throttled France's already weakened and defenceless transatlantic trade. Such energies as a new republic beset by European enemies could spare for faraway colonies were now devoted to recovering control in the former 'Pearl of the Antilles', where planters had called in the British to protect them against the rebels. But agents sent out to coordinate the effort rapidly concluded that the only way to restore order was to abolish the one thing the planters had sought British help to preserve: slavery itself. In August and September 1793 the abolition of slavery in the colony was proclaimed. Rather than disavow its agents, on 4 February 1794 the Convention confirmed the abolition and extended it to all French dominions. Dressed up as it was as the overdue fulfilment of the principles of human freedom and equality proclaimed in 1789, this, the first general slave emancipation ever, was no altruistic gesture. It was merely a recognition of the colonial situation on the ground. The same Jacobins who gave themselves the credit were bitter in denouncing the Amis des Noirs for stirring up slave discontent in the first place, and so undermining the nation's commercial prosperity. They had no more idea than the Amis themselves how the lucrative luxuries of the tropics could be produced without slave labour. Only on the question of compensation to planters for lost human property did the Jacobin Convention solve one of the great paralysing conundrums of abolition. No compensation was offered.

There was a revolutionary precedent for uncompensated abolition of property in human beings. On the night of 4 August 1789, one of the first proposals which opened the torrent of suppressions and renunciations was for the abolition of serfdom. This one was not drowned out. And, although problems of definition over the next few months gradually whittled down the numbers benefiting from unredeemable emancipation,[17] the Revolution permanently destroyed all remnants of personal bondage to a lord or to the soil.

And yet serfdom in recognizably medieval forms had long disappeared in France. Most of it had gone by the sixteenth century. One way of defining the Ancien Régime in the countryside might be as the time of feudalism without serfdom, when lords retained rights over properties but no longer over persons. As with everything about the Ancien Régime, however, exceptions, anomalies, and relics persisted, so that even in the eighteenth century various forms of personal subjection or bondage to the soil could still be found under the French crown, particularly in eastern areas of the kingdom added since the sixteenth century at the expense of rulers in whose realms serfdom was still normal. Nobody really knew how many people were involved. Eighteenth-century polemicists, anxious to demonstrate the pervasiveness of the evil they were denouncing, pushed the number as high as one and a half million. The Duke de la Rochefoucauld told the Constituent Assembly that he thought it was no more than 140,000; whereas more recent historical estimates have moved it back again towards the million mark.[18] Possibly, therefore, there were as many or more serfs in France as there were slaves in her overseas colonies. But estimates depend on how serfdom is defined. The best known definition was the holding of land in mortmain (*mainmorte*), which meant that it could never be sold or alienated, and could only be passed on to a child living under the parental roof. The holders of such lands were called *mainmortables,* a term often used as a synonym for serf. In return for their tenure, they might be subject to a wide variety of duties and payments to their lords, normally including several days a week of forced labour (*corvée*). They and their family might not be allowed to marry outside the lordship without their lord's permission (*formariage*). They might also be subject to forced repatriation by the lord or loss of lands if they left the domain (*droit de suite; échute*). Anyone who married such a serf automatically took on the same status.

However burdensome all this was, defenders of French serfdom pointed out that it was far from the same as slavery. Serfs were not chattels. Usually they remained free to give up their holdings and the servile status that went with them. It was also harder to dispossess servile tenants than freer feudal vassals.[19] Yet for much of the eighteenth century the plight of serfs commanded far more public interest and sympathy than that of slaves beyond the seas. Over the last decade of his life, Voltaire (d. 1778) waged a sustained public campaign to alleviate the burdens of serfs belonging to a monastery in Franche Comté, luridly invoking the inhumane conditions of their lives. Yet at this very moment other monasteries were seeking ways of freeing their serfs on the grounds that they cultivated their lands, not to mention those of their lords, carelessly and inefficiently. By now this was fashionable economic doctrine, and Adam Smith's remarks of 1766 on the inadequacies of slave labour were extended by him to the work of serfs, too. And in 1779 Louis XVI decided formally to abolish serfdom on all lands in the royal domain. In the preamble to the edict, the King expressed the hope that his example would encourage other lords to do the same, but few did. The Parlement of Besançon, which had more serfs within its jurisdiction than any other, held out for nine years before registering the edict into law. When it came to drafting *cahiers* in 1789, only 9 per cent of peasants thought serfdom worth mentioning—perhaps reflecting how few serfs there were, and how localized their distribution. But almost a third of the overwhelming urban *cahiers* of the Third Estate (28 per cent) condemned serfdom as an inhuman relic of the dark ages, and called for its abolition.[20] On the night of 4 August 1789, uncompensated abolition of serfdom was carried by acclaim, as self-evidently just. But murmurs of disapproval were heard when isolated deputies argued for the logic of extending this emancipation to slaves overseas.[21]

To equate serfs with slaves was certainly loose usage, but the parallel was often drawn. Deciding lawsuits concerning the legitimacy of slavery in Europe, both French and English judges felt obliged to consider whether the serfdom of medieval times showed that some sort of slavery had once been lawful. Elsewhere in Europe, however, serfdom had never died out as it had in England, or shrunk into ambiguity, as in France. East of the Rhine, in fact, serfs could be found in many regions, and further east, beyond the Elbe, unfree labour formed the bedrock of the social structure. In these serf economies, manorial lords cultivated their demesnes, or 'dominical' land as it was known throughout the Habsburg realms, with unpaid serf labour (*robot* or, in Russia, *barschina*). They might also exact other dues in cash or kind. Serfs in return held plots of 'rustical' land for their own use during the days in the week when they were not working for their lords. Thus, so far from a time of feudalism without serfdom, the Ancien Régime in central and eastern Europe was the age of what many historians have called 'second serfdom', originally imposed in the sixteenth and seventeenth centuries by lords desperate to overcome the scarcity of labour. Even here it was often unclear how close their status was to slavery. When in 1763 Frederick II of Prussia proclaimed the abolition of serfdom in Pomerania, he used the word *Leibeigenschaft,* bodily subjection. The reaction of Pomeranian landlords was to claim that no such thing existed. They did not own the persons of their vassals, but merely customary contractual rights to their labour.[22] Twenty years later, the same word used by Joseph II brought a similar response in Styria.[23] The status of these peasants, therefore, was much closer to France's *mainmortables,* notionally at liberty to abandon their holdings and the servile status that went with it. But the usual arbiters of this were the lords' own courts, which habitually upheld their right to pursue vassals who quitted their tenures without permission, and to punish all sorts of defiance or disrespect with scarcely restricted violence.

The power of lords over their 'subjects' (*Untertanen*) was much more extensive in Poland than in German or Habsburg territories, as Joseph II found when he tried to extend his reforms to newly annexed Polish Galicia. Even so, around a quarter of the Polish rural population held free tenures on the eve of the old Commonwealth's disappearance.[24] It was in Russia that serfdom came closest to slavery. Slavery, in fact, was an established institution in Russia, the only place in Europe where it was unambiguously recognized by positive law. Serfdom was originally quite distinct from it. But the same scarcity of labour which drove enserfment further west led landlords to whittle away peasant independence, and under the Assembly Code of 1649 (*Sobornoe Ulozhenie*), the absolute power of serf owners was confirmed, and any meaningful distinction between serfs and slaves disappeared. Subjects no longer had the right to leave their lords: most of the Code's provisions on the peasantry concerned the right of lords to pursue and recover fugitives. And, although the primary bond of the serf was still to the soil, the Code gave their masters extensive powers to move them about, lease them out, mortgage them, or buy and sell them. As a British traveller wrote in 1710: 'The peasants are perfect slaves, subject to the arbitrary power of their lords, and transferred with goods and chattels: they can call nothing their own.'[25] Arguably, indeed, the situation of Russian serfs was worse than that of colonial slaves, since in addition to working unpaid for their masters, they were liable to direct taxation and lifetime conscription into the armies. It is true that a substantial minority of Russian peasants, perhaps 40 per cent in 1762, were not privately owned serfs, but 'state peasants' under the direct jurisdiction of the autocrat. But this authority was no less arbitrary, and Catherine II, notoriously, transferred them by the thousand into the hands of her favourites and lovers.

Like slaves, serfs had certain perilous ways of resisting or defying their lords. They could deliberately perform their work slowly, or spoil it. Or like the maroons who infested the wooded hills of the West Indies, they could attempt escape. In many parts of Germany, the air of towns was deemed to confer freedom, but further east towns were increasingly small and scattered, and in any case extensively populated by serf domestics. But beyond the heartlands of Russia were the open steppes of the Ukraine, peopled by nomadic Cossacks constantly reinforced by fugitives, where agriculture was positively prohibited as the gateway to subjection. Much of the extension of Russian authority into these regions over the seventeenth and eighteenth centuries was driven by the determination of serf owners to close this vast escape route from servitude.

The most spectacular form of resistance was outright rebellion. Serfs rebelled far more frequently than colonial slaves—perhaps because they knew, or cherished mythical memories, that they were supposed to have at least minimal rights. When they voiced grievances they invariably called them abuses of a regime not challenged in itself. But lords went in fear of peasant unrest, and when rebellions were put down they were punished with a savagery no less severe than that meted out to rebellious slaves in the colonies. The nearest serf equivalent of the great Saint-Domingue slave uprising came in Russia in 1773–4, when Cossack resistance to ever-encroaching central power spilled over into more settled regions of serfdom and provoked violent anti-landlord outbreaks the length of the Volga. The rebel leader Pugachev openly exhorted the peasantry to slaughter their lords, and perhaps 3,000 perished before the uprising was put down, with exemplary brutality, by military force. The Empress Catherine professed to deplore serfdom, and in the first decade of her rule she had encouraged discussion of how it might be replaced. All that now stopped. The very mention of reform had only seemed to stir the peasantry up, and in the aftermath of the *Pugachevshcina* the rights of owners were comprehensively reinforced. News of the French Revolution only strengthened the Empress's determination to brook no changes. When in 1790 a radical nobleman, Alexander Radischev, criticized serfdom in his satirical *Journey from St Petersburg to Moscow* she declared him 'worse than Pugachev'. Briefly condemned to death, he spent the years until the Empress died in Siberian exile.

Radischev's strictures on serfdom were by now commonplaces further west. Interestingly, however, one of his avowed inspirations was Raynal, and the *Journey* makes frequent comparisons between serfdom and colonial slavery, even castigating the sugar consumed by serf-owners as the shameful product of oppression. But otherwise he made two main criticisms. One was that serfdom was inhuman, tyrannical, and contrary to the natural freedom and equality of mankind. The other was that it was inefficient. He had read Adam Smith, and endorsed with picturesque examples the Scotsman's contention that 'the experience of all ages and nations...demonstrates that the work done by slaves, though it appears to cost only their maintenance, is in the end the dearest of any. A person who can acquire no property can have no other interest but to eat as much and to labour as little as possible'.[26]

Both these criticisms were regularly invoked in public justifications by rulers seeking to mitigate serfdom in other parts of eastern Europe. But behind them lay a much more practical concern: the peasant as taxpayer. Ultimately the state was in competition with lords in tapping the resources of the peasantry. In serf economies where lords relied extensively on forced labour, these services limited the ability of subjects to generate taxable income. In the Habsburg lands initial attempts to restrict the number of days of *robot* that lords could demand were made in the late seventeenth century. The issue became more urgent in the mid-eighteenth after military defeats at the hands of the Prussians spurred plans for more effective unlocking of the monarchy's capacities. In 1767 the powers of Hungarian lords over their serfs were circumscribed in a new rural code called the

Urbarium. The occasion for issuing it, in the teeth of noble opposition, was a widespread uprising in 1765–6. It was no secret that similar plans were being discussed for other territories, and rumours of impending alleviation played their part in sparking an even more serious rebellion in Bohemia in 1775. The appalled Empress Maria Theresia wished to respond by abolishing serfdom entirely, but was dissuaded by her normally impulsive son Joseph II. After her death in 1780, now ruling alone, the Emperor did issue a stream of measures allowing serfs freedom of movement and the right to buy their plots 'as natural law and the public weal demand' because 'the right of property…as experience shows, will give a new boost to the diligence, hard work, and industry of the subject'.[27] Amid the confusion caused by these changes, yet another great revolt broke out in Transylvania late in 1784, in which as many as 4,000 landlords were killed before troops restored order. The Emperor was undeterred. It reinforced his conviction that reform was urgent. Within a year personal serfdom had been abolished throughout Hungary and Transylvania, and plans were being laid for a comprehensive conversion of serf tenures into rented plots, on terms quite deliberately framed to ruin landlords. The land-survey on which this policy was to be based took several years to complete, and by the time the new policy was promulgated in 1789 the Emperor, his health breaking down, had run into so much opposition on so many issues throughout his dominions that he was unable to enforce it. When he died the next year, it was abandoned by his brother and successor. Serfdom under the Habsburgs saw no further substantial reform for another half-century, although folk-memory would long celebrate Joseph as the peasants' friend.

As in Russia, the spectacle of popular power driving France into chaos and terror did much to scare the authorities into reactionary intransigence. The times were now too disturbed to make incautious social experiments. Frederick II of Prussia dismissed serfdom as a 'barbarous custom' and spent much of his reign making piecemeal efforts, by example on royal domains as much as by legislation, to limit the labour services owed by peasants to their lords. But they came to an end when he died in 1786, and the great Prussian lawcode issued in 1794 re-emphasized the subjection of serfs to their lords. Only in two important states was serf emancipation not arrested or set back by counter-revolutionary panic. In the Alpine Duchy of Savoy its ruler the King of Sardinia freed his own serfs as early as 1762 and authorized peasants and landlords to agree rates for redemption. If they failed to agree the crown would impose its own terms. After some vicissitudes the scheme made steady progress from 1778, and by 1790 around half the serfs in Savoy had been freed. This operation was closely watched from across the border in France, an inspiration alike to economic thinkers and administrators speculating on how to end *mainmorte*, and eastern peasants in its grip, regularly informed by seasonal migrants from the Alpine valleys. In 1789 disturbing news flowed the other way, and the royal response was to appease the peasantry by trying to accelerate rather than retard the process of emancipation. True acceleration came, however, in 1792, when republican French troops invaded and, in accordance with what were now French principles, abolished the remnants of serfdom and ended all outstanding redemption payments.

The first act of serf emancipation in Europe had occurred in Denmark in 1702, when a particularly burdensome form operative in certain islands (*vornedskab*) was abolished.

But with the introduction of universal compulsory militia service in 1733 (*stavnsband*), which made lords responsible for providing quotas of recruits, Danish peasants were tied to the soil as effectively as any in Europe. Yet by the 1770s dissatisfaction with what were seen as its adverse effects on agriculture led to the establishment of a series of commissions to consider alternatives. Their work was much retarded by political instabilities, but a Great Agrarian Commission established in 1786 produced proposals two years later to phase out the militia system over twelve years and give peasants freedom of movement. Under the Danish crown, accordingly, the years of the French Revolution were marked by the steady and unviolent dismantling of the agrarian Ancien Régime.

Denmark was a slaving power, too. It had several small sugar colonies in the Virgin Islands, and Danish slave traders transported almost 74,000 Africans across the Atlantic over the eighteenth century. And, just as the Danes had been the first to decree an abolition of serfdom, they were also the first to announce the prohibition of trade in slaves in 1792. This was a miscalculation. They thought they were merely keeping in step with an expected British prohibition which did not materialize. And because it was not to come into force until 1803, the effect of Danish prohibition was to give the trade a final vigorous lease of life as demand for slave imports boomed across the Caribbean in islands now taking advantage of the distressed French colonies. The disintegration of the French Ancien Régime in the Caribbean, in fact, reinvigorated its competitors. The British recaptured the European re-export market in colonial luxuries, and the slavers of Liverpool and Bristol carried more captives across the Atlantic than ever before. The Spaniards, for the first time, began to see the potential for large-scale slave cultivation in the biggest Caribbean island of them all, Cuba. The chaos in Saint-Domingue, though it scared them, reinforced rather than dented the faith of non-French planters and merchants in slavery. It also helped to postpone the success of abolitionists, though borne along by a massive groundswell of public opinion, in winning parliamentary backing for outlawing the British slave trade. And, to increasing numbers of the French, it underlined the folly of having abolished slavery at a moment of weakness in 1794. In terms of regaining at least the nominal allegiance of rebellious Saint-Domingue, emancipation had worked. British invaders were driven out, and the black leader who eventually emerged, Toussaint L'Ouverture, governed in the name of the Republic. But when the British made peace with the new consular regime of Napoleon Bonaparte in 1802, and returned Martinique as part of the bargain, the way seemed open for a restoration of the vanished glories of the French Atlantic economy. The British had kept slavery going during their occupation of Martinique, and a large military expedition was sent by Napoleon to Saint-Domingue to re-establish direct control with every intention of reintroducing slavery. Toussaint was captured, and the prospects for success looked good until news arrived that slavery was to be restored throughout French territories. Black cooperation with the French turned into determined resistance, and disease completed the débâcle for the invaders. Links with France were severed once more when war between Britain and Napoleon resumed in 1803. The next year the overthrow of the Ancien Régime in Saint-Domingue was completed with the establishment of the Republic of Haiti, a black state with no slaves. But the French took until 1825 to recognize the independence of their former colony, and slavery in those they retained was not abolished until 1848.

Slavery and serfdom, therefore, together underpinning so much of the economic Ancien Régime, survived the challenges of revolution. Only serfdom in France (already a dwindling relic) and slavery in Haiti disappeared for good. Elsewhere, both systems of servitude reached their zenith. And although both had begun by then to come under attack, the initial impact of the French Revolution was to arrest or retard chances of emancipation as terrified governments and propertied elites witnessed what mayhem freedom could unleash. But for all the comparisons often made, then and since, between the two systems of subjection, they cannot be pressed too far. Despite the spectacular prosperity built on the backs of colonial slaves, revolts among them were relatively rare and did not threaten social structures in Europe. Persistent serf unrest did. After all, although the number of black slaves across the oceans exceeded three millions by this time,[28] that number was dwarfed by tens of millions of European serfs. And even if most of the latter, being Russians, were chattels subject to conditions not far from animals and condemned to hereditary servitude, they had not been transported from another continent and a diversity of cultures in order to produce cash crops for luxurious consumption in a third. Many serfs retained some residual rights connected to the lands they occupied.[29] They were presumed to be economically self-sufficient and they were not marked out as servile by the colour of their skin—even if the appearance of most of them made their status clear enough.

What serfs and slaves did have in common was the obligation to work unpaid, subjection to the largely unchecked power of their masters, and little prospect for them or their children of ever being freed. In the nineteenth century, over the course of three generations, all this would change. Their descendants would become free men and women. Freedom brought its own problems: the claims of defenders of slavery and serfdom that emancipation would not necessarily improve the everyday lives of those released from bondage cannot be dismissed out of hand. There is not much evidence, however, of regret, among those set free, for the Ancien Régime which had held them and their ancestors in hopeless servitude.

Notes

1. Arthur Young, *Travels in France during the Years 1787, 1788 and 1789*, ed. Constantia Maxwell (Cambridge, 1929), 58 (26 Aug. 1787).
2. Ibid. 115, 21 Sept. 1788.
3. Ibid. 99, 16 Aug. 1788.
4. Quoted in John Lough, *France on the Eve of the Revolution: British Travellers' Observations, 1763–1788* (London, 1987), 94.
5. Sue Peabody, *'There are No Slaves in France': The Political Culture of Race and Slavery in the Ancien Regime* (New York, 1996).
6. Ibid. 55.

7. Pierre H. Boulle, *Race et esclavage dans la France d'Ancien Régime* (Paris, 2007), 196.
8. Erick Noël, *Être noir en France au xviiie siècle* (Paris, 2006), 81–93.
9. Robert Louis Stein, *The French Slave Trade in the Eighteenth Century: An Old Regime Business* (Madison, Wis., 1979), 211.
10. Except, briefly, St Lucia.
11. Stein, *French Slave Trade*, 39.
12. *De l'Esprit des Lois* (1748), bk. xv.
13. Bk. iii, ch. 2.
14. Though dated 1770 on the title-page.
15. Seymour Drescher, *Abolition: A History of Slavery and Antislavery* (Cambridge, 2009), 152–3.
16. Gabriel Debien, *La Société coloniale aux xviie et xviiie siècles: Les Colons de Saint-Domingue et la Révolution. Essai sur le Club Massiac (août 1789–août 1792)* (Paris, 1953).
17. John Markoff, *The Abolition of Feudalism: Peasants, Lords and Legislators in the French Revolution* (University Park, Pa., 1996), 460–2.
18. Thierry Bressan, *Serfs et mainmortables en France au xviiie siècle: La Fin d'un archaisme signal* (Paris, 2007), 196.
19. Pierre de Saint-Jacob, *Les Paysans de la Bourgogne du Nord au dernier siècle de l'Ancien Régime* (Paris, 1960), 422–5.
20. Markoff, *Abolition of Feudalism*, 43.
21. Patrick Kessel, *La Nuit du 4 août 1789* (Paris, 1969), 157–8.
22. Jerome Blum, *The End of the Old Order in Rural Europe* (Princeton, 1978), 227.
23. Derek Beales, *Joseph II*, ii. *Against the World, 1780–1790* (Cambridge, 2009), 244–55.
24. Markus Cerman in Peter H. Wilson (ed.), *A Companion to Eighteenth Century Europe* (Oxford, 2008), 55.
25. Quoted in Lindsay Hughes, *Russia in the Age of Peter the Great* (New Haven, 1998), 161.
26. *Wealth of Nations*, bk. iii, ch. 2.
27. Quoted in Beales, *Joseph II*, ii. 254.
28. Including the USA: Robin Blackburn, *The Making of New World Slavery: From the Baroque to the Modern 1492–1800* (London, 1997), 377.
29. M. L. Bush in M. L. Bush (ed.), *Social Orders and Social Classes in Europe since 1500: Studies in Social Stratification* (London, 1992), 136–57.

Bibliography

Blackburn, Robin, *The Making of New World Slavery: From the Baroque to the Modern, 1492–1800* (London, 1997).
—— *The Overthrow of Colonial Slavery 1776–1848* (London, 1998).
Blum, Jerome, *The End of the Old Order in Rural Europe* (Princeton, 1978).
Boulle, Pierre H., *Race et esclavage dans la France d'Ancien Régime* (Paris, 2007).
Bressan, Thierry, *Serfs et mainmortables en France au xviiie siècle: La Fin d'un archaisme signal* (Paris, 2007).
Bush, M. L. (ed.), *Serfdom and Slavery: Studies in Legal Bondage* (London, 1996).
Drescher, Seymour, *Abolition: A History of Slavery and Anitislavery* (Cambridge, 2009).
Dubois, Laurent, *A Colony of Citizens: Revolution and Slave Emancipation in the French Caribbean, 1787–1804* (Chapel Hill, NC, 2004).

Geggus, David, 'The French Slave Trade: An Overview', *William and Mary Quarterly*, 58 (2001), 119–38.
Godechot, Jacques (ed.), *L'Abolition de la féodalité dans le monde occidental* (2 vols. Paris, 1971).
Klein, Herbert S., *The Atlantic Slave Trade* (2nd edn. Cambridge, 2010).
Lentz, Thierry, and Branda, Pierre (eds.), *Napoléon, l'esclavage, et les colonies* (Paris, 2007).
Mackrell, J. Q. C., *The Attack on 'Feudalism' in Eighteenth Century France* (London, 1973).
Markoff, John, *The Abolition of Feudalism: Peasants, Lords, and Legislators in the French Revolution* (University Park, Pa., 1996).
Noël, Erick, *Être noir en France au xviiie siècle* (Paris, 2006).
Peabody, Sue, *'There are no slaves in France': The Political Culture of Race and Slavery in the Ancien Régime* (New York, 1996).
Popkin, Jeremy, *You are All Free: The Haitian Revolution and the Abolition of Slavery* (Cambridge, 2010).
Stein, Robert Louis, *The French Slave Trade in the Eighteenth Century: An Old Regime Business* (Madison, Wis., 1979).

PART IV
RELIGION

CHAPTER 17

THE ESTABLISHED CHURCH

NIGEL ASTON

The universal experience and practice of mankind [prove] that civil government cannot subsist without regard to the will of God, or, in other words, without the sanctions of religion.
(Edmund Gibson, *The Dispute Adjusted about the Proper Time of Applying for a Repeal of the Corporation and Test Acts*, 1733)

CHURCH AND STATE

ANCIEN Régime Europe had an ineradicably Christian character that was publicly embodied and expressed in its established churches. It was and remained a divided continent confessionally after the Peace of Westphalia (1648) with the churches of the Reformation established (sometimes precariously) in Scandinavia, Britain, Switzerland, much of Germany, and parts of eastern Europe; Roman Catholicism predominated elsewhere except within Russia and inside the Ottoman Empire where various forms of Orthodoxy were the primary form of Christian expression. Irrespective of confessional variations, every European state *c*.1700 exhibited and upheld an established church, at once a fundamental component and final sanction of its institutional life. The concept of establishment found different legal expression from state to state, from a kingdom the size of France to the tiny principalities of Protestant Germany and the Swiss cantons, and it was not necessarily the confession of the majority population, as the instances of early modern Ireland and Bohemia indicate. At its heart was the sense of a church whose rights and privileges were protected against encroachment and infringement, which enjoyed an ecclesiological monopoly (or quasi-monopoly) within a polity, and which expected and demanded the loyalties and support of subjects (and, in some cases, citizens) much as a monarch might. In return, the church offered mediatory access to the means of grace in word and sacrament that would uniquely bring men and women safely through the perils of this world into the harbour of divine salvation. Since the conversion of Constantine in the fourth century, church leaders had recognized that they needed the cooperation of the state—and sometimes the coercive powers available to it—to bend the fallen hearts and minds of humankind to see what was good for their eternal well-being. And, despite the state's origins as an agency of necessity in a fallen world, the church (Christ's bridegroom and with a continuous history longer than any monarchy) sanctified the state as a way both of protecting itself, and ensuring obedience to the state at risk of personal damnation to those who would resist. Classically articulated, the relationship between church and state was thus one in which both offered each other mutual support and protection and were the stronger for it, acting as, in the words of W. R. Ward, 'public statements of the relation of the community to God'.[1] It was also a providential combination, divinely ordained, and celebrated in annual, official (liturgically prescribed) observances such as, in later Stuart England, mourning the execution of Charles I (30 January), celebrating the Restoration of the monarchy (29 May), and giving thanks for the state's deliverance from the Gunpowder Plot (5 November). Kingship was right at the heart of establishment with the prince's status defined as *jus reformandi*, meaning that it was he who decided which creed his members should confess. In most Protestant countries, kings were supreme heads or governors of national churches; in Catholic ones, coronation rites set them apart from other mortals symbolized in anointing ceremonies and admission to holy communion in both kinds. In both the doctrine of royal supremacy in church as in state was central to political thought and practice. Subjects must fear God and honour the King as St Paul had instructed, and when they broke the law and were duly punished, the clergy were usually at hand to drive home the awful majesty of the occasion.

Confessional Churches and Limited Toleration

Of course, at any point in history this alliance had been erratic, variable, and lop-sided and it was particularly so from the mid-seventeenth-century until the demise of the Ancien Régime. Pressures came from two directions: from the state itself and from a changing climate of opinion—call it Enlightened opinion—that considered the institutional power of established churches to be excessive and viewed any religious monopoly as undesirable and a threat to human freedom of action. Sovereigns had always been inclined to confront and infringe the rights of churches when policy dictated it and, during the 'long' eighteenth century, it frequently did. Limited legal toleration had been stipulated within the Empire under the Peace of Westphalia where the standard arrangement (an amended and updated version of the 1555 Augsburg principle of *cuius religio, eius politico*) was that each territory would have one of three recognized confessions authorized as the dominant church, i.e. there were three privileged churches with equal status. Thus, after 1648, non-Catholics at Strasbourg shared the official status of members of the cathedral chapter and Catholics and non-Catholics rotated in the see of Osnabrück. However, crucially, each territory would also permit limited rights for religious minorities existing in the year 1624. In the later seventeenth century, embattled Protestant rulers defending Europe against French—and therefore Catholic—aggression, began to take up the idea; famously, the electors of Brandenburg were Calvinist but they accepted Lutheran domination in Prussia and protected Lutherans against the Calvinist majority in Cleves. It made increasing political sense in the next century. Monarchs sponsored it when it suited them, from William III in England in 1689 to Joseph II within the Habsburg Empire almost a century later. Their actions commonly caused consternation at senior levels of church hierarchies and yet these were powerless to stop a determined monarch and his ministers from proceeding.

The concept of establishment was not being purposefully dissolved but it was being modified to authorize minorities to worship freely while still withholding full participatory rights in the state. The numbers benefiting from such a concession may have been small (about 2,500 dissenting places of worship had been licensed in England *c.*1710) and yet its symbolic significance was immense, breaching as it did the principle that participation in the life of the state was co-terminal with and dependent upon membership of the church. From 1689 the church courts in England became powerless to compel attendance at services and their powers declined speedily (though less so than was once claimed). It could be, as in England, that civic rights for dissenters (only Trinitarian Protestants in this case) seeking public office of some kind required them to take holy communion in an Anglican church at least once a year. This 'Occasional Conformity' was lambasted as arrant hypocrisy and an abuse of the sacraments by high church Tories but Whigs saw it as a way of demonstrating their commitment to religious liberty. Nevertheless, despite the huge pressure from Enlightenment protagonists after *c.*1750, most monarchs had no interest in introducing religious toleration on any other basis than that of expediency and dynastic advantage. It remained normative to restrict the holding of public office and the practice of leading professions to those conforming to the established religion of a realm.

Thus in pre-revolutionary France (as in England) legitimacy as a subject was conferred through the reception of the Catholic sacraments. Within state boundaries, it was a golden rule—reinforced by the traumatic experience of the Thirty Years War—that religious dissidence must be avoided at all costs and that toleration was a sign of state weakness rather than strength and, where it existed at all, to be kept within strict bounds. Preferable by far for monarchs to uphold the established church in their realm (on their own terms of course) and have it inculcate obedience to the powers providentially ordained of God. Thus it was not until after the death of the emperor Charles VI in 1740 that the Habsburgs ceased to make Tridentine Catholicism the touchstone of political loyalty in their extensive realms, the so-called *Pietas Austriaca*, allying the church, the monarchy, and the political establishment. This duty of obedience was transmitted not just by preaching but by the physical presence of the churches in the lives of every European.

Physical Presence

One crucial, visual expression of religious establishment was its built heritage. No other institution in early modern Europe, certainly no monarchy, could compete with the range, scale, and ubiquitous presence of the church from the palace to the parish, all testifying to its continuing contemporary importance. Much of this medieval inheritance had been damaged by Protestant iconoclasts and zealots in the century after the Reformation but, after c.1630, the Reformed Churches in settled polities such as the United Provinces, as the paintings of Pieter Jansz Saenredam (1597–1665) disclose, had imposed their own ordering on their (originally Catholic) medieval built heritage in ways that expressed a confident confessional identity.[2] Lutheran Protestants, by comparison, usually with the endorsement of princes, had been doctrinally more comfortable making minimal modifications to fittings and fixtures of their pre-Reformation churches and, by the late seventeenth century, most were in a good state of repair. That was in part a remedying of damage inflicted during the Thirty Years War, just as the Church of England had to confront the depredations inflicted on church buildings in the Civil Wars of the 1640s and 1650s. More losses followed the Great Fire of London in 1665 that necessitated a rebuilding programme for fifty-two churches in the City of London from Sir Christopher Wren's Office of Works that displayed the latest trends in Anglican design and provided for worship that laid equal stress on word and sacrament. Wren's St Paul's cathedral (completed 1709) gave London the finest purpose-built worship space of any Protestant polity, one that was paid for by the Stuart state through a Coal Tax with ring-fenced funds. Catholic monarchs were also committed to ambitious building schemes that reflected dynastic glory as well as religious dedication in churches such as the Karlskirche for the Emperor Charles VI in Vienna, the basilica of Superga overlooking Turin for Victor Amadeus II of Savoy (basking in his new title of king of Sardinia), and the huge complex of monastery and palace constructed at Mafra in Portugal between 1717 and 1730 for John V by a labour force of 50,000.

These were all admittedly trophy designs and yet this commitment to new building and maintenance of existing fabrics found expression across all dominions, not least at parish level, for it was here that most men and women encountered the established church. Here they were baptized, catechized, married, and buried, and, above all, worshipped; here they met their priest, their neighbours, and their God. And they did so in buildings that, taking Europe as a whole, when not brand new were probably in a better state of repair than at any previous point in history. This was often down to the painstaking discharge of his duties by their landlord, in whose gift the cure of souls might lie. That high-born landlords paid for improvements and upkeep reflected well on themselves and was a debt to their ancestors whose tombs were often lavishly displayed inside churches. It was also, in a neglected sense, a visible sign of their commitment to the well-being of an established church that in return conferred the blessing of scripture and tradition on their position at the apex of society. Frequently, a manor could belong not to an individual but to a corporate institution, a cathedral, a monastery, or a college.

Established Churches and Land Ownership

Despite the appropriation of vast swaths of ecclesiastical (especially monastic properties) land by Protestant polities during the Reformation, all the established churches remained major landowners in Ancien Régime Europe. It was the basis of their independent corporate power and made possible the lavish lifestyles enjoyed by many of those at the upper end of the hierarchies. In Castile, the church owned no less than one-seventh of the region's agricultural and pastoral lands and in Bavaria it was over half and here, as well as elsewhere, parishioners were obliged to pay tithe to their parish priest (or the principal landowner who would offer a proportion of that income to the incumbent). As the beneficiaries of increasing agricultural prices, parish clergy of all denominations tended to become more comfortably off. Compulsory tithe payment generated considerable resentment and not just in times of dearth. In Ireland (where the established church represented no more than 15 per cent of the population) agrarian discontent such as the 'Whiteboy' disturbances of the 1760s often took the form of cattle maiming, rick burning, and even murdering tithe collectors.

High levels of propertied possession generated considerable annual individual and corporate revenues. In late seventeenth-century France the annual income of the Gallican Church from landed wealth based on about one-sixth of the cultivable area of the country was estimated at 270 million *livres,* considerably in advance of anything available to Louis XIV from the crown's landed estates, financial vindication of its juridical standing as the First Estate of the realm.

Established churches had built up their wealth steadily over the centuries thanks in no small measure to the bequests of the faithful. The right of mortmain (land held in perpetuity) was increasingly seen by lay critics as an obstacle to agricultural progress, yet prelates clung to it even as princes such as Joseph II of Austria legislated against it. While it was in theory vulnerable to continued secular incursions, secular rulers largely recognized that a prosperous and prestigious national church reflected well on monarchy and was its essential institutional complement. Rather than mounting any general offensive, they selectively targeted ecclesiastical landowners, notoriously the Jesuits in the mid-eighteenth century. Monarchies were sensitive to charges that they might be engorging themselves at the expense of religion and in the reallocation of Jesuit lands, for instance, many went to other religious orders (whose acquiescence in dispossession had its origins in sensing that they stood to be big beneficiaries). As is now recognized, monasticism in the late eighteenth century successfully reinvented itself with the assistance of monarchy. The Commission des Réguliers in France was set up in 1766–8 to investigate the health of the religious orders in the state and its recommendations (including a reduction in the number of religious houses) helped focus energies and consolidate resources in a largely cooperative rather than confrontational manner. When there were obstacles to implementing recommendations, the secular clergy leading the Commission had no hesitation in using state resources to impose their preference. In Spain in 1776 a national vicar for the Franciscans was forced on the order by the crown, which subsequently extended this provision to the Trinitarians, Carthusians, and Augustinians in the 1780s.

Monarchy and Religious Establishment

Whatever the scale of religious establishment in early modern Europe, it had an intrinsic monarchical dimension irrespective of confessional allegiance, as one might expect in a society where the idea of the state as an entity distinct from dynastic patrimony was only gradually emerging. Thus saints days associated with the royal family were always splendid occasions for official rites. The future Louis XVI was born on 23 August 1754, and the feast of St Louis of France (two days later), was his name-day, and eagerly kept after he became king in 1774. In Bohemia and other parts of the Empire, the dynasty sponsored the cult of St Wenceslas. Here, as elsewhere, there was a strong connection between national saints and the rites of the chivalric orders for whose ribbons noblemen universally competed. Palaces and courts throughout this period were the centres of rituals and display that had religion at the heart of them and the daily attendance of the monarch and his family at the court chapel was a focus for displaying the centrality of religious observance to the life of the realm. At Versailles, it was no coincidence that the chapel (the last major part of Louis XIV's palace to be completed, consecrated in 1710) dominated the palace's roof-line. Royal households contained a full complement of ecclesiastics—there were about 200 attendant on Louis XV—whose physical proximity to the King nicely represented the degree of influence they were likely to enjoy. Royal almoners, confessors, and chaplains were prized appointments in an established church's *cursus honorum* and they frequently competed with ministers and other laity about the court in advising monarchs on patronage questions. For across the continent, appointments to bishoprics and cathedral chapters belonged in practice almost exclusively to crowned heads. Polities that were Roman Catholic acknowledged the primacy of the papacy in spiritual matters but were otherwise watchful of pontifical intrusion into the affairs of their 'national' church and expected the papacy to confirm senior nominations with minimal fuss. Jurisdiction was a non-negotiable matter and bishops, jurists, and academics were quick to react to any perceived breaches. 'Independence' of the Holy See was the hallmark of a mature Catholic polity classically embodied in the Gallican liberties of the French church that were ringingly reaffirmed in the articles promulgated by the General Assembly of 1682. And, as if there could be any doubt about royal supremacy, matins in France ended with the saying of the responsary 'Domine salvum fac regem', a prayer (Psalm 19: 10) for the welfare of the King, a reminder to the ordinary parishioner (who was likely to have only seen the face of his monarch on the side of a coin), that rulership was providentially ordained and to be loyally upheld by subjects. The same presumption was made for Protestant sovereigns whose extensive writ within the church had been confirmed by the Reformation. The persons of kings (and queens regnant) were sacred as people marked out for government by heredity and law and they had that position confirmed in the sanctifying rite of coronation. Once accorded, that status did not easily allow a king to undermine a church or threaten its established status for he would have taken an oath to protect it. The subsequent conversion of a sovereign or the descent of a throne to a family line with a different allegiance was best avoided at all costs. In England, the Roman Catholic proselyte James II received a magnificent Anglican coronation in 1685 and yet his deliberate use of the prerogative to undermine the privileges of the church (for which his father had died a martyr in 1649) fatally weakened the loyalty of the church hierarchy and made possible his 'abdication' and the Glorious Revolution of 1688; in Germany, princely conversions could threaten the stability of the 1648 settlement, and Protestant church establishments had to hang on (which they were very capable of doing), as when the duchy of Württemberg passed to a Catholic, Karl Alexander, in 1733. His sudden death four years later put an abrupt end to using ducal power to the advantage of his new communion. As many as fifty-one German princes became Catholic proselytes during the seventeenth and eighteenth centuries, correctly identifying the Roman Church as an uncompromising supporter of royal authority.

CLERGY IN THE SERVICE OF THE STATE

James I of England may have been of the opinion 'No bishop, no king', yet it was possible for Protestant denominations that rejected the principle of episcopacy to serve the state loyally, as many of the King's English and Scottish subjects—who looked to Calvinist Geneva as their lodestar—would have asserted. Yet they had to argue their way around Calvin's theory of resistance to ungodly rulers to do so and the experience of the British Civil Wars (1639–51) confirmed Anglican apologists in their view that the theocratic leanings of sectarians were irrepressible and that the restored monarchy (1660) had to exclude all clergy who rejected episcopal government as the bedrock of establishment. The principle was for thirty years enforced in Scotland too. Then it had to be hastily dismantled by William III after the Revolution of 1689 when he found that the majority of Episcopalians would not recant their oaths to James II. The eighteenth-century established Church of Scotland was solidly Presbyterian yet unflinchingly loyal to the Hanoverian crown and watched over by the Lord High Commissioner, the King's personal representative to its General Assembly. French Huguenots of the same era worked hard if covertly (the Reformed religion had been outlawed in the country after the revocation of the Edict of Nantes, 1685) to impress the same point on the Bourbon crown. They were up against the insistence of the court *dévots* and most bishops that they were intrinsically republican in their politics and potential fifth columnists at times of national emergency when invasion threatened (as during the first half of the Seven Years War, 1756–63).

The bishops of the French church not only taught their clergy and people to respect the rights and privileges of kings, they often took office within the state themselves. This was a choice that made much practical sense; bishops usually amassed abundant administrative experience in the government of a diocese (or a province if they were archbishops) and were often members of great noble families that moved naturally in and out of royal circles from one generation to the next. For Richelieu and Mazarin in the seventeenth century, and for Fleury and Brienne in the eighteenth, to serve as first minister was a legitimate ambition for them that (in the first three cases at least) conferred considerable benefit on the realm. Other prelates served as heads of the provincial Estates in the *pays d'états* such as Burgundy, Brittany, and Languedoc and did their best to ensure that royal wishes were respected and taxation granted. They were thus well positioned to act as intermediaries between the centre and the periphery, central government and the localities. They could have a decisive impact on dynastic selection, as in Spain during the late 1690s when Cardinal Fernández de Portocarrero of Toledo (1635–1709) pressurized Charles II to make a will in favour of the crown passing to the French Bourbons. The reward for meritorious service to the crown could commonly be promotion to a more lucrative diocese. In England, bishops also filled high executive office until well into the eighteenth century. Charles I in the 1630s had the archbishop of Canterbury, William Laud, as his leading adviser on policy in the Privy Council, while William Juxon, bishop of London, served as Lord Treasurer. This precedent was too embarrassing for the restored monarchy to use for a long time after 1660 until Robert Harley appointed the bishop of Bristol, John Robinson (a former envoy to Sweden), as Lord Privy Seal in 1711. Thereafter, though archbishops of Canterbury often attended Privy Council meetings, their direct influence on ministerial policy-making tailed off, though in Spain, as many as nine of the twelve presidents of the Council of Castile in 1700–51 were clerics. The parish clergy locally imitated what prelates did for the state at this exalted level. In England, more and more clergy were appointed justices of the peace in the eighteenth century, enforcing the criminal laws against malefactors who might be their parishioners (thus setting up a potential clash between their pastoral and judicial duties); in France parish priests were charged with keeping a register of births, marriages, and deaths so that the lives of all the King's subjects were charted from beginning to end. Nowhere did clergy perform harder in the service of the state than in Lutheran polities such as the newly formed kingdom of Prussia (1701) where they acted as army chaplains, taught at the Cadet School in Berlin, and ran the military orphanage at Potsdam.

As monarchies increased in power so they might move to limit episcopal powers. In every diocese in Denmark and Norway, kings after 1662 appointed an administrative officer above the bishop who took over duties that had previously belonged exclusively to the Lutheran Church. The performative use of the clergy in early modern monarchies may point up the deficiencies in bureaucratic structures but it also dramatically underlines the point that no state could function smoothly without the participation of this key cadre: state life was simply impossible without them. Witness their continuing involvement in Roman Catholic countries in poor relief and hospital provision, with the latter so often staffed by members of female religious orders. The monasteries, too, remained centres of practical help for the hungry and destitute at times of harvest failure.

The Churches and Educational Provision

Until well into the eighteenth century, the churches upheld by a monarchy were the main educational provider in every European state, usually to the legal exclusion of any competing sect. It was in this setting that the catechism was imparted (according to the dominant confession) and subjects instructed in their duties towards God and their ruler. According to John Locke's influential *Some Thoughts concerning Education* (1693) (which appeared in at least twenty-one English editions and in many other European languages), children's minds were a blank sheet on which ideas and knowledge could be imparted, and obedience to higher authority was paramount. Clerical domination of elementary school teaching was a consequence of their own higher level of education, though a non-beneficed priest, member(s) of a religious order, or even a layman, might often discharge responsibilities in the classroom. They would be trusted to teach religion, reading, and writing, to prepare their charges to accept whatever position in life God had placed them in, and to accept His will meekly. Early modern monarchies had no cadre of officials able to undertake these basic duties at parish level and it says much for the mutual trust that church and state had for each other that this sort of staffing continued throughout the period. Those children who were in a position to continue to a secondary school where grammar and mathematics were taught were being prepared by their teachers to be useful subjects of their sovereign in positions of minor authority as befitted the superior education (commonly in Latin) they were receiving. Beyond that, a small minority progressed to higher education where classical culture (presented through a Christian prism) was fundamental to the curriculum in most universities until well into the eighteenth century.

The links between universities and church establishments were basic and these institutions were both heavily staffed by the clergy and (particularly in Protestant regimes) trained young men to enter the ecclesiastical profession. The two English universities were primarily staffed by men in holy orders who were teaching undergraduates of whom a high proportion would end up taking holy orders, while in France their equivalents would commonly register at an elite and fashionable seminary such as St-Suplice in Paris (the Trent decrees had required a seminary in each diocese). In some polities, notably the United Provinces and Scotland, the universities were also strongly involved in forming students to enter the lay professions of medicine and law, somewhat diluting the clericalist culture that predominated elsewhere.

The majority of universities had medieval origins and like most corporate bodies were firmly wedded to their privileges. These could on occasion be deployed in a manner that might be deemed inimical to state interests. Thus the Sorbonne in Paris (its powerful theological faculty) proved a thorn in the side of Louis XV's ministers until the 1750s for its questioning of and often overtly hostile attitude to the bull *Unigenitus* (1713), ironically in part because the bull could be read as implying that the Pope had a superior power over monarchs. When state security was judged at stake, governments were capable of threatening to encroach on university statutes, as in the late 1710s and late 1740s when successive Whig administrations stood ready to reduce the corporate privileges of Oxford University because of its attachment to Jacobitism in the wake of the '15 and the '45 rebellions.

Charles III of Spain (1759–88) was similarly concerned to increase the power of central government over the numerous universities and colleges in both Old and New Spain, with the crown thus leading the way in curriculum reform and new forms of academic institutional life. The expulsion of the Jesuits did not in itself solve the problem of modernizing higher educational provision and governance (though it released a lot of empty buildings for state use) and yet, in responding to royal initiatives such as the decree of February 1771 aimed at restoring the colleges to their original purpose, the King called in a prelate, Felipe Bertrán, bishop of Salamanca, to be his chief college inspector. In Tuscany—a small state of about one million people—Catholic reform was not a new current but Duke Peter Leopold viewed himself as an 'external bishop' interfering in clerical education and prescribing reading lists. Even the papacy under Pius VI was ready to support such regalian educational initiatives, as the 1777 *Motu proprio* brief suggested.

By that date most Catholic regimes were involved in imposing reforms on seminaries and establishing decisive episcopal control. Bishops were expected to act on royal initiatives, whatever their personal views. They were not all keen when Joseph II controversially abolished all the small seminaries in the Austrian Empire and concentrated ordinands in larger institutions, the general seminaries. One way of overcoming the legal obstacle posed by privilege was to establish new institutions whose primary function would be to produce graduates who would normally move on in to bureaucratic life (or sometimes the state church). Before the Thirty Years War, rulers founded their own universities to promote their chosen faith and to train administrators and clergy for their territory. This was a policy that particularly endeared itself to several German Protestant princes who founded universities at Halle (1694), Göttingen (1734–7), and Erlangen (1743). These were prestige projects for the monarchies that endowed them rather than partnership projects of church and state together, and they became powerhouses of Enlightenment thought through the displacement of the scholastic curriculum and the employment of internationally celebrated scholars such as Wolff and Thomasius who were heavily influenced by the practical aspects of Pietist teachings. Their success reflected the inroads being made after *c.*1750 into the domination of academic life by the ordained ministry and the acquiescence (and frequently the encouragement) of the state in this trend. It coincided with a gradual widening of voluntary educational provision.

In England this often took the form of Sunday Schools that worried some Anglican apologists after the outbreak of the French Revolution because the children of Methodists and dissenters often learnt alongside boys and girls whose parents attended their parish church exclusively and it was thought that this mingling might allow subversive Jacobin principles to spread insidiously. 'Schools of Jacobinical religion and Jacobinical politics abound in this country in the shape of charity Schools and Sunday Schools', asserted the bishop of Rochester. The only answer was (the time-honoured device of) clerical control and inspection.[3]

An Unequal Alliance?

The alliance of church and state was foundational to the ideology and functioning of early modern Europe and yet it was never an alliance of equals and became less so over this period. This was an era in which the claims of canon law were constantly being whittled down. The churches could be pinned down by lawyers working sometimes for the state (as in Venice) or for magistrates (as with the French parlements) determined to insist on the primacy of civil law over any canonical prescriptions. Lutherans accepted that princely protection compromised institutional independence and yet had been open about this point since the Reformation while their religious rivals struggled with it. Thus in Sweden, church and state were almost co-terminous: it was not until 1951 that a Swede was allowed to withdraw from membership of the Church of Sweden without becoming a member of another denomination. All established churches looked to the agencies of the state for patronage and protection of their privileges and property. This was a fair presumption given that the state was customarily seen as the civic expression of the community's religious commitment. Usually, those supportive duties were discharged honourably. As Lord Chief Justice Raymond in the trial of the deist Thomas Woolston for blasphemous libel in 1729 remarked: 'Christianity is a parcel of the common law of England ... now, whatever strikes at the very root of Christianity, tends manifestly to the dissolution of civil government.'[4]

Sometimes, however, they were abused and when that happened the sanctions available to the clergy were relatively few (the ultimate penalty of excommunication was used sparingly by the Roman Catholic Church, though as late as 1663 the theologians of the Sorbonne upheld the right of the Pope to discipline the King), partly because there were always priests ready to align themselves with the government and hope for career benefits that way. Confrontation was not to be undertaken lightly as the state could be predatory in seizing ecclesiastical assets, as the Reformation experience had shown, and as would be seen again in France in 1789-90 in the aftermath of the Revolution and in the Holy Roman Empire in the early 1800s when huge swaths of monastic lands were secularized. Indeed, the church was expected to be self-sacrificial when the royal state was in crisis. It was a privilege of Catholic monarchs to confiscate church plate in wartime, always allowing one paten and chalice in each parish church so that mass could be celebrated, which explains why there is hardly any French church plate left which dates from before the War of the Spanish Succession. Similarly, the Church of England permitted Charles I to melt down its precious communion sets for emergency coinage during the first Civil War (1642–6).

The churches were thus vulnerable to their protector turning on them and exploiting the inequality built into the relationship. Yet, outside some Protestant city-states, it would be an exaggeration to deem the working arrangement blatantly 'Erastian' (named after the sixteenth-century Swiss physician, Thomas Erastus), that is, one in which a state led by a godly ruler governed and disciplined the church to the point of denying it any independent sphere. In the period c.1550–1750, as they came to write their own histories, the Protestant churches across Europe developed an institutional self-confidence and a sense of what was 'theirs' vis-à-vis the prince that they could stand firm against perceived encroachment on their corporate entitlement. They were willing to bend but where the state appeared to be involving itself in spiritual affairs then sparks would fly. Of course, Protestants could disagree among themselves on these matters and much would depend on how far they subscribed to the doctrine of a church visible and militant in this world, divinely ordained as the bride of Christ, the church of the Apostles and the Fathers predating the state in its origins, and seamlessly joined to the church triumphant in heaven. These were the cherished beliefs of the high church party in the Church of England during the reign of Queen Anne who dominated the lower house of Convocation, the clerical assembly recalled in 1701. One of the reasons behind the clamour for its reconvening had been the sense that the new Williamite state of the 1690s was all too ready to betray the sacerdotal identity of the established church, to treat it as a *de facto* department of state and to stuff it with Whig latitudinarians. After enjoying an Indian summer of favour under Queen Anne these 'high fliers' took up the same themes again after 1714 when the low churchmen basked in Hanoverian favour and one of their number, Benjamin Hoadly, newly promoted bishop of Bangor, preached a sermon before George I insisting that Christ's assertion that 'my kingdom is not of this world' made any claim for the visibility of the church on earth a nonsense. The fury of the high churchmen (and that of many moderate Whigs) was such that in 1717 the government suspended the Convocation of Canterbury's authority to conduct business. If, for the remainder of the century, that situation was just about acceptable to the Anglican clergy, it was only because the Whig custodians of the state showed themselves trustworthy guardians of the church to the point of defending the Test Act on the Walpolian principle of letting sleeping dogs lie. No wonder that William Warburton, in his *Alliance between Church and State* (1736), could present it as a matter of 'civic utility' while, significantly, as a Whig beneficiary, denying that church and state were interchangeable.

The clergy of the Church of England had abandoned their right to tax themselves in 1664 shortly after the monarchy was restored; the clergy of the Church of France preserved theirs until the Revolution as a vital means of leverage in their often fraught relations with the Bourbon state. And they had retained a national forum in the shape of General Assembly of the Clergy of France, though unlike Convocation this body was almost exclusively representative in practice of the bishops and higher clergy. The

Assembly contributed to the fiscal needs of the monarchy by offering a so-called 'free gift' (*don gratuit*) at its regular five-yearly meetings (extraordinary assemblies were occasionally summoned between times), based on its own allocation of a tax burden on the clergy. The cooperation of the General Assembly could never be taken for granted and, even when it was not in session, there were two clerical agents-general in office ever alert to possible infringements of the First Estate's privileges. In 1749, Machault d'Arnouville, the Controller-General, had attempted to subject the First Estate to comparable direct taxation burdens to those on the King's lay subjects and encountered insuperable resistance in the General Assembly. This august body afforded opportunities for the clergy to bring subjects of concern insistently to government notice. More commonly, the remonstrances they issued concerned official indulgence of disputative minorities such as Jansenists and Huguenots, although, from the 1750s, the irreligious publications of the *philosophes* figured prominently, with the clergy insisting on the indispensable role of religion in the defence of order and the preservation of authority.

REGALIANISM AND THE PAPACY

The formidable control exerted by monarchs over their 'national' churches within the Roman Catholic world came at the cost of papal authority. Throughout this period the papacy was institutionally on the defensive, able to capitalize on the status of Rome as the most sacred Christian city in Europe and the centre of Roman civilization previously, and yet otherwise ill-equipped to counteract the chipping away of pontifical power. It was in tune with the times that the annual bull *In Coena domini* tacitly asserting the Roman Church's right to its autonomy and immunities was quietly put aside in 1769. There was no more poignant symbol of this slippage than the long journey of Pius VI to Vienna in 1782 to try and persuade Joseph II to modify his aggressive reformist policies towards the church in the Habsburg lands. Pius came away with nothing to show for his troubles, a kind of Road to Canossa in reverse. Joseph was determined not to compromise on any of the regalian rights he deemed inherent in his office. Over a century previously Louis XIV had found it slightly harder to make headway with his claims. In the 1670s (partly to finance the costs of the war with the Dutch starting in 1672) he sought to extend the temporal regalian rights of the crown to draw the revenues of vacant bishoprics to cover the whole of France. Most of the bishops fell into line, with the exception of those occupying the small sees of Alet and Pamiers. They successfully appealed to Innocent XI and he upheld them. The result of his determination to resist Louis XIV was thirty-five vacant sees in France by the late 1680s as a result of his refusal to institute bishops on Louis's terms and French violation of papal property in both Rome and Avignon. A settlement only became possible after Innocent's death in 1689 and, significantly, no eighteenth-century Pope ever played out such a game of aggressive brinkmanship with either Louis XV or Louis XVI. In Spain the securing of the throne by the Bourbon dynasty in 1700 (internationally recognized in 1713–14) led to successive monarchs wanting to enjoy the equivalent regalian powers over the church as those enjoyed by their French cousins. This objective was achieved by diplomacy rather than excessive intimidation and, on the whole, crown and papacy worked harmoniously together. Thus in 1724, encouraged by Philip V, Innocent XIII issued a papal bull *Apostolici Ministerii* to reassert the principles of Tridentine discipline among secular and regular clergy. Two concordats with the papacy were subsequently signed—in 1737 and 1753—signalling the formidable extent of the control of the established church alloted to Phillip V (1700–46), Ferdinand VI (1746–59), and Charles III (1759–88), especially in Granada and the American empire. Charles required royal authorization for the introduction of papal documents into Spain and went on to reduce further the power of the Inquisition. Newly equipped with almost universal patronage over the most important benefices, the King was a thoroughgoing religious reformer and used his new powers constructively through a caucus of talented prelates, reforming diocesan structures and establishing ten new seminaries. It was in line with this policy that in 1767 the Council of Castile sent a circular to the bishops ordering them to curb abuses and superstition in their dioceses. For his pains he was hailed by many clerics as a king in the manner of David and Solomon.

Mid-eighteenth-century Spain was the archetypal regalian monarchy and there was no more obvious symbol of that tendency than the expulsion of the Jesuits from the monarchy in 1767. This Society from its inception in the 1530s had been the warmest ally of the papacy and accumulated large amounts of property that were looked on covetously both by kings and other religious orders. The time was ripe in the 1750s for a full-scale assault on this powerful institution for, by that date, the Catholic Reformation inaugurated by the Council of Trent was finally over, and the *raison d'être* of the Jesuits had in a sense passed. Expulsion and abolition was in the interest of Catholic monarchies across Europe as a calculated act of state. The first moves occurred in Portugal where Joseph I (1750–77) resented the extent of their wealth and trade in South America. In 1757 his minister the Marquês de Pombal used talk of Jesuit-inspired revolt against the house of Braganza to destroy the Society and assert the power of the crown. Pombal moved fast during the vacancy following Benedict XIV's death in 1758 to strip the Jesuits of all their Portuguese possessions. Anxious not to jeopardize their own chances of preferment, the leaders of the Portuguese church did little to stop him and Pombal's insistence that the Jesuits had prior knowledge of an assassination plot against Joseph I in September 1758 completed his successful campaign. Other states followed the Portuguese example. In France the Jesuits had become the *bêtes noires* of Jansenists, *philosophes*, and *parlementaires* alike and Louis XV was content to accept the advice of his former mistress, Mme de Pompadour, and his principal minister, the Duke de Choiseul, leading to a decree dissolving the Society in France in 1764. Interestingly, the French Jesuits had refused an offer whereby they would reconstitute themselves as a purely French Society operating under their own vicar-general within the Gallican church. The Jesuits were expelled throughout Spain and its Empire in 1767–8, and in Naples and Parma in 1768. Clement XIII's death in 1769 had saved the Jesuits from outright abolition but that was more than his successor, Clement XIV (1769–74) could manage. This Franciscan friar had only been elected as a result of diplomatic lobbying from the Bourbon and Habsburg powers to secure a candidate who would do their bidding (Joseph II of Austria and his brother Peter Leopold of Tuscany even made an unofficial visit to the conclave). The Pope worked hard to improve strained relations with Catholic kings but the price of this was the passing of *Dominus ac redemptor* in 1773 suppressing the Jesuits. Securing the election of the right candidate for the throne of St Peter was a tried and tested diplomatic resort of the Catholic powers and operated throughout this period. Most of the cardinals had their royal patrons and knew where their obligations lay when they went into conclave. Their intransigence, usually exercised on behalf of cardinals to either the French or the imperial cause, could lead to compromise candidates emerging as the only means of breaking the impasse. Thus in autumn 1700, during the mortal illness of the last Habsburg king of Spain, Charles II, it took a forty-six-day conclave before all sides turned to Cardinal Giovanni Francesco Albani, the preferred choice of the *zelanti*, those who wanted a politically neutral Pope who would prioritize the interests of the church. As Clement XI (1700–21), Albani found himself in the position of so many successful papal candidates: hemmed in by powerful monarchies leaving them with limited means of exerting the force of their office unless it was by exploiting dynastic rivalries and using their individual gifts of personality to constructive effect. Papal preferences at a time of international conflict counted for less and less, as Clement XII experienced during the War of the Polish Succession (1733–8) when he backed first one candidate and then the other without achieving any shift in the balance of power in Italy to papal advantage. And yet the major monarchies still saw it as in their best interests to devote time and money to getting their man placed on the throne of St Peter: in 1740 it took six months to get (the outstanding) Benedict XIV (previously archbishop of Bologna) elected into office.

In more or less every Catholic state during the eighteenth century, the papacy found its scope for independent manœuvre reduced to almost a nullity. In France, Roman bulls and briefs could not be published without consent, and where papal collation to benefices was required, it had to be given automatically or risk precipitating a diplomatic showdown. In Germany, anti-curialism (which dated back to the middle ages) had become the default setting of most Catholic states during the War of the Spanish Succession, and was reactivated by such apologists as Paul Joseph Ritter von Riegger, Professor of Canon Law at Vienna University. Most German lay rulers had at their disposal the power of the *Placetum*, holding up the publication of papal decrees until it had been established that they were in accordance with the interests of the state. German expressions of ecclesiastical nationalism reached their culmination in Febronianism, an extreme championing of the rights of local bishops against the Holy See, derived from the pseudonym of Nikolaus von Hontheim, suffragan bishop of Trier (1701–90), who, for a time in the 1760s, was shaping up to be another Martin Luther. Despite its condemnation by Clement XIII in 1764, the Febronian tendency reached its high-water mark in the Punctuation of Ems (1786), a statement of Catholic reformism issued by the three ecclesiastical electors and the archbishop of Salzburg, directed in the first instance against all the papal nuncios in Germany.

Conclusion

The 1780s were a decade in which the established churches in much of Europe were on the defensive against monarchies determined to pursue reformist policies that too often conflicted with ecclesiastical interests. In the Habsburg Empire, Joseph II's wholesale schedule of state reordering included religious institutions that by the end of the decade had driven scores of bishops and clergy into open alliance with the Emperor's opponents from the Austrian Netherlands to Hungary; in France, there was fury that Louis XVI's ministers were ready to concede limited civil toleration to Huguenots without adequately hearing the representations of senior clerics. As in the Empire, prelates and priests together aligned themselves with the 'patriotic' opposition to the rationalizing policies of 'enlightened' monarchies and joined in the clamour for the convening of the Estates-General. They took their revenge in a spectacular snub to the government in 1788 when the General Assembly of the Clergy rejected the demand from the Principal Minister, Loménie de Brienne (who was himself an archbishop!) for a *don gratuit* when the state was on the verge of bankruptcy. Even the Church of England leadership could not take the support of Pitt the Younger's government for granted when there was a nationwide lobbying among dissenters for repeal of the Test and Corporation Acts in the late 1780s. Meanwhile in Ireland, growing numbers of their brother bishops were convinced that the Cabinet and Dublin Castle between them were moving to confer rights on Roman Catholics that would fatally undermine the Protestant Ascendancy and the established status of the Church of Ireland. This was the position in 1789. Ten years later, the position was very different. Governments had abandoned confrontational attitudes in favour of conciliating ecclesiastical establishments and were relying on them to speak up for the status quo in church and state. The difference had been made, of course, by the outbreak of the French Revolution, dechristianization in France, and the outbreak of the revolutionary war in 1792. One did not have to agree entirely with Edmund Burke's wake-up call in his *Reflections* to see that there was a fundamental cultural challenge to the European order that threatened the privileged place accorded the Christian Church since the conversion of Constantine. In these very different circumstances, the 1790s was a decade in which clergy heeded the call to speak out in pulpits and pamphlets in defence of the 'Old Order' on condition that governments respect the vested interest of the churches in the status quo. Rulers realized as much themselves, with the result that whereas the French Republic in 1795 declared itself officially without religion, virtually everywhere else church and state moved closer together. Even in France, the new arrangement lasted for less than a decade as Napoleon Bonaparte saw that ruling the French would be so much easier if he did it in conjunction with the church rather than in opposition to it. Hence the negotiation of the Concordat in 1801. And yet, in conformity with the underlying trend of the two previous centuries, it was on his terms not those of the church.

Notes

1. W. R. Ward, *The Churches under the Ancien Regime* (Cambridge, 1999), 2.
2. Gary Schwartz and Marten Jan Bok, *Pieter Saenredam: The Painter and his Time* (London, 1990).
3. Roger D. Lund, 'Irony as Subversion: Thomas Woolston and the Crime of Wit', in Roger D. Lund (ed.), *The Margins of Orthodoxy: Heterodox Writing and Cultural Response 1660-1750* (Cambridge, 1995), 187.
4. Deryck W. Lovegrove, *Established Church, Sectarian People: Itinerancy and the Transformation of English Dissent, 1780-1830* (Cambridge, 2004), 126-7.

Bibliography

Bergin, Joseph, *Church, Society and Religious Change in France, 1580-1730* (New Haven, Conn., 2009).

Callahan, William J., and Higgs, David, *Church and Society in Catholic Europe of the Eighteenth Century* (Cambridge, 1979).

Chadwick, Owen, *The Popes and European Revolution* (Oxford, 1981).

Dickson, P. G. M., 'Joseph II's Reshaping of the Austrian Church', *Historical Journal*, 36 (1993), 89-114.

Gibson, William, *Enlightenment Prelate, Benjamin Hoadly, 1676-1761* (Cambridge, 2004).

Hope, Nicholas, *German and Scandinavian Protestantism 1700-1918* (Oxford, 1995).

Lynch, J., *Bourbon Spain, 1700-1808* (Oxford, 1989).

McManners, John, *Church and Society in Eighteenth-Century France* (2 vols. Oxford, 1998).

Maxwell, Kenneth, *Pombal, Paradox of the Enlightenment* (Cambridge, 1995).

Printy, Michael, *Enlightenment and the Creation of German Catholicism* (Cambridge, 2009).

Stumberg, Martha Mel, *Piety and Politics: Imaging Divine Kingship in Louis XIV's Chapel at Versailles* (Newark, Del., 2002).

Sykes, Norman, *Church and State in England in the Eighteenth Century* (Cambridge, 1934).

Van Kley, Dale K., *The Damiens Affair and the Unraveling of the Ancien Régime, 1750-1770* (New Haven, Conn., 1984).

Ward, W. R., *The Churches under the Ancien Régime* (Cambridge, 1999).

CHAPTER 18

POPULAR RELIGION

ROBIN BRIGGS

POPULAR religion, along with the wider field of popular culture, has only been a recognized subject for historical investigation for a relatively short time; the bibliography is virtually non-existent before 1970. Even so, a term that was at first accepted as comprehensible and useful has rapidly come to be seen as highly problematic. Among the multiple reasons for concern, two in particular stand out. Historians now recoil from any suggestion that there was a single or coherent phenomenon that could be labelled in this way, while detailed research has largely destroyed the notion of a clear frontier between 'official' and 'popular' beliefs and practices. These discussions have been particularly lively in the case of France, where the nature of religious change under the Ancien Régime raises important issues with wide relevance, and the documentation is unusually rich. As the debate has evolved some early interpretations that suggested an outright conflict between old and new religious styles, and between the elites and the people, have been largely abandoned. Along with them has gone the view that there was a massive process of acculturation, with a largely alien set of religious values being imposed from above. Such ideas are now seen as excessively crude and oversimplified, with their implications of binary oppositions and stark contrasts. In consequence, this chapter is not about some monolithic entity that can be named as 'popular religion'; instead it must deal with a messy and complex set of changes, conflicts, and compromises. That once said, there is a problem of popular belief which any serious analysis of the period must confront, and which cannot be argued away by logical or semantic quibbling.

In the seventeenth and eighteenth centuries a high proportion of the French population had little or no formal education, so that many of them remained functionally illiterate. These men, women, and children belonged to an inherited culture of a kind familiar to anthropologists, within which religion was largely pragmatic and communal, mobilizing divine power to protect individuals, animals, and crops, while its ceremonies acted as containers for group loyalties. Until this point the Catholic clergy themselves had rarely done more than challenge a few excrescences of such ways of thought. Over the seventeenth century a major reform movement not only created many new religious orders with a vocation for pastoral work, but brought about dramatic changes in the training and attitudes of the parish priests.[1] In theory at least the reformed clergy were committed to an individualized and purified religion. As expounded by the writers of moral and pastoral theology, this Tridentine Catholicism was an alarmingly austere creed, very remote from the comforting certainties of the traditional faith. Its literal application would certainly have created a reprobated category of popular belief, in which superstition, idolatry, and even diabolism were to be found. Some missionaries gave graphic expression to this view when they described the French countryside as a new Indies, whose populations needed evangelizing as much as the American Indians or other savages. One Capuchin friar, Yves d'Evreux, went so far as to say of the Tupinamba of Brazil: 'I believe that they are much easier to civilize than the common run of our French peasants'.[2] Although similar trends and phenomena can be identified across virtually the whole of Catholic Europe, at the national level France does appear to have witnessed the most intensive and sustained of all these campaigns to instil a drastically purified version of the Christian faith.

Protestant observers, whether local or foreign, found no difficulty in explaining this tendency. It was the need to contend with a powerful challenge from the Huguenot minority that had driven French Catholics into cleaning up their act and making an attempt to steal their rivals' clothing. For historians this now looks to be a wholly inadequate interpretation of the Catholic reform as a whole, yet it may retain considerable value in accounting for aspects of the French situation. The conventional view among articulate French Catholics in the late sixteenth and early seventeenth centuries was that the Protestants had only won extensive support among the laity because the Catholic secular clergy had proved quite unable to compete with the committed and well-educated ministers who spread the heresy.[3] Such a blanket condemnation of the parish clergy was patently exaggerated, but as so often it was the perception of the problem that was crucial; it lay behind a massive pastoral, educational, and disciplinary effort that changed almost every aspect of the relationship between the church and the people. Change does not have to mean transformation, however, so that many continuities can be found just beneath the surface. The unquestioned success—admittedly achieved over a very long period—was in transforming the education and lifestyle of the secular clergy. Before the reform *curés* and *vicaires*, especially in the rural parishes, were normally local men who learnt their trade through a form of apprenticeship, often to a relative. One acerbic later commentator would describe some survivals of this type as nothing more than 'peasants dressed in black', a very revealing derogatory remark.[4] After most dioceses brought in a property qualification for ordination in the late sixteenth century, the really decisive step was the slow imposition of seminary training as the indispensable route for would-be clerics. Although financial considerations always severely limited the time ordinands spent at the seminary, entry depended on a previous commitment to a Latinate education, a significant investment of both time and money that excluded poor children.

The implementation of this change was roughly coterminous with the long personal reign of Louis XIV (1661–1715); the internal disputes which afflicted the Gallican church from these times were linked to it in complicated ways, and had their own impact on pastoral matters. The first wave of reform, however, was led by new types of religious orders (even if some were rejuvenated versions of older foundations). The Jesuits were only the most celebrated of many orders which chose to work outside the cloister, as missionaries, preachers, and educators. They taught in the seminaries and in the colleges which provided secondary education, the latter now completely dominated by the teaching orders. The Ursulines and other feminine orders offered unprecedented provision for teaching girls, while France pioneered forms of lay sisterhood whose members took on vital roles in social welfare and primary education. Over the seventeenth century the church succeeded in multiplying the agencies through which its messages were transmitted to all social groups, and in imposing a much more unified set of values and ideas through all levels of the clergy. At the same time French society was becoming more stratified and hierarchical, as both economic trends and royal policies sharpened the divisions between haves and have-nots. The elites were marked out as never before by literacy, formal education, and a distinctive culture. There was an obvious synergy here, which led to the identification of the popular as the opposite of the polite, a great amalgam of largely rural cultural backwardness and inferiority. Although the term 'popular religion' was not in use under the Ancien Régime, a looser notion of the type can be detected in many writings and phrases of the time. At one level, therefore, this was a construction by those who wished to mark their own distance from their inferiors, and to assert their own rationality.

As will become apparent in what follows, clerical attitudes were never so simple or so uniform as any rapid sketch might imply. There are particular dangers of exaggeration here because the materials available to the historian may be abundant, but they are also distinctly one-sided. A mildly caricatured view would assert that the church, aided and abetted by the ruling groups, embarked on a great repressive campaign against traditional religious practices. Distinctions between sacred and profane were enormously sharpened, whether these applied to time, space, objects, or persons. The concept of superstition was elaborated and used to condemn a wide range of behaviour that had previously been tolerated, while a pastoral style built around the fear of hellfire was linked to discipline through the confessional box. One extreme interpretation (subsequently disowned by the historian concerned) suggested that the result was to disrupt a previously unified popular culture to the point where it survived only as a set of fragmented local usages.[5] A series of massive (and very valuable) studies by Jean Delumeau has set out the arguments and prescriptions found in the clerical literature of the day, to give a rather dismal picture of a religion based on guilt, sin, and fear.[6] The underlying suggestion here is that the Catholic reform was a deviation from more humane and balanced understandings of Christianity, which bears a heavy responsibility for alienating many of the faithful, so that pious illusions about the pre-revolutionary age of faith must be discarded. There is indeed some truth in these views, which identify real dangers and defects in the reform programme, especially as it was stated on paper. Yet they are ultimately misleading, unless balanced by more subtle understandings of how matters played out in reality across more than a hundred dioceses and around 35,000 parishes.

Both the reform and its reception were far more ambiguous than these broad-brush treatments in primary colours would imply.

The key shifts demanded by modernizing theologians and disciplinarians can be summarized under two main headings. The individual Christian was made more important at the expense of the community and the family, while true faith was to be suitably internalized, rather than resting on external observances. A vast enterprise of conversion was implied here, resting on better instruction, above all through the use of catechisms, and on intensified self-examination through the practice of regular confession. Meanwhile the boundaries between sacred and profane, and between the licit and the illicit, were to be defined by ecclesiastical fiat. In all this the printed word was crucially important, even if much of the instruction of the laity must ultimately rely on word of mouth. Reforming bishops issued books of diocesan instructions—*rituels* and *statuts synodaux*—and either prescribed specific catechisms or produced their own. There were guides for parish priests, then great collections of *cas de conscience*, covering a breathtaking range of possible and fanciful sins. Towards the end of the seventeenth century the *curés* were widely organized into monthly study groups, the *conférences ecclésiastiques*, some of which in their turn generated multi-volume publications. One obvious way for a French publisher to become rich in this period was to have contracts with several dioceses, turning out large numbers of the standard texts, notably service books and catechisms. Religious publishing covered a much wider range than this, of course, from devotional works such as the writings of François de Sales and his emulators, through theology and hagiography, to cheap popular texts on miraculous events and the lives of saints. As time went on there was also a new strain of increasingly violent polemic, leading to intensified censorship, noisy condemnations, and underground publications.[7] These dissentions came to centre on just what the reform should mean for the laity, and developed into one of the most dangerous fissures within the Ancien Régime as a whole. They also went a long way to determining just what effect the changes would have on the general population, not least because they led the royal government to intervene.

The massive output of new religious literature worked together with some dominant intellectual trends of the time to encourage very unbalanced positions. One such was the 'science' of casuistry, of which the Jesuits were the most celebrated exponents. The moral theologians concerned were trying to find ways of making the new demands for a personalized religion acceptable to the mass of the population, quite rightly sensing that some kind of accommodation was necessary if the whole effort was not to break down. Unfortunately this degenerated into displays of misplaced ingenuity, whose effect was to declare many forms of morally dubious conduct exempt from any sanction, and to turn even major offences into venial sins. Although Pascal's devastating satire of these writings in the *Lettres provinciales* was often unfair on details, it caught the tone of such advice so well that it was virtually unanswerable. Even without these polemical fireworks, the casuists were bound to provoke a reaction; in France this took the form of a rigorist moral teaching that could never have been seriously applied at the parish level.[8] Where the laxists had vied with one another to argue away whole categories of sin, their adversaries competed to see who could draw up the most demanding and rebarbative creed, one which only an elect minority could ever aspire to follow. With predictable if depressing logic this led to the conclusion that the great majority of the population must be doomed to eternal damnation. Although there are good reasons to suppose that many clerics thought otherwise, such dissent was almost wholly silent in the face of apparent unanimity at the formal level. We should not be surprised, however, to find that the church was simultaneously giving a very different impression through most of its everyday practice. Sunday mass, the sacraments, and the multiple forms of communal religious activity all emphasized the inclusive aspects of the Catholic faith. They were also associated with the very conservative social message of the church, that men should be content with the station in which God had placed them, which could hardly be separated from a notion that passive obedience ought to be enough to win salvation. This dichotomy would persist right through to the revolutionary period, allowing huge ambiguities to permeate the whole situation.

Where we can find early evidence for local feelings about reform in the church, as with the lists of grievances prepared for the Estates-General of 1614, the emphasis is precisely on the need for a dutiful and resident clergy.[9] Priests needed to be on the spot to baptize children and provide the last rites for the dying, while parish life largely functioned around the liturgical calendar for which clerical leadership was essential. These were issues on which everyone could agree, alongside the need to put churches back into better physical shape and provide the objects and vestments necessary for the decent celebration of divine service. Church and community came together here around common objectives, ones which provided an ongoing focus for activism, while behind them there was the powerful idea that those who showed proper respect for God and his house might expect his protection. The regular visitations, by bishops or their agents, which were one of the main agencies of reform, were much more concerned with these pragmatic matters than they were with changing deeply ingrained mental habits or attacking popular culture. Those who made most noise about ignorance or residual paganism, in the formative decades of the Catholic reform, were almost always members of an urban clerical intelligensia with little direct experience of ministering to rural populations. However, these more radical demands for a great conversion programme did gradually penetrate more deeply, and during a period roughly coterminous with the reign of Louis XIV a high proportion of bishops made serious efforts to apply such ideas in their dioceses. There were still very significant local variations, because the Gallican church retained a strongly cellular structure within which bishops enjoyed remarkable freedom of choice. Just how many *curés* and *vicaires* had been properly co-opted as willing supporters of a campaign to evangelize their flocks is simply impossible to know; the marked rise in the social and educational level of this group meant that at least a significant minority must have aspired to play this role. Meanwhile the expansion of the new religious orders, with their commitment to action in the world, made it possible to launch a sustained missionary effort covering much of the kingdom. It can well be argued that for the first time the church was in a position to turn a set of aspirations dating back to at least the Lateran Council of 1215 into something like a reality, now that it had finally created a body of clergy equal to this demanding task.

It is from the comments in journals and similar documents kept by individual *curés* that we can best form an opinion of religious life in their parishes. Those who recorded their opinions gave a very consistent picture of the peasantry; they were stubborn and secretive, well used to evading or frustrating external power, whether it was that of the state, the landlords, or the church. Not only were they often drunken or violent, they stole when they could and were adept at petty chicanery, although comments on their sexual morality were more ambiguous. For the most part they were deeply attached to the church, even if unreliable at attending services, and enthusiastic about processions, pilgrimages, and other communal rituals. Their other moral failings were compensated by a notable inclination to be charitable to the less fortunate. It was hard work to keep catechism classes going, while congregations paid little attention even to short homilies during Sunday mass, which one could safely repeat after a year to two without anyone noticing. As for the apparently powerful mechanism of annual confession, as Easter approached the *curé* was swamped by the demand; in any case his penitents concealed as much as they could from him or pretended ignorance of the rules. Around 1700 a priest whose living was in the admittedly backward region of the Sologne described his parishioners (for the benefit of his successor) as 'baptized idolaters'.[10] Here as elsewhere they were obstinately determined to maintain local shrines to saints of their own devising, and expected the priest to sustain a wide range of protective rituals without much regard for their orthodoxy. The gulf between this picture and the idealized vision of a personal faith that brought a change of lifestyle might well have been thought unbridgeable. Yet there are reasons to think that clerical pessimism only tells a very partial story, based as it was on some unduly rigid ideas, and emanating from a minority of priests.

Very few of those who wrote about confessional practice gave any sign of understanding the circumstances in which ordinary *curés* had to operate; in fact most of the test cases to which they applied their minds were much more relevant to the privileged groups, and in particular to the clergy themselves. Any notion of a regime of scrupulous self-examination, backed up by guidance from the confessor, with the ultimate sanction of the refusal of absolution, was bound to collapse at the village level. What seems to have been encouraged, on the other hand, was an older and more relevant tradition, that of using Easter confession as a mechanism for reconciling enemies and restoring harmony in the community. Missions developed this further, with a special emphasis on getting people to settle long-standing quarrels. The favoured technique here was to combine intense hellfire sermons, and even dramatic performances showing the fate that awaited the ungodly, with much gentler treatment in the confessional booths. In the short term at least many notable successes appear to have been scored, although the local clergy might grumble that hardened sinners got off lightly at the hands of confessors who did not know the whole story, and would not be around to see if repentance was sustained. These protests were part of a wider grievance, that people were allowed to evade the system by finding compliant external confessors, which looks very unrealistic when one considers the obvious defects of parish practice. One has to suspect that the *curés* were displacing their dissatisfaction with the broader situation through this much reiterated complaint, while of course they must have understood why parishioners would have found it easier to confess to strangers. One of those who expressed such sentiments was Alexandre Dubois of Rumegies in the northern diocese of Tournai; he was strongly attracted by the austere Jansenist theology, and was very critical of the behaviour of his flock. Yet after suggesting that their love for worldly goods was the reason why they proved to be cruel, addicted to blasphemy, and obstinate, he went on in a quite unexpected fashion to state:

> Nevertheless there are certainly many honest people among them, and a large proportion of whom one could only speak well, in particular of nearly all the parishioners that they are very charitable towards the poor. I believe that God will save them by this means.[11]

These sentiments were wholly at odds with the rigorist position Dubois generally admired, but they appear as a triumph of charity and common sense over dogma; it seems likely that the great majority of clerics would have agreed with him, and that there was an instinctive resistance to the notion that the great majority of believers were destined for hell.

It would appear that there were dioceses where bishops (usually those with Jansenist sympathies) did manage to push significant numbers of their clergy into serious efforts at discipline and evangelization in the decades either side of 1700; it has also been argued that a long-run effect in terms of alienation from the church can be perceived in some of these cases. As in many other respects, the papal bull *Unigenitus* of 1713 marks a frontier here, because one of its ambiguous successes was in identifying a large group of clerical dissidents. The crown had already begun to favour candidates with safe opinions as its nominees for bishoprics, something that now became absolutely standard practice under Louis XV. *Unigenitus* itself had effectively ruled out a whole range of practices that were linked to greater lay participation, so the church itself had in effect scaled back its ambitions. Clerical stances would become ever more defensive as the eighteenth century wore on, with impious writings, Enlightenment philosophy, and economic change all seen as forces undermining true faith. The hierarchy and the *curés* alike continued to demand better conduct, using such means as they could to attack irreligious behaviour, but whatever enthusiasm there had ever been for educating the people disappeared. With it, one might think, went any hope of spreading a new religious style, based on understanding and individual commitment, to significant groups beyond the privileged elites. An extreme version of the conservative position was expressed in a popular set of sermons first published in the 1760s, by a *curé* named François-Léon Réguis, who thought that faith was best maintained by illiteracy, while children who went to school corrupted one another and became disinclined to work. Yet he had to admit that those pious peasants who never missed a procession or a service

> get up at night to strip our gardens, steal our fruit and harvest our grapes. They have herbs blessed to treat their sick animals, but these animals eat our young corn, ruin our harvests, destroy our woods. They are devout when in church, they pray at length, put their hands together, kiss the earth; but when they leave they go to the tavern where they get drunk and have their mouths full of nothing but oaths and crude words.[12]

Like many others, Réguis repeatedly failed to make the connection between such age-old patterns of behaviour and his insistence that the laity were best off when they learnt no more than the basic elements of the faith, then did as the clergy told them.

The loss of dynamism in the eighteenth century was in truth all too predictable, for many reasons. The sheer scale of the responsibilities accumulated by the church, and often thrust on it by the royal government, put immense strains on even so wealthy and relatively well-manned an institution. At every level clerics had to make choices about where they should concentrate their efforts, and these naturally evolved towards the areas which gave most satisfaction to themselves and to others. The *curés* of the eighteenth century generally enjoyed the esteem and respect of parishioners whom they allowed to continue with a largely external faith, while they themselves often acted as benevolent local notables and defenders of the secular rights of the community. In its own terms this was a great success story, which helps to explain why Catholicism survived the Revolution as well as it did, and why one of Napoleon's shrewdest moves was to re-establish the links between church and state. By then, of course, few adherents of the church would have doubted that Réguis and his like had been right; the traditional faith of the people had proved far more reliable, in their eyes, than the more advanced doctrines associated with those social elites which had also produced the men who ultimately launched strident campaigns for the end of 'fanaticism' and clerical power. What the Revolution also exposed was one of the most serious gaps in pastoral efforts under the Ancien Régime, the relative neglect of the growing urban proletariat. This is perhaps the biggest unwritten story of the period, largely because the records are so sparse; it is almost as if these social groups had dropped out of sight for most of the clergy. The inflexible parish structure was partly to blame, with enormous populations sometimes developing within individual units, and the sprawling suburbs of major cities notably ill served. Large inflows of migrants meant that there was a far less stable social pattern to underpin religious life, so it appears that for the poor there was a 'take it or leave it' quality to religious observance, even though there was an abundance of ceremonies and rituals theoretically available to them. If the system of hospitals and poor relief institutions brought municipal and clerical authorities together in many worthwhile efforts, those who engaged in such charitable work had few illusions about the spiritual state of many of their charges.

Even in the time of Louis XIV, when reforming efforts were at their highest, the zealots who made up the cutting edge of the reform movement often displayed a deep pessimism about the results of their campaign. There was a certain self-imposed quality about this, because they had allowed their own rhetoric to saddle them with impossibly high aims; arguably their images of the minority of the just and the narrow path to salvation may have prepared them unconsciously to accept such failure as virtually inevitable. They were bitterly aware that avarice and hedonism were widespread among the educated elites, whose behaviour hardly suggested that better religious instruction necessarily led to a change of life.[13] Where the urban poor were concerned, both clerical and lay authorities gravitated naturally towards a repressive policy, even if the idea of a 'great confinement' in punitive institutions is a massive exaggeration. Hospitals and their like tended to come more under lay control in the eighteenth century, partly because the great financial crash associated with the 'System' of John Law in 1720 left many foundations permanently impoverished. Perhaps the most imaginative scheme for improving the state of the urban proletariat, the free schools organized by Jean-Baptiste de la Salle, had already run into serious opposition around 1700, when the most powerful argument used by hostile clerics was the bizarre one that children educated purely in French would be unable to enter the church. Although the Salesians did survive these attacks, their promising expansion was reversed, never to resume before the Revolution.[14]

Throughout the system those in authority seem to have subscribed to a vision of the people as childish and irresponsible, readily tempted by every opportunity for idleness, self-indulgence, and misbehaviour. In the rural parishes too there was a natural alliance between the clergy and the wealthier minority, the group who dominated the communal assemblies and also controlled the funds for maintaining the church. No *curé* could easily decide to set himself against this dominant element; in any case for most of them it was axiomatic that the social order should be maintained, so these were the natural allies to whom they looked.[15] One of the most significant disciplinary successes of the period would have reflected a common interest here. The church was able to eliminate the old practice of treating the betrothal ceremony (the *fiançailles*) as the start of cohabitation, by allowing only a very short gap between this and the wedding proper. As with some other measures to repress both irregular marriages and sexual misbehaviour, property-owners had their own reasons to favour better control. Betrothal was however an unusual case, because a simple change in the formal rules was sufficient to alter practice; most vexed problems were much harder to tackle. Marriages themselves were a case in point, since these crucial rites of passage were surrounded by a whole range of festive customs which rigorists strongly disliked. Much of this activity was orchestrated by youth groups, a powerful force in traditional culture (yet strangely absent from most of the literature on the subject of popular religion) whose style was especially well adapted to defy outside interference. The clergy instinctively retreated into asserting their control over what happened in and around the church, where greater sobriety was imposed, while most of them were apparently happy enough to attend the feast and bless the marriage bed. One doubts whether they normally thought it necessary to follow the gloomy advice some rigorists offered, that they accompany these blessings with warnings about concupiscence and reminders of mortality.[16]

The most widespread form of organized religious activity outside clerical control was that associated with the confraternities, and in the south the penitents. Essentially these were lay fraternities which held regular processions and masses, might have their own chapels or shrines, organized social gatherings, and assisted in various ways with the funerals of members. A bewildering variety of such associations existed, with a much wider range of activities, while old ones sometimes disappeared as others were created; towns might have numerous bodies of this kind, some of them overlapping with guilds. The confraternities were unpopular with the hierarchy, always suspicious of anything that smacked of local independence, but they were much too deeply rooted to be eliminated. It did however prove possible to reduce their numbers in many places, perhaps only reinforcing a natural tendency in that direction, and to foster a more elitist structure within them. At the same time *curés* might found new ones as stimuli to local devotion, sometimes with notable success.[17] These were legal organizations, with individual rules and financial arrangements, which fell under the authority of the royal courts. Other forms of communal activity were less formal, and often even more disliked as dangers to morality or good behaviour. The winter spinning-bees or *veillées*, gatherings for story-telling and singing as well as handiwork, were regularly denounced as occasions where young people (in particular) mingled in an improper style. As with many such conflicts, it is impossible to tell whether these complaints led to much in the way of intervention; the assumption must be that few parishes saw much change in their long-standing customs. Dancing had rapidly become one of the obsessions of reforming clerics, whose irritation must have been increased because the normal occasions for it were Sundays and holidays. This was another deeply ingrained part of local culture, so if suppression worked for a time in one village it probably only displaced the dancers to an adjoining parish. Worst of all, in clerical eyes, were the taverns, many of which remained open during Sunday mass in defiance of innumerable prohibitions, keeping a significant proportion of male parishioners away from the services. Drunkenness was blamed, no doubt with some justice, for everything from violence to the ruin of families. The most that was ever achieved here was to compel some innkeepers to close during the main Sunday services, a modest result that was rarely sustained for long.

The church certainly aimed to establish some basic control over sacred time and space. Various marginal or disruptive activities were driven out of the churches, and even the parish assemblies increasingly took place in special porches built up against the church. Burials were excluded from the church itself in favour of the cemetery, then in the later eighteenth century the cemeteries themselves were often moved to more remote sites on public health grounds. Although conflicts over these issues were quite common, parishioners (or at least the elites) usually seem to have ended up by accepting that there were good reasons for imposing better order in such matters, showing some enthusiasm to beautify their churches and improve their equipment. For their part the clergy often contented themselves with these advances in their own restricted area, rather than seeking an impossibly high degree of conformity everywhere. Eighteenth-century visitation records show a very marked tendency to concentrate on the state of the church and of formal religious observances, with much less attention to wider disciplinary and even educational questions than had been evident in the earlier period. Some late seventeenth-century bishops had acquired formidable reputations as *dénicheurs de saints*, as they went round removing the statues of local saints devoid of any canonical status—in at least one case the parishioners promptly dug up the condemned image from its resting place in the graveyard and resumed their devotions.[18] In the later period the favoured episcopal move was to reduce the number of holidays, alleging that they encouraged debauchery and prevented the poor from earning their living; this policy was probably much more to the taste of the market-oriented elites than of the general population.

Saints' days were frequently the occasion for processions and pilgrimages. In towns these consolidated parish loyalties, while providing occasions for formal reassertions of the social hierarchy, at the risk of occasional confrontations in which dignity could easily be lost (and with clerical groups as not infrequent participants). Village feast-days, processions, and pilgrimages were simpler affairs, much more obviously tied to the agrarian and ritual calendars, and to the protection of the community. As usual the unstable mixture of sacred and profane elements worried the clergy, but it was hardly possible to prevent pilgrims taking refreshment in taverns, or the young men engaging in traditional battles with their counterparts from nearby villages. Pilgrimages also allowed for individual responses to illnesses and other troubles, with a wide range of healing shrines attracting visitors who might come from very considerable distances. If some of these were ancient, others were new creations bolstered by stories of miraculous events or the discovery of sacred objects; both local clergy and the regular orders might be deeply involved in promoting these centres.[19] Any notion that a rationalist clergy was trying to take the magic out of religion tends to crumble when these extensive activities are taken into account. Famous shrines offered cures for rabies, venereal disease, infertility, and virtually every other conceivable malady.[20] The pilgrims brought ex votos, usually representations of the sick person or the relevant part of the body, which festooned the shrines; the lame or paralysed would (somewhat dangerously) celebrate recovery by leaving their crutches behind. At a local level there were innumerable sanctuaries where still-born infants were alleged to revive for long enough to receive baptism, so that they became eligible to enter heaven. Meanwhile the clergy still offered exorcism as a standard treatment for mental illness, which could extend to a much wider range of disorders, and carried out a range of similar rituals to protect buildings and livestock, or to anathematize plagues of pests. The widespread conviction that bellringing could ward off hail and thunderstorms became a bone of contention, however, as the principle of the lightning-conductor became understood among the educated, and it was noted that bellringers routinely became the victims of lightning strikes.

In a routine fashion the church provided sacramentals, such as holy water and blessed bread, that were believed to carry protective power with them. These were prophylactics that also featured in a whole range of medical practices, in many of which both regular and secular clergy participated. Although they had clearly become more critical in their attitudes to intercessory powers, and now declined to support some popular beliefs, the logical basis for such discrimination was often far from obvious. The writers who analysed popular superstitions, like Jean-Baptiste Thiers and Pierre Lebrun, were themselves largely defeated by the task of establishing or explaining where the frontier should be drawn between licit and illicit practices; they were driven back to relying on authority, in the form of previous ecclesiastical decisions, rather than on real differences in kind.[21] From the perspective of an ordinary believer it must have seemed that the clergy were rather capricious about what they would agree to do, not to say inconsistent among themselves. Meanwhile many of the achievements of the Catholic reform might be seen as enhancing the special status of the priests and thereby reinforcing their claims to hold unusual power. Relics and processions were regularly employed in times of drought or flooding, or to seek intercession against animal epidemics and the like. In late eighteenth-century Paris, whenever a member of the royal family was feared to be dying, the relics of St Geneviève were brought out and special sessions of forty-hour prayers organized, in an obvious attempt to secure divine intervention. When the unpopular Louis XV died someone remarked to a Jansenist *curé* that the prayers did not seem to have done much good, attracting the devastating response 'Why are they complaining? He's dead isn't he?'[22] In the early 1730s the Jansenist cause itself had become entangled with a great outburst of the miraculous, in the shape of the *convulsionnaires* who established themselves in the cemetery of St Médard and claimed to have obtained many spectacular cures. This turned out to be something of an own goal, despite all the trouble it caused the authorities, because it divided opinion among the Jansenists themselves, and alienated sympathizers among the educated elites in the capital.[23]

What such episodes demonstrated was that both the church and the believers remained convinced that religious observances were directly linked to the fates of individuals and the larger community. As modern anthropologists working on Africa would say, religion was built around a triad of explanation, prediction, and control. It was only a relative handful of austere theologians and lay zealots who sought to repudiate at least some part of this intuitive logic, to replace it by the religion of the hidden God, whose decisions none should presume to influence or understand. A rarefied faith of this type stood no chance of winning widespread support, while it was permanently at odds with the whole great liturgical and ceremonial cycle of the Christian year. If large sections of polite society were coming to find something alien or embarrassing about aspects of popular devotion, this is more plausibly explained in terms of broader intellectual trends, themselves based more on the fashion of the times than on any coherent system. Popular credulity became an easy target for elite criticism, with the unattractive implication that the common people were inferior beings, naturally incapable of responding to a rational faith. Pierre Bayle suggested that his readers would 'concede to me that it is easy to persuade the people of certain false ideas which are in accord with the prejudices of childhood or the passions of the heart, as are all the pretended rules about omens'. Nicolas Malebranche shared this pessimistic vision, going on to affirm that 'popular applause for a particular opinion on a difficult question is an infallible sign that it is false'. An even harsher view came from the seventeenth-century moralist Pierre Nicole, in a chapter forbiddingly entitled 'That the world is almost entirely composed of stupid people who think about nothing.' He wrote 'of what do most working people think? About their work, eating, drinking, sleeping, securing what is owed them, paying the *taille*, and a few other objects. They are as if unaware of everything else, and their habituation to turning within a little circle renders them incapable of conceiving anything outside it.' The attempt to inform these 'mechanics' about the rules of religion and morality is doomed to failure; 'either they don't hear at all, or they forget in a moment what has been said to them, and their mind returns immediately within that circle of gross objects to which it is accustomed. If their nature is infinitely removed from that of beasts, as the latter truly is, they are very little different from our common idea of animals.' The group thus condemned is very wide, 'For this number of the stupid includes, even in Christianity, nearly all working people, almost all the poor, most women of low condition, all children.

All these people think of almost nothing during their life, beyond satisfying their bodily needs, finding the means of life, of buying and selling, and even on these objects they only form very confused thoughts.'[24]

A less brutal view would be that although peasants and artisans did indeed occupy a different religious world to that of Jansenists like Nicole, it was still a surprisingly rich and complex one. Enough scraps of evidence survive to demonstrate that members of the labouring classes thought about a much wider range of topics than others recognized, often in ways that their social superiors would have found uncomfortable. Since they were (with some justice) very suspicious of outsiders, their apparent stupidity when questioned about their formal religious knowledge should not be taken at face value, while their range of practical skills and their ability to create survival strategies in a harsh world both fit very poorly with the idea that they were merely ignorant and confused. Over the territory of France as a whole one could argue that they had largely succeeded in getting the kind of church they wanted, by a mixture of resistance and accommodation. Power in the parishes was shared between the lay elites and a respectable, remarkably dutiful clergy, whose members performed a wide range of services for the state and the community. The relationship between the *curés* and their flocks was in general a mutually supportive one, as reflected in the common eighteenth-century image of 'the good priest', a mixture of wise counsellor and dispenser of charity. Most priests seem to have found this role so congenial that they did little more than grumble about the persistent religious and behavioural defects they were largely powerless to remedy. Their own position was shot through with ambiguities and ambivalences that made it virtually impossible for them to carry through the kind of thoroughgoing reform that some enthusiasts had hoped to see. As great defenders of the established order they naturally preferred that the lower classes should be passive followers of a largely routinized faith, safe in the belief that regular performance of their Christian duties was sufficient to keep them in line for ultimate salvation. Meanwhile the development of polite disdain towards superstition and credulity might provide a new motive to repress public displays of this kind, but fear of exposing the people to the 'spirit of the century' inhibited any notion of spreading rational thinking through education. If the church had become a limited ally of rational approaches, this was rather because clerics were among the sharpest observers of the everyday problems of the poor, and of the harsh social and economic environment with which they had to struggle. Moves to eliminate superfluous holidays and to reposition graveyards away from the churchyards did not represent a wider commitment to any general Enlightenment project.

Religion therefore continued to function as a fundamental element in the lives of all but the most unstable elements in the French population, according to some very traditional rules. There is much evidence that ordinary people wholly accepted the orthodox link between terrestrial existence and the world to come, believing that those who lived wicked lives and died unrepentant would be suitably punished. That was why the rites of passage, especially baptism and extreme unction, were so important to them, and why the vast majority made their annual Easter communion. Where religion impacted most strongly on everyday life, however, was in a rather different register, that of a great arsenal of supernatural power to which one might appeal for protection or cure. Much of this too was perfectly orthodox, for all but a few extreme and unrepresentative clerical zealots. The church endorsed a multiplicity of rituals, shrines, and pilgrimages, while it routinely handed out objects that carried sacred power with them. If there was a growing tendency to restrict such claims, by stigmatizing unauthorized devotions or applying much more critical standards to alleged miracles, local practice realigned itself easily enough, where it did not simply continue unabashed. Behind it all was that universal tendency to believe that there was no such thing as simple misfortune; when things went wrong this was imputed to a human cause, for even the devil rarely operated except through mundane allies. These beliefs had underlain the persecution of supposed witches, although most of the relevant authorities had been too sceptical for this to gather much force even in the decades around 1600, and by the 1670s the monarchy had put a complete stop to legal prosecutions in France. Since there is abundant evidence to show that witchcraft was still widely feared in parts of rural France in the late twentieth century, its prevalence in the intervening period has to be accepted. This was less a question of lurid beliefs about women engaging in nocturnal rituals than a much more basic fear of secret local jealousies, perhaps more commonly associated with men, so that it was the ill-will of rivals which took this menacing form. A shadowy world of magical operators, the witch-doctors known as *devins*, flourished as a result. Their techniques adroitly mixed claims to personal power with a whole range of remedies drawing on the powers of local saints, together with rituals that appropriated Christian symbols, formulae, and sacramentals.

Protective magic of this type was normally invoked by individuals to cope with crises affecting their own family. When children sickened or animals died mysteriously the natural response was to call in the specialist who might identify the human cause; then either counter-magic or coercive pressure might remove the spell. Although one of the effects of the Catholic reform was to make the *curés* far more reluctant than in the past to take any part in such processes, the church seems to have been almost powerless to prevent its sacral charge being incorporated into this schema. Nor could it do much to undermine beliefs in lucky and unlucky days, a variety of supernatural signs used for predictions, or other forms of fortune-telling. When more general disasters occurred, in the form of bad weather, harvest failures, or human and animal epidemics, the church did normally respond with special ceremonies parading relics and invoking divine intervention. Even when such performances were accompanied by warnings against facile assumptions, these are unlikely to have made much impression on the average participant. Whatever attempts were made to redefine Christianity as a demanding personal creed, which almost by definition was only accessible to an educated elite, popular religion under the Ancien Régime therefore remained a very different animal. Beneath a veneer of greater external conformity the mass of the population found consolation and protection from a very traditional faith, a blurred yet sustaining compound of animism, multivalent sacred power, and popular moralism. These resources interacted with the approved practices and beliefs along a series of fluid boundaries, so that no clear distinctions can ever be drawn. This infinitely flexible faith was certainly not the 'fanaticism' denounced by excitable revolutionaries after 1789; it did however meet so many needs that it would prove virtually indestructible.

Notes

1. For a superb overview see J. Bergin, *Church, Society and Religious Change in France, 1580–1730* (London, 2009).
2. Yves d'Evreux, *Suitte de l'histoire des choses plus mémorables advenues en Maragnan, ès années 1613 & 1614* (Paris, 1615), 68.
3. B. Dompnier, *Le Venin de l'hérésie: Image du protestantisme et combat catholique au xviie siècle* (Paris, 1985).
4. J.-B. Thiers, *L'Avocat des Pauvres* (Paris, 1676), 337.
5. R. Muchembled, *Popular Culture and Elite Culture in France, 1400–1750* (London, 1985). Unfortunately the much more nuanced study that followed has never been translated: *L'Invention de l'homme moderne: Sensibilités, mœurs et comportements collectifs sous l'Ancien Régime* (Paris, 1988).
6. See esp. J. Delumeau, *Sin and Fear: The Emergence of a Western Guilt Culture, 13th–18th Centuries* (London, 1990).
7. There is a very full coverage in the first 2 vols. of H.-J. Martin and R. Chartier (eds.), *Histoire de l'édition française* (4 vols. Paris, 1982–6).
8. I explored this process at greater length in 'The Sins of the People: Auricular Confession and the Imposition of Social Norms', in R. Briggs, *Communities of Belief: Cultural and Social Tensions in Early Modern France* (Oxford, 1989), 277–338. See also the brilliant short account by J.-L. Quantin, *Le Rigorisme chrétien* (Paris, 2001).
9. Y. Durand (ed.), *Cahiers de doléances des paroisses du bailliage de Troyes pour les états généraux de 1614* (Paris, 1966).
10. This was Christophe Sauvageon, whose *Mémoires* are expertly put in context by G. Bouchard, *Le Village immobile: Sennely-en-Sologne au xviiie siècle* (Paris, 1972). Quotation p. 341.
11. *Journal d'un curé de campagne au xviie siècle*, ed. C. Platelle (Paris, 1965), 77.
12. G. Besse, 'La Représentation du "peuple" chez un prédicateur: François-Léon Réguis 1725–1789', in *Images du peuple au xviiie siècle* (Paris, 1973), 159–76. Quotation pp. 170–1.
13. This is very well described in A. Tallon, *La Compagnie du Saint-Sacrement (1629–1667): Spiritualité et société* (Paris, 1990).
14. Y. Poutet, *Le xviie siècle et les origines lasalliennes: Recherches sur la genèse de l'œuvre scolaire et religieuse de Jean-Baptiste de La Salle (1651–1719)* (Rennes, 1970).
15. For an excellent case study see B. Restif, *La Révolution des paroisses: Culture paroissiale et Réform catholique en Haute-Bretagne aux xvie et xviie siècles* (Rennes, 2006). This can be complemented by the book by P. Goujard (n. 17 below).
16. I have written on this in 'The Church and the Family in Seventeenth-Century France', *Communities of Belief*, 235–76.
17. P. Goujard, *Un Catholicisme bien tempéré: La Vie religieuse dans les paroisses rurales de Normandie, 1680–1789* (Paris, 1996); see also B. Restif (n. 15 above).
18. This was an image of St Antoine at Sennely; Bouchard, *Le Village immobile*, 299–300.
19. G. Provost, *La Fête et le sacré: Pardons et pèlerinages en Bretagne aux xviie et xviiie siècles* (Paris, 1998) is an outstanding local study.

20. For a superb and very amusing example see A. Boureau, 'Adorations et dévorations franciscaines', in R. Chartier (ed.), *Les Usages de l'imprimé (xve–xixe siècle)* (Paris, 1987), 25–81.
21. J.-B. Thiers, *Traité des superstitions selon l'Ecriture sainte* (Paris, 1679), and P. Le Brun, *Histoire critique des pratiques superstitieuses* (Paris, 1702).
22. J. McManners, *Church and Society in Eighteenth-Century France* (2 vols. Oxford, 1998), ii. 125.
23. B. R. Kreiser, *Miracles, Convulsions, and Ecclesiastical Politics in Early Eighteenth-Century Paris* (Princeton, 1978).
24. These are taken from an enormous collection of similarly depressing views cited in Pierre Ronzeaud, *Peuple et représentations sous le règne de Louis XIV: Les Représentations du peuple dans la littérature politique en France sous le règne de Louis XIV* (Aix-en-Provence, 1988). Bayle (*Pensées sur la Comète*, 1682) is cited on p. 129, Malebranche (*De la recherche de la vérité*, 1675–6) on p. 135, Nicole (*Essais de morale*, 1671, ch. 9) on p. 134.

Bibliography

Bergin, J., *Church, Society and Religious Change in France, 1580–1730* (London, 2009).
Briggs, R., *Communities of Belief: Cultural and Social Tensions in Early Modern France* (Oxford, 1989).
Châtellier, L., *The Europe of the Devout: The Catholic Reformation and the Formation of a New Society* (Cambridge, 1989).
—— *The Religion of the Poor: Rural Missions in Europe and the Formation of Modern Catholicism, c.1500–c.1800* (Cambridge, 1989).
Delumeau, J., *Sin and Fear: The Emergence of a Western Guilt Culture, 13th–18th Centuries* (London, 1990).
Greyerz, K. von (ed.), *Religion and Society in Early Modern Europe, 1500–1800* (London, 1984).
Hoffman, P. T., *Church and Community in the Diocese of Lyon, 1500–1789* (London, 1984).
Kaplan, S. L. (ed.), *Understanding Popular Culture: Europe from the Middle Ages to the 19th Century* (New York, 1984).
Luria, K. P., *Territories of Grace: Cultural Change in the Seventeenth-Century Diocese of Grenoble* (Berkeley, Calif., 1991).
McManners, J., *Church and Society in Eighteenth-Century France* (2 vols. Oxford, 1998).
Tackett, T., *Priest and Parish in Eighteenth-Century France: A Social and Political Study of the Curés in a Diocese of Dauphiné, 1750–1791* (Princeton, 1977).

CHAPTER 19

JANSENISM

THOMAS O'CONNOR

Introduction

JANSENISM was given a name only in the 1640s but originated as a sixteenth-century theological current in Spanish Flanders, where it was part of the Catholic response to the intellectual and pastoral challenges thrown up by the Reformation. It gradually outgrew its university origins and, by the 1640s, had come to represent a distinct and contested renewal tendency in Flemish and French Catholicism. Although Antoine Arnauld (1612–94), the greatest Jansenist so-called, claimed that Jansenism was the product of its critics' febrile imaginations,[1] there was nothing illusory about its capacity to create enemies. Detractors distrusted its positive theological method and suspected its dogged determination to impose St Augustine as the church's unique theological yardstick. Most of all they objected to its conviction that opposition to the authority of church or state was, on occasion, the sincerest form of loyalty.[2] Among the fiercest anti-Jansenists were the Jesuits, who actually coined the terms 'Jansenist'[3] and 'Jansenism'.[4] Thanks to their persistent antipathy, Jansenism gained an even more fearsome reputation than it deserved and, in this sense, the movement was their creation. As the incarnation of the Society's dread and horror, Jansenism came to assume a potent virtual existence.[5] In this form it attracted the approval of the Jesuits' many foes and became a rallying point for the enemies of the Society's friends at court and in Rome. In the seventeenth and eighteenth centuries, the tendency knew many metamorphoses,[6] attracting supporters not only in Flanders,[7] its original heartland, but also in France,[8] Ireland,[9] the British Catholic diasporas,[10] Spain,[11] the Italian peninsula,[12] the Empire,[13] and further afield.[14] In the period before the French Revolution its theological passions cooled and the tendency aligned itself with a range of largely aristocratic interests impatient of perceived state and church authoritarianism. In France, some Jansenists made common cause with proscribed Jewish and Protestant minorities in the 1780s and what might be called 'leveller' elements of Jansenist ideology appeared in the grievances of lower clergy, in the clerical *cahiers* of 1788–9 and in the Civil Constitution of the Clergy (1790). As a movement within Catholicism, Jansenism did not outlive the old regime, though it did survive in the nineteenth-century romantic imagination as a figure of tragic failure and defiant heroism alternately.

In the twentieth century the movement enjoyed fairly consistent attention from historians. Its treatment, particularly at the hands of Lucien Ceyssens OFM and his school recaptured the violence of the polemics that marked the movement's origins, development, and diversification. It also revealed the complexity of the phenomenon and the extent to which its defence, in Rome and in various European courts, was orchestrated in much the same way as the assaults it suffered. Overall, however, Ceyssens tended to present Jansenism both as a victim of Roman *Realpolitik* and as a tragically aborted version of the Catholic reform.

His conclusions were not unproblematic. It could be argued, for instance, that he tended to overlook Jansenism's role within the divided household of early modern Catholicism, particularly from the point of view of the challenge it posed to institutions, like the papacy, which struggled, not always self-interestedly, to prevent their quarrelling charges coming to blows or worse. Other modern historians might be criticized for extrapolating categories more at home in the later seventeenth- and eighteenth-century manifestations of the phenomenon back to the sixteenth and early seventeenth century, thereby bestowing a conceptual order on the historical complexity of the phenomenon that is unconvincing if not misleading. Also, they have tended to cast the late sixteenth- and early seventeenth-century papacy, Society of Jesus, and Roman Inquisition as undifferentiated monoliths with clearly defined anti-Jansenist strategies. This underestimates the conflicts of interest and internal feuding that so compromised their effectiveness as agents of authority.

Popular understandings of Jansenism, however, have remained impervious to these debates. In spite of the the travails of generations of historians, the term 'Jansenism' retains an old-fashioned sulphurous connotation in the popular mind, especially in English-speaking countries, where it remains stubbornly associated with sexual repression and general human pessimism.

The First Jansenism

Those first labelled as Jansenists were a group of Catholic university clergy who, in execution of the will of the recently deceased theologian bishop of Ypres, Cornelius Jansen (1585–1638),[15] published a book called *Augustinus de gratia*. This was ostensibly an act of pietas but, in fact, concealed a propagandist purpose. For many years, Jansen, his editors, and the theological tendency they represented had been concerned about the direction of the Catholic renewal. In particular, they doubted the scriptural and patristic authenticity of the Jesuits' pastoral and educational ideology and were anxious to correct it according to the theology of grace outlined in the later, anti-Pelagian works of St Augustine, the greatest of the Western fathers.

The reaction to *Augustinus*'s appearance was predictably stormy,[16] with the local Jesuits taking particular offence. For them, *Augustinus* was another episode in the long-running struggle for ideological supremacy between theirs and alternative versions of the Catholic renewal. There was something to this view. Jansen, like generations of Louvain theologians before him, had espoused an Augustinian theology, with a pessimistic religious anthropology that was at odds with the more optimistic view of man preferred by the Society and derived from their rereading of Thomas Aquinas.[17] This was a significant difference that lay at the heart of how the early modern mind understood the relationship between God and man, faith and reason, the spiritual and the temporal. Both Augustine and Aquinas agreed that human nature was vitiated by Adam's sin of disobedience. This primordial tragedy had opened up a gulf between creator and creature and posed the question of how the chasm might be bridged. Here the Protestant reformers had stolen a march on the old church. No human effort, they said, could span the rift but only the forgiveness of sin through divine initiative, that is God's gift or grace. This understanding of grace, soundly scriptural and based on Augustine, had many devotees within the old church, who, although they had no intention of abandoning Rome, recognized the authenticity of the Protestant position on grace. The Council of Trent (1545–63) convened to reconcile these differences within the old church and to reaffirm its role as mediator *par excellence* between God and man.[18]

Like Luther and Calvin, the Council fathers admitted the persistence of concupiscence even in the baptized. However, they also rejected Luther's *simul iustus et peccator* and reaffirmed the church's mediating role, particularly through the eucharist and the priesthood. Succeeding generations of pastors and theologians strove to interpret the Tridentine blueprint. To this end, Jansen's most important Louvain precursors, Michael Baius (1513–89) and John Hessels (d. 1566), engaged Protestant reformers in polemical debate. Baius believed that Luther and Calvin had misread scripture and deformed the fathers. An authentic Catholic theology of grace, he held, would be sufficient to bring the reformers back to the Catholic fold. From its vantage point in Rome, the recently founded Inquisition (1542)[19] took a dim view of Baius's activities, which appeared protestantizing. In 1567, Pius V (1566–72), in his bull *Ex omnibus afflictionibus*, censured seventy-nine propositions, which expressed in a general way the doctrinal views of Baius.[20]

Baius was willing to accept papal reprimands, but his devotion to Augustine, his readiness for polemics, and his apparently 'protestant' understanding of grace made him vulnerable to accusations of insubordination and heresy. Over time, Baianism developed into a bogey for those church interests that chafed under the doctrinal authority of Augustine and saw an enhanced teaching and disciplinary role for the papacy as essential to the Catholic renewal. Battle lines, however, were not always clearly drawn. Louvain Augustinians and their Dominican allies were as prepared as their opponents to enlist the Roman magisterium for their own purposes. For their part the Jesuits were divided on their attitude towards Baianism, particularly during the period 1580–1620. However, it remains true that many in the Society did hold that Baius and other Catholic Augustinians, like the Protestant heretics, had overstated the gulf between God and sinful man. They believed that divine grace built on rather than superseded human nature in the process of salvation.

Although this was essentially a difference of emphasis within the broader Catholic tradition, it provoked substantial disagreements. Theologies of grace were at the heart of early modern religious renewal models and to a siginificant degree influenced their practical effectiveness. The religious anthropology of the Jesuits and their allies permitted them to present their pastoral and educational mission in terms of divine grace triggering latent human potential. This proved to be an attractive model for many, particularly as it created the impression of permitting individuals to participate in their own salvation and instilled a sense of personal responsibility. Little wonder that Jesuit educational initiatives and mission activity in Protestant Europe and among non-Christian populations in Asia and the Americas enjoyed success and benefited from the Society's canny self-promotion. The more pessimistic Augustinian anthropology, on the other hand, ascribed the preponderant agency to divine grace, understood as an external, remedial force. In the conversion process, the contrite human subject ceded to intrusive divine grace. From this viewpoint, education and mission activity could appear rather more elitist affairs. This is not to suggest, of course, that Baius and Jansen were any less concerned than the Jesuits to bring the masses into the Catholic fold. However, the success of the Jesuits' devotional models of piety as opposed to the Jansenists' more elitist, and demanding, sacramental models probably caused the latter to become more exclusive, with educational philosophies emphasizing divine election rather than human effort. Augustinians like Baius fretted over the sort of Christian emerging from the Jesuit schools and missions. Furthermore, although the Jesuits were no less concerned about quality of education than their Jansenist opponents, they were rather more successful in producing quantity. It was probably envy as much as ideological differences that caused Jansenists to doubt if church fathers like Augustine would recognize Jesuit-educated Catholics as co-religionists.

Baius's anxieties were shared by many. They resonated strongly with traditional opponents of the Jesuits, like the Dominicans. In 1584, Domingo Bañez OP (1528–1604), a Salamanca professor, published a work which envisaged the human individual as a moral instrument driven by an overwhelming divine impulsion. In response Luis de Molina SJ (1535–1600) published *Liberi arbitrii cum gratiae donis…concordia*.[21] This book crystallized the theological and pastoral tendency called Molinism,[22] which became characteristic of the Jesuits' interpretation of Trent, at least until it was quietly dropped by the Society's Father General, Acquaviva, in 1612–13. Molina attempted to reconcile divine omnipotence with human free will in terms of a carefully defined divine foreknowledge. Although his was by no means a full-blooded defence of human freedom, it presented a theological system where the individual was in a way personally responsible for his salvation.[23] It provided the Jesuits with a tailor-made theological vocabulary with which to defend their educational and pastoral programmes against Augustine-inspired alternatives.

Opposition to Molinism was, among other things, an attack on the Society's privileges and was influenced by its troubled relations with the Spanish Inquisition. The violence of the anti-Jesuit attack probably helped the Society to overcome (at least for a while) its internal divisions, especially those between Belgian and Roman Jesuits (over the Lessius affair) and also between its Spanish heartland and an increasingly Romanized generalate. However, by the 1590s this conflict was no longer a mere question of competing renewal models within early modern Catholicism or the great religious orders. Henceforth it also concerned Catholic orthodoxy's capacity to manage internal dissidence and loyal opposition. It would be no easy matter to reconcile the sometimes inconvenient authority of church fathers, especially St Augustine, with the new pastoral and political needs of the age and with the papacy's attempts to manage a church in turmoil.

The papacy had been struggling to redefine its directive role in the church since the fifteenth-century conciliar crisis. Although the founding of the Inquisition in 1542 expressed an authoritarian and bureaucratic understanding of its task, the Council of Trent harked back to a consensus-seeking understanding of that duty. Faced with the developing crisis over Molinism, Pope Clement VIII (1592–1605) attempted to apply a conciliar-style remedy to the festering grace problem. He summoned the Salamanca controversy to Rome and set up a special mini-council, the *Congregatio de auxiliis*, to examine the issues raised.[24] It edged towards a condemnation of Molina and a stricter definition of the disputed matter along Augustinian lines.[25] However, Clement, who would emerge later as the darling of pro-Jansenist historians, died in 1605, without issuing the condemnation so feared by the Jesuits. Paul V's election gave the embattled Jesuits a crucial breathing space. Sensitive to the pressures now on the Jesuits, vulnerable to Spanish influence, and impatient of the conciliar approach to the problem, he disbanded the Congregation and opted to have the Roman Inquisition manage the question. It would never loosen its grip on this poisoned chalice. Although the Augustinian tendency had had powerful friends in the Inquisition in the late sixteenth century, as the seventeenth century wore on its officers sympathized more and more with the Jesuits and their supporters. In 1611 the Inquisition published a decree forbidding publications on the grace question without papal permission. In 1625 it renewed this order, with the approval of Urban VIII (1633–44). During these crucial years, the Jesuits ingeniously circumvented Roman prohibitions and interpreted continuing pontifical silence on the grace controversy as approval for Molina and the Society's generally laxist position on sacramental practice. Accordingly, their pastoral and educational models were allowed to grow in popularity, particularly in Iberia, the Italian peninsula, France, Bohemia, and the Low Countries.

Augustinians looked askance at Jesuit progress and it was with the intention of critiquing Molinism that Jansen prepared *Augustinus*. The controversy provoked by its appearance might have fizzled out had the local Jesuits remained aloof. However, stung by the book's critical even aggressive tone, particularly in the preface, and anxious to settle old scores with Louvain university, they launched a spirited attack on *Augustinus*.[26] In the following months Jesuit correspondents flooded the Brussels and Cologne nunciatures, the Roman Inquisition, and the Jesuit Father General with denunciations that painted Jansen, his book, and his associates in the lurid colours of schism and heresy.

Jansen's defenders responded in kind. In the crucible of these ill-tempered exchanges Jansenism was forged. At this time, Francesco Albizzi (1593–1684) was assessor of the

Roman Inquisition and its most influential officer.[27] He responded positively to Jesuit lobbying and gave ear to their accusations against Jansen. Because of his legal background, Albizzi tended to abstract *Augustinus* from its theological and historical context and to see it solely in terms of papal authority, understood in a rather authoritarian and bureaucratic way. Given the papacy's increased marginalization from the diplomatic manœuvring to end the Thirty Years War, senior Roman officers like Albizzi were sensitive to doctrinal challenges and more intolerant than usual of internal dissent. Once support for *Augustinus* was reckoned in Rome as disobedience to papal authority, Jansenism assumed a form in the Roman bureaucratic mindset that subsequent real and imagined versions of the phenomenon would fail to dislodge. In these crucial years, the anti-Jansenist lobby proved more adept, partly thanks to Albizzi, in mobilizing papal authority for their purposes.

It was on Albizzi's advice that the susceptible Urban VIII issued the bull *In eminenti* condemning *Augustinus*. It appeared in 1643.[28] To have effect, the bull required registration by ecclesiastical and civil authorities in Flanders, France, and elsewhere. In Louvain, Jansen's supporters successfully persuaded the university to seek clarification of the bull.[29] Rome feared that Jansenism might emerge from its theological cradle in the university to cause trouble in the local church and state.[30] Albizzi intervened decisively, activating sympathetic interests in Flanders. Taking their cue from the assessor, the Flemish and Cologne nuncios, and all but two of the Flemish bishops, they moved against Jansen's supporters. By the mid-1650s they had been hounded into abjuring their objections to the bull and sublimating their dislike of Molinism into a campaign against moral laxism.[31]

The containment of Flemish Jansenism by the Inquisition and the Jesuits was facilitated by the tendency's failure to take root among parish clergy and laity and by its inability to forge durable alliances with legal and political elites. When appropriately solicited by the Inquisition, the Brussels administration easily disarmed potentially troublesome alliances between university Jansenists and the politically disgruntled. It was a different story in France. There the Inquisition's efforts to win authoritarian purchase had been poorly rewarded. For Rome, the Bourbon state proved an unreliable ally in matters of doctrinal and pastoral discipline. In any case, Bourbon authority was itself subject to important constraints, imposed by the great corporate bodies like the parlements, universities, estates, and clerical assemblies. Functioning in tension with one another and the monarchy, they vigorously defended their privileges against encroachments by secular and religious authorities. For elitist religious interest groups like the Jansenists, the inter-corporate stresses that characterized the French baroque state offered useful opportunities, initially for manipulation and later for outright colonization.

The French Catholic religious interest, connected with Jean Duvergier de Hauranne, Abbé de Saint-Cyran (1581–1643), empathized with Jansen's theology. Jansen and Saint-Cyran were old friends, and since his own religious conversion in the early 1620s,[32] Saint-Cyran had developed a personal and pastoral renewal model in the strict

Augustinian tradition. It was the fruit of his years of experience as spiritual director to elite religious communities, like the nuns of the convent of Port-Royal, but was also indebted to Aquinas and to the founder of the French Oratorians, Cardinal Pierre de Bérulle (1575–1629). His activities did not initially attract great public attention in France. However, Saint-Cyran's rigorism concerning reception of the sacraments caused some of the religious under his direction to refrain from receiving holy communion regularly. This set him at loggerheads with the local Jesuits and St Vincent de Paul's Lazarists. It also soured his relations with Richelieu, who preferred laxer penitential practice and, in any case, was anxious for sacramental uniformity, following the Jesuit model.

When *Augustinus* appeared in a French edition in 1641 its reception in Paris helped define Saint-Cyran's position. It blended Flemish doctrinal with French moral/ascetical Augustinianism and associated an influential French religious constituency with the Flemish campaign to keep the book in circulation, thereby linking Saint-Cyran, in Roman eyes, with Flemish Jansenism. He was an old man at this stage but his energetic *protégé*, Antoine Arnauld, took up the defence of *Augustinus* with enthusiasm.

It was Arnauld who gave French Jansenism its distinctive stamp with the publication of *De la fréquente communion* in 1643. This work developed and popularized Saint-Cyran's theories of personal conversion as a coherent model for religious renewal. The book proved attractive to younger clergy in the Sorbonne and raised the hackles of senior staff there, who resented Arnauld's influence. In the parishes, it provided sympathetic clergy and associated lay elites with a reliable guide to a rigorist confessional practice that was unbeholden to the Jesuits. Arnauld's book thereby helped French Jansenism make the transition from its cradle in the universities and aristocratic religious communities to Parisian parishes and beyond. It formed a constituency among the Franciscans. By 1647 it was rumoured that a Jansenist mission was active in Ireland.[33] Three years later attempts to implement Arnauld's pastoral programme were under way in Cour-Cheverny, near Blois, under the direction of the indefatigable John O'Callaghan (1605–54).[34]

Arnauld's supporters were never numerous but they were vocal and well-connected. His popularity alarmed the bishops and set Jesuit networks buzzing. The government was also concerned, particularly as the Frondes were channelling *parlementaire*, noble, and clerical discontent against Mazarin's ministry. Arnauld was no political conspirator but some of Mazarin's enemies, who defended traditional liberties against state encroachment, were among his supporters. The cardinal minister took careful note, biding his time. It was at the height of the *parlementaire* Fronde, in 1649, that the first serious attack was made on Arnauld. With government support, his opponents in the Paris theology faculty isolated five theological propositions, allegedly contained in *Augustinus*, and proposed them for examination for heterodoxy. This was an ingenious move. It associated Arnauld's work with Jansenism, and reduced them both to a convenient set of doctrinal propositions. This reflected general censorial practice in the early modern period as much as ecclesiastical *Realpolitik*. Ostensibly, this flattered the faculty by permitting it to act as doctrinal judge; at the same time it reassured the Inquisition by pressurizing Jansenists with the threat of an eventual appeal to Rome. More fundamentally, however, it permitted the government and its ecclesiastical allies to use adherence to a dogmatic formula as a litmus test not only for spiritual but also for temporal obedience. This focused the debate on the rights of conscience and liberties *vis-à-vis* duties to church and state.

Embattled Jansenists opposed the more in the name of university, ecclesiastical, and personal privileges and sought the support of the parlement and the university administration. They garnered only mediocre support in the faculty of theology, where the religious orders had largely swung in behind the government and its allies. Outside the faculty, political instability had rendered the bishops and most of the clergy wary of dissent. Further, Mazarin's opportunistically ultramontane religious policy was well viewed in Rome. This emboldened one of Arnauld's old enemies Issac Habert (1598–1668), bishop of Vabres, to request Pope Innocent X (1644–55) to condemn the propositions identified by the faculty. Eventually over ninety of his episcopal colleagues signed this petition, with hardly more than a dozen dissenting. From the Roman perspective, the strength of the episcopal majority, coupled with Mazarin's endorsement, proved decisive. Innocent X acquiesced. On 31 May 1653 the bull *Cum occasione* condemned the Five Propositions. This apparent pontifical capitulation to French state and church interests appalled Jansenists and Mazarin's successful campaign to impose the bull in France rekindled their potential for political dissidence. Anti-Jansenist tracts like the Abbé Jean Filleau's *Relation juridique de ce qui s'est passé à Poitiers touchant la nouvelle relation des Jansénists* (1654) capitalized on this and painted the movement as a seditious threat to the state and as a heretical assault on the church.

Propaganda like Filleau's definitively blackened Jansenism's reputation with the Bourbon state and its dependent elites, while *Cum occasione* finished the movement as a viable universal renewal alternative to either Molinism or its avatars. Over time, state and church harassment transformed Jansenism into an increasingly isolated and persecuted minority. In the long term it was Jansenism's greatest tragedy, perhaps, to allow itself to internalize these imposed designations and to pose as suffering 'friends of the truth'.[35] This exacerbated the tendency's elitist character which, when coupled with the intellectual archaism engendered by its devotion to Augustine, increased Jansenists' isolation within the universal church.

Ironically, it was Jansenism's virtual existence as perceived threat to state security and church orthodoxy that enabled it to survive both Mazarin and *Cum occasione*. After 1653 a string of high-profile episodes convinced both state and church that Arnauld's clique was politically and ideologically dangerous. In 1653, for instance, the Jansenist Roger du Plessis, Duke of Liancourt was refused absolution by the curate in Saint Sulpice because he had failed to break off relations with Jansenist Port-Royal.[36] Arnauld came to his defence, deploring arbitrary excommunication and attacking the moral theology and pastoral practice of the Jesuits. Crucially, although he accepted the Pope's right (*droit*) to condemn the Five Propositions, Arnauld refused to comment on the fact (*fait*) of whether or not they were in *Augustinus*. This was a typical early modern interpretative ploy and had been used successfully by the Jesuits in the *De auxiliis* debates.

Much more than intellectual hair-splitting, this distinction was a sharp rebuke to church and state agents who believed that papal authority and government intervention could on occasion override historical fact and impose on conscience. The denial of absolution at Saint Sulpice was interpreted by important clerical and lay interests outside Jansenist networks as unwarranted ecclesiastical interference in the dispensing of a religious entitlement. Accordingly, when the faculty of theology initiated an examination of Arnauld's defence of Liancourt,[37] sixty-four doctors objected.[38] There was an appeal to the parlement to annul the examination, which, although later successfully overturned, was initially accepted. Blaise Pascal's intervention in the affair brought the controversy to a wider public. His first three *Provinciales*, which began to appear in early 1656, were attempts to save Arnauld from condemnation in the Sorbonne; the remainder attacked Jesuit laxism. Their success did provide respite for the Jansenists. However, their enthusiastic reception by the public alerted church authorities and state officials alike to the potency of properly pitched propaganda in transposing troublesome theological quarrels into the political domain. This outward thrust of Jansenism to new readerships was accompanied by a downward flow to a more popular public with the occurrence of the first alleged miracles associated with the tendency.[39]

Arnauld was expelled from the Paris theology faculty in February 1656 but his disappearance did little to assuage fears of Jansenism. Indeed, the movement, having lost its voice in the faculty, was ever more prone to fantastic reimagining by its enemies. The Assembly of the Clergy petitioned the new Pope Alexander VII (1655–67) to clarify the bull *Cum occasione*. He obliged with the bull *Ad sanctam* (1656), which stated that the Five Propositions were in *Augustinus* and that they had been condemned in the sense intended by Jansen. Initially the parlement objected to the bull's registration but a *lit de justice* saw it through in November. A formulary or oath of adherence was attached to ensure maximum inconvenience for Jansenist consciences. Arnauld had no option now but to argue that the Pope was mistaken in saying that the propositions, understood in the condemned sense, were in *Augustinus*. Although this was by no means an attack on papal infallibility, which even the staunchest papal supporter at the time would not stretch to include a papal bull, for most of Arnauld's supporters this defiance was a bridge too far.

State and church harassment of the French Jansenists continued unabated in the late 1650s and early 1660s. In response to reports that Jansenists were using Arnauld's distinction between 'fact' and 'right' to create conscientious wriggle room, Alexander VII published the bull *Regiminis apostolici* (1665), condemning Arnauld's famous dichotomy. A formulary was drawn up to give this decision effect among the French clergy. When it was proffered to the old nuns of Port-Royal, they refused to sign. Their resistance found an echo in the decision of a number of bishops to promulgate the bull subject to a proviso that maintained Arnauld's distinction. This breach in episcopal support for the new bull perturbed the government and triggered calls to discipline the dissenting prelates. In January 1667 the Roman Inquisition condemned the offending ecclesiarchs and prepared disciplinary action. For the majority of French bishops this reeked of Roman authoritarianism and, as Gallican sentiment waxed, support for the beleaguered Jansenist bishops grew. This development alarmed Rome. The new Pope, Clement IX (1667–69), who feared a Gallican schism, was keen on a pacific resolution and Louis XIV, preparing for war, was himself willing to compromise. The recalcitrant bishops were invited to republish the bull and sign an uncontroversial formulary. This arrangement, which forced no retraction and left the quarrel intact, eventually reconciled even the most rigid Jansenists. In early 1669 the so-called 'peace' of Clement IX became fact. More a truce than a settlement, it allowed the sleeping dogs of conscience to lie.

The Second Jansenism

In the ensuing lull, Louis XIV's bad relations with the papacy, especially during the *régale* controversy in the mid-1670s, allowed Arnauld and his entourage to rebuild their reputation in Rome. Accordingly, they focused their literary efforts on refuting Protestantism, sedulously testifying to their horror of schism. This was something of a golden age of Jansenist literary production, which spanned scripture, liturgy, apologetics, pedagogy, and moral teaching. Their attacks on laxism were appreciated in Rome where Innocent XI was enamoured of rigorism. So sterling were Arnauld's services to the papacy during the French *régale* crisis that he was obliged to quit France for the Spanish Netherlands in 1679. There he was joined by Jacques-Joseph Duguet (1649–1733) and Pasquier Quesnel (1634–1719). Under the latter's influence Arnauld's doctrinal positions mellowed into Thomism, particularly with regard to the idea of freedom understood as the capacity to choose between alternatives rather than the mere absence of coercion. This was hardly strict Jansenism in the original Louvain mould and was suggestive of how little, for all the vitriol, really separated the Jansenists from their Molinist enemies.

Quesnel's and Arnauld's intellectual evolution caused disquiet among the newer generation of Jansenists who tended to be ideologically narrower than their predecessors. Dom Gabriel Gerberon (1628–1711), for instance, clove to what he believed to be the stricter theological tradition of the tendency's origins.[40] His nostalgia for the early days, which became characteristic of the third generation of Jansenists, encouraged a spate of Jansenist histories from Serry[41] and others. Quesnel too contributed to this Jansenist reinvention, especially following the deaths of Arnauld and his irenic collaborator, Pierre Nicole (1625–95), in the 1690s.[42] On the other side, fresh generations of anti-Jansenists, like the Jesuit Michel Le Tellier (1643–1719), confessor to Louis XIV, contested these accounts and ensured that the polemical tensions, which were essential to Jansenism and indeed the Gallican church in general, remained taut.

This second Jansenism was, however, much more than a historical controversy. Thanks to the ministrations of certain clergy, it had put down roots in Parisian parishes like Saint-Jacques du Haut-Pas and Saint-Merry. It had also gained adepts in some religious orders like the Benedictines, the Daughters of the Holy Infant, and the Oratorians, especially in their Paris seminary, Saint-Magloire, home to Jacques-Joseph Duguet and

Jean-Baptiste Etemare (1682–1771). Although the numbers of Jansenist clergy remained small, there was sympathy for their brand of confessional rigour, sacramental piety, and doctrinal primitivism among a broader swath of ecclesiastics. These included Louis Antoine de Noailles (1651–1729), who, as bishop of Châlons, had warmly recommended to his clergy Quesnel's *Nouveau Testament en français avec des réflexions morales sur chaque verset* (1671). When Noailles was translated to the French capital in 1695, Paris Jansenists assumed they had a new friend in high places and brazenly republished a work by the well-known Jansenist Martin de Barcos (1600–78). Noailles's Augustinian sympathies did not prevent him condemning the book in 1696, thereby earning the opprobrium of the Jansenists. It was probably from Gerberon's entourage that a 1698 pamphlet originated which pointed out Noailles's apparent inconsistencies. More trouble followed in 1701 when he tacitly supported a Sorbonne decision to approve the granting of absolution to a penitent who had maintained a respectful silence on the question of the 'fact' of Jansen. Rome's disapproval of this decision forced Noailles into a humiliating climbdown that further compromised his standing with the government.

The archbishop's strain of Gallicanism, suspect in Rome and unpopular with the opportunistically ultramontane government, made him enemies on all sides. Events took a serious turn in the early 1700s. Following the accession of Philip of Anjou, grandson of Louis XIV, to the Spanish throne in 1700, Quesnel, who had remained in Spanish Flanders after Arnauld's death, became the object of government harassment. Shortly after his arrest in Brussels in 1703 Quesnel fled custody but his papers, including over 1,000 letters, were confiscated. Following scrupulous examination by the Jesuits, a report on their contents was communicated to the police.[43] Predictably, it revealed the existence of an international Jansenist network of allegedly seditious intent.[44] Louis XIV, whose regime was already wary of Jansenism's primitivist philosophy of history, also recognized in the affair an opportunity to curry favour with Rome. The King requested Clement XI to deliver a new bull to dispel the putative Jansenist threat. The Pope reluctantly acquiesced in 1705 when the bull *Vineam Domini* unambiguously disapproved respectful silence. Initial episcopal and *parlementaire* demurral infuriated the King and perplexed the Pope. Noailles was obliged to demonstrate his loyalty by moving against the aged Jansenist community in Port-Royal. The old nuns' refusal to conform led to their dispersal, the closure of the monastery, and its physical dismantling between 1707 and 1710. Noailles and, behind him, the King, may have been hoping for a propaganda victory, but exactly the opposite occurred. The petty cruelties of the manœuvre achieved martyr status for Port-Royal.

Noailles was now in an impossible position. Torn between his genuine Gallican sympathies, his sense of duty to the church, and his Augustinian proclivities, he fell foul of virtually every ideological constituency in French Gallicanism. His episcopal colleagues were especially opportunistic, using his recommendation of Quesnel's *Reflexions* against him at court and in Rome. The King grew increasingly concerned at the growing divisions among his bishops. He decided to request a bull against Quesnel from Clement XI hoping, in this way, to impose unity on his episcopate by flushing out dissidents and exposing Jansenists. The bull *Unigenitus*, when it was eventually published in 1713, consisted of a condemnation of 101 propositions, moral and theological, allegedly taught by Quesnel. For the King, acceptance of the bull was to be a pure act of obedience but important interests scrupled, leading to a standoff between Louis and key state constituencies, notably the Paris parlement. Under procurators-general such as Guillaume-François Joly de Fleury (1675–1756) and Henri-François d'Aguesseau (1688–1751) it proved especially truculent, positing the possibility that the Pope had erred in a point of doctrine. The bishops were divided, with Noailles petitioning Rome for clarification. Pro-Jansenist works like *Hexaples, ou les six colonnes sur la Constitution Unigenitus* (Amsterdam, 1714) enjoyed a wide circulation and penetrated a reading public beyond the narrowly theological. Royal browbeating eventually produced the reluctant acquiescence of bishops and parlement but the experience revealed that dissidence, far from being the apanage of Jansenists, was endemic in church and state. Piqued by the opposition, Louis XIV contemplated calling a Gallican church council to remove Noailles and condemn opponents of the bull.

The King's death intervened and the regent Philippe of Orléans judged it more prudent to ride the tiger of Jansenist dissent than to muzzle it. In a conciliatory mood he nominated Noailles to head the Conseil de Conscience which dealt with religious affairs. Seconded by the Abbés René Pucelle (1655–1745), Antoine Dorsanne (1664–1728), and (now Chancellor) Henri-François d'Aguesseau, Noailles released imprisoned Jansenists and generally slackened persecution. The regent came to regret his initial indulgence when, in 1717, four bishops appealed officially against *Unigenitus* to a general council of the church. This appeal eventually won the support of only about 3 per cent of the French clergy, including Noailles, but they were an active minority. For them, the Pope had erred in a matter of faith and it was their duty to appeal to a higher authority, in this case, a general council. Rome was infuriated and retaliated by refusing to invest French bishops.

Rome's indignation placed pressure on the regent. As the affair dragged on he employed sterner counter-measures, including the isolation of the most vulnerable of the original four episcopal appellants, Jean Soanen of Senez (1647–1740). This backfired badly, installing another hero in the increasingly crowded Jansenist pantheon. Noailles meanwhile remained ambiguous towards the appeal. His vacillating attitude aroused ferociously divisive loathing among anti-Jansenists. It also permitted the 'jansenization' of up to half of the parish clergy in Paris.[45] It was not until his death in 1729 that the government had the opportunity to move decisively against the appellants. The new archbishop, Charles-Gaspard du Luc Vintimille (1655–1746), obtained a royal declaration proclaiming *Unigenitus* a state law and barring those who refused to accept it from ecclesiastical office. With the support of the Cardinal de Fleury (1653–1743), Louis XV's chief minister, the French bishops blocked Jansenist priests from exercising pastoral ministries. By 1730 hundreds of clergy had been removed and the ban was later extended to educational establishments.

Fleury did manage to drive Jansenists out of parishes, seminaries, and the university, but he was powerless to silence them. From 1728 and in spite of continuous government harassment, the acerbic and often vindictive *Nouvelles ecclésiastiques* published samizdat for an increasingly disgruntled network of dispersed Jansenists.[46] As persecution pushed them from the public sphere and threatened the very survival of the movement, Jansenists became obsessed with the tendency's historical record. Memoirs were drawn up, personal accounts committed to paper, and full-scale histories appeared, particularly after mid-century.[47] This feverish literary activity reconstructed historical Jansenism in the virtual reality of memory. There 'Port-Royal' began to function as a powerful symbol of heroic resistance in the face of unjust oppression. In this form it proved more than a match for the extravagant imaginings of its adversaries and gained admirers far beyond the confines of the church.

'Jansenisms'

This was just as well as, under the pressure of persecution, Jansenism was now suffering some extraordinary mutations. Although in its first and second generations the movement was sober in tone and not given to enthusiastic expression, some influential third-generation members, like Duguet and later Etemare, had more millenarian proclivities. Both were figurists, who believed that the scriptures contained representations or figures for the present and the future, which explained current events and foretold those to come. In particular, they searched the scriptures to discover the meaning of the ongoing controversies over Quesnel and *Unigenitus*. More zealous Jansenists used scriptural passages to justify rejection of royal and ecclesiastical efforts to have the bull accepted and observed. The increasing popularity of figurism accompanied allegedly miraculous phenomena in the late 1720s and early 1730s.[48] A series of extraordinary events occurred at the tomb of the recently deceased Jansenist deacon François de Pâris (1690–1727) in the parish of Saint-Médard. These disturbed both church and state authorities who intervened to prevent access to the city-centre graveyard. Repression pushed these phenomena underground where they acquired more extravagant physical expression in convulsionism.

For Jansenists of the old school, the convulsionists were an embarrassing distraction from the real battle, which was still raging for the soul of the church. Although Fleury's campaign to remove Jansenists from key pastoral and educational positions had been quite successful, a large Jansenist constituency remained, none the less influential for being largely clandestine. Following the cardinal's death in 1743, ecclesiastics like the new archbishop of Paris, Christophe de Beaumont (1703–81), harried the Jansenists ever more provocatively. Failing to draw lessons from the failures of his predecessors, Beaumont unwisely ventured into the sensitive domain of private conscience when he encouraged his clergy to refuse the last rites to Jansenists who failed to produce certificates (*billets de confession*) attesting confession to an authorized priest. As in the 1650s and the 1700s, the denial of the sacraments was seen by many as an exercise in clerical despotism. By the early 1750s, parlement, already in defiant mood over fiscal issues, objected to the certificates on the grounds that the matter was leading to public disorder at funerals. This escalated into a general legal strike when Louis XV refused to accept *parlementaire* remonstrances on the matter and Beaumont continued to demand the *billets*. *Parlementaire* Jansenists were few in number, perhaps no more that fifteen or so out of 200 functioning magistrates. However, they were expert in grafting their own grievances onto *parlementaire* protests. Jansenist magistrates like Claude Mey (1712–96), Gabriel Nicolas Maultrot (1714–1803), and particularly Louis-Adrien Le Paige (1712–1802) not only influenced but actually spoke for their confrères in the language of the *billets* dispute.[49] When the government finally managed to cajole the magistracy back to the bar, parlement was the stronger and more confident for the confrontation. Damiens's attempt on the king's life (1757) furthered strengthened its hand. This encouraged the magistrates, egged on by Le Paige and his colleagues, to treat Jesuit misdemeanours as contrary to inherited Gallican tradition and injurious to the state. The suppression of the Jesuits in France in 1764 was, to an important degree, the symbiotic achievement of *parlementaire* Jansenists and the wider magistracy.[50]

This was, however, something of a pyrrhic victory for the Jansenists. The steel of *parlementaire* contestation entered its soul, giving it a political *élan* that was worlds away from the movement's theological and pastoral origins. Bereft of familiar old enemies like the Jesuits and *Unigenitus*, which was no longer a state law, it found it difficult to forge a new identity that was appropriate to contemporary preoccupations and yet faithful to its historic roots. To some extent, the movement, through its colonization of *parlementaire* grievance, now assumed the role of policing the clergy, as the affair of the condemnation of the *Actes de l'Assemblée du clergé de France* (1765) reveals. In this way, *parlementaire* Jansenism achieved, in a somewhat ersatz form, what its elitist, archaist originators had sought: the opportunity to impose its theology and discipline on the church. This, however, was a secularized Jansenism, virtually indistinguishable from Gallicanism and dependent on *parlementaire* whim.

Chancellor Maupeou's attempted reform of the magistracy in 1771 was vigorously opposed by magistrates of Jansenist hue and seems to have somehow radicalized them. In print they developed a political discourse that was only remotely inspired by the sacraments controversy and increasingly critical of the monarchy's failure to respect the traditional privileges of the various French state corporations.[51] In Le Paige's case, this critique was innocent of seditious intent. He believed that the state's problems could be solved by the more efficient functioning of the existing system. However, his thinking and that of Jansenist colleagues like Noël de Larrière (1738–1802), Henri Jabineau (1724–92), and Gabriel-Nicolas Maultrot gradually developed to embrace the idea of the formal subordination of the church to the state. *Nolens volens*, this set an axe to the very root of the old regime. However intolerant the Bourbon monarchy had been of ecclesiastical independence, it had relied on the church to maintain, with the parlements and other corporations, the institutional tensions which were the life's blood of the old regime. Any slackening of these tensions was potentially fatal to the Bourbon state. This, however, was exactly what *parlementaire* Jansenism was recommending in its demands for church reform. Needless to say this evolution cut it off definitively from its roots in the historical tendency. Critical as they were of the exercise of papal authority, Le Paige's

Jansenist predecessors could never have conceived of the church without its spiritual independence.

In this context, the Civil Constitution of the Clergy (1790), by absorbing the church into the state, marked the demise of both the old regime and Jansenism. By provoking the creation of a political and clerical counter-revolution it also, arguably, compromised the Revolution.[52] Jansenists, whether *parlementaire* or otherwise, were, however, only apparently responsible for this. It was true, of course, that among the clergy who joined the Third Estate in June 1789, there were a few clerics who might be described as 'janséni-sant'. However, the new Constitution was not a Jansenist creation and actually served to split what remained of the tendency. Although Le Paige accepted it and a few clergy of faintly Jansenist hue, like Henri Grégoire (1750–1831), actually served under it, Maultrot demurred and Jabineau launched *Contre-Nouvelles Ecclésiastiques* in opposition.

Small convulsionist groups survived into the nineteenth century and a sprinkling of 'jansénisant' clergy associated with the Constitution and critical of the Concordat, survived until the 1840s. They were but the shadow of their old regime ancestor. More significant, however, was the romantic consecration of Port-Royal as memory and symbol. Grégoire's *Ruines de Port-Royal*, which first appeared in 1801, set the tone. It owed little to the historical record of the Port-Royal community and much to the author's need to find a Jansenist precedent, however forced, for the religious reforms of the Revolution. With the publication of Sainte-Beuve's *Port-Royal* in 1860, the destroyed Jansenist monastery gained a literary and historical form that remained largely intact until the middle of the twentieth century.[53] For Sainte-Beuve, Port-Royal was grand tragedy whose dramatic conclusion came with *Unigenitus*. Generations of scholars followed his lead and it was not until the middle of the last century that Jansenism's eighteenth-century avatars came into scholarly focus. Augustin Gazier's *Histoire générale du mouvement janséniste depuis ses origins jusqu'à nos jours* (1923) despite its partiality, was the key text in this development. Although denominational historiography continued to present Jansenism as, at best, the black sheep of the Catholic family, the phenomenon, from the 1950s, also attracted increasing interest from political and cultural historians and from historians of religion. The meticulous archival work of Jean Orcibal and of Lucien Ceyssens set the precedent for the historiographical, and some of their critics would say doctrinal, normalization of the movement. Gradually Jansenism emerged from partisan ideological ghettos to assume its place as another component, if a rather extraordinary one, of the European Ancien Régime. In the process, the phenomenon lost nothing of its capacity to excite intellectual passions, as recent exchanges over its role in the origins of the French Revolution reveal.[54] Nor have new sources ceased coming to light: research has only begun to feel the impact of the opening to the public of the Roman Inquisition's archives (1999). The exploitation of this documentation will undoubtedly help rebalance research towards the religious origins and ecclesiastical significance of the tendency.

The current revival in the study of Jansenism is not without its challenges, many of which are linked to the present focus on the eighteenth-century and politicized manifestations of the phenomenon. Their description as simply 'jansenist' can create an exaggerated sense of the tendency's agency, particularly with regard to its putative role in the unravelling of the old regime. It can also create a deceptive coherence, not only between the different 'jansenisms' of the mature old regime but also between eighteenth-century varieties in general and their more staid seventeenth-century ancestors. Jansenism and anti-Jansenism were complex, multi-faceted phenomena, which, as historical terms, have always been and remain potent yet difficult heuristic devices. They continue to challenge historians and to intrigue because, both as historical phenomena and as historiographical ideas, they straddle the border between the religious and political worlds of the old regime. Perhaps the recovery of their passionately religious origins will guard against absorbing the religious into the political and ensure an appropriate appreciation of a regime which took these distinctions for granted and moved between the two worlds with unselfconscious ease.

Notes

1. Antoine Arnauld, *Le prétendu ennemi de Dieu et de la foi réfuté par le Sieur de Saint-Victor* (Lille, 1680), 9.
2. Jean-Louis Quantin, 'Avant et après *l'Unigenitus*: Sur les mutations du jansénisme dans la France du xviiie siècle', in Daniel Tollet (ed.), *Le Jansénisme et la Franc-Maçonnerie en Europe centrale aux xviie et xviiie siècles* (Paris, 2002), 172.
3. The adjectival form is quite common in Latin from 1641. See e.g. André Judoci SJ to Adrien Crom SJ, Brussels, 9 July 1641, cited in Lucien Ceyssens, *Sources relatives aux débuts du jansénisme et de l'antijansénisme 1640–1643* (Louvain, 1957), 150; Jérôme Séguin, *Sommaire de la théologie du sieur Arnauld* (n.pl., 1643), 65.
4. The proper noun appears to have originated somewhat later as a French neologism. See Jean Brisacier, *Le jansénisme confondu dans l'avocat du Sr Callaghan* (Paris, 1651).
5. A[rchivio] C[ongregazione] D[ella] F[ede], S[anctum] O[fficium] S[tanza] S[torica], St F1–F7.
6. Emile Appolis, *Entre jansénistes et zelanti: Le 'Tiers Parti' catholique au xviiie siècle* (Paris, 1960); Monique Cottret, *Jansénismes et Lumières: Pour un autre xviiie siècle* (Paris, 1998).
7. The voluminous work of Lucien Ceyssens OFM is essential. For an introduction see his edited *Sources relatives aux débuts du jansénisme et de l'antijansénisme*, and subsequent volumes in the series. See also Léopold Willaert SJ, *Les Origines du jansénisme dans les Pays-Bas catholiques*, i. *Le Milieu: Le Jansénisme avant la lettre* (Bruxelles, 1948); Jean Orcibal, *Jansénius d'Ypres (1585–1638)* (Paris, 1989); and Mathijs Lamberigts (ed.), *L'Augustinisme à Louvain* (Louvain, 1994).
8. For France, the best single-volume introduction is still Louis Cognet, *Le Jansénisme* (Paris, 1961).
9. Thomas O'Connor, *Irish Jansenists: Politics and Religion in Flanders, France, Ireland and Rome* (Dublin, 2008).
10. Ruth Clarke, *Strangers and Sojourners at Port Royal* (Cambridge, 1932).
11. María Giovanna Tomsich, *El jansenismo en España: Estudio sobre ideas religiosas en la segunda mitad del siglo XVIII* (Madrid, 1972); Joël Saugnieux, *Jansénisme espagnol du xviiie siècle: Ses composantes et ses sources* (Ovideo, 1975).
12. Pietro Stella, *Il Giansenismo in Italia* (3 vols. Rome, 2006).

13. Wilhelm Deinhardt, *Der Jansenismus in Deutschen Landen: Ein Beitrag zur Kirchengeschichte des 18. Jahrhunderts* (Munich, 1929); Daniel Tollet (ed.), *Le Jansénisme et la franc-maçonnerie en Europe centrale aux xviie et xviiie siècles* (Paris, 2002).
14. Elisa Luque Alcaide, 'Debates doctrinales en el IV Concilio Provincial Mexicano (1771)', *Historia Mexicana*, 55 (2005), 5–66.
15. Orcibal, *Jansénius d'Ypres*.
16. Cognet, *Le Jansénisme*, 33–4.
17. Jean Orcibal, 'Qu'est-ce que le Jansénisme?', in *Études d'histoire et de littérature religieuse, xvie–xviie siècles* (Paris, 1997), 291–2. This article was originally publ. in 1953.
18. Adriano Prosperi, *Tribunali della coscienza: Inquisitori, confessori, missionari* (Turin, 1996), 117–34; Alain Tallon *Le Concile de Trente* (Paris, 2000), 47.
19. Andrea del Col, *L'Inquisizione in Italia dal XII al XXI secolo* (Milan, 2006), 257–341.
20. See Bruno Neveu, *Érudition et religion aux xviie et xviiie siècles* (Paris, 1994), 413ff.
21. (Lisbon, 1588).
22. Henri De Lubac, *Surnaturel: Études historiques* (2nd edn., Paris, 1991), 146.
23. Catherine Maire, *De la cause de Dieu à la cause de la nation* (Paris, 1998), 20.
24. The best account of the Congregation, from a Jansenist perspective, is F. Jacobus Hyacinthus Serry (Le Blanc), *Historia congregationum de auxiliis divinae gratiae sub summis pontificibus Clemente VIII et Paulo V libri quatuor* (Louvain, 1700). The work was violently criticized. See Liévin de Meyer SJ, *Historiae Controversiae...* (Venice, 1756).
25. Cognet, *Le Jansénisme*, 15.
26. Ceyssens, *Sources relatives aux débuts du jansénisme et de l'antijansénisme*, pp. xxix–xxxi.
27. Lucien Ceyssens, *Le Cardinal François Albizzi 1593–1684* (Rome, 1977), 96.
28. Lucien Ceyssens, *La Première Bulle contre Jansénius: Sources relatives à son histoire* (2 vols. Brussels, 1961–2).
29. Lucien Ceyssens (ed.), 'Verslag over de eerste jansenistisch deputatie van Leuven te Rome 1643–46', *Bulletin de l'Institut Historique Belge de Rome* (Brussels, 1942–3), 31–111.
30. ACDF, SO, SS, St St F1b, ff 741–3.
31. Franziskus Deininger, *Johannes Sinnich: Der Kampf der Löwener Universität gegen den Laxismus* (Düsseldorf, 1928).
32. Jean Orcibal, *Jean Duvergier de Hauranne, abbé de Saint-Cyran et son temps (1581–1643)* (Louvain and Paris, 1947), 212–48.
33. René Rapin, *Mémoires* (3 vols. Paris, 1865), i. 410–11; Clarke, *Strangers and Sojourners at Port-Royal*, 188.
34. O'Connor, *Irish Jansenists 1600–70*, 196–217.
35. Peter Campbell, *Power and Politics in Old Regime France 1720–45* (Cambridge, 1996), 196.
36. See Jacques M. Gres-Gayer, *Le Jansénisme en Sorbonne 1643–1656* (Paris, 1996), 140, 142, 144.
37. For the theological background see Jacques M. Gres-Gayer, *En Sorbonne, autour des Provinciales: Édition critique des Mémoires de Beaubrun (1655–1656)* (Paris, 1997), 1–38.
38. Gres-Gayer, *Le Jansénisme en Sorbonne*, 148.
39. Jean-Louis Quantin, 'La Vérité rendue sensible: Port-Royal entre l'histoire et le miracle, de l'*Augustinus* à la *Perpétuité*', in *Chroniques de Port-Royal*, 46 (1997), 119–36; B. Robert Kreiser, *Miracles, Convulsions and Ecclesiastical Politics in Early Eighteenth-Century Paris* (Princeton, 1978).
40. Dom Gabriel Gerberon, *Histoire générale du Jansénisme* (3 vols. Amsterdam, 1700).
41. Pasquier Quesnel, *Histoire abrégée de la vie et des ouvrages de Mons. Arnauld* (Cologne, 1697); Serry, *Historia congregationum de auxiliis divinae gratiae*; Maire, *De la cause de Dieu*, 40–1.

42. See his *Justification de M. Antoine Arnauld contre la censure d'une partie de la faculté de théologie de Paris* (Liège, 1702).
43. Michel, *Jansénisme et Paris*, 194–5.
44. H. J. Susteren, *Causa Quesnelliana sive Motivum Juris* (Brussels, 1704).
45. Michel, *Jansénisme et Paris*, 249–94.
46. René Taveneaux, *La Vie quotidienne des Jansénistes* (Paris, 1973), 227–47.
47. Claude-Pierre Goujet, *Mémoires pour servir à l'histoire de Port-Royal* (3 vols. n.pl., 1734); Dom Charles Clemencet, *Histoire générale de Port-Royal* (10 vols. Amsterdam, 1755–7); René Cerveau, *Nécrologie des plus célèbres défenseurs et confesseurs de la vérité* (n.pl., 1760–78).
48. Catherine-Laurence Maire, *Les Convulsionnaires de Saint-Médard: Miracles, convulsions et prophéties à Paris au xviiie siècle* (Paris, 1985). A more recent but uneven account of the phenomenon can be found in Brian E. Strayer, *Suffering Saints: Jansenists and Convulsionnaires in France, 1640–1799* (Brighton, 2008), 206–90.
49. See his *Lettres historiques sur les fonctions essentielles du Parlement, sur le droit des pairs et sur les lois fondamentales du Royaume* (Amsterdam, 1753–4).
50. Dale Van Kley, 'Jansenism and the International Suppression of the Jesuits', in Stewart J. Brown and Timothy Tackett (eds.), *The Cambridge History of Christianity*, vii. *Enlightenment, Reawakening, Revolution, 1660–1815* (Cambridge, 2006), 302–28.
51. Le Paige, *Requête des Etats Généraux* (1772).
52. Dale Van Kley, *The Religious Origins of the French Revolution: From Calvin to the Civil Constitution, 1560–1791* (New Haven, Conn., 1996), 362.
53. Charles-Augustin Sainte-Beuve, *Port-Royal* (5 vols. Paris, 1860).
54. Dale Van Kley, 'The Rejuvenation and Rejection of Jansenism in History and Historiography: Recent Literature on Eighteenth-Century Jansenism in French', *French Historical Studies*, 29 (Fall, 2006), 649–84.

Bibliography

Appolis, Emile, *Entre jansénistes et zelanti: Le 'Tiers Parti' catholique au xviiie siècle* (Paris, 1960).

Ceyssens, Lucien, 'Que penser finalement de l'histoire du jansénisme et de l'antijansénisme?', *Revue d'Histoire Ecclésiastique*, 88 (1993), 108–30.

Clarke, Ruth, *Strangers and Sojourners at Port Royal* (Cambridge, 1932).

Cognet, Louis, *Le Jansénisme* (Paris, 1961).

Doyle, William, *Jansenism: Catholic Resistance to Authority from the Reformation to the French Revolution* (London, 2000).

Gres-Gayer, Jacques, *Le Jansénisme en Sorbonne* (Paris, 1996).

Kreiser, B. Robert, *Miracles, Convulsions, and Ecclesiastical Politics in Early Eighteenth-Century Paris* (Princeton, 1978).

Maire, Catherine, *De la cause de Dieu à la cause de la Nation: Le Jansénisme aux xviiie siècle* (Paris, 1998).

O'Connor, Thomas, *Irish Jansenists: Politics and Religion in Flanders, France, Ireland and Rome* (Dublin, 2008).

Orcibal, Jean, *Jansénius d'Ypres (1585–1638)* (Paris, 1989).

Stella, Pietro, *Il Giansenismo in Italia* (3 vols. Rome, 2006).

Taveneaux, René, *Le Jansénisme en Lorraine, 1640–1789* (Paris, 1960).
Van Bavel, J., and Schrama, M. (eds.), *Jansénius et le Jansénisme dans les Pays-Bas: Mélanges Lucien Ceyssens* (Leuven, 1982).
Van Kley, Dale, *The Religious Origins of the French Revolution: From Calvin to the Civil Constitution, 1560–1791* (New Haven, Conn., 1996).
Willaert, Léopold, *Les Origines du jansénisme dans les Pays-Bas catholiques*, i. *Le Milieu: Le Jansénisme avant la lettre* (Bruxelles, 1948).

CHAPTER 20

DISSENT AND TOLERATION

MARISA LINTON

Religious toleration was one of the most controversial subjects of this period.[1] By the seventeenth century there were relatively few non-Christians in Europe. The largest communities of non-Christians were Jews and gypsies, both of whom suffered periodic persecution. But most of the debate around toleration was waged between Christians—Catholic and Protestant. Religion was the social cement that held society together. For that cement to do its work Christian theologians of whatever denomination argued that it had to be all of the same kind, and linked indissolubly to the monarch, who was seen as God's representative on earth. There were two principal sets of arguments for the necessity of religious uniformity. The first was about belief, and the conviction that one's own religion was the 'true religion', and that any other religion was heretical and could not lead to salvation. It therefore was the duty of the devout to stamp out heresy, a task said to be justified by the phrase in the gospel of St Luke *compelle intrare* (compel them to come in). The second set of arguments was political, and revolved around the idea that uniformity was needed to prevent social unrest and even civil war. This was a very real fear. The Reformation had led to a traumatic period of upheaval, and to religious wars, particularly in France, the German states, and the northern territories of the Holy Roman Empire.

The Peace of Augsburg in 1555 was a treaty between the Holy Roman Emperor Charles V, and those German princes who had adopted the Lutheran faith. It acknowledged the right to existence of Lutherans, and thus gave a legal status to the Reformation in the German states. Each prince would determine the religion of his people. This was expressed as the principle of *cuius regio, eius religio* (the lord of the realm determines the religion of his realm). But no provision was made for Calvinism, which had only recently come into existence, and the situation of Lutherans remained problematic. Renewed war broke out in 1618. This was the Thirty Years War: its causes were complex, but religious conflict between Catholics and Protestants was a major factor. The Thirty Years War was finally brought to an end by the Peace of Westphalia in 1648. The Peace emphasized the growing importance of the sovereign state. It included amongst its provisions the recognition of the legitimacy of Calvinism. It was a pragmatic measure which helped to prevent a renewal of the religious wars, and brought about a decline in the persecution of religious minorities. There were limitations to the settlement that it wrought, however, and it had less effect beyond the boundaries of the Holy Roman Empire.

Religious differences continued to generate tension throughout the seventeenth and eighteenth centuries.[2] The spectre of the Reformation and the religious wars of the sixteenth century continued to haunt the Catholic Church. As one historian puts it, the memory of that traumatic period provided 'a graphic illustration of how religious heresy led to political upheaval, of how dissent from the one true faith could unravel into the tangled web of internecine conflict and bloody civil war'.[3] Religious identity was linked closely with political loyalty to a sovereign or state. State authorities showed little acceptance of the idea that a king's subjects might have liberty of conscience and yet still be loyal citizens of the state. Though the incidence of burning heretics at the stake became a rare occurrence even in the countries where the Inquisition operated, and outright persecution diminished during the eighteenth century, people who belonged to religious minorities continued to be heavily discriminated against in most countries, and were confronted by problems regarding both their right to worship and their legal existence.

France: Huguenots and Jansenists

The purpose of the Edict of Nantes of 1598 which granted toleration to the Huguenots (French Calvinists) was to bring about an end to the wars of religion that had torn France apart. At that time the Huguenots constituted a well-armed fighting force. Even so the Edict gave only limited toleration: the right to worship for Huguenots was confined to specific towns and noble estates where their communities already existed. It was a pragmatic measure, designed as a way of ensuring peace rather than as an acknowledgement of the moral right of a religious minority to coexist in France. Over time the Catholic authorities made it increasingly difficult for the Huguenots to practise the religious liberty which they enjoyed in theory.[4] Eventually this theoretical liberty ceased altogether with the Revocation of the Edict of Nantes in 1685 (set out in the Edict of Fontainebleau). Louis XIV's decision to withdraw toleration for the Huguenots was partly motivated by his religious convictions, but his primary reasons were political. The Huguenots constituted a sizeable minority, and it was feared that they constituted a threat to the political and social stability of France—that they were an 'enemy within'. It was said that the French Protestants had republican tendencies and were anti-monarchical.[5] Thus the Duke de Saint-Simon claimed that the Calvinist community after the Edict of Nantes had established 'a separate, well organised republican government... in a word, a state within a state'.[6] In the sixteenth century both the authorities and ordinary Catholic communities who lived alongside Huguenots had feared that the Huguenots were plotting conspiracies against them. Such fears persisted long after the Huguenots had ceased to pose a military threat.[7] These characterizations of Protestants as the 'enemy within' were not borne out by events: few Protestants had taken part in the Fronde rebellion (1648–53), and studies reveal peaceful coexistence between Protestants and Catholics.[8] Ironically, it was the Revocation of the Edict of Nantes that fuelled the resistance of many Protestants, and alienated them from the Catholic state. Also, in the period leading up to the Edict, the implementation of the infamous *dragonnades* (enforced conversions by dragoons) to force Protestants to give up their faith inspired terror in the Huguenots and caused outrage in Protestant states abroad. The *dragonnades* contributed to the Protestant image of Louis XIV as a tyrant.

The Edict ordered that Huguenots be prohibited from practising their faith, and that their churches should be closed. Their children were ordered to be baptized as Catholics. Huguenot ministers were banished, and those who stayed risked being sent to the galleys. The Catholic state denied that Protestants still existed in France, and instead called them *nouveaux convertis* (new Catholic converts); a fiction which meant that they were denied separate legal status and were entirely subject to Catholic courts.

In 1724 a 'Declaration concerning religion' was issued which codified and tightened the legislation against the Huguenots. It stated that Catholicism was the only religion existing in France. Protestant clergy who preached the faith could be liable to execution. People who attended Protestant services could be sent to the galleys, perpetually imprisoned, and even executed. Protestants were not allowed to hold public office. Their children must be baptized within twenty-four hours of their birth by a Catholic priest. Many Protestants were forcibly taken to houses of conversion run by the Catholic clergy. Exclusion from the sacraments of the Catholic Church meant exclusion from civil identity. Marriages conducted by Protestant clergy were not accepted in French law, and constituted a felony. This meant that children of such marriages were legally designated as illegitimate and could lose their rights to inherit their parents' property.

Although these measures were designed to ensure religious conformity, and to put an end to the perceived menace of a religious minority, its effects backfired on the French authorities. Many Huguenots went into voluntary exile: approximately half a million left France between 1685 and 1760, and fled to different parts of Europe, and even to Russia and America. A second consequence was the outbreak of the revolt of the Camisards against Louis XIV in the isolated and mountainous Cévennes region in the south. The worst of the fighting here took place between 1702 and 1704. Brutal measures taken against the Protestants of this region—including the *dragonnades*—led to them taking up arms. For the most part the revolt of the Camisards was a peasant movement; many of their clergy had been lost to them through Catholic persecution. The leaders of the revolt, known as 'the prophets' were inspired by millenarian beliefs. Most of the Protestant nobles tried to keep out of the Camisard war, and had scant sympathy for the violence and prophesying of the peasants. Nonetheless, the government held Protestant nobles to be responsible and thought that they were secretly conspiring to lead the revolt. A number lost their lands, and even their lives, as a consequence.[9]

Another religious minority group that suffered severe hardships in France in the eighteenth century was that of the Jansenists. This movement of Catholic reform was regarded as just as threatening to church and state as Protestantism, and consequently was persecuted. That very persecution provoked a response that raised theological and civil issues that proved dangerous for the monarchy. Jansenism was an austere and puritanical movement within Catholicism. It began in the early seventeenth century and rapidly became established in France. The tenets of Jansenism recalled in some ways those of Calvinism; but the Jansenists remained fiercely Catholic, and wanted to reform the Catholic Church from within, rather than leave the church as the Protestants had done. Indeed, during the seventeenth century Jansenists were generally hostile to the Calvinists (from whom they wanted to distinguish themselves) and spoke out in support of the Revocation of the Edict of Nantes. This situation changed, however, when in 1713 the Pope issued the bull *Unigenitus,* condemning a series of doctrines called Jansenistic as heretical. Henceforth those who persisted in these beliefs risked exclusion from the sacraments of the Catholic Church, and thus from civil existence.

Some Jansenists chose to resist the acceptance of *Unigenitus* as a law of the state in the principal law courts, the parlements. They formed what became increasingly known as a *parti janséniste*, articulating the case for their religious and civil rights through legal challenges. In organized pamphlet campaigns they appealed to public opinion, using arguments that were couched in a new kind of language, one based on notions of citizenship and civic rights.[10] They claimed that members of religious minorities could also be virtuous citizens.[11] Dale Van Kley, the historian who has done more than anyone else to bring about a reassessment of the political importance of Jansenist protest in the years leading up to the French Revolution,[12] has demonstrated how Jansenists contributed to the development of political ideas that helped to prepare the ground for the French Revolution, by deploying a political language and terms of debate that helped to conceptualize and justify the idea of civic rights.[13]

England

Seen from France, England seemed like a land of toleration. That was the view put forward by Voltaire, who admired the plurality of religious faiths there: 'This is the country of sects. An Englishman, as a free man, goes to Heaven by whatever road he pleases...If there were only one religion in England, there would be danger of tyranny; if there were two, they would cut each other's throats; but there are thirty, and they live happily together in peace.'[14] Voltaire put forward this exaggerated vision of English tolerance, partly as a way of challenging the official lack of toleration in France, but seen from across the Channel the reality looked rather different.

The situation of religious minorities in England had a long and complex history. Since the Reformation Catholics had been the group most feared and the most discriminated against, largely because it was thought that their loyalty was to a foreign power—to Rome. As a consequence of large-scale repression Catholics constituted rather less than 1 per cent of the population in the seventeenth century.[15] The English Civil War took place against a backdrop of renewed religious fervour and antagonism:

John Morrill refers to it with some justice as, 'England's war of religion'.[16] New Protestant sects came into being and, despite some restrictions, flourished during the brief period of the English Republic. Cromwell himself was reasonably open to religious minorities (excepting Catholics) and in 1655 readmitted Jews to England. The justification for this was millenarian: the conversion of the Jews would fulfil biblical prophecy, and signal the second coming of Christ. Following the restoration of the Stuart monarchy in 1660, 'Dissenters' was a term used to describe those Protestants (including Baptists, Presbyterians, and Quakers) who refused to accept the reinstatement of episcopacy and the Church of England prayer book. The Test and Corporation Acts of 1673 and 1678 required anyone who wanted to take public office, either civil or military, to take an oath of allegiance and supremacy. They were also obliged to deny any belief in transubstantiation, and to receive the sacrament according to the forms of the Anglican Church. By these means Dissenters and Catholics were excluded from public office.

When William III came to the throne in 1688 he was heralded as the great champion of toleration. Most historians of the period see this as an exaggeration. John Miller argues that toleration in England came about 'almost by accident...as the result of a sordid behind-the-scenes political deal' to shore up the power of the Anglican Church.[17] The Anglican establishment needed the support of the Dissenters to outmanoeuvre James II's attempts to secure toleration for Catholics. The Toleration Act of 1689 was limited in scope. It was designed specifically for Protestant Dissenters. It excluded Catholics, Jews, and Unitarians. (Catholics did not obtain the right to public worship until 1791, when the threat posed to Christianity by the French Revolution encouraged greater acceptance of other Christian groups.[18]) Even Protestant Dissent was not officially legalized by the Toleration Act. According to the provisions of the Act, Dissenters who took the oaths of supremacy and allegiance and made a formal declaration against transubstantiation would not face penalties for refusing to attend services within the Church of England; but the penal laws against Dissent remained on the statute book. Dissenters could serve as ministers or teachers, and they had their own places of worship, though these had to be licensed and the doors kept unlocked during meetings.

Toleration in England may have been inspired by pragmatic politics rather than liberal philosophy but its effect was to make persecution for the most part a thing of the past—except sporadically for Catholics. In practice there was more toleration in England than was provided for by the strict letter of the law. The jury system encouraged greater toleration of dissidence and freedom of speech. Another factor was the relative freedom of the English press. The lapse of the Licensing Act in 1695 meant an effective end to pre-publication censorship, though the Blasphemy Act of 1697 remained in force and was occasionally used, for example, in the case of Thomas Woolston.[19] Whilst the Toleration Act gave religious toleration to Protestant Dissenters in practice, they were still excluded from public office. The Test and Corporation Acts remained in force. Dissenters continued to campaign for their civil rights, and Dissent remained officially a crime until the Mansfield verdict of 1767.[20] Some Dissenters did get around the Test Act by 'occasional conformity', that is, by carrying out the minimum requirement of church attendance and communion in order to qualify themselves for office. From 1727 the terms of the first Test Act were made less harsh, but it remained law until 1828. Only then were Catholics and Dissenters able to obtain public office.

The Toleration Act was thus a practical measure, based largely on political expediency. But England also provided some of the major theorists of religious toleration. Amongst these, one of the most significant and certainly most influential figures was John Locke. His wrote his *Letters on Toleration* whilst in exile in the Dutch Republic, though it was not published until after his return to England in 1689, and therefore followed the 'Glorious Revolution' that brought William III to England. Locke's approach to religious toleration was pragmatic, intellectually coherent, and closely related to his ideas about the proper functioning of society and politics. He argued that religious belief was outside the sphere of the civil magistrate. It was the role of the magistrate to ensure the peace and stability of society. Intervention in the religious faith of individuals was only acceptable where they constituted a threat to society. He denied that Dissenters constituted any such threat. Locke's toleration had its limits, but his reasons for withholding toleration were less about theology than politics. Thus, he argued against the toleration of Catholics, on the grounds that their first loyalty was to a foreign power, the Pope. Nor did he accept that atheists should be tolerated, regarding that their rejection of divine authority made them morally and socially subversive, and their oaths of loyalty to the state could not be trusted.[21]

Locke still held to some form of revelation as a basis for his faith. But the English deists went further. Their leading writers were John Toland, author of *Christianity not Mysterious* (1696), and Matthew Tindal, who wrote *Christianity as Old as the Creation* (1730). They took a comparative approach to their study of religion, arguing that there was a common core of truth to all religions, of which the main features were love of God and love of one's fellows. These constituted the basis of natural religion, and were fundamental truths. These core truths were revealed through nature. Everything else, from dogmas to sacred texts, from the priesthood and liturgy to sacred rituals, was contingent and therefore inessential. Toland was also the author of a still more radical text; this was his *Reasons for Naturalising the Jews in Great Britain and Ireland*, published in 1714. He is credited with being the first writer to coin the phrase 'the emancipation of the Jews'.[22] He took the radical position that Jews should have unconditional rights.[23] His arguments were based not only on utility (toleration for Jews would be economically advantageous) but also on morality. He said: 'My Purpose at present then, is to prove that the *Jews* are so far from being an Excrescence or Spunge (as some wou'd have it) and a useless member in the Commonwealth, or being ill subjects, and a dangerous people on any account, that they are as obedient, peaceable, useful, and advantageous as any; and even more so than many others', adding that the Jews had 'infinitely more charity than the bulk of *Christians*'.[24] Toland was one of very few people before the French Revolution who argued that Jews should be treated as equal citizens, without any conditions. Most of those who wanted toleration for Jews thought in terms of 'assimilation'—that is, that Jews should live more like Christians, with a view to ultimately becoming Christian.

FRANCE: THE *PHILOSOPHES*

Within France the battle for toleration was not led only by Huguenots and Jansenists: opposition to Catholic autocracy also emerged from quite a different direction—that of the *philosophes*. The *philosophes* were moved by quite different concerns than those of religious minorities. Whereas Huguenots and Jansenists wanted the right to worship freely, the *philosophes* were motivated by their belief in liberty of conscience as a natural right. They were also for the most part profoundly anticlerical, and opposed the power of the Catholic Church over many aspects of people's lives. The most famous case in which the *philosophes* became involved was that of the Calas Affair. In 1762 a Protestant merchant, Jean Calas, was tortured and executed by order of the Parlement of Toulouse for the alleged murder of his son, who had converted to Catholicism. Voltaire became convinced that Calas was innocent, and that he had received an unfair trial due to his religion.[25] Voltaire's *Traité sur la tolérance* (1763) took up the challenge of Calas's case and blazoned the injustice of it across Europe. Voltaire went further than the particular facts in Calas's case to make a passionate and articulate defence of the principles of religious toleration. Here he was bringing the case for toleration to a new moral authority—that of public opinion.[26] He said that Calas had been denied civic rights—rights which Voltaire said were due to Calas as a citizen, regardless of his religious beliefs. Stripped of these rights, Calas had 'no defence but his virtue'.[27] Natural law, according to Voltaire, should be the basis of human law: 'All over the earth the great principle of both is: Do not unto others what you would that they do not unto you. Now, in virtue of this principle, one man cannot say to another: "Believe what I believe, and what thou canst not believe, or thou shalt perish".' The supposed right of intolerance, he said, was 'the right of the tiger; nay, it is far worse, for tigers do but tear in order to have food, while we rend each other for paragraphs'.[28]

Ironically the Calas Affair was something of an anomaly. From the 1750s onwards the actual position of Protestants in France had been easing; though they were still officially not tolerated, authorities were increasingly turning a blind eye to Protestant practice. In regions where the Protestants were numerous (primarily in the south, in Dauphiné, Poitou, Provence, and Languedoc) they openly held services (in the open air rather than in churches) without hindrance by the authorities. Even so, the last Protestants sentenced to the galleys were not freed until 1775.[29]

The traditional view of the *philosophes* is of fearless campaigners for religious and civil freedoms.[30] But their primary motive was hostility to the Catholic Church and its institutionalized power over people's lives. This did not incline them to sympathize with other religious beliefs. It was not easy for devout believers of whatever religion to make common cause with *philosophes* who were sceptical about the value of any organized religion—or even of religion at all. Nor were the Enlightenment thinkers the only reason for the greater tolerance of the eighteenth century. According to R. R. Palmer's classic work of 1939, *Catholics and Unbelievers in Eighteenth-Century France*, the chief reason why the eighteenth century was more tolerant was that the church itself was of less importance. There were two reasons for this: first, the growth of the state meant that secular authorities were taking over some of the functions which previously had been the province of the church. The second reason was the growth in acceptance of the scientific revolution; a sense that the world was knowable and understandable outside the explanatory framework of revealed religion. This did not make people into atheists in most cases, but it made the consolations and explanatory systems of the church less central. By the middle of the eighteenth century most educated people accepted Newton's universe.[31] Palmer showed that the Enlightenment philosophers were far from enjoying a monopoly on concepts we would think of as 'modern', such as toleration. A considerable number of the clergy in eighteenth-century France were humane, educated, and thoughtful men, who endorsed toleration within certain limits; whilst the *philosophes* themselves were sometimes lacking in toleration towards their own opponents. Voltaire, for example, routinely used ridicule and vituperative comments as weapons against those who disagreed with his views. There is much to support Palmer's argument that some sections of the Catholic clergy valued tolerance, but it is helpful to read Palmer in common with a more recent work, McMahon's *Enemies of the Enlightenment,* which reminds us that the reverse was also often true. McMahon examines what is known as the 'counter-Enlightenment' and demonstrates the strength of opposition maintained amongst many Catholics to new ideas, including toleration.[32]

THE DUTCH REPUBLIC

The Dutch Republic was home to some of the leading theorists of religious toleration in the later seventeenth century. A key figure in the early debates was Pierre Bayle. He was by birth a Protestant from the south of France who, anticipating the Revocation of the Edict of Nantes, kept his religious faith, but left France and moved to Rotterdam. In 1686, in reaction to the Revocation, he wrote a *Philosophical Commentary on the Words, 'Compel Them to Come In'.* In this work he argued that to compel people to adopt a faith they did not believe was both immoral and irrational.[33] In his *Dictionnaire historique et critique* (1697) he argued for the possibility of a society of virtuous atheists, which implied that morality could exist outside organized religious belief. Nonetheless, Bayle remained a Calvinist, arguing that reason was not enough, it was necessary to have faith. He sought to distance himself from a more radical figure—the materialist philosopher Spinoza. Spinoza was part of a community of Jews of Portuguese extraction, who had settled in Amsterdam. He lapsed from his faith, and was rejected by his community, who considered his ideas to be unacceptable. He went further down the path of scepticism than almost all of his contemporaries. According to Justin Champion, Spinoza's writings were consciously based on philosophy rather than religion, and expressed 'a republican civic agenda' based on the 'defence of a freedom to think rather than a right to worship'.[34] The implication of Spinoza's theory was that rational philosophy was sufficient in itself: there was no need for any religious belief. It was a deeply controversial, but revolutionary, idea that was to influence certain Enlightenment thinkers, such as the English deists.[35]

Ironically, the fairly tolerant regime that had been established early on in the Dutch Republic, together with the existence of thriving community of Enlightenment theorists there, caused something of a reaction against toleration in the later years of the eighteenth century. Dutch Calvinists were particularly alarmed by the circulation of ideas about 'freethinking'.[36] From the 1760s onwards there were bitter debates between pro- and anti-Enlightenment groups. It took the Batavian Revolution to fully separate church and state in the Republic and achieve widespread toleration through legislation in 1796.[37]

The Habsburg Empire

The religious situation in the Holy Roman Empire was complex, as it included within its confines so many different peoples, many of whom were members of religious minorities. The Peace of Westphalia had brought the wars of religion to an end. But it was seen as a temporary measure: a sticking plaster over the wounds of the Thirty Years War. As Joachim Whaley states, 'the Peace of Westphalia was not intended to promote toleration in any straightforward sense but rather ensure that peace would prevail until the divided Christian Churches were re-united'.[38] In the years that followed, the Habsburgs made strenuous efforts to reinforce Catholic uniformity in all those lands where they were able to exert direct control. Maria Theresia, who came to the Austrian throne in 1740, had a reputation as being much more of a reformer than her predecessors. Her reign is seen as launching a period of 'Enlightened Absolutism' in the Empire. But in matters of religion she was a staunch defender of the Catholic faith. She wrote to her son, Joseph, to advise him not to read the works of the French philosophes because of their opposition to Catholic beliefs. She deported thousands of her Bohemian Protestant subjects. She was particularly hostile towards the many Jews in Vienna. Her Patent for the Jews of 1764 was very restrictive. Such toleration as they had was based on their economic contribution—they were obliged to pay an annual tax of toleration (the *Toleranzgeld*). But after her death the Habsburg Empire went through some extraordinary changes of policy regarding religious minorities within its boundaries. Her son Joseph II introduced a Patent of Toleration (1781), followed by another the following year. Together they provided a radical reconfiguration of the position of religious minorities in the Habsburg Empire. They gave toleration to the three most important religious minorities: Protestants, Greek Orthodox Christians, and Jews (and even Unitarians—though not atheists and deists). There were limits to this toleration, particularly for the Jews; those in Vienna labouring under fewer restrictions than those in Bohemia, Hungary, and Galicia. Joseph's intention regarding the Jews was that of 'assimilation' rather than 'toleration'.[39] In instituting these changes

Joseph was not motivated solely —or even chiefly—by Enlightenment ideals. He was persuaded that toleration would bring economic and trade benefits. It would also have strategic political benefits: by ending religious unrest it would help to unify the Empire and thus make it a greater power. To his great disappointment, Joseph's policy of toleration may have appeased religious minorities in the Empire, but it antagonized many of his devout Catholic subjects who reacted with suspicion and outrage. Joseph's successor, his brother Leopold II, who reigned from 1790 to 1792, was a more moderate man, who by acting more circumspectly, managed to preserve most of Joseph's religious reforms. But when Leopold was succeeded in turn by the less intellectually able, and more reactionary, Francis II, the situation had been radically changed by the progress of the French Revolution. Austria went to war with the French in April 1792. In October 1793 the revolutionaries took the step of executing the Emperor's aunt, Marie Antoinette: he would never forgive such an act. Thereafter the Habsburgs set their faces firmly against any radical and libertarian ideas associated with revolutionary politics.[40]

Spain

Southern Europe was much more antithetical to the idea of toleration than northern Europe. Spain is a curious case. The Iberian peninsula had once been home to a significant numbers of Muslims and Jews, and people there had long coexisted with other religions, often—though not always—peaceably. The Spanish had been used to the presence of non-Christians. But this came to an end at the time of Isabella of Castile and Ferdinand of Aragon, whose marriage unified Spain under one crown. The Jews were expelled from Spain in 1492. In the same year the Muslims were expelled from Granada, their last stronghold in the Iberian peninsula. The remaining Muslims were forced either to flee or to convert to Christianity, becoming known as *moriscos*. In the early seventeenth century their descendants, too, were forced to leave. Thus the unification of Spain was made partly through acts of intolerance. Once the last significant groups of non-Christian were forced out of Spain, a process which Henry Kamen attributes largely to the growing centralization of the state, there was no longer any particular reason for Spain to take seriously the issue of toleration.[41]

The Spanish Inquisition had a great notoriety (partly from Protestant propagandists); nonetheless it did not act arbitrarily, but in accordance with established procedure, and was fairly rigorous about evidence (by the standards of the time). Heretics were given the opportunity to recant their heresy and thereby save their lives.[42] The penalties handed out by the Inquisition, which in some cases led to burning alive, were extreme; but by the eighteenth century this was rarely carried out and *autos da fe* were no longer held in public. There were very few Protestants in Spain. The majority of the victims of the Inquisition were *conversos*, that is, Jews who had converted to Catholicism but about whom the church still nurtured suspicion. Though the recourse to the Inquisition declined during the eighteenth century, Spain continued to be a deeply conservative country. Indeed, it was not until the 1960s that practical toleration came about in Spain, and it was only fully legally instituted when the Spanish constitution was drawn up after Franco's death in 1975.[43]

THE ITALIAN STATES

Like Spain, the Italian states were fairly solidly Catholic. Here also, without a sizeable religious minority to press for toleration, it was less of an issue than in northern Europe. In addition, Italy was the home of the papal states, the epicentre of the Catholic faith. The Inquisition was a powerful force in the Italian states and the Roman Congregation of the Index regularly compiled indices of prohibited books that Catholics were not permitted to read. Many of the core works of the Enlightenment featured on this list of banned books, including Voltaire's *Traité sur la tolérance*. On the face of it, Italy was antithetical to both the Enlightenment and to toleration. But the eighteenth century saw a steep decline in the activities of the Italian tribunals of inquisitors, which led to their being moribund and eventually to their closure, beginning with the Neapolitan Inquisition in 1746. Many of the officially banned books were in practice widely available. There was a robust trade in prohibited literature, particularly in the Venetian Republic.[44] In contrast to Spain, the Italians were reasonably tolerant of Jews, who lived in significant numbers in cities and major towns. Although the debates on toleration lacked the urgency and intensity of Enlightenment writers in northern Europe, the parameters of the discussion changed in the eighteenth century. There was a growing sense that discussion of differences rather than persecution of those of different faiths was the proper way to proceed. As Pilati, author of *On the Reform of Italy*, put it in 1767: 'Those who disagree with us now believe themselves to be in the right and to be on the road to truth, just as we believe ourselves to be. Therefore, instead of persecuting them let us seek to persuade them from their errors.'[45] The writers of the Italian Enlightenment increasingly used such arguments to make the case for toleration of other religious faiths. There was no inclination, however, to extend such toleration to deists or atheists. Even staunchly Catholic intellectuals in Italy were prepared to concede that some toleration was acceptable, and some of the arguments they used were not dissimilar to those of the *philosophes*. Pope Benedict XIV went so far as to correspond with Voltaire. Some of the strongest arguments for toleration were put forward by Jansenists such as Pietro Tamburini, who stated in his 1783 work *On Ecclesiastical and Civil Tolerance* that the church's use of violence and terror to enforce religious conformity had the opposite effect—faith cannot be commanded by fear. Therefore the church should use gentle means of persuasion.[46]

France: The Position of the Jews

The *philosophes* opposed the persecution of the Jews, but some remained suspicious of them: Voltaire was especially hostile.[47] In eighteenth-century France Jews were fairly well situated in contrast to many other parts of Europe, partly because the French old regime was based on the monarchy's recognition of particular corporate rights and privileges. Jewish communities were for the most part organized into recognized corporative groups, and as such had some protection under the law—though they had to pay additional taxes to get it. Thus, until the 1780s the Jews of Alsace were subject to a special tax known as the 'body-toll'. There were about 3,500 Sephardic Jews living in the region of Bordeaux: most were fairly wealthy and quite integrated. There were an additional 30,000 Askenazic Jews, mostly in Alsace and some in Lorraine, and around 500 more in Paris.[48] These were often very poor, and laboured under considerable discrimination, as well as hostility from the local peasantry. The emancipation of France's Jews would become a touchstone by which to judge the authenticity of the French revolutionaries' commitment to the principles of liberty and equality.[49]

The French Revolution

In the years immediately before the outbreak of the French Revolution, the French monarchy was increasingly influenced by a rising tide of public opinion in favour of rights for Protestants. Through the Edict of 1787, imposed on the Paris parlement by enforced registration, Louis XVI's government established the principle of toleration for France's Protestants. The Edict's strongest advocate in the generally hostile Paris Parlement was the noted Jansenist magistrate Robert de Saint-Vincent, speaking in defence of the rights of Protestants. The Edict gave Protestants civil rights, including the recognition of their marriages, and the right to register the births of their children, together with the right to hold and bequeath property. This gave them *de facto* toleration. The Edict stopped short of full toleration for Protestants: they still were not given the right to public worship; they were not permitted to establish their own clergy; and they were still excluded from public office.[50]

When the French Revolution broke out in 1789 one of the founding acts of the revolutionaries was to set out a Declaration of the Rights of Man and of the Citizen (26 August 1789). Article 10 of the Declaration stated: 'No one must be troubled on account of his opinions, even his religious beliefs, provided that their expression does not disturb public order under the law.'[51] Full toleration was granted to Protestants on 24 December 1789. In 1790 descendants of Huguenots who had fled or lost property were awarded compensation by the state.[52]

The Abbé Grégoire (a Jansenist sympathizer) published a *Motion en faveur des Juifs* in October 1789. He was a keen advocate of rights for Jews, but within certain limits. He thought that emancipation would help the Jews to assimilate, and eventually to abandon their own culture, language—even their religious beliefs—and become Christian.[53] There was still considerable hostility in the new National Assembly to equal rights for Jews. From the point of view of staunch Catholics such as the Abbé Maury (who thought that Jews were irretrievably corrupt), the question of the emancipation of the Jews was bound up with the fate of the Catholic Church. He viewed the prospect of rights for Jews as presaging the overthrow of the church. There was a tendency in this period to see opposition in terms of conspiracy. The revolutionaries saw politics in this way, as did the opponents of the Revolution.[54] Staunch supporters of the monarchy and the Catholic Church thought that the Revolution itself was the result of a concerted conspiracy by *philosophes*, Protestants, Jansenists, and others to overthrow the church along with the monarchy.[55] This conviction made the reactionary group in the Assembly even more hostile to revolutionary reforms.

In October 1789, Robespierre (then an obscure deputy in the Assembly) used the Declaration of the Rights of Man to argue the principle that all citizens, including Jews, should have civil and political rights:

> All citizens, whoever they are, have the right to aspire to all levels of office-holding. Nothing is more in conformity with your declaration of rights, in the face of which every privilege, every distinction, every exception must disappear. The Constitution establishes that sovereignty resides in the people, in all the individuals of the people. Therefore each individual has the right to participate in making the law which governs him and in the administration of the public good, which is his own. If this is not so, then it is not true that all men are equal in rights, that every man is a citizen.[56]

The debate had now gone much further than 'toleration'. The issue at stake was whether all citizens, regardless of their religious beliefs, should have equal political rights. Robespierre's words were met with heated opposition from many of the Right of the Assembly. The question of the Jews continued to be unresolved for some time. In January 1790 the Sephardic Jews were given equal rights as citizens, followed by the Askenazic Jews in September 1791. France was the first European country to give equal rights to its Jewish population. It is a sad irony then, that a hundred years later, France should be the country where the Dreyfus Affair took place.

Notes

1. There is often confusion about the use of the terms 'tolerance' and 'toleration' and whether or not they are interchangeable. Properly speaking the term 'tolerance' refers to attitudes, whilst the term 'toleration' refers to social and political practices.
2. A classic study of this subject is that by Henry Kamen, *The Rise of Toleration* (London, 1967). More recently there have been two major collective publications on toleration in Europe: on the earlier period there is Ole Peter Grell and Bob Scribner (eds.), *Tolerance*

and Intolerance in the European Reformation (Cambridge, 1996); and on the period from the late 17th to the late 18th cent., Ole Peter Grell and Roy Porter (eds.), *Toleration in Enlightenment Europe* (Cambridge, 2000). See also Richard H. Popkin and Mark Goldie, 'Scepticism, Priestcraft, and Toleration', in Mark Goldie and Robert Wokler (eds.), *The Cambridge History of Eighteenth-Century Political Thought* (Cambridge, 2006), 79–109.

3. Darrin M. McMahon, *Enemies of the Enlightenment: The French Counter-Enlightenment and the Making of Modernity* (Oxford, 2001), 44.
4. On the Edict of Nantes and its longer term legacy, see Ruth Whelan and Carol Baxter (eds.), *Toleration and Religious Identity: The Edict of Nantes and its Implications in France, Britain and Ireland* (Dublin, 2003).
5. See Geoffrey Adams, *The Huguenots and French Opinion, 1685–1787: The Enlightenment Debate on Toleration* (Waterloo, Ontario, 1991), 9–10.
6. Cited by Adams, ibid. 39.
7. Penny Roberts states that fears of Protestant conspiracies which began in the 16th cent. continued into the 17th cent., after the Protestants had ceased to pose a genuine threat: Penny Roberts, 'Huguenot Conspiracies, Real and Imagined, in Sixteenth-Century France', in Barry Coward and Julian Swann (eds.), *Conspiracies and Conspiracy Theory in Early Modern Europe: From the Waldensians to the French Revolution* (Aldershot, 2004), 55–69, esp. 66.
8. See Gregory Hanlon, *Confession and Community in Seventeenth-Century France: Catholic and Protestant Coexistence in Aquitaine* (Philadelphia, 1993).
9. On this subject, see W. Gregory Monahan, 'Between Two Thieves: The Protestant Nobility and the War of the Camisards', *French Historical Studies*, 30 (2007), 537–58.
10. For a more extended examination of the debate about religious toleration in 18th-cent. France, see Marisa Linton, 'Citizenship and Religious Toleration in France', in Grell and Porter, *Toleration in Enlightenment Europe*, 157–74.
11. On the relationship between religion, virtue, and citizenship, see Marisa Linton, *The Politics of Virtue in Enlightenment France* (Basingstoke, 2001).
12. Amongst the major works by Dale Van Kley on the political impact of the Jansenists in the second half of the 18th cent., see Dale Van Kley, 'The Jansenist Constitutional Legacy in the French Prerevolution, 1750–1789', *Historical Reflections/Réflexions Historiques*, 13 (1986), 393–454; *The Damiens Affair and the Unraveling of the Ancien Régime, 1750–1770* (Princeton, 1984); *The Jansenists and the Expulsion of the Jesuits from France, 1757–1765* (New Haven, Conn., and London, 1975). For the political role of Jansenism in the 1720s and 1730s, see Peter R. Campbell, *Power and Politics in Old Régime France, 1720–1745* (London, 1996), ch. 9.
13. Van Kley's conclusions are brought together in Dale Van Kley, *The Religious Origins of the French Revolution* (New Haven, Conn., 1996), and summarized in Dale Van Kley, 'The Religious Origins of the French Revolution, 1560–1791', in Peter R. Campbell (ed.), *The Origins of the French Revolution* (Basingstoke, 2006), 160–90. See also Monique Cottret, *Jansénisme et lumières: Pour un autre xviiie siècle* (Paris, 1998).
14. Voltaire, *Letters on England*, cited on website. 'Liberty, Equality, Fraternity: Exploring the French Revolution': http://chnm.gmu.edu/revolution/d/272/
15. See John Miller, 'Pluralism, Persecution and Toleration in France and Britain in the Seventeenth Century', in Whelan and Baxter, *Toleration and Religious Identity*, 170.
16. John Morrill, *The Nature of the English Revolution* (London, 1993), pt. 1.
17. Miller, 'Pluralism, Persecution and Toleration', 178.

18. On the continuation of hostility towards Catholics during the 18th cent., see Colin Haydon, *Anti-Catholicism in Eighteenth-Century England: A Political and Social Study* (Manchester, 1993).
19. On the Blasphemy Act, see Martin Fitzpatrick, 'Toleration and the Enlightenment Movement', in Grell and Porter, *Toleration in Enlightenment Europe*, 45.
20. For a discussion of this verdict and its implications, see Fitzpatrick, 'Toleration and the Enlightenment Movement', 30–1.
21. For further reading on Locke see the chapters in John Horton and Susan Mendus (eds.), *John Locke: 'A Letter Concerning Toleration' in Focus* (London, 1991), esp. Maurice Cranston, 'John Locke and the Case for Toleration', and J. Waldron, 'Locke: Toleration and the Rationality of Persecution'; also, John Dunn, *The Political Thought of John Locke* (Cambridge, 1969); John Marshall, *John Locke: Resistance, Religion and Responsibility* (Cambridge, 1994); and Jeremy Waldron, *God, Locke, and Equality: Christian Foundations in Locke's Political Thought* (Cambridge, 2002).
22. See Justin Champion, 'Toleration and Citizenship in Enlightenment England: John Toland and the Naturalisation of the Jews', in Grell and Porter, *Toleration in Enlightenment Europe*, 133–56.
23. For a thoughtful consideration of this argument, and a comparison of Toland's views with those of the Abbé Grégoire, see Alyssa Goldstein Sepinwall, *The Abbé Grégoire and the French Revolution: The Making of Modern Universalism* (Berkeley, Calif., 2005), ch. 3.
24. Cited in Sepinwall, *Abbé Grégoire*, 62–3.
25. On this subject see David Bien, *The Calas Affair: Persecution, Toleration and Heresy in Eighteenth-Century Toulouse* (Princeton, 1960).
26. There is a growing literature on the important topic of public opinion in the 18th cent. A good introduction is offered in: James Van Horn Melton, *The Rise of the Public in Enlightenment Europe* (Cambridge, 2001).
27. Cited in Lynn Hunt (ed. and tr.), *The French Revolution and Human Rights: A Brief Documentary History* (Boston, 1996), 38–9.
28. Ibid. 39–40.
29. Nigel Aston, *Religion and Revolution in France, 1780–1804* (Basingstoke, 2000), 61–72.
30. A fuller account of the relationship between the Enlightenment and toleration can be found in many of the chapters in Grell and Porter, *Toleration in Enlightenment France*, particularly the chapters by Martin Fitzpatrick, 'Toleration and the Enlightenment Movement', 23–68; Robert Wokler, 'Multiculturalism and Ethnic Cleansing in the Enlightenment', 69–85; and Sylvana Tomaselli, 'Intolerance, the Virtue of Princes and Radicals', 86–101. It is notable that these historians take contrasting views of the value of Enlightenment interventions on toleration.
31. R. R. Palmer, *Catholics and Unbelievers in Eighteenth-Century France* (Princeton, 1939), 5–11.
32. McMahon, *Enemies of the Enlightenment*.
33. For a detailed study of the life and thought of Bayle, see Hubert Bost, *Pierre Bayle* (Paris, 2006).
34. Justin Champion, 'Toleration and Citizenship in Enlightenment England', in Grell and Porter, *Toleration in Enlightenment Europe*, 135.
35. On the importance of Spinoza and his influence on radical Enlightenment thought, see Jonathan Israel, *Radical Enlightenment: Philosophy and the Making of Modernity, 1650–1750* (Oxford, 2001); and on Spinoza's theory of toleration contrasted with that of Locke, see

Jonathan Israel, 'Spinoza, Locke and the Enlightenment Battle for Toleration', in Grell and Porter, *Toleration in Enlightenment Europe*, 102–13.

36. On disputes about toleration in the Dutch Republic in the 18th cent., see Ernestine van de Wall, 'Toleration and Enlightenment in the Dutch Republic', in Grell and Porter, *Toleration in Enlightenment Europe*, 114–32.
37. For a detailed investigation of the specifically Dutch context of the Batavian Republic and its ideology, see Annie Jourdan, *La Révolution batave: Entre la France et l'Amérique (1795–1806)* (Rennes, 2008).
38. Joachim Whaley, 'A Tolerant Society? Religious Toleration in the Holy Roman Empire, 1648–1806', in Grell and Porter, *Toleration in Enlightenment Europe*, 175–95.
39. Ibid. 187.
40. For detailed accounts of toleration and reform in the Holy Roman Empire, see Whaley, 'A Tolerant Society?'; Karl Vocelka, 'Enlightenment in the Hapsburg Monarchy: History of a Belated and Short-Lived Phenomenon', in Grell and Porter, *Toleration in Enlightenment Europe*, 196–211; and, more generally on political reform, H. M. Scott, 'Reform in the Habsburg Monarchy, 1740–1790', in H. M. Scott (ed.), *Enlightened Absolutism: Reform and Reformers in Later Eighteenth-Century Europe* (Ann Arbor, Mich., 1990), 145–87.
41. Henry Kamen, 'Inquisition, Tolerance and Liberty in Eighteenth-Century Spain', in Grell and Porter, *Toleration in Enlightenment Europe*, 250–8.
42. The major revisionist work on the Spanish Inquisition is Henry Kamen, *The Spanish Inquisition: A Historical Revision* (New Haven, Conn., 1998).
43. Kamen, 'Inquisition, Tolerance and Liberty', 257.
44. See Nicholas Davidson, 'Toleration in Enlightenment Italy', in Grell and Porter, *Toleration in Enlightenment Europe*, 230–49.
45. Cited ibid. 236.
46. Ibid. 239–40.
47. On Voltaire's attitude to the Jews and what this revealed about his concept of toleration, see Adam Sutcliffe, 'Myths, Origins, Identity: Voltaire, the Jews and the Enlightenment Notion of Toleration', *Eighteenth Century*, 39/2 (1998), 107–26. More generally on Enlightenment attitudes, see Arthur Hertzberg, *The French Enlightenment and the Jews: The Origins of Modern Anti-Semitism* (New York, 1968). Hertzberg takes a largely negative view of Enlightenment attitudes towards the Jews, which he sees as paving the way to the anti-Semitism of the 20th century. For a critique of Hertzberg's position, see Gary Kates, 'Jews into Frenchmen: Nationality and Representation in Revolutionary France', in Ferenc Fehér (ed.), *The French Revolution and the Birth of Modernity* (Berkeley, Calif., 1990), 103–16. Kates argues strongly that Hertzberg's position is based on a 'distorted view of French revolutionary politics' (ibid. 114).
48. See Nigel Aston, *Religion and Revolution in France, 1780–1804* (Basingstoke, 2000), 72–80; and Kates, 'Jews into Frenchmen', 108–10.
49. A strong defence of the record of the French revolutionaries on the rights of Jews is presented in Robert Badinter, *'Libres et égaux': L'Émancipation des Juifs, 1789–1791* (Paris, 1989); whilst a more cautious judgement is offered in Shanti Marie Singham, 'Betwixt Cattle and Men: Jews, Blacks, and Women, and the Declaration of the Rights of Man', in Dale Van Kley (ed.), *The French Idea of Freedom: The Old Regime and the Declaration of Rights of 1789* (Stanford, Calif., 1994).
50. On debates about toleration in the early stages of the French Revolution, see Raymond Birn, 'Religious Toleration and Freedom of Expression', in Van Kley, *The French Idea of Freedom*, 265–99.

51. Cited in John Hardman (ed.), *The French Revolution Sourcebook* (London, 1999), 118.
52. Aston, *Religion and Revolution in France*, 245.
53. For a detailed study of the Abbé Grégoire's views on Jewish assimilation, see Sepinwall, *Abbé Grégoire*, esp. 66–77, 94–5, and 231–2.
54. On belief in conspiracy during the French Revolution see Timothy Tackett, 'Conspiracy Obsession in a Time of Revolution: French Elites and the Origins of the Terror, 1789–1792', *American Historical Review*, 105 (2000), 691–713; and Peter R. Campbell, Thomas E. Kaiser, and Marisa Linton (eds.), *Conspiracy in the French Revolution* (Manchester: Manchester University Press, 2007).
55. McMahon, *Enemies of the Enlightenment*, 77–83.
56. Maximilien Robespierre, 'On the Right to Vote', 22 Oct. 1789, in *Œuvres complètes de Robespierre*, ed. Marc Bouloiseau, Albert Soboul, *et al.* (10 vols. Paris, 1910–67), vi. 131.

Bibliography

Adams, Geoffrey, *The Huguenots and French Opinion, 1685–1787: The Enlightenment Debate on Toleration* (Waterloo, Ontario, 1991).

Bien, David, *The Calas Affair: Persecution, Toleration and Heresy in Eighteenth-Century Toulouse* (Princeton, 1960).

Birn, Raymond F., 'Religious Toleration and Freedom of Expression', in Dale Van Kley (ed.), *The French Idea of Freedom: The Old Regime and the Declaration of Rights of 1789* (Stanford, Calif., 1994).

Campbell, Peter R., *Power and Politics in Old Regime France, 1720–1745* (London, 1996).

—— Kaiser, Thomas E., and Linton, Marisa (eds.), *Conspiracy in the French Revolution* (Manchester, 2007).

Grell, Ole Peter, and Porter, Roy (eds.), *Toleration in Enlightenment Europe* (Cambridge, 2000).

Hanlon, Gregory, *Confession and Community in Seventeenth-Century France: Catholic and Protestant Coexistence in Aquitaine* (Philadelphia, 1993).

Haydon, Colin, *Anti-Catholicism in Eighteenth-Century England: A Political and Social Study* (Manchester, 1993).

Hertzberg, Arthur, *The French Enlightenment and the Jews: The Origins of Modern Anti-Semitism* (New York, 1968).

Kamen, Henry, *The Rise of Toleration* (London, 1967).

—— *The Spanish Inquisition: A Historical Revision* (New Haven, Conn., 1998).

Linton, Marisa, *The Politics of Virtue in Enlightenment France* (Basingstoke, 2001).

Marshall, John, *John Locke: Resistance, Religion and Responsibility* (Cambridge, 1994).

Palmer, R. R., *Catholics and Unbelievers in Eighteenth-Century France* (Princeton, 1939).

Van Kley, Dale, *The Religious Origins of the French Revolution* (New Haven, Conn., 1996).

Whelan, Ruth, and Baxter, Carol (eds.), *Toleration and Religious Identity: The Edict of Nantes and its Implications in France, Britain and Ireland* (Dublin, 2003).

PART V
CULTURE

CHAPTER 21

EDUCATION

DORINDA OUTRAM

THE history of education is enmeshed with the growth and final crisis of the Ancien Régime. The rapid expansion of the state, and the vigour of international competition in the eighteenth century, interlocked with educational change. Struggles between church and state for the control of schools and pupils were vital for the making of well-trained armies and docile peasants. The vast and complex international intellectual movement known as the Enlightenment is incomprehensible without a history of education. Across Europe, and over national boundaries literacy, fluent readers, access to books and newspapers, were necessary to form what Kant called, exactly, the *Leserwelt,* the world of readers, in his famous essay 'An Answer to the Question, What is the Meaning of Enlightenment?' and which others have called 'public opinion'.[1] It has also often been posited that the child stood at the heart of the Enlightenment. Struggles to make links between sensory impressions, ideas, and thoughts, and personhood were often projected onto the fresher sense impressions of the child. Educationalists were also well aware that education trained the affect of the child and thus culture as a whole.

It is from sectarian conflicts under the French Third Republic that the history of education has evolved many of its traditional themes: institutions, literacy, ideologies, religion, curriculum, personnel, and young and not so young learners. Yet in the modern era, it was the 1970s that saw an explosion of writing on the history of education, and a concerted attempt by historians of many countries, such as Roger Chartier, François Furet, Jacques Ozouf, Dominique Julia, and Jacques Revel in France, Marina Roggero in Italy, or Wolfgang Neugebauer in Germany, to link modern historical methods with the history of education, society, and politics.[2] Above all, however, it was the publication in 1977 of a study on literacy, *Lire et écrire: L'Alphabétisation des Français de Calvin à Jules Ferry* by François Furet and Jacques Ozouf, which marked the largest breakthrough of this historiographical era. The book used results gained from researches in the 1880s of the education inspector, Louis Maggiolo, who directed a vast survey, mainly on the pre-revolutionary period, on the signs of literacy such as the ability to sign a name on marriage certificates and wills. Taking this as an index of literacy, he argued for the existence of 'two Frances' separated by a line drawn from Geneva to St Malo in Brittany. France north of that line was much more literate than that to the south and west. 'There was in fact one France which became literate in the Ancien Régime, and another that, on the contrary, owed its admission to written culture to the nineteenth century' (p. 45). Furet and Ozouf confirmed the distinction between the 'two Frances', but drew on a wider range of sources than had Maggiolo, from the census to the army's information on conscript literacy. They argued, in a controversial field, for a link between the ability to read and write, and the ability to sign one's name.

Less attention, however, was paid in the 1970s to the way in which education became part of the world of the ever-expanding political and social reforms of the Ancien Régime. The eighteenth century saw almost continuous warfare. Fierce international competition forced the states involved to perform feats of social engineering in order to create the skilled bureaucratic class which could modernize their armies and their state apparatus to face renewed military crises, and the pastors who could convince their congregations of the rightness of the arrangements of throne and altar. Educational institutions were vital to this process. In fact, it can be said that the presence of the state had such a strong propulsive force in the shaping of educational structures and ideas that we can describe the history of education in one sense as part of the rise and redefinition of the state under the Ancien Régime.

The new capacity of educational institutions created by the state to reach deep into society also allowed them to strengthen the attachment to church and state of sometimes restive subjects. This was especially important because the eighteenth century was not only the age of the Enlightenment, but also an age of mass poverty, famine, and revolt. The Pugachev revolt in Russia (1773–4) and the famine which afflicted Bohemia in 1774 and caused large-scale peasant rebellion, are only the most famous of those which dotted the eighteenth century. They accelerated from the 1770s on, in what Franco Venturi has called the 'Crisis of the Old Regime'.[3]

A major turning point was the decade immediately following the global Seven Years War (1754–63). Most European states that participated in the war ended financially drained, and hampered by old-fashioned political structures in the mobilization of their country's resources, including its manpower. In the ferocious international competition of the eighteenth century, it was crucial that the population of the state should be numerous, healthy, educated to the limits indicated by their social class, and indoctrinated in state educational programmes in the love of order, religion, good morals, and loyalty to the ruler. As the Austrian educational reformer Sonnenfels put it: 'Observe the major goal of public education, the true source of love for the fatherland: to instil into the hearts of children the certainty that their welfare is inseparably joined to the welfare of the state, and that the laws are wise, and lawbreakers unfortunate and foolish people.'[4]

Under such pressures, most monarchies, such as Austria, Prussia, Portugal, Spain, the kingdom of Piedmont, and Saxony, with the perennial exceptions of Britain and France, embarked on comprehensive reform programmes to which the reshaping of education was integral. As never before, monarchies announced their responsibilities for education, nearly always attempted to make school attendance compulsory, and announced their responsibility for school buildings and teacher training. As Empress Maria Theresia of Austria said, 'Education must always be a *politicum*', a matter of state.

Other problems also shape the character of the decade after the end of the Seven Years War with its accelerating educational initiatives. Most notable was the struggle between the Catholic monarchies and the Jesuit order. Jesuits had come to dominate education at the university level (for example, at the University of Vienna), and the colleges, such as the Parisian college Louis-le-Grand, which prepared for university entrance, included some professional training, and offered a full humanistic education.[5] In some parts of Europe, the Jesuits even came to play a considerable role in primary education. The charges against the Jesuits, a religious order vowed to loyalty to the Pope, and teaching throughout Catholic Europe and its colonies, were two. They were accused of having supported an Indian rebellion in the Portuguese possession of what is now Paraguay. Secondly, the primary loyalty of the order to the Pope also worried many secular monarchs. What ideologies of papal supremacy, in an age where monarchs were increasingly concerned with matters of jurisdiction and loyalty, might they not be teaching their charges? The Jesuits were in control of over 700 schools in Europe and many universities, the nurseries of hopefully loyal bureaucrats for the secular monarchies, so this was not an idle worry.

All over Catholic Europe these concerns came to a head at approximately the same time, not accidentally during the decade after the end of the Seven Years War when many states were still reforming themselves, and seeking desperately to mobilize available resources. The order was expelled from Portugal in 1759, France in 1764, and Spain and Naples in 1767, and the Pope was persuaded in 1773 to abolish the order altogether. The monarchies eagerly fell on the vast Jesuit possessions. Each devoted some of these new resources to constructing a state educational system. The Austrian monarchy devoted almost all these new resources to this purpose, developing a system of compulsory education in city and country elementary schools, with a new curriculum emphasizing rational belief in God and respect for the ruler,[6] while the Italian kingdom of Sardinia/Savoy and the even smaller grand-duchy of Parma also moved in the same direction.[7]

The expulsion of the Jesuit orders from the states of Catholic Europe was not only a chance to build new institutions, but also to introduce a more modern curriculum than the Jesuit staples of rhetoric, logic, and scholastic philosophy. It was a chance to introduce the study of the sciences, history, and modern languages, alongside the study of Latin and Greek which were of course mandatory in education. Yet this was a time when that culture began to change. At the University of Vienna, for example, the Jesuits' special privileges were curtailed, and they lost control of the philosophy and theology faculties as early as the later 1750s, just as the movement against them was beginning to gather momentum.[8] The expulsion of the Jesuits, perhaps the most profound break between Baroque and Enlightenment education, was a chance to craft a new culture for the elites and would-be elites who frequented the colleges and universities. It was also the first real opportunity in Europe to found a secular educational system in Catholic lands.

The Seven Years War and the expulsion of the Jesuits thus bracket the most important era in the history of education in the later eighteenth century. Both are intimately tied up with the vicissitudes of the Ancien Régime itself. For Catholic countries, Jesuit possessions were the difference between being able to construct an often long-desired state educational system or not. France however, whilst taking many individual former Jesuit schools and colleges under state control, failed to put a national educational system in place, in spite of the well-known calls for a national system of education by, among many others, the magistrates La Chalotais (*Essai d'Education nationale, ou plan d'études pour la jeunesse*, 1763) and Guyton de Morveau (*Mémoire sur l'Education publique*, 1764).[9]

But what happened in the Protestant states? With the perennial exception of Great Britain, the Protestant states, in spite of the draining debts of the Seven Years War, also moved with remarkable unanimity towards the same construction of state educational systems. Both Catholic Savoy and Lutheran Prussia, for example, like many other smaller German states, sent out at the end of the war, in 1763, state decrees on teacher training, on the enforcement of compulsory schooling, and engineered a massive expansion of schools at the village level aiming to teach the basic literacy needed by recruits to the army, and by the peasant farmer – often one and the same person. All this implies that while the seizure of the Jesuit possessions may have been a sufficient condition for the making of new state educational systems, it was not a necessary one. The European-wide push towards the new educational systems came from the push towards recovery from the Seven Years War. The seizure of Jesuit property only affected Catholic states, whereas almost every state in Europe was trying to recover from its participation in what had been the first global war. In that recovery educational structures and practice were everywhere seen as vital. Theories of education, such as that of Jean-Jacques Rousseau in his famous 1762 book *Emile, or on Education*, hardly intervened at all in the problems of mass education faced by the European states.

However, for all the importance of the new state educational systems, it is as well to remember that throughout Europe education for all social classes was often largely domestic and familial in character, at least for part of the school years. This is certainly the setting, for example, of John Locke's 1693 *Some Thoughts Concerning Education*, a work whose influence is difficult to overestimate, whose context is that of a middle-class boy receiving education at home from a tutor. It is worth noting that Locke's schoolboy, alone among the children discussed in the major educational texts of the time, is not expected to become a perfect human being, just one capable of living 'with civility', that is, decently in society. It is noticeable that the boy is also expected to respond to social pressures to guide his behaviour. In other words society is his second tutor, not an educational institution or a teacher. At the other end of the social scale, apprentices in the skilled trades learnt by doing, and lived in their masters' households.[10] Midshipmen learnt their profession on board ship. Upper-class children were taught at home by private tutors, even if the boys and sometimes girls later attended a boarding school,[11] or the boys a university. Richard and Maria Edgeworth, probably the most influential educators of the English-speaking world in the later Enlightenment, envisaged the children around whom they wove their advice to parents, as living at home, and made many of their observations in *Practical Education* (1798) and the six volumes of *The Parents' Assistant* (1796–1800) of children from within their own family.[12]

New toys and books appeared. Dolls' houses (doubly domestic, a house inside a house) were seen for the first time, accompanied by new educational aids to be used in the home, as well as a new class of books aimed at a child audience.[13] In the German lands in particular, children's newspapers, like the *Kinderfreund: Ein Wochenblatt* (Leipzig, 1780–2), or the *Leipziger Wochenblatt für Kinder* (1773–83), appeared, containing fairy stories, fables, moral commentaries, and information about nature. Some parents produced their own teaching aids. Middle and upper class children, whose parents could afford the books and teaching aids, began to develop a culture of their own through this commercial explosion.[14] Professional educationalists such as the famous Joachim Campe, in the little German state of Hesse-Darmstadt, produced a best-selling version of *Robinson Crusoe* aimed at children (as the original had not been). Campe was also the director of a printing house, sponsored by the Grand Duke, which published nothing but books for children, from school books to nursery tales. That such a printing house could exist shows the extent of the market for child-oriented writing. The books published by Campe held fast to the ideals of the school founded by the so-called *Philanthropin* in Dessau, which emphasized forming the child as autonomous, a world-citizen, alert to the world, through the training of hand and eye. Riding, gardening, carpentry were all taught to train the faculties.[15]

What did these books and teaching aids aim to teach? Books were often aimed at pure pleasure, with moral lessons very much to the rear, as the title of the *Anecdotes of Miss Lydia Lively. Intended to Improve and Amuse the Rising Generation* (London, 1787) makes very clear. Many of them, however, were surrogate tutors, like the publications by John Newbery which taught science through the common Enlightenment method of written dialogues between child and tutor. Another noticeable feature of children's books was that they now began to contain, not the theology and scripture stories which were emphasized in the children's books of the early part of the eighteenth century, but to replicate the way in which knowledge itself was beginning to be split up into specialized subject-matter. Children's reading matter by the late century was divided between such subjects as natural history, history, geography, and mythology. Children could read travel accounts, and possess short books, designed to be carried in the coat pocket, to enable identification of flowers and birds. Their knowledge could be gathered together by an entirely secular book, such as August Ludwig von Schlozer's *Vorbereitung zur Weltgeschichte für Kinder* (editions between 1779 and 1806). Middle-class children were also taught new and increasingly fashionable scientific subjects, such as the workings of electricity, by books describing experiments which could be performed in the home, such as the *Sammlung elecktrischer Spielwerke für junge Electricker*, published by Georg Heinrich Seiferheld from 1787 to 1799.

It must therefore never be forgotten that education, while vital to the Ancien Régime state and carried out through its many different institutions, was also often domestic in character, and was accompanied, for the middle class, by a newly capitalist creation of toys, books, and educational apparatus.[16] As Marina Roggero has pointed out, the child's encounter with the printed word might well come from other places than the school.[17] Little chap books, hymnals, and almanacs could be just as important.[18] Roggero estimates for Piedmont that even at the end of the Ancien Régime, and in spite of the emergence from the Piedmontese normal school of professional teachers, the majority of the population lived 'amphibiously' between the world of the spoken word and that of the written.[19] None of the European states could teach all of its subjects all of the time, or could fully institutionalize education.

The large numbers of private schools also made impossible the search of the state to impose universal compulsory education. The private schools began from the ground up with the *petites écoles* of France, or the *Winkelschulen* (literally, 'corner schools') in the German states, which taught the 3Rs to a motley group of often unruly pupils, both girls and boys, drawn from the peasantry and the lower classes in the towns.[20] The *petites écoles* were often taught by the religious orders who dominated primary education, such as the Oratorians and the Fathers of the Christian Schools, but there was no lack of secular teachers.

Private schools, whose numbers increased rapidly on the eve of the French Revolution, ranged from fly-by-night institutions to the well-respected and long-standing that competed with the local college on almost equal terms and sometimes with greater success in attracting the well-to-do and well-born of the district. They avoided the crises of the 1760s and 1770s caused by the expulsion and dissolution of the Jesuits, and offered a different curriculum. The new curriculum, in a rejection of the Jesuit mould, would contain subjects such as modern languages, science and modern history, accounting and navigation.[21]

No Ancien Régime state held the monopoly of education. Nor, in most states, was it clear who was to be educated and to what degree. Debate raged under the Ancien Régime in all countries, even those whose governments only weakly involved themselves in the creation of national educational systems, such as France, or even more so England, on the fit between social class and formal education. The Academy of Châlons, in France, for example, announced a prize competition in 1779 on the theme 'What would be the best plan of education for the people?'[22] Among the elites and semi-elites, such as the *philosophes* of the Enlightenment, many held the view, as did Diderot, paradoxically himself the son of a mere master cutler, that the spread of formal education could only further destabilize society. Peasants, labourers, and townspeople of the lower classes in particular, it was argued, would be particularly harmed by exposure to education in colleges and universities, or the social ascent made possible by entry into the professional schools for pastors and bureaucrats. Education beyond the level of the *petites écoles* would, it was thought, produce displaced members of the lower classes who could find no outlets or positions which would absorb their talents, and whose example would disturb social order by the envy of others of their social class. Their labour would also be lost to the economy.

It has to be said that many peasants had the same views. Advanced education would not improve their fortunes if a member of the family removed his labour to a profession in the town. The sober conservatism of the peasant in particular meshed with the prejudices of the *philosophes*. This influenced the character of the Enlightenment, undermining its universalist, progressivist claims when it came up against the reality of social class.

Diderot, like many other thinkers, was strongly concerned that their works should not reach the lower social classes. He wrote to his publisher, 'There are... some readers whom I don't want, and never shall; I write only for those with whom I could talk at my ease.'[23]

If one objective of state educational systems was to keep social order, while at the same time instilling what we would see as minimal literacy amongst peasants and town workers, it involved the Ancien Régime in a profound contradiction. Why, in an age where many, including influential Enlightenment thinkers, regarded popular literacy as unnecessary or even dangerous, did most rulers try to promote universal literacy on an unprecedented scale? The answer to this seeming conundrum may well be that considerations of the survival of the monarchy in both cases took precedence, for their rulers and their civil servants, over the complaints of the *philosophes*. The interest of these states in reaching deep into society by initiatives, largely successful in the Austrian case (less so in Prussia), to widen compulsory schooling, shows that in spite of the ravages of the Seven Years War, the states had increasing power, and an increasing capacity to see 'society' as a whole, rather than still being confined with the 'society of orders'.

Prussia's debts, for example, after the end of the Seven Years War were enormous and the maintenance of the army, even in peacetime, absorbed 75 per cent of state revenues. No windfall from departing Jesuits was to be expected in this Lutheran state and there was for the years of the war little space to manœuvre in the direction of the reform of education.[24] It was not until after the end of the Seven Years War in 1763 that Prussia was able to begin to institute a state system of education which would build on the initiative of Frederick William I. Like the Austrian, the Prussian government under Frederick II assumed, in spite of its massive debts, financial liability for its new state school system. The monarchy built schools, and opened normal schools for teacher training. The costs of erecting an educational system taking in the whole of the social order, and particularly the peasant, were important enough consciously to add to the massive financial burden of the war. In the same way, compulsory education and school reform marked the culmination of a process whereby universal literacy was instituted as a desirable social goal, in spite of the caveats of the *philosophes* who saw popular literacy as a social danger.

One very big difference between Austria and Prussia, however, was the influence in the latter of Pietism, a militant offshoot of Lutheranism. Based on the individual call to salvation, Pietism was a sect which placed great emphasis on a religion of the heart. Their ideology of religious inwardness meshed with the wish of the monarchy that subjects internalize their loyalty to the crown. First supported by Frederick William I, the father of Frederick II, Prussian Pietism stood near the Calvinist monarchy against the established Lutheran Church, and was undoubtedly the strongest force behind the Prussian monarchy's policies of educational reform and innovation. It was on schools that the Pietists' campaign for moral and spiritual reform was focused. They promoted popular literacy on an unprecedented scale. They helped to create a new profession in Prussia, that of the professional schoolmaster, by giving the first instruction in teaching methods in normal schools. Frederick II strongly supported Pietism's educational objectives, allowed Pietist ideas to dominate education in the Prussian monarchy, and promulgated an edict under their influence compelling attendance in rural schools. By the end of the Seven Years War, the Pietists had taken over the new (1694) University of Halle, and established a famous orphanage where more than 1,000 children were educated in skilled crafts, the scriptures, literacy, and numeracy.

Pietists used a far stronger disciplinary model than had ever been used by the village schoolmasters whom they replaced. As their leader August Franke wrote:

> Youth do not know how to regulate their lives and are naturally inclined toward idle and sinful behaviour, when left to their own devices. For this reason it is a rule in this institution that a pupil will never be allowed out of the presence of a supervisor. The supervisor's presence will stifle the pupil's inclination to sinful behaviour and slowly weaken his wilfulness.[25]

The student, under constant surveillance, would internalize not only the order and discipline so necessary to the subjects of a military state, but also the Pietists' variety of religious belief which emphasized inward conviction and Bible study. It should be noted that the spread of reading and compulsory education was not intended to be a project of social ascension.[26] Reading was to allow pupils to read the Bible and the textbooks which extolled loyalty to church and state. There was no intention of leading orphans, peasants, and poor boys in the cities to better themselves, by leaving their own social class.

An exception to this was the theology schools, such as that at the University of Halle. To recruit Pietist teachers and ministers badly needed to fill parishes which would otherwise be filled by orthodox Lutherans, the theology faculties became centres of social ascension, making them very different from, for example, the Milan Collegio delle Provincie, or the French technical schools founded by the monarchy.[27]

The Austrian situation was very different. The Jesuit windfall, following the dissolution of the order in 1773, was accompanied by funds confiscated by the Emperor Joseph II from monasteries, and put to use to found state teacher training schools, and to commission standardized textbooks.[28] Even earlier, the Empress Maria Theresia, following on the slow reforms of the 1740s, had issued the *Allgemeine Schulordnung* of 1774, immediately following dissolution of the Jesuit order. The first major Catholic educational reformer, Johann Ignaz Felbiger, the only major educational thinker of this era to advise both Catholic and Protestant monarchs, followed royal policies which emphasized universal literacy. Felbiger concentrated on the village schools where reading, writing, and the catechism were to be taught. For the first time, children were taught as a group rather than individually. They were, unsurprisingly, taught to be good Catholics and good subjects. They were, as Felbiger wrote, 'creatures of God, instruments of His holy will, and good members of the Church' (and also) 'honest subjects of their ruler, useful members of the state, and also a vessel for earthly happiness'.[29] How long the contradiction between universal literacy and political and social quiescence could have been maintained is another question.

Royal policies also involved social engineering at the other end of the social scale. The relentless demands of war led to pressure to extract the most possible of each country's resources. This could not be done without an expanding bureaucracy. In each European state (again with the exception of England), whether Protestant or Catholic, similar measures were taken to solve the problem. In the German states *Ritterakademien* were founded, mostly serving the minor nobility and scholarship boys drawn from the sons of army officers. Often, their pupils came from all over Europe. Their curriculum, beside the obligatory Latin and Greek, was composed of practical subjects fitting them for state service, subjects like forestry, mining, law, science, and modern languages. The curriculum of the *Akademien* had little or nothing to do with that of the old Jesuit schools, nor yet with the humanistic curriculum of the colleges and universities of the German lands. In 1737, the same year as the foundation of Yale, and of the Prussian *Allgemeine Schulordnung*, a new university was founded in the Hanoverian town of Göttingen. This university began the trend of teaching 'modern' subjects, and acted as a training ground for pastors and bureaucrats.[30] Numbers of students in the twenty-eight universities in the German states tripled by 1789, while English and French universities continued to stagnate with very low numbers of undergraduate admissions.[31] A mining school, the training ground of Alexander von Humboldt, was opened in the kingdom of Saxony, at Freiburg-im-Breisgau, followed by the French École des Mines in 1783. Rulers knew well the value of these institutions. In the grand-duchy of Württemburg, for example, the Grand Duke's palace opened directly into the *Ritterakademie*, named the Karlsschule after him, and the ruler was prone to make unannounced visits that showed both his wish to remind the *Akademie* of the purpose of its existence, and also minutely to oversee its teaching.

At the same time, throughout Europe, more specialized schools in new professions useful to the state began to be founded. In an age of war, it is not surprising to see the foundation of military schools. The schools represented an attempt to develop a new, more professional military, aware of the mathematics, engineering, and military history important to their trade. In France, the artillery school at Grenoble was founded in 1720, that of Besançon in 1736, and the most famous, Mézières, was established in 1749 and reorganized as a school of military engineering in 1762. It should be noted, however, that, yet again, the Ancien Régime did not equate the education of a military elite with any projects of social engineering. As Roger Chartier has remarked, Mézières was not a school where social ascension was to be looked for. The conditions for entry into Mézières, for example, included the stipulation that the entrant should be born a noble or be a son of a high-ranking army officer. The same can be said for the Collegio delle Provincie in the kingdom of Sardinia.[32] Just as much as in the case of the village schools of Austria and Prussia, the facilitation of social ascent was not part of the policy behind the military schools.

Where do England and France stand in this 'grand narrative?' Each seems to consistently take an outlier position. It is difficult, however, to find any continuities between them. Britain emerged triumphant from the Seven Years War, while France was the heaviest loser among the great powers. Yet neither responded to the Seven Years War with the building of a state education system, as did Austria and Prussia, most of the smaller German states, Tuscany. and the kingdom of Sardinia. Even tiny Parma's grand duke drafted a *Costituzione per i nuovi reggi studi*, immediately the Jesuits left the state in 1768.

Portugal and Spain made valiant efforts in the same direction, after they expelled the Jesuits in 1759 and 1767 respectively.[33]

France profited by the expulsion of the Jesuits, but did not devote these resources to the formation of new educational institutions, nor develop strong educational policies, unlike the revolutionary regime which succeeded it. French education was dominated by the religious orders, in which the school was regarded as inseparable from Catholic education, and the repression of heresy.[34] The monarchy was largely interested in the schools from the same point of view. The Edict of Fontainebleau, revoking that of Nantes in 1685, prohibited Protestant schools, and decrees in 1724 laid down parental obligations to send children to school, and authorized the raising of a special tax for financing village schools. Given the pull of the rhythms of the agricultural year, it is likely that these decrees remained a dead letter. But their intention of the repression of heresy was clear.

English education also remained largely unchanged. Protestant England had finished its plundering of church property already in the Reformation, and much of these new resources had already gone, via private donors, into the foundation of numerous grammar schools (secular secondary schools with a classically based curriculum frequented by all ranks of the middle class), endowed elementary schools, and Oxford and Cambridge colleges. The Church of England, founded as a result of the Reformation, took over much education at the level of the village school, taught by schoolmaster or mistress, or the parson and curate, and not answerable to the state. The two English universities of Oxford and Cambridge were expanded overwhelmingly by large-scale private donations in the late fifteenth and sixteenth century, and by the eighteenth century had fallen into a sharp decline. Each admitted less than 150 students a year.[35] There was little feeling that the monarchy ought to intervene to construct a compulsory education system, or that it should have the objective of universal literacy. Most education was in fact, except the grammar schools, run by the Church of England. Not surprisingly, given the presence of so many schools, literacy was high.

Secular private schools were also numerous. Very like the *écoles privées* in France, their curriculum, apart from the obligatory Latin and Greek, was full of practical subjects and they usually ran a modern syllabus of French, geography, and modern history. The same thing went for the colleges founded to give advanced education to Dissenters, or Protestants outside the Church of England who were excluded from the two English universities on religious grounds.

For all these reasons, it is probably impossible to conduct a direct comparison between the English and French cases under the Ancien Régime. At the level of the state, so crucial to the construction of educational systems in central Europe, the differences continue. The English monarchy came ever more quickly under the control of Parliament in the eighteenth century and effectively lost control of much of its income. By itself, it was in no position financially or politically to found a state educational system, and this is what separates it from states such as Prussia and Austria. States whose monarchs had no powerful representative bodies to contend with lay in a totally different relationship to both their populations and their bureaucracies. On the other hand, the French monarchy in the later part of the century, weakened by France's losses in the Seven Years War, struggled relentlessly for political and financial control with its legal and representative bodies, the parlements, and certain provincial estates. It was this struggle, vital for the financial survival of the monarchy, and one of the forerunners of revolution, which was to the forefront of policy, not the creation of a national educational system leading to universal compulsory school attendance and mass literacy. In general, universities stagnated,[36] and education below this level was left to the teaching orders: Jesuits before 1762, when they were expelled from France, and the religious orders specializing in teaching peasants and the poor after that date. Of these the Fathers of the Christian Schools and the Oratorians, and the Ursulines for girls, were the most prominent.

How successful were these schools in teaching the minimal skills of reading and writing? (Arithmetic was then taught separately.) The measurement of literacy of any kind is a slippery matter. Historians, however, agree that by the end of the eighteenth century, a global increase in literacy, however defined, had taken place for both men and women throughout western and central Europe and in England, and this in spite of the fact that in rural areas, all over Europe, the school could be deserted for at least a third of the year, the harvesting and sowing months, as children's labour was necessary in the fields. The universality of child labour rendered problematic any attempt by either state or teaching orders to achieve mass literacy,[37] yet for unknown reasons, still literacy increased.

In the case of France the major push towards literacy came not from the state but from the teaching orders. Each order believed in the importance of the school in repressing heresy and teaching literacy. It was not from the monarchy but from the teaching orders that the pressure came for mass literacy in France. Standardized reading was emphasized: 'uniformity must be the rule for all, without departing in any way from received practice; thus, the same signs are to be used in lessons, the same method for reading, writing and arithmetic; the same manner of coaching for the catechism, of saying prayers and hearing them, of assembling and dismissing children; the conduct of schools should be an unvarying rule for all'.[38] But can the schools and the schools alone account for the start-up of the literacy process which clearly accelerated all over Europe in the final decade of the Ancien Régime? Can it explain the different rates of literacy observed for men and for women throughout the eighteenth and nineteenth centuries, and throughout France and other European countries?

Girls' schools played an increasingly large role in the network of schools. Yet nothing could better express normal attitudes to the education of women than the prize essay subject of the Academy of Besançon in 1777: 'How might the education of women contribute to making men better?' Women's education always, from the highest to the lowest social strata, focused on their future roles as wives and mothers. Nonetheless, a great deal changed in this period, especially in France. Teaching orders specializing in the education of girls, such as the Ursulines, the Apostolat des Filles pieuses, or the Sisters of St Vincent de Paul, mostly founded at the end of the seventeenth century, multiplied, and *petites écoles* for girls run by nuns thus became numerous for the first time, both in town and country, though with significant variations according to the wealth or poverty of each region. In a large town such as Châlons-sur-Marne, for example, there were three

Ursuline schools, five free schools for girls, four convents taking female boarders, and three schools kept by lady teachers trained in the Séminaire des Dames régentes; Grenoble in 1789 had five free schools for girls, and four convents taking female boarders.[39] Even in Prussia, without the benefit of teaching orders, girls' schools grew in number, and girls were allowed to take part not only in classes on the domestic crafts, and reading and writing and religion, but also French, history, and geography.[40]

However, this European expansion in girls' education still left women with educational curricula which were less rigorous, narrower in definition, and always taken up to some extent with the domestic arts. Controversy broke out over the extent to which women and girls were rational creatures and thus could benefit from education. Women writers pointed out the extent to which women's education reproduced Enlightenment struggles over rationality. This controversy began with Fénelon's *De l'Education des filles* (1687). As Mary Astell wrote in 1701 in *A Serious Proposal to the Ladies*, 'For since God has given women as well as men intelligent souls, why should they be forbidden to improve them?' This agenda had altered little by the end of the century, when Catherine Macaulay in her 1790 *Letters on Education* protested against 'that degrading difference in the culture of the understanding which has prevailed for several centuries'. She argued that 'there is but one rule of right for the conduct of all rational beings'. In other words, a unitary 'reason' cannot be divided into female and male reason without undermining the very concept, one of the most important of the Enlightenment. Macaulay also attacked Rousseau on the same grounds for his support of a 'sexual difference in character'. Macaulay's views were echoed in Mary Wollstonecroft's *Vindication of the Rights of Women* (1792), which also emphasized the danger for the Enlightenment of a dual standard both for mental achievement and for virtue.

Early feminist writers, however, were far from holding the field in theoretical writings over education. In spite of addressing themselves mainly to the middle class, they wrote about problems which afflicted all girls and women in education. Other educational theorists, however, such as Jean-Jacques Rousseau in *Emile*, wrote as though the expansion of education and the bitter struggles to educate manpower in most European states were not happening just as they were writing, and as though the educational plans of La Chalotais, Guyton de Morveau, Gabriel François Coyer, and Rolland d'Erceville, all arguing for national systems of education, had never appeared. The English philosopher John Locke, for example, addressed himself in *Some Thoughts Concerning Education* (1693) to the comfortable English middle class, and posited as his subject the bringing up of a single young boy, pointing out the dangers of school education, while the focus of all educational reform plans in Europe was the school.

Basing his comments on watching a friend's child, Locke was also, however, bringing together his work in his thoughts on the way that personhood and physical sensation come together. Locke believed that the foundation of all knowledge, and the precondition of formal education was the mixture of meditation and sense impressions. In the educational thinking of the Ancien Régime, the body played a central role. Education developed via the stimuli received by the senses. It has often been pointed out that the child stood at the centre of Enlightenment thinking, because it was on the child that the

Enlightenment focused its obsession with finding links between perception and personhood. John Locke, for example, famously viewed the child as a blank slate, to be written upon by the work of sensation. These sensationalist ideas implied that the training of these sense impressions was vital in the bringing up of the child. On them were based both the training of moral principles, and substantive knowledge. As Locke wrote, 'The little and almost invisible impressions on our tender infancies have very important and lasting consequences...I considered (children) only as white paper or wax, to be moulded and fashioned as one pleases.'

Locke's book, though isolated from European concerns, had real results. His idea that the foundation of all future knowledge was based on the education of the senses, was appropriated by the Enlightenment and applied to the physical objects it produced for children. Locke's influence was not merely philosophical. The optical toys which in this period trained ocular perception are only one example of the way in which Lockean ideas influenced actual child-rearing practices. Locke repeatedly emphasized the importance of toys for learning, with their emphasis on handling, and seeing closely, as well as the teaching of gardening to strengthen the senses. Locke also, very practically, goes outside his philosophical theses, and sees his pupil as being shaped by the pressures of society. To the friend to whom this book was addressed, he argues for the training effect of 'good company', 'it being of greater force to work upon him than all you can do besides'.

Locke's work, however, extraordinary as its influence was, produced no new institutions. In that, he followed the pattern of English education in the Enlightenment. However, a plethora of new institutions, and the appearance of the first professional educationalists was one of the most striking features of the German Enlightenment. We have already seen the foundation of new universities, and of the *Ritterakademien*. Educationalists like Joachim Campe, with his writing and publishing and Johann Basedow in his famous school the *Philanthropin*, of which Campe was briefly director, concentrated their attention on the child. Campe published the first dictionary of pedagogy in German, and wrote and published best-selling works for children.[41] A plethora of books on education followed, such as Samuel Bauer's *Ein Handbuch für Erzieher*. In Basedow's school, physical punishment was not allowed, and carpentry, gardening, and other crafts were encouraged. Even a playful element entered schoolwork with the frequent presentation of plays, riding, and sports. Basedow's school, however, was not for the lower classes. It was a place for the retraining of the middle and upper classes into world-citizens, and autonomous human beings. It was a place which foreshadowed the remaking of elites characteristic of the revolutionary era.

Undoubtedly, however, the best known educational theorist of this period was the Genevan Jean-Jacques Rousseau, himself a notoriously incompetent private tutor. His 1762 *Emile, or on Education* was widely read, although less widely put into practice. Like other educational theories of the time, apart from those in Germany, the book advocated no new educational institutions and has little to do with the contemporary crisis of French education and its relation to the church/state relationship. Colleges in fact are attacked by Rousseau.

Emile is educated from infancy by a tutor. (Emile's parents play little role in the book.) Rousseau believed that Emile should be taught to perceive only things, not be corrupted by the slippery nature of words. To this end, he allows Emile to be taught to read only at the age of adolescence, and allows him only one book, Daniel Defoe's *Robinson Crusoe*, willing him to follow Crusoe's example of brave autonomy (Emile is educated in solitude) and the importance of being able to make useful objects. The rest of his education proceeds along lines common to Locke and the German reformers, in largely training the senses with gardening and woodwork. He is also trained to have reciprocal feelings with other people, without reading, exhortations, or conversations with his tutor. Enraged by the theft of vegetables from his garden, for example, he learns from experience the nature of private property. The child, out in all weathers, is physically hardened. In spite of these revolutionary ideas, Rousseau strongly argues that education should be appropriate to social class, and he attacks the teachings of Locke, especially the idea that children should be talked to as though rational beings.

From the child to the institution, education under the Ancien Régime intervened both in the Enlightenment and in the history of the war-torn states of the eighteenth century. Many thousands of children across Europe were taught basic literacy, in new state schools which emphasized diligence, uniformity in teaching, and loyalty to the state. Far fewer, but at elite levels, were educated in ways which reflected the teachings of John Locke, Joachim Campe, and Jean-Jacques Rousseau, and 'the new world of children', to use J. H. Plumb's phrase. Each constructed a new form of childhood subjectivity, pivotal to the construction of culture and to the state.

Notes

1. Rolf Engelsing, *Der Burger als Leser: Lesergeschichte in Deutschland, 1500–1800* (Stuttgart, 1974).
2. Lawrence Stone, *The Family, Sex, and Marriage in England, 1500–1800* (New York, 1977); Roger Chartier and Jacques Revel, 'Université et société dans l'Europe moderne: Position des problèmes', *Revue d'Histoire moderne et contemporaine*, 35 (1978), 353–74; G. Ricuperati and M. Roggero, 'Istruzione e società in Italia: Probleme e prospettiva di recerce', *Quaderni storici*, 38 (1978), 640–65.
3. Franco Venturi, *The End of the Old Regime in Europe, 1768–1776: The First Crisis* (Princeton, 1979).
4. B. Becker-Cantarino, 'Josef von Sonnenfels and the Development of Secular Education in Eighteenth Century Austria', *SVEC* 167 (1977), 29–47.
5. R. R. Palmer, *The School of the French Revolution: A Documentary History of the College of Louis-le-Grand and of its Director, Jean-François Champagne, 1762–1814* (Princeton, 1975).
6. James Van Horn Melton, *Absolutism and the Eighteenth Century Origins of Compulsory Schooling in Prussia and Austria* (Cambridge, 1988).
7. Ernesto Lama, *I classici della pedagogia italiana; Il pensiero pedagogico dell'Illuminismo* (Turin, 1958); Brambilla, *Il sistema scolastico di Milano: Professioni nobili e professioni borghesi dall'età spagnola alle riforme teresiane* (Bologna, 1982); Marina Ruggero, *Insegnar lettere: Richerce di storia dell'istruzione in età moderna* (Turin, 1992).

8. Jean Egret, 'Le Procès de Jésuites devant les parlements de France (1761-1770)', *Revue Historique* (1950), 1–17.
9. Charles R. Bailey, 'Attempts to Introduce a "System" of Secular Secondary Education in France, 1762-1789', *SVEC* 167 (1977), 105–24.
10. Dominique Julia, 'L'Éducation des négoçiants français au xviii*e* siècle', in F. Angiolini and Daniel Roche (eds.), *Cultures et formations négoçiantes* (Paris, 1995).
11. Erasmus Darwin, *A Plan for the Conduct of Female Education in Boarding Schools* (Derby, 1797).
12. Mitzi Myers, ' "Anecdotes from the Nursery" in Maria Edgeworth's *Practical Education* (1798): Learning from Children "Abroad and at Home" ', *Princeton University Library Chronicle*, 60 (1999), 220–50.
13. Jill Shefrin, ' "Make it a Pleasure and Not a Task": Educational Games for Children in Georgian England', *Princeton University Library Chronicle*, 60 (1999), 251–75; J. H. Plumb, 'The New World of Children in Eighteenth Century England', *Past and Present*, 67 (1975), 64–93.
14. Lady Elinor Fenn, *The Art of Teaching in Sport* (London, c.1790); Andrea Immel, ' "Mistress of Infantile Language": Lady Elinor Fenn, her Set of Toys, and the "Education of Each" Movement', *Children's Literature*, 25 (1997), 215–28; Rudolf Dekker, *Childhood Memory and Autobiography in Holland* (London, 2000); Ariana Buggerman, 'The Cultural Universe of a Dutch Child: Otto Van Eck and his Literature', *Eighteenth Century Studies*, 31 (1997), 129–34.
15. Hanno Schmitt (ed.), *Visionare Lebensklugheit: Joachim Heinrich Campe in seiner Zeit, 1746–1818* (Wiesbaden, 1996).
16. Anke Te Heesen, *The World in a Box: The Story of an Eighteenth Century Picture Encyclopedia* (Chicago, 2002).
17. Marina Roggero, *L'alfabeto conquistado: Apprendere ed insegnare nell'Italia tra Sette ed Ottocento* (Bologna, 1999).
18. Geneviève Bollème and Alphonse Dupront (eds.) *Livre et société dans la France du xviii*e* siècle* (Paris and The Hague, 1965).
19. *Alfabeto conquistado*, 19.
20. Harvey Chisick, 'School Attendance, Literacy, and Acculturation: Petites Écoles and Popular Education in Eighteenth Century France', *Europa*, 3 (1979), 85–221; Bernard Grosperrin, *Les Petites Écoles sous l'Ancien Régime* (Rennes, 1984); Wolfgang Neugebauer, *Absolutischer Staat und Schulwirklichkeit in Brandeburg-Preussen* (Berlin, 1985); Michel Vovelle, 'Y a-t-il eu une révolution culturelle au xviii*e* siècle? A propos de l'éducation populaire en Provence', *Revue d'Histoire moderne et contemporaine*, 22 (1975), 89–141; Paul Butel, 'L'Instruction populaire en Aquitaine au xviii*e* siècle', *Revue d'Histoire moderne et contemporaine*, 54 (1976), 12–31.
21. Philippe Marchand, 'Un modèle éducatif original à la veille de la Révolution: Les Maisons d'éducation particulière', *Revue d'Histoire moderne et contemporaine*, 22 (1975), 549–67.
22. Grosperrin, *Petites Écoles*.
23. Jean-Pierre Belin, *Le Mouvement philosophique de 1748 à 1789* (Paris, 1913), 73.
24. Melton, *Absolutism*, 232–4.
25. Quoted ibid. 43.
26. Harvey Chisick, *The Limits of Reform in the Enlightenment: Attitudes towards the Education of the Lower Classes in Eighteenth Century France* (Princeton, 1981).
27. Marina Roggero, *Il sapere e la virtù: Stato, università e professioni nel Piemonte tra Settecento ed Ottocento* (Turin, 1987); Anthony La Vopa, *Prussian School Teachers: Profession and*

Office, 1768-1848 (Chapel Hill, NC, 1985), 'Vocations, Careers, and Talents: Lutheran Pietism and Sponsored Mobility in Eighteenth Century Germany', *Comparative Studies in Society and History*, 28 (1986), 256-86, *Grace, Talent, and Merit: Poor Students, Clerical Careers and Professional Ideology in Eighteenth Century Germany* (Cambridge, 1988); Roger Chartier, 'Un recrutement scolaire au xviiie siècle: L'École royale du génie de Mézières', *Revue d'Histoire moderne et contemporaine*, 20 (1973), 353-75.
28. Melton, *Absolutism*, 233.
29. Ibid. 102.
30. Charles McLelland, 'German Universities in the Eighteenth Century: Crisis and Renewal', *SVEC* 167 (1977), 169-89.
31. L. W. B. Brockliss, *French Higher Education in the Seventeenth and Eighteenth Centuries: A Cultural History* (Oxford, 1987); Dominique Julia, Jacques Revel, and Roger Chartier, *Les Universités européenes du xviie au xviiie siècle: Histoire sociale des populations étudiantes* (Paris, 1986); Frederick B. Artz, *The Development of Technical Education in France, 1500-1850* (Cambridge, Mass., 1966).
32. Roggero, *Il sapere e la virtù*.
33. Richard S. Tompson, 'English and English Education in the Eighteenth Century', *SVEC* 167 (1977), 65-79: Lama, *I classici della pedagogia*.
34. Furet and Ozouf, *Lire et écrire*.
35. Chartier and Revel, 'Université et société.'
36. Brockliss, *French Higher Education*.
37. Ludmilla Jordanova, 'Conceptualising Childhood in the Eighteenth Century: The Problem of Child Labour', *British Journal for Eighteenth Century Studies*, 10 (1987), 189-99.
38. Furet and Ozouf, *Lire et écrire*, 79.
39. Roger Chartier, Marie-Madeleine Compère, and Dominique Julia (eds.), *L'Éducation en France du xviie au xviiie siècle* (Paris, 1976), 245.
40. Ibid. 619-20.
41. Schmitt, *Visionare Lebensklugheit*.

Bibliography

Artz, Frederick B., *The Development of Technical Education in France, 1500-1850* (Cambridge, Mass., 1966).

Bollême, Geneviève, and Dupront, Alphonse (eds.), *Livre et société dans la France du dix-huitième siècle* (2 vols. The Hague, 1965).

Brambilla, E., *Il sistema scolastico di Milano: Professioni nobili e professioni borghesi dall'età spagnola alle riforme teresiane* (Bologna, 1982).

Brockliss, Lawrence, *French Higher Education in the Seventeenth and Eighteenth Centuries: A Cultural History* (Oxford, 1987).

Chartier, Roger, Compère, Marie-Madeleine, and Julia, Dominique (eds.), *L'Éducation en France du xviie au xviiie siècle* (Paris, 1976).

Chisick, Harvey, *The Limits of Reform in the Enlightenment; Attitudes towards the Education of the Lower Classes in Eighteenth-Century France* (Princeton, 1981).

Engelsing, Rolf, *Der Burger als Leser: Lesergeschichte in Deutschland 1500-1800* (Stuttgart, 1974).

Findlen, Paula, *Contest for Knowledge: Debates over Women's Learning in Eighteenth-Century Italy* (Chicago, 2005).

Furet, Francois, and Ozouf, Jacques, *Lire et écrire: L'Alphabétisation des Français de Calvin à Jules Ferry* (Paris, 1977). Tr. as *Reading and Writing: Literacy in France from Calvin to Jules Ferry* (Cambridge, 1982).

Grosperrin, Bernard, *Les Petites Écoles sous l'Ancien Régime* (Rennes, 1984).

Julia, Dominique, Revel, Jacques, and Chartier, Roger (eds.), *Les Universités européennes du xviie au xviiie siècle: Histoire sociale des populations étudiantes* (Paris, 1986).

La Vopa, Anthony, *Prussian School Teachers: Profession and Office, 1768–1848* (Chapel Hill, NC, 1985).

Melton, James Van Horn, *Absolutism and the Eighteenth-Century Origins of Compulsory Schooling in Prussia and Austria* (Cambridge, 1988).

Neugebauer, Wolfgang, *Absolutischer Staat und Schulwirklichkeit* in *Brandenburg-Preussen* (Berlin, 1985).

—— *Schule und Absolutismus in Preussen* (Berlin, 1985).

Roggero, Marina, *Il sapere e la virtù: Stato, università e professioni nel Piemonte tra Settecento ed Ottocento* (Turin, 1987).

—— *Insegnar lettere: Ricerche di storia dell'istruzione in età moderna* (Turin, 1992).

—— *L'alfabeto conquistato: Apprendere ed insegnare nell'Italia tra Sette e Ottocento* (Bologna, 1999).

Schmitt, Hanno (ed.), *Visionare Lebensklugheit: Joachim Heinrich Campe in seiner Zeit, 1746–1818* (Wiesbaden, 1996).

Trenard, Louis, 'Culture, alphabétisation et enseignement au dix-huitième siècle', *Dix-Huitième Siècle*, 5 (1973), 139–50.

Willey, Thomas E., 'Kant and the German Theory of Education', *SVEC* 167 (1977), 543–67.

CHAPTER 22

SOCIABILITY

PIERRE-YVES BEAUREPAIRE

In 1767 the Abbé François-André-Adrien Pluquet published *De la Sociabilité* in two volumes with the Parisian printer Barrois. But the term had first been used in Spain at the end of the previous century, when Francisco Gutierrez de los Rios, Count de Fernan Nuñez, used it to refer to living in society. Dominique Poulot has called the town of the age of Enlightenment the 'sociable town',[1] with its classic range of forms and places for meeting together: academies, reading rooms, cafés, collections open to a select public, fraternities facing the secularization of society, salons, rapidly proliferating masonic lodges, *musées*, and, at the end of the old order, clubs. If we think first about the eighteenth century when coming to the Ancien Régime, it is worth remembering at the outset that the century of Enlightenment did not invent sociability. Fraternities rooted in the middle ages remained very numerous; academies had spread over the seventeenth century; and, as recent research has shown, like those other forms salons clearly reflected the aristocratic and fashionable ways of the seventeenth century. Even masonic lodges, for all their astonishing and sustained growth in the eighteenth century, laid claim, even as they transformed it, to the heritage of the craft guilds and confraternities of the middle ages and the earliest modern times.

Even so, it is undeniable that the last century of the Ancien Régime brought new departures in sociability, akin to those in the circulation of free, direct, and useful information. Contemporaries sought to create frameworks for association less subject to the obligations required by the authorized sociability of rulers or the church. They still sought protection, for it vouchsafed autonomy in exchange for tribute paid in published form to the glory and generosity of the protector through dedications or other marks of honour, but the emphasis was on the principle of voluntary belonging. This meant that statutes and rules did not come from outside, as in a charter, but rather were planned, elaborated, and adopted from within. The members accepted them voluntarily: nobody had imposed them. This principle of individuals voluntarily joining a group marked a fundamental break from traditional sociability, but it kept within continuity in observing the rules and distinctions of the Ancien Régime, as was shown in the artificial equality of interpersonal relations found in the salons, and the respect given to outside titles and qualities within masonic lodges.

Beyond a taste for conviviality and being together, voluntary sociability meant free acceptance of belonging, temporarily or otherwise, to a peer group meeting under its own rules. The rise of sociability reflected both the expansion and growing authority of the private sphere, but also its ability to offer in return, to a public sphere manifestly troubled and unbalanced, a more harmonious way of social organization.

Since the end of the 1960s, Ancien Régime sociability has been at the heart of research in cultural history and the social history of cultural practices. Major works have given stimulus and direction to this research. First published in 1966, Maurice Agulhon's *Pénitents et francs-maçons de l'ancienne Provence* not only fostered the production of monographs on fraternities and masonic lodges, the sociology of their recruitment, and the blending of one form of sociability into another, but also drew attention to the social, material, cultural, and religious practices of their members.[2] The author underlined structural affinities between forms of sociability which it would be wrong to contrast distortingly as opposed paradigms of old and new at the end of the Ancien Régime, in terms of fraternities versus masonic lodges. He outlined the shape of a change which anyway fitted in with research findings on the 'revolutionary transition' of the years 1770–1820, in which masonic lodges accommodated themselves to what was possible in sociable terms under the Ancien Régime, reconfiguring it but not tearing it apart. They were certainly rivals to the confraternities (though beginning merely as a particular type among them), but they also allowed them to adapt to the demands of 'social intercourse'. This approach, with its preferred emphasis on practices, is still today the hallmark of French historians studying sociability. But it has made them slow to take account of the pioneering work of Georg Simmel, one of the founding fathers of modern sociology, who studied sociability as the 'ludic form of social activity'.[3] Significantly, in 1984, in the 3rd edition of *Pénitents et francs-maçons*, Agulhon admitted that Simmel's works had been unknown to him during his research. Yet Simmel had been interested in both sociability and secrecy.[4] Even today, Simmel is not widely read among historians, in contrast with Jürgen Habermas or Norbert Elias, who also took a long time to be recognized and then challenged.

The thesis of Daniel Roche on *Le Siècle des Lumières en province: Académies et académiciens provinciaux 1680–1789* (1978)[5] and then his articles collected in *Les Républicains des lettres: Gens de culture et lumières au xviiie siècle* (1988)[6] studied cultural and academic sociability. They portrayed academic and learned sociability as a national 'social fact', going beyond Paris to take in provincial cities in all their diversity and individual development, to offer a sociology of their members, studying them by age and generational evolution, through their links and overlapping affiliations with other forms of sociability. Daniel Roche insists on the necessity of studying 'personal relations' and tracking individuals. 'It is a vast field of study' he wrote in an article on business and culture in Enlightenment France, 'cultural societies, masonic lodges, correspondence networks and institutions of Enlightenment, all in turn allow us to grasp the reality of cultural engagement among businessmen.'[7]

Taking us back to the work of Augustin Cochin on *sociétés de pensée*, François Furet in *Interpreting the French Revolution* (original French edition, 1978) and then his pupil Ran Halévi in *Les Loges maçonniques dans la France d'Ancien Régime: Aux origines de la sociabilité démocratique* (1984)[8] saw in the emergence of masonic lodges the coming of a 'democratic sociability' which undermined the foundations of the Ancien Régime and pointed towards the Revolution. But since the impact of the work of the German philosopher and sociologist Jürgen Habermas—late and exceptional though it was, *The Public Sphere* appearing in 1962—the emphasis has all been on the impossibility of thinking about Ancien Régime sociability outside the context of the public sphere, to the point where the two sometimes appear synonymous. A 'political public sphere' still called 'bourgeois' shook off the control of the absolutist state, that is the 'sphere of public power', and of court society: this was why it was called 'bourgeois'. The bourgeois public sphere can be understood first of all as being the sphere of private persons coming together as a public. The development of a voluntary, unofficial sociability, its growing autonomy, made possible the emergence of a critical public, where individuals who recognized each other as equals used their reason collectively. Masonic lodges, a crucible of bourgeois sociability freed of the model of court society, were at the heart of this productive process. Nowadays, notably influenced by literary history, research is increasingly focusing on publication strategies aimed at identifying a public.[9]

Salons: Taste Fashionably Displayed

The description *salon* was adopted in the nineteenth century, for contemporaries preferred to call them 'societies'. Salons served to emphasize the domestic sphere where the hostess, whom American gender historians call a *salonnière*, received those invited to her eponymous society. Male hosts, like Baron d'Holbach, were unusual, but some were run by couples; for example Mme Helvétius was supported by her husband Claude-Adrien Helvétius, tax farmer, freemason, materialist philosopher, and literary man in his own right. 'Society' strongly emphasized the bond between the members of the salon, its sociable nature.

Lemonnier's painting *An Evening at Mme Geoffrin's in 1755*, is one of the most classic representations of Ancien Régime sociability, even though it is generally forgotten that it has no historical authenticity.[10] But here private space meets public, the literary and fashionable worlds are grouped to immortalize a blossoming social interchange, where literary pastimes, *News of the Republic of Letters* to paraphrase Pierre Bayle, and the European realm of manners and taste come harmoniously together, with nobody feeling inhibited by norms of social behaviour to which they submit voluntarily. The identification of those who are there and those who are not, of the expected faces from literary cosmopolitanism and from the aristocracy, is reassuring: Enlightenment is at its pinnacle, Paris is its preferred scene, its salons sought after by the whole of literary and taste-forming

Europe. Yet we need to go beyond simply observing this scene to analyse the functioning and logic of salons.

Beacons of Ancien Régime sociability, the most important salons were a driving force of the European realm of manners and taste, were widely known outside, and integrated with what Lucien Bély calls princely society (*la société des princes*), and the world of courts.[11] If the best known were those of the Marquise de Lambert, Mme du Deffand, Mlle de L'espinasse, Mme Geoffrin, or Mme Necker, there were many others whose discussions, less dependent on writers or newssheets (privately circulated periodic chronicles such as Grimm's *Correspondance littéraire*), were less in the public eye but at local level took an active part in elite sociability and in fashionable literary life. At their various levels, these societies marked themselves out and gave themselves the right to decide who was worthy to belong to them. As Antoine Lilti writes,[12] 'It was this central position which empowered them, for frequenting salons could lead to election to academies. Here again, it was not so much as "literary salons", institutions of the republic of letters, but as hybrids, solidly embedded in fashionable life and court networks, that salons could function in such a way. They could thus be active in the literary world, but also be linked to the king, his counsellors and ministers who held the keys to institutional academies.' Salons were not institutions of the republic of letters, but by their integration into the sociability of the Ancien Régime upper crust and its fashionable life they could promote candidates for academies even if the final decision was not theirs.

Salons also permitted foreigners in Paris to take part in fashionable cosmopolitan life. With the rise of travel and a culture of mobility, plenty of foreigners wished to visit them. A successful Grand Tour would demand recognized entry into fashionable circles and marks of esteem to be treasured: letters of recommendation, gifts, frequent invitations, promised correspondence. Salon entries ranked alongside visits to aristocrats and the great names of Enlightenment, but carefully calibrated: sometimes secondary provincial figures from the republic of letters would have to do. It was a cosmopolitan universe not without limits or hierarchies: a foreigner who failed the first social test upon entry to a salon need not count on his host's indulgence. He would have the greatest trouble in recovering social momentum. If he showed himself not master of the rules of fashion and taste, he found himself excluded. Good taste and ease of manner were the rule of social life, and what the most recent research on sociability has clearly demonstrated is the importance and vitality of traditions passed down from the seventeenth century. We must abandon the old-fashioned idea that salons were the first signs of bourgeois sociability escaping from the aristocratic values of the *Grand Siècle*. Those whom Greek antiquity designated *Kaloi Kagathoi*, the fine and the good, were sure of possessing, through birth, education, and mastery of etiquette, that subtle blend of the innate and the acquired, the keys to Pierre Bourdieu's 'legitimate culture'. Marshal de Richelieu summed it up in a letter to Mme Favart on 30 August 1768: 'The first talent of all in company, is to be sociable; and when there are superiors in this company, never to transgress the laws of subordination.' Those who deluded themselves that in the eighteenth century the world of Molière's *Le Bourgeois Gentilhomme* was over learnt their error the hard way. Thus the financier La Reynière tried to enter high society by buying himself a mansion on the Champs Elysées.

But when he refused to receive the Viscount de Narbonne in his salon, it was considered very bad taste. La Reynière then expected to be challenged to a duel by the young aristocrat. But the latter preferred the weapon of symbolic humiliation to the sword. By making the financier look ridiculous, Narbonne showed his command of the ways and codes of high society, and demonstrated besides the inequality of their respective social positions: La Reynière was not his peer, and did not deserve the sword.

Embodying the fashionable sociability of the Ancien Régime, Parisian salons were often described in the letters and travel journals of foreign visitors, illustrating suggestively how contemporaries saw these French-style societies imitated throughout Europe, even when they thought French men of letters unbearably pretentious. From this viewpoint the letters to Pietro Verri (1728–97), the pillar of the journal *Il Caffè*, from his younger brother Alessandro (1741–1816), who accompanied Cesare Beccaria on his triumphal journey to Paris on the invitation of the Abbé Morellet, are particularly fruitful. Significantly, he happily emphasizes the domestic and material aspects of salon sociability:

> The houses I visit are the following: Baron d'Holbach, Mademoiselle d'Espinasse where I always meet d'Alembert, Madame Necker, Countess de Boufflers, the Portuguese ambassador. All is perfectly easy everywhere. We eat wonderfully. Much conversation, though I say little, as is my way; argument is free, but the tone is always one of good company. I have made the acquaintance of M. Marmontel: he is a decent sort, somewhat crude in his ways, but all in all an excellent fellow (…) As for d'Alembert, he seems to me to be the greatest and the best of all the philosophers. Direct and agreeable as an angel in conversation. I really love him. (27 Oct. 1766)

Although not concealing from his brother the real pleasure he took in this social life, he cast a critical eye on the fashionable and aristocratic codes which were then current in this society but rooted still broadly in a model inherited from the previous century: 'I went to dine at the Countess Boufflers. She is a woman of the highest wit, much seen with the Prince de Conti. Accordingly she is much respected. Our Morellet and Marmontel behave in her presence with much modesty. This is a woman who can get you a pension. But this fawning air disgusts me. Nothing can be done about it. I shall only go there rarely.' At a time when scientific and technical progress were accelerating and universally praised in the name of human progress, men of science were particularly sought after in salons, especially when they were entertaining and knew how to conduct themselves. D'Alembert himself noticed this: 'In England, it was enough for Newton to be the greatest genius of his age: in France he would have been expected also to be agreeable.'

Old and new aristocratic elites were at home in the salon of Mme Geoffrin, at the smart private theatre of the Duke d'Orleans, at balls, at amateur or subscription concerts, at the Palais Royal, or at carefully orchestrated public philanthropic occasions—generosity had to be seen, but those expected to witness its scale, the selflessness, and the names of those involved should, as good breeding required, keep a good and respectful distance. As for the men of letters who realized the value of salons to get themselves known and recognized, secure protection and sinecures, they had to remember

Richelieu's letter. The lesson was clear: the myth of equality governing social relations in polite society did not make inequality of rank disappear. For his part, Voltaire wrote to Mme du Deffand: 'One must be a man of the world before being a man of letters. That's the merit of President Hénault. You would not know that he works like a Benedictine monk.' Mme de Genlis said the same. 'A man of letters must live in the best society: if he devotes four hours a day to it, he will be left with enough time to work and think about what he has seen.'

In the salons, those portals to high society, *faux-pas* and lapses of taste were scarcely allowed: ridicule punished them implacably, and the deadly news of them soon got about; the gate was shut, as Mme Geoffrin put it, to the would-be entrant who could not show on his first appearance his command of the codes of polite behaviour, his ability to fit in to a symbolic organization governed by fictional equality, the language of friendship, discreet benevolence, and gratitude. As Charles Collé, himself a great source on the best company for literary distractions, put it, the disinterested benevolence given to a literary man was a 'protective politeness', not free, but on the contrary presuming something in return, the discreet but recurrent manifestation of acceptance of the norms governing the world of high society. Similarly, women seeking their own participation in this literary and fashionable sociability, must first of all show their acceptance of these norms: their role was to be hostess; if they dreamt of writing, it must be in a genre deemed secondary, feminine, meaning letter-writing. Woe betide those who did not understand this, such as Mme du Bocage or Mme de Beauharnais. Women who played the wit or sought literary distinction were the target of repeated ridicule and symbolic humiliation. It was only after having disarmed criticism and suspicion that others might imperceptibly loosen the clamp, manage the norms, and win some autonomy. It worked very well for Mme Geoffrin, whose communication strategy was remarkable. In 1766 it enabled her skilfully to transform, in the eyes of Parisian society, a more or less fruitless journey to Poland in the hope of becoming a mentor to King Stanislas-Augustus Poniatowski, into a successful European tour: notably, she was received by the Empress-Queen Maria Theresia, her son Joseph II, and Prince Kaunitz. Beyond individuals, it was the universality of the Parisian model of polite sociability which was recognized among princes, from Vienna to Warsaw.

Academies between Tradition and Modernization

In 1734 the *Dictionnaire de Trévoux* defined the French meaning of *Académie*: 'An academy is an assembly of the learned, who hold meetings between themselves on matters of erudition.' It was different from the English or Latin usage, which 'employ this term (academy) to mean what we call a University... But writing in French the two things, so different in our language, must be kept distinct. A university is a body made up of doctors, of bachelors aspiring to a doctorate, of regents teaching in colleges, and of young people and scholars studying under these regents.' And academy meant above all a small learned circle which from the informal in the early seventeenth century (the 'early academism' noted by Simone Mazauric and numbering more than seventy according to Alain Viala) became institutionalized from mid-century onwards. We think of course of Richelieu commissioning Valentin Conrart and his friends in 1634 to set up an Academy to define and illustrate the French language, and then of the creation of the Royal Academy of Sciences in 1666 on the initiative of Colbert.

From the end of the seventeenth century to the mid-eighteenth academic foundations multiplied, as d'Alembert, himself perpetual secretary of the Academy of Sciences, bore witness in the article *Académie*, which he wrote for the *Encyclopédie*: 'The number of academies is increasing by the day; and without examining here whether it be useful to let such establishments proliferate so strongly, we can at least not disagree that they are contributing in part to the spread and maintenance of taste for letters and study. Even in towns with no academies, literary societies are forming which do much the same thing.' In fact, provincial academies numbered around forty at the end of the Ancien Régime (more than two-thirds of provincial capitals had them) not to mention numerous literary and learned societies in the west, north, and centre of the kingdom.

Traditional historiography emphasized the exhaustion of the academic movement over the last two decades of the Ancien Régime, in contrast to the rise of a sociability more independent of state power, notably in the form of reading rooms and masonic lodges. This was also the context of an expanding body of 'museums' (*musées*) which organized public lectures and offered more practical and useful lessons than the work of academies, in response to academic stagnation and to the reluctance of academicians to commit to more advanced forms of the production and diffusion of knowledge. It was noticed that academies were pondering the value of their own roles towards the end of the Enlightenment. There was the well-known diatribe of Jean-Paul Marat in 1791 on the uselessness of academies called *Modern Charlatans, or, Letters on academic charlatanism* where he says among other things: 'The study of the sciences which so rarely begets true wisdom almost always drags behind it the credulity of superstition'; 'You will be surprised by the confidence of these gentlemen in the wisdom of the age, and at the interminable compliments they pay themselves on the progress of reason, and on the reign of truth' (letter ii). But we can too readily overlook that this former household doctor to the Count d'Artois had once dreamt of academic recognition...

This viewpoint is not wrong, but nevertheless it partially obscures the variety and the ambiguities of what academics did. When we go back to contemporary statements we need to be careful to situate them in their precise political, intellectual, institutional, and social context. Take the case of Voltaire. The twenty-fourth letter in *Lettres philosophiques* is traditionally described as a frontal attack on the French Academy. Whilst the Newtonian Royal Society promoted the diffusion of research, in contrast the French institution practised above all the art of the polished compliment: 'One day, an important thinker from that country asked me for the transactions of the French Academy; it does not have transactions, I replied; but it has printed 60 or 80 volumes of compliments.' Nor was Voltaire kinder about the Academy of Sciences: 'The Royal Society of London is without two of the things that men find most necessary, rewards and rules. Membership of the Academy means a secure small fortune in Paris for a geometer or for a chemist: whereas in London it costs money to be in the Royal Society. Whoever in England says, *I like the Arts*, and wishes to be in the Society can get in at once.'[13] Voltaire, however, often unjust but always lucid, was far from condemning the whole academic movement. At the end of his article 'Académie' in his *Philosophical Dictionary* he recognized that: 'Academies in the provinces have given rise to emulation, promoted work, accustomed young people to good books, blown away ignorance and prejudice in some towns, inspired politeness and so far as is possible driven out pedantry.' Voltaire did not disdain praise from academies or invitations to be an associate of European academies. And of course his supporters controlled the French Academy at the end of the Ancien Régime.

We should stress the central role of the Royal Academy of Sciences as an example of the legitimation of knowledge and those who possessed it, the publicizing of experiments, knowledge, and organization in the scientific field—although it is too early still to talk of a discipline in the modern sense. From 1699, article 31 of its rules entrusted it notably with expertise in scientific discoveries and gave it the goal of deciding which sciences and works were useful to the monarchy: 'The Academy will examine, if the king so orders, all machines for which a privilege is sought from His Majesty. It will certify whether they are new or useful, and the inventors of those which are approved will be required to deposit a model with it.'

The social conservatism of a number of provincial academies was an indisputable reality. The delights of *otium*, that aristocratic leisure which allowed commitment as an amateur, disinterested and not seeking mean material profit, to the cult of the muses and practice of the arts, did not sit well with the constraints of *neg-otium*, the mercantile life where time was money. Merchants (*négociants*), when they showed the desire, were most often accepted with lip-service in provincial academies, in contrast to representatives of the nobility of the parlements or the upper clergy who had an 'innate' vocation to sit in these well-padded narrow circles or to put together collections of curiosities. There was an obvious bond between aristocratic sociability and the academic movement; it helps to modify any hasty if not distorting distinction between the relaxed salon, where talk was free and unconstrained among those present, and the academic session, supposedly stilted and sclerotic towards the spirit of innovation. Similarly, we need to abandon looking at the academic movement in terms of administration and events, only noticing the dates when letters-patent and royal recognition were obtained. Under the Ancien Régime academic institutionalization was essential to the process of recognizing the public utility of a place of sociability, but it should not obscure the process or the essence of this sociability. Thus, to get the full flavour of the academic movement in Dijon under the Ancien Régime, we need to bring out the influence of President Bouhier and his deep attachment to the freedom of those who met at his house, the autonomy of 'his' society. This model of social intercourse, allowing a flexible association of activities and membership of many groups, could be found and recognized throughout Europe. It was precisely what made the elites of the age feel at home everywhere: in salons as in lodges, in academies as in societies given to amateur theatricals and music making.

Before seeing academies as opposed to the new sociability, it should also be stressed that academies were at one in emphasizing public utility, educational priorities, and their role as cultural intermediaries. The model case is Dijon again. In 1770 the magistrate Legouz de Gerland offered to establish at his own expense a 9,000 square metre botanical garden, hothouses, and a public lecture series on botany. The Academy accepted, and the Count de Buffon himself—a great man born in the province who lent legitimacy and protection—endorsed the operation: 'he will be delighted to contribute in some way to stocking the botanical garden'. Then followed the process of institutionalization: letters-patent were obtained in 1772 and regulations drawn up fixing the duties and rules of recruitment of the professor of botany. The 'publication' of the benefactor's personal initiative, of its acceptance by the academic body, and recognition of its public value by the monarchical authorities, crowned the enterprise and brought harmoniously together the happy stages it had all gone through and the support which had enabled it to succeed. On 20 June 1773, a public session of the Academy was held at the botanical garden, and an inaugural lecture. The magistrate founder, the perpetual secretary of the Academy, and the professor of botany all took turns to speak. The secretary's address, a true Enlightenment credo, throws remarkable light on the importance of the creation in terms of spreading knowledge and of public utility:

> Foundations that can dispel ignorance, that source of all ills, are worthy of the greatest favour. They are above all most precious to humanity when the art of healing is in view. We can see many like this in France, and the art is taught with the greatest success in Paris, in Montpellier, in Rouen...most of the academies established in different provinces are still involved in accelerating its progress...But. despite the number of schools dedicated to this teaching, and despite the efforts of academies, occasions for learning are far from abundant as they ought to be in the interests of society...there should be set up, at least in every provincial capital, establishments designed to giving free instruction to those who wish to devote themselves to the practice of the different parts of medicine, establishments where there would be lessons on anatomy, the history of diseases, childbirth, surgical operations, chemistry, pharmacy, medical matters or botany...So this garden will be of enormous value, because medical men have always complained of not being able to use the plants, even indigenous ones, that they need.

In these circumstances, *musées* were not only rivals to academies, they complemented them in stressing their educational function, their openness to new disciplines, including practical ones, accelerating the assimilation of the utilitarian perspectives signposted by the Enlightenment. The creation of *musées* bears witness to the desire of the reforming elites of the end of the Ancien Régime to renew the field of academic sociability by offering a structure alongside official sociability, with its social and cultural conformism, open to non-Catholics and to the world of trade. Thus from its very foundation in 1783 the *musée* of Bordeaux paid supportive homage to trade 'first of the arts, so beneficial and so despised', whereas the Academy still undervalued *negotium*. *Musées* sought to open themselves to a wider public, offering lectures in mathematics, chemistry, physics, anatomy, foreign languages, drawing... to such an extent that they sometimes became veritable institutions of free higher education. They published collections of work and sometimes even journals. *Musées* therefore were a response to the cultural thirst of a talented middle class, which could cultivate the muses in these select but not exclusive circles. As vehicles of education and philanthropic aims, their philosophy seems close to that of the more dynamic masonic lodges, which sought the patronage of the elites but blossomed on the outer edges of the Ancien Régime establishment.

Freemasons were a sign of real convergence and complementarity in terms of sociability. They gave decisive impetus to the foundation of different *musées*. In Paris the Nine Sisters Lodge, derived from Helvétius's plan for a Lodge of the Sciences and defining itself as a 'society of freemasons cultivating the sciences and fine arts' was behind the Société apollonienne (1780), soon to be the Paris *Musée* of Court de Gébelin, whose rival was none other than the scientific *musée* and future *lycée* of Pilâtre de Rosier. In Bordeaux, 55 of the 150 members of the musée are identifiable as freemasons, but Johel Coutura thinks that in fact most members were in both. It is noteworthy that when plans for *musées* came to nothing for lack of support from the provincial intendant or municipal elites, freemasons were still behind societies with comparable ambitions. This is what happened with the Collège des Philalèthes at Lille, the Société des Philalèthes at Metz, or even the Cercle des Philadelphes, the only academic structure in the colonies, midway between an academy and a *musée*, sustained by the freemasons of Saint-Domingue who endowed it with a particularly far-reaching network of correspondents. Thus masonic lodges appear as the crossroads of Ancien Régime sociability and not as an instrument for its destruction. Descendants of the world of confraternities, they were not clubs, they sought the patronage of the powerful but organized themselves beyond the power of the state, parading their aim of enlivening sociable life even as they demonstrated its fears about the decay of social bonds.

From Fraternities to Masonic Lodges

The success of freemasonry was unparalleled within Ancien Régime sociability. The first lodge whose story can be archivally documented dates from 1725 in Paris, but it is clear that British freemasons were found in France by the end of the seventeenth century, performing individual initiations, and that throughout the century there were very many masonic clusters in various stages of formality which saw no necessity to seek recognition (or had been refused it) from what was at first called the 'centre of union', then the Grand Lodge and then from 1771 to 1773, the Grand Orient of France. These unevenly constituted kernels of sociability were often very active, but having no administrative correspondence with the Parisian centre, most often little is known about them except when they are mentioned in some private correspondence. On the eve of the Revolution, there were around 900 masonic lodges, with 40,000–50,000 members in a kingdom of

28.5 million inhabitants (in comparison, France today has around 120,000 freemasons for 64 million inhabitants). But the success is all the more remarkable if we remember that freemasonry enjoyed no official recognition from the authorities, despite various attempts to achieve it under Louis XV. It had plenty of effective protection, and its development met no obstacles after the end of the 1740s. The numerous professions of loyalty, faithfulness, and social conformity which it made to the sovereign and his representatives were very well received. Masonic sociability, an urban phenomenon, was particularly active in the great seaports and judicial and military capitals, but it could be found right down to very modest townships like Saint-Paul de Fenouillet in the province of Roussillon. The smartest lodges, often welcoming both sexes ('lodges of adoption' are spoken of, or ladies' masonry), did not hesitate, either, during the summer or judicial vacations to meet in the country in the pleasure mansion of one or other of their members for hunting parties, balls, literary relaxation, or amateur theatricals, games of skill. In fact, lodge activity was not simply a matter of what was strictly masonic, such as the practice of symbolic rituals, ceremonies of reception into the masonic order for new initiates, or of promotion in grade.

In 1966, Maurice Agulhon's pioneering study on penitents and freemasons revealed the structural kinship and formal analogies between fraternities of Provençal penitents and masonic lodges, and demonstrated a distinct slippage among the elites of the one towards the other in the course of the second half of the eighteenth century. Coming between fraternities before and *cercles* after the Revolution and the First Empire, lodges brought about a seamless change in sociability: laicization and individualization of activity and commitment, autonomization of the social sphere with respect to the constraining powers (political, municipal, and religious authorities), but also politicization in the sense of playing a public part notably through changes in Christian benevolence and lay philanthropy. Such an analysis brings out how malleable the so-called traditional Ancien Régime forms of sociability were, and their ability to transform themselves in response to the expectations of those who belonged or might do. Certainly, in the case of the Provençal penitents, we see the *major et sanior pars* moving over to freemasonry, just as the Brotherhood of Saint-Sébastien abandoned the 'Noble sport of archery' (games of skill in chivalric style) for the lodges. But it was not a question of rupture, or of departure without thought of returning. Sociability needs to be conceived as networks, simultaneous overlapping membership was the thing, and according to the reputation of a body and its dynamism, the influence of its members which attracted or put off new ones, and all sorts of other more or less chance causes, courses were followed which were not final. If a fraternity managed to adjust the level of its recruitment in terms of civil qualities, then the representatives of urban elites might well agree to return, or in any event to remain honorary members.

The Provençal case was not alone. In Avignon (Claude Mesliand), in Savoy (Jean Nicolas), in Le Puy-en-Velay (Pierre Yves Beaurepaire), in the south around Toulouse (Michel Taillefer), extensive links have been discovered between masonic lodges and fraternities of penitents, with interesting variations. In Toulouse, where in spite of a fragile financial situation and a certain spiritual decline, fraternities managed to retain an enviable social composition, they held back the drift towards lodges, nevertheless not losing good relations with the freemasons, whom they welcomed to their chapels for regular masses and funeral services. In fact it is the way these structures complemented one another as much as competition between them which stands out. Nor could their members have been less than aware of structural similarities: these were male societies, friends who recognized each other as brothers after co-optation and a ritual admission, peers who elected their officers in full awareness of outside hierarchies, and who practised festive sociability and Christian charity.

However, there existed plenty of other fraternities besides penitents, whose geographical ambit did not go beyond the southern provinces. Craft fraternities, fraternities of prayer, pious and charitable foundations variously named Brotherhoods of the Holy Sacrament (not to be confused with the Company of the same name) have thus been studied in the provinces of the northern half of the kingdom, and notably in Normandy, where their presence was massive—more than a thousand charities and fraternities in Upper Normandy alone. Earlier analyses seem to be confirmed. Simultaneous membership of lodges and fraternities was no problem, but seemed complementary, widening the spread of social relations. It was greater with the attractions of sociability, and we always find a core of persons in most local institutions, from the reading room to the lodge via the vestry (in charge of the buildings and funds of a parish) and the fraternity, and these individuals brought in members of their own networks of contact. But the key to the interaction or the blending of the two structures lay in their social composition. If there was an imbalance against urban elites inside a fraternity, whether as a result of members leaving or the entry of new members of a lower social rank, the lodge would frequently bring back defectors. Conversely, if a fraternity managed to recover its social level, then representatives of the elites would return (for example, in the Brotherhood of the Holy Sacrament in Le Havre before the Revolution) without necessarily leaving the lodge, thanks to cross-affiliation, which was at its strongest when social composition was at its most homogeneous and relations were not altered by personal incompatibilities.

Sketching out a history of forms of masonic sociability under the Ancien Régime, we can distinguish two periods while emphasizing the permanence of masonry in the register of voluntary sociability as it became less religious over the eighteenth century. In the middle of the century, masonic sociability spread throughout France, Europe, and the colonial world on a grand scale, lodges proliferated, sometimes too quickly for the number of potential brothers or initiates. The foundation on 6 November 1744 of the first Catalan lodge, in Perpignan, at the very edge of the French kingdom, reflects the movement of expansion. Its original name (about which there remains some doubt, St John or St John and St Peter, like the one it adopted when it was reconstituted by the Grand Lodge of France on 18 May 1772, St Peter and St Paul) belongs to the then dominant register of saintly names. But in 1782, when masonic sociability had forged a powerful identity, the Catalan Lodge wrote to the Grand Orient of France to ask to be reconstituted under the name of Sociability 'in place of that of St Peter and St Paul which it had received when it was previously constituted'. This was the only French lodge to adopt this name, but the choice is a good example of the evolution of the smartest masonic sociability. This lodge was in fact often seen as the 'nobles' lodge', and, confident in its social pre-eminence within the province, it described itself as 'made up of almost the whole of the best Nobility of Roussillon which takes pleasure in setting an example of regularity of manners and virtue'. At the same moment, one of the most brilliant Parisian lodges, the Amis réunis (United Friends) a lodge of farmers general of taxes, leading Protestant bankers, international financiers, amateur musicians, and distinguished foreigners, was giving thought to the nature of the loftiest masonic sociability. It consigned the result of this thinking to its 'golden book', a rare and precious piece of evidence since lodges generally preferred books of minutes. The brothers 'wished to form a society of friends rather like an English club', adding in the margin 'clubs meaning coteries in French', and then on the next page, 'a coterie of respectable people'. And so there emerged a high-society masonry with pleasure gatherings, female affiliates (*loges d'adoption*), smart theatricals, and carefully orchestrated charitable displays. It was exactly what Ancien Régime elites expected.

In understanding Ancien Régime sociability, the Habermas model, stimulating though it is, remains for all that a theoretical model which must be questioned in the light of social practices. For in bringing out an all-conquering 'high society masonry' with its involvement in the display of taste and distinction, and in fashionable entertainment, yet not to the point of losing identity thanks to the basic difference conferred by the bond of a shared initiation, we see the persistence of an aristocratic model dominant beyond the narrow circle of the smartest lodges.

Notes

1. Dominque Poulot, *Les Lumières* (Paris, 2000), 419.
2. Maurice Agulhon, *Pénitents et francs-maçons de l'ancienne Provence: Essai sur la sociabilité méridionale* (Paris, 1966; 2nd edn., 1984).
3. Georg Simmel, *Sociologie et épistémologie*, (French tr. Paris, 1991); *Sociologie: Études sur les formes de la socialisation* (1908; French tr. Paris, 1999).
4. Lilyane Deroche-Gurcel, 'La Sociabilité: Variations sur un thème de Simmel', *L'Année Sociologique*, 43 (1993), 159–188; Deroche-Gurcel and Patrick Watier (eds.), *La Sociologie de Georg Simmel* (Paris, 2002).
5. 2 vols. The Hague, 1978.
6. Paris, 1988.
7. Ibid. 289.
8. *Cahiers des Annales* 40 (Paris, 1984).
9. Hélène Merlin, *Publique et littérature en France au xviiie siècle* (Paris, 1984).
10. The factitious construction of this work, whose proper title is 'La lecture de l'Orphelin de Chine chez Mme Geoffrin', is subjected to a critical deconstruction by John Lough, 'Lemonnier's Painting "Une soirée chez Madame Geoffrin en 1755"', *French Studies*, 45 (1991), 268–78, and in *Recherches sur Diderot et l'Encyclopédie*, 12 (1992), 4–18.
11. Lucien Bély, *La Société des princes, xvie–xviiie siècles* (Paris, 1999).
12. *Le Monde des Salons: Sociabilité et mondanité à Paris au xviiie siècle* (Paris, 2005).
13. *Lettres Philosophiques*, letter xxv.

Bibliography

Agulhon, Maurice, *Pénitents et francs-maçons de l'ancienne Provence: Essai sur la sociabilité méridionale* (3rd edn., Paris, 1984).

Beaurepaire Pierre-Yves, *Le Mythe de l'Europe française au xviiie siècle: Diplomatie, culture et sociabilité au temps des Lumières* (Paris, 2007).

—— *La France des Lumières 1715–1789* (Paris, 2011).

Brockliss Laurence W. B., *Calvet's Web: Enlightenment and the Republic of Letters in Eighteenth-Century France* (Oxford, 2002).

François, Étienne (ed.), *Sociabilité et société bourgeoise en France, en Allemagne et en Suisse, 1750–1850: Actes du colloque de Bade-Hombourg (1983)* (Göttingen and Paris, 1986).

Goodman, Dena, *The Republic of Letters: A Cultural History of the French Enlightenment* (Ithaca, NY, 1994).

Jouhaud, Christian, and Viala, Alain (eds.), *De la publication entre Renaissance et Lumières* (Paris, 2002).

Habermas, Jürgen, *The Structural Transformation of the Public Sphere: An Inquiry into a Category of Bourgeois Society* (Cambridge, Mass., 1991).

Kors, Alan Charles, *D'Holbach's Coterie: An Enlightenment in Paris* (Princeton, 1976).

La Vopa, Anthony J., 'Ideas and Society in Eighteenth-Century Europe', *Journal of Modern History*, 64 (1992), 79–116.

Lilti, Antoine, *Le Monde des salons, sociabilité et mondanité à Paris au xviiie siècle* (Paris, 2005).

McClellan James, III, *Science Reorganized: Scientific Societies in the Eighteenth Century* (New York, 1985).

Roche, Daniel, *Le Siècle des Lumières en province: Académies et académiciens provinciaux, 1680–1789* (2 vols. Paris and The Hague, 1979).

—— *Les Républicains des lettres: Gens de culture et Lumières au xviiie siècle* (Paris, 1988).

CHAPTER 23

PATRONAGE

MARK LEDBURY

In the past twenty-five years, and since what some have called the 'cultural turn' in historical studies, the subject of how various regimes sponsor and exploit the arts in the service of personal, dynastic, political, or national aims has moved from the fringe to a more central place in the frames of understanding of historical moments, and this is particularly true of the Ancien Régime in France. In the work of Tim Blanning, Peter Burke, Roger Chartier, and Colin Jones, among others, we note new attention to the details of how Ancien Régime institutions and individuals used the arts and artists as tools of statecraft.[1] This trend in historical writing has coincided with a more rigorous and intense engagement with the mechanisms and details of collecting and patronage among art historians, many of them influenced to a greater or lesser degree by the pioneering studies of Francis Haskell and his students, and more recent studies such as that of Martin Warnke on *The Court Artist*.[2]

At the same time, political patronage (and clientage) has become a key topic for historians seeking to understand the complex power and privilege networks of the Ancien Régime; the work of Sharon Kettering and Peter Campbell among others has developed the area of political patronage studies in sophisticated ways.[3] However, as Kettering herself points out, it is difficult to map these models of political patronage onto the cultural realm, indeed there is an assumption in the historiography that political patronage as a model of actual government receded in the face of a new bureaucratic absolutism with the advent of Louis XIV. Despite the nuanced studies of Kettering, and Campbell on Fleury, showing political patronage–clientage networks of traditional stamp to be alive and well throughout the seventeenth and eighteenth centuries, a sense that Louis XIV created a new modern, bureaucratic state less dependent on these networks still influences the accounts of many historians, particularly in the French tradition, as most eloquently restated by Emmanuel Le Roy Ladurie.[4] Hence an apparent paradox: the same Louis XIV brand of absolutism that diminished the importance of political patronage made the state sponsorship of artists, and artistic patronage more generally, a vital part of its political strategy.

This chapter, like many of the other contributions to this book, will focus on the last century and a half of the Ancien Régime. However, for art historians, one of the first and most important events in the history of the attempt to transfer the cultural sophistication of the Italian Renaissance courts to France, and in doing so to create a powerful sense of France as culture-state, occurred at an earlier moment with the policy of Francis I, first in the Loire valley and then, most intensely, at the hunting lodge/palace of Fontainebleau (1528 and after). At Fontainebleau, Francis enticed significant artists away from Italy and created the kind of complex architectural, decorative, and iconographic ensembles that he and his entourage knew from the grand courts of Renaissance Florence, thus setting a pattern for complex cultural-political intervention and for the intense focus on a courtly château-space as centre of experiment in patronage.[5] Francis I also began urban renewal in Paris and his policies, continued to some extent by Henry II (1547–59), must be seen as significant in the formation of an *expectation* that French monarchs would inscribe their power on the visual fabric of their dwelling spaces, whether these be individual rooms, palaces, city squares, or whole kingdoms. Henry IV's significant impact on the city of Paris (through the creation of *places*, through deals with urban property entrepreneurs, for example) must also be seen as a key model, a part of the cultural memory of all future kings, and thus a tremendous influence on the grand urbanist/visual, architectural schemes of later years.[6]

Vaux and Versailles

For the sake of brevity and concentration of argument, these highly significant moments in the history of Ancien Régime artistic patronage must remain as 'back story'. Nevertheless, in the light of recent scholarship, this chapter will not begin quite in the expected place (1682 in Versailles) but rather at a moment immediately before the creation of the Versailles with which we are familiar. The most thoroughgoing of recent reappraisals of Versailles as a cultural phenomenon has been the work of Claire Goldstein, who has set out to demonstrate through an analysis of literature, theatre, visual art, and garden design, that in many ways certain key patterns of patronage—the creation of a space outside the city, the assembling of major talents in all fields of artistic creation—the encouragement of a certain kind of atmosphere of freedom, and the use of seductive spectacle—were crucial parts of the intense but short-lived experiment of Nicolas Fouquet at Vaux-le-Vicomte, in the late 1650s and early 1660s, before Fouquet was disgraced, put on show trial, and ultimately banished.[7] Goldstein argues that although Vaux effectively set a precedent and provided a model for Versailles, it fundamentally represented a very different spirit of patronage as a creative act, an assembly of diverse artistic talent in a space of experiment and excellence, one which Louis XIV's Versailles both copied and destroyed. In this Goldstein follows such scholars as Marc Fumaroli and Alain Niderst who propose Vaux as a project committed to diversity, equality, liberal ethos, and a sense of peaceful coexistence—a reaction, an antidote even, to the regimes of Mazarin and Richelieu.[8] Further, it has been argued, Vaux represented a specifically cultural-nationalist agenda, the 'manifesto of a France reconciled with itself, and finally the perfect mother and mistress of its own arts' (Fumaroli, *Poet and the King*, 175). In this aim it foreshadows later projects by individuals and institutions, and even the creation and promotion in the later eighteenth century of what Colin Bailey has termed *Patriotic Taste*.[9]

Notwithstanding Claire Goldstein's fresh and original analysis of what Versailles owes to Vaux, it would be fair to say that Versailles became the epicentre of efforts to marshal the arts to the service of political and dynastic agendas, and that the organization of the arts under Louis XIV set a pattern for the whole of Europe. Cultural history has in the past decades argued that this was not the froth on the top of warfare, but integral to the entire functioning of politics and society in absolutist France (and Europe more widely). Versailles has proved a key centre for cultural histories of the reign of Louis XIV, and the studies of Jean-Marie Apostilidès, Louis Marin, and Peter Burke particularly focused on the *function* of the various spectacles and performances hosted at Versailles in the creation and sustaining of a political project around the King's image.[10] Louis XIV's reign had something of what the anthropologist Clifford Geertz described as the 'theatre state' about it.[11] Cultural historians argue that Louis's power and image, his status, was created not just by force of arms, or by bureaucratic organization, or financial reform, but by and through his use of a cultural vocabulary, a manipulation of ritual, visual, and symbolic forms and gestures. *Le Roi Machine* (to use Apostilidès's terms), and his hypnotic, engrossing, as well as coercive court culture at Versailles was, for a time at least, a central space of power and authority in France and Europe. It was not just the site of power, it spoke that power.[12] The right to watch the King's *grand* or *petit lever* became a marker of status, and ascending the *escalier des ambassadeurs*, foreign dignitaries would be overawed by the assemblage of carefully constructed representations of victory, homage, luxury, and magnificence. As Nivelon so clearly perceived in his description of the staircase, created out of multiple types of French marble and which combined images of Louis's victories with trompe-l'œil representations of peoples of the world paying homage, the *escalier* actually blurred representation with desired reality, by making homage to the great king the theme of the decorative scheme.

> When the great king descends this staircase, followed by all the princes and princesses, this makes for such a grand and superb spectacle that one would think all peoples are rushing to honor him as he passes, and to see the finest court in the world—so artfully are the natural and the represented mixed in this ensemble.... this will be seen as one of the most magnificent spaces in all Europe.[13]

To some extent, our model of understanding of the relationship between power and culture in the Ancien Régime is still under the 'spell' of Versailles as experiment in government by culture. Such a view, of course, then produces the other dominant narrative of patronage in the Ancien Régime—that of the movement from a magnificent, centralized, court-based culture of appearances reaching its apogee at the moment of Louis

FIGURE 23.1. J.-M. Chevolet, *l'Escalier des Ambassadeurs*, engraving, c.1674

XIV's splendour, to a disputatious, fragmented cultural sphere in which absolutist certainties were gradually erased by the increasing power of the marketplace and of public opinion by the end of the Ancien Régime. The narrative has become even more powerful in the wake of the powerful influence of the Habermas thesis of the growth of a modern public space, which has influenced many cultural histories, including Robert Darnton's extraordinary corpus of work on the growth of a certain kind of literary public sphere in France.[14] In the visual arts, the basic thesis of a new crucible of contest in which art is received by the end of the century is at the heart of recent and highly influential works such as Thomas Crow's *Painters and Public Life in Eighteenth Century Paris* (probably the single most important book on the visual arts in the public sphere published in the last twenty years) and Roger Chartier's *The Cultural Origins of the French Revolution*.[15] This is the powerful, if teleological, narrative of the gradual erosion of monarchical control over the arts, as the Bourbon monarchy's grip on power weakened and individual monarchs (guided or misguided by their powerful favourites or venal courtiers) consequently or concurrently lost their grip on the symbolic realm until they were finally ousted by a new republican image-making machine in the revolutionary process.

In the light of new research, however, this narrative must be nuanced, if not entirely rethought. Firstly, scholars have seen shifts occurring many decades before the Revolution. Jay Caplan has recently argued, with the help of analyses of certain moments in the late reign of Louis XIV and in the Regency, that at the death of Louis XIV and even before it, the power of the monarch to impose cultural standards and representations faded fast.[16] Caplan, and others, see a visualization of this transfer of cultural power in Watteau's famous and remarkable *Shop Sign of Gersaint* with its apparent 'packing away' of the portrait of the King (scholars debate whether the King is going in or coming out, however).

The more salient point is that painters such as Watteau and their allies and patrons were already becoming part of a sophisticated, commercial culture of the city that challenged and even 'discounted' Versailles very early in the eighteenth century, and displaced elite sociability and its cultural representations from Versailles to Paris.[17] This was even more the case for theatrical life, whose centre of gravity shifted definitively to Paris in the post-Louis XIV moment.[18]

But, more importantly, there are reasons to doubt the effectiveness of absolutist image-building even in its heyday. Even at the highest points of Louis's power and glory, neither Versailles nor any other monarchical site was ever what Louis XIV hoped it would be, a space of total mastery and dominance. Instead, Louis's ever-developing Versailles, in common with all elaborate systems of patronage and image-building, was both a composite and a compromise: Versailles as a complex of buildings and gardens was in a permanent state of flux, renewal, and renovation, not just in Louis XIV's reign but right up until the Revolution, with decisions being made on the basis of commodity, practicality, and the basic needs of comfort and physical dynastic expansion as much as, and in some cases at the expense of, statecraft.[19] The extent to which the court was a human network, a system, rather than a series of gravitationally fixed planets revolving obediently round the Sun King, has been beautifully revealed by Emmanuel Le Roy Ladurie's latest edition of the Memoirs of the Duke de Saint-Simon, whose often acerbic

FIGURE 23.2. Antoine Watteau, *Shop Sign of Gersaint*, 1721, oil on canvas. Charlottenburg Palace, Berlin

commentaries on the community forced together in Versailles are themselves an indictment of the impossibility of pressing complex human entities into grand schemes.[20] The complexities and impossibilities of Versailles have been teased out in Gérard Sabatier's recent and monumental *Versailles ou l'image du Roi*.[21] The acts of reuse, repurpose, and destruction at Versailles (whether this be the melting down of silver crafted at enormous expense for the war effort in 1669, the abrupt changes in iconographical scheme of major suites of rooms, or the theatrical use of the *escalier des ambassadeurs* by Pompadour in the 1740s and then its demolition in 1752) are redeployments and erasures rich in resonance for modern historians, probing what might be called the *contingency* of all attempts to harness art to political agendas.

We do well to remember that the structural 'firm grip' on the arts that the Colbert–Louis XIV axis created via the academies and via control over public art did not lead to mastery of political image-making or public opinion in the way desired or intended. As Peter Burke details, transitions between moments of absolute control of art's making and response to periods characterized by the buffeting of monarchical plans via political and financial difficulties and the vagaries of public opinion are swift, and can happen within the space of months, let alone a long reign or a century and a half. In Burke's view, Louis XIV's royal programme of allegory and symbolic representation in paintings, decorations, and ballets, for example, was already undermined in the later years of his reign by the disparity between early glory and more recent 'less than glory', and by the coming of a scientific and knowledge revolution that shaped reception of the image in the high-born and city circles in which the image of Louis XIV was supposed to resonate.[22] Burke also shows how already after the revocation of the Edict of Nantes and the subsequent persecutions and expulsions of Protestants, a lively counter-image, a desacralizing image of the King, was soon at play. Rochelle Ziskin's work on the Place de nos conquêtes shows just how fickle, problematic, and difficult to fix were representations of majesty.[23] The Place de nos conquêtes—then Place Louis Le Grand and ultimately Place Vendôme—was conceived by Louis XIV to be a monumental tribute to celebrate the conquests of his reign, and would be the space of concentration of French cultural authority (via the housing behind its façades of the Academies that Colbert had been gradually establishing and reorganizing from the early 1660s). It was also to be the model for a wide-scale diffusion of the message of the crown's domination, via plans for squares in cities throughout the kingdom. Moreover, the plan to host in the square a 'Residence for Ambassadors' would make all special envoys and ambassadors from European rivals the witnesses of the glorious ceremonial that defined the centre of power. And at the centre, an imperial equestrian statue of Louis XIV would express the authority and presence of the monarch in Paris, even when the court itself was in Versailles. So far, so absolute. However, the history of the development of the plans for the *place,* and that of the reception of the statue, are a sorry and for us salutary tale of how problems with finance, but more especially problems with what might be called 'reception', and the fickle and quickly changing intellectual and political scene, derail the grand and well-worked out plans for massive public patronage projects. After the financially disastrous League of Augsburg War, the repercussions of the disastrous campaigns and the fallout from the revocation of the Edict of Nantes had created entirely new conditions of reception for vast public works of art. Now the statue in the Place des Victoires was thought inappropriate and ridiculed outright and Louis XIV ordered that the new equestrian statue be portrayed without any pomp. Eventually the entire design of the square was rethought, and the grandiose academic and ambassadorial aims entirely changed. Even the new place 'Louis le Grand', of far more self-contained design, soon took on its popular nomenclature, Place Vendôme.[24]

We might then propose that that these vacillations, changes of plan, moments that come and go, ideas that are modified, politically inspired changes of mind and matter, are in fact typical of what might be called the system of monumental patronage in the Ancien Régime—a constant *va et vient* between certainties of absolutist will, control, and ceremony, and the uncomfortable intrusion of complex events, a new world of ideas, of public and political challenge. Within every project of significant political patronage of the visual or plastic arts lay the tension of reception, the possibilities of scabrous misreading and rereading, the awareness of how a project might interact with currents of rumour and other forms of viral, ungovernable 'opinion'. It reminds us that the moment of absolute control of the image was fleeting, often lying only in the plan, the idea, and usually fading by the time these plans made it into physical instantiation and despite all the measures and institutions (strict decrees and academies, for example) that could help the crown control the image-makers.

As Ziskin has reminded us

> Louis XIV... abandoned several significant projects and even dismantled one of the most acclaimed. He left the east facade of the Louvre incomplete, allowed the colossal Arc de Triomphe du Trône to remain a model, realized only four of a larger projected series of triumphal portals, and demolished the first incarnation of the Place Vendôme.[25]

Thus we might want to claim that the relationship of crown to artists (corporately or individually) often involves a complex jostling of identities and desires, powers and wills, and takes place within a network of power relations that is never entirely within the control of the powerful organs of monarchical authority. And despite the compelling story of Louis XIV's glory and the abundant evidence of failure that seems to haunt Louis XVI, we cannot plot a straight line of decline in cultural glory from 1661 to 1789. Indeed, Jean Locquin's influential and triumphalist narrative of history painting in France plots a gradual ascension of quality and seriousness of painting culminating in 1785, and although there is much to debate in his century-old thesis, it could be argued that at no point was the crown's effectiveness in its mission control over the agenda and production of painting stronger than during the tenure as *Directeur des Bâtiments du Roi* of the Count D'Angiviller between 1774 and 1789, a moment in which a generation of painters were disciplined and shaped to create visual and sculptural monuments to France's glory, all this occurring during the (otherwise highly challenged) reign of Louis XVI.[26]

It is perhaps more helpful to postulate two models of patronage for the Ancien Régime—one loosely a 'Vaux' model (following Goldstein) in which a person of wealth and influence gathers to them the products of advanced and fashionable artists of various types in an immersive cultural milieu often bringing musicians, artists, decorative artists, and writers together, resulting in a particular mode, idiom (some would say style). The aims here might be aesthetic, political, and 'nationalist', but they are 'soft' in the sense that they operate through the lubricants of money, and through networks of friendship and particular associations between patrons and artists. We will see this as a frequent and important phenomenon in court and city at various moments of the Ancien Régime. We might then oppose this to a 'Versailles' model of large-scale royal patronage of public art, which has what might be called 'hard' cultural political aims— explicit agendas, specific audiences and targets, and clearly articulated messages about the power and prestige of the ruling monarch.

This dual model replaces the well-known 'good and bad patron' opposition with what might be called 'liberal' and 'coercive' models of patronage itself. One might further argue that the Vaux model can never really last, and the Versailles model can never fully succeed. The Versailles model of patronage is a constantly fraught, tense process, full of complex personal and corporate battles fought in corridors and on canvas, paper, or in the fabric of the city as the image of the Bourbon monarchy and of France is 'at play'. The Vaux model is doomed to be the temporary conjunction of talent, money, self-interest, and generosity, an alignment that leads to sparkling moments and leaves a stylistic legacy, but has no political staying power, based as it is around key personalities whose time in the limelight is itself limited by their position in court networks, or by social and financial change.

One famous moment in the history of patronage in France somehow bridges both models and in recent years has fascinated historians as it did the Goncourts and other nineteenth-century chroniclers. That is of course what might be called the 'Pompadour Moment'—the period of the ascendancy of Jean-Antoinette Poisson, the Marquise de Pompadour, Louis XV's official and primary mistress from 1745 to 1750 and then confidante, friend, and adviser until her death in 1764. The recent exhibition at Versailles and at London's National Gallery did much to refocus our attention on the wide variety of important ways in which 'la marquise' shaped a cultural sphere which both furthered her aims and inspired remarkable and important works of art.[27] If we take, for example, her marshalling of sculptors, painters, and decorators as well as architects and garden designers to work at the now destroyed Château de Crécy, we can recognize the desire for a 'Vaux-like' space of culturally alive festivity. If we explore her deep and continuing attachment to François Boucher, we see a complex relationship of mutual admiration and need that is emblematic of the most positive and productive patron–artist relations forged at Vaux. Her keen and constant interest in French porcelain manufacture and her patronage of the fledgling manufacture of Vincennes/Sèvres made a huge difference to its prestige and branding (witness the number of new designs bearing her name). She was highly active and engaged with theatre and music, and a particularly accomplished stage performer. But the diverse evidence of her interventions in and support of art and artists indicates that her patronage of so many different branches of the arts was part of the creation of a utopian and patriotic space, one dedicated not just to her as centre of some kind of constantly mobile *Gesamtkunstwerk*, but to France as the centre of sophisticated and advanced culture. She was well acquainted with Voltaire and the *philosophes*, with the most 'contemporary' of musicians, actors, and playwrights, and with the most talented *modern* painters in all genres. We are so accustomed to Rococo, through the eyes of the neo-classical generation, thus labelling it, as decadent, that we miss just how fresh and exciting were some of Pompadour's tastes in painting and decorative art (*pace* Donald Posner).[28]

Yet there was a sense, too in which Mme de Pompadour's particular form of patronage also fell into the Versailles pattern. As Colin Jones points out, she was obliged to create multiple images and repeatedly to perform in order to maintain status *vis-à-vis* other factions at court.[29] As she did so, she constantly battled a tide of negative image-making in gossip, pamphlets. and other attacks from various factions at court who objected to her on the grounds of rank and influence.[30] Part of her strategy to place herself at the centre of court culture and battle her court enemies was astute image crafting, achieved in the Louis XIV manner, by control over visual, musical, and dramatic spectacle at Versailles. She created the *théâtre des petits cabinets* in 1747, established its rules, repertoire, and became one of its principal performers, ably assisted by professional actresses and talented courtiers.[31] These spectacles were designed to enrapture and to impress, as surely as the *Plaisirs de l'Isle enchantée* had been, and forged an identity, a complex, mobile, and sophisticated one, which her portraits by Boucher and others also helped to create.[32] Despite her efforts though, this identity was never stable or fully controllable, and always at the centre of court and wider cultural storms, as her spectacular self was always (even more so than Louis XIV's) vulnerable to gossip, unfavourable interpretation, and vicious attack in the 'information society' of the eighteenth century.[33] In my view it is as a key example of the tension between 'Vaux'—genuinely interested and committed patronage of talented and modern artists—and 'Versailles'—the attempt to spectacularize and overwhelm audiences and fix an image of power—that Madame de Pompadour's patronage should be most compelling and interesting to historians.

Academies as the Locus of State Patronage

The academy system was one of the great organs of state patronage of the visual and plastic arts, and of culture more generally. The creation of a network of arts organizations whose goals were to reorganize creative forces around new and absolutist principles has been central to our accounts of the art and culture in the Ancien Régime for many years.[34] Indeed there is something monumental about the fundamental reorganization of cultural professionals into state-sponsored and tightly controlled entities. However, few historians dwell on the highly complex, embattled origins of the Académie

Royale de Peinture et de Sculpture, despite the fact that since at least the synthetic, sometimes opinionated, but richly documented account of Vitet in 1861, we have a blow-by-blow account of the years between the academy's founding in 1648 and its refounding under the close supervision of Colbert in 1663.[35] Again, beneath the surface of the academy as an instrument of absolutist power lies a seething history of acts of rebellion, retribution, generous patronage (the Ratabons, Testelins, etc.), and heated territorial jealousies and resistances from long established guilds and artisan companies. Moreover, as with the grand schemes of Versailles, the plans for pedagogy, statutory change, and the transference of cultural doctrines in the academy met with all sorts of resistance.[36] To be glib, one could say that while it was a struggle to take the painters out of the guilds, it was even harder to take the guilds out of the painters— academy histories are punctuated by acts of proud rebellion and artistic self-assertion like those that marked the academy's founding in the face of guild power, but also by behaviours that remind us of the endurance of those very same older guild structures of self-perpetuation and self-regulation that somehow survived the transition into the new academy frame. Disputes over rights, letters-patent and even over much more minute details of statutes arise frequently within academies—witness the painful explusion of Abraham Bosse, a key academy member who fell out with it over a complex dispute about letters-patent and became one of its earliest and harshest critics. In his treatment we see already the nascent sense of *inside and outside* which remained vital to the academic dynamic. When the artist Jean-Baptiste Greuze submitted his reception piece, his now infamous *Septimius Severus and Caracalla* in 1769, hoping to be accepted as a history painter and thus eligible for academic honours of the highest rank, he was refused, and accepted into the academy, to his great humiliation, only as a genre painter. We have tended to see this as stiff inflexibility on the part of the monolithic academy in the face of radical innovation, but from the existing accounts, it is clear that in fact, at the heart of the matter was not the painting but the painter. The painters of the academy didn't actually like Greuze very much. He had been an arrogant and troublesome student, was favoured above other painters by the regime of the Directeur des Bâtiments, the Marquis de Marigny, and played off that favour to circumvent academic politesse. He had thus irritated the community of the academy—and his partial rejection was a community action in defence of its ethics, power, and freedom to select its peers.[37] Another incident from the same years, this time at the Académie Royale d'Architecture, demonstrates even more directly a battle of wills, this time not between academy as corporate entity and an 'upstart' student, but between crown and academy. The architect Charles de Wailly, who had worked for and gained favour with the Pompadour/Marigny administration, was nominated by the court as a member of the first class of architects directly (there being a vacant place in this category). The other architects protested that according to the statutes, he must, first, be placed in the second class and then it would be up to the architects themselves to promote him to the first. The crown insisted on the first-class status: the architects once again resisted, appealing directly to the Count de Saint Florentin at Versailles. In reaction, Marigny wielded his power in the King's name, threatening the revocation of all the architects' *brevets* as academicians and the closure of the academy. This was a mini *lit de justice* and the rebellious academicians were forced to climb down.[38] However, the bad blood and tension between court and academy continued, and when the post of secretary to the academy became free, the Marigny administration snubbed the popular insider and influential historiographer and theorist of the academy, Julien David Le Roy, the architects' candidate and the obvious choice for the role, and instead plucked out of the air a writer and distinct outsider, Michel-Jean Sedaine (who had been an *entrepreneur de bâtiments* but never trained as an architect).[39] This led to rancour and a very uncomfortable few years for Sedaine, but also demonstrated that the power of appointment and promotion was at the centre of a struggle between competing authorities—the corporate identity of the architectural professionals in the academy and the will of the crown. The relative court neglect of the Academy of Architecture right through to the end of the Ancien Régime (charted in the many complaining memoranda of Sedaine and others to the various administrations) may have its origin in the sense of friction that was caused by academies being at once tools of the state's culture apparatus and professional bodies with a strong sense of corporate identity, and a strong internal network of loyalty and friendships.

These are two (of many) examples of persistent *internal* frictions within the academic structures set up by the crown. There were *external* tensions generated by the interface between the academies and public life more generally. We have seen how the circulation of pamphlets, gossip, and opinion eroded the ability of powerful monarchs and court figures to create enduring and unambiguous public images. It is perhaps the Academy of Painting that has garnered the most attention in this regard because the meeting point of aspiration, control, and reception was so public, so visible—the salon exhibitions which were sponsored by the academy and held, from 1737 on, in public and on a regular basis (eventually every two years) opening on the feast day of St Louis (25 August) and running usually until the end of September (see Figure 23.3).

This public space of interaction—spectatorship was wide and, as far as we can tell, mixed—produced new forms of textual interaction and response: the beginnings of a discourse of engaged art criticism.[40] Art was indeed subject to scrutiny in ways which were often brutal and distinctly unconnoisseurial and, in Crow's view, the art that excited the audiences of the 1780s was an art that, although produced by official policy and under the tutelage of the academy, was formally disruptive and chimed with other forms of growing resistance, dissent, and disruption in the public sphere, even if it was not explicitly recognized as radical practice. Bernadette Fort took another angle, exploring the many satirical pamphlets in the form of dialogues, and coming to the conclusion that a form of Bakhtinian carnivalization of official art was taking place.[41] These frameworks of understanding are different, but both tend to point to the public sphere as corrosive of state-endorsed official arts policy.

Because of this, and because of David's later revolutionary utterances about the illiberality and aristocracy of the academy, we have thus opposed criticism (liberal) to academies (conservative and restrictive). However, just as our vision of academic doctrine is being radically revised by current historians, so we must look more carefully at the 'liberal' side of this opposition. If we were to look at the satirical exuberance of

FIGURE 23.3. *Vue du Salon de 1785*, Pietro Martini

salon criticism in the light of recent work by Antoine de Baëcque and Elisabeth Bourginiat, we might actually be tempted to reflect on the variety of (far from uniquely liberal) political standpoints that might be analysed in the wittily mocking pamphlets that were often anonymously published to accompany the salon.[42] Certainly we cannot see all salon pamphleteers as seditious underminers of the political status quo. What we can more firmly and unambiguously trace is a sense of the new *weight* of the public as an entity, in the discourse surrounding the arts. The sheer volume of public interest in the arts gives fuel to critics with specific moral, ethical, and ultimately political agendas. The early pioneer of art critical discourse, La Font de Saint-Yenne, invoked a morally high-minded, sensitive, and expectant public as he railed against Boucher or advocated for new public spaces for art. Part of what makes Diderot's aesthetics political was his crusading advocacy of Greuze as moral painter and his biting attacks on Boucher's laxity—painters' works were being used as part of a public critique of standards of public life, of fiscal and moral probity, no matter whether the assessments either critic made about these particular artists were justified or accurate.[43] The impact of opinion-formers and opinion-makers in print certainly resonated and provoked attempts by artists and administrators to act against pamphleteers.[44] To an extent, the atmosphere of the theatre *parterre*, that space *par excellence* of contest, dissent, and cabal, did start to pervade the response to visual art in the later decades of the Ancien Régime.[45] David and other painters of the 1780s came to understand and build into their practice a sense of a crucible of reception, that of necessity needed to take on board the pressure of the *parterre* as well as the exigencies of the *loges*—the 'official' patrons and sponsors of their art.⁴⁶ Thus, to an extent, like the musicians and composers whom James Johnson describes in *Listening in Paris*, artists in late Ancien Régime France had to adapt to a more self-confident and economically empowered public which was less in thrall to being told what it should and should not like, and more active, less predictable, and less dutiful in its consumption of culture.⁴⁷

Market Realities: Forms of Patronage

We must not lose sight either of the fact that artworks, decorative ensembles, even buildings are, then as now, marketable and to an extent market-dependent commodities. Naturally this has introduced a new and complex aspect to our thinking about patronage of the arts in the Ancien Régime: to what extent did the marketplace (seen as metaphor for a complex system of trade of goods of all kinds, and the expansion of a capitalist economy of luxury) interfere with or cohere with what we have traditionally seen as the heavy hand of autocratic control of the institutions of art by court and royal authority? If the academies were created in part to defeat the guilds or at least rob them of their prestige, then how did these relatively young structures cope with the demands of the growing and ever more sophisticated marketplace for cultural goods? If one source of tension in our understanding of patronage of art in the Ancien Régime is the conflict between pressures of the court and pressures exerted by the public, then another is certainly a new intensity of commerce and trade in art and luxury objects, and thus a widespread understanding of art as luxury, as commodity, as an exchangeable good in a larger system of trade which was transnational, driven by the flow of capital and not beholden to any one centre of authority, and associated with cities and ports, not with the centres of court life. From cultural historians of decorative art such as Carolyn Sargentson we have learnt how complex and far reaching was the web of commercial use and reuse of items of luxury in eighteenth-century France.⁴⁸ Dealers, auctioneers, and a whole series of new arts middlemen emerged who were both financial and aesthetic intermediaries. Among these the most prominent were the entrepreneurs who became key advisers to the rich and high-placed, such as Paillet, Basan, and Jean-Baptiste Pierre Lebrun, but they were part of a wider network covering a large spectrum of visual 'product' from cheap prints to expensive colour engravings to all kinds of oil painting.⁴⁹ The rapidly expanding market gave artists some new possibilities and strategies as well as setting them new challenges, but it also challenged the authority of a court-controlled, bureaucratic, and 'patriotic' system.

The artist Jean-Honoré Fragonard's artistic trajectory tells us much in this regard because of his involvements with key court patrons, the academies, and the growing group of rich bankers and tax farmers who sought out his work. Due to the powerful patronage (in a political sense) of François Boucher, whose studio he had joined three years earlier, he was able to enter the *Prix de Rome* competition in 1752, at the age of 20, despite not being an academy pupil. He won, and then became part of the young academic elite groomed at the *École des Élèves Protégés* for three years. He then went off to Rome in 1756, having already begun to work for private patrons. On his return he continued to produce work (in landscape and genre) for sophisticated private collectors while working on a large-scale history painting, the *Corésus and Callirhoë* (*Le grand prêtre Corésus se sacrifice pour sauver Callirhoë* 1765: Paris, Louvre) to be his *morceau d'agrément*, his provisional acceptance piece into the academy. At the salon of 1765, the critics loved it, the administration saw in Fragonard a new great hope of official history painting, and the crown, through the agency of the *Directeur des Bâtiments*, Marigny, bought it and even commissioned a pendant. However, they neglected to actually pay Fragonard for the painting for years; and perhaps disillusioned by this, perhaps tempted by the rise in his stock in the public sphere, Fragonard never sent another ambitious history painting to the salon.[50] Instead he worked mainly on commissions from wealthy tax farmers and other high-profile public patrons including Madame du Barry, for whose residence at Louveciennes he created the extraordinary ensemble known today as the *Progress of Love* and installed at the Frick collection in New York.[51] He continued to work for himself, and his friends, producing the extraordinary *figures de fantaisie* and illustrations for Don Quixote seemingly for his own amusement. He also continued to clash with patrons: quarrelling with the actress and courtesan Marie Madeleine Guimard, falling out of favour with Madame du Barry, getting into a legal dispute with the financier, *amateur*, patron, and collector Jacques-Onésyme Bergeret de Grancourt on whose considerable dime he had travelled to Italy again in 1773.[52] It was only in the revolutionary years that he re-entered the official realm, through David's patronage, and became an administrator and arts bureaucrat.

The socially and politically engaged reformist and anti-financier journalist and writer Louis Sébastien Mercier saw Fragonard as being exploited by unscrupulous tax farmers, and regretted the loss of Fragonard as a national asset in these terms:

> He only started to do these little paintings [for private patrons] because of the disgust he felt over his treatment around the Callirhoée,—he got paid too little and too late—to the point where because he didn't get paid he had to pawn his shirt—that's how we lost the Rubens of France.[53]

Mercier is being rhetorical, of course, in his highlighting of both the failures of the crown's arts administrators and the greed of the financiers who exploited the impoverished artist. In reality, Fragonard's complex career demonstrates two things: the academy and its exhibition were a strategy, but not an end for Fragonard, who used the public renown he achieved in 1765 (which, although it didn't bring him immediate riches brought him huge public and aesthetic 'capital') to free himself from the academic honours system and pursue what can only be described as an independent and self-directed career, though he continued to exploit his long-time links with the learned and fabulously wealthy financier-patrons who provided an alternative axis of patronage. Thus we might conclude that turning one's back on the academy and constructing a portfolio career (producing ensembles for patrons and selling individual works, for example) was a serious alternative strategy for the highly gifted artist by this point in the century and, therefore, that the monopoly on talent that the academy had sought throughout its existence was being eroded not by any direct political challenge but by the possibilities for alternative revenue streams offered to the most talented painters. In the face of these new patron–client relationships, the successful and sought-after artist did not have to remain the subordinate supplier, but could in fact assert his will and independence.

Further, as recent studies have shown, private patronage—the commissioning and purchasing of works of art by private individuals—was not simply to be seen (as it was by Mercier) as the triumph of luxury over higher values in the plastic art. Indeed, as Colin Bailey has persuasively argued, many important patrons and purchasers of art in the eighteenth century were explicitly committed to the furthering of a 'patriotic' project of sponsoring art by ambitious living artists which reflected the glories of France. Bailey's intriguing thesis is that a number of key individuals from the patrician class (from aristocratic, financier, and *parlementaire* backgrounds) did not collect in order to associate themselves with luxury and opulence, but out of what La Live de Jully called 'a national investment' in reviving a glorious French school of painting and through it the cultural prestige of the nation.[54] This would in some ways make these collectors the inheritors not just of the Pompadour project but Fouquet's Vaux. In the wake of military defeat, financial crisis, and uncertain political times, they actively sought to foster art as a means of national glory and cultural self-definition.

Naturally enough, this patrician class was accused by the revolutionary actors of everything but patriotism, and we thus must not be tempted to see their often lavish spending on the arts as entirely altruistic—these men pursued pleasure and luxury and distinction as they made their purchases and sponsored their artists. In fact, the highborn courtiers and wealthy tax farmers who make up most of Bailey's sample of collectors of contemporary art in the later eighteenth century were the target of critique from within the arts themselves. The discourses that emerged out of cultural phenomena such as the experimental genre of stage play we call the *drame*—which was pioneered in theory by Diderot and made into stage reality by Sedaine, Beaumarchais, and Louis-Sebastien Mercier on the stages of the Opéra-Comique, Théâtre Italien and occasionally the Comédie Française, tended towards the advocacy of simple, agriculture- or commerce-based virtues and made a spectacle of unadorned virtue and simple lives.[55] In this context visual and decorative art was problematic, because unlike text, or even music, it was both luxury good and purveyor of ideological messages. How could a painting or decorative ensemble be patriotic if it was part of a culture of luxury and consumption that was itself corrupt? The glaring gaps between popular suffering and the luxurious, art-filled lives of the rich were a major cause of revolutionary complaints and of popular retaliatory actions. Furthermore, when David and his colleagues were thinking through how to integrate the arts into revolutionary aims and rhetoric, they were well aware of the tarnished reputation of both academy and market structures for art, and this determined revolutionary administrators of the arts to organize art and artists through structures and mechanisms that were open (the experiment with entirely 'open' salons) or that would harness art to the public good (the creation of the Louvre) or promote civic engagement and revolutionary virtues (the Concours de l'An II).[56] Suspicion of Bourbon uses of imagery, combined with demands for virtue in the public sphere and for public ownership of art and its institutions, decisively shaped revolutionary reorganization of the arts, even though the newly formed organizations looked superficially similar to those that had preceded them.

Ordinary People and the Arts

In the story of the patronage of the visual arts in the Ancien Régime, though, it is somewhat telling that the ordinary peasant, artisan, or worker in Paris can only play a part as a member of that complex and somewhat phantasmatic composite entity known as *the public*. Until recently we paid little attention to habits of patronage and consumption that pertained at modest levels of income and status. But from illustrations and accounts in the contemporary press, we know of the multiplicity of print enterprises in the Rue Saint Jacques and the shops and vendors of visual material on the bridges (particularly the Pont Notre-Dame), and we also have some evidence from *inventaires* to show that many households were adorned with imagery and that later in the century, there was a trend away from devotional imagery towards secular themes.[57] The meaning of this widespread deployment of increasingly secular images in domestic space is so far largely unstudied and there remain many questions about how and why the image circulated in and adorned many modest homes. There is certainly an argument, though, that the end of the Ancien Régime saw a trend towards what might be called the democratization of visual pleasure and the spread of a general taste for the visual and the decorative—part of what Pardailhé-Galabrun analysed as the trend to increased *confort*.

All this is a far cry from claiming that the beginnings of a modern moment of widespread image-saturation of homes across the demographic spectrum are to be located in the Ancien Régime. And indeed, one of the defining features of the patterns of patronage in the Ancien Régime is the sense of visual art as an elite and privileged language, one which might be encouraged, owned, and manipulated at the centres of wealth and power. From this perspective, it is difficult to resist seeing the entire network of arts patronage and all its expensive institutions in the Ancien Régime as somehow the most evident sign of the regime's lack of modernity. On the other hand, if we think of the ways in which the arts have been exploited for personal and national prestige, from Napoleon to Mitterrand, we could take the opposite view: the creation of identity through a complex web of performance and spectacle is, in fact, one of the enduring legacies of the Ancien Régime to political cultures of more modern times.

Notes

1. Roger Chartier, *The Cultural Origins of the French Revolution: Bicentennial Reflections on the French Revolution* (Durham, NC, 1991); T. C. W. Blanning, *The Culture of Power and the Power of Culture: Old Regime Europe, 1660–1789* (Oxford, 2002); Milton Cummings,

The Patron State: Government and the Arts in Europe, North America, and Japan (New York, 1987); Peter Burke, *Fabrication of Louis XIV* (New Haven, Conn., 1992).

2. Martin Warnke, *The Court Artist: On the Ancestry of the Modern Artist* (Cambridge and New York, 1993); Francis Haskell, *Patrons and Painters: A Study in the Relations between Italian Art and Society in the Age of the Baroque*, rev. and enlarged edn. (New Haven, Conn., 1980); Cummings, *Patron State*.

3. Peter Campbell, *Power and Politics in Old Regime France, 1720–1745* (London and New York, 1996); Sharon Kettering, *Patronage in Sixteenth- and Seventeenth-Century France* (Aldershot, 2002).

4. Emmanuel Le Roy Ladurie, *The Ancien Régime: A History of France, 1610–1774* (Oxford, 1996), 42 and following, in which he argues that the 'Patronage state' came to be replaced by 'The predator state, founded on modern fiscal exactions'.

5. On Fontainebleau and Francis I's cultural politics, see exh. cat., Galeries nationales du Grand Palais (France) and Réunion des musées nationaux (France), *L'École de Fontainebleau* (Paris, 1972); Louis Dimier, *Le Château de Fontainebleau et la cour de François Ier* (Paris, 1930); exh. cat., Château de Blois (Blois, France), *François Ier: Images d'un roi, de l'histoire à la légende* (Paris, 2006).

6. On this subject see Hilary Ballon, *The Paris of Henry IV: Architecture and Urbanism* (Cambridge, Mass., 1991).

7. Claire Goldstein, *Vaux and Versailles: The Appropriations, Erasures, and Accidents that Made Modern France* (Philadelphia, 2008).

8. Ibid. 14. See also Marc Fumaroli, *The Poet and the King: Jean de la Fontaine and his Century* (Notre Dame, Ind., and Chichester, 2002); Alain Niderst, *Madeleine de Scudéry, Paul Pellisson et leur monde* (Paris, 1976).

9. Colin Bailey, *Patriotic Taste: Collecting Modern Art in Pre-revolutionary Paris* (New Haven, Conn., 2002).

10. Burke, *Fabrication of Louis XIV*; Jean-Marie Apostolidès, *Le Roi Machine: Spectacle et politique au temps de Louis XIV* (Paris, 1981); Louis Marin, *Portrait of the King* (Minneapolis, 1988); Gérard Sabatier, *Versailles, ou, La Figure du roi* (Paris, 1999).

11. Clifford Geertz, *Negara: The Theatre State in Nineteenth-Century Bali* (Princeton, 1980).

12. See the very useful review article, Alain Guéry, 'Review: Versailles, le phantasme de l'absolutisme (note critique)', *Annales. Histoire, sciences sociales*, 56 (2001), 507–17.

13. Claude Nivelon, *Vie de Charles Le Brun et description détaillée de ses ouvrages*, ed. Lorenzo Pericolo, École Pratique des Hautes Études, 86 (Geneva, 2004), 472 (my tr.).

14. Robert Darnton, *The Forbidden Best-Sellers of Pre-Revolutionary France* (New York, 1995); Jürgen Habermas, *The Structural Transformation of the Public Sphere: An Inquiry into a Category of Bourgeois Society* (Cambridge, Mass., 1989).

15. Thomas E. Crow, *Painters and Public Life in Eighteenth-Century Paris* (New Haven, Conn., 1985); Chartier, *Cultural Origins of the French Revolution*.

16. Jay Caplan, *In the King's Wake: Post-Absolutist Culture in France* (Chicago, 1999).

17. See Crow, *Painters and Public Life*, for a subtle account of Watteau's relationship with the Crozat circle, and with a patronage network; see also Andrew McClellan, 'Watteau's Dealer: Gersaint and the Marketing of Art in Eighteenth-Century Paris', *Art Bulletin*, 78 (Sept. 1996), 439–53.

18. Caplan, *In the King's Wake*; see Henri Lagrave, *Le Théâtre et le public à Paris de 1715 à 1750* (Paris, 1972).

19. On the history of Versailles see esp. Pierre de Nolhac, *Versailles et la cour de France: La Création de Versailles* (Paris, 1925). Pierre de Nolhac, *Versailles au xviiie scièle* (Paris, 1926);

Pierre Verlet, *Le Château de Versailles* (Paris, 1985); William Newton, *L'Espace du roi: La Cour de France au Château de Versailles, 1682–1789* ([Paris], 2000); Sabatier, *Versailles*.

20. Emmanuel Le Roy Ladurie, *Saint-Simon and the Court of Louis XIV* (Chicago, 2001).
21. Sabatier, *Versailles*.
22. Burke, *Fabrication of Louis XIV*.
23. Rochelle Ziskin, 'The Place de Nos Conquêtes and the Unraveling of the Myth of Louis XIV', *Art Bulletin*, 76 (Mar. 1994), 147–62.
24. For the subsequent history of the Place, see Rochelle Ziskin, *The Place Vendôme: Architecture and Social Mobility in Eighteenth-Century Paris* (Cambridge, 1999); exh. cat., Action Artistique de la Ville de Paris, *La Place Vendôme: Art, pouvoir et fortune* (Paris, 2002).
25. Ziskin, 'Place de Nos Conquêtes', 147.
26. Jean Locquin, *La Peinture d'histoire en France de 1747 à 1785* (Paris, 1912).
27. Xavier Salmon, Helge Seifert, and Humphrey Wine (eds.), *Madame de Pompadour et les arts* (Paris, 2002).
28. Donald Posner, 'Mme. de Pompadour as a Patron of the Visual Arts', *Art Bulletin*, 72 (Mar. 1990), 74–105. Posner argued that Pompadour was not to any great extent either an innovator or a taste-changer, but mostly a consumer of already established trends.
29. Colin Jones and the National Gallery, *Madame de Pompadour: Images of a Mistress* (London [and New Haven, Conn.], 2002).
30. Thomas E. Kaiser, 'Madame de Pompadour and the Theaters of Power', *French Historical Studies*, 19 (1996), 1025–44.
31. On Pompadour's theatre the still fundamental study is Adolphe Jullien, *Histoire du théâtre de Madame de Pompadour dit Théâtre des petits cabinets* (Paris, 1874).
32. On the complexity of Pompadour's gendered identity, see Melissa Hyde, 'The "Makeup" of the Marquise: Boucher's Portrait of Pompadour at her Toilette', *Art Bulletin*, 82 (Sept. 2000), 453–75.
33. The provocative anachronism of the term is Darnton's. See Robert Darnton, 'An Early Information Society: News and the Media in Eighteenth-Century Paris', *American Historical Review*, 105 (2000), 1–35.
34. Nikolaus Pevsner, *Academies of Art, Past and Present* (New York, 1973 [1940]), *Academies, Museums, and Canons of Art* (New Haven, Conn., 1998); Anton W. A. Boschloo *et al.* (eds.), *Academies of Art between Renaissance and Romanticism* (The Hague, 1989).
35. Louis Vitet and Ludovic Vitet, *L'Académie royale de peinture et de sculpture* (Paris:, 1861).
36. One of the most interesting of modern chroniclers of the administrative life of the Academy of Painting and Sculpture is Reed Benhamou. See her 'Discipline and Punishment in the Académie Royale de Peinture et de Sculpture', in Anne Goldgar and Robert L. Frost (eds.), *Institutional Culture in Early Modern Society* (Leiden and Boston, 2004), 247–77; her forthcoming book on statutory change in the Academy will further reveal the complex workings of the organization.
37. On this incident see exh. cat., and Musée Greuze, Tournus, *Greuze et l'affaire du Septime Sévère* (Paris, 2005).
38. See Archives Nationales, Maison du Roi, O^1 1073–219 and sqq., Archives de l'Institut B18 (7). Also Wolfgang Schöller, *Die 'Académie royale d'architecture' 1671–1793: Anatomie einer Institution* (Cologne, 1993), 284–7.
39. On this appointment see Mark Ledbury, *Sedaine, Greuze and the Boundaries of Genre* (Oxford, 2000).

40. On the visitor numbers for the salons, some of the best extrapolations are in Udolpho van de Sandt: 'La Fréquentation des salons sous l'Ancien Régime, la Révolution et l'Empire', *Revue de l'Art*, 73 (1986), 43–8. On the salon as a public space and on engaged criticism, see Crow, *Painters and Public Life*. See also Bernadette Fort, 'Voice of the Public: The Carnivalization of Salon Art in Prerevolutionary Pamphlets', *Eighteenth-Century Studies*, 22 (1989), 368–94.
41. Ibid.
42. For an analysis of the significance of this work, see Jeremy D. Popkin, '"Post-Absolutism" and Laughter in Eighteenth-Century France', *Eighteenth-Century Studies*, 35 (2002), 295–99. For an argument about the complex political status of genres of mocking banter, see Élisabeth Bourguinat, *Le Siècle du persiflage, 1734–1789* (Paris, 1998).
43. On La Font de Saint-Yenne, see Étienne Jollet (ed.), *La Font de Saint Yenne: Œuvre critique* (Paris, 2001). On Diderot, see esp. exh.cat., Musée de la monnaie (France), *Diderot et l'art de Boucher à David: Les Salons, 1759–1781. [Exposition] Hôtel de la Monnaie, 5 Octobre 1984–6 Janvier 1985* (Paris, 1984).
44. On censorship and anonymity see esp. the important work by Richard Wrigley, *The Origins of French Art Criticism: From the Ancien Régime to the Restoration* (Oxford, 1993). See also Bernadette Fort (ed.), *Les Salons des 'mémoires secrets' 1767–1787* (Paris, 1999).
45. On the parterre and theatre as part of political culture, see Jeffrey S Ravel, *The Contested Parterre: Public Theater and French Political Culture, 1680–1791* (Ithaca, NY, 1999).
46. See Crow, *Painters and Public Life*. M. Ledbury, '"Vous aves achevé mes tableaux": Michel-Jean Sedaine and Jacques-Louis David', *British Journal for Eighteenth-Century Studies*, 23 (2000), 59–84.
47. James H. Johnson, *Listening in Paris: A Cultural History* (Berkeley, Calif., 1995), 92–4 and sqq.
48. Carolyn Sargentson, *Merchants and Luxury Markets: The Marchands Merciers of Eighteenth-Century Paris* (Malibu, Calif., 1996).
49. The most important work on dealers in Paris in the later Ancien Régime is Patrick Michel, *Le Commerce du tableau à Paris dans la seconde moitié du xviiie siècle* (Paris, 2008). On the market for paintings in Europe, see the new studies by Hans van Migroet, which tend to show just how large were the flows of paintings into a large cross-section of homes in Europe in the 18th cent. Hans J. van Migroet and Neil de Marchi. *Mapping Markets for Paintings in Early Modern Europe 1450–1750* (PLACE, 2006). See also E. Duverger, 'Réflexions sur le commerce d'art au xviiie siècle' *Stil und Ueberlieferung in der Kunst des Abendlandes*, iii (Berlin, 1967).
50. On the *Corésus* see esp. Jean Cuzin, *Jean-Honoré Fragonard: Life and Work. Complete Catalogue of the Oil Paintings* (New York, 1988). Sergiusz Michalski, 'Jean-Honoré Fragonards "Koresos und Kallirhoe": Opferungsszene und "Theatre des ombres"', *Artibus et Historiae*, 16/31 (1995), 189–207. Daniel Rabreau (ed.), *Corésus et Callirhoé de Fragonard: Un chef-d'œuvre d'émotion* (Bordeaux, 2007).
51. On Fragonard's life and career, see Cuzin, *Jean-Honoré Fragonard*; for the aftermath of the Coresus, see Mary D. Sheriff, 'For Love or Money? Rethinking Fragonard', *Eighteenth-Century Studies* (1986), 333–54; Mary Sheriff, *Fragonard: Art and Eroticism* (Chicago, 1990).
52. On Bergeret and other amateurs and patrons, see Charlotte Guichard, *Les Amateurs d'art à Paris au xviiie siècle* (Seyssel, 2008).
53. Bibliothèque de L'Arsenal, Mercier Ms 15083, fo. 3 (my tr.).

54. See Colin Bailey, *Patriotic Taste: Collecting Modern Art in Pre-revolutionary Paris* (New Haven, Conn., 2002).
55. On the *drame*, see Félix Gaiffe, *Le Drame en France au xviiie siècle* (Paris, 1910). Alain Ménil, *Diderot et le drame: Théâtre et politique* (1st edn., Paris, 1995). On the various rhetorics which critiqued nobility before 1788, see John Shovlin, 'Toward a Reinterpretation of Revolutionary Antinobilism: The Political Economy of Honor in the Old Regime', *Journal of Modern History*, 72 (Mar. 2000), 35–66.
56. On art and the French Revolution see esp. Régis Michel, *Aux armes et aux arts! Les Arts de la Révolution: 1789-1799* (Paris, 1988). On the origins of the Louvre, see Andrew McClellan, *Inventing the Louvre: Art, Politics, and the Origins of the Modern Museum in Eighteenth-Century Paris* (Cambridge, 1994).
57. Annik Pardailhé-Galabrun, *The Birth of Intimacy: Privacy and Domestic Life in Early Modern Paris* (Philadelphia, 1991), esp. 195–200.

Bibliography

Apostolidès, Jean-Marie, *Le Roi-Machine: Spectacle et politique au temps de Louis XIV* (Paris, 1981).
Bailey, Colin, *Patriotic Taste: Collecting Modern Art in Pre-revolutionary Paris* (New Haven, Conn., 2002).
Crow, Thomas E., *Painters and Public Life in Eighteenth-Century Paris* (New Haven, Conn., 1985).
Fort, Bernadette, 'Voice of the Public: The Carnivalization of Salon Art in Prerevolutionary Pamphlets', *Eighteenth-Century Studies*, 22 (1989), 368–94.
Gaiffe, Félix, *Le Drame en France au xviiie siècle* (Paris, 1910).
Goldstein, Claire, *Vaux and Versailles: The Appropriations, Erasures, and Accidents that Made Modern France* (Philadelphia, 2008).
Guichard, Charlotte, *Les Amateurs d'art à Paris au xviiie siècle* (Seyssel, 2008).
Johnson, James H., *Listening in Paris: A Cultural History* (Berkeley, Calif., 1995).
Jones, Colin, and the National Gallery, *Madame de Pompadour: Images of a Mistress* (London, 2002).
Kettering, Sharon, *Patronage in Sixteenth- and Seventeenth-Century France* (Aldershot, 2002).
McClellan, Andrew, *Inventing the Louvre: Art, Politics, and the Origins of the Modern Museum in Eighteenth-Century Paris* (Cambridge, 1994).
Michel, Régis, and Bordes, Philippe (eds.), *Aux armes et aux arts! Les Arts de la Révolution: 1789-1799* (Paris, 1988).
Newton, William, *L'Espace du roi: La Cour de France au château de Versailles, 1682-1789* (Paris, 2000).
Pardailhé-Galabrun, Annik, *The Birth of Intimacy: Privacy and Domestic Life in Early Modern Paris* (Philadelphia, 1991).
Ravel, Jeffrey S., *The Contested Parterre: Public Theater and French Political Culture, 1680-1791* (Ithaca, NY, 1999).
Sabatier, Gérard, *Versailles, ou, La Figure du roi* (Paris, 1999).
Sargentson, Carolyn, *Merchants and Luxury Markets: The Marchands Merciers of Eighteenth-Century Paris* (Malibu, Calif., 1996).

Schöller, Wolfgang, *Die 'Académie royale d'architecture' 1671–1793: Anatomie einer Institution* (Cologne, 1993).
Wrigley, Richard, *The Origins of French Art Criticism: From the Ancien Régime to the Restoration* (Oxford, 1993).
Ziskin, Rochelle, *The Place Vendôme: Architecture and Social Mobility in Eighteenth-Century Paris* (Cambridge, 1999).

CHAPTER 24

THE PUBLIC SPHERE

THOMAS E. KAISER

IN SEARCH OF THE 'SHADOWY PHANTOM'

'Does the public exist?' asked Louis-Sebastien Mercier in 1782. 'What is the public? Where is it? By which organs does it manifest its will?' If locating 'the public' proved difficult for Mercier more than two centuries ago, the task has not become substantially easier in the intervening years, notwithstanding repeated efforts of historians, literary scholars, and sociologists to give shape to what some of Mercier's contemporaries imagined as a 'shadowy Phantom'. Of all these attempts, none has been so influential as Jürgen Habermas's *Structural Transformation of the Public Sphere*, first published in German in 1962 and in English translation in 1989. This study established the paradigm within which virtually all subsequent research on 'the public' and the debates it inspired have been conducted, and in any analysis of 'the public sphere' in the Old Regime, it is the virtually inescapable place to begin.[1]

According to Habermas, there were two incarnations of the 'public', or as the English translation renders it 'public sphere', under the Ancien Régime. The first arose during the sixteenth and seventeenth centuries, when the royal state gradually absorbed powers and rights previously exercised by semi-public corporations, localities, and individuals. This institutional reshuffling, in Habermas's view, entailed a fresh division between the 'public' and 'private' realms. 'Public', according to Habermas, came to mean state-related and denoted the sphere occupied by a 'bureaucratic apparatus with regulated spheres of jurisdiction' that exerted 'a monopoly over the legitimate use of coercion'. 'Private', by contrast, denoted the sphere occupied by those who held no office and were for that reason 'excluded from any share in public authority'. The result of this disjunction, Habermas contended, was that previously autonomous, empowered elites were stripped of their 'public' functions by a faceless bureaucratic state. Bourgeois intellectuals and administrators were recruited to engage their critical faculties on behalf of the prince. Nobles became virtual conscripts of the royal court, where they bore passive witness to the ceremonial 'representations' staged by the monarchy to legitimate itself.[2]

Beginning in the late seventeenth century, Habermas argued, a second 'public sphere' took shape 'within the tension-charged field between state and society'. In part, this second 'public sphere' resulted from the progressive depersonalization of the state, which had alienated certain aristocratic elements from the royal court and led to their integration with other elites in various urban sites such as the salons—semi-formalized gatherings held in private homes, where the high-born rubbed shoulders with fashionable, if not always well-heeled intellectuals. But for Habermas the development of the second 'public sphere' was principally a product of an expanding commercial capitalism, which, notwithstanding the admixture of alienated court nobles, indelibly class-typed the second 'public sphere' as 'bourgeois'. According to Habermas, the social nature of this new 'bourgeois public sphere' allowed for the public articulation of previously private bourgeois family values in public settings. But that was only one of its novel features. Whereas the first 'public sphere'—centred in the royal court—had been exclusive, hierarchically structured, and essentially passive in the face of state 'representation', the 'bourgeois public sphere' had a widely inclusive membership, which, by pushing public scrutiny of state operations far beyond their previously circumscribed legal limits, created a free-fire zone of critical exchange that in turn engendered an autonomous 'public opinion'. In England, a nation that enjoyed a relatively wide freedom of expression, 'public opinion', according to Habermas, began to play a political role by the early eighteenth century. In France, 'public opinion', nurtured for decades within Parisian salons and focused originally on aesthetic matters, became intensively political only when the finance minister Jacques Necker published the state budget in 1781. Despite continued efforts at censorship, 'civil society' found its authentic voice in the 1780s, as 'the sphere of a public that eventually also engaged in a critical debate of political issues now definitely became the sphere in which civil society reflected on and expounded its interests'. It was out of the contradictions generated by the two 'public spheres', Habermas concluded, that the French Revolution erupted in 1789.[3]

In the nearly half-century since it was published, *The Structural Transformation of the Public Sphere* has been the object of intense and extensive scrutiny, and a number of its propositions have been critiqued and revised in light of further research.[4] In particular, the notion of a 'bourgeois public sphere' has been attacked on many grounds—among them, its outdated Marxist class analysis, its chronology, its gender-blindness, and its Kantian idealization of what was in reality a much less enlightened and much less open public debate than Habermas imagined. Do these objections now make Habermas's treatment of the 'public sphere' obsolete? In some respects, certainly, but at a minimum Habermas asked some probing questions that are still worth posing, and his book provided a framework within which it is still useful to ponder them. What was 'the public'? How was 'the public' conceived? How did it change over the Ancien Régime? What authority did it command? These are the principal questions that this chapter will address.

The 'Public Sphere' in the Seventeenth Century

Habermas's two 'public spheres' were *ex post facto* constructs, but this was certainly not true of '(the) public', a term in common use since the fourteenth century. What was meant by it? As indicated by expressions like *voies publiques* (public roadways)—to say nothing of *femmes publiques* (prostitutes)—'(the) public' denoted that which was owned or used by society in general as opposed to that which was owned or used exclusively by individuals and/or their families. With the expansion of the royal state in the sixteenth and seventeenth centuries, 'the public', as Habermas argued, increasingly came to be associated with its various agencies—as in the expression 'public treasury'—and with the King—as in the phrase, 'the prince is a public good'. At the same time, it is now clear that Habermas overestimated the extent to which 'the public' was encapsulated by the royal state. The sixteenth-century jurist Jean Bodin affirmed that the royal domain constituted part of 'the public', yet also argued that 'the public' extended well beyond the property and powers inherent in the royal *dignitas*. 'Beyond sovereignty', he affirmed, 'there must be something common and public', examples of which included customary laws and urban marketplaces, walls, and streets. Although some historians have alleged that the King had become the only acknowledged 'public person' by the reign of Louis XIV, this 'person' was in fact no more equivalent with 'the public' than he completely embodied the 'state'. Even Bishop Bossuet, the Sun King's premier apostle and apologist of mature 'absolutism', distinguished between his royal patron and the 'public'; thus, in his celebrated *Politique tirée des propres paroles de l'écriture sainte*, he insisted that 'the prince is not born for his own sake, but for [the good of] the public'. To be sure, the interests of the King and the 'public good' were often equated during Louis XIV's reign and remained closely associated in official government discourse until the end of the Ancien Régime. But as David Kammerling-Smith has shown in his study of the language of economic policy-making in the Bureau of Commerce, the gap between the crown and the 'public' had become sufficiently wide by the early eighteenth century to allow expressions like 'neither in the interests of the King, nor of the public good' to creep into government discourse.[5]

That the monarchy was not isomorphic with 'the public' makes sense in view of the latest mapping of Ancien Régime institutions. Far from levitating itself into its own separate sphere as absolutist ideology suggested and Habermas and his generation believed, the royal state was in reality shot through with particularist claims on its powers and revenues exercised by a variety of corporate groups—for example, nobles, clergy, guildsmen, venal officeholders. As David Potter puts it, 'the Absolute monarchy was...the vehicle in which a substantial political elite rode in order to control the machinery of order, power, patronage and private interest'; and it would thus be 'fatal to regard the crown as in any sense divorced from the complex structure of the French political society'. Within this perspective, even the reign of Louis XIV no longer appears to be a paradigmatic instance of the centralization and rationalization of power. Rather, it presents a much muddier picture of a royal state built upon the consolidation of the rights and corporate status of state officeholders. Finding the 'public' in this mass of conflicting jurisdictions is no simple task. For although its interests might command respect, 'the public' had no clearly defined shape, no single institutional setting, and no single set of recognized legal rights. Many might speak in its name, yet no one, the King included, monopolized its authority.[6]

All this is apparent from the growing seventeenth-century debate on the phenomenon of public opinion, whose existence was acknowledged well before the age of the Enlightenment. To be sure, public opinion was more poorly regarded in official circles during the seventeenth century than it would be in the eighteenth. To many philosophers in this period, opinions of any sort constituted an inferior form of knowledge, and when they bore the stamp of popular approval, they were all the more suspect. 'The applause of the people for some opinion in a difficult matter', the philosopher Nicolas Malebranche wrote dismissively, 'is an infallible sign that it is false.' Yet it would be altogether too hasty to infer from this condescension that contemporaries dismissed opinion as irrelevant to politics or social and cultural affairs generally. In Blaise Pascal's formulation, opinion was 'queen of the world', and many of his contemporaries acknowledged it as such. It would be equally mistaken to accept without qualification Habermas's view of the seventeenth-century 'public' as an audience lacking an autonomous critical faculty. Much as ministers and cultural elites might bemoan the situation—the scholar Jean Mabillon called it 'one of the diseases of our century'—they were well aware that the reign of *la critique* had become an undeniable reality by the end of the seventeenth century. Mass communications engendered by the invention of the printing press certainly allowed established elites to consolidate their rule, but, by the same token, publication of anything was an invitation to criticism that would more likely than not be shared. 'There are no readers', insisted the poet and critic Nicolas Boileau, 'who do not express their opinion on writings that have been published ... [For] what is it to publish a work? Is it not in some measure to say to the Public, "judge me"?' Fallible as the verdicts of public opinion might have appeared in some quarters, the notion that public opinion constituted some sort of tribunal was in place well before the age of the Enlightenment.[7]

Royal ministers like Cardinal Richelieu were well aware of the dangers of public opinion, but they were no less aware of the opportunities for exploiting it. 'A good reputation', Richelieu recognized, 'is especially necessary to a prince, for if we hold him in high regard, he can accomplish more with this name alone than a less well esteemed ruler can with great armies at his command.' Protecting the King's reputation required the close policing of public expression, and to this end the monarchy severely punished slanders and libels (*mauvais discours*) upon the King as offences against his very majesty (*lèse-majesté*). But the silencing of negative opinion could only accomplish so much. For this reason the King's ministers adopted other strategies—most notably, the rectification of public opinion through the sponsorship of royal encomiums, state ceremonies, and artistic performances replete with tropes of glory. Reflecting the allegedly god-like status of the ruler, these panegyrics no doubt powerfully influenced minds and discourse regarding the King. Yet their rhetorical impact was lessened by the well-known fact that they had been arranged and paid for by the royal object of their acclamations. Thus, for example, even a monarchist like Jean Bodin advised readers to regard Philippe de Commines's flattering portrait of Louis XI with caution since Commines had been 'endowed by the King with great riches and honour'. To those with deep reservations about the entire absolutist enterprise like the Baron de Montesquieu, all court-sponsored works were suspect, among them histories written by scholars 'who surrender their good faith for a meager pension' and thereby 'mislead posterity'. This is why Louis XIV's more astute advisers recommended that court historians avoid fulsome praise of the monarch and allow readers to reach their own politically correct conclusions by means of an invisible rhetorical hand. 'It is necessary to praise the king in all parts,' advised Paul Pellisson,

> but, as it were, without adulation, by means of a narrative [recounting] all that he has been seen doing, saying, and thinking, [a narrative] that appears disinterested, but is lively, piquant, and stately, avoiding in its expressions all that recalls the panegyric. To win more credence, one ought not accord him the epithets and magnificent eulogies that he merits; one must extract them from the mouth of the reader by means of things themselves...One undoubtedly hopes that His Majesty approves and agrees to this plan...But it must not appear to have been authorized.

Another subtle strategy for eliciting politically correct opinion was to circulate well-doctored accounts of the nation's alleged euphoric reaction to ceremonies honouring the King. For example, in addition to erecting nearly twenty equestrian statues of the Sun King in cities around France, the government published official newspaper reports describing 'how everywhere there is a rush to erect statues to him', thereby inviting readers to align their reactions with those of the public. Coached or not, public responses to royal performances and propaganda do seem to have been genuinely enthusiastic for most of Louis XIV's reign—that is, until protracted war, heavier taxes, and religious persecution made the Sun King so unpopular that his funeral had to be held at night to prevent an unseemly riot.[8]

Even in the halcyon days of the early and middle reign, Louis XIV's propagandists could not be assured that the public would faithfully absorb the messages imparted to it, just as, Orest Ranum points outs, the crown could not guarantee public acceptance of a government-sponsored work of literature. When the public assembled in such boisterous venues as the theatre, it not only judged officially sanctioned dramas with a lack of 'good taste' that drove erudite critics to despair, but also voiced its opinions with such outcries, booing, foot-pounding, and whistling—not to mention physical abuse of the actors—that they could hardly be misconstrued. Still more unbounded were the frequent volleys of unpoliceable political street songs, which even under the Sun King mercilessly satirized the highest and mightiest of the realm in the most disrespectful terms imaginable. One notable target was Mme de Maintenon, the King's mistress and later morganatic wife. She was publicly scorned in street songs as a 'witch' and a 'whore' in libels that reportedly offended Louis XIV even more than those directed against himself.

By the early eighteenth century, the situation had gotten sufficiently out of hand for the police to post spies (*mouches*, or *mouchards*) in many Parisian venues to monitor expressions of such opinion and report them to the secretary of state for the King's household, who occasionally communicated them to the King. This surveillance would hardly have been considered necessary if the public had not made independent political judgements or if those judgements had not posed some serious danger to established authority.[9]

The royal court—the closest approximation to a paradigmatic public—obviously provided a more sedate and far better controlled environment for expression than did the theatres and the street. Assembled there were the most prestigious elements of society, whose prestige and conspicuous deference to the King provided powerful validation of the monarchy's propaganda. 'In everything [Louis XIV] says,' recorded one observer, 'he speaks like an oracle, even [when talking] about the most frivolous things. At table and where he is obliged to converse, he talks gravely, and clearly when he opens his mouth, all the courtiers who surround him lower their head and approach him as closely as they can to hear him.' But even at court there were lingering suspicions that the politically correct message was not sinking in. Indeed, in light of the profoundly cynical view of human nature held by most royal advisers, there was reason to fear that the unintended effect of government propaganda and display was to drive sycophants with unorthodox and possibly dangerous opinions to hide their true sentiments behind a mask. Hence, Jean de La Bruyère's classic description of the courtier as a deep dissembler, who 'disguises his passions, contradicts his heart, [and] speaks, acts against his [true] sentiments'. Hence, too, the repeated warnings by Richelieu and other royal counsellors of the corrupting, disarming methods of flatterers, which, notwithstanding the supposedly penetrating gaze of the monarch, made it necessary for the King not merely to avoid them, but also to banish them from the court. In the eyes of the King's ministers, the true opinions of such individuals might be deplorable, but there could be no denying the ability of individuals to form and communicate them among the public.[10]

As the example of the court demonstrates, by creating new publics to further the interests of the King, the monarchy paradoxically provided new sites for potential intrigue and dissent and new 'tribunals' capable of rendering 'verdicts' on its operations—welcome or not. One of the most influential of these 'tribunals' developed as a result of the monarchy's increasing dependency on court bankers to finance its operations. In an absolute monarchy like France, convincing this financial interest that the monarchy represented a good credit risk was no simple matter. For the King had the power to 'reassign' revenues reserved for debt servicing, and the crown's spotty history of loan repayment—not to mention, outright debt renunciation—gave prospective creditors good grounds to fear that their loans might not be secure. If financiers doubted the creditworthiness of the monarchy, court financiers were in turn regarded with great suspicion by the monarchy and the public, which was also justified, since they expertly bilked the crown out of every *sou* they could lay their hands on. Despite these mutual suspicions, the increasingly costly military ventures of Louis XIV forced the monarchy to tap into ever larger reservoirs of credit, which made scrutiny and judgement of its financial operations by court financiers virtually inescapable. Early in the reign, the ill-fated finance minister Nicolas Fouquet acknowledged the need to establish 'so impeccable a reputation for keeping one's word' that the King's creditors 'believe they are not running the slightest risk' in lending money to him. His successor, Jean-Baptiste Colbert, likewise instructed the King that royal credit rested upon 'the opinion of the public regarding the good condition of his finances'. Of course, good intentions were only fitfully translated into sound policy, but at least the King's ministers had few delusions about the likely result of a default, which would lead, Colbert predicted, to 'nearly universal bankruptcy'. In the end, such vulnerability made the monarchy as dependent upon its creditors as the creditors were upon the crown for investment opportunities. As one anonymous memoir put it in 1717 amidst the Regency government's struggles to cope with the financial crisis left by Louis XIV, it was unfortunate that the monarchy's debt was 'extraordinary'. But it was altogether 'vexatious' that 'the public is fully informed about this state of affairs, which increases distrust and completely discredits all the claims on the king'.[11]

A second site provided by the monarchy for a public to crystallize and assert leverage on the crown was the royal judiciary. As David Bell has persuasively argued, the notion of the public as a tribunal drew strength from the operations of the royal sovereign courts, notably the parlements. The parlements had little choice but to acknowledge the King as the fount of justice in their formal pronouncements, and they were subject to exile when the King decided they had overstepped their proper limits in remonstrating against his edicts. Yet they also claimed a certain independent authority based on their alleged descent from ancient assemblies of their countrymen, while the venality of their offices provided *parlementaires* with a layer of legal protection against outright dismissal. This margin of autonomy—considerably narrowed under the Sun King but widened thereafter—allowed the parlements to argue with some credibility that they represented a public interest which the King's ministers had overlooked or even betrayed when setting and administering royal policy. In other words, the parlements effectively asserted the right to speak not only *for* the King, but also *to* him; and they represented enough of a challenge to royal authority to have made it politically wiser for the King to negotiate with the parlements in most circumstances than to ride rough-shod over their sometimes noisy protests.[12]

Beyond the parlements, as Sarah Hanley has recently shown, the publication of royal edicts and compendia of previous court decisions created a non-professional judicial 'public sphere' among the French population already in the early seventeenth century. These publications—directed explicitly to the 'public' for its own use—not only empowered ordinary individuals to pursue litigation in the courts, but also gave rise to the circulation of judicial memoirs (*factums*), in which litigants laid out their cases before the public at large and elicited public judgement on them. Thanks to a loophole in the laws, *factums* escaped regulation by state censors, and they provided the medium for conducting a vibrant exchange of ideas and arguments on private matters and their legal implications across many social sectors. 'Hawked in the streets, read by the literate, or aurally communicated to the illiterate in Paris and regional cities,' Hanley writes, *factums* exposed 'the multifarious workings of law, touching all in civil society', thereby generating a new public space. 'Juridical in contour, this public space was staked out by law, lawyers, and litigants, shaped by writers, listeners, and readers of *factums* recounting lawsuits, and populated with competing voices that moulded public opinions on social entitlements (material and symbolic), rights guarded by civil law.' Thus, long before the eighteenth century, the state created a setting and provided the means whereby private matters could be given public expression, debate, and commentary.[13]

To sum up: any satisfactory account of the public and public opinion through the reign of Louis XIV must take into account the variegated, corporate nature of Ancien Régime society and state in which the public enjoyed an uncertain status. Broad as were its claims to sovereignty, the monarchy—if by that term is meant the King and his ministers—was not the only mouthpiece of the public, which, even in the face of vigorous royal censorship, found ways of expressing its opinion in alternative forms and settings. Because there was no single institutionalized representation of the public nor any one public voice, it is not surprising that the public was perceived in starkly different ways: often, to be sure, as an extension of the royal court, but sometimes as a tribunal that rendered autonomous verdicts, sometimes as an irresistible torrent, and sometimes as little more than the rabble. Each of these images persisted into the eighteenth century, when the nature of the public and its opinion would be scrutinized and debated all over again.

A New Public Sphere?

According to Habermas, at the end of the seventeenth century a second 'public sphere' began to materialize that differed from the first 'public sphere' in three critical ways. (1) Unlike the first 'public sphere', the second comprised primarily non-aristocratic elites, whose size and influence expanded greatly in the eighteenth century. (2) Whereas the first 'public sphere' had been closed to debate of many political and religious issues, the new 'public sphere' promoted rational inquiry into all realms of knowledge and practice and facilitated the free exchange of ideas. (3) Whereas in the first 'public sphere' the conduct of 'public' affairs had been conducted beneath a shroud of secrecy, advocates of the new 'public sphere' demanded greater transparency based on the notion that an informed citizenry and laity was indispensable for the successful administration of public affairs. Inclusiveness, free inquiry, and transparency were values and practices championed by the Enlightenment, and it was undoubtedly the Enlightenment—especially in its Kantian mode—that Habermas had in mind when elaborating upon the new 'public sphere'. But how much Habermas's picture captured social and political reality and to what extent it distorted and idealized that reality remain unclear. In light of what we now know, is it more accurate to conceive of the eighteenth century, to paraphrase Kant, as an enlightened age, or is it more accurate to conceive of it more narrowly, as did Kant himself, as an age of the Enlightenment? Does it make sense, in short, to speak of a new 'public sphere' in the eighteenth century? Certainly there have been many historians working directly or indirectly under Habermas's influence who have thought so, and even if they have generally abandoned his 'bourgeois' class-typing of the 'new public sphere', they make a strong case in his defence on at least three counts.

First, as they have amply demonstrated, literacy and the book trade greatly expanded across Europe, although not uniformly across all classes, professions, regions, religious groups, or genders. In France, the literacy rate roughly doubled in the last century of the Old Regime, moving from 29 to 47 per cent among men and from 14 to 27 per cent among women. Among servants, too, literacy was on the rise, the Abbé Jean-Baptiste Dubos observing already at the turn of the seventeenth century that in Paris 'a petty bourgeois will not employ a lackey or even a cook who cannot read or write'. As literacy and personal wealth expanded, so did the number and size of personal libraries. This expansion was limited neither to the capital nor to the rich; in the urban areas of western France, the percentage of personal estates of less than 500 *livres* containing books rose from 10 to 25 per cent between the late seventeenth and middle eighteenth centuries. Authors and their publishers responded to the growing demand for books and periodicals despite heavy-handed state censorship of printed matter. If nothing else, the economics of the marketplace motivated entrepreneurial men of letters to find ways of evading censorship laws, as evidenced by the booming trade in prohibited books—among them, less than edifying gossip sheets and scandalous novels, but also great Enlightenment classics. That so many of these works, including the pornographic ones, had a critical, even subversive edge and/or explored the lives and affairs of the middle class, argue many historians, was no accident. Less dependent upon the patronage of princes and the church than previous writers, their authors—some of whom claimed to speak for the public—were freer to engage the views—and pander to the arguably less discriminating tastes—of a wider range of readers. The result was a more free-wheeling debate of hitherto proscribed topics that Habermas identified as one of the cardinal features of the new 'public sphere'.[14]

Another sign of the emergence of a new 'public sphere' highlighted by some historians was the emergence of a new, more egalitarian sociability that developed in sites outside the royal court. Court sociability, as Daniel Gordon puts it, involved 'a constant sense of "above" and "below"', which 'served the double purpose of imbuing the king with sovereign power and the nobility with ceremonial honor'. But by the second half of the eighteenth century, it is alleged, Versailles had lost its importance as the central site of 'the public'. 'The word *court* no longer awes us as it did in the time of Louis XIV,' wrote Mercier. 'It is no longer the source of prevailing opinions; it no longer decides all sorts of reputations; we no longer say with ludicrous emphasis, *the court has judged thusly*. We overrule the judgements of the court; we say aloud that it understands nothing.' Such statements and other evidence have persuaded many historians that, apart from attendance at certain ceremonies that remained *de rigueur* for maintaining their status, court nobles were leaving Versailles for Paris and other urban centres. As they mingled with bourgeois elites, they cultivated a more egalitarian form of social exchange in such venues as cafés—which in Paris increased from 380 in 1723 to nearly 2,000 in 1773—masonic lodges—which increased nationally from approximately 60 in 1750 to more than 300 by

1770— and above all the salons. "The public", writes Gordon in a reprise of Habermas, 'makes its appearance... as a sphere of independent judgment, a sphere in which individuals interact, define each other, and evaluate each other without reference to the hierarchies observed elsewhere in the regime.'[15]

Not surprisingly, many historians view these new centres of social interaction as incubators of the Enlightenment. Stressing the role played by the salons generally and the salon hostesses in particular in generating the Enlightenment 'project', Dena Goodman argues that because of their gendered education, the *salonnières* were specially equipped to moderate debate and reconcile opposing male opinions in a way that made salons models for other Enlightenment social sites and a template for enlightened public opinion in general. That women performed such functions, in her view, belies the claims of some historians that the 'new public sphere' was essentially and irredeemably gender-typed masculine. To be sure, women suffered terrific disadvantages when they 'went public' in arenas like government, the church, and the art world, and their rights of entry to the 'public sphere' in general were vigorously contested by misogynists like Jean-Jacques Rousseau. But, as Goodman and a raft of other historians have shown, these serious strikes against them did not prevent women from ultimately exercising considerable public influence, not only as salon hostesses, but also in such varied roles as court powerbrokers, convent directors, and authors. Nor did their inferior legal status prevent women, even at their domestic stations, from acting in myriad ways that connected them to public affairs. By negotiating contracts, lobbying for causes, exchanging letters, buying, reading, discussing, and even authoring books, women could heavily influence public outcomes. In the end, there may be no stronger evidence of the active role women did, in fact, play in the 'public sphere' than the loud, repeated claims of misogynists that by so frequently transgressing their allegedly God-given, naturally ordained gender roles, women were wreaking havoc on the morals of their age. 'An insistence that the public sphere was intrinsically masculinist,' observes James Van Horn Melton, '...obscures its multiple guises and narrows the range of attitudes and outcomes it could generate.'[16]

A third claim made in support of Habermas's notion of a new eighteenth-century 'public sphere' is that the eighteenth-century public and public opinion—understood as the rational distillation of colliding private opinions—acquired an unprecedented, almost unchallengeable discursive authority in arenas from the arts to religion to politics. Just why or how this investment of authority occurred—and why across such a broad range of activities—remains an open question. For Keith Baker the new political 'public sphere' arose rather suddenly around 1750 in response to a particular crisis of absolute authority. Before the mid-eighteenth century, Baker argues, there was no 'public politics' in the sense that any contestation over or discussion of political issues outside the royal entourage was regarded as illegitimate. But a series of noisy and disruptive controversies—beginning with the refusal of sacraments controversy in the 1750s and extending through the debates over liberalization of the grain trade in the 1760s and the Maupeou coup of the 1770s—shattered the 'absolutist mold' of politics. The result was the invention of a 'new system of authority in which the government and its opponents competed to appeal to "the public" and to claim the judgment of "public opinion" on their behalf'. Notwithstanding its increasing evocation, this 'public', Baker insists, had no sociological referent. The 'public' and its 'opinion', he contends, have to be understood as purely ideological constructs that carried weight inasmuch as they implicitly contradicted the absolutist notion that the King was the sole 'public person', while pointing away from the chaotic politics of faction, which in French eyes recalled the traumas of the sixteenth-century religious wars and the troubling instability of English politics. To the extent that the monarchy was seduced into embracing this new form of politics after 1750, Baker suggests, it fell into a trap. For despite the monarchy's efforts to win favourable 'verdicts' in the court of public opinion, the qualities it had long claimed for itself—orderliness, stability, irresistibility, and universality—were inexorably transferred to the rhetorical figure of 'the public', a process that accelerated as the crown fell under increasing public indictment for arbitrariness, instability, and moral turpitude—in a word, for 'despotism'.[17]

Do these three arguments clinch the case for the existence of a new enlightened 'public sphere' in the eighteenth century? In my view, that case needs to be restated and qualified in a number of significant ways, given what has already been said about the first 'public sphere' and other evidence.

First, as regards the origins of the new 'public sphere', the argument that the politics of public opinion suddenly emerged during the mid-eighteenth century in response to a particular crisis of—and in antithesis to—absolutism no longer appears tenable. As we have seen, well before the eighteenth century, the monarchy, while never coincident with the 'public' or recognized as such, had played a critical role in its creation. This point has been underscored by David Bell, who takes the long, Tocquevillean view that 'the public' arose principally as the result of the bureaucratic and communication networks erected by the monarchy to administer the nation. Long before the Enlightenment, ministers like Richelieu had understood that the state could not rule by force alone, that it depended upon public 'credit', financial as well as moral, which inescapably meant—even under the reign of Louis XIV—submitting itself to judgement before the, or at least a, 'public'. When during the John Law affair of 1716–20, the monarchy tried and failed to incorporate the public at large within the circle of its financial creditors through forcible acceptance of government paper money, it revealed not only the limits of its ability to orchestrate public response to its initiatives but also the power of 'public opinion'—a term long in use among financiers—to determine public outcomes. When during the same period the Jansenists, in association with the parlements and the barristers, resisted the crown's efforts to enforce the papal bull *Unigenitus* levelled against them, they explicitly and successfully appealed to the 'public' through a wide network of underground publications. Notable in both these instances is the way in which the government's missteps fanned fears of encroaching 'despotism', thereby initiating a process that made possible—though certainly not inevitable—the Revolution of 1789. It is undoubtedly true that after 1750 rhetorical appeals to the public increased and the authority of public opinion grew. But by then, the monarchy and the public had been tangled in a tumultuous embrace for a very long time.[18]

If so, the claim that institutions like the salons operated in a new 'public sphere' distinct from and in opposition to the monarchy—that they 'symbolized an emerging civil society that was increasingly coming to view itself as autonomous from the state'—also needs some major qualification. Just as in the seventeenth century the state did not inhabit an elevated 'sphere' of its own, nor was it disconnected in the next century from many institutions that some historians working within the Habermasian paradigm have all too readily consigned to an autonomous social realm—among them, the salons. Antoine Lilti's recent, exhaustive study has demonstrated that, far from constituting a world apart from Versailles in its membership, sociability, and intellectual orientation, the salons were in fact what many contemporaries said they were, namely, antechambers to the court. 'Nothing', he shows in opposition to the claims of Gordon and Goodman, 'is more false than to imagine the salons as spaces cut off from the court and the political battles that took place there.' If the salons enjoyed a somewhat more relaxed etiquette than Versailles, the same social markers that were used to define status at court counted in the salons of Paris as well, which is hardly surprising since the salons were heavily populated by court nobles forever on guard against any slight to their rank. On the basis of very narrow evidence, Lilti comes to the debatable conclusion that the salons should not be considered part of the 'public sphere'. Yet he does show effectively how the salons served as springboards for advancing the careers of aspiring public figures like Jacques Necker, which suggests that in so far as the court belonged to the 'public sphere', so too did the salons that served as its antechambers.[19]

A second cautionary point worth pondering is that, although in some quarters the public was imagined as a unitary tribunal capable of distilling reason and consensus from the mass of conflicting individual opinions, this representation competed with others that were far less likely to induce confidence in its verdicts; not everyone was willing to bow before a god that could not be visualized in some concrete form. In the face of conflicting claims to speak for 'the public', some observers drew the conclusion that there was no omnibus 'public' capable of rendering unimpeachable judgements in all matters, but rather multiple 'publics', each inclined to render particular judgements according to its own more or less well-informed lights. 'If there is a French public,' wrote one critic in 1740, 'there is also an English public, an Italian public, a German public; in a word, ... there are as many publics as there are nations in the world and ... I could not please one without appearing ridiculous to the others.' Approval by a variety of national publics might appear to have validated the taste and discernment of them all; but by the same token, conflicting verdicts—and there were many—threatened to invalidate the judgement of each one. Within every nation, moreover, the public—notwithstanding its image as a crucible of reconciliation—did not always appear to speak univocally. Some critics, such as Jean-François Marmontel, thought they heard the authentic, unified voice of the French nation in the murmurings of the theatre *parterre*; but others detected little more than discordant shouting. Although he disagreed with his even more sceptical colleagues who claimed that the public was nothing but a 'shadowy Phantom, which never existed, and will never exist', one critic cast enough contemporary 'doubts upon the existence of a public' to pronounce the death of a once vibrant theatrical public opinion. 'Success', he wrote, 'is no longer the work of the public; it is the fruit of the intrigues of individuals... Each group has pretended to be the true public... Division has made good taste problematical... and the authority of a legitimate public has lost its unity.'[20]

These doubts expressed about the unity and integrity of the public suggest that at least to some observers the politics of public opinion, far from offering an attractive alternative to the corrupt rough-and-tumble of English political culture, suffered from many of the same defects. Here, we are faced with a paradox that historians have not sufficiently recognized: the greater the authority acquired by the public in some circles, the more those who stood to lose or gain by its political or aesthetic judgements had reason to hijack it. This danger was by no means purely hypothetical, nor—as can be seen from the previous quotation—did it go unnoticed. At court, ministerial factions routinely used the police to plant rumours among the public in order to sully the reputation of their enemies or to restore that of embattled political allies in the eyes of the King. As Jean-Louis Favier described the practice, in addition to 'memos, notices, [and] leaflets that a minister can use at will to spread smears and the most atrocious calumnies against those he wants to ruin', the police 'is also very useful for supporting and sometimes saving a man in place. It is by this means that the king can be made to interpret, however one thinks best, "the talk of Paris" and what one tells him is "the public voice".' Favier was in an excellent position to know how the 'public voice' was manipulated. For as an experienced hired pen of the 'devout party', he was undoubtedly familiar with that court faction's circulation of sexually defamatory verses against their enemy—Louis XV's mistress, Mme de Pompadour—as a means for demonstrating to the King how much the 'public' loathed her and thereby obtaining her dismissal. Undoubtedly, this sort of defamatory campaign had impact. But it is equally true that even some relatively low-born political observers understood how this game was played. Indeed, they occasionally factored that knowledge into their judgements of what the public 'really' thought as opposed to what interested parties, seeking falsely to speak in the name of the public, claimed it believed. Thus, when the hated chancellor René-Nicolas de Maupeou tried to discredit the young and still popular Marie Antoinette in 1774, a crowd reportedly burnt him in effigy crying 'let us avenge our charming queen against whom this despicable man has dared to speak disparagingly and spread libels!' Even those like Mercier who retained faith in the ultimate rectitude of public opinion recognized how cynically it could be exploited. 'Tell a man in office that "the public disapproves [of him]," he will respond, "I, too, have my public, which approves [of me], and I will consort with that one." Another [official] will say, "the public—I make it speak as I wish; I have merely to impress upon it this or that view." '[21]

In the worlds of painting, literature, and the theatre, public opinion was likewise subverted by artists who employed claques to hail their work and/or assail the work of their rivals—practices that were not beneath the likes of notables such as Voltaire and Diderot. 'There is no author so wretched', commented one critic, 'that he does not shamelessly proclaim that his works have pleased you [the Public], that they are esteemed by the Public, that they enjoy the admiration of the Public, etc.' Given the widespread recognition of such practices, it is scarcely surprising that public judgements of artistic works were often met with disdain. 'The public, the public', acidly responded one critic when told that 'the public' did not share his judgement of a particular work, 'how many fools does it take to make a public?' If some observers respected the public for its discernment, others respected it merely for its power, much as had the King's ministers in the seventeenth century. 'A man spoke of the respect that the public merited. "Yes," replied M..., "the respect that comes from prudence. Everyone despises fish-mongers. But who would dare offend them while crossing the marketplace?" ' Jean-Jacques Rousseau took comfort in the thought that the fickleness of the public's *opinions* made them resistant to subversion, corruption, and control. But whether that resistance extended to *public opinion* was not clear. According to most observers, public opinion as embodied in any of its concrete manifestations merited respect only inasmuch as the 'public' that judged was composed of the well-informed and incorruptible. This was not a big group by most contemporary calculations, and for this reason respect for the judgements of the public tended to vary, as Richard Wrigley wryly puts it, 'in direct proportion to its intangibility'.[22]

A third reason to question the case for a new 'public sphere' relates to its alleged inclination to embrace and promote the Enlightenment and other progressive movements. That the Enlightenment and the critique of the Ancien Régime generally were enormously facilitated by the expansion of the reading public and the book trade cannot be disputed. Yet as James Melton has persuasively argued, eighteenth-century public opinion was not nearly so 'enlightened' and uniformly critical of established ideas and institutions as Habermas and his followers have indicated. In fact, much of that 'opinion' was traditionalist, if not downright reactionary in matters of religion, politics, and art. The orthodox may have inwardly abhorred the widening world of print, but they were hardly prepared to abandon the 'public sphere' to their *philosophe* enemies and did what they could to impress their opinions upon it. Hence, for every later eighteenth-century journal that was favourable to the views of the *philosophes*, at least three circulated that were openly hostile. If by 1770 the Enlightenment tide seemed to be rising, in that year alone ninety works rose to the defence of orthodox religion. What made so many of these works effective, Darrin McMahon contends, was neither their erudition nor their theological sophistication, but, to the contrary, their lack of learning and want of fine-grained argumentation. Indeed, some of them were no more than diatribes against the Enlightenment, warning of its dangers to society, the state, social mores, and the salvation of humankind. Moreover, although conservative in their main thrust, these polemics cleverly invoked certain themes advanced by the republican wing of the Enlightenment that served their authors' purposes. Thundering alongside Rousseau and Gabriel Bonnot de Mably against the alleged decline of contemporary morals, these jeremiads evoked fears of an imminent, violent Armageddon, with the *philosophes* and their fellow-travellers cast as the new servants of Satan.[23]

In the face of such masterful conservative appeals to and manipulation of public opinion, it is not surprising that the *philosophes* were often struck and depressed by the deep-rooted nature of 'prejudice' and 'superstition'. Indeed, some of them sadly came to the conclusion that 'public opinion' was not their most reliable ally. 'Public opinion', declared

Pierre Le Brun in 1788, 'is the queen of kings, but if it lacks reason, justice, and truth for its foundation, it is but a blind despot, a fanatical tyrant that will be the torment and misfortune of those it governs.' 'Public opinion', declared Bon de Saint-Flocel even more emphatically, 'is the source of all the evils, all the abuses, all the crimes that today ravage humanity. It is a monstrous mixture of prejudices, errors, and superstitions… If men are everywhere crushed under the weight of despotism and anarchy, if they are everywhere slaves of tyrants and priests, if they are everywhere victims of violence or ruse, it is public opinion that has subjugated them.' The hyperbolic character of these judgements make them exceptional for their time. But they do point up an important historical truth: namely, that whereas Habermas contended that the eighteenth-century 'public sphere' was inherently an instrument of progressive change rather than a bulwark of orthodox continuity, a fairer conclusion would be to say that it was—and was perceived to be—both.[24]

Conclusion

Has the 'public sphere'—like so many other once fashionable heuristic constructs—suffered the death of a thousand qualifications? After nearly a half-century of debate and discussion, there can be no doubt it has lost the sharp edges Habermas originally gave it; but that loss does not invalidate the 'public sphere' as a tool of historical analysis so much as it obligates us to keep in mind its multiform, protean nature. The 'public' has become increasingly hard to define because, in the light of recent research, the sociological entity to which that term refers stands out less boldly from the patchwork quilt of private persons, corporations, and state agencies that constituted the Ancien Régime.[25] This is why in tracking the various incarnations of the 'public'—both as it was and as it was perceived—one must not focus exclusively on the state in the seventeenth century or on civil society in the eighteenth, but rather keep both firmly in view over the entire course of the Ancien Régime. Just as the monarchy never incorporated the entire public, nor did it ever monopolize the public voice, even under Louis XIV. Moreover, inasmuch as the monarchy—in order to finance and administer the kingdom and validate its own propaganda—provided fresh opportunities and sites for the public to gain leverage, the King's ministers unwittingly engendered a sorcerer's apprentice that increasingly escaped their masters' control.

This hardly means that the monarchy ceased to be a major player in the 'public sphere' during the eighteenth century. Just as its long reach extended into institutions of civil society that have been erroneously typed as distinctly counter-cultural, so did the crown continue to sponsor propaganda on its own behalf—some of it intellectually innovative, and, up to a point, influential—in the face of attacks from Jansenists and barristers in particular. The outcome was a 'public sphere' that remained largely closed to the popular underclass, but at least partly open to almost everyone else. No single party could convincingly claim complete ownership of the 'public sphere': neither the monarchy, nor its critics; neither the Jansenists, nor the Jesuits; neither the *philosophes*, nor their enemies; neither men, nor women. This openness bred a volatility which belied the often repeated claim that public opinion provided a reliable mechanism for the rational—and national—reconciliation of conflicting views. Such became evident when, in the late 1780s, the monarchy, desperate for national sanction of its financial reforms, once again provided new sites for the articulation of 'public opinion', in this instance, the Assembly of Notables of 1787 and the Estates-General of 1789. However high the hopes that the nation would then speak univocally through a 'union of orders', the result was not reconciliation, but rather a bitterly contested revolution the like of which France had never before witnessed.[26]

Notes

1. Louis-Sébastien Mercier, *Tableau de Paris* (new edn., 12 vols. Amsterdam, 1782–8; Slatkine repr. 1979), vi. 303 (tr. mine), as are all those that follow except where indicated; Roland Puchot, comte des Alleurs, *Avis au public* (n.pl., 1740); Jürgen Habermas, *Structural Transformation of the Public Sphere*, tr. Thomas Burger and Frederick Lawrence (Cambridge, Mass., 1989).
2. Habermas, *Structural Transformation*, 11, 18.
3. Ibid. 141. 69.
4. The critical literature is too vast to be cited here. For one useful collection of critiques that also includes Habermas's responses, see Craig Calhoun (ed.), *Habermas and the Public Sphere* (Cambridge, Mass., and London, 1992).
5. For an extended discussion of '(the) public', see Hélène Merlin, *Public et littérature en France au xviie siècle* (Paris, 1994), ch. 1; Alain Rey, Marianne Tomi, and Chantal Tanet (eds.), *Dictionnaire historique de la langue française* (2 vols. Paris, 1992), ii. 1665–6; Jean Bodin, *Les Six livres de la République* (Paris, 1577), 15; Keith Michael Baker, *Inventing the French Revolution: Essays on French Political Culture in the Eighteenth Century* (Cambridge, 1990), 114; Jacques-Bénigne Bossuet, *Politique tirée des propres paroles de l'Écriture sainte* (Paris, 1709), 91; cited in David Kammerling-Smith, 'Le Discours économique du Bureau du Commerce, 1700–1750', in Charles Loïc, Frédéric Lefebvre, and Christine Théré (eds.), *Commerce, population et société autour de Vincent de Gournay (1748–1758): La Genèse d'un vocabulaire des sciences sociales en France* (Paris, forthcoming).
6. See, among a large literature on the subject, William Beik, *Absolutism and Society in Seventeenth-Century France: State Power and Provincial Aristocracy in Languedoc* (Cambridge, 1985), and Roger Mettam, *Power and Faction in Louis XIV's France* (Oxford and New York, 1988); David Potter, *A History of France: The Emergence of a Nation State, 1460–1560* (New York, 1995), 90.
7. J. A. W. Gunn, *Queen of the World: Opinion in the Public Life of France from the Renaissance to the Revolution*, in *SVEC* 328 (Oxford, 1995); cited ibid.; ibid. 66–77; Dom Jean Mabillon, *Traité des études monastiques* (Paris, 1691), 184; on the phenomenon of *la critique*, see Reinhard Koselleck, *Critique and Crisis: Enlightenment and the Pathogenesis of Modern Society* (Oxford, 1988); Nicolas Boileau Despréaux, *Œuvres complètes* (n.pl., 1966), 6.
8. Armand Jean du Plessis, Cardinal de Richelieu, *The Political Testament of Cardinal Richelieu*, tr. Henry Bertram Hill (Madison, Wis., 1961), 119; among many studies, see Orest

Ranum, *Artisans of Glory: Writers and Historical Thought in Seventeenth-Century France* (Chapel Hill, NC, 1980); Sarah Hanley, *The 'Lit de Justice' of the Kings of France: Constitutional Ideology in Legend, Ritual, and Discourse* (Princeton, 1983); Peter Burke, *The Fabrication of Louis XIV* (New Haven, Conn., and London, 1992); Jean Bodin, *Method for the Easy Comprehension of History*, tr. Beatrice Reynolds (New York, 1945), 46; Montesquieu, *Persian Letters*, tr. C. J. Betts (Harmondsworth and New York, 1973), 145, 267; Paul Pellisson-Fontanier, 'Projet de l'histoire du Roy Louis XIV à M. Colbert', in *Lettres historiques de Monsieur Pellisson* (3 vols. Paris, 1729; [Slatkine Reprints, 1971]), iii. 328–9 [423–4]; Burke, *Fabrication*, 92–6.

9. Ranum, *Artisans*, 112; for one despairing comment, see Jean-Baptiste Dubos, 'Documents de critique musicale et théâtrale: Dix lettres extraites de la correspondance entre Ladvocat et l'abbé Dubos (1694–1696)', ed. Jérome de la Gorce, *xviie siècle*, 129 (1983), 282–3; on the world of the theatre, see the delightful Henri Lagrave, *Le Théâtre et le public de 1715-1750* (Paris, 1972).

10. On the demonization of Louis's mistresses, see Thomas E. Kaiser, 'Louis *le Bien-Aimé* and the Rhetoric of the Royal Body', in Sara E. Melzer and Kathryn Norberg (eds.), *From the Royal to the Republican Body: Incorporating the Political in Seventeenth- and Eighteenth-Century France* (Berkeley, Calif., 1998), 147–51; id., 'The Monarchy, Public Opinion, and the Subversions of Antoine Watteau', in Mary Sheriff (ed.), *Antoine Watteau: Perspectives on the Artist and the Culture of his Times* (Newark, NJ, 2006), 71. Despite my profound differences with the author regarding the social status of the public monitored and its role in political dissent, there is much useful information on police spying in Arlette Farge, *Subversive Words: Public Opinion in Eighteenth-Century France*, tr. Rosemary Morris (University Park, Pa., 1995); Jean-Baptiste Primi Visconti, *Mémoires sur la cour de Louis XIV*, ed. Jean-François Solnon (Paris, 1988), 100; Jean de La Bruyère, *Les Caractères, ou les mœurs de ce siècle* (Paris, 1962), 221.

11. Richelieu, *Political Testament*, 111–12; cited in Germain Martin and Marcel Bezançon, *L'Histoire du crédit en France sous le règne de Louis XIV* (Paris, 1913), i. 63; Jean-Baptiste Colbert, 'Lettre', in *Lettres, instructions et mémoires de Colbert*, ed. Pierre Clément (8 vols. Paris, 1861–82), ii/II. 526–7; ibid. ii/I, p. ccxlii; this symbiotic relationship is stressed in Daniel Dessert, *Argent, pouvoir et société au Grand Siècle* (Paris, 1984); Anon., 'Mémoire, 26 December 1717', Bibliothèque Nationale Joly de Fleury Ms. 566, 175; on the notion of 'credit' in this period, see Thomas E. Kaiser, 'Public Credit: John Law's Scheme and the Question of *Confiance*', *Proceedings of the Annual Meeting of the Western Society for French History*, 16 (1989), 72–81.

12. David A. Bell, 'The "Public Sphere," the State, and the World of Law in Eighteenth-Century France', *French Historical Studies*, 17 (1992), 912–34.

13. Sarah Hanley, 'Social Sites of Political Practice in France: Lawsuits, Civil Rights, and the Separation of Powers in Domestic and State Government, 1500–1800', *American Historical Review*, 102 (1997), 27–52; ead., 'The Pursuit of Legal Knowledge and the Genesis of Civil Society in Early Modern France', in Anthony J. Grafton and J. H. M. Salmon, *Historians and Ideologues: Essays in Honor of Donald R. Kelley* (Rochester, 2001), 71–86; ead., 'The Jurisprudence of the *Arrêts*: Marital Union, Civil Society, and State Formation in France, 1550–1650', *Law and History Review*, 21 (2003), 1–40; Hanley, 'Social Sites', 34.

14. Roger Chartier, *The Cultural Origins of the French Revolution*, tr. Lydia G. Cochrane (Durham, NC, and London, 1991), 69; Émile Gigas (ed.), *Choix de la correspondance inédite de Pierre Bayle (1670-1706)* (Copenhagen, 1890), 285; Chartier, *Cultural Origins*, 69; Robert

Darnton, *The Forbidden Best-Sellers of Pre-Revolutionary France* (New York and London: Norton, 1995); *id.*, *The Devil in the Holy Water or the Art of Slander from Louis XIV to Napoleon* (Philadelphia, 2010); Simon Burrows, *Blackmail, Scandal and Revolution: London's French Libellistes, 1758–1792* (Manchester and New York, 2006).

15. Daniel Gordon, *Citizens without Sovereignty: Equality and Sociability in French Thought, 1670–1789* (Princeton, 1994), 87–8; Mercier, *Tableau*, iv. 261; William Ritchey Newton, *L'Espace du roi: La Cour de France au château de Versailles 1682–1789* ([Paris], 2000); Daniel Roche, *France in the Enlightenment*, tr. Arthur Goldhammer (Cambridge, Mass., and London, 1998), 461; Margaret C. Jacob, *Living the Enlightenment: Freemasonry and Politics in Eighteenth-Century Europe* (New York and Oxford, 1991), 205. For an excellent survey embracing three national contexts, see James Van Horn Melton, *The Rise of the Public in Enlightenment Europe* (Cambridge and New York, 2001); Gordon, *Citizens*, 100.

16. Dena Goodman, 'Public Sphere and Private Life: Toward a Synthesis of Current Historiographical Approaches to the Old Regime', *History and Theory*, 31 (1992), 1–20; *ead.*, *The Republic of Letters: A Cultural History of the French Enlightenment* (Ithaca, NY, and London, 1994); Joan Landes, *Women and the Public Sphere in the Age of the French Revolution* (Ithaca, NY, and London, 1988). Among a large and growing literature on women writers, see Elizabeth C. Goldsmith and Dena Goodman (eds.), *Going Public: Women and Publishing in Early Modern France* (Ithaca, NY, and London, 1995), and Carla Hesse, *The Other Enlightenment: How French Women Became Modern* (Princeton, 2001); Melton, *Rise of the Public*, 274.

17. As Richard Wrigley has observed in *The Origins of French Art Criticism from the Ancien Régime to the Restoration* (Oxford, 1993), 108, 18th-cent. art critics 'indicted academic corruption and misconduct by virtue of the same criteria—Nature, Truth, the Public—as were being used by adversaries of the government and court'; Baker, *Inventing*, 172, 193–6.

18. David A. Bell, *Lawyers and Citizens: The Making of a Political Elite in Old Regime France* (New York and Oxford, 1994), 12–13; see e.g. Colbert's campaign to convince investors to buy shares in the East Indies Co. and the backlash engendered by the monarchy's forsaken promises to them. Kaiser, 'Public Credit', 74; Thomas E. Kaiser, 'Money, Despotism, and Public Opinion: John Law and the Debate on Royal Credit', *Journal of Modern History*, 63 (1991), 1–28; Bell, *Lawyers and Citizens*, ch. 3; Dale Van Kley, *The Religious Origins of the French Revolution: From Calvin to the Civil Constitution, 1560–1791* (New Haven, Conn., and London, 1996), ch. 2; Catherine Maire, *De la cause de Dieu à la cause de la Nation: Le Jansénisme au xviiie siècle* (Paris, 1998), ch. 8. The crown was neither insensitive nor unresponsive to the use of 'public opinion' by its critics. See Thomas E. Kaiser, 'The Abbé de Saint-Pierre, Public Opinion, and the Reconstitution of the French Monarchy', *Journal of Modern History*, 55 (1983), 618–43; *id.*, 'The Abbé Dubos and the Historical Defense of Monarchy in Early Eighteenth-Century France', *Studies on Voltaire and the Eighteenth Century*, 267 (1989), 77–102; *id.*, 'Rhetoric in the Service of the King: The Abbé Dubos and the Concept of Public Judgment', *Eighteenth-Century Studies*, 23 (1989), 182–99.

19. Melton, *Rise of the Public*, 273; Antoine Lilti, *Le Monde des salons: Sociabilité et mondanité à Paris au xviiie siècle* (n.pl., 2005), 364.

20. Alleurs, *Avis*, 5. Earlier in the century, the Abbé Dubos had developed a sophisticated theory regarding the varying abilities of different 'publics' to make artistic and political judgements based on their different ranges of experience—see Kaiser, 'Rhetoric'; Jeffrey S. Ravel,

The Contested Parterre: Public Theater and French Political Culture, 1680–1791 (Ithaca, NY, and London, 1999), ch. 6; cited in Wrigley, *Origins*, 103.

21. Jean-Louis Favier, 'Précis des faits sur l'administration de M. de Choiseul', ed. Jules Flammermont, *La Révolution française: Revue d'Histoire moderne et contemporaine*, 36 (1899), 445; Thomas E. Kaiser, 'Madame de Pompadour and the Theaters of Power', *French Historical Studies*, 19 (1996), 1025–44; id., 'The Drama of Charles Edward Stuart, Jacobite Propaganda, and French Political Protest, 1745–1750', *Eighteenth-Century Studies*, 30 (1997), 365–81; Alfred d'Arneth and Auguste Geffroy (eds.), *Correspondance secrète entre Marie-Thérèse et le comte de Mercy-Argenteau* (3 vols. Paris, 1874), ii. 232; Mercier, *Tableau*, vi. 303.

22. Thomas E. Crow, *Painters and Public Life in Eighteenth-Century Paris* (New Haven, Conn., and London, 1985), 14; Alleurs, *Avis*, 8; Sébastien-Roch-Nicolas Chamfort, *Caractères et anecdotes de Chamfort* (Paris, 1924), 8; ibid. 140; Jean-Jacques Rousseau, 'Lettre à M. d'Alembert', in *Du Contrat Social* (Paris, 1962), 182; Wrigley, *Origins*, 104; cf. Crow, *Painters*, 19, who remarks upon 'the disparity between a public evoked in abstract terms and an actual audience whose behavior can only be characterized as a collection of vagrant individual responses'.

23. Melton, *Rise of the Public*, 11–12; Daniel Mornet, *Les Origines intellectuelles de la Révolution française, 1715–1787* (Lyon, 1989), 240; Darrin M. McMahon, *Enemies of the Enlightenment: The French Counter-Enlightenment and the Making of Modernity* (Oxford and New York, 2001), ch. 1.

24. [Pierre Le Brun] in *Journal général de l'Europe: Politique, Commerce, Agriculture*, 138 (18 Nov. 1788), 113–14; [Bon de Saint-Flocel], *Journal des princes; ou Examen des journaux & autres Ecrits périodiques, relativement aux Progrès du Despotisme* (London, 1783), 1–2.

25. Of course, for those like Keith Baker who view the 'public' merely as an ideological/discursive construct, this sociological indeterminacy poses no particular concern.

26. On the hopes for a 'union of orders' and their disappointment, see Kenneth Margerison, *Pamphlets and Public Opinion: The Campaign for a Union of Orders in the Early French Revolution* (West Lafayette, Ind., 1998).

Bibliography

Baker, Keith Michael, *Inventing the French Revolution: Essays on French Political Culture in the Eighteenth Century* (Cambridge, 1990).

Calhoun, Craig (ed.), *Habermas and the Public Sphere* (Cambridge, Mass., and London, 1992).

Chartier, Roger, *The Cultural Origins of the French Revolution*, tr. Lydia G. Cochrane (Durham, NC, and London, 1991).

Chisick, Harvey, 'Public Opinion and Political Culture in France during the Second Half of the Eighteenth Century', *English Historical Review*, 117 (2002), 48–77.

Darnton, Robert, *The Forbidden Best-Sellers of Pre-Revolutionary France* (New York and London, 1995).

Farge, Arlette, *Subversive Words: Public Opinion in Eighteenth-Century France*, tr. Rosemary Morris (University Park, Pa., 1995).

Goodman, Dena, 'Public Sphere and Private Life: Toward a Synthesis of Current Historiographical Approaches to the Old Regime', *History and Theory*, 31 (1992), 1–20.

Gunn, J. A. W., *Queen of the World: Opinion in the Public Life of France from the Renaissance to the Revolution*, SVEC 328 (Oxford, 1995).

Habermas, Jürgen, *Structural Transformation of the Public Sphere*, tr. Thomas Burger and Frederick Lawrence (Cambridge, Mass., 1989).

Hanley, Sarah, 'Social Sites of Political Practice in France: Lawsuits, Civil Rights, and the Separation of Powers in Domestic and State Government, 1500–1800', *American Historical Review*, 102 (1997), 27–52.

Kaiser, Thomas E., 'Money, Despotism, and Public Opinion: John Law and the Debate on Royal Credit', *Journal of Modern History*, 63 (1991), 1–28.

Landes, Joan, *Women and the Public Sphere in the Age of the French Revolution* (Ithaca, NY, and London, 1988).

Melton, James Van Horn, *The Rise of the Public in Enlightenment Europe* (Cambridge and New York, 2001).

Mornet, Daniel, *Les Origines intellectuelles de la Révolution française, 1715–1787* (Lyon, 1989).

Ozouf, Mona, ' "Public Opinion" at the End of the Old Regime', *Journal of Modern History*, 60 (1988), 1–21.

PART VI

SOLVENTS?

CHAPTER 25

ENLIGHTENMENT

THOMAS MUNCK

The Enlightenment, as a historical term, is intimately linked to the Ancien Régime: both describe historical constructs that once seemed more French than European, at least in origin, and although the term 'Ancien Régime' acquired its meaning only in retrospect (from the perspective of 1790), both were originally used by historians to denote something which had come to an end by 1789. The Enlightenment was the intellectually innovative and emancipatory process which, depending on your definition of the Ancien Régime itself, either modernized the political and social structures of the early modern state, or helped to undermine it and to precipitate the upheaval of the French Revolution. In effect, the Enlightenment was both part of, and a direct response to, the Ancien Régime itself—breaking with older intellectual and religious traditions, criticizing long-established institutions, and encouraging at least the elite to rethink the world around them. In accordance with prevailing historiographical trends, historians of the Enlightenment tended to focus on those major writers who fitted within this narrative, and who stood out because of the striking originality and the brilliance of their reasoning: Montesquieu (1689–1755), a prominent member of the Parlement of Bordeaux and subtle critic of Ancien Régime society and politics, both in his *Persian Letters* (1721) and in his treatise *The Spirit of the Laws* (1748); Voltaire (1694–1778), master stylist of the French language and powerful campaigner against many of the abuses of the old order; Rousseau (1712–78), an outsider from Geneva whose *Discourse on Inequality* (1755), *La Nouvelle Héloïse* (1761), and *Emile* (1762) each appeared to challenge the fundamental assumptions of contemporary readers and in effect question the old order; and Diderot (1713–84), whose work on the *Encyclopédie* (1751–65/72) provided the Enlightenment with its greatest and most widely read work of reference. To this list, of course, should be added a large number of less remarkable but still very gifted writers, scientists, and polemicists, who between them critically reassessed most forms of knowledge, and fuelled those brilliant and unpredictable intellectual debates which made Ancien Régime France such a productive and exhilarating environment.

Recent research has in no way diminished either the stature or significance of the French Enlightenment, but has changed its context both in time and place. The chronological framework has widened, to take more account not only of the formative stages in England and in the Netherlands from the middle of the seventeenth century onwards, but also of developments in the last decades of the eighteenth century. Geographically, in addition to Scotland and the German-speaking lands, fresh light has been thrown on the role of the North American colonies, Ireland, Italy, Russia, the Balkans, and other areas with distinctive but significant developments of their own. As we shall see in this chapter, the trend in the 1980s to compartmentalize these into 'national' variants risked understating the extent to which eighteenth-century Europe really was both cosmopolitan and multilingual: in fact study of translation and transmission processes across Europe has revealed levels of selective adaptation and creative paraphrasing of ideas to suit different cultural and linguistic contexts, going well beyond mere imitation of French cultural influences. Such research, moving away from the 'great works' of the period towards a more comprehensive range of writings (including, for example, journals and newspapers), has also tended to bring out the fact that (as noted elsewhere in this volume) Ancien Régime society was more fluid and less segregated than traditional assumptions about deference and social hierarchy have allowed. These trends—recognition that distinct components of 'enlightened' thinking evolved in different ways which did not all culminate in the anti-French reaction of the early 1790s, and greater awareness of the permeability of both geographic and social barriers—have ensured that research on the processes of enlightening has broadened very significantly.

Interestingly, changing perceptions of the mechanisms and impact of the Enlightenment have not altered our understanding of its key intellectual concerns as much as one might expect. Challenges to formal religious authority and inherited beliefs can still, albeit in modified form, be regarded as central to enlightened thinking: strident anticlericalism may have been unique to France, culminating in its uncompromising dechristianization campaigns of 1793, but the (grudging) acceptance of religious pluralism, alongside hesitant acceptance of limited toleration, in France as elsewhere, suggests a gradual recognition not only that faith and reason could no longer easily be harnessed in the same cause, but also that some degree of separation of church and state might be both unavoidable and even beneficial. Cautious emancipation from the dictates of faith in turn fostered other reassessments. What we might loosely call the science(s) of man (moral philosophy, ethics, psychology, political economy, history, anthropology, ecology, and aspects of jurisprudence), combining systematic empirical observation with theoretical speculation, in turn fostered detailed scrutiny (without preconditions) of the realities of human existence rather than its teleological aspirations. There were major new developments in natural history, geology, chemistry, and physics, all with the capacity to change perceptions of the role of man. Systematic observation in the natural sciences, medicine, and political economy also led to a striking recognition that governments should take full responsibility for social policy and 'improvement'—with implications across areas and issues (such as poor relief and the management of underemployment) where previously most governments had followed merely reactive policies. Analysing these priorities as part of mainstream enlightened thinking has enabled historians to develop further insights into the period with respect to notions of identity and nationality, race, gender relations and the role of women in society, and the related issues of citizenship and political participation. In the process, historians may have made a cohesive and succinct definition of the Enlightenment ever more elusive; but its critical versatility, as well as its 'blind spots', have become clearer, and our perception of the Ancien Régime itself has changed.

Access to New Ideas

There was no eighteenth-century consensus on a programme or definable outcome to which a label such as *enlightenment* might be ascribed; and despite continuing fascination with all matters of rank and status during the Ancien Régime, there were no effective means of restricting the impact of new ways of thinking solely to the higher levels of society. The means by which new ideas were disseminated and discussed, and especially the innovative uses of print technology, ensured rapidly widening access, especially in urban society and in the more prosperous parts of Europe. The French use of the term *philosophes*, applied self-referentially by the group of liberal thinkers associated with the *Encyclopédie*, is liable to convey too restrictive a definition of the Enlightenment, both by implying some kind of unity of purpose (which did not exist), and by (deliberately) claiming exclusive ownership of intellectual innovation and reason. In fact variants of the word 'light' were used widely across western and central Europe, to denote the processes whereby individuals might (originally, in the seventeenth century, in a religious sense) 'see the light', or gain a new understanding. Significantly, the French equivalent, when used in the philosophical sense in the eighteenth century, was always in the plural: *les lumières*. The German term *Aufklärung* gained common currency, notably as a result of the discussion initiated in a Berlin journal in 1783—but as Kant made clear in his contribution the following year, the word meant no more than a process of clarification, a kind of self-education whereby the individual gained the intellectual autonomy and confidence required to make up his own mind.[1] Such a process was potentially within the reach of everyone: formal education, though it might help, was not (at least in the original religious context) an essential precondition, but the ability to read usually was.

The original eighteenth-century keywords were overshadowed during the late nineteenth and twentieth centuries, when the formalization of the historical discipline resulted in more explicit periodization and labelling. By the early twentieth century, the Enlightenment itself had become institutionalized as a period in intellectual history, its main (French) protagonists held up as philosophers working almost independently of their age, nourished at most by the high society of salons, literary networks, and academies. However, if we revert to Kant's conceptual framework, we have a better chance of seeing Enlightenment (without the definite article) more as an open-ended process, a way of handling questions, which had the potential of affecting everyone in some way, and was liable to alter the way society interacted. Nearly all the major thinkers of the period were acutely aware of how to communicate with readers of diverse social background. We need only contrast Montesquieu's fictional best-seller, *The Persian Letters* of 1721, with his weightier treatise published twenty-seven years later, to see that popular accessibility need not preclude profound content. In reality, it is difficult to find a major eighteenth-century writer who did not 'popularize' in one way or another: David Hume's first major publication (1740) famously did not sell well, but he gained a wide readership for his historical writing, and was able to make his last (posthumous) book, *Dialogues concerning Natural Religion*, both controversial and dangerously readable. Rousseau was even more a master of self-projection, particularly keen to emphasize the extent to which he spoke for the ordinary man. Diderot was too cautious to publish his most provocative writings in his own lifetime, but he knew how to write for a wide audience. So did Beaumarchais, the irrepressible Louis-Sébastien Mercier (with his acute sense of making new words, and using old ones differently), Lessing, Beccaria, not to mention the growing host of novelists and pamphleteers. Burke was deeply disappointed when his florid *Reflections on the French Revolution* (1790) was trounced in the best-seller list by Paine's populist two-part tract *Rights of Man* (1791–2). No less important, a growing number of women were able to contribute without having to disguise their identity: Mary Wollstonecraft remains an excellent example of the self-educated outsider who eventually managed to earn an independent living as translator, reviewer, and campaigner.

Determining the wider social impact of specific components in Enlightenment thinking is a major challenge in current historical research.[2] Separate chapters in this volume discuss education, sociability, and the public sphere, all of which can help provide answers. In the present context, however, two closely related points need to be emphasized, both to do with diffusion in print: the spread of reading skills, and the development of new forms of publication designed for the wider market. Of the two, reading ability is the most difficult to quantify. We know that many eighteenth-century schools paid more attention to religious rote learning than to key practical skills such as reading unseen text. But attempts by historians to measure adult reading skills by means of a proxy such as their ability to sign (for example, their marriage contract) is clearly misleading: reading and writing were taught as two distinct skills, and there is every indication that the extent of reading skills amongst women, in particular, has been substantively underestimated because they were rarely expected to write. Current research has confirmed that adequate reading skills were much more prevalent in urban than in rural society, in wealthier compared with poorer regions, and in the northern half of Europe compared with the south. It is also clear, however, that the use of some kinds of reading material by the middling and lower sorts in the more literate parts of later eighteenth-century Europe was almost certainly greater than traditionally assumed. Paris, London, the Dutch cities, Hamburg, and Leipzig may have been exceptionally lively in this respect, but there is no doubt that many other places, from Dublin, Edinburgh, and Stockholm in the north, to Geneva, Neuchâtel, and Prague further south, also experienced a massive growth in the quantity and types of print intended for a wide readership. In southern and eastern Europe, religious as well as economic priorities may have placed less emphasis on reading, but cities such as Naples and Milan are now also being mapped onto the print market.

Historians of print have long since noted that part of this demand is reflected not just in the huge growth in overall output, but also in the striking shift towards smaller format and cheaper reprints of all kinds of books in the second half of the eighteenth century, particularly noticeable with regard to novels and other forms of fiction, plays, travel literature, almanacs, and even some history. Much of what was published has little or nothing to do with Enlightenment: folktales, the 'blue books' of popular reading, devotional literature and collections of sermons, sensational stories, and ephemera continued to constitute a major part of eighteenth-century sales. Tracking changes in demand is difficult, not least because we can never be sure who the buyers really were. Nevertheless, the rates of reprinting, piracy, and translation, as well as deliberate efforts to provide the cheapest possible edition by saving on paper, does provide some evidence of what was read at the less wealthy end of the market. Equally significant in the present context, however, is the huge growth in newspapers, journals, and other periodical publications. Recognizable newssheets first appeared in the German lands and the Netherlands in the late sixteenth century, usually providing narrative summaries of events mixed with sensationalism. By the late seventeenth century, however, the quantity and range of output increased noticeably.

The market for actual news changed rapidly after the peace settlements of 1713–21: in London, for example, Stamp Act records indicate that the output of legally sold newspapers trebled between 1712 and 1750, and by 1790 there were not only fourteen dailies but even (since 1779) a Sunday paper. In the Netherlands, printers not only chose to cater for local readers, but also sustained an impressive production of French-language papers such as the *Gazette d'Amsterdam* and the *Gazette de Leyde*, designed for the international quality market. In Sweden, abolition of press censorship by parliament in 1766 enhanced an already varied range of domestic papers responding to ever-growing demand for domestic and foreign news, advertisements, and financial information. In France itself, despite continuing censorship restrictions which severely limited what could be published regarding the main domestic political and religious controversies of the day, the demand even for such restricted information resulted in rapid growth both in Paris-based papers and provincial advertisers (*affiches*). A fivefold increase in the number of titles over the period 1745–85 turned into a flood of new launches after the collapse of formal restrictions in 1788–9: alongside pamphlets, newspapers became one of the vital ingredients in the French Revolution over the next years. For readers who wanted the biggest choice of newspapers, however, the northern part of the Holy Roman Empire was the best place of all: historians have been struck by the very large number of titles there, as well as the exceptionally large print-runs for the most famous amongst them—such as the bi-weekly *Hamburgische Correspondent*, which by the end of the century required up to twelve printing presses (operating in parallel) in order to meet a demand of upwards of 30,000 copies.

Despite the absence of any major developments in printing technology in this period, the typical eighteenth-century newspaper was very simple to produce, and highly adaptable. It usually consisted of a standard single sheet (somewhat larger than modern A4), often folded once to produce four pages. Printed on both sides of the paper, sometimes laid out in two columns on each page in order to make a compressed typeface more readable, it was quick to make and distribute, and easy to pass round amongst friends or make available as an extra service in coffee-shops and at barbers. Although the original idea was to summarize news from different cities, usually without any political slant other than a generally patriotic one, the balance and content could be adjusted in each issue, depending on demand. The format lent itself to significant experimentation and new genres, the most distinctive of which was the essay-centred journal often referred to as the 'moral weekly'. Its prototype, *The Tatler* (launched in 1709 by Richard Steele), in fact appeared three times a week and was an immediate success because of its combination of light-hearted entertaining stories (narrated as if by a neutral observant bystander), news, comment, and advertisements. After just two years, Steele brought *The Tatler* to an end, but then joined forces with Joseph Addison to produce the even more successful daily *Spectator*. The tone remained invariably moderate, its editors at pains to emphasize that the paper would maintain standards of sociability such that it could be left around the house and read by 'respectable' people as well as by their servants, and in particular by women. Seemingly an instant success in the growing British consumer market, the format was soon imitated in the Netherlands and elsewhere, constituting a highly flexible, witty, and attractive genre accessible to all. Such ventures, alongside newspapers, helped make habitual reading a normal daily activity.

One other, more specialized, type of periodical publication developing in this period has attracted less systematic interest: the literary review. This, too, grew from seventeenth-century origins, in imitation of the French official *Journal des Sçavans* (1665) and especially Pierre Bayle's famous *Nouvelles de la république des lettres* (1684). But although initially very academic, this genre, too, evolved to accommodate a broader readership, not least because review journals could serve (in countries with effective censorship restrictions) as a means of discussion-by-proxy of contemporary issues as reflected in recent publications. The most important Danish review journal, *Kiöbenhavnske Lærde Efterretninger* (Copenhagen Learned News) sustained continuous weekly publication from 1721 right through to the Napoleonic period, and offered a digest of new publications in Danish and in other European languages, increasingly mixed with comments on experiments, reports on practical inventions, general discussions, and such other material as the editors thought might be of interest to general readers. More ambitiously, the Berlin publisher and book trader Friedrich Nicolai launched his *Allgemeine deutsche Bibliothek* in 1765 with the specific intention of reviewing all new German-language publications (other than dissertations and collections of sermons): remarkably, he maintained this plan right through to 1792, and the journal survived until 1806 despite the upheavals in Europe.[3]

Other forms of publication served the rapidly growing market of the later Ancien Régime. Particular examples can serve to illustrate how even French restrictions could be evaded: first, the serial *Histoire de l'Académie des Sciences*, which the long-lived secretary of the official French academy, Fontenelle (1657–1757), used deliberately to make new scientific work accessible through non-technical language (suitable for the kind of audience that might also attend popular science demonstrations); secondly, the austere Jansenist periodical *Nouvelles ecclésiastiques*, started in 1728 and survived to the end of the century even though it remained prohibited; and finally Fréron's avowedly anti-*philosophe* review, the *Année littéraire* (1754–76), popular even in court circles because it was designed to appeal to those readers who were afraid that radical Enlightenment might undermine the very fabric of traditional society. No doubt most of these periodicals initially had only very limited appeal outside their intended circle (the wealthier levels of society). Even so, personal study of the original 'great works' of the Enlightenment was no longer a necessary precondition for active engagement in contemporary debate: some of the key ideas, accompanied by an often selective discussion of practical implications, were available through the reviews and (in even more diluted but sometimes still recognizable form) in the more general press. Significantly, these journals could enhance international awareness of new works well before translations became available, in effect enhancing the market for all kinds of print.

Cultural Contexts, Translation, and Transmission

When the debate on 'Enlightenment in national context' surfaced amongst English-speaking scholars in the early 1980s, it paved the way for a reassessment of the distinctive emphases and processes of enlightening in different parts of Europe. The Germans (often subdivided between those of the Protestant north and Catholic south) were characterized as more moderate in their criticisms of both church and government than the French, less iconoclast and provocative, and more practical in terms of working for change from within the system. Scottish writers seemed more interested in civic society and moral philosophy, less directly concerned to engage with the politics of their day. Similar generalization also seemed viable for other parts of Europe, encouraging historians to explain these in terms that might fit cultural (or even state) boundaries. As has been noted since then, however, the term 'national' is itself problematic for the eighteenth century. Before the 1770s, few observers had any clear concept of what national identity meant—not surprisingly, since the prevalence of dynastic conglomerates ensured that nation and state hardly ever coincided. In any case, one might question the value of grouping, say, Voltaire and Diderot together as part of one identifiable set, or even Lessing and Kant. Where should we locate Rousseau, or for that matter Beccaria? Does the cultural profile of Hamburg in this period have anything significant in common with that of, say, Berlin, other than the language? Do the religious divisions within several of the larger political units in Europe make cultural coherence inherently improbable?

Once we accept that there was no cohesive Enlightenment programme, and probably not even a single 'French Enlightenment' or 'Protestant German Enlightenment', the task of explaining why there were such indisputably substantial geographic and cultural differences in enlightened thinking becomes more complicated. Some distinctive trends may in part be explained in terms of particular political structures and social systems, the degree of control exercised by the church, the strengths of censorship and legal enforcement, the impact of domestic and overseas economic growth on consumer choice, and, for the individual writer, the availability (or otherwise) of copyright protection, author's rights, patronage, or formal employment. Most fundamentally of all, we might need to focus on the specific role of language itself, in shaping the processes of enlightening across Europe and North America. Surprisingly, and in contrast to literature specialists, only a few historians have tackled this last aspect at all systematically. The distinctive linguistic interests of a few eighteenth-century observers such as Herder (1772), Hamann, or the French revolutionary reformer Henri Grégoire (whilst he was directly involved in reform, 1790–4) have of course been studied, but few full-scale comparative analyses have been attempted other than those of Peter Burke and especially Fania Oz-Salzberger.[4]

It has long been recognized that Latin was retained as the language of choice in specific fields of science such as botany (all the publications of Linnaeus, for example), but otherwise declined rapidly as the language of international communication, no doubt because it was accessible only to traditionally trained scholars, and in any case did not lend itself well to the forms of expression which eighteenth-century writers and readers demanded. For most other types of writing, French naturally took over as the *lingua franca* of the early eighteenth century: accessible to the educated elite all over Europe, and carrying the undisputed cachet of cultural sophistication and political dominance, the French language had the additional benefit of large-scale printing and distribution by the effectively uncensored Dutch. After around 1750, however, the situation became more complicated. Nearly all the major works of the European Enlightenment continued to appear quickly, somewhere, in French translation, but French ceased to be the standard intermediary language linking other language communities. German became more significant as a vehicle across central and eastern Europe (as it already had been for some time in Scandinavia), and, significantly, knowledge of English began to spread. With the common ground of Latin disappearing, the handicap associated with minority languages was likely to be aggravated: translation from peripheral to major languages was rare, and significant work in Spanish, Swedish, or even Italian, was often ignored and forgotten simply because of the language barrier.

These overall trends can be measured in various ways, not just through the publication- and translation-data available from the book industry itself, but also through the innovative development of language instruction material and multilingual dictionaries designed for non-specialized readers. An interesting transitional example is the Swedish–English–Latin dictionary published in Stockholm by Jacob Serenius in 1741 (its original version had a Latin title-page, the revised and extended version of 1757 significantly had an English one): there, Latin is used to help explain those nuances of English which an educated Swede might otherwise have difficulty in grasping. As we would expect in an age acutely aware of the finer points of language colouring, there was a growing interest all over Europe in the quality of professional translation. In for example the literary reviews of the time, we can observe major arguments whether translators should try to adhere closely to the original, or should work more freely in order to create something that might match the expectations of the target readership (occasionally leading to outright bowdlerization). As Oz-Salzberger has emphasized, sensitive translations could help develop the actual potential of minority languages, and might even help create new literatures and linguistic identities in those parts of Europe where the market had not previously been buoyant. The international reputation of Shakespeare, for example, dates from this period.[5] Equally, some writers who used minor languages failed to become recognized abroad either because a translation was not published, or because it was of poor quality.

By the second half of the eighteenth century the speed and efficiency of the European translation-network was becoming impressive, but there are still some surprises in store for historians trying to map the pathways of individual works. It is clear from surviving records of the book trade, and from the holdings of private libraries, that elite readers had no difficulty gaining access to the French (and in some areas German) versions of the major texts. Translations into other languages must therefore be assumed to have been intended primarily for the wider market, for those readers who lacked the means or the skills to access the French version easily. This would explain why a very large publication such as the *Encyclopédie* was never translated, whereas much of the new fictional output of the early eighteenth century was: thus Defoe's *Robinson Crusoe,* Swift's *Gulliver's Travels,* Richardson's *Pamela,* and the plays of Voltaire, Mercier, and Beaumarchais quickly became part of the shared European-wide heritage. It is striking, however, that Montesquieu's *Persian Letters,* despite the book's huge success on the western market, did not get translated into Dutch, Swedish, or Danish—the only trace in Scandinavia being a few extracts anthologized half a century after the original had appeared. Even if the book might have been deemed dangerously critical of authoritarian monarchy in Denmark, such caution would have been unnecessary in Sweden. Montesquieu's much more theoretical classic of 1748, *The Spirit of the Laws,* was used widely in its original French version across much of Europe, quickly rendered into English and German, and finally in 1771 also translated both into Dutch and into Danish (but not into Swedish). It is strange that Mandeville's provocative *Fable of the Bees* failed to be translated by his Dutch compatriots (or indeed by the Germans and Scandinavians), while the Scandinavians had to do without Mercier's light-hearted *The Year 2440*.

Predictably, most foreign translators studiously avoided the more controversial works of David Hume, La Mettrie, and those scrupulously untraceable texts that we now know were penned by the Baron d'Holbach. Rousseau's works were rendered into English and German usually within a year or two of publication, but had to wait until the 1790s for the first Dutch or Danish translations, even longer for a Swedish rendition. Beccaria (1764), by contrast, appeared in French, English, Dutch, and Swedish within a few years, but not in German until 1778 and not in Danish until the later 1790s. Ferguson's *Essay on the History of Civil Society* (1767) naturally suited the German market (1768), but took fifteen years to appear in French, twenty-two to Swedish, and was not translated into Dutch or Danish at all. Even more remarkably, none of Adam Smith's major work appeared in Swedish. We might also note that neither Kant nor Herder appear to have been regarded as widely marketable in translation, while Radishchev went virtually unnoticed outside Russia. Some of these gaps may have been the result simply of failed initiatives, idiosyncratic publishers, or other accidents, or they may reflect the modest demand for certain types of academic and philosophical writing outside the well-educated elite; but they may also reflect substantial differences in the priorities and interests of the Enlightenment across various parts of Europe which have still not been explored as fully as they deserve to be.

Knowledge, Reason: Questioning the Old Order?

The Enlightenment affected both the search for new empirical knowledge, and the theoretical explanations that might help rationalize these findings. In the sciences, for example, we need only look at Buffon's multi-volume *Natural History* from 1749, Priestley's and Lavoisier's work on oxygen and combustion in the 1770s, or Hutton's on geology and geological time (published 1784–95), to realize how such research had the capacity not only to change the parameters of scientific understanding, but might also reinforce ideas of natural evolution, and challenge a literal reading of biblical time. Inevitably, conflicts arose when older established authority appeared to be so undermined that traditional intellectual systems might be in danger of collapse. This had already begun to happen during the seventeenth-century 'intellectual revolution', when the work of Descartes, Hobbes, Newton, Locke, and others opened up questions which continued to challenge their followers a century later. Some confrontations with authority seemed rather contrived, as in the so-called quarrel of the ancients and moderns (1690s) which pitted traditionalists (relying on the authority of classical Greece and Rome, as interpreted in the renaissance) against those who felt that modern empiricism, mathematical modelling, and reasoning held real innovative potential. This particular controversy soon appeared to exhaust itself, but the underlying issues did not go away. The great *Critical Dictionary* of Pierre Bayle (1697) eloquently demonstrated the erosive potential of philosophical scepticism, whilst examination of the Bible by scholars such as Baruch Spinoza (1670) and Richard Simon (1678–92) started a systematic review of that text, not as a clear and irrefutable divine statement, but rather a conglomerate compilation reflecting the work of many authors and an extremely complicated history of its own.

As we have already noted in Part IV, belief and religious faith were subject to recurrent questioning and doubts, but so were the increasingly contentious problems of how faith might relate to reason, and how ethics and moral philosophy might work within a more mechanistic understanding of humankind itself. The Enlightenment's most extreme challenges to religious belief came in a string of publications around mid-century, notably La Mettrie's overtly materialist tract *Man Machine* (1747), Condillac's *Treatise on Sensations* (1754), Helvetius's *Essay on the Mind* (1758), and d'Holbach's *Christianity unveiled* (1761). All caused storms of protest, first in France, and soon also in those parts of Europe capable of accessing the texts or getting a hint of their content from reviews. Many of the *philosophes* themselves reacted against the materialism and sensationalism of such books, which seemed to prove what some churchmen had always feared: that French Enlightenment led straight to hedonism, immorality, the destruction of faith, and the collapse of order. But even if ways could be found to demolish the extreme views of these particular authors, the far more sophisticated sceptical arguments constructed by David Hume in his various major works and essays published between 1739 and 1779 posed challenges regarding the source and reliability of knowledge which even the greatest minds of the age had difficulty responding to effectively.

The hugely influential *Encyclopédie* edited by Diderot did not help. His co-editor for the early volumes, the mathematician d'Alembert, had used the *Preliminary Discourse* at the start of the first volume (1751) to proclaim boldly the value of empirical knowledge and scientific understanding—and both were presented, in great abundance, in each volume as they appeared. But d'Alembert also included a detailed classificatory map of all human knowledge where religion was demonstratively banished to a remote corner. The whole project soon acquired a formidable momentum of its own, involving around 160 contributors, and eventually running to 17 large folio volumes of around 1,000 pages each (with another 11 volumes of magnificent illustrative plates published later). An unenforced ban imposed in 1752 (after the appearance of the second volume) was good publicity for the venture, and the number of subscribers tripled to over 4,000 by 1754; yet the precariousness of the whole enterprise became clear when the remaining 10 volumes of text were suppressed in 1759 (eventually appearing all together, with a false imprint, in 1765). It is clear that the *Encyclopédie* explored, as no other publication of the Enlightenment, the sensitive boundaries of what was permissible within the Ancien Régime and what was not. Diderot himself authored many of the most controversial articles, but expected his readers to follow cross-references and leads in order to get most out of the work. Complementary articles (such as *tolérance* and *intolérance*) were often used to put forward quite incompatible ideas, and to distract the hard-worked censor. Taken as a whole, the *Encyclopédie* stands as a true reflection of the French Enlightenment: inconsistent and uneven, both moderate and deeply subversive, absorbing and elusive, idealistic and practical—yet fundamentally innovative in subjecting all areas of knowledge to close scrutiny, and making free use of cross-cultural comparisons in ways that seem to suggest that truth itself was relative.

Not surprisingly, the purpose and validity of censorship came in for close scrutiny all over Europe. Originally intended to secure consistent orthodoxy in matters of religious belief, censorship during the early modern period had naturally been extended to cover all aspects of the state and government, the creative arts, the stage, and most other forms of substantive communication. Few believed in total freedom of expression, and even where pre-publication censorship as such had collapsed (primarily in Britain and the

Netherlands), the laws relating to libel, blasphemy, and sedition were used to full effect. The *philosophes* themselves did not campaign for total freedom, but did want a more consistently liberal and proportionate system of checks. In France, Ancien Régime institutions were too hierarchical (and arguably too weak) to enable controlled reform in this area to take place, and it took the Revolution to bring censorship (briefly) to an end. Elsewhere in Europe, however, debate about freedom of expression acquired significant momentum from the 1760s, challenging some of the fundamental assumptions of secrecy, exclusivity, inequality, and deference which seemed so fundamental to the Ancien Régime itself. This is perhaps most clearly illustrated in the first state to abolish formal pre-publication censorship, Sweden (1766). The Swedish parliamentary government of the 'Age of Liberty' (1719–72) was unique in Europe both for its transparency and its social inclusiveness, but this had been achieved at a price. Swedish political culture was by mid-century highly conservative, even defensive, and in the opinion of many contemporaries excessively prone to corruption and manipulation (not least by foreign powers). Already from the 1750s, this led to a detailed and thorough debate (in print) about transparency, accountability, and the public interest, in which censorship inevitably figured very prominently. Although some historians have been sceptical about the stability of the Swedish system, there is no doubt that the abolition of censorship there in 1766 was part of a process which, although truncated by Gustavus III after the royalist coup of 1772, nevertheless ensured a more lively and wide-ranging public engagement with domestic political issues than in any of the traditional monarchies of Europe. The contrast is all the more striking if we note the initially much less productive abolition of censorship in Denmark in 1770, or the more limited experiments in the Austrian Habsburg lands in 1781 which were soon partially rescinded. Clearly, Ancien Régime monarchy and complete freedom of expression did not fit comfortably together. More fundamentally, some feared that the traditional old order, which so far had seemed stable and permanent, might risk unravelling if access to information brought greater demands for accountability.

Enlightened Reform: The 1780s and Beyond

To those primarily interested in the history of ideas, the Enlightenment may seem to have come to an end with the death of the older generation of (especially French) contributors, between 1755 and the 1770s. However, a glance at the American colonies, Ireland, much of central Europe, not to mention turbulent prerevolutionary France itself, would suggest otherwise. The emphases shifted somewhat in the 1770s, towards more contemporary affairs, politics, political economy, and the other social sciences, creating the basis for a broader agenda of domestic reform and economic development. But if we look at the plays and fiction of this period, we are reminded that there was also a strong interest in human nature itself. Especially in the German-speaking areas there was a marked turn towards the inner workings of the mind and its darker emotional turmoil (as in the *Sturm und Drang* movement and the early romantic writings of Goethe and Schiller). Equally, the work of Edmund Burke and Thomas Paine, Beaumarchais and Condorcet, Mendelssohn and Kant, not to mention many writers whose output has since been relegated to the margins of the canon of 'great works' of the Ancien Régime, shows that none of the critical momentum of contemporary thinking had been lost. Study of the increasingly diverse press of the later decades of the eighteenth century indicates that what Kant described as a process of 'enlightening' took a greater variety of forms amongst the wider public than ever before. No doubt a closer look at the 1780s and 1790s will tend to reinforce the more inclusive definition of Enlightenment adopted by many historians in recent years; but doing so also enables us to understand more clearly the relationship between Enlightenment, the Ancien Régime, and revolution.

The twenty years up to 1795 brought a succession of challenges to the social and political assumptions underpinning the Ancien Régime. The American war of independence forced both British and French participants to reflect on their own strategies and aims; but even more, the process of constructing a new political system attracted observers as if to a huge public experiment. By contrast, the persistent weakness of the French monarchy became increasingly obvious to all European observers: the Maupeou crisis (1770–4) involved unprecedented public exposure in print, while much of the ensuing remedial work by a string of highly talented ministers touched on nearly all aspects of government. Dramatic reform initiatives in other parts of Europe (notably the Austrian Habsburg lands including Lombardy, many of the other component states of the Holy Roman Empire, and Denmark after 1784) were carried out in ways which not merely made lively public engagement in current affairs unavoidable, but in some cases came to rely on public opinion as a means to successful implementation. Equally striking, though slightly less comprehensible to western Europeans, were the traumatic efforts to salvage the Polish-Lithuanian Commonwealth, and efforts by Catherine II to impose reforms on Russia. The impact of all this is clearly reflected in the increasingly politically oriented press of the 1780s: not only in the long-running *Gazette de Leyde* and other quality periodicals noted above, but also in such new initiatives as the Göttingen professor August Schlözer's highly informative *Staats-Anzeigen* (1782–93), von Schirach's respected but conservative *Politische Journal* (1781–1804), several new Dutch-language papers launched at this time, or the Danish monthly *Minerva* (from 1785). Journals often had to operate under very complicated circumstances: thus the *Berlinische Monatsschrift* (from 1783) appeared to be an independent publication, but in reality it was the unofficial organ of the highly influential secret *Mittwochsgesellschaft* (Wednesday society), a society whose monthly meetings brought together some of the greatest minds of the Prussian Enlightenment. They were not allowed to report their discussions formally, but by accepting the constraints of absolutism they enjoyed a significant measure of direct influence on government through the protection of Frederick II. It is clear that the editors of many other journals worked out ways of achieving considerable freedom of expression, provided they accepted that some fundamentals of the existing order were not up for debate.

Our understanding of the late Enlightenment in France itself has been transformed in recent years, not least in terms of the circulation of ideas, communication through print, and the development of public debate. What has also become clearer, however, is the extent to which ideological battles were fought out around the successive ministers who tried to give Louis XVI some sense of direction. A glance at the career of one of the last true *philosophes*, the Marquis de Condorcet (1743–94), is in this respect particularly instructive. First making an impression in the 1760s as a mathematician and *protégé* of d'Alembert, Condorcet gained personal contact with many older *philosophes* through the brilliant salon of Julie de Lespinasse. Frequented by intellectuals of all kinds, from Voltaire to Condillac, unconventional churchmen such as Raynal and de Brienne, influential holders of public office such as Malesherbes and Turgot, this salon even had an occasional visit from Diderot, the Baron d'Holbach, and David Hume. By then, the *philosophes* were themselves irretrievably divided by the charges of atheism raised against some of the *encylopédistes*, and by disagreements over their own role in the shaping of the agenda for reform. Condorcet, while continuing his work in mathematics, also became directly involved in politics, notably as adviser to Turgot (finance minister 1774–6) and as a key participant in the French Royal Academy of Sciences. His *Lettres d'un théologien* (published anonymously in 1774) marked the start of his public commitment to a whole raft of contemporary non-scientific issues: the abuse of power by the French clerical establishment, the inadequacies of current monarchical assumptions about political representation and 'national' consensus, the need for constitutional reform recognizing the natural rights of all Frenchmen regardless of status, the desirability of both religious toleration and universal education, and the need to give women civic equality. To Condorcet, natural and civic rights (liberty enshrined in law, the right to property, the right to political participation) were not something a benevolent government could grant, but an essential and unconditional prerequisite of civilized society to which all humans were entitled. This made him an impatient campaigner for reform, both before the Revolution (as in his demand for elected provincial assemblies, 1788) and during it (as member of the *Cercle social*, and as deputy in both the Legislative Assembly and the Convention). Characteristically, he was revising a work first planned in 1772 when he was arrested and died early in 1794: his *Esquisse*, a sketch for a larger book on the *Progress of the Human Spirit* which was never completed, reiterated his belief in the capacity of humanity to improve its own condition by means of what he described as 'social mathematics' (social science)—a message extraordinarily at odds with the trajectory of the Revolution itself by this stage.[6]

The late Enlightenment is remarkable in that it produced several examples of that rare type of original thinker who could also for a while engage directly in contemporary politics and social reform. Condorcet counted amongst his friends the equally irrepressible Tom Paine (who himself barely escaped the guillotine), and he may perhaps be best understood alongside other tireless critics of the old order such as the English prison-reformer John Howard (1726–90), or the Norwegian lawyer Christian Colbiørnsen (1749–1814), who drove enlightened reform in Denmark from 1786. All of these had moved well beyond the abstract intellectual Enlightenment of mid-century, but all retained its core ideals, even as they attempted to make them work in practical ways. Their belief that human society, for all its flaws, could benefit from orderly and rational reform may seem optimistic and in some cases unrealistic. But in their perseverance they not only gave sharper focus to what some historians have seen as the link between Enlightenment and 'modernity', they also demonstrated at a very practical level that the Ancien Régime itself was not inherently moribund, and that the Enlightenment had not run out of steam.

Conclusion

To some observers, events in France from 1791 seemed to demonstrate yet again what critics had already said against the *Encyclopédie* in the 1750s: that Enlightened thinking was materialist, ungodly, hedonistic, and fundamentally destructive of social order. Such a judgement of course fails to recognize the sheer range and diversity of enlightened thinking: even within the French-speaking world, Voltaire, Diderot, and Rousseau reacted to these accusations in fundamentally different ways. But we can now recognize that, at least outside France, Enlightenment was not generally perceived to be inherently incompatible either with religious belief and idealism, or with the more adaptable style of government of the later eighteenth century which could engage with public opinion. A genuine interest in broader education, in the availability of verifiable and independent information, and in the relaxation of traditional censorship and other restraints on freedom, are all indicative of an active commitment to 'improvement' of some kind both amongst those in power and amongst those taking an interest in public affairs. Yet as many would-be reformers also discovered, the old order was surprisingly resilient, and change (even when generally accepted as beneficial) was quite difficult to implement within existing structures. In any case, even though enlightened thinking fostered new research in the social sciences, it never considered the kind of revolutionary social levelling advocated by radicals in England in the late 1640s and early 1650s. Some exponents of Enlightenment did explore new ideas on political representation—even turning to republicanism in their search for solutions in France after 1791. But the older generation of theorists such as Rousseau would have been astonished to see the use to which their ideas were put by 1793, and in the eyes of the rest of Europe what happened in France by then was a negation, not an implementation, of what Enlightenment meant.

To the historian, too, the Enlightenment has presented a succession of challenges that look set to continue, not only bringing new insights into the Ancien Régime itself, but also making simple definitions more problematic. Just as the Enlightenment is no longer exclusively French, attempts to define it within 'national' contexts, although very instructive, have proved inadequate. In the 1980s and 1990s postmodernists challenged the very concept of Enlightenment, seeing it as little short of a western liberal conspiracy of power and manipulation which sought to impose new European orthodoxies, and a false sense of progress, on everyone else. The ensuing debate has been productive, both in fostering a better understanding of the significance of language itself as a historical variable, and in encouraging historians to come more fully to grips with the social and political context within which the contributors to the Enlightenment worked and their ideas were received. However, the postmodernist challenge fundamentally misunderstood its target. As we now see it, the Enlightenment was deeply rooted in the Ancien Régime itself, with all the complexity, inconsistencies, and self-contradictions that that entailed; but it was also itself postmodernist *avant la lettre*, in so far as it was more effective at questioning apparent truths, and recognizing the manipulative power of ideas, than it was at constructing any solid or universal replacements. Arguably, the very absence of a single or coherent message was its true strength: the lack of simple answers entailed acceptance of plurality, and recognition that neither truth nor power was immutable or absolute. It also allowed the Ancien Régime to develop in unexpected directions—perhaps even ensuring that, when revolution came, only France had to endure successive upheavals in search of an acceptable consensus.

Notes

1. J. Schmidt, *What is Enlightenment? Eighteenth-Century Answers and Twentieth-Century Questions* (Berkeley, Calif., 1996).
2. The case made by J. Israel, *Enlightenment Contested: Philosophy, Modernity, and the Emancipation of Man 1670–1752* (Oxford, 2006), 863–71, that the Enlightenment provided the foundations for 'modernity', has not provided the basis for a consensus among historians: see notably the historiographical reviews by A. J. La Vopa, 'A New Intellectual History? Jonathan Israel's Enlightenment', *Historical Journal*, 52 (2009), 717–38, and by A. Lilti, 'Comment écrit-on l'histoire intellectuelle des Lumières? Spinozisme, radicalisme et philosophie', *Annales ESC*, 64 (2009), 171–206.
3. P. E. Selwyn, *Everyday Life in the German Book Trade: Friedrich Nicolai as Bookseller and Publisher in the Age of Enlightenment 1750–1810* (Philadelphia, 2000).
4. P. Burke, *Languages and Communities in Early Modern Europe* (Cambridge, 2004); F. Oz-Salzberger, *Translating the Enlightenment: Scottish Civic Discourse in Eighteenth-Century Germany* (Oxford, 1995). On the geography of Enlightenment, see also R. Butterwick and S. Davies (eds.), *Peripheries of the Enlightenment*, SVEC (2008/01); and C. W. J. Withers, *Placing the Enlightenment: Thinking Geographically about the Age of Reason* (Chicago, 2007).
5. F. Oz-Salzberger, 'The Enlightenment in Translation: Regional and European Aspects', *European Review of History*, 13 (2006), 385–409.
6. K. M. Baker, *Condorcet: From Natural Philosophy to Social Mathematics* (Chicago, 1975).

Bibliography

Barker, H., and Burrows, S., *Press, Politics and the Public Sphere in Europe and North America, 1760–1820* (Cambridge, 2002).
Censer, J. R., *The French Press in the Age of Enlightenment* (London, 1994).

Clark, W J. Golinski, J., and Schaffer, S. (eds.), *The Sciences in Enlightened Europe* (Chicago, 1999).

Darnton, R., *The Business of the Enlightenment: A Publishing History of the Encyclopédie 1775–1800* (Cambridge, Mass., 1982).

Farge, A., *Subversive Words: Public Opinion in Eighteenth-Century France* (Cambridge, 1994).

Goodman, D., *The Republic of Letters: A Cultural History of the French Enlightenment* (Ithaca, NY, 1994).

Gordon, D. (ed.), *Postmodernism and the Enlightenment: New Perspectives in Eighteenth-Century French Intellectual History* (New York, 2001).

Hesse, C., *Publishing and Cultural Politics in Revolutionary Paris, 1789–1810* (Berkeley, Calif., 1991).

Israel, J., *Radical Enlightenment: Philosophy and the Making of Modernity* (Oxford, 2001).

—— *Enlightenment Contested: Philosophy, Modernity, and the Emancipation of Man 1670–1752* (Oxford, 2006).

—— *Democratic Enlightenment: Philosophy, Revolution, and Human Rights, 1750–1790* (Oxford, 2011).

Melton, J. Van Horn, *The Rise of the Public in Enlightenment Europe* (Cambridge, 2001).

Munck, T., *The Enlightenment: A Comparative Social History 1721–94* (London, 2000).

Porter, R., *Enlightenment: Britain and the Creation of the Modern World* (London, 2000).

—— and Teich, M. (eds.), *The Enlightenment in National Context* (Cambridge, 1981).

Robertson, J., *The Case for the Enlightenment: Scotland and Naples 1680–1760* (Cambridge, 2005).

CHAPTER 26

TECHNOLOGICAL CHANGE

CHRISTINE MACLEOD AND
ALESSANDRO NUVOLARI

Introduction

DURING the eighteenth century Europeans embarked on a revolutionary phase of economic growth and social change, the full environmental costs of which we are only just beginning to recognize. Breaking free from an essentially subsistence economy to embrace the market and long-distance trade, they led the world into sustained economic growth. This has allowed the unprecedented phenomenon of long-term population increase in tandem with a rising standard of living; previously one type of gain had always been at the other's expense, as never before had it been possible to expand an economy fast enough to accommodate both.[1] The causes of this shift into sustained (if ultimately unsustainable) economic growth are still debated, but there can be no doubt that the fundamental driver has been technological change. In this chapter, we will explore the nature of those new technologies and reasons why Europeans began to invest (literally and metaphorically) in technical innovation.

At the core of Europe's economic growth was its discovery of new resources and the techniques necessary to exploit them. Medieval Europe's principal resource had been its land. Wealth and power in feudal society rested on the tenure of land, and everyone's livelihood was totally dependent on it.[2] Agriculture and the processing of its produce employed the vast majority of the population: it fed, clothed, and shod them (in woollen, linen, and leather garments) and it provided them with fuel (wood), kinetic energy (fodder for horses and oxen, supplemented by watermills and windmills), and timber, the primary structural material for buildings, ships, tools, and furniture. Largely self-sufficient, farmers rarely bought anything other than metal goods (smelted with wood or charcoal) and locally produced earthenwares. Transport was expensive, and the small trading sector dealt overwhelmingly in luxury items for the rich minority. Medieval Europe's technology was by no means unsophisticated (as witnessed by its cathedrals), but its gains in land productivity tended to be labour-intensive and more hands (or horses) meant more mouths to be fed from a resource that was subject to diminishing returns. In many parts of Europe, particularly in the south and east, major elements of this organic technology persisted long into the twentieth century, before being overtaken by new methods powered by, or made with or from, fossil fuels.

Yet, since the late fifteenth century (when Europe finally recovered from the serial depredations of plague and bad harvests), its population has grown exponentially while simultaneously enjoying rising levels of material comfort. Although this new trend was scarcely visible before 1750, population increase became (worryingly) evident thereafter and widespread improvements in living standards followed about a century later. Initially, this European achievement was facilitated by technologies that allowed international trade and the conquest and settlement of other continents—ocean-going sailing ships and navigational instruments, guns, horses, and agriculture, not forgetting the leg-irons and chains that disciplined its slave labour. From these new trades emerged the desire for exotic groceries (sugar, tea, coffee, chocolate, tobacco) and new consumer goods (cottons, silks, porcelain, etc.) that could be imitated by Europe's craftsmen.[3] Subsequently, this growing demand provoked the mechanization of industrial and agrarian processes, powered by new, underground sources of energy that were independent of the land surface—coal, and later, oil, gas, and the electricity generated chiefly from fossil fuels—and the manipulation of new chemicals also largely derived from minerals. It created a demand for many new skills (e.g. in engineering or mining) and rendered others obsolete.

Historians are still discussing what, at this juncture, prompted Europeans increasingly to turn to innovation as their preferred means of resolving problems and improving their material conditions. Undoubtedly, the world-view of late medieval Europe was seriously destabilized from several directions. Renewed contact with the ideas and technologies of the ancient Greeks and Romans during the renaissance, the Copernican 'revolution' in astronomy, the 'discovery' of the New World and increasing communication with the Far East, and the challenge to authority posed by the Reformation, all suggested there were alternative, perhaps better, ways of doing things and new knowledge to be obtained through experiment, ingenuity, and bravado. Within Europe, the demands of emerging nation-states for novel types of expertise and the migrations of craftsmen generated by the wars of religion and waves of persecution consequent upon the Reformation, not to mention the stimulus both politics and religion gave to the multiplication of printing presses, all promoted the dissemination and cross-fertilization of ideas.

The Contours of Technical Progress, c. 1300–1800

Technological change was central to the process of European expansion and development of international trade. Without critical improvements in navigational techniques and instrumentation, in ship design and production, and in firearms, the process of European expansion would have been impossible. The origins of many of these improvements remain obscure; undoubtedly some were Asian. For example, the magnetic compass was evidently in use by 1300 but the precise date and place of its invention are unknown. Its adoption promoted the systematic use of instrumentation and *portolans* (nautical charts with detailed indications of winds, tides, depths, etc.). Similarly, the origins of the caravel and the carrack (the first successful oceanic ship designs) are unclear. Both designs represent a remarkably fruitful marriage between Mediterranean and Nordic maritime traditions, which emerged from a continuous phase of empirical tinkering (reinforced by imitation and exchanges of best practices) around 1300.[4] Very rapid progress in shipbuilding techniques and ship design continued throughout the seventeenth and eighteenth centuries, mostly thanks to empirical improvements, although there were attempts, especially in France under Colbert, to introduce a more scientific approach to naval architecture.[5] This trajectory culminated in the late eighteenth-century 'ship of the line' (a warship equipped with up to 100 guns)—an artefact of almost unparalleled sophistication. During the Napoleonic Wars, Britain's Royal Navy undertook the construction and maintenance of these ships in its own dockyards, which pioneered early forms of mass production that employed machine tools and other specialized machinery. These naval dockyards were easily the biggest industrial establishments of the time, far ahead of other large-scale industrial employers, such as mines and breweries.[6]

Such technical improvements were facilitated by expansion in both mercantile and military navies. During 1500–1780, western Europe's merchant fleet grew from approximately 200,000 tons to over 3 million tons, almost a tenfold increase per inhabitant (see Table 26.1). Considering that throughout the same period most European economies experienced relatively sluggish growth of income per head, this evidence points to shipbuilding as one of the continent's most dynamic industries.[7]

By contrast, very limited progress was attained in land transport during the early modern period. As Fernand Braudel remarked: 'Napoleon moved no faster than Julius Caesar.'[8] During the eighteenth century, the expansion of inland waterways facilitated the bulk transport of low value to volume goods, such as timber, coal, ores, and grain, while road-building programmes (both state and private) and improvements to carriages expedited the circulation of people, posts, and news. The installation of optical

Table 26.1. The West European merchant fleet, 1500–1780

Year	Total fleet (000s tons)	Tonnage per 1000 inhabitants
1500	200–250	3.2–4
1600	600–700	7.7–9
1670	1000–1100	12.8–14.1
1780	3372	30.7

Source: Van Zanden (2001: 82)

telegraph posts, primarily for military purposes, and the intense excitement generated by early ballooning that was consequent upon the Montgolfier brothers' successful experiments in 1783, testify to the demand for greater speed and range. Until, however, the construction of national railway and electric-telegraph networks in the mid-nineteenth century, everyday communications remained slow and expensive and markets overwhelmingly local.[9]

The second critical area of strategic importance for Europe's ascendancy was weaponry. Its adoption of gunpowder was coupled with a rapid development of firearms. The emergence of nation-states and the almost continuous military competition between them produced a strong, steady demand throughout the continent. Although gunpowder had been a Chinese invention, when the Portuguese reached China in the early sixteenth century their guns were greatly superior to those that met them. Since then, the production of artillery, firearms, and gunpowder in Europe experienced sustained productivity growth. Possibly even more important than that were inventions which improved the fighting performance of firearms, such as the flintlock, the paper cartridge, and the bayonet, making it possible to replace pikemen with soldiers carrying guns. According to Parker, the rapid spread of increasingly destructive weaponry, combined with the growing size of armies, produced a European 'military revolution' that was crucial to its expansion. In order to survive, the newly emerging European states had to mobilize and manage armies and navies of unprecedented size and destructive capacity. In this way, the West's recently acquired technological edge in weaponry was coupled with substantive organizational advantages.[10]

The emergence of a distinctive European pattern is also to be found in power generation. While the watermill was known at least from Roman times, its widespread adoption began during the middle ages. Initially, the product of determined attempts by feudal lords to enforce their seigniorial rights (the monopoly of milling was one of the most ancient and widespread),[11] the use of watermills expanded from the primary method for grinding corn to a variety of applications, such as metal manufacturing, 'fulling' woollen cloth, paper making, food and drink production, etc.[12]

Makkai's estimates of the growth of water power in pre-industrial Europe suggest a process of moderate but steady growth in horsepower per head (Table 26.2), but other counting exercises indicate a more rapid increase.[13] His estimate of the power output of watermills around 1800 is probably also too low: according to Reynolds, the average power of eighteenth-century water-wheels was between 5 and 7 HP.[14]

The mechanical energy produced by water and windmills represented only a very small share of the total,[15] which continued to be supplied principally by human and

Table 26.2. Number and power of European water-wheels, 1200–1800

Year	No. of water-wheels	Average power (HP)	HP per head
1200	300,000	2	0.008
1800	750,000	3	0.012

Source: Makkai (1981: 178); see also Malanima (2009: 74).

animal muscle until the mid-eighteenth century. Nonetheless, it is important to acknowledge the increasing availability of inanimate sources of power, for a wide range of production activities, before the classical period of the industrial revolution.

Power from inanimate sources was rapidly becoming indispensable in the mining sector. The seventeenth century saw intensive growth in Europe's extractive industries (coal, iron, tin, and copper), which emphasized the problem of mine drainage. Without effective technical solutions to this problem the exploitation of deep ore deposits would have been impossible. Consequently, while European engineers increasingly focused on the design and improvement of water-powered mining pumps, it was in response to this challenge that the early steam engines were developed in south-western England by Savery and Newcomen c.1700. Estimates by Kanefsky and Robey indicate that 48.6 per cent of all the steam engines installed in Britain during the eighteenth century were used for mining purposes (pumping water or hauling ore to the surface).[16]

Traditional accounts of British industrialization have tended to conflate the economic significance of steam-power technology with its early development.[17] For example, Rostow dated Britain's take-off to the years 1783–1802, linking it explicitly with the commercialization of the Watt engine. However, the diffusion of steam power, even in a precocious coal-abundant user such as Britain, was a long and protracted process. Table 26.3 reports Kanefsky's estimates of the use of steam in comparison with wind and water power in manufacturing and mining, at various dates between 1760 and 1907.

It shows that, as late as 1830, steam power was yet to become the predominant source of power.[18] The early phases of industrialization were accommodated by the expansion and 'stretching' of the traditional mixture of water, wind, animal, and human power.[19]

Although still in its early stages, another technological trend that characterized the early modern European economy was the increasing use of machinery for productive processes. From self-regulating cathedral clocks to Gutenberg's printing press and William Lee's stocking knitting-frame, these sophisticated mechanisms were indicative of the highly developed mechanical skills and ingenuity available in renaissance Europe wherever new degrees of precision or levels of output were sought. It was only, however, once such mechanisms were harnessed to inanimate sources of power in the late eighteenth century that their capacity to expand and cheapen production began

Table 26.3. Sources of inanimate power in use (HP) in Britain (mainly mining and manufacturing)

Year	Steam	(%)	Water	(%)	Wind	(%)
1760	5000	5.88	70 000	82.35	10 000	11.76
1800	35 000	20.59	120 000	70.59	15 000	8.82
1830	160 000	47.06	160 000	47.06	20 000	5.88
1870	2 060 000	89.57	230 000	10.00	10 000	0.43
1907	9 659 000	98.14	178 000	1.81	5000	0.05

Source: Kanefsky (1979: 338).

to be fully realized. With access to rapidly growing markets in Africa and America as well as at home, Britain's cotton textile industry pioneered numerous attempts to mechanize production.[20] Devices invented to increase the productivity of domestic ('proto-industrial') spinners and weavers, such as Hargreaves's spinning jenny and Kay's flying shuttle, were quickly surpassed by the factory-based machines driven by water or steam: Arkwright's water-frame, Crompton's spinning mule, Cartwright's power loom, and Peel's cylindrical cotton-printing machinery. These prototypes showed the way to a generation of entrepreneurs, who hurried not only to install them but also to improve and diversify them, to extend their use to other fibres, and, in some cases, to manufacture them.

The machine-making industry became a major source of innovation, both increasing its own productivity by the development of powered machine-tools and helping to disseminate mechanization throughout the industrial sector and, later, agriculture. By the early nineteenth century, its customers included the paper and printing industries, which were meeting the burgeoning demand for everything from stationery and tracing paper to newspapers, books, and pamphlets by installing water- and steam-powered machinery and presses. Machine-makers recruited many skilled workers from the horological and instrument-making trades, where accurate methods of cutting and shaping metals (and grinding glass) were highly prized. In their turn, these trades, hitherto dependent on a small, luxury market for scientific instruments and watches, found new opportunities to diversify their products and expand: transport projects and maritime trade required numerous surveying and navigational instruments; the fiscal state invested heavily in measuring equipment; manufacturers experimented with thermometers or pyrometers; and middle-class households increasingly expected to own clocks, microscopes, barometers, globes, and (soon) pianos. Vital to industrialization, the instrument trades remained, however, workshop-based and unmechanized. The introduction of the dividing engine in the late eighteenth century, the greater division of labour, and the steady accretion of skills gradually increased their productivity but expansion came chiefly through the entry of new firms.[21]

While metal-working and glass-making skills were indigenous to early modern Europe, the import of Asian luxuries, such as Indian silks and fine cottons or Chinese porcelain triggered the search for techniques to replicate them and capture the market. One strategy was to discover and copy the secrets of Asian manufacturers. Intensive experiments with different clays and kilns, for example, led in 1710 to the establishment of Europe's first hard porcelain manufacture at Meissen in Saxony. Together with a few rival factories across the continent it largely ousted China in supplying this exotic luxury to the wealthy. Another strategy was to develop new ceramic bases and glazes in imitation of porcelain but, by employing cheaper materials and more efficient methods of production, to manufacture a distinctly European product for a middle-class market. One of its most successful exponents was Josiah Wedgwood, the Staffordshire potter whose high-quality stoneware incorporated fashionable neo-classical designs. It was produced with an extensive division of labour that minimized the need for skilled workers, and was marketed through innovative techniques, including a West End showroom, newspaper advertisements, and celebrity endorsements. Where Wedgwood led, many others followed. Matthew Boulton, prominent in the Birmingham 'toy' trades, simultaneously reorganized the production and marketing of small metalwares. Birmingham workshops thrived by experimenting with new finishes, such as silver plating, 'ormolu' and lacquered ('japanned') papier mâché.[22]

THE ORGANIZATION OF INNOVATION

The economic and military rivalry between the newly emerging European nation-states of the early modern period led gradually to the creation of a number of new institutions whose ultimate goal was the improvement of national innovative performance.[23] This point has been aptly summarized by Rosenberg and Birdzell:[24] 'In the West, the individual centres of competing political power had a great deal to gain from introducing technical changes that promised commercial or industrial advantage and hence greater government revenues, and much to lose from allowing others to introduce them first.'

In this respect, the institutional reform that has received most attention from historians is undoubtedly the creation of patent systems. The roots of this institution are to be found in the proprietary and exclusionary attitudes towards technological knowledge and skills that had emerged within the medieval guild system.[25] Early modern technology was, fundamentally, a matter of 'expert' knowledge and skills.[26] Consequently, the diffusion of technology was tightly linked with the migration of skilled workers.[27] Furthermore, there seems to have existed a widespread awareness among governments and other authorities of the key role of this migration in the process of technology transfer, because, from the late middle ages, a growing number of laws tried to restrict the emigration of skilled craftsmen. At the same time, governments introduced measures aimed at attracting or suborning skilled workers from other countries. One of the commonest policies was that of awarding special patents or 'privileges' to the importers of new technologies, which conceded them incentives such as the exclusive right (for a limited amount of time) to the use of the specific body of knowledge and skills they brought with them.[28]

In 1474 the Venetian government enacted a statute that codified such previously *ad hoc* practices. This contained, in an embryonic form, several features of modern patent laws. In particular, Venetian grants depended on the applicant's ability to fulfil certain criteria, rather than being subject to the discretion of the authorities: the invention should offer something of recognized 'usefulness' for the state and it should not already have been made or be known within the boundaries of the Republic. Thus, the two fundamental criteria for awarding the grant were established as *utility* and *novelty* (which remain in modern patent systems). The Venetian model of protection and exclusive privileges spread rapidly to other states, such as the Netherlands, England, and France (where they coexisted with more direct means of rewarding inventors) . This is hardly surprising, since the objective of import substitution represented a key component of the mercantilist model of political economy. Privileges of invention, by encouraging the immigration of foreign craftsmen and skilled workers were, in fact, a particularly effective measure for achieving this goal.[29]

The evolution of privileges of invention in England is of particular interest.[30] Here, they were tarred by association with the crown's licences of monopoly, which by interfering with established trades triggered a series of protests that culminated in the Statute of Monopolies of 1624. Yet Parliament made an explicit exemption in the Act to allow the crown to continue granting patents for new inventions.[31] The Statute also introduced a fixed term of fourteen years (corresponding to twice the normal term of an apprenticeship). The exclusive focus on the protection of inventions has led legal historians to consider the Statute of Monopolies as the first modern patent law. Following this cue, Nobel laureate Douglass North argued that its enactment, by creating an appropriate set of property rights over inventions, constituted the indispensable precondition behind the acceleration of technical progress that defined the industrial revolution.[32]

In fact, the relationship between patents and innovation during the early modern period was not straightforward. If we limit ourselves to the British case, it is surely true, as suggested by Dutton and Sullivan,[33] that some of the investments in the development of new technologies (including the large 'research and development' projects of the water-frame, spinning jenny, power loom, and steam engine) envisaged their commercial exploitation within the coverage of patent protection. However, before the mid-nineteenth century most inventive activity was undertaken outside the purview of the patent system, as becomes evident through a systematic comparison of patent records with industrial histories and other sources. First mover advantages and secrecy, in many fields, were effective tools for appropriating economic returns from inventive activities. This evidence of widespread technical change outside the patent system suggests that views such as North's, which have ascribed to the patent system a critical role in triggering industrialization, are probably wide of the mark. Moreover, the relationship between patents and innovation is confounded by the sometimes negative impact of patents on the *subsequent* improvement of any given invention, as witnessed by Watt's prolonged patent for the separate condenser (1769), which for two decades frustrated the further refinement of steam power, in particular the development of Hornblower's compound engine.[34]

If the development of patent systems is traditionally regarded as an institutional change that promoted innovation, the resilience of guild systems after 1500 is frequently seen as an institutional obstacle to the development of new technologies.[35] This view has been recently challenged by several scholars, including Epstein who argues that, in a world of largely tacit technological knowledge, some features of the guild system, such as apprenticeship regulations, were an effective means of transmitting and consolidating technical skills.[36] Epstein contends that the overall contribution of the guild system to technological progress in early modern Europe was positive. In fact, the traditionally negative judgement of craft guilds is based on a number of documented instances of guild opposition to the introduction of specific inventions. Epstein invites us to be extremely careful in drawing generalizations from these cases. These episodes, rather than demonstrating an outright hostility to innovation *per se*, show the guilds' opposition to *a specific form of technological progress* (typically the use of capital-intensive and labour-saving devices). By contrast, skill-enhancing and capital-saving inventions were often promptly adopted and developed by the guilds. In fact, guild regulations and practices, by emphasizing the 'collective ownership' of skills and technical know-how, actively promoted the sharing of technical knowledge, with favourable effects on the rate of innovation.[37] Since guild inventions typically took the form of incremental improvements and refinements to current processes and products, they tend to be much less visible in the historical records. Epstein's revisionist view has been refined by Belfanti, who argues that patents and guild prerogatives ought to be seen as two instruments of technology policy that were consciously used in tandem by mercantilist states. The guild system offered a way of preserving, protecting, and gradually enhancing the repertoire of skills and technical know-how in existing trades, whereas patents were a means for importing new manufactures and technologies from abroad. In most cases, in order to receive a patent or privilege, the inventor was required to reveal the secrets of his invention to some authority or directly to a guild or his indigenous apprentices. In this way, a newly imported technology could be absorbed into the guild system.[38]

Awareness of the critical role of technology for economic and military competitiveness led to the implementation of a number of other measures intended to stimulate inventions or encourage technology transfer. The awarding of prizes for specific technical attainments (which amounts to a form of technological procurement) is a case in point. For example, during the eighteenth century Britain, Spain, and France instituted prizes for inventions that would allow a correct determination of the longitude at sea. In other cases, innovative projects and ideas were frequently discussed and implemented within the purview of the large 'military-industrial' complexes of Ancien Régime states as, for example, block-making machinery at the Portsmouth dockyards, or the pioneering attempt to introduce interchangeable-parts manufacturing into the production of muskets in France following the humiliating defeat the Seven Years War. Nor should we forget the concomitantly intense industrial espionage, which again reveals the deep concern of these governments with the prevention of technological lacunae that could irreparably damage the power of the state.[39]

Another critical institutional novelty in the area of knowledge production that has attracted historians' attention is the emergence of 'open science'. The term 'open science' refers to the set of norms that, since the scientific revolution of the seventeenth century, governs the procedures of scientific inquiry, which is perserved as a collective undertaking based on the progressive accumulation of research findings. Accordingly, they require the timely publication of new research findings, which permits other practitioners both to rigorously check the validity of results and to build on them in new inquiries. In this system, the chief incentive is represented by the rewards attached to the enhancement of the scientist's reputation when his/her claims of priority in a new discovery are acknowledged by the relevant peer community. Paul David has traced the origins of open science norms to the aristocratic patronage system of arts and science of the renaissance courts,[40] which arose, he suggests, from two motives. The first was utilitarian, a reflection of the growing appreciation that scientific modes of inquiry could offer solutions to technical problems. Men of science were frequently called on by their aristocratic patrons to provide expertise and advice on military matters, building projects, transport systems, etc. The second motive was ornamental, since their achievements (if not susceptible of immediate application) could enhance the prestige of their patrons, in much the same way as those of artists and men of letters. Reputational contests (for example, solving mathematical challenges), the establishment of priority claims, and the publication of research findings (enhanced by the growing circulation of printed books) gave to the men of science of the renaissance the opportunity of signalling their talents, and to their aristocratic patrons the possibility of performing some screening of this not so transparent market on the basis of reputation. Again, it is interesting to note that the emergence of an effective institutional arrangement in the field of knowledge production is related to Europe's political fragmentation, which provided the environment for competitive displays in the fields of arts and sciences between royal and aristocratic patrons.

The Sources of Technological Change

The sources of technological change and its impact on the economic development of Europe are highly contentious issues. Despite the growing prestige of the 'experimental philosophy' in early modern Europe, historians of science and technology have generally concluded that scientific discoveries had a very limited impact on technological progress at this time. Indeed, the causal connection probably ran in the opposite direction, with technological developments more often setting the natural philosophers' research agenda. The invention of the steam engine, for example, stimulated the development of modern thermodynamics. Long after the seventeenth-century scientific revolution, technologies were still improved largely through trial-and-error procedures and accumulated rules of thumb.[41] In an important challenge to this view, Musson and Robinson argued in 1969 that, in Britain at least since the early eighteenth century, the connections between science and technology were not tenuous but rapidly became stronger and more direct. They pointed to the interests of leading entrepreneurs, such as Matthew Boulton and Josiah Wedgwood, in scientific enquiries; highlighted the emergence of scientific societies, open to individuals from different walks of life, for the discussion of scientific findings and experiments; and specified a number of inventions in the engineering and chemical industries to which the contribution of a scientific insight or perspective on a practical problem was crucial. Their case has been recently elaborated by Joel Mokyr, who introduces the concept of 'industrial enlightenment' to connect the scientific revolution of the seventeenth century with the industrial revolution of the late eighteenth.[42]

In a nutshell, Mokyr's 'industrial enlightenment' is a cultural revolution with profound implications for the procedures for discovering technical improvements. He contends that the Baconian ideal of employing natural philosophy ('science') for the solution of technical problems became progressively articulated through three interrelated changes. First, there was a drastic reduction in the costs of accessing extant bodies of knowledge (thanks to the expanding publication of scientific and technical works, including more systematic descriptions and representations of the functioning of artefacts); secondly, a systematic effort to account for the functioning of artefacts using existing scientific theories and, when necessary, as in the case of the steam engine, trying to develop new explanatory theories; thirdly, a concerted attempt to create a 'public sphere' for the fruitful interaction between scientific researchers and practitioners confronted with technical problems. Taken together, these developments supposedly amounted to a knowledge revolution which dramatically increased the productivity of inventive activities. Since Mokyr recognizes that the *direct* contribution of science to technology may have been very circumscribed, he suggests the concept of 'useful knowledge' to define the knowledge base underlying all the techniques mastered by a society. 'Useful knowledge' is a much broader set than scientific knowledge, containing not only systematic knowledge about natural phenomena but also other types of practical knowledge about the properties of the natural world that may potentially have a bearing on the design of artefacts. The main achievement of the 'industrial enlightenment' was to establish the conditions for a self-sustaining process of accumulation of 'useful knowledge'. Accordingly, Mokyr emphasizes more the adoption of a scientific method and attitude as the key to improvements in technology than the direct contribution of scientific knowledge.

One of most telling examples of this approach is John Smeaton's research on water wheels. In 1759, through a systematic series of experiments, which measured changes in efficiency in response to variations in the design of a scale model, Smeaton showed that Antoine Parent's theory of water-wheel efficiency was inaccurate and established the superiority of overshot wheels. He used this method, again in the early 1770s, to improve significantly the fuel efficiency and operation of the Newcomen engine. As Cardwell remarks,[43] Smeaton's method of *parameter-variation* represents a cornerstone of modern engineering design. Its power lies in permitting the identification of sound design principles, even in the absence of an accurate scientific understanding of the functioning of an artefact.

Although Mokyr's approach undoubtedly helps to illuminate the role of science as a source of technical advances, we would raise three concerns. The first is methodological. There may be evidence, especially in the British case, of many forms of exchange and communications between the 'world of science' and the 'world of technology'. However, *by itself* this type of evidence provides no proof of the existence of significant causal linkages. For example, James Watt had frequent discussions and exchanges on the properties of steam with Joseph Black, then professor of the University of Glasgow (where Watt was working as a maker of scientific instruments), who was conducting research on the nature of heat. Yet, a careful reading of the evidence indicates that these exchanges probably did not play a critical role in Watt's invention of the separate condenser. This implies that the assessment of the exact contribution of science to technology in this phase needs to be done case by case, by means of detailed reconstructions of inventive processes.

Secondly, Mokyr's concept of 'industrial enlightenment' implies a rather drastic change (a 'knowledge revolution') taking place during the eighteenth century. However, as our survey has shown, since at least the late middle ages a more general 'culture of improvement' permeated Europeans' attitude towards technology. Hence, both the seventeenth-century scientific revolution and the adoption of more systematic approaches to inventive activity should be seen as *ramifications of earlier changes in the general cultural outlook of European societies*. In this perspective, the ascendancy since the renaissance of beliefs advocating the subordination of nature to man and celebrating humanity's increasing ability to manipulate natural forces were the product of the peculiar European attitude towards technical improvements of which Mokyr's 'industrial enlightenment' was itself symptomatic.[44] Thirdly, Mokyr's concept of 'industrial enlightenment' threatens to underestimate the role that the mechanical arts, rules of thumb, and other forms of empirical and tacit knowledge not susceptible of being fully articulated and codified, continued to play in the generation of innovations well into the nineteenth century.

Another stream of literature attempts to account for inventive activities by linking them to the economic endowments of different locations. In this approach, inventions are conceptualized as creative responses either to shortages or relative abundances of specific production factors.[45] A recent example is Robert Allen's exposition of Britain's rise to technological leadership during the eighteenth century.[46] Allen argues that Britain's success in developing steam engines and mechanizing textile production and other industries reflected its peculiar wage and price structure (in particular, its high wage economy, created by success in long-distance trade). With coal abundant, the search for technical solutions to problems of power-supply (especially for mines drainage) was, from a very early date, focused on the employment of steam. While there were other attempts to develop steam engines in Europe, such as the steam-powered vehicle for transporting artillery developed by Cugnot in France around 1770, it was only in the British context that a substantial capital investment in the development of a successful steam engine was likely to generate large economic returns. Likewise, the mechanization of cotton spinning. In this case, Britain's relatively high wages (especially in comparison with India, then the leading producer) spurred inventive efforts towards contriving labour-saving machines, such as the spinning jenny and the water-frame. Similarly, it may be argued that Abraham Darby's invention of smelting iron with coke was motivated by the increasing price of charcoal relative to coal. Allen's insistence on the embedding of inventive activities in very specific economic contexts opens an interesting and still largely unexplored research agenda on the border between economic history and the traditional history of technology.[47]

However, the adoption of a new technology involves much more than the direct assessment of the costs and benefits of different pieces of equipment as assumed in the profitability calculations, based on current factor prices, carried out by Allen. In most cases a wider range of factors, such as the availability of skills to operate the new technology, expectations concerning future technological developments, and the overall compatibility of the new technology with complimentary pieces of equipment and other contingent production activities, will affect the choice-of-technique context, making the individual adoption of a new technology the outcome of a complex decision-making process. Hence it remains to be seen whether Allen's economic approach to the study of eighteenth-century technological breakthroughs can be fully integrated into accounts that also recognize the influence of these other factors in the explanation of timing, rate, and direction of inventive activities.[48]

While Allen's analysis highlights the critical role of the economic context in which inventive activities took place, it also tends to minimize the role of scientific insights as *autonomous sources* of invention (partially excepting the appreciation of atmospheric pressure as fundamental to the Newcomen engine). Inventions such as the Newcomen engine (which allegedly required almost ten years of experiments) or Arkwright's water-frame were essentially imaginative new combinations of extant components, such as a rocking beam, a boiler, and a piston cylinder-apparatus in the former, or a new arrangement of spindles, rollers, and flyers in the latter. The real novelty was the unprecedented amount of resources invested in bringing these ideas into practice (and it was to capture the profits of such investments that pressure was mounting for the introduction of more effective patent systems).[49] Previously, most technologies developed through the long-term accumulation of incremental improvements arising through processes of *learning by doing* and *learning by using*.[50] Of course, this form of technical improvements continued to complement the deliberate search for innovations.

Interestingly enough, both Mokyr's and Allen's accounts recognize that essential to the great eighteenth-century breakthroughs in power technologies, textile machinery, and metallurgy was the existence of a pool of sophisticated mechanical skills that transformed designs into practical contrivances. In our view, the precise identification of the factors accounting for the development and consolidation of this strong base of mechanical skills throughout Europe during the Ancien Régime period is indeed one of the most pressing research issues for historians of technology.

Conclusions

Recent research in economic history has been characterized by a renewed debate on western Europe's economic performance during the eighteenth century. The traditional view held that, on the eve of the industrial revolution, it had already 'forged ahead' of the rest of the world, attaining a sizeable lead in its material standards of living. By contrast, the revisionists' account denies any significant differences between western Europe and other advanced locations (especially China) before the eighteenth century, contending instead that the 'great divergence' was the product of subsequent industrialization.[51]

Whatever the outcome of this debate on relative living standards, the historical record suggests that in Europe, since the late middle ages, a number of specific technological trends were already emerging. It is unlikely that these trends (in weapons and transport systems, in power usage, in the mechanization of some production processes) were strong enough to exert a major impact on economic performance before the mid-nineteenth century. Nonetheless, they were critical because of their transformative nature, which put Europe on a steeper path of technological progress, enabling its manufacturers to seize the opportunities presented by expanding markets and trade.

Our survey also points to the emergence of a number of specific institutional arrangements governing the generation and exploitation of technical opportunities. By virtue of this peculiar 'organization of invention', by the eighteenth century technological changes and their application in the economy assumed increasingly the character of a regular and steady flow. Remarkably, most of these institutional changes had a very clear mercantilist imprint, and ultimately were an outcome of Europe's geo-political environment of fierce competition between independent nation-states.[52] These considerations show that accounts of the rise of western Europe which give exclusive emphasis to minimal state intervention, the definition and security of property rights, and the unfettered operation of markets, etc. run the risk of delivering a 'Whig history' which is not warranted, at least in the history of technology.[53] The Ancien Régime state played a significant role in promoting the generation of new technologies, through its pursuit of military supremacy and the wealth to underpin it, but, above all, we would agree with Habakkuk[54] that, 'It is probable that the most important of the conditions which made Europe the cradle of economic advance originated very far back in its history'. Industrialization constituted a change of gear, not a change of direction.

Notes

The financial support of the Netherlands Organization of Scientific Research (Veni Grant 'Inventive activities, patents and the Industrial Revolution') is gratefully acknowledged.

1. See G. Clark, *A Farewell to Alms: A Brief Economic History of the World* (Princeton, 2007) for a discussion of the general significance of the Malthusian model for human history before 1800.
2. E. A. Wrigley, *Continuity, Chance and Change: The Character of the Industrial Revolution in England* (Cambridge, 1988).
3. Maxine Berg, 'In Pursuit of Luxury: Global History and British Consumer Goods in the Eighteenth Century', *Past and Present*, 182 (2004), 85–182.
4. Carlo M. Cipolla, *Guns and Sails in the Early Phase of European Expansion, 1500–1700* (London, 1965); F. C. Lane, 'The Economic Meaning of the Invention of the Compass', *American Historical Review*, 68 (1963), 605–17; Fernand Braudel, *The Structures of Everyday Life* (London, 1981), 403.
5. G. B. Naish, 'Ships and Shipbuilding', in C. Singer, A. J. Holmyard, A. R. Hall, and T. I. Williams (eds.), *A History of Technology*, iii (Oxford, 1957), 471–99; J. Goodman and K. Honeyman, *Gainful Pursuits: The Making of Industrial Europe, 1600–1914* (London, 1988), 157; C. Fox, *The Arts of Industry in the Age of Enlightenment* (New Haven and London, 2009), 48–69; David McGee, 'From Craftsmanship to Draftsmanship: Naval Architecture and Three Traditions of Early Modern Design', *Technology and Culture*, 40 (1999), 209–36, has noted that, before 1800, the direct impact of science on improvements in ship design was very limited. L. D. Ferreiro, *Ships and Science: The Birth of Naval Architecture in the Scientific Revolution, 1600–1800* (Cambridge, Mass., 2006), argues for a more positive role for science in the development of naval architecture.
6. Fox, *The Arts of Industry*, 116–30; J. Coad, *The Portsmouth Block Mills: Bentham, Brunel, and the Start of the Royal Navy's Industrial Revolution* (Swindon, 2005); J. Brewer, *The Sinews of Power: War, Money and the English State, 1688–1783* (London, 1989), 36; D. C. Coleman, 'Naval Dockyards under the Later Stuarts', *Economic History Review*, 6 (1953), 134–55.

7. J. L. Van Zanden, 'Early Modern Economic Growth: A Survey of the European Economy, 1500–1800', in M. Prak (ed.), *Early Modern Capitalism: Economic and Social Change in Europe, 1400–1800* (London, 2001), 80–6.
8. *Structures of Everyday Life*, 424.
9. S. P. Ville, *Transport and the Development of the European Economy, 1750–1918* (New York, 1990); D. R. Headrick, *When Information Came of Age: Technologies of Knowledge in the Age of Reason and Revolution, 1700–1850* (Oxford, 2000), ch. 6.
10. Geoffrey Parker, *The Military Revolution: Military Innovation and the Rise of the West 1500–1800* (Cambridge, 1988); P. T. Hoffman, 'Prices, the Military Revolution and Western Europe's Comparative Advantage in Violence', *Economic History Review* 64 (2011), 39–59. For a more cautious assessment of the role of western military advantage in European expansion in the period 1500–1800, see P. J. Marshall, 'Western Arms in Maritime Asia in the Early Phases of Expansion', *Modern Asian Studies*, 13 (1980), 13–28.
11. E. M. Carus-Wilson, 'An Industrial Revolution of the Thirteenth Century', *Economic History Review*, 11 (1941), 39–60, also argued that the rapid spread of fulling mills in England during the 13th cent. was linked with attempts by landlords to establish new, profitable seigniorial monopolies.
12. T. S. Reynolds, *Stronger than a Hundred Men: A History of the Vertical Water Wheel* (Baltimore, Md., 1983), 69–96.
13. L. Makkai, 'Productivité et exploitation des sources d'énergie (xiie–xviiie siècles)', in S. Mariotti (ed.), *Produttivitá e tecnologie nei Secoli xvii e xviii* (Florence, 1981), but see Reynolds, *Stronger than a Hundred Men*, 123–5. The population of Europe (including Russia) in 1800 is generally estimated to have been around 187 million.
14. Reynolds, *Stronger than a Hundred Men*, 174. For Britain c.1800, J. W. Kanefsky, 'The Diffusion of Power Technology in British Industry, 1760–1870' (University of Exeter, Ph.D. thesis, 1979), 220, estimates the average power for watermills as 10 HP.
15. P. Malanima, *Pre-Modern European Economy* (Leiden, 2009), 84–6.
16. J. W. Kanefsy and J. Robey, 'Steam Engines, in Eighteenth Century Britain: A Quantitative Assessment', *Technology and Culture*, 21 (1980), 181.
17. Esp. W. W. Rostow, *The Stages of Economic Growth: A Non-Communist Manifesto* (Cambridge, 1960); *How it All Began: Origins of the Modern Economy* (London, 1975); and somewhat more cautiously D. S. Landes, *The Unbound Prometheus: Technological Change and Industrial Development in Western Europe from 1750 to the Present* (Cambridge, 1969).
18. Kanefsky, 'Diffusion of Power Technology'. G. M. Von Tunzelmann, *Steam Power and British Industrialisation to 1860* (Oxford, 1978), ch. 6, and N. F. R. Crafts, 'Steam as a General Purpose Technology: A Growth Accounting Perspective', *Economic Journal*, 114 (2004), 338–51, provide independent assessments of the contribution of steam power technology to productivity growth in Britain, concurring that it became significant only after 1840.
19. E. A. Wrigley, *Energy and the English Industrial Revolution* (Cambridge, 2010), 36–46, 91–101. In an important article, R. B. Gordon, 'Cost and Use of Water Power during Industrialization in New England and Great Britain: A Geological Interpretation', *Economic History Review*, 36 (1983), 240–59, shows that as late as 1840, even in the most developed industrial areas, only a limited fraction of the potentially usable water-power sites had been exploited. This contradicts the idea that steam power was a necessary response to an energy crisis in the 18th-cent. economy.
20. R. Friedel, *A Culture of Improvement: Technology and the Western Millennium* (Cambridge, Mass., 2007), 102–28, 218; J. Inikori, *Africans and the Industrial Revolution* (Cambridge, 2002).
21. N. Rosenberg, *Perspectives on Technology* (Cambridge, 1976), chs. 1, 8; C. MacLeod, 'Strategies for Innovation: The Diffusion of New Technology in Nineteenth-Century British

Industry', *Economic History Review*, 45 (1992), 285–307; A. D. Morrison-Low, *Making Scientific Instruments in the Industrial Revolution* (Aldershot, 2007), 249–96.

22. J. Gleeson, *The Arcanum* (London, 1998); M. Schonfeld, 'Was there a Western Inventor of Porcelain?', *Technology and Culture*, 39 (1998), 716–27; Friedel, *Culture of Improvement*, 243–8; Berg, 'In Pursuit of Luxury'.

23. One of the first scholars to note the positive role of European political fragmentation on economic performance and technical progress was Edward Gibbon: 'Europe is now divided into twelve powerful, though unequal kingdoms, three respectable commonwealths, and a variety of smaller though independent states.... *In peace, the progress of knowledge and industry is accelerated by the emulation of so many active rivals*: in war, the European forces are exercised by temperate and undecisive contests.' *Decline and Fall of the Roman Empire*, ch. 38 (emphasis added).

24. N. Rosenberg and L. E. Birdzell, *How the West Grew Rich: The Economic Transformation of the Industrial World* (New York, 1986), 137.

25. P. O. Long, 'Invention, Authorship, "Intellectual Property" and the Origins of Patents: Notes towards a Conceptual History', *Technology amd Culture*, 32 (1991), 846–84.

26. A particularly revealing example of the 'tacit' nature of technological knowledge is the case of the water-powered silk throwing mill developed in northern Italy. The famous treatise *Nuovo Teatro di Macchine e Edificii* by Vittorio Zonca published in 1607, with subsequent edtions. in 1621 and 1656, contained a quite detailed description and a drawing of the apparatus. Yet the successful transfer of this invention to England *c*.1710 was possible only after nearly two years of industrial espionage by John Lombe. See C. M. Cipolla, *Before the Industrial Revolution: European Society and Economy, 1000–1700* (London, 1976), 174.

27. In many cases, migrations of skilled craftsmen resulted from the forced migrations of religious minorities, which proved to be one of the main drivers of the spread of technological know-how across early modern Europe, as with the emigration ofHuguenots from France in the late 17th cent.: see W. C. Scoville, 'Spread of Techniques: Minority Migrations and the Diffusion of Technology', *Journal of Economic History*, 11 (1951), 347–60; 'The Huguenots and the Diffusion of Technology', *Journal of Political Economy*, 60 (1952), 294–311, 392–411. For the emergence of Geneva and London as leading centres of clock-making, one of the most technically sophisticated industries of the time, see C. M. Cipolla, *Clocks and Culture, 1300–1700* (London, 1967).

28. Cipolla, *Before the Industrial Revolution*, 174–81; Long, 'Invention, Authorship'; C. M. Belfanti, 'Between Mercantilism and Market: Privileges for Invention in Early Modern Europe', *Journal of Institutional Economics*, 2 (2006), 319–38.

29. C. May and S. K. Sell, *Intellectual Property Rights: A Critical History* (Boulder, Colo., 2006), 59, 63; L. Hilaire-Pérez, *L'Invention technique au siècle des lumières* (Paris, 2000); Belfanti, 'Between Mercantilism and Market', 326.

30. For the influence of the Venetian model on the first concessions of monopoly privileges as a reward to inventors during the reign of Elizabeth I, see J. Phillips, 'The English Patent as a Reward for Invention: The Importation of an Idea', *Journal of Legal History*, 3 (1982), 71–9.

31. C. MacLeod, *Inventing the Industrial Revolution: The English Patent System, 1660–1800* (Cambridge, 1988), ch. 1.

32. D. C. North, *Structure and Change in Economic History* (New York, 1981), 164–6.

33. H. I. Dutton, *The Patent System and Inventive Activity during the Industrial Revolution* (Manchester, 1984); R. J. Sullivan, '"England's Age of Invention": The Acceleration of

Patents and of Patentable Invention during the Industrial Revolution', *Explorations in Economic History*, 26 (1989), 424–52.
34. MacLeod, *Inventing the Industrial Revolution*, ch. 6; C. MacLeod and A. Nuvolari, 'Patents and Industrialization: An Historical Overview of the British Case, 1624–1907' (UK Intellectual Property Office, 2010), http://www.ipo.gov.uk//pro-ipreseach/ipresearch-policy-economic.htm. On the case of the Hornblower engine, see H. S. Torrens, 'New Light on the Hornblower and Winwood Compound Steam Engine', *Journal of the Trevithick Society*, 9 (1982), 21–41.
35. J. Mokyr, *The Lever of Riches* (Oxford, 1990), 191, 258–60.
36. S. R. Epstein, 'Craft Guilds, Apprenticeship, and Technological Change in Preindustrial Europe', *Journal of Economic History*, 58 (1998), 684–713.
37. Liliane Hilaire-Pérez has termed the knowledge-sharing practices of the guild system 'open technique' institutions. For a detailed case study, see her 'Inventing in a World of Guilds: The Case of Silk Fabrics in Eighteenth Century Lyon', in S. R. Epstein and M. Prak (eds.), *Guilds, Innovation and the European Economy* (Cambridge, 2008). On the shared and distributed character of a large body of premodern technical knowledge, see also S. R. Epstein, 'Property Rights to Technical Knowledge in Pre-Modern Europe, 1300–1800', *American Economic Review*, 94 (2004), 382–7.
38. C. M. Belfanti, 'Guilds, Patents, and the Circulation of Technical Knowledge: Northern Italy during the Early Modern Age', *Technology and Culture*, 45 (2004), 569–89.
39. S. T. McCloy, *French Inventions in the Eighteenth Century* (Lexington, Ky., 1952), 176; Coad, *Portsmouth Block Mills*; K. Alder, *Engineering the Revolution. Arms and Enlightenment in France* (Chicago, 1997); J. R. Harris, *Industrial Espionage and Technology Transfer: Britain and France in the Eighteenth Century* (Aldershot, 1998).
40. P. A. David, 'The Historical Origins of Open Science: An Essay on Patronage, Reputation, Commo n Agency Contracting in the Scientific Revolution' , *Capitalism and Society*, 3 (2008), 1–103.
41. A. R. Hall, 'Engineering the Scientific Revolution', *Technology and Culture*, 2 (1961), 333–41; P. Mathias, 'Who Unbound Prometheus? Science and Technological Change, 1600–1800', in P. Mathias (ed.), *Science and Society 1600–1900* (Cambridge, 1972).
42. J. Mokyr, *The Gifts of Athena: Historical Origins of the Knowledge Economy* (Princeton, 2002). For a more comprehensive discussion we refer the reader to a special issue of *History of Science* for 2007 (45/2) which is entirely devoted to a comprehensive appraisal of On the critical role that different forms of empirical and tacit knowledge not susceptible of being fully articulated and codified played in the generation of innovations in this historical phase, see Fox, *The Arts of Industry*, and on the mutual interactions between 'expert' knowledge and other forms more susceptible of systematic codification in different technical fields, see the essays collected in L. Roberts, S. Schaffer, and P. Dear (eds.), *The Mindful Hand: Inquiry and Innovation from the Late Renaissance to Early Industrialization* (Amsterdam, 2007).
43. D. S. L. Cardwell, *The Fontana History of Technology* (London, 1994), 194; see also W. G. Vincenti, *What Engineers Know and How they Know it: Analytical Studies from Aeronautical History* (Baltimore, Md., 1990), 137–69.
44. D. S. Landes, *The Wealth and Poverty of Nations* (New York, 1998), 58–9; A. Maddison, *Contours of the World Economy, 1–2030 AD* (Oxford,: 2007), 307–20.
45. Max Weber argued that from the 17th cent., in connection with the formation of a capitalistic outlook, inventive activities became increasingly focused on cost reductions, thereby

marking a discontinuity with earlier periods. 'If one scrutinizes the devices of the greatest inventor of pre-capitalistic times, Leonardo da Vinci... one observes that his urge was not that of cheapening production but the rational mastery of technical problems as such': *General Economic History* (London, 1981), 311–12.

46. R. C. Allen, *The British Industrial Revolution in Global Perspective*: (Cambridge, 2009), and R. C. Allen 'Why the Industrial Revolution was British: Commerce, Induced Innovation and the Scientific Revolution', *Economic History Review*, 64 (2011), 357–84. How Commerce Created the Industrial Revolution and Modern Economic Growth' (University of Oxford mimeo, 2006).

47. See also C. MacLeod, 'The European Origins of British Technological Prominence', in L. Prados de la Escosura (ed.), *Exceptionalism and Industrialisation: Britain and its European Rivals* (Cambridge, 2004), 111–26.

48. G. Dosi, 'Sources, Procedures, and Microeconomic Effects of Innovation', *Journal of Economic Literature*, 26 (1988), 1142–3; U. Gragnolati, D. Moschella, and E. Pugliese, 'The Spinning Jenny and the Industrial Revolution: a reappraisal', *Journal of Economic History*, 71 (2011), 455–60, revise some of Allen's computations and argue that the Spinning Jenny could be also profitably adopted in the French economic context. For Allen's response, see R. C. Allen, 'The Spinning Jenny: a Fresh Look', ibid., 461–4.

49. The development costs of Hargreaves's spinning jenny were probably in the region of £500. While the development of Richard Arkwright's water-frame cost about £13,000 (for both figures, Allen, *British Industrial Revolution*, 191, 203. In the field of steam engineering, the development of the Newcomen engine required about ten years of experimentation (L. T. C. Rolt and J. S. Allen, *The Steam Engine of Thomas Newcomen* (Hartington, 1977), 39–43), whereas the costs of developing Watt's engine were probably in the region of £10,000–£13,000. These are all remarkable figures, taking into account that the yearly salary of a skilled craftsman in the second half of the 18th cent. was around £50: F. M. Scherer, 'Invention and Innovation in the Watt-Boulton Steam Engine Venture', *Technology and Culture*, 6 (1965), 169–70.

50. K. G. Persson, *Pre-Industrial Economic Growth, Social Organisation and Technological Progress in Europe* (Oxford, 1988).

51. Landes, *Unbound Prometheus*, ch. 1; K. Pomeranz, *The Great Divergence: Europe and the Making of the Modern World Economy* (Princeton, 2000).

52. E. L. Jones, *The European Miracle: Environments, Economies and Geopolitics in the History of Europe and Asia* (Cambridge, 3rd edn., 2003).

53. D. C. North and R. P. Thomas, *The Rise of the Western World: A New Economic History* (Cambridge, 1973); North, *Structure and Change in Economic History*. A somewhat similar argument for the case of British state intervention in the economy during the 18th cent. has been proposed by Brewer, *Sinews of Power*, and by P. K. O'Brien, 'The Nature and Evolution of an Exceptional Fiscal State and its possible significance for the precocious commercialization and Industrialization of the British economy from Cromwell to Nelson', *Economic History Review* 64 (2011), 408–46. For a revealing study of the impact of government interventions on the early mechanization of the English cotton spinning industry, see P K O'Brain, T. Griffiths, and P. Hunt, 'Political components of the Industrial Revolution: Parliament and the English cotton textile industry, 1660–1774, *Economic History Review*, 44 (1991), 395–423.

54. H. J. Habbakuk, 'The Historical Experience of the Basic Conditions of Economic Progress', in L. H. Dupriez and D. Hague (eds.), *Economic Progress* (London, 1955), 86.

Bibliography

Allen, R. C., *The British Industrial Revolution in Global Perspective* (Cambridge, 2009).

Berg, M., 'In Pursuit of Luxury: Global History and British Consumer Goods in the Eighteenth Century', *Past and Present*, 182 (2004), 85–142.

Brewer, J., *The Sinews of Power: War, Money and the English State, 1688–1783* (Cambridge, Mass., 1988).

Cardwell, D. S. L., *The Fontana History of Technology* (London, 1994).

Clark, G., *A Farewell to Alms: A Brief Economic History of the World* (Princeton, 2007).

Cipolla, C. M., *Guns and Sails in the Early Phase of European Expansion, 1400–1700* (London, 1965).

—— *Before the Industrial Revolution: European Society and Economy, 1000–1700* (London, 1976).

Fox, C., *The Arts of Industry in the Age of Enlightenment* (New Haven and London, 2009).

Friedel, R., *A Culture of Improvement: Technology and the Western Millennium* (Cambridge, Mass., 2007).

Goodman, J., and Honeyman, K., *Gainful Pursuits: The Making of Industrial Europe, 1600–1914* (London, 1988).

Hilaire-Pérez, L., *L'Invention technique au siècle des Lumières* (Paris, 2000).

Jones, E. L., *The European Miracle: Environments, Economies and Geopolitics in the History of Europe and Asia* (3rd edn. Cambridge, 2003).

Landes, D. S., *The Unbound Prometheus: Technological Change and Industrial Development in Western Europe from 1750 to the Present* (Cambridge, 1969).

—— *The Wealth and Poverty of Nations* (New York, 1998).

MacLeod, C., *Inventing the Industrial Revolution: The English Patent System, 1660–1800* (Cambridge, 1988).

——MacLeod, C., and Nuvolari, AS., 'Patents and Industrialization: An Historical Overview of the British Case, 1624–1907' (UK Intellectual Property Office, 2010), http://www.ipo.gov.uk/pro-ipresearch /ipresearch-policy-economic.htm.

Maddison, A., *Contours of the World Economy, 1–2030 AD* (Oxford, 2007).

Mokyr, J., *The Lever of Riches* (Oxford, 1990).

—— *The Gifts of Athena: Historical Origins of the Knowledge Economy* (Princeton, 2002).

Persson, K. G., *Pre-Industrial Economic Growth: Social Organization and Technological Progress in Europe* (Oxford, 1988).

Pomeranz, K., *The Great Divergence: Europe and the Making of the Modern World Economy* (Princeton, 2000).

Rosenberg, N., and Birdzell, L. E., *How the West Grew Rich: The Economic Transformation of the Industrial World* (New York, 1986).

Rostow, W. W., *The Stages of Economic Growth: A Non-Communist Manifesto* (Cambridge, 1960).

—— *How it All Began: Origins of the Modern Economy* (London, 1975).

Van Zanden, J. L., 'Early Modern Economic Growth: A Survey of the European Economy, 1500–1800', in M. Prak (ed.), *Early Modern Capitalism: Economic and Social Change in Europe, 1400–1800* (London, 2001).

Ville, S. P., *Transport and the Development of the European Economy, 1750–1918* (New York, 1990).

Wrigley, E. A., *Continuity, Chance and Change: The Character of the Industrial Revolution in England* (Cambridge, 1988).

—— *Energy and the Industrial Revolution in England* (Cambridge, 2010).

CHAPTER 27

REVOLUTION

MICHAEL RAPPORT

IN 1814, as the Napoleonic Empire teetered on the brink of destruction, Bertrand Lhodiesnière, a veteran revolutionary from Normandy, told his fellow-citizens that when the Bourbon monarchy returned, 'you will have to pay tithes and feudal dues again, and after dark, they will make you keep the frogs quiet so that milord and milady can get a good night's sleep'.[1] This dire warning reflected how far French society had changed since the collapse of the absolute monarchy in 1789. There had been no set programme of radical reform right at the start. Yet the force of circumstances combined with the revolutionaries' ideology to create an impetus which left no area of eighteenth-century life untouched. The elected representatives of the people, the National Assembly, were confronted with the challenge of restoring order to the country, tackling the monarchy's financial woes and establishing a viable political framework for the kingdom. The founding deeds of the French Revolution were therefore at once a pragmatic response to the crisis and an expression of the new order's fundamental principles.

The first dramatic break with the past came in the night of 4 August 1789. In an emotional session pregnant not only with symbolism, but also with real transformative potential for the whole kingdom, the National Assembly abolished what it called 'feudalism'. The deputies, many of them property owners, were urgently trying to pacify the insurgent countryside by renouncing seigneurial rights, but, emboldened by a potent brew of alarm and idealism, they went even further. In a crescendo of zeal, they renounced one privilege after another, levelling individual, corporate, and provincial privileges which made up the very fabric of social differentiation in the Ancien Régime. The tithe, seigneurial justice, and venality were abolished, alongside other vestiges of 'feudalism'. A popular uprising had spurred France's revolutionary elite into razing the old order, leaving the Revolution with the immense task of building a new regime.

The principles which were meant to guide the revolutionaries in this next challenge were expressed in the Declaration of the Rights of Man and the Citizen on 26 August. 'Men are born and remain free and equal in rights', the first electrifying article rang out. These rights included 'liberty, property, security and resistance to oppression'. 'Liberty' was defined as the freedom to do anything which did not infringe the rights of others. There would no longer be any distinctions of birth, but only those based on 'public utility', meaning that positions were now open to anyone with the talent and the education. Sovereignty no longer rested with the King, but with the nation. Civil rights were guaranteed: arbitrary arrest was proscribed (condemning the notorious *lettres de cachet*) and freedom of opinions ('even religious ones') was upheld. All citizens were to enjoy the presumption of innocence in law. The contentious fiscal privileges were now null and void, since taxation would be divided amongst all citizens according to ability to pay. Taken together, the actions of the National Assembly in August were a statement of radical intent: the Ancien Régime was to be rooted out and France was to be rebuilt anew. The hierarchical society of orders, in which status had been determined by the amount of privilege one enjoyed, was to be replaced by an egalitarian, national community in which all shared the same fundamental rights. The Ancien Régime ended in France not only because it had collapsed financially and politically, but also because the Revolution had torn out its ideological and moral underpinnings, replacing them with the foundations of a society based on an egalitarian ideal of individual citizens living under the same law, framed by a more representative form of politics.

Among the losers was the monarchy itself. No longer could a French king declare with any great confidence, as Louis XV had in 1766, that 'the rights and interests of the nation...repose only in my hands'.[2] In the future, every subsequent regime—and not only in France—had in some way to confront and adapt to the counter-claim that legitimate authority emanated from the people. Theoretically absolute and divinely ordained before 1789, Louis XVI was forced to rule as a constitutional monarch, sharing power with the National Assembly before 10 August 1792, when he (and with him the monarchy itself) was overthrown. On 22 September the Republic was proclaimed and 'Louis the Last', as some hopeful revolutionaries dubbed him, was guillotined on 21 January 1793. Monarchy did not disappear forever from France, however: Napoleon restored it under a different, imperial name in 1804. The Bourbons came back in 1814, only to be overthrown in 1830 and replaced by another dynasty, the Orléanist line, which was in turn toppled in 1848. The French rid themselves of their last monarch, Emperor Napoleon III, in 1870 and have lived without one ever since. Yet the Revolution could not only be destructive. It also had to build up a new civic order: practical reasons of political and social stability demanded it, but at the same time the revolutionaries were guided by the implications of the principles proclaimed in August 1789.

The revolutionaries began by trying to reverse the monarchy's centralizing impulses and creating a system of local government which would be accountable to the electorate. The decree of 22 December 1789 abolished the old *bailliages, sénéchaussées,* and *généralités* and replaced them with eighty-three *départements*, roughly equal in size and each with its own administrative seat, the *chef-lieu*. The departments were divided into districts, split in turn into communes (larger cities had sections), each with elected officials. Departments took over the tasks of the Ancien Régime intendants: education, social welfare, policing, taxation, the enforcement of legislation (including conscription), and the gathering of information for the central government. Districts were to act as the conduits between the department and the communes and to oversee the implementation of the laws in the latter. The emphasis on local accountability barely survived the crisis of the mid-1790s. From the spring of 1793, the Convention sent out 'representatives on mission' to the departments, acting with its full authority to mobilize local society for the war effort and crush counter-revolution. The law of 14 frimaire (4 December 1793), strengthened the authority of the central government by, amongst other things, abolishing the departments' elected general councils and appointing in every commune a 'national agent' answerable to Paris. Unsurprisingly, 'Jacobinism' remains to this day a term synonymous with the heavy hand of central government over local autonomy. The Thermidorian regime and Directory softened some of the more intrusive elements of the Terror, but they never returned to the original spirit of the revolutionary reforms. In Napoleon's hands, the system became more than ever the instrument of state power. In 1800, Bonaparte introduced the prefects, one for each department. Although the prefect is often described as a resurrection of the Ancien Régime intendant, he was stronger since there were no longer any institutions which could offer serious opposition. These 'small-scale emperors' were answerable only to Napoleon, who gave them considerable authority to carry out his orders. This was a political centralization to which the Bourbons could only have aspired. As Alexis de Tocqueville observed in the mid-nineteenth century, in administrative terms the French Revolution did not break with the Ancien Régime, but rather consummated the ambition of the absolute monarchy.[3]

In return the Revolution at least offered representative government and protection to rights of all citizens, but in practice some citizens were politically more equal than others. Most of the revolutionary leadership in 1789 believed strongly that power should be exercised by those who were educated enough to understand politics and who had enough wealth to have a stake in the stability of the new order. The Abbé Emmanuel Sieyès, whose pamphlet *What is the Third Estate?* had so vigorously rallied the opposition to noble privilege in early 1789, argued in July that the new constitution should distinguish between those citizens who were 'active' and those who were not: all inhabitants of the country were to enjoy the basic rights of citizens, 'the protection of their person, property and freedom, etc.', but 'not everyone has the right to take an active part in the election of public officials; not all are active citizens'.[4] In the revolutionary constitutions of 1791 and 1795, the suffrage was restricted to adult males paying certain levels of taxation, representing 60 per cent of adult males in 1791 and a mere 20 per cent in 1795. In both constitutions voting was indirect: to be chosen as an elector and then as a deputy, one had to be even wealthier. Even the more democratic elections for the National Convention, held after the fall of the monarchy in August 1792, excluded domestic servants, those who had no regular income, and who had not lived in the same district for at least a year. Direct and universal male suffrage was enshrined in the constitution of 1793, applicable to all males over 21 years old, provided they lived in the same district for six months, but it was never implemented because the constitution was suspended during the Terror. In fact, the elections to the Estates-General in 1789 had been more inclusive, with William Doyle suggesting that they were 'the most democratic spectacle ever seen in the history of Europe...nothing comparable occurred again until far into the next century'.[5] The Napoleonic constitution granted universal male suffrage in 1800, but it was used in plebiscites aimed at strengthening the dictatorship, and in indirect elections for a parliamentary system which had little real power.

The Revolution therefore introduced parliamentary government to France, but it was only 'an apprenticeship in democracy',[6] the first step towards modern, democratic politics, not its consummation. François Furet has controversially argued that the values and practices of democracy were not definitively embedded in France until the consolidation of the Third Republic in the 1870s, which he describes as 'the French Revolution coming into port'.[7] A continuing focus of research, therefore, are the ways in which the people entered politics *outside* the formal processes, namely in the dramatic expansion in civil society, which had been developing since the mid-eighteenth century, but which in the Revolution flowered with the collapse of censorship, empowering a wide cross-section of French society. The press flourished: at the beginning of 1789, there were eighty newspapers in circulation, but some 2,000 new titles appeared over the next three years, with readership trebling. This expansion in journalistic enterprise did not go unchecked: many contemporaries feared that unrestrained freedom of expression merely encouraged moral degeneracy and fomented civil strife. How public opinion could and should be 'policed' therefore remained a preoccupation in the new order. During the Terror, writers defined as 'enemies of liberty' were classified as 'suspects' under the law of 17 September 1793 and later, after the fructidor coup in 1797, monarchist newspapers were shut down. The weight of institutionalized censorship, however, was not felt fully until the Napoleonic regime: in 1811 the number of Parisian journals was restricted to four, and the departments to one each.[8] The 1790s also saw political associations flourish: clubs combined sociability with the clamour of debate on a scale not seen again in France until 1848. The most famous were the Jacobin clubs, which became less exclusive in their membership as the revolution progressed. The more democratic 'popular societies', with their artisanal backbone, spread rapidly during the crisis of 1792–4, so that in all there were 6,000 political clubs across France. Popular political mobilization also reached its peak in these years thanks to the wider franchise, with the opening of urban sections, or wards, to all male citizens: it is estimated that 10 per cent of all men regularly attended their local assemblies in Paris; a remarkable level of commitment given the heavy economic pressures of the time.[9]

As historians since the 1980s have emphasized, this expansion in political participation occurred within a cultural environment which was itself transformed, as the revolutionaries sought self-consciously to break with France's Ancien Régime past.[10] A new political culture emerged, encompassing the ideology, rhetoric, symbols, and assumptions which lay behind them, as well as the practice of politics itself. It was adopted then (and subsequently) by those who sought to harness the Revolution's liberating promise. In their attempts to secure the support of all French citizens, the revolutionaries deployed the full arsenal of culture and communication: education, newspapers, pamphlets, public festivals, theatre, opera, music, painting, sculpture, and architecture. A practical measure, but also symbolic of the break with the past, was the decimal system of weights and measures, announced on 1 August 1793 and put into practice two years later, which continues to expand its empire today (provoking surprisingly virulent protests from devotees of other systems). There was also an explosion in visual messages, including mass-produced engravings of revolutionary events, personalities, and allegorical messages. More widespread still were revolutionary images and messages found in the most banal, everyday items—on stamps, games, playing cards, ladies' fans, paper money, coins, official certificates and letterheads, and items of clothing, including the red Phrygian bonnet.[11] There is still room for more research on the ramifications of such material culture—not least who was making a living from what appears to have been a veritable industry.

The new political culture encouraged the protests of those who remained excluded from formal politics, challenging older assumptions in the process. Women may not have been enfranchised, but some tested the limits of citizenship through journalism, demonstrations, petitions, and political societies. Feminists like Théroigne de Méricourt, Olympe de Gouges, and Claire Lacombe adopted the ideas and language of the Revolution itself to press their points home. De Gouges adapted the Declaration of Rights of 1789 to proclaim that 'Woman is born free and remains equal to man in rights'.[12] Women attended the political debates of the revolutionary assemblies, cheering or heckling from the public galleries, and did the same in political clubs. They also established their own societies, the most famous being the Parisian Club of Republican Revolutionary Citizenesses, but this was one among thirty others which sprang up across France between 1789 and 1793. Political mobilization cut across gender boundaries. All this was enough to alarm the Jacobin regime, which closed down women's political associations in October 1793. In this respect, at least, the predominant eighteenth-century attitudes towards gender held firm: women's roles were meant to be restricted to those of the nurturing mother, supportive wife, or dutiful daughter.[13] Yet the ideological and rhetorical framework left by the French Revolution, such as its ideas of rights and citizenship, including the very term *citoyenne*, enabled women to stake a claim to a place equal to men in the new civic order.[14]

The Revolution did emancipate other groups. Protestants had been granted civil liberties by the monarchy in 1787, with legal recognition of their baptisms, marriages, and property and inheritance rights, but they could not hold municipal or judicial office. The Revolution gave Protestants full citizenship on 24 December 1789. This opened up the issue of emancipating all non-Catholics—and it was clear from the debates that not everyone in the Constituent Assembly considered Jews to be naturally French. The ensuing arguments delayed the recognition of Jews as citizens until 27 September 1791. The question of rights was also applicable to the black population, free and enslaved, of the French overseas empire. Emancipation there was forced by events: the enslaved blacks of Saint-Domingue (Haiti) rebelled against the white population in August 1791. Free men of colour (mixed race) were given political rights in March 1792, but slavery was formally abolished on 4 February 1794 only when it became clear that it was the sole means of securing the loyalty of the insurgents in the bitter colonial war against the British and the Spanish. The freedom was short-lived. Napoleon restored slavery in 1802 and stripped all blacks of their political rights, but while he could enforce this on Martinique and Guadeloupe, the determined Haitian insurgents took up arms again and won their independence in 1804—creating the longest-surviving republic in the western hemisphere after the United States. Slavery would only be definitively abolished in the rest of the French overseas empire in 1848.[15]

While the Revolution fell significantly short of its liberating promise, it was radical in its assault on the privileges enjoyed, in particular, by the former First and Second Estates of the realm, the Catholic clergy and the nobility. For the revolutionaries, national sovereignty meant that there could be no privileged corporations, orders, or castes which divided the sovereign nation: everyone had to be equally citizens. Despite harbouring some fashionable eighteenth-century anticlericalism, however, the revolutionaries initially had no desire to attack Catholicism as a whole. There was an impulse to reform the church—a goal supported by many of the clerical deputies themselves—but the burden of the national debt inherited from the Ancien Régime ensured that the Revolution developed into a frontal assault, the consequences of which would poison French politics until the second half of the twentieth century. The revolutionaries believed sincerely in freedom of conscience, rejecting the clerical deputy Dom Gerle's motion on 12 April 1790, which would have proclaimed Catholicism the state religion 'with the exclusive right of public worship'. In a radical breach with the old order, the state itself was to be secular: clerical influence was steadily squeezed out of education and the registration of births, marriages, and deaths—previously the task of the parish priest—was handed over to the municipal authorities on 20 September 1792. Since it was axiomatic to most deputies that ecclesiastics had to perform useful social services, on 13 February 1790 monasteries and convents not engaged in educational and charitable work were closed down and monastic vows decreed null and void. The resulting dispersal of monks and nuns removed an important Ancien Régime institution from France's social landscape.

Yet if some clerics fumed about all this 'national apostasy', the truly devastating hammer-blow came in the form of the Assembly's nationalization of ecclesiastical property. Church estates (up to a sixth of all the agricultural land in France) could not be ignored by the revolutionaries who were trying to navigate the state out of its financial crisis. On 2 November 1789, ecclesiastical property was decreed 'at the disposal of the nation', to be auctioned off to raise money. The activities of the church would now have to be funded by the state, which gave the revolutionaries the opportunity for root-and-branch reform. It came in the shape of the Civil Constitution of the Clergy of 12 July 1790. In a radical overhaul of France's ecclesiastical structures, no single parish was to have fewer than 6,000 souls, but their priests were to be salaried by the state. All sinecures, such as cathedral chapters without pastoral responsibilities, were suppressed. Bishoprics were to coincide with the eighty-three departments, effectively abolishing fifty-two episcopal sees and the archbishoprics. Most radically of all, parish priests and bishops were to be elected by the local citizens. While these reforms removed some of the most glaring abuses, many otherwise supportive clerics were disturbed by the fact that the Pope was not consulted (and he remained strangely silent until it was too late) and by the election of priests, since voters might have included Protestants, Jews, and deists. Meanwhile the election of bishops destroyed the Gallican church's long-defended rights over appointments, which it had shared with the King. Into this tense situation fell the bombshell of the clerical oath on 27 November 1790, by which all priests and bishops would have to swear an oath of loyalty to the Constitution (intended at this stage to include the Civil Constitution of the Clergy), or face dismissal, albeit with a pension. The Assembly expected the oath to represent an overwhelming endorsement of the Civil Constitution by the parish clergy, but just over half of them took the oath—becoming known as 'constitutional' priests—and some 10 per cent of those retracted when the Pope finally declared his opposition to the reforms in April 1791. Those who refused to take the oath, the non-jurors or 'refractories', often had the vocal support of their parishioners, angry over what was developing into a full-blown assault on the church. Non-jurors now emerged as the moral centre of local, popular opposition to the Revolution.

French society had been torn down the middle. The schism was especially bitter because refractory priests rallied their flocks to the counter-revolution—and the Revolution gave the church its martyrs. After the fall of the constitutional monarchy in August 1792, the revolutionaries enacted punitive measures against refractories, deporting those priests who refused to take a new oath. Some were brutally slaughtered in the September Massacres. During the Terror, the clergy as a whole—constitutional and non-juror alike—came under sustained assault. Seven per cent of all the official death sentences were handed down against clerics. Meanwhile, in some areas overzealous local authorities led popular militants in a campaign against religious belief itself. In this 'dechristianization' campaign of the autumn of 1793, priests were forced to renounce their vocation, churches were closed to worship and became the venues for atheist ceremonies celebrating 'reason'. This was accompanied by an onslaught of 'vandalism' (the term comes from this period) against religious symbols. Churches, streets, and towns were renamed to erase any religious associations and given titles evoking secular, republican values. In this climate, the Convention further stressed the break with the past on 7 October by introducing a new calendar to replace the Gregorian version, with 'Year One' dated from 22 September 1792, the birth of the French Republic. A month later, a law allowed local authorities to ban the public practice of religion if they so wanted. Yet this was about as far as the Convention was willing to go. The revolutionary government feared that the iconoclasm was alienating far too many people from the Republic—and it was, moreover, led by the extreme left-wing opposition. The clampdown began in December, beginning with a decree reiterating the freedom of religious belief. This did not prevent state-sponsored efforts to erect a more secular, rationalist code of morality as an alternative to Catholicism, the short-lived cult of the 'Supreme Being', celebrated by the Convention in June 1794. After the Terror, church and state were formally separated by a law of 21 February 1795. No public displays of worship were allowed, the state would support no religion, but the law would otherwise protect the free practice of any faith—behind closed doors. Officially, France had travelled a long way from the confessional state of the Ancien Régime. Yet the new law permitted a Catholic resurgence. The devout—often led by women—seized the opportunity to reopen churches and to encourage their intimidated priests to emerge from hiding. This reconstruction of the church prepared the ground for one of the more lasting pieces of revolutionary legislation, the Concordat signed by Napoleon Bonaparte, as First Consul, and Pope Pius VII, in July 1801.

The Concordat, the compromise which lasted until 1905, declared Catholicism to be 'the religion of the majority of French citizens', explicitly accepting the legitimacy of religious minorities, while also ensuring that the state itself remained secular. The Pope recognized the nationalization and sales of church lands, but in return the state would salary some 3,500 parish priests and the bishops who, as under the old Gallican Church, would be appointed by the head of state, but bend to the spiritual authority of the Pope. Clerics would declare their loyalty to the government, offer prayers for the state, and preach obedience to the laws. These arrangements allowed most souls on either side of the Republican–Catholic divide to make an uneasy peace.[16]

The nobility was equally storm-tossed. The loss of seigneurial rights dealt a considerable blow to their income (reducing it by up to 60 per cent in some areas), although the impact varied from one region to the next, according to the extent to which they were financially dependent upon these privileges. The principle of fiscal equality signalled a dramatic leap in the nobility's tax liabilities: under the Ancien Régime nobles expected to pay 10 per cent of their income to the state in peacetime, but the Revolution's new land tax, the *contribution foncière* was set at 16 per cent, to which should be added the various 'patriotic contributions' and the forced loans of 1793 and 1799 imposed on the wealthiest citizens. While the financial screws tightened, the abolition of manorial courts stripped the nobles of their judicial authority over the peasantry. With the highest positions of every branch of the state now open to merit rather than birth, nobles also lost their preferment in receiving appointments. The abolition of the parlements, pinnacle of the legal ladder, in August 1790 tore away the constitutional shield which had protected their privileges. By then, the nobles had already lost the hereditary status, titles, and coats of arms and other signs of nobility, which were abolished on 19 June 1790. The old Second Estate no longer had any legal existence. After the fall of the monarchy, the ex-nobles were disenfranchised, banned from the primary electoral assemblies in December 1792, from the surveillance committees in March 1793, and then included in the Law of Suspects of 17 September 1793, unless they could demonstrate active loyalty to the Revolution. By the law of 26–7 germinal II (15–16 April 1794), they were classed alongside foreigners—a further sign of their legal exclusion from the national order—in being expelled from political clubs, sectional assemblies, and banished from Paris and important maritime and frontier towns, although in practice the revolutionary government 'requisitioned' (and therefore exempted) hundreds of ex-nobles when they offered useful services to the Republic. Nine per cent of the official death sentences during the Terror were passed on nobles. After the Terror, they were subjected to a further round of persecution in the wake of the left-wing coup of fructidor (September 1797). In November, a decree excluded all ex-nobles from public office and ordered their deportation. In July 1799, the Law of Hostages empowered departmental authorities to arrest the families of ex-nobles and *émigrés* in 'disturbed' areas.

One course open to the hard-pressed aristocracy (and indeed the clergy) was to emigrate, although precise figures as to how many noble families were affected have been hard to pin down: estimates range from anywhere between 5 and 25 per cent. Flight came at a price. From August 1792, the property of *émigrés* became *biens nationaux*, to be sold off like church land, a penalty hurting perhaps as many as 12,500 families. Yet the figures also suggest that the vast majority mostly lived discreetly in the provinces, avoiding conflict with the new authorities, so that they and their estates, if not their legal status, survived. Relief came with the rise of Napoleon in November 1799. He was keen to base his authority upon the support of a unified elite and one of his earliest acts was to repeal the Law of Hostages. From 1800, the *émigrés* were allowed to return, provided they accepted that the land which they had lost was irredeemably so. In 1808, Napoleon went so far as to establish an imperial aristocracy, but since the essential criterion for an award of a title was state service and wealth, the majority (58 per cent) came from the bourgeoisie, while only 22 per cent had noble pedigrees from the Ancien Régime. The rest had artisan or peasant origins. Moreover, the privileges of the old aristocracy were not restored and imperial nobility was only hereditary in so far as the title-bearer was able to acquire enough land which qualified as a *majorat* (an entail, which could not be sold or divided, allowing the property to be passed on intact within the same family), but less than half of the Napoleonic nobility succeeded in doing that. Additionally, a son who failed to match his father's record of state service could lose his title. Napoleon's nobility, therefore, tried to encapsulate some of the core revolutionary values of utility, service, and merit, while embodying an emphasis on property rather than birth, but it represented a retreat from the Revolution's more radical egalitarianism.

Still, the old regime nobility survived as an important social and political force deep into the nineteenth century. By 1815, noble families still held 80 per cent of their original landholdings and they managed to recover yet more up to 1830. This recovery cost some nobles dear, saddling them with long-term debts and the integrity of their estates was no longer guaranteed, since the Revolution abolished the various forms of primogeniture in March 1790, after which all children had to receive an equal share of the inheritance. This was less radical than it at first appeared, since primogeniture under the Ancien Régime had only applied to fiefs associated with a title: all other property, including that belonging to the nobility, could be divided up among heirs, thus guaranteeing all children a share of the inheritance. In any case, the revolutionary legislation was significantly modified by the Napoleonic Code of 1804, which allowed parents to show more favour to one heir and entitled them to transform some of their property into an entail, or *majorat*. Landownership and old habits of deference ensured that the nobility clung onto their political influence for generations.[17]

Yet the aristocracy no longer had a monopoly of social or political pre-eminence. With the abolition of privilege, they now shared this with others who were just as wealthy, particularly bourgeois landowners. It has been argued that prior to 1789 these rich bourgeois and nobles were fusing into a common elite, with a shared culture in the Enlightenment and similar economic interests in land and commerce.[18] This view of a prerevolutionary common elite in all but name—which effectively denies the 'Marxist' view of the Revolution as essentially the result of a clash between two antagonistic classes, the bourgeoisie and aristocracy—has not won universal acceptance among historians, some of whom, without necessarily being 'Marxist', point to the evidence of a more distinctively 'bourgeois' public sphere which was gradually being infused with a commercial spirit worthy of a capitalist society. There is no doubt that there was a burgeoning middle class outside the elites, but whether or not this heterogeneous group of professionals, officeholders, small-scale merchants, and investors actually had a class-consciousness of its own is still being debated.[19] This middling sort certainly played a leading role in the Revolution (and it remained active throughout the nineteenth century) but it appears that a reconstituted version of the elite which had existed before 1789, with its wealth and influence grounded in landed property—the *notables*—emerged in control of France's political fortunes. Wealth, education, and state service became the basis of an elite which was composed of the rich, noble and non-noble alike, divided by politics rather than by status. The *notables* held sway over national politics, punctuated by the 1848 Revolution, until the consolidation of the Third Republic in the 1870s.[20]

Much of the revolutionary leadership may have been recruited from the professional middle class, but as a broad group the latter did not necessarily benefit from the upheaval. The assault on privilege carried off a venerable Ancien Régime tradition, venality—the sale of offices, by which the state raised money and through which non-nobles had clambered their way towards an aristocratic title. The compensation offered by the revolutionaries, moreover, was based on the exaggeratedly low valuations made for tax purposes back in 1771 and paid in the inflation-ridden *assignats* (paper redeemable against *biens nationaux*). Venality was a far-reaching old regime practice, but the scale of the abolition was largely ignored by historians until very recently. Yet by 1794 the revolutionaries had suppressed 60,000 venal posts, compensating their owners to the tune of 805 million *livres*—an immense achievement and one which consolidated the professionalization of the civil service.[21] In the assault on privileged corporations, the legal and medical professions were simply opened up to all-comers with minimal qualifications. In the law, a commitment to the free administration of justice combined with the revolutionaries' suspicion of corporatism, so that barristers (*avocats*) lost their monopoly of pleading in court and their order was abolished. *Procureurs* (solicitors) and notaries lost their offices with the abolition of venality. Henceforth, all legal practitioners were called equally *hommes de loi*. Napoleon eventually reconstituted legal orders and licensing—but barristers had to wait until 1810 for that to happen.[22] The medical profession has enjoyed less attention from historians, perhaps because (apart from some notable exceptions like Joseph-Ignace Guillotin and Jean-Paul Marat) few doctors engaged in national politics, but also because the history of clinical medicine does not fit easily into the timescale of the French Revolution. Yet the profession was regarded by the revolutionaries as an essential part of the new order, since ill-health, old age, and disability were recognized as both causes and symptoms of poverty. Still, the medical profession initially stumbled under the impact of the Revolution because hospitals, which had been formally run by the church, were plunged into crisis. The Constituent Assembly considered ambitious plans for a national health system as part of a wider attack on poverty. A structure was finally put into place in 1803 (and it lasted until 1892), but it was a two-tier system, with qualified doctors for those who could pay and free, but less thoroughly trained, medical officers for the poor. While this fell short of the egalitarian plan initially presented to the Constituent Assembly, the medical profession was no longer associated with religious charity, but was intimately bound up with state-sponsored programmes of public health and became a central element in the type of society the revolutionaries wanted to create. Despite some excellent work on medicine, doctors, and patients,[23] the comprehensive medical history of the French Revolution has yet to be written.

The peasantry expected a lot from the assault on privilege, but after all the National Assembly's abolitions and renunciations of 4 August, they would be disappointed. The definitive decree of 11 August proclaimed that 'the feudal regime' was destroyed 'in its entirety'. Yet 'feudalism' was carefully defined to mollify the worst fears of the landowners. Seigneurial rights and dues relating to personal servitude, such as labour obligations (the *corvées*) and various forms of *mainmorte* (which restricted the peasant's ability to leave the manor, or prevented a vassal from freely disposing of his land) were to be abolished without compensation. The gibbet (for meting out manorial justice) and irritants such as the lord's personal church pew and weather vane, were finally abolished in April 1791. All other seigneurial impositions were subject to redemption payments by the peasants because, as a decree of 15 March 1790 explained, they related to the lord's property rights. Yet the distinction was not entirely clear, either to local officials or to disappointed and angry peasants. The hated *banalités*, monopolies by which peasants were obliged to use the lord's wine and olive presses, his mill and bread ovens, though formally abolished, continued in practice in some places, where they could be shown to have originated in a contract. The tithe remained until the National Assembly had worked out how it was going to support the clergy. In 1790, it was to be paid to the state and, the following year, to the landlords. Harvest dues were held to be the price of the original grant of the peasant's land. Eventually, the more radical Convention abolished all seigneurial rights and dues without compensation on 17 July 1793. As far as the peasants were concerned, therefore, the August decrees did not entirely abolish 'feudalism'. Moreover, the revolutionary emphasis on individual property rights brought an assault on communal traditions such as *vaine pâture* (the custom of free grazing of animals on unenclosed fields) and common land. The revolutionaries were practical enough to compromise over *vaine pâture*—the Rural Code of 28 September 1791 allowed it to continue (and it remains the basis of grazing rules today), but the division (*partage*) and enclosure of common land, permitted from June 1793, was more controversial. *Partage* benefited wealthier farmers over their poorer neighbours, for whom the acquisition of a small plot of land was paltry compensation for the loss of the literally vital opportunities offered by the commons for grazing, foraging, and gleaning. Where *partage* occurred, the hard-pressed rural poor sold off their share to the richer peasants at the first opportunity.[24]

Yet the Revolution still represented a material gain for the peasantry, particularly where labour services (as in eastern France) or *banalités* were especially onerous. The outright abolition of seigneurialism in 1793 eliminated some 100 million *livres* of impositions on the peasantry at a stroke. Peasants were no longer subject to the caprice of manorial justice, but were equal to their landlords in the eyes of the law, able to appeal directly to the new civil courts. This was a great step in integrating the peasants as free citizens of the state rather than as subjects of a local lord.[25] Peasant control over their own land was entrenched by the revolutionaries' conception of individual property rights, an important step in a country where up to 40 per cent of the land (albeit with dramatic regional variations) was in peasant hands in 1789. This proportion expanded during the Revolution, although not as dramatically as the peasantry might have hoped. Many farmers simply could not profit from the sales of *biens nationaux*, because they were not auctioned off in small, affordable parcels. The beneficiaries of the sales were often bourgeois townsfolk and in some areas the resulting intrusion of urban values seemed to threaten the delicate balance of social relations in the village, a factor which helped to push the Vendée and Brittany into counter-revolution in 1793.[26] *Émigré* property was auctioned in smaller lots in 1793—and this time the poorest peasants received a voucher worth 500 *livres* to compete in the auctions. None the less, this was as far as the revolutionaries were willing to go towards redistributive justice. In March 1793 the Convention decreed the death penalty for anyone who urged an 'Agrarian Law', meaning the forcible redistribution of property. The 'Ventôse Laws' of February 1794 proposed to seize the property of 'enemies of the revolution' and to use it to 'indemnify' indigent patriots, but this was primarily a political move to outflank the revolutionary government's left-wing opponents and remained a dead letter.

The extent to which the peasants expanded their property varied from one region to the next. George Lefebvre's then ground-breaking work on the department of the Nord suggested that over half the land auctioned was acquired by the peasantry—one third of them first-time property-owners. More recent work has shown that, in Alsace, peasant landownership expanded by a fifth. Yet in Brittany and the Haute-Marne, most of the pickings—85 per cent of them in the latter—were snatched up by bourgeois bidders.[27] The cumulative effect of future local studies will begin to offer a broader perspective as to how peasant landowning was affected by the Revolution. So far it seems that, while their precise effects varied from one locality to another, the revolutionaries' reforms had a direct impact on every village.[28] The long-term economic effects are debatable. The pressure on agrarian land grew along with the number of smallholders in the first half of the nineteenth century, retarding economic development. Yet peasants were no longer subject to seigneurial dues, which would have swallowed up perhaps a quarter of their income. Although a direct link is by no means clear, this may help to explain a rise in life expectancy between the 1780s and the 1820s, a phenomenon unique in Europe at precisely a time when one might expect war and social dislocation to have had the opposite effect.[29]

The assault on privilege also shook up life for the urban population. Even today, historians disagree as to whether or not guilds were actually abolished on 4 August, so confusing were the events of that night. All ambiguity was removed in February 1791, when abolition was made explicit: the guilds had disappeared for good. Harder to pin down were the illegal but (prior to 1791) tolerated *compagnonnages*, the brotherhoods of apprentices and journeymen. With the abolition of the guilds, there was a real danger that the journeymen might exploit the weakness of the master craftsmen and push for better conditions. When these workers began to hold meetings, form clubs, and, in some cases, go on strike, the National Assembly reacted on 14 June 1791 with a law proposed by Isaac-Guy-Marie Le Chapelier, reiterating the abolition of corporations. The right to assemble peacefully, Le Chapelier argued, did not mean that people of the same trade could gather and form associations, for this was to establish a separate corporation, which was unconstitutional. Consequently, all workers were forbidden from establishing labour organizations for collective bargaining or petitioning. Unlike the guilds, the *compagnonnages* persisted clandestinely in defiance of the law, seeking to control wages and work for their members, re-emerging more openly, though still illegally, after 1815. Artisanal politics then developed, shaped by republicanism and socialism, but punctuated by government repression. The 1848 Revolution would see only a short-lived emergence of legalized workers' organizations. Trade unions were tolerated under Napoleon III from 1864, but it was not until twenty years later that they were formally legalized. It was only from then that the modern structures of French labour politics were allowed to take shape uninterrupted, though not painlessly.[30]

The French Revolution did not forge a new, working-class consciousness, either: in this respect, the continuities from the old order remained dominant. The notion of a working class still belonged to the future in the pre-industrial world of the late eighteenth-century city, with its divisions of labour, its subcontracting (*marchandage*), its close, but often fraught, relationships between masters and journeymen and its struggling master-craftsmen trying to protect their economic independence from the commercial pressures of the day. The urban militants of the 1790s adopted the term *sans-culottes*, which obscured the variegated nature of the popular movement, but which could be adopted by anyone who felt a common interest with the artisans in their opposition to the social elites. Despite the fine work already carried out by historians, especially on Paris,[31] the complex relationship between the city environment, economic developments, and popular politicization in urban France—particularly in the larger provincial cities—remains a still fertile field for research.

In their quest for a new civic order, the revolutionaries had to construct viable social institutions which corresponded with the ideal of transforming French people into citizens, while offering workable, practical solutions to the social problems of the day. Foremost amongst the latter was poverty. The revolutionaries—and the Jacobins in particular—had fine intentions in this area. The Constituent's dogged Comité de Mendicité sought to replace Ancien Régime methods of poor relief, grounded in religious ideas of charity, with a nationwide system of *bienfaisance*, state assistance given to the poor as a right via municipal or district *commissions de bienfaisance*, created in May 1791. This aid applied only to those who were clearly unable to earn an honest living: the aged, the sick, and the disabled. By contrast, malingerers, vagabonds, and professional beggars were to be imprisoned in the harsh *dépôts de mendicité*: poor relief should not be so generous that it encouraged idleness. While the revolutionaries had not, therefore, escaped eighteenth-century attitudes towards poverty, they did seek radical solutions to the problem. The Jacobins opened a *Grand Livre de Bienfaisance Nationale* in each rural department to forge ahead with a system of relief funded by the central government. Like all good revolutionary intentions, the scheme was never allowed to make its full impact, because the demands of the war, including pensions for the wounded and for veterans, syphoned off money intended for social welfare. The Jacobin system was abolished by the Directory, which by the law of 30 November 1797 threw the responsibility squarely back onto the shoulders of the local *commissions de bienfaisance*. Yet an important shift had been made in that government, whether local or national, was now regarded as the most rational provider of welfare. Above all, the revolutionaries questioned the effectiveness and humanity of hospitals and the poorhouse. Run by the church, they ran with high costs and housed the destitute alongside the sick and the dying. Their finances were severely squeezed by the nationalization of church lands and the demands of the war, while the Revolution's anticlericalism chased off the nuns who served as nurses. Although the hospitals clung on, they were no longer the principal source of poor relief.[32] Rather, they began to be transformed into medical establishments. The French Revolutionary Wars created an urgent need for well-trained doctors to treat the bloodied masses of wounded soldiers and hospitals began their evolution into centres for clinical training. In December 1794 the Convention established three *écoles de santé* attached to hospitals in Paris, Montpellier, and Strasbourg.[33]

The revolutionaries were no less ambitious in trying to forge a state education system on the ruins of schooling formerly provided by the church. Ambitious schemes went through various mutations in the early 1790s, driven by the political ideologies of those in power, including the 'Jacobin' plan for a free, universal, and compulsory system of primary education. Yet these ideas foundered on the rapid turnover of regimes, the lack of money, and peasant hostility. A universal, free, and compulsory system of primary education was eventually established in the 1880s. The Revolution's record in secondary and higher education was happier. Building on the secondary schools established in 1795, the *écoles centrales*, Napoleon created the *lycées* in 1802. They became a lasting feature of the French education system, as did the examination essential for university entrance, the *baccalauréat*, which was first introduced in 1809 and has tormented *lycéens* ever since. The universities were abolished by the Convention in 1793, but replaced by specialist institutions of higher education, including the Natural History Museum (1793), the Medical Schools (1794), the École Normale (1795, for teacher training), and the famous engineering school, the Polytechnique (1795). To this day, these form part of the elite crust of French higher education.[34]

Like the lawyers that so many of them were, the revolutionaries saw a rational, equal, and fair legal system as essential to the new civic order. They were also sincere in their pursuit of more equitable and humane ways of dispensing justice. The penal code of 25 September–6 October 1791 abolished the prosecution of 'imaginary crimes', such as heresy, sacrilege, magic, and witchcraft. Penalties aimed at both punishing and 'correcting' the guilty. Torture to obtain a confession had already been abolished in 1780, but it was now banned outright as a form of punishment. Breaking on the wheel, the pillory, mutilations, branding, flogging, and the so-called *amende honorable* were abolished. Capital punishment was kept for a limited number of crimes (treason, murder, arson, and counterfeiting money), but everyone condemned to death would be executed by beheading, a right previously reserved for nobles. For this brave new world of egalitarian judicial killing, Joseph Guillotin proposed the use of a decapitation machine which would guarantee a quick and (experts assumed) painless end: the 'guillotine' was introduced on 20 March 1792. Otherwise there was a scale of other punishments: hard labour, imprisonment, deportation, civic degradation (for men with full citizenship rights), and the *carcan*—an iron collar to be worn by condemned women and others without the full rights of citizenship.

The courts, criminal and civil, were to be transparent, uniform, equal, and free for all, a break with the Ancien Régime system, which was paper-ridden, slow, and costly. Serious criminal cases were heard by the departmental criminal tribunals—and tried by jury. The accused could only be brought before such a court after a preliminary investigation by a district judge (the prototype for France's modern-day—and controversial—*juge d'instruction*) and once a grand jury had arraigned the defendant. Judges were to be elected. In civil law, quarrelling citizens were to be encouraged to seek reconciliation first, before going to court. A free and compulsory system of arbitration was established and, where that failed, every district had an elected justice of the peace, as well as a *bureau de paix*, to make formal judgments. The basic principles of the legal system laid out by the National Assembly were retained—albeit in modified form—by Napoleon in the Civil Code of 1804, the Codes of Civil Procedure (1806) and Criminal Procedure (1808), and the Penal Code of 1810, but the institutional framework did not come out unscathed. The lower judicial institutions, including the justices of the peace, were reduced in number, so that they became less localized. Judges were no longer elected, but were appointed by Napoleon for life. The Emperor disliked juries, since they were unpredictable, but they survived even when criminal tribunals were abolished in 1811, for they were retained by the new assize courts. Trial by jury had become a permanent feature on the French judicial landscape, with all the civic responsibility and public engagement with the legal process which that implied.[35]

The revolutionary attack on privilege in the legal system had some radical implications for women. Frenchwomen were not politically emancipated, but the revolutionaries saw no inconsistency in expanding their legal rights within the family.[36] On 20 September 1792, the Legislative Assembly introduced one of the most radical divorce laws in European history. Men and women were allowed to divorce on equal grounds, including mutual consent, insanity, physical abuse, abandonment, incompatibility, and conviction of a crime bearing a penalty considered to be a mark of 'infamy'. The process was cheap and accessible: perhaps up to 100,000 divorces took place up to 1803. Depending upon the region, two-thirds to three-quarters of the initiators were women: it was they who made the most of the new law to escape from unhappy marriages. Women's rights to family property were also strengthened: in April 1791, the Constituent Assembly decreed that intestate inheritances had to be divided equally between all children, male and female. In March 1793, the Convention extended this law to all inheritances, making it retroactive to July 1789—and this was enforced through the courts. The laws on divorce and inheritance together altered relationships within the family, weakening the legal authority of both husbands and fathers, and gave women more rights as individuals, along with the ability to assert those rights in court. The Civil Code of 1804 reversed some of the more liberal aspects of the legislation, but a divorce law survived in France until 1816, when the restored Bourbon monarchy abolished it. The Napoleonic law on inheritances allowed parents to allocate between a quarter and a half of their estate to one heir (depending upon the total number of children), but the other heirs, male and female, still had to have an equal share of the remainder.[37]

The revolutionary transformation of politics and society left France a nation divided for more than a century and a half. The old certainties of the Ancien Régime—the King and Catholicism—were no longer able to unite French society. Yet the new order created by the French Revolution was divisive: no nineteenth-century regime before the Third Republic was able to forge a broad enough consensus about the place of the Revolution and its ideals in French society to survive for more than two decades. King Louis XVIII, Louis XVI's brother who came to the throne at the fall of Napoleon in 1814, wrote that 'I must not be a king of two peoples',[38] meaning that his task was to heal the schism between those who accepted the principles of the French Revolution and those who rejected them. Yet the restored Bourbon monarchy failed to do so, as did every subsequent regime until after 1870. This political and cultural struggle, alongside social developments and international crises, explains why since 1789 France has had no less than 'three monarchies, two empires, five republics and fifteen constitutions'.[39] There could never be any question of extirpating all of the revolutionary inheritance. The Count de Villèle, King Charles X's principal minister, may have bemoaned that 'the bonds of subordination are so loosened everywhere...the evil is in our mores, so influenced are we still by the Revolution',[40] but conservative governments could only go so far in their assaults on the legacy of the French Revolution. Charles X himself provoked a liberal backlash, culminating in his own downfall in 1830, when he attacked the freedom of the press, bolstered the position of the church, tried to introduce primogeniture in order to prevent the impoverishment of the nobility, and sought to indemnify the *émigrés*. As Charles's older and wiser brother Louis XVIII had better understood, there could be no restoration of the Ancien Régime without alienating important elements within French society and destabilizing the political order. Moreover, every successive regime found too much use in the new institutions to slash and burn the entire revolutionary inheritance. Legacies such as the administrative system, the prefects, and even parliamentary government seemed to offer more effective ways of governing the country, managing public opinion, and integrating the elites than the uneven patchwork of Ancien Régime institutions. Yet while every regime could adopt the Revolution's administrative structures and legal institutions, its political culture and ideology were another matter. Memories of the upheaval of the 1790s ran deep on both sides of the political divide and the great struggles of the nineteenth century were fought with reference to this inheritance. For some, the Revolution represented the Terror, anarchy, and the assault on the church; for others, it gave all people the promise of emancipation and human rights. Furthermore, there were bloody internecine struggles within the latter camp in the nineteenth century, as liberals, radicals, and socialists fought over how far the revolutionary legacy could be pushed towards greater democracy and social justice. The controversies continue to smoulder, flaring up at symbolic moments such as the bicentennial celebrations in 1989. In particular, the religious schism of the 1790s had left Catholicism associated with counter-revolution and monarchy (although no longer these days), while republicanism remains to this day equated with a staunch attachment to *laïcité*, or secularism, which partly explains the present-day emotions unleashed by the issue of whether or not Muslim women have the right to wear veils in public. So the Ancien Régime may well never have returned, contrary to the fears so eloquently expressed by Bertrand Lhodiesnière in 1814. But the Revolution ensured that the French people lived—and in many ways continue to live—with the aftershocks from its collapse in 1789.

Notes

I dedicate this chapter to my excellent friend Jane Laverick: a tribute to a specialist in the flamboyant early modern period from a writer working on the sartorially challenged French Revolution. My thanks also go to Bill Doyle, for some crucial points of information which have improved this article. All errors, however, are my own original creation.

1. Quoted in M. Lyons, *Napoleon Bonaparte and the Legacy of the French Revolution* (Basingstoke, 1994), 278.
2. Quoted in K. M. Baker (ed.), *The Old Régime and the French Revolution* (Chicago, 1987), 49.
3. A. Forrest, *Paris, the Provinces and the French Revolution* (London, 2004), 80–2, 190–1; M. Lyons, *France under the Directory* (Cambridge, 1975), 161; M. Biard, *Les Lilliputiens de la centralisation: Des intendants au préfets. Les Hésitations d'un 'modèle français'* (Seyssel, 2007), 265; Tocqueville, *Ancien Régime*, ch. 2.
4. Quoted in M. Crook, *Elections in the French Revolution: An Apprenticeship in Democracy, 1789–1799* (Cambridge, 1996), 30.
5. W. Doyle, *The Oxford History of the French Revolution* (Oxford, 1989), 97.
6. Crook, *Elections, passim*.
7. F. Furet, *Revolutionary France, 1770–1880* (Oxford, 1992), 537.
8. K. M. Baker, *Inventing the French Revolution: Essays on French Political Culture in the Eighteenth Century* (Cambridge, 1990), 167–99; R. Chartier, *The Cultural Origins of the French Revolution* (Durham, NC, 1991); P. McPhee, *The French Revolution 1789–1799* (Oxford, 2002), 85; C. Walton, *Policing Public Opinion in the French Revolution: The Culture of Calumny and the Problem of Free Speech* (Oxford, 2009), 198 and *passim*. See also J. D. Popkin, *Revolutionary News: The Press in France, 1789–1799* (Durham, NC, 1990).
9. Forrest, *Paris, the Provinces*, 111–12.
10. See e.g. L. Hunt, *Politics, Culture, and Class in the French Revolution* (Berkeley, Calif., and London, 1984); M. Ozouf, *Festivals and the French Revolution* (Cambridge, Mass., 1988);

C. Lucas (ed.), *The French Revolution and the Creation of Modern Political Culture*, ii. *The Political Culture of the French Revolution* (Oxford, 1988).
11. See E. Kennedy, *A Cultural History of the French Revolution* (New Haven, Conn., and London, 1989); J. Leith, 'Ephemera: Civic Education through Images', in P. Jones (ed.), *The French Revolution in Social and Political Perspective* (London, 1996), 188–202.
12. L. Hunt (ed.), *The French Revolution and Human Rights: A Brief Documentary History* (Boston and New York, 1996), 125.
13. See e.g. the speech by the government spokesman, Jean-Baptiste Amar, ibid. 137.
14. J. N. Heuer, *The Family and the Nation: Gender and Citizenship in Revolutionary France, 1789–1830* (Ithaca, NY, 2005), 49; D. Godineau, *The Women of Paris and their French Revolution* (Berkeley-Los Angeles and London, 1998), 101–7.
15. For the revolution in the colonies and the questions of slavery and the slave trade, see Y. Benot, *La Révolution française et la fin des colonies 1789–1794* (Paris, 1987); R. Blackburn, *The Overthrow of Colonial Slavery, 1776–1848* (London, 1988); C. L. R. James, *The Black Jacobins: Toussaint L'Ouverture and the San Domingo Revolution* (London, 1938); C. L. Miller, *The French Atlantic Triangle: Literature and Culture of the Slave Trade* (Durham, NC, 2008); N. Nesbitt, *Universal Emancipation: The Haitian Revolution and the Radical Enlightenment* (Charlottesville, Va., 2008); J. D. Popkin, *Facing Racial Revolution: Eyewitness Accounts of the Haitian Insurrection* (Chicago, 2007).
16. On the trials, tribulations, and resurgence of the clergy, see N. Aston, *Religion and Revolution in France 1780–1804* (Basingstoke, 2000); J. McManners, *The French Revolution and the Church* (London, 1969); M. Vovelle, *The Revolution against the Church: From Reason to the Supreme Being* (Cambridge, 1991); O. Hufton, 'The Reconstruction of a Church 1796–1801', in G. Lewis and C. Lucas (eds.), *Beyond the Terror: Essays in French Regional and Social History, 1794–1815* (Cambridge, 1983), 21–52.
17. For the struggles and survival of the nobility, see R. Forster, 'The Survival of the Nobility during the French Revolution', in D. Johnson (ed.), *French Society and the Revolution* (Cambridge, 1976), 133–5; A. Crubaugh, *Balancing the Scales of Justice: Local Courts and Rural Society in South-West France, 1750–1800* (University Park, Pa., 2001); J. Dunne, 'The French Nobility and the Revolution: Towards a Virtual Solution to Two age-old Problems', *French History*, 17 (Mar. 2003), 96–107; P. Higonnet, *Class, Ideology and the Rights of Nobles during the French Revolution* (Oxford, 1981); Lyons, *Napoleon Bonaparte*, 171–3; D. M. G. Sutherland, *France 1789–1815: Revolution and Counterrevolution* (London, 1985), 367, 374, 387. For a more recent work on noble attitudes and responses, attuned to the latest work on ideas of the 'nation', see Jay M. Smith, *Nobility Reimagined: The Patriotic Nation in Eighteenth-Century France* (Ithaca, NY, 2005).
18. C. Lucas, 'Nobles, Bourgeois and the Origins of the French Revolution', in Johnson, *French Society and the Revolution*, 90–7, 124–30, and W. Doyle, *Aristocracy and its Enemies in the Age of Revolution* (Oxford, 2009).
19. See the exchanges between Colin Jones and Sara Maza, which is scholarly debate at its best: witty, well-researched, and mutually respectful. C. Jones, 'The Great Chain of Buying: Medical Advertisement, the Bourgeois Public Sphere and the Origins of the French Revolution', *American Historical Review*, 101 (1996), 13–40; S. Maza, 'Luxury, Morality and Social Change: Why there was no Middle-Class Consciousness in Pre-Revolutionary France', *Journal of Modern History*, 69 (1997), 199–229. See also C. Jones, 'Bourgeois Revolution Revivified: 1789 and Social Change', in C. Lucas (ed.), *Rewriting the French Revolution: The Andrew Browning Lectures, 1989* (Oxford, 1991), 69–118, and S. Maza, *The Myth*

of the French Bourgeoisie: An Essay on the Social Imaginary, 1750–1850 (Cambridge, Mass., 2003).
20. R. Tombs, *France 1814–1914* (London, 1996), 441.
21. W. Doyle, *La Vénalité* (Paris, 2000), 110–23; W. Doyle, *Venality: The Sale of Offices in Eighteenth-Century France* (Oxford, 1996).
22. M. P. Fitzsimmons, *The Parisian Order of Barristers and the French Revolution* (Cambridge, Mass., 1987), 54–6, 180–2.
23. See e.g. Dora B. Weiner, *The Citizen-Patient in Revolutionary and Imperial Paris* (Baltimore, Md., 1993). I am grateful to my friend Professor Dave Andress for pointing me to this book.
24. P. M. Jones, *The Peasantry in the French Revolution* (Cambridge, 1988), 81–103, 128–32, 137–54; G. Lefebvre, 'La Révolution française et les paysans', *Études sur la Révolution française* (2nd edn., Paris, 1963), 343.
25. J. Blum, *The End of the Old Order in Rural Europe* (Princeton, 1978), 440–1; Jones, *Peasantry*, 89, 122–3.
26. C. Petitfrère, 'The Origins of the Civil War in the Vendée', in Jones, *French Revolution in Social and Political Perspective*, 339–58. See also D. M. G. Sutherland, *The Chouans: The Social Origins of Popular Counter-Revolution in Upper Brittany, 1770–1796* (Oxford, 1982).
27. G. Lefebvre, *Les Paysans du Nord pendant la Révolution française* (Bari, 1959), 514–25; Jones, *Peasantry*, 154–61, 165.
28. See the study of six villages in very different parts of France: P. M. Jones, *Liberty and Locality in Revolutionary France: Six Villages Compared, 1760–1820* (Cambridge, 2003).
29. T. J. A. Le Goff and D. M. G. Sutherland, 'The Revolution and the Rural Economy', in A. Forrest and P. Jones (eds.), *Reshaping France: Town, Country and Region during the French Revolution* (Manchester, 1991), 76; P. McPhee, *A Social History of France, 1789–1914* (2nd edn., Basingstoke, 2004), 100–1; D. Andress, *French Society in Revolution, 1789–1799* (Manchester, 1999), 163–4.
30. M. P. Fitzsimmons, *The Night the Old Regime Ended: August 4, 1789, and the French Revolution* (University Park, Pa., 2003), 178–210; McPhee, *Social History of France*, 130; Tombs, *France*, 160.
31. A. Soboul, *The Parisian Sans-Culottes and the French Revolution 1793–4* (Oxford, 1964), 33–4; W. H. Sewell, *Work and Revolution in France: The Language of Labor from the Old Regime to 1848* (Cambridge, 1980); R. M. Andrews, 'Social Structures, Political Elites and Ideology in Revolutionary Paris, 1792–4', *Journal of Social History*, 19 (1985–6), 71–112; M. Sonenscher, 'Artisans, *Sans-Culottes* and the French Revolution', in Forrest and Jones, *Reshaping France*, 108–9; D. Garrioch, *The Making of Revolutionary Paris* (Berkeley, Calif., and London, 2002).
32. A. Forrest, *The French Revolution and the Poor* (New York, 1981), 34–95.
33. C. Jones, 'Picking up the Pieces: The Politics and the Personnel of Social Welfare from the Convention to the Consulate', in Lewis and Lucas, *Beyond the Terror*, 62–3.
34. Lyons, *France under the Directory*, 84–95; Lyons, *Napoleon Bonaparte*, 103–10.
35. R. Allen, *Les Tribunaux criminels sous la Révolution et l'Empire 1792–1811* (Rennes, 2005), 275–6.
36. S. Desan, *The Family on Trial in Revolutionary France* (Berkeley, Calif., 2004), 312–13. See also B. Rose, 'Feminism, Women and the French Revolution', in Jones, *French Revolution in Social and Political Perspective*, 253–68.

37. Desan, *Family on Trial*, 93–100, 137, 141–2, 175–6; R. Phillips, 'Women and Family Breakdown in Eighteenth-Century France: Rouen 1780–1800', *Social History*, 2 (1976), 197–218.
38. Quoted in G. de Bertier de Sauvigny, *The Bourbon Restoration* (Philadelphia, 1966), 150.
39. Tombs, *France*, 3.
40. Quoted in Forster, 'Survival of the Nobility', 144.

Bibliography

Andress, David, *French Society in Revolution, 1789–1799* (Manchester, 1999).

Aston, Nigel, *Religion and Revolution in France 1780–1804* (Basingstoke, 2000).

Crook, Malcolm, *Elections in the French Revolution: An Apprenticeship in Democracy, 1789–1799* (Cambridge, 1996).

Desan, Susan, *The Family on Trial in Revolutionary France* (Berkeley, Calif., 2004).

Doyle, William, *The Oxford History of the French Revolution* (Oxford, 1989).

—— *Venality: The Sale of Offices in Eighteenth-Century France* (Oxford, 1996).

Fitzsimmons, Michael P., *The Night the Old Regime Ended: August 4, 1789, and the French Revolution* (University Park, Pa., 2003).

Forrest, Alan, *The French Revolution and the Poor* (New York, 1981).

—— *Paris, the Provinces and the French Revolution* (London, 2004).

Godineau, Dominique, *The Women of Paris and their French Revolution* (Berkeley-Los Angeles and London, 1998).

Jones, Peter M., *The Peasantry in the French Revolution* (Cambridge, 1988).

Kennedy, Emmet, *A Cultural History of the French Revolution* (New Haven, Conn., and London, 1989).

Lyons, Martyn, *Napoleon Bonaparte and the Legacy of the French Revolution* (Basingstoke, 1994).

McPhee, Peter, *Living the French Revolution* (Basingstoke, 2009).

Maza, Sarah, *The Myth of the French Bourgeoisie: An Essay on the Social Imaginary, 1750–1850* (Cambridge, Mass., 2003).

Woloch, Isser, *The New Regime: Transformations of the French Civic Order, 1789–1820s* (New York and London, 1994).

PART VII
TEST CASES

CHAPTER 28

THE NAPOLEONIC REGIMES

MICHAEL BROERS

The Napoleonic regimes, the Consulate of 1799–1804, and then the First French Empire from 1804 to 1815, have always proved baffling. Napoleon was anything but a convenient stereotype, and it stands to reason that his political creation soon comes apart in the hands of those who think in neat categories. This is not to say that close scrutiny cannot shed light on them, or even produce a reasonable definition of 'Napoleonism'. It is to say, however, that the path is not straight. Nevertheless, the fundamental role played by the Consulate and Empire in shaping modern Europe makes it all the more desirable to attempt to define them, if possible.

True to this convoluted spirit of enquiry, any examination of the nature of Napoleonic rule, whether in the context of defining the Ancien Régime or not, must be undertaken with a cardinal caveat always in mind: The choice of the plural—Napoleonic regimes—is not pedantic. Napoleonic rule was ever evolving during its short life. Hence its slippery nature.

It would be absurd to argue that the Consulate and the First Empire had nothing to do with the old order, or with the Revolution, for that matter. Obviously, they contained elements of both. The real point is to try to ascertain to what extent one predominated over the other, and, if so, whether this was by design or circumstance. Conversely, it must be asked if neither predominated, but if 'Ancien Régime' and 'Revolution' were rather held in balance by each other or, indeed, if both aspects of the past were eclipsed by something new. Accordingly, the relationship between the Napoleonic regimes and the old monarchy might best be approached through a set of questions. Did Napoleon and his collaborators wish deliberately to restore the Ancien Régime? This must entail exploring what they considered the Ancien Régime to be, in the first place. Second, did they almost inevitably end up salvaging and restoring the Ancien Régime, as much through *la force des choses* as by design? To accept this, even in part, may appear at first sight to be untenable, because old regimes are just that—old—and a restoration of such an organic growth would seem impossible in the space of a decade and a half. Yet, to sweep such a possibility aside is to ignore the durable analysis of Tocqueville, for, as he reminded his own generation, the French failed to shatter the foundations of the Ancien Régime, for all their best efforts in 1789. The third question sets out to test what is, perhaps, the most generally agreed definition of Napoleonic rule, that it was a meditated blending of the old order and the Revolution. This would confirm Napoleon's avowed policies of *ralliement* and *amalgame* as his permanent, unaltered *raison d'être*.

There are two defiant rejoinders to these three approaches, all of which to some degree acknowledge the importance of the old monarchy in Napoleonic calculations. One is that the Consulate and Empire, for all their outward trappings, were really the continuation of the Revolution by other means. This was certainly the view of most contemporary opponents of French hegemony, from the great chancelleries of Europe to the mountain lairs of Spanish *guerrillas* and non-juring Italian monks. Such an interpretation must encompass the possibility that the men of the 1790s were capable of redefining their Revolution by their own lights, and in terms somewhat different from those in which the revolutionary legacy has come down to the contemporary world. Finally, there is the prospect that the essence of the Napoleonic regimes represent something altogether new in the political culture of modern Europe; that they managed to break with the past, both that of the *longue durée* and of the 1790s. After all, in the wake of so unparalleled a life and career as that of Napoleon Bonaparte, anything is possible, even the choice of not having to choose.

An Attempted Restoration?

There has always been a powerful current of thought that sees in Napoleon little more than the return of the monarchy. When assessing the regimes in this way, however, two things must be borne in mind, and seldom are. First, which aspects of the old order were to be restored, and which left buried under the rubble of the revolutionary decade? There are two levels on which this case is made. The first is the public face Napoleon chose to give his rule, through the creation of a hereditary monarchy and the trappings that went with it. The other is his ready recourse to absolutist rule, in practice as well as appearance.

The most immediately obvious 'symptoms' of restoration were the transformation of the Republic into a hereditary empire in 1804, the refoundation of a court, particularly with its reliance on Bourbon forms of etiquette, and the creation of an imperial nobility. The court, dating *de facto* from 1802, collapses the Consulate into the Empire, causing Jacques-Olivier Boudon to see a monarchical restoration being planned carefully in gradual stages, well before 1804, with the coronation, the institution of the hereditary principle, and the creation of the offices of *Grandes Dignités* as but the culmination of a well-meditated process.[1] The regime's official tone is the most blatant evidence for a willed restoration, albeit without the real dynasty, as Napoleon rebuffed entreaties from Louis XVIII in 1800. On one hand, that entreaties were made at all is a clear sign that monarchists detected empathy with the Brumarian regime at a very early stage. Beside this, however, is the fact that they were quickly and rudely disappointed. It did not take Chateaubriand long to abandon Bonaparte nor, in truth, was the papacy long in following him.

The symbolism of the coronation shows, if anything, how mixed were Napoleon's own feelings about what sort of monarchy he wanted to create. The ceremony owed nothing to the old order, whatever the daily routine of the court might be like. As Luigi Mascilli Migliorini has pointed out, it took place in Notre Dame—the national arena, as it were— not in Reims or even St Denis; those of its invocations that were not Merovingian or Carolingian were, in fact, drawn from the era of Francis I, the costumes most obviously.[2] Its core was imperial, its setting was national; its attire evoked less the Ancien Régime, than the spirit of 'new monarchy' associated with the renaissance. Even the old order had been young once.

The other obvious aspects of the imperial regime that evoked the old order were the creation of the imperial nobility and the institution of the *majorats*. These extended aristocratic privileges beyond the milieu of the imperial family, who did enjoy their own fiefs and special judicial privileges. There are two things to note about both the new titles and the *majorats* that offer less a clear definition of their relationship to the Ancien Régime than a window on the ambiguous nature of the Napoleonic state. The *majorats* were all located outside France, as were the fiefs of the imperial family; this indicates at least two contradictory things. On the one hand, it shows clearly how firm the principle of the abolition of feudalism was within France, and, indeed, within all those lands under direct French rule before 1806; even the Emperor did not dare toy with the idea of violating this within these boundaries. Conversely, the fact that Napoleon had to keep them confined to the outer empire, mainly in central Germany, might be interpreted as a sign that Napoleon knew he was reverting to Ancien Régime mores in this, and that he had to keep it well away from the French, even those who benefited from them. Perhaps what is most approximate to the ways of the old order in the case of the *majorats* is the very fact that, through them, the Empire resurrected the kind of 'exceptions and inequalities' so typical of the pre-1789 world. The creation of the imperial nobility raises less of a problem on an institutional or political level than the *majorats*. Noble title went with the appropriate level of public service, pure and simple, and what distinguishes it from traditional nobility is far more important than any artificial resemblance on this level at least: imperial titles carried no legal privileges or exemptions from taxation; very few of them were hereditary. They could in no way form the basis or the goal of a 'social project', as was the case before 1789.

The Legion of Honour, and even the new imperial titles, were rapidly assimilated into the ethos—arguably more supposed than real—of a meritocratic political culture. Indeed, the closer a seemingly 'restored' entity is inspected, the more 'revolutionary' it emerges in essence. Howard Brown made this telling point, with respect to the special military tribunals created early in the Consulate, to deal with banditry and insurrection, which are often equated with the monarchy's provostial courts: 'Unlike the provostial courts of the ancien regime...the special tribunals held their trials in public, provided the accused with a defence lawyer, permitted oral debate, and relied on moral proof for conviction. These were all basic features of the revolutionary system of justice.'[3] The leap from the particular to the general is also clear, here. The Revolution had swept away inquisitorial justice, and Napoleon confirmed this, no small refutation of the old order.

Most of the case for a 'willed' restoration rests on appearance, ceremonial, and Napoleon's personal behaviour. The evidence is too disjointed to formulate a comprehensive argument beyond that of personal taste, and even then, particularly in the case of the coronation, the messages sent out were very mixed. Carolingian ceremony rubbed shoulders with trappings of the renaissance New Monarchy. The personification of power does not, really, sit easily with the concept of divine right kingship and Napoleon was too shrewd, and too much a man of his times—secular, cynical, and, above all, insecure—to couch his own claim to leadership in 'hallowed, traditional' terms. Napoleon wielded a more powerful authoritarianism than that of the old monarchy— there was no scope for a new Bodin in a secular regime—but not a restoration of the essence of traditional authority. Louis XVIII was quite right when he told Napoleon that he, alone, could guarantee this. The way in which Napoleon often chose to rule is a more complex matter, however.

Calm historicism is all very well. At the time, all these acts caused great dismay among former revolutionaries of all hues of moderation or radicalism, as did the creation of the Legion of Honour and the revival of noble titles. Thus, the deeper question remains. The increasingly hierarchical character of French society under Napoleon, and the virtual end of parliamentary politics, coupled to the Concordat and the readmission of the nobility to the public sphere in general, perhaps more than into high office in individual instances, are the most powerful and profound indicators of a change after 1799. A form of monarchy was apparent in 1802, and entrenched by 1804, none the less, whatever the views of purists. The regime 'at work', if not at its official coronation, looked the part. These are far more powerful grounds for a reversion to traditional monarchy than those often invoked, notably by dwelling on the symbolism of the coronation, or of Napoleon's revival of the Gallican Liberties in his quarrel with Pius VII after 1809. All this certainly meant casting aside much of the Revolution in favour of an autocratic regime, yet it is not enough to argue that the entrenchment of authoritarianism equates readily with a restoration. It is beyond doubt that whatever elements of the old order that re-entered French public life did so on Napoleon's terms; it is less clear that those terms were at one with even the old order as embodied by the regime of Louis XIV.

When Napoleon confronted the religious issue, he did so as a Gallican and a Jansenist, influences that become evident when it is recalled what the Concordat did not restore, something which becomes more important over time than what was allowed to return in Catholic worship. Social necessity dictated the re-establishment of organized religion, but the Catholicism of the Consulate and Empire reflected only one strand of the rich, varied piety of the old order. As is so often the case with Napoleonic 'restorations', what was not restored is probably more revealing than what was. The regular church did not return, partly as a result of the confirmation of the sales of *biens nationaux*, but even more because the contemplative life was incompatible with the new order. All regulars were not cloistered monks or nuns, any more than all Ancien Régime regulars were idle, but none returned. Of the colourful church calendar, only the barest bones survived; of the six High Days still permitted, one—the Assumption—was intended to be overshadowed by the new holiday of 'St Napoleon'—carefully positioned less to correspond with Napoleon's birthday, than to avoid spring, the time of the old *fête du Roi*. Confraternities shrank to one per parish, tightly controlled by the *curés*, their right to process confined to inside the parish church. Civil marriage remained the only legal contract, nor did baptism return in place of registration at the *mairie*. This was a very Jansenist restoration, at best, on very Gallican terms. Nor did it last long. Pius was already turning against Napoleon by 1805, as these terms were extended along with the Empire, to new areas. By 1809, it was in tatters; if Pius's own declaration is to be credited, the breach with Rome had far more to do with the Concordat, itself, and its extension beyond the borders of 1801, than the seizure of the papal states or the divorce.

The Ancien Régime did not speak with one voice, and the Napoleonic regimes seemed able to answer only to one of them, and that—the voice of the Maupeou–Terray–Calonne faction—was hardly representative of the world of the old monarchy. If Napoleon's policies and behaviour pointed backwards with any consistency, they were towards an Ancien Régime idealized by Voltaire in *The Age of Louis XIV*, rather than that discerned as the natural state of prerevolutionary France by Montesquieu in *The Spirit of the Laws*. The reality of the late Ancien Régime has been encapsulated in the words of William Doyle thus: 'Privileged, self-perpetuating oligarchies...had made the whole of prerevolutionary society a chaotic, irrational jungle of special cases, exceptions, and inequalities.'[4] Napoleon was willing to revive only that part of the Ancien Régime set on destroying exactly this anarchic pluralism.

Nevertheless, at a more subjective level, the deeper question remains: why bother? Why did Napoleon choose to use the titles he did? Why did he also allow the old nobility to use theirs again, even if he never conceded them any of their former privileges? Something of these deeper currents is reflected in the regime's resurrection of that almost ritually execrated practice, the *lettre de cachet*, rechristened the 'administrative measure' or the *mesure de Haute Police*, for a more bureaucratic age. It made a return, and was deployed, less through a desire to extend the police state into the family, than at the behest of families and communities exasperated, and often terrified, by those beyond the normal reach of the law—just as under the old order.[5] Be it a craving for noble status or peace within families and communities, such urges were considered deeply rooted in an earlier political culture, and appeased accordingly, in defiance of revolutionary principles.

LA FORCE DES CHOSES: RESTORATION AS PRAGMATISM

The whole tenor of Tocqueville's thesis is the immovability of the centralized French state, and its ability to reassert its ethos over the whole breadth of society, before, during, and after the Revolution. His goal, unachieved, was to have the third, and final, volume of his history of modern France show these forces at work under and through Napoleon. The power and continuing influence of Tocqueville's thoughts are reason enough to explore the view of the Napoleonic regimes as being led by instinct and circumstances to revive much of the old order. Napoleon and Tocqueville shared an ingrained sense that France could only be governed by a centralized authoritarian regime, even if they held this belief for utterly different reasons. Put another way, did Napoleon's 'star' lead him back to the age of Louis XIV whether he liked it or not?

This approach helps to explain the impulse behind the relentless centralization and professionalization of the structures of power. Seen thus, the regime became a mixture of the old order and the Revolution, but only because the revolutionaries themselves had been unable to shake off such basic instincts. The Terror had revived a quasi Conseil du Roi in the Committee of Public Safety; the Directory had hardened the Representatives on Mission into crypto-intendants, as well as proto-prefects, through the national agents. Here, both Napoleon and the post-1792 revolutionary regimes appear closer to the Ancien Régime paradigm of Louis XIV than did the monarchy itself in its last phases, and the aberrational period the becomes the reign of Louis XVI—save for his brief collaboration with Brienne over the Plenary Court—and the Revolution until 1791, after which older political norms fitfully re-emerged until definitively reasserted after Brumaire.[6]

At an even deeper level, if Tocqueville is correct in his belief that the irrecusable characteristic of the French as a nation was the preference for equality over liberty, then Napoleon only pushed post-Brumarian France the way it was going to fall. If so, Napoleon simply ran into the *masses de granit*, in the manner of a brick wall, and accepted that the Revolution could not eradicate the essence of French society. The real power of this interpretation lies in how it resolves the seeming incongruity of equating a regime that made no secret of its insecurity, nor its intrinsic lack of legitimacy, with anything resembling an old order. Napoleon's new court, his aching for a dynastic solution to his problems, the creeping Bourbon nomenclature, could never hope to restore the old order. That it takes time—centuries perhaps, generations, at least—for an 'old order' to evolve makes the idea of a Bonapartist restoration a contradiction in terms. However, if Napoleon's regime is perceived as tapping into, of surrendering to, the immovable elements of French society so deeply rooted in history, then assimilating the old and new regimes becomes obvious, as opposed to ridiculous.

However, in truth, Napoleon respected only one definition of the Ancien Régime, the 'Calonne paradigm', as it were. If a restoration it was, the increasing authoritarianism and centralization of the Consulate quickly disappointed and disaffected most militant royalists, even disregarding dynastic loyalty. Chateaubriand despaired of its censorship and the death of parliamentary politics, as well as its ill-disguised secularism; *Chouannerie* lingered on, to be defeated by arms and concessions over conscription, not the Concordat; there was little for the *parlementaires* or their version of old order, in the Napoleonic settlement, except jobs for their sons on Napoleon's terms in the service of his Code. The trappings of the Empire, all of which failed to cloak even more rigid political institutions, often intensified their alienation, rather than mellowed it. The old families stayed away from the new *lycées*, with their militaristic, ahumanist curriculum.

There were *ralliés*, to be sure. Their presence in the regime was, indeed, a sign of changed times, as was their willingness to offer passive acquiescence during the crucial period of pacification in the early Consulate marks. To a degree, there was a interest shared with the new regime in 'ending the French Revolution'.[7] This much can be said with some certainty: If the distinction between counter- and anti-revolution is accepted as generally valid in defining resistance to, and resentment of, the Revolution in the 1790s,[8] counter-revolutionaries could gain something from the Napoleonic settlement. Nonetheless, the question remains of the extent to which their *ralliement* was born of enthusiastic empathy, or a pragmatic acceptance of *faute de mieux*. Anti-revolutionaries, on the other hand, had nothing to hope for, but much to lose, from regimes intent on enforcing taxation, conscription, and legal and administrative uniformity with unheard of ruthlessness, and at hitherto unimagined levels of efficiency.

The legal classes encapsulate many of the contradictions those who had formed the backbone of the Ancien Régime found in trying to come to terms with the new order. Most of them welcomed the creation of a structured hierarchy of courts, and the reintroduction of professional standards and training. However, that hierarchy and those processes of training were now wholly under state control; the legal classes were now no longer a caste, but an open profession ordered by the state.[9] The nature of the *cours impériales*, and the circumstances surrounding their creation in 1810, are quite revealing of the contradictions involved. Napoleon has often been accused of attempting to resurrect the parlements through the *cours impériales*, and the archives leave no doubt that he actively sought to attract ex-*parlementaires* and their sons into the magistracy at this time. However, 1810 also saw the second massive purge of the magistracy—the first came in 1807—which, in reality, saw the removal from service of many men who had actually made their careers in the parlements. In terms of the resorts they served and their relationship to the lower courts, there are valid comparisons with the parlements; they were there to influence, to improve the quality of jurisprudence in the *tribunaux de première instance* and to strengthen the principle of hierarchy throughout the magistracy. Here, the Napoleonic reforms might readily be interpreted as appealing to the innate conservatism of a very conservative element of the Ancien Régime, of recognizing the necessity of accommodating the ingrained realities of French society. Nevertheless, this was not how many among the magistracy saw it. The Parisian Bar, in particular, chafed at state control, and, in truth, Napoleon harboured a distrust of lawyers that was most atypical of the Ancien Régime elites.[10]

The experience, and reactions, of the legal classes mirrors a wider phenomenon in the relationship of French society to the Napoleonic regimes, and it reduces the dilemma of definition to its very core: was Napoleonic policy a deliberate attempt to mix the old and the new, or was it about forcing the old into new forms? Of subjugating the useful elements of the old order into entirely new structures? Did *ralliement* and *amalgame* represent the realization that he could not leave the past behind, or were they about taming the Ancien Régime in the service of the Revolution?

Ralliement and *Amalgame*: A Synthesis of the Old and New Régimes?

There was a touch of Social Darwinism *avant la lettre* in Napoleon. He respected most in French society what had managed to survive the Revolution, which is not quite the same thing as accepting what might appear eternal and immovable, for more of the revolutionary innovations survived and prospered than were compatible with a restoration. If one, single element confirms this, it is the Civil Code, enshrining as it did equality before the law, freedom of conscience, the abolition of primogeniture, and a whole legal system that swept away inquisitorial methods in favour of the open, public trial. The Code, of itself, confirms a commitment to the new order more emphatically than the fiction of plebiscites or the dry, Roman-esque constitutionalism that 'entrusted the Republic to an hereditary Emperor'.

On another level, the revolutionary conflagration had proved that the *notables*, as quite distinct from the nobility, were the mass of granite on which France reposed. Nevertheless, the provincial nobility comprised a considerable part of the *notables*,[11] and Napoleon had to accommodate them. Initially, much the same attitude applied to the church. Catholic worship and the refractory clergy had survived assaults by successive revolutionary regimes that make the *dragonnades* of the *Grand Siècle* pall into insignificance. Hence, Napoleon applied not only a degree of restoration, but a policy of genuine *amalgame* towards the non-jurors. They had won the same respect from the First Consul as the equally obstinate rebels of the western departments, the men Napoleon himself called 'the giants of the Vendée'. Yet this attitude did not last long. The avowedly monarchical regime of the later years found itself more openly and bitterly at odds with the traditional enemies of the Revolution than had the Consulate.

In practice, *amalgame* could only work if different stripes of opinion found their own niches within the structures of the Consular regime. Jacques-Olivier Boudon interprets the re-establishment of associational life as a return to prerevolutionary corporatism, as the manifestation of Napoleon's realization that the society of individuals created by the Revolution was unworkable.[12] These policies might be better explained as part of a search for balance, not only because of the very uncorporatist state control they operated under, but by their composition. This was true from the apex of the state—where Fouché's police, composed in great part of ex-Terrorists, jostled with Talleyrand's ex-noble diplomats—to the parishes, where jurors and non-jurors, alike, were accommodated in areas where they were likely to find most local sympathy. Regional privilege returned in the matter of conscription, so serious was the quest for a broadly based regime, but at the extremes of politics: the only regions to receive artificially light quotas were revolutionary Paris and the western departments of the *Vendée militaire*. All of this was accompanied by a ruthless campaign of internal pacification that, if it aimed to be non-partisan, was inevitably directed more at royalism than the left, but in the longer term. When that campaign, and the wars of 1805–7, proved successful, the newly created Empire emerged in a more secure, but also very different set of circumstances.

Napoleon's rule rested on shifting currents; priorities and original policies predicated on a degree of political and social equilibrium were swamped by new realities. Mme de Staël was doubtless right in her acerbic insight into the nature of the Consulate: that it spoke with a forked tongue, the twin prongs of which were Cambacérès, the regicide, who invoked a 'revolutionized' France, and Lebrun, a royal bureaucrat, who talked of a France reunited to her glorious past. Citing Stäel, Pierre Serna emphasizes 'the ceaselessly ambivalent language' of the Consulate in its early days.[13] This does not quite fit the realities of the later Empire, however. Frédéric Bluche addresses this directly, citing the years 1804–7, those of the early Empire, as the only moment when the twin inheritances of the Ancien Régime and the Revolution were truly in equilibrium in what he terms 'the Napoleonic schema'. This was the moment when the political process was most in harmony with Napoleon's own, complex instincts.[14] The Bourbon and revolutionary baggage were evenly balanced in both hands.

However, there is still a problem of definition, even in so lucid an exposition as that of Bluche. Should this balance be interpreted, as he suggests, in terms of the centrist elements of Bonapartism, or was it really about neutralizing the extremes of Jacobinism and reaction? Bluche interprets *ralliement* and *amalgame* as symptoms of the insecurity of the Napoleonic regimes, and of their unending, almost desperate quest for legitimacy.[15] Mme de Staël, by contrast, saw them as a cynical, finely calibrated balancing act, to neutralize as many potential sources of opposition as possible. Staël quickly came to hate Napoleon with a vengeance, so much so that she never felt the need to give much thought to what the Consulate or the Empire were actually like; 'Oriental despotism' was usually enough for her. However, she knew what they were not—they were not the old order:

> Bonaparte hit upon the idea of making the counter-revolution work to his advantage by preserving nothing that was new in the state, save himself. He re-established the throne, clergy, and nobility: a monarchy, but without legitimacy or bounds; a clergy preaching only despotism; a nobility composed of old and new families, but with no power in the state, who were merely an ornament for absolute power.[16]

Staël loathed Napoleon enough to have called him a closet royalist or a crypto-Tarquin, had she thought for a moment it would have done him real harm, but she had too clear a grasp of contemporary politics to waste her breath. A despot her foe may have been, but he was no monarch of the old regime, nor did she accuse him of it.

Both Staël and Bluche are correct, but two further questions—at the very least—remain, unanswered by both views. Neither chose to take into account the possibility that the Napoleonic regimes were just that—different regimes—or that their policies evolved. The Empire's solutions to the quest for legitimacy were very different to those of the new, nervous, Consulate. After years satiated by military and diplomatic success, to say nothing of the successful implementation of the Civil Code, the new educational system, and the consolidation of a remarkably efficient bureaucracy, the Empire evolved a different view of the problem from that of a new, nervous regime, born of defeat and desperation.

In broader, more structural terms, there were even more profound changes at work in French society. The policies of the Consulate had come together to give shape to a France of two extremes, more generational in nature than political or economic. The regime was meant to rest on the provincial *notables*, the masses of granite—conservative, passive, stable—the beneficiaries, and targets, of *ralliement*. Napoleonic economic and social policies all sought to foster their interests. *Amalgame*, however, had created something quite contrary to this inert, parochial world. By 1804–7, the new *lycées*, military academies, and the university were producing a new, genuinely imperialist generation of administrators and soldiers in Napoleon's chosen mould, and their job was to move and to act. This is why Tocqueville's appraisal of the overwhelming power of continuity is not unassailable, at least until 1814. New forces had been unleashed by the Revolution, and moulded under Napoleon. All the contradictions and paradoxes of this powerful, dynamic regime were ultimately reflected in the composition of its elites.

The New Regime: Permanent Revolution by Other Means?

Mirabeau infamously advised Louis XVI as early as 1789 to leave the revolutionaries to their reforms, as they would make him a more absolute monarch than any of his predecessors. If Louis failed to take this to heart, Napoleon certainly did. Valérie Huet, with the coolness of the historian, compares the First Consul with neither Cromwell nor Julius Caesar, but with Octavian, noting slyly that Bonaparte knew it was better to appropriate the Republic than to restore the monarchy.[17] This he could do, as Louis XVI could not, because Napoleon was part-and-parcel of the Revolution. He was less its heir than its product, and the difference is crucial. Just because the way forward had changed course, it did not mean there was any going back. Napoleon saw, from beginning to end, that what made him powerful, and what gave his power its best hope of legitimacy among the French—if not abroad—was the work of the Revolution. Too much had been won, especially for a man with autocracy ingrained in him, to risk restoring what had so spectacularly failed its own architects. As one of the revolutionary generation, himself, Napoleon knew how the Revolution had been redefined by those who had initiated it. He could work through what later generations and contemporary foreign radicals could not bear to contemplate: that equality was more important to the revolutionaries than liberty, and that saving the principles of equality embodied in the Civil Code, to say nothing of the *biens nationaux*, far outweighed a free press or a powerful parliament. He went too far, but for the majority of the *masses de granit* this scarcely mattered until after 1812. Napoleon saved what mattered of the Revolution for most contemporary revolutionaries; he knew it was not elitist moderates like Staël who counted within the ranks of the left, but provincial Jacobins and Girondins, harried by royalist bandits, and the 'immortals' of the Plain, Thermidor, and

Fructidor, who knew elections meant upheaval. This is the main point in claiming that, above all else, Napoleon was a man of his times.

The first sign of knowing how to go forward, away from the old order, came immediately after Brumaire. The Consulate was a precarious regime at its inception, and Napoleon displayed his originality in extricating it from the dangers surrounding its birth. He reversed the logic followed by the Second Directory. Whereas the Directory operated from an increasingly narrow, if politically reliable, base at the ideological centre of French politics, Napoleon's twin prongs of *ralliement* and *amalgame* sought, in complete contrast, to embrace as much of the political extremes as were willing to cooperate. Pierre Serna has argued, convincingly, and with originality, that *ralliement* represents Napoleon's new and fundamental contribution to French political culture, 'the ideological force…invented by Bonaparte'.[18] Even his purges were even-handed. This was a very different approach to politics to that of the revolutionaries, and although the essence of *ralliement* may have amounted to a somewhat passive acceptance of the new regime, *amalgame* entailed active participation in its institutions and administration. If this was a 'return' to anything, it was, arguably, to the hopes of 1795, shorn of their parliamentary methods.

As Bluche has pointed out, although Napoleon's instincts were anti-parliamentary, authoritarian, and even monarchical, this did not mean he sought a restoration: 'Dictatorship and the stifling of liberties do not signify political reaction'; otherwise, as Bluche notes, the Terror would find itself well to the right of the restored monarchy under Charles X.[19] It is thinking of the most wishful kind to deny any links between authoritarianism and the radical wing of the French Revolution. *Dirgisme* has been part-and-parcel of the modern left ever since. Thus, Napoleonic dictatorship can quite plausibly be defined as a regime of the revolutionary left. For the Spanish historian Jesus Pabón, as for Bluche, the key to Napoleon's responses to revolutionary anarchy were not those of a reactionary, nostalgic for the old order or a return to some sort of lost normalcy, but those of a soldier. Pabón discerned clearly that what Napoleon loathed was disorder, which again should not be equated too readily with either reaction or opposition to the reforms of the Revolution.[20] Liberty is inimical to order in such circumstances; equality is not. His authoritarianism, in Bluche's words, was that of 'A leader (who became) over the years, more sure of himself, more and more (and too) confident of his military and civil ability (to rule), conscious of his power and cleaving to his star.'[21] There is much truth in this, and there is little of the reactionary here, haunted by a sense of loss in the wake of revolution.[22] Rather, he was the boldest of empire-builders.

Too often, the 'imperial aspect' of the Napoleonic regimes is neglected and misunderstood when trying to assess their nature. Empire was an exhilarating reality for contemporaries, more than just an alternative title to that of 'king'. At the very moment Napoleon might best be argued to have turned his regime into an imitation of the old monarchy, from 1807 onwards, in fact, his lieutenants—the young auditors of the Council of State, together with a host of French administrators, magistrates, and gendarmes, his own brothers, sisters, and in-laws—were bringing the whole panoply of revolutionary reforms, the Code above all, to some of the most inhospitable terrain in Europe. On the borders of the empire, a new generation of men formed in the *lycées,* the university, and the military academies relearnt the values of 1789, and the attitudes of 1792–3, in the 'thousand Vendées' of Italy and Spain, and in the truly feudal societies of Illyria, northern Germany, and Andalusia. Napoleon may well have intended these young civil servants to move the regime away from the baggage of the 1790s, as will be examined below, but their practical experience brought them back to many of the original tenets of the Revolution, whatever was aspired to in Paris. Bismarck is often said to have quipped that 'Russia should always look east; there, she stands for civilisation.' When the Napoleonic empire looked south, east, and north, it stood for the Revolution.

The true nature of even the most paradoxical regime is usually revealed in a crisis. Just as the unprecedented tide of the Revolution threw the crown and the Second Estate into an alliance that would have been unthinkable as late as 1788, so the Hundred Days—or, more accurately, his time on Elba—proved to Napoleon that the true, unalterable nature of his regime was revolutionary. It was the same for his embattled servants, on the far-flung frontiers and hinterlands of the Grand Empire, well before the final *dénouement*. However, it had not always been thus. It is arguable that Napoleon had a vision of his own, and that others shared it, and that its *raison d'être* was to escape the past, royalist and revolutionary alike.

The Fourth Dynasty: A Truly New Regime?

Official historians, and Napoleon, himself, elaborated a view of French history which saw absolutist centralization under an hereditary dynasty as inevitable, but only after each dynasty had exhausted itself, having failed to grasp the spirit of a new age; the Bourbons were baffled, and then battered, by the Enlightenment, whereas the Bonapartes were at one with it, and so could move forward with the French of their era.[23] It is always dangerous to take Napoleon at his word, especially as he expounded so many. Pabón got this exactly right, with enviable acumen, when he said that Napoleon's pronouncements can be of value to historians only when they are matched by his actions.[24] During the late Empire, he remarked that he knew his son would have to govern differently from him. When his attitude to personnel changes, professional formation, and the role of key institutions are brought together, actions emerge that underpin this assertion.

Each time Napoleon abandoned an attribute of the Revolution, he is assumed to be turning backwards, to thoughts of monarchical restoration; each time he sets himself against a facet of the old order, he is seen as the heir of the Revolution. Either way, Napoleon and his collaborators are seldom credited with any originality. Thus, it must be asked whether the Napoleonic regimes, and the late Empire, in particular, were bent on moving on from both their inheritances, towards something essentially, if hardly entirely, new and different? What of Napoleonic exceptionalism?

Claims for originality are generally based on initiatives that bore some fruit later in the century or beyond. The 'liberal empire' of 1815 was, undoubtedly, a sane if cynical response to the loss of *notable* support for the regime from 1812 onwards, and Napoleon's calculations were correct in these months, insofar as they foreshadowed many of the norms of the parliamentary regimes of the early nineteenth century. Luigi Mascilli Migilorini reveals how the Hundred Days was the period of his long rule that Napoleon used to underpin so much of his memoirs, and so made his whole political career, including his conception of himself as 'the people's king' appear forward-looking.[25] In similar vein, the Napoleonic regimes have been portrayed at their most innovative in the context of the plebiscites and the manner in which Napoleon 'personalized' power. There is great truth in this; Mascilli Migilorini has pinpointed the novel means plebiscites provided as the 'short-circuit representative basis of one-many', which allowed the Consulate to break with the narrow alternatives of Revolution or restoration, as well as making it into something different from an administrative monarchy on eighteenth-century lines.[26] This is a real insight, for Mascilli Migilorini has done most among historians to break the stranglehold of the 'either/or' conception of Napoleonic government. Steven Englund also discerns this when he says that Napoleon's power, 'both consular and imperial, pointed to something new: a form of democratic authoritarianism'.[27]

Nevertheless, there is evidence that Napoleon was already looking forward—away from both Revolution and reaction, well before his belated 'learning curves' on Elba and St Helena. His vision was neither liberal in the accepted nineteenth-century sense, nor democratic in that of the twentieth. Nor did it prevail, but this need not deny either its originality or its will to break with the past, both the proximate of the Revolution, and the *longue durée* of *le Grand Siècle*.

There would seem to be two periods that provide a window on Napoleon's mind, moments when he was able to do what he wanted, which do not quite correspond with Bluche's dates. The first is his Presidency of the Cispadane/Cisalpine Republic, 1796–7 which represents, effectively, his political apprenticeship; the second is roughly the years 1807–11, when the Empire was at its apogee. These were the times in his career when Napoleon was relatively unshackled by the need to appease the French revolutionary factions or pander to the past. The character of the regimes he shaped at these two points had much in common, but a comparison also shows how Napoleon's ideas had evolved over time, and to accept continuity and change as equal, integral parts of the Napoleonic regimes.

General Bonaparte created his own country in northern Italy in 1796–7, free from the grip of Paris. The sister republic had a *de facto* 'President'—Bonaparte—set over its Directory, whose members were chosen by Bonaparte, just as were the members of the upper house of its bicameral legislature. The warning signs should have been clear to Sieyès and company, two years hence, but they were not. The differences between his constitution and that of his own country were soon exposed as more important than the similarities, in terms of the structures of power, to the lasting regret of many of his early collaborators. Isser Woloch concludes that the Revolution meant very little to Napoleon, a quite different assessment from many other historians, but by pointing directly to his ability to outmanœuvre the Directorial elite, Woloch has provided powerful evidence of Napoleon's capacity to move his regime forward in an original direction.[28] Perhaps more significant in trying to untangle the nature of 'Napoleonism' is that the authoritarian regime Bonaparte created in Italy did not at all resemble the old order it replaced, nor did its dictatorial character impede the path of radical reform encapsulated by 4 August 1789. Howard Brown's formulation of 'liberal authoritarianism' as the hallmark of the early Consulate was already there for all to see over the Alps. In Milan and even more at Mombello are many of the constants of the Napoleonic regimes—powerful executive organs, subordinate legislatures, uncompromising administrative and social reforms, unbendingly uniform centralization.[29] Bonaparte had to work with what he found in Italy to create his state, and he outlined this with arresting clarity: 'There are, at present, three parties in Lombardy: 1. Those who will let the French lead. 2. Those who want liberty, and show this desire by their impatience. 3. The friends of Austria and the enemies of the French. I support and encourage the first, contain the second and repress the third.' Only his attitude to the third, when translated to France, would change under the Consulate. All three parties had their drawbacks as allies, however, and as time moved on, Napoleon sought to change things. Henceforth, he would produce his own men.

Staël noted with acidic intelligence of the early *ralliés* to the Consulate, that 'The revolutionaries and the royalists...did not believe themselves bound irrevocably to the fate of their master.'[30] Napoleon knew this, too, and sought to move the world on a generation as quickly as possible, to marginalize those he first had to court. *Les enfants du siècle* were hewed from different stone from the *Brumairiens*. The real 'high point' was 1810–11 when the Empire was at peace everywhere but Spain, and these years—those of the 'Grand Empire'—were their golden age. In this brief *conjoncture* of peace and European hegemony, *les enfants du siècle* rose through the ranks of a truly imperial administration with a rapidity unthinkable under the old order. Their task was to enforce the system honed in France since 1800, and, regardless of their backgrounds, this they did. In these years, so often regarded as stagnant, Napoleon found the men so craved by Eugène de Beauharnais, 'men whose personal interests are bound and at one with the state, not those whose private interests are merely reflected by that state's'. They were meant to be Napoleon's men, and through their most eloquent spokesman, Stendhal, they emerged as such, although If being a *Napoleonide* also meant being, in no small measure, a grateful heir of the Revolution, but not being its slavish imitator.

AN ANCIEN RÉGIME: YES OR NO?
A PLEBISCITE *EN SOI*

In the last analysis, both the Consulate and the First Empire owed more to the Revolution than to the Ancien Régime, and more to enlightened absolutism than either, but above all, they show Napoleon to be very much his own man, for all that he was a man highly attuned to the context of his own times. There is much to be said for Luigi Mascilli Migliorini's argument that the exceptional nature of the Revolution left its children with no compass, other than their own experience and that of remote, principally Roman, antiquity. The thrust of the *Mémorial* of St Helena was the originality of the Napoleonic regimes, and the uniqueness of the experience of an entire generation of Frenchmen; its conscious model was Caesar's *Gallic Wars*, for only antiquity could provide a sufficiently original vantage point to assess both the recent past and the future.[31] Steven Englund is also right, when he asserts that Napoleon could never be Louis XIV, not because he looked forward, but because his regime was rooted in a Revolution that had destroyed almost all of the old order.[32] Huet, by comparing the First Consul to Octavian, perhaps hits the mark best: if there is a key, it may be to see the Napoleonic regimes as quick to appropriate, and even swifter to move on. It would not last; the *masses de granit* were reconverted to parliamentary liberalism after 1812, and *les enfants du siècle* banished to the margins, but while Napoleon held sway, the new forces prevailed. There were, indeed, elements of the Ancien Régime in both Napoleonic regimes, but they belonged to the vision of the narrowest of its cliques, the frustrated proponents of the *thèse royale*. Above all, no vision but their own—imperialist, reforming, aggressive, optimistic—could never do for men with such ambition as Napoleon and *ses enfants du siècle*. The true oracle remains Stendhal.

Notes

1. Jacques-Olivier Boudon, *La France et l'Empire de Napoléon* (Paris, 2006), 43–52.
2. Luigi Mascilli Migliorini, *Napoleone* (Rome, 2002), 235.
3. Howard G. Brown, *Ending the French Revolution: Violence, Justice and Repression from the Terror to Napoleon* (Charlottesville, Va., and London, 2006), 347.
4. William Doyle, *The Ancien Regime* (Basingstoke, 2001), 3.
5. Michael Sibalis, 'Prisoners by *mesure de Haute Police* under Napoleon I: Reviving the *lettres de cachet*', *Proceedings of the Annual Meeting of the Western Society for French History*, 18 (1991), 205–13.
6. P. M. Jones, *Reform and Revolution in France: The Politics of Transition, 1774–1791* (Cambridge, 1995); John Hardman, *French Politics, 1774–1789* (London, 1994).
7. Brown, *Ending the French Revolution*, passim.
8. The two terms were first and best distinguished from each other and defined in: Colin Lucas, 'Résistances populaires à la Révolution dans le Sud-Est', in Claude Langlois (ed.), *Mouvements populaires et conscience sociale (xvie–xixe siècles)* (Paris, 1985), 117–35; Roger Dupuy, *De la Révolution à la Chouannerie* (Paris, 1988).
9. Michael Fitzsimmons, *The Parisian Order of Barristers and the French Revolution* (Cambridge, Mass., 1987), 130–1.
10. Fitzsimmons, *Parisian Order of Barristers*, 154–61.
11. Louis Bergeron and Guy Chaussinand-Nogaret, *Les 'Masses de granit': Cent mille notables du Premier Empire* (Paris, 1979).
12. Boudon, *La France et l'Empire*, 71–2.
13. Pierre Serna, *La République des Girouettes* (Paris, 2005), 474–5.

14. Frédéric Bluche, *Le Bonapartisme: Aux origines de la droite autoritaire, 1800–1850* (Paris, 1980), 90.
15. Ibid. 26.
16. Madame de Stäel, *Considérations sur la France*, cited in François Furet, *Revolutionary France, 1770–1880* (Eng. tr. Oxford, 1995 edn.), 249.
17. Valérie Huet, 'Napoleon I: A New Augustus?', in Catherine Edwards (ed.), *Roman Presences: Receptions of Rome in European Culture, 1789–1945* (Cambridge, 1999), 53–69, 54.
18. Serna, *La République*, 468.
19. Bluche, *Bonapartisme*, 88–9.
20. Jesus Pabón, *Las ideas y el sustema Napoleonicos* (Madrid, 1944), 12–13.
21. Bluche, *Bonapartisme*, 89.
22. Peter Fritzsche, 'Specters of History: On Nostalgia, Exile, and Modernity', *American Historical Review*, 106 (Dec. 2001), 1587–1618.
23. June Burton, *Napoleon and Clio: Historical Writing, Teaching and Thinking during the First Empire* (Durham, NC, 1979).
24. Pabón, *Las ideas*, 14.
25. Migliorini, *Napoleone*, 440.
26. Ibid. 178–9.
27. Steven Englund, *Napoleon: A Political Life* (New York, 2003), 222.
28. Isser Woloch, *Napoleon and his Collaborators: The Making of a Dictatorship* (London and New York, 2001).
29. Melchiore Gioa won the *concorso* for the Cisalpine constitution not because he advocated Italian unity, but for his emphasis on centralization.
30. Cited in Serna, *République*, 475.
31. Mascilli Migliorini, *Napoleone*, 434–4.
32. Englund, *Napoleon*, 221.

Bibliography

Alexander, Robert S., *Napoleon* (London, 2001).
Bergeron, Louis, and Chaussinand-Nogaret, Guy, *Les 'Masses de granit': Cent mille notables du Premier Empire* (Paris, 1979).
Bluche, Frédéric, *Le Bonapartisme: Aux origines de la droite autoritaire, 1800–1850* (Paris, 1980).
Boudon, Jacques-Olivier, *La France et l'Empire de Napoléon* (Paris, 2006), 43–52.
Brown, Howard G., *Ending the French Revolution: Violence, Justice and Repression from the Terror to Napoleon* (Charlottesville, Va., and London, 2006), 347.
Burton, June, *Napoleon and Clio: Historical Writing, Teaching and Thinking during the First Empire* (Durham, NC, 1979).
Dwyer, Philip (ed.), *Napoleon and Europe* (London, 2001).
Ellis, Geoffrey, *Napoleon* (Harlow, 1997).
Englund, Steven, *Napoleon: A Political Life* (New York, 2003).
Geyl, Pieter, *Napoleon: For and Against* (London, 1986 edn.).
Huet, Valérie, 'Napoleon I: A New Augustus?', in Catherine Edwards (ed.), *Roman Presences: Receptions of Rome in European Culture, 1789–1945* (Cambridge, 1999), 53–69.
Migliorini, Luigi Mascilli, *Napoleone* (Rome, 2002).

Pabón, Jesus, *Las ideas y el sustema Napoleonicos* (Madrid, 1944).
Woloch, Isser, *The New Regime: Transformations in the French Civic Order, 1789–1820s* (New York, 1994).
—— *Napoleon and his Collaborators: The Making of a Dictatorship* (London and New York, 2001).
Woolf, Stuart J., *Napoleon's Integration of Europe* (London, 1991).

CHAPTER 29

REFORMED AND UNREFORMED BRITAIN, 1689–1801

JULIAN HOPPIT

As close neighbours, Britain and France naturally had much in common in this period. Both were composite states where Christianity was a major, if often contested, feature of everyday life; much authority was exercised by monarchs and nobles; slow yet marked economic change occurred; striking intellectual developments were experienced; and nationalism, militarism, and imperialism flourished. Proximity and similarity inevitably led to their histories being interwoven, not least by waging war against one another time and again. Yet if France was an Ancien Régime, Britain was not.[1]

Very few historians have argued otherwise. Indeed, only one has attempted to do so in a more-or-less concerted way. J. C. D. Clark, in a book first published in 1985, with a significantly revised 2nd edition in 2000, argued for a fundamental continuity in the nature of *England's* regime between the Glorious Revolution of 1688 and the Great Reform Act of 1832.[2] In his view, during that period Ancien Régime England was a 'confessional state' with 'three essential characteristics: it was Anglican, it was aristocratic, and it was monarchical. Gentlemen, the Church of England, and the Crown commanded an intellectual and social hegemony.'[3] In practice his focus was particularly upon certain beliefs and ideas. A fundamental point of departure was that 'Traditional society looked, above all, to two ideals: the ideal of a Christian, and the ideal of a gentleman.'[4]

Clark's book elicited a good deal of discussion and debate.[5] Many reviewers applauded his emphasis upon the significance of religion in eighteenth-century England, and his book has had a lasting impact in that regard. Also uncontested was Clark's emphasis upon the need to place England within its full European context, not least because he followed an existing historiographical lead that others have further developed independent of Clark's general thesis.[6] Few, however, believed that he had persuasively shown that England was indeed an Ancien Régime. For example, O'Gorman argued, rather, that

> Eighteenth-century Britons...conceived of themselves less within *ancien régime* perspectives than within their direct opposite. The cluster of organizing concepts which meant so much to ordinary Englishmen cannot be contained within what is normally understood as an *ancien régime* model of social and political life: the freeborn Englishman, the Anglo-Saxon constitution, the freedom of the press, the virtues of a protestant nation, the Glorious Revolution.[7]

Many other criticisms were voiced, often relating to the implications of the observation that 'If the English went to Italy to see Antiquity, foreigners came to England to see modernity.[8] Clark defended his thesis vigorously, but confessed that he used the concept of an Ancien Régime more rhetorically than practically, 'to negate former reifications in terms of bourgeois modernity'.[9] But he has not held to this important concession, continuing to use the concept in the second edition of his book, which sought 'to outline a social order which preserved its hegemony despite repeated internal challenge (and sometimes armed insurrection)' and 'what is addressed under [ancien régime] is a hegemonic set of ideas which provided the ideological framework within which changes happened'.[10]

Clark's premise and argument are unpersuasive. It is highly questionable to characterize a regime largely on the basis of certain elements of what has been called public doctrine. A regime, in the normal politico-social sense of the word, is the mixture of institutions and ideas, including culture, by which people are actually governed.[11] Clark's focus is much narrower, being largely unconcerned with institutions, the practice and experience of government, or large bodies of relevant ideas. Nor is he much concerned to establish the means by which the doctrines he explores became allegedly hegemonic, inevitably so given his dependence upon printed sources. Nor, finally, is Clark right to argue that the changes he sees taking place between 1828 and 1832 radically reconstituted the regime, presumably from *ancien* to *moderne*.

Clark is certainly not alone in using the idea of an Ancien Régime so loosely that it is robbed of utility. As is well known, the term was invented to help clarify what the revolutionaries in France were reacting to from 1789. However, it has been employed in many different ways.[12] At its most simple it was the previous or old mode of government; it was no more than what had gone before. Such a general definition allows the term to be applied very widely, for all previous regimes are thereby *ancien*. In much the same vein, the term has also been used adjectivally, as in 'ancien régime Europe', by which is usually meant the period of Louis XIV and his two successors (1643–1793), or some part thereof. But, except to be somewhat evocative, there is little point in such broad approaches, for they employ Ancien Régime merely as a loose *label*.[13] A slightly more sophisticated form of this involves comparing or juxtaposing the pre- and post-1789 regimes. In particular, the 'modernization' or 'rationalization' undertaken by the revolutionaries is contrasted with an Ancien Régime often deemed to have been traditional and feudal, chaotic and capricious. But such a contrast is liable to be teleological—the pre-1789 regime is not seen in the round or in its own terms—or value laden—establishing 'modern' and 'rational' government was a good thing—or both, quite apart from the fact that defining 'modernity' and 'rationality' is so problematic as to make them of highly questionable value.[14]

The applicability of the idea of an Ancien Régime to different states can only be tested by defining it. It might, for example, be deemed to constitute certain key elements, such as feudalism and privilege, or certain structures of authority. The approach here follows the latter, more analytical option. Arguably, Tocqueville gave the term its most significant and useful form as a *concept*. To him it comprised those broad features within political society—the interplay of institutions, social classes, and ideals or culture—that collapsed rather unexpectedly, strikingly quickly, and, for a while, utterly. It is important to note that he was particularly interested in exploring the development of profound contradictions within French political society from the middle of the seventeenth century. These were the product of change not stasis; he described a process and analysed a dying organism. His interpretation has of course been challenged by many subsequent studies. Yet if his emphasis upon the threats faced by the traditional aristocracy in the face of increasing centralization has, at different times, been superseded by an emphasis upon class, fiscal crises, nationalism, religion, the public sphere, and so on, his stress upon the need to identify the inherent tensions within French political society has not. He was right to argue that central to the Ancien Régime was that attempts to change the distribution of authority so alienated significant interests that the whole of French political society was brought to the edge of a great precipice.

Britain was not an Ancien Régime in this period because, despite its many similarities to France, its political society retained authority and legitimacy as it changed to altered circumstances. In large part this was because of major changes in the half-century after the collapse of the authority of Charles I. Between 1642 and 1660 civil war, regicide, and republicanism did turn the world upside down. It was not just that some old institutions were swept away, such as the Court of Wards, but that assumptions about the nature of government were changed forever. There was, of course, a sharp reaction after the Restoration in 1660, but political society in Britain was now on a different footing to that before the outbreak of civil war. However, this produced contradictions, especially regarding the relationship between faith, citizenship, and political authority. Dramatic tensions emerged between the overwhelmingly Protestant political nation and Charles II (1660–85) and James II (1685–8) when they both clearly turned towards France and Rome in the 1670s. The 'Glorious Revolution' of 1688–9, which saw the Roman Catholic James forced from his throne into exile in France, was only possible because in England he had lost the confidence of his natural, but utterly Anglican, allies: his two daughters; the Church of England; much of the judiciary; Oxford and Cambridge universities; and the landed elite. They had been petrified that he was undertaking a revolution in church and state, towards Catholicism and absolutism.

The Glorious Revolution may not have been glorious, especially in Ireland, but it was a revolution. Crucially, parliament came to provide the focal point for absolute authority and decision-making. Doyle has argued that the crucial characteristic of Ancien Régime societies was the 'intense confusion of powers and perpetual overlaps of unequal jurisdiction, in which the king, so far from imposing an unchallengeable authority, was constantly bargaining with his subjects at a number of different levels'.[15] After 1688 this was no longer the case within England, nor after 1707 within Scotland, though it did remain true of Ireland for most of the eighteenth century. The Glorious Revolution changed the distribution of central political power towards parliament as a forum for decision-making between commons, peers (secular and spiritual), and monarch, with legislation coming to play a very much larger part in political society, central and local. Absolute authority, frequently exercised, was now found in parliament, limiting the significance of overlapping jurisdictions that undoubtedly existed. As Blackstone, the great jurist, put it in 1765, parliament

> hath sovereign and uncontrollable authority in making, confirming, enlarging, restraining, abrogating, repealing, reviving, and expounding of laws, concerning matters of all possible denominations, ecclesiastical, or temporal, civil, military, maritime, or criminal: this being the place where that absolute despotic power, which must in all governments reside somewhere, is entrusted by the constitution of these kingdoms.[16]

After 1688, in order to manage parliament better, executive authority gradually shifted to a cabinet and departments of state and away from the court and privy council. Working with and through parliament became essential to executive government. The failure of the crown to use its power to veto legislation after 1708 partly indicates its success in managing the legislature, but also signifies its realization that such a right was no longer generally deemed reasonable.

The revolutions in the seventeenth century transformed the nature of political authority in Britain, allowing most major challenges in the following century to be addressed successfully. Certainly there were failures: American Independence in 1776 and Irish rebellion in 1798 made very clear that disastrous contradictions could develop. Importantly, however, both were largely extra-British crises that led to pressure on political authority in Britain, but not its collapse or a general sense of its illegitimacy. Challenges within Britain most usually led to change, not contradiction, and a new workable consensus. How?

Schematically, in this period Britain's regime came periodically under extreme pressure from six main sources: competing claimants to the throne; the religiously disaffected; acute fiscal strain; the elite's enthusiasm for oligarchy; new economic interests; and resistance to English imperialism. All of these had been experienced before 1688, but they took on a new significance thereafter, not least by often intermingling. In what follows there is only space to sketch their nature and how British political society reacted to them. The conclusion argues that it is best to see Britain's regime in this period as neither *ancien* nor *moderne* but, rather, as flexible and negotiated amongst a wide range of political participants.

In Britain, uncertainties about the relationship between faith, citizenship, and office-holding grew dramatically following the Reformation in the sixteenth century. Paradoxically, though monarchs now headed the church and were notionally the absolute fount of authority, the prevalence of anti-Catholicism meant that monarchs lacked full freedom of choice in the religion of either themselves or their people. James II discovered this to his cost in 1688. William III (1689–1702) may have been Dutch, Calvinist, and detached, but he was Protestant and married to Mary II (1689–94), James's eldest daughter. In 1714, following the Act of Settlement of 1701, the throne once again ignored strict lines of hereditary descent to pass from the now childless Anne (1702–14), James's youngest daughter, over dozens of legitimate but Catholic claimants, to the Lutheran George of Hanover (1714–27) and his heirs.

Not all within Britain were prepared to abandon their oaths to James II after 1688, or their belief that the succession was a matter for God alone. For a generation, the nonjuring schism was an important feature, but more of a threat was posed by attempts to restore James and his heirs. Jacobitism was more extensive and powerful than used to be thought, but when all is said and done it did fail. It is telling that a plot to assassinate William III in 1696 led to a huge wave of enthusiasm towards him. A large number of minor Jacobite plots were also snuffed out without great difficulty. Even two major armed risings in 1715–16 and 1745 unequivocally failed. Both posed substantial threats to the governments of the day, but neither commanded enough military power or popular support to succeed. Whatever complaints there were about foreign-born kings and their foreign ways, the failure of the two risings confirmed that enough within Britain preferred the revolution constitution to the old order; limitations on the political independence of the crown were valued subtly, but deeply.

The second pressure that the regime faced was from the religiously disaffected. If in 1688–9 the political nation had decided that it was to be governed by a Protestant regime, there was uncertainty about whether it had to be more narrowly Anglican.[17] William III and George I were not and in Scotland Presbyterianism was very strong. Indeed, varieties of Protestantism vied with one another for supremacy and legitimacy, a contest which can be traced back to the sixteenth century and which became bitterly intense during the era of the civil wars and interregnum. Partly in reaction to the chaos of that period, the Restoration religious settlement led in England to the imposition of Anglicanism both as the state religion and as a requirement for much officeholding. Religious orthodoxy and unity were seen then as essential to good government, and to be enforced by legislation such as the Test and Corporation Acts (1672 and 1661 respectively). But it meant that many honest, educated, wealthy, and God-fearing Protestants were thereby denied full citizenship. William III attempted to resolve this immediately by widening the definition of the Church of England to bring most Protestants within its compass. Yet this 'comprehension' was defeated in parliament, and in 1689 only a more limited 'toleration' to worship by Protestant dissenters was enacted. Such a toleration was, nonetheless, a major step, for it legalized many different variants of Protestant belief and somewhat subverted the hegemony of the Church of England. But dissenters were still disadvantaged and had either to accept their political exclusion or conform, fully or partially. In fact, many suspended their principles once a year to take communion at the parish church to bring them within the pale. Though this 'occasional conformity' was lambasted by staunch Anglicans, it was only formally legislated against between 1711 and 1719. From 1727 Indemnity Acts were passed in most years effectively to allow Protestant Nonconformists to hold office without fear of prosecution, even though the Test and

Corporation Acts remained in force. This was nothing more than a fudge, a realization that strongly held divergent views on fundamental matters of faith had to be accommodated if the regime was to function effectively. (This was at one with the fact that the Glorious Revolution had established Presbyterianism as the state religion in Scotland and that the same religion received a state subsidy in Ireland, even though the (minority) Church of Ireland was the established Church.) Cries for the repeal of the Test and Corporation Acts did not become loud until new radical, rights-based, ideologies developed in the 1770s and 1780s, but for decades it is striking that Britain had had no *cause célèbre* to rival Jean Calas or the Chevalier de la Barre.

Throughout the seventeenth and eighteenth centuries central government was under considerable pressure to finance its ambitions, mainly military. This is the third challenge to be considered. In the 'Stop of the Exchequer' in 1672, Charles II effectively defaulted on the crown's debts; in the 1690s the government was deemed such a poor risk that it could often only borrow money in the markets at more than twice the legal maximum set by the usury laws; in 1720, mimicking John Law's efforts in France, the 'South Sea scheme' to reschedule the national debt collapsed; and from the late 1750s there were widespread fears of a certain, perhaps imminent, state bankruptcy, with even Adam Smith amongst the pessimists. Yet the state avoided financial catastrophe by finding the ways to tax its people heavily without encountering significant resistance and making concessions only when marked resistance was occasionally encountered within Britain, as in the 'Excise crisis' of 1733. Several factors explain this: a dependence on an excise levied at point of production rather than point of sale (and so somewhat hidden from view and difficult to avoid); the relatively trivial privileges and exemptions granted to the propertied, including the church; the relative efficiency of the state's bureaucracy; the use of parliament rather than the crown to authorize and audit revenue raising; and separating out the expenses of the crown, the 'civil list', from those of the state more generally. A highly sophisticated fiscal system was created, not least in the creation of a funded national debt—that is, loans raised with the parliamentary promise of specified future stream of taxes for their repayment. This allowed Britain generally to wage wars with conspicuous success, becoming a great power by 1713 and an imperial power with global reach by 1763. It speaks volumes that, despite its success in the American War of Independence (1775–83), it was the French not the British state which went bankrupt.

The fourth main challenge to Britain's regime came from the growth of oligarchy, itself the reaction to the political divisions experienced under William and Anne. After the Restoration, bitter memories of the civil wars and interregnum united England's elite in a deep unease about the threat to order and property from the bulk of society. James's Catholicism began to strain that unity in the late 1670s, but the Glorious Revolution broke it, opening up major opportunities for the people to contest the course of public policy and the nature of governance. The scale of the issues was, of course, huge: establishing a working relationship between religion and politics; agreeing the monarchical succession; and funding and fighting two major wars against France. Little wonder that in England the electorate, encouraged by the 1694 Triennial Act (requiring general elections at least every three years), was highly active. Moreover, politics spread more generally, particularly through addresses (over 4,300 to the crown between 1689 and 1714), petitions, and print. Annual sessions of parliament encouraged petitions to be sent to Westminster in substantial numbers, while the collapse of pre-publication censorship in 1695 (the authorities could not cope with the growing torrent of printed words) led to an explosion of broadsides, pamphlets, and books, the numbers of works published annually in Britain rising from about 1,300 in the 1670s to around 2,000 in the 1700s. Many of these works were deeply corrosive: lies, satire, and irony were commonplace.[18] Resistance to the Hanoverian succession in 1715, including riots, squibs, and an armed rising, made plain just how fine was the line between order and chaos.

This turmoil deeply unsettled the social and political elite, but by 1725 it had been significantly contained. Most visibly, the Septennial Act of 1716 now required general elections only every seven years. But not only did they now become infrequent, they became much more costly and, thereby, exclusive. The growing influence of the traditional elite over constituencies led to the proportion of seats being contested shrinking from a peak of 44 per cent in the general election of 1705 to a low point of 19 per cent in 1761. Second, both George I and George II committed themselves to one-party, Whig, rule. The Tories had long been less than wholly enthusiastic about the Hanoverian succession and the Jacobite rising of 1715–16 allowed them to be tarred with the brush of sedition. Major and minor offices of state became out of bounds to them. Moreover, their high church allies also lost some of their voice when Convocation, the church's representative assembly, was prevented from meeting after 1717 and Francis Atterbury, the Jacobite bishop of Rochester, was sent into exile in 1723 after a show trial. Third, the authorities became increasingly skilled in using the press to present their policies, particularly Robert Harley, effectively prime minister, 1710–14, and Robert Walpole, usually said to be Britain's first prime minister, 1721–42. Fourth, the scope for popular agitation was circumscribed in 1715 when the Riot Act empowered the authorities to disperse a crowd of as little as twelve people with lethal force. This was at one with a huge growth in capital punishments in the period, the so-called 'Bloody code', best symbolized by the passage of the 'Black Act' in 1723 that specified the death penalty for over fifty offences. Finally, Britain avoided major war between 1713 and 1740 and so some of the stresses and strains that had beset the previous generation.

The argument then is that the challenges faced before 1714 led in the first instance not to overwhelming contradictions, but, at its upper levels, to a markedly more oligarchic regime. However, that regime might itself have led to irresolvable problems. Certainly critiques of oligarchy began to mount in the 1760s: that most of those who had the vote were unable to exercise it; that the House of Commons lacked sufficient independence from peers and crown; that successive Whig ministries offered monotonous, unprincipled, visions of the public good; that the central state retained far too many redundant yet expensive offices filled on the basis of connection rather than ability; and that the law was oppressive.[19] The youthful George III (1760–1820) was clear that this did not constitute good governance, with deep rifts opening up between him and the Whig establishment. Yet in practice, oligarchy had not and did not mean tyranny was common. Critically, the press remained remarkably vital, bounded by the law of libel rather than a state-appointed censor. It drew strength from other aspects of a developing urban culture, notably clubs and coffee-houses.[20] The sense of the people was also periodically expressed loudly and effectively, for example in 1733 to defeat Walpole's rather pragmatic proposal to shift the balance between customs and excise, or in 1753–4 to urge the repeal of the Jewish Naturalization Act. Third, the Riot Act notwithstanding, the crowd remained an important factor in the eighteenth-century polity: exclaiming against moving food out of a region, or novel ways of marketing; breaking down contested enclosures or turnpikes; or challenging new working conditions or lower wages. Last, but not least, some semblance of natural justice was preserved via trial by jury, judicial interventions, and royal pardons. Legal fictions to ameliorate the bloody code became commonplace.

In the middle of the eighteenth century, Britain's executive and legislature certainly appeared oligarchical and exclusive. But, in addition to the qualifications just offered, there were also many other sites of authority within the political regime which were much more participatory, communitarian, and inclusive, albeit often within a framework of responsibilities that had a statutory basis. In particular, parishes, boroughs, and counties were important founts of government. In 1700 there may have been around 50,000 parish officers in England, or an average of about five per parish. Parish constables, overseers of the poor, and churchwardens might undertake a large amount of business, with vestries an important forum for debate and decisions. In nearly 200 boroughs there were mayors, aldermen or councillors, chamberlains, recorders, clerks, coroners, and bailiffs. For the forty English counties, justices of the peace (JPs) were pivotal, having both judicial and administrative functions—in 1702 there were over 5,000, by 1761 perhaps 10,000, though far from all of these were active. All these officers, from the parish constable to the JP, were male, local, unsalaried, and amateur, often simply taking their turn to administer authority for the good of their community. In places there was a growing reluctance to do this, with the rich increasingly unwilling to undertake the labour of being JPs, and boroughs having to resort to paid officials, but in many places the system remained more or less intact until the early nineteenth century. There was a profound antipathy towards the growth of central powers, with local autonomy highly prized. Even much later Beaumont, Tocqueville's colleague, believed that 'there is not a parish in England which does not constitute a free republic'.[21] The language here is very telling.

Arguably, the most important aspect of local government was in the administration of the Poor Laws, whereby a rate was levied on the better-off parishioners to aid the impoverished. The Poor Law was indeed a remarkable element of Britain's political society, fundamentally changing the nature of that society across the seventeenth century and distinguishing it from most of Europe. By statute, it obligated all parishes to provide some care for its poor, a requirement the poor quickly came to appreciate and voice, often being ready to remind those in authority of their duty, perhaps weaving together legal, Christian, and paternal ideals. Naturally the well-to-do criticized the system, looking to alter it in the hope that the costs would be reduced and the behaviour of the poor improved. But it was difficult for them simply to ignore it, or always get their own way when disputes arose. A triangular relationship existed between the poor, the vestry, and the local JPs, helping in the process to create legitimacy in the fundamental social inequalities which existed, as well as articulating a particular sense of community.

The fifth challenge to Britain's political society came from the direction of economic change. Economically, England began to diverge from much of the rest of Europe from the early seventeenth century. The sway of the market had increased significantly in the previous century, with agriculture becoming visibly more market orientated. This produced labour, raw materials, and capital to be used elsewhere. A more productive symbiosis between farming and manufacturing developed, most obviously in the textile trades scattered across many of the nation's agricultural regions. Overseas trade also expanded strongly, mainly with Europe, though a vital foothold was secured in New England at the start of the seventeenth century. In the final third of that century as many as 400,000 crossed the Atlantic from Britain and Ireland, while English merchants began to ship huge numbers of slaves from Africa to the Caribbean. Consequently, England's ports, market towns, and capital flourished, even before the period of the 'classic' industrial revolution (1760–1830). In 1600 about 8 per cent of Britain's population lived in towns of 5,000 or more, but by 1750 this had increased to 21 per cent. This was very different to the rest of Europe where the proportion only rose from 11 to 12 per cent. London in particular exploded. In 1600 the capital had accounted for 5 per cent of England's population and was smaller than Paris. By 1700 it had more than doubled in size to 490,000, now accounted for 10 per cent of the nation's population, and had overtaken Paris in size.

Once upon a time it was argued that such changes led to competing class interests that erupted into civil war in 1642. Such an analysis has become deeply unfashionable—and few have seen economic interests as central causes of the Glorious Revolution. Yet economic changes did pose profound questions for the regime after 1688, in particular whether a political culture so highly committed to the sanctity of landed property would make space for other interests. It was certainly conceivable that financiers, merchants, and industrialists could have found themselves not only excluded from power, but even from access to the political authority they might have sought to further their interests. This did not happen for three main reasons. First, the landed were highly commercialized, sharing many sentiments with the non-landed elite. Most embraced a spirit of change and improvement in an effort to maximize their rents. On their land they had mines dug, fields enclosed, and streets built, as well as investing in infrastructural changes and the national debt. Peers as well as cotton masters were capitalists. Second, landowners embraced an increasingly vibrant urban social scene, thereby bridging a major potential divide. London became a favoured haunt in winter; spas such as Bath became places of polite resort; and in many towns assembly rooms, theatres, clubs, and concerts flourished in what has been called England's 'urban renaissance'.[22] Finally, if landowners dominated political power they left room for other important economic interests. This crucial point needs detailing a little.

As has been seen, the Glorious Revolution was unquestionably a victory for the political nation over James II, leading to institutional changes. These centred on the fact that at Westminster parliamentary sessions now took place at least annually, usually at more or less the same time, and for long enough to allow a substantial amount of business to be conducted. Parliament became the focal point for the airing of alternative views of the public good, giving rise to a period of intense party strife. But, more importantly, it allowed parliament to consider increasing numbers of legislative proposals, many of which came from very particular economic interests.

In the 200 years before 1688 some 2,700 Acts were passed by the Westminster parliament, excluding the constitutionally troubled years 1642 to 1660. But in the next 112 years over 13,600 Acts were passed. That is to say, the annual rate of legislation increased nearly tenfold. Three-quarters of all legislation was specific and local in its concerns. All complexions of the propertied turned to Westminster to obtain unquestionable authority to further their interests: to enclose fields, turnpike roads, dig canals, establish hospitals, and so on. Critically, parliament was reluctant either to pass general legislation, or to pass catch-all legislation for specific matters. Parliament preferred bespoke legislation on a case-by-case basis, with all the time, trouble, and uncertainty entailed, because it remained extremely cautious about enhancing the interests of one person or group, for fear of eroding interests elsewhere. That is to say, it struggled not to view change as a zero-sum game. Even so, it did create thousands of what the Webbs dryly called 'statutory authorities for special purposes', not only for infrastructural developments (roads, rivers, canals, bridges, harbours), but also urban improvements such as paving and lighting and institutions such as hospitals, schools, and charities and did legislate for major changes of property rights.[23] All this was central to the profound economic and urban change in Britain in the century after the Glorious Revolution. Each new authority was usually small and initiated locally, but collectively many hundreds were created between the Glorious and French revolutions, significantly recasting the nature of authority in certain fields. In that way Parliament was a resource, a use right, available to many of the propertied in eighteenth-century Britain, providing a 'reactive state' as part of the larger whole.[24]

The final challenge to Britain's political society came from resistance to England's imperial ambitions, particularly from Scotland, Ireland, and the Thirteen Colonies in North America. In 1603, James VI of Scotland succeeded Elizabeth I (1558–1603) on the English and Irish thrones, thereby creating the composite monarchy of Britain and Ireland that survived until 1922. Scottish national identity derived considerable strength from the fact that the royal house of Stewart could be traced back to the fourteenth century. Thus there was armed support in Scotland for James II and his heirs until the middle of the eighteenth century—though the strength of Presbyterianism in Scotland also meant that the revolution settlement in 1689 was more radical there. Similarly, opinion north of the border reacted strongly against the English decision in 1701, made without consulting the Scots, that the Hanoverians were to succeed the childless Anne whenever she died. But, strong and articulate though that opinion was, it was overcome by an incorporating union in 1707, by which the Edinburgh parliament was dissolved and the Scots given limited representation at Westminster. Again divisions within Scottish society were vital here. Enough Scots wished to be part of a British state, not least those who feared being excluded from the vibrant economy to the south. After 1707 Britain had a single unified state which many Scots were happy to play an active part in. The national polity, the dimensions of the fiscal-military state, and the meanings of nationhood were all thereby profoundly changed.

Ireland lacked the same sense of shared history as Scotland, but had embraced James II because most Irish were Catholics. They hoped that he might be able to reverse the assaults on their rights and property that Cromwell had devoted such attention to. It was entirely predictable, therefore, that when James sought to reclaim his realms by force of arms he headed to Ireland. But his defeat at the Boyne in 1690 and the final victory of the Williamites in the following year fatally compromised the position of the Catholic majority. In the ensuing generation they were robbed of yet more land and rights as a 'Protestant Ascendancy' was constructed on the backs of the 'penal laws'. It might be expected that such injustices would have produced considerable resistance to the English and their allies in Ireland. But before the French Revolution it rarely did, at least not actively. In part that was because the Dublin parliament remained under a significant element of scrutiny by the privy council in London—thereby preventing or containing some of the excesses that might otherwise have been perpetrated by Ireland's Protestant minority. Deep divisions also existed in that minority, most importantly between the Church of Ireland and Ulster Presbyterianism. Catholics also found ways to work within the system, helped by the extent of landlord absenteeism. For example, they were often the middlemen responsible for negotiating land rentals, with long leases, often for three lives, on very small farms, thereby limiting what landowners could actually do.

Scotland and Ireland did substantially challenge English political society and it is telling that ultimately those challenges were contained by the unions of 1707 and 1801. English expansionism was certainly an important part of this, but the unions did change English political society in important ways. (Wales, to a considerable extent already incorporated within the English system, offered no such challenge.) The challenge mounted in the Thirteen Colonies after 1763 was not contained in those ways. It was more concerted, much better articulated—the quality of discourse and theory was remarkably high—and distant. The distance mattered not simply because of the difficulties it posed for Britain to win the War of Independence (1775–83), but because Britain's political elite were sometimes badly misinformed. Not least was the belief in London that the most vociferous opponents of British policy formed only a small, unrepresentative, phalanx and that a loyalist majority in the colonies would stand up and be counted the moment the imperial government asserted itself. Attachment to the idea of parliamentary supremacy also hindered a resolution of the tensions. Thus monarch, ministers, and parliament in Britain were unwilling to make the concessions or retreats that they were usually prepared to make at home when faced by such a grave challenge to their authority. International isolation nailed shut the coffin of this phase of empire.

The loss of the Thirteen Colonies did not lead to the sudden demise of British political society but, rather, to its slow reform. Questions that had begun to be asked about the nature of the regime in the 1760s now became more considered and concerted than ever, significantly stimulated by ideas about rationality, reason, and rights. An 'age of reform' can be discerned from around 1780, with keen attention being paid to the extent within the regime of corruption and cronyism, inefficiencies and inequalities. Those proposing change were not tilting at windmills: there were meaningless well-paid offices, awarded with regard to questionable standards of 'merit'; the distribution of the vote and the nature of parliamentary constituencies was unequal and inconsistent; religious disabilities were ridiculous and unfair; the criminal law was a mess; and trade regulations were often byzantine. Reformers and radicals were skilled at articulating these deficiencies, not least through use of the language of 'old corruption'. But it should be remembered that it was in their interests to paint the existing order as old and disordered, as unreformed and stuck in its ways. In fact, as has been seen, British political society was more open to change than reformers were inclined to say, though critically they overwhelmingly sought reform within, not revolution from below or without.

Clark's argument that England's regime remained Anglican, aristocratic, and monarchical between 1688 and 1832 can be set against the profound changes shown to have taken place in reaction to six structural pressures to which the regime was subjected in the period. England and Britain were increasingly multi-confessional; much power was exercised by the middling sort at the local level; parliament was available to a very wide range of propertied interests; many amongst the higher reaches of the landed elite disengaged from local governance; and the monarch's power was weakened by dilution, expectation, circumscription, and overstretch (to the Dutch republic (1689–1702), Hanover (1714–1837), and empire). Put differently, the church courts, the House of Lords, the privy council, and the court all diminished in relative significance in this period. The huge rise of the exercise of authority through parliament was very striking, while the emergence of the office of prime minister, of cabinet government, and of an annual 'budget', nicely point to profound changes at the executive level.

Tocqueville did not put it in those terms, but he was clear that France and Britain were very different before 1789. Often drawing telling comparisons between the two (he had visited England and Ireland, corresponded with some leading intellectuals in England, and had an English wife), he thought of England that, 'If we forget the old names and disregard the old forms, we find, from the seventeenth century on, the substantial abolition of the feudal system, the mixing of classes, a displaced nobility, and an open aristocracy. Wealth has become power, there is equality before the law, equal taxation, a free press, open debate; all these are new principles of which medieval society was ignorant.'[25] This was too rosy a view, and palpably inaccurate in places, but to Tocqueville, as for other French historians in the early nineteenth century, if England had had an Ancien Régime it was to be found before the execution of Charles I and the establishment of a republic in 1649 following years of bloody civil war. He rightly believed that the Restoration of 1660 was not the re-establishment of the Ancien Régime.

If, then, Britain was not an Ancien Régime after 1688 how might it be characterized? Fundamentally, power was more widely distributed, negotiated, and flexible than Clark assumes. Together these maintained the regime's authority and legitimacy, even in the face of very profound challenges. Burke's famous dictum, that 'A state without the means of some change is without the means of its conservation', is not the whole of the story, for, as Tocqueville pointed out, change can lead to irreconcilable differences.[26] Though it was sometimes a very close-run thing, in Britain the state changed sufficiently in step with society in this period to retain its authority and legitimacy, not least because wide sections of the propertied used it for its own ends.

Power within Britain's regime emanated from many different points, with each having a degree of autonomy from, but also dependence upon, the others. In the old language of a 'mixed and balanced constitution', these layers comprised executive, legislature, and judiciary, blending several forms of government: monarchical, aristocratic, democratic, and juridical. But local authorities (trusts and commissions as well as local government) certainly need to be added to this. Though the central state was able to exercise much more power in 1801 than in 1688, there had also been a huge expansion of authority at the local level. Sir John Bowring was exaggerating only a little when he told Tocqueville that 'England is a country of decentralisation. We have got a government, but we have not got a central administration. Each county, each town, each parish looks after its own interests.'[27] Distrust of the central state remained an important part of the consciousness of the British through the period, providing, in Goldie's telling phrase, an 'unacknowledged republic'. In a very real sense, authority was widely distributed, though with parliament providing a generally agreed ultimate site of sovereignty.

The widely scattered nature of authority was partly born of fear and anxiety, particularly of what had happened under Charles I and his sons and what was thought to be happening in Bourbon France. There was also a lingering sense amongst the propertied that the fabric of society might unravel all too easily. This consequently produced a willingness to concede and negotiate where necessary.[28] 'Management' not proclamation or diktat best summarizes the regime's culture, certainly after 1688. This was most obviously the case with the increasing resort to legislation, where different sides of a question, different conceptions of the public good, could be considered both within and without Westminster. It is notable, therefore, that between 1660 and 1800 some 33 per cent of attempts at legislation there failed. Negotiation can be seen in many other parts of political society also, not least in the reminders uttered by the poor to their superiors to do their duty and enforce the law, as well as in the operation of the criminal justice system. More generally, public opinion, as expressed through a remarkably vibrant urban and print culture, did make the authorities aware of a wider range of views of what was and what was not reasonable.

Together, the distribution of authority and an attachment to a high degree of negotiation created a regime that had the flexibility to change in the face of wider developments. Often enough the changes were small and unremarkable—though they could be substantial, as in the unions of 1707 and 1801. In large part this was because of the prevalence of a conservative cast of mind amongst the propertied, one that looked to change on pragmatic rather than theoretical grounds. Nonetheless, it is striking just how often there were major changes, in 1688–9, 1707, 1714, 1776, and 1801. While, therefore, an 'age of reform' can indeed be identified in Britain between 1780 and 1850, where change became more 'principled', it would be wrong to characterize the preceding era as generally static and 'unreformed'.

Political society in Britain changed subtly yet profoundly from 1689 to 1801. But there was not much method to this. Henry Fielding, novelist and JP, put it nicely in 1751:

> There is nothing so much talked of, and so little understood in this Country, as the Constitution. It is a Word in the Mouth of every Man; and yet when we come to discourse of the Matter, there is no Subject on which our Ideas are more confused and perplexed. Some, when they speak of the Constitution, confine their Notions to the Law; others to the Legislature; others, again, to the governing or executive Part; and many there are, who jumble all these together in one Idea. One Error, however, is common to them all: for all seem to have the Conception of something uniform and permanent, as if the Constitution of England partook rather of the Nature of the Soil than of the Climate, and was as fixed and constant as the former, not as changing and variable as the latter.[29]

This gave Britain's regime a somewhat unsettled and uncertain disposition. Power could also be exercised very capriciously, while the high level of inequality made many feel oppressed and excluded. But a revolutionary moment akin to France in 1789 was avoided, despite the tremendous stresses and strains experienced in the late eighteenth and early nineteenth centuries: caused by dramatic population growth, mushrooming towns and cities, an infant industrial revolution, class formation, challenging new ideas, and two bloody, long, and expensive wars against revolutionary and Napoleonic France. As has been seen, British political society was far from poorly prepared to deal with those new challenges. And so the story of change continued.

Notes

I am grateful for comments on a draft of this paper at a seminar at Lille, especially from Renaud Morieux, Anne Bonzon and Jean-Pierre Jessenne, and by Stephen Conway.

1. The focus of this essay is upon England, but England and Scotland had the same monarch from 1603 and their parliaments were merged in 1707. I tend, therefore, to write 'England' when discussing the pre-1707 period, 'Britain' the later period.
2. *English Society, 1688–1832: Ideology, Social Structure and Political Practice during the Ancien Régime* (Cambridge, 1985); *English Society, 1660–1832: Religion, Ideology and Politics during the Ancien Régime* (2nd edn., Cambridge, 2000), 25. Note the change in title from the 1st edn.
3. Clark, *English Society, 1688–1832*, 7.
4. Ibid. 93.
5. The fullest and most perceptive review was Joanna Innes, 'Jonathan Clark, Social History and England's "Ancien Regime"', *Past and Present*, 115 (1987), 165–200. He replied in 'On Hitting the Buffers: The Historiography of England's Ancien Regime. A Response', *Past and Present*, 117 (1987), 195–207.
6. e.g. Stephen Conway, 'Continental Connections: Britain and Europe in the Eighteenth Century', *History*, 90 (2005), 353–74.
7. F. O'Gorman, 'Eighteenth-Century England as an *Ancien Régime*', in S. Taylor, R. Connors, and C. Jones (eds.), *Hanoverian Britain and Empire: Essays in Memory of Philip Lawson* (Woodbridge, 1998), 30.

8. Roy Porter, 'Georgian Britain: An Ancien Régime?', *British Journal for Eighteenth-Century Studies*, 15 (1992), 142.
9. J. C. D. Clark, 'Reconceptualizing Eighteenth-Century England', *British Journal for Eighteenth-Century Studies*, 15 (1992), 136.
10. Clark, *English Society, 1660–1832*, 25.
11. Pierre Goubert defines a regime even more broadly as 'a society, a law, institutions, methods of government, mental attitudes, almost a "civilization"': *The Ancien Régime: French Society, 1600–1750*, tr. Steve Cox (London, 1973), 15. This seems too lax.
12. François Furet, 'Ancien Régime', in F. Furet and M. Ozouf (eds.), *A Critical Dictionary of the French Revolution*, tr. A. Goldhammer (Cambridge, Mass., and London, 1989), 604–15.
13. A good example is the unhelpful use of the phrase '*ancien régime* of identity' in Dror Wahrman, *The Making of the Modern Self: Identity and Culture in Eighteenth-Century England* (New Haven, Conn., and London, 2004).
14. A useful, relevant, discussion of the concept of modernity is Alan Houston and Steve Pincus, 'Introduction: Modernity and Later-Seventeenth-Century-England', in Houston and Pincus (eds.), *A Nation Transformed: England After the Restoration* (Cambridge, 2001), 1–19.
15. W. Doyle, 'The Union in a European Context', *Transactions of the Royal Historical Society*, 6th ser. 10 (2000), 168.
16. William Blackstone, *Commentaries on the laws of England* (4 vols. Oxford, 1765–9), i. 156.
17. 'Anglican' and 'Anglicanism' only become current terms in the 19th century, but they are used here as a convenient shorthand.
18. Mark Knights, *Representation and Misrepresentation in Later Stuart Britain: Partisanship and Political Culture* (Oxford, 2005), 117.
19. John Brewer, *Party Ideology and Popular Politics at the Accession of George III* (Cambridge, 1976).
20. Peter Clark, *British Clubs and Societies c.1580–1800: The Origins of an Associational World* (Oxford, 2000). Habermas's ideas are also relevant here. For a recent discussion see Peter Lake and Steve Pincus, 'Rethinking the Public Sphere in Early Modern England', *Journal of British Studies*, 45 (2006), 270–92.
21. Quoted in S. Drescher, *Tocqueville and England* (Cambridge, Mass., 1964), 91.
22. Peter Borsay, *The English Urban Renaissance: Culture and Society in the Provincial Town, 1660–1770* (Oxford, 1989).
23. Sidney and Beatrice Webb, *Statutory Authorities for Special Purposes* (London, 1922).
24. Lee Davison, Tim Hitchcock, Tim Keirn, and R. B. Shoemaker, 'The Reactive State: English Governance and Society, 1689–1750', in Lee Davison, Tim Hitchcock, Tim Keirn, and R. B. Shoemaker (eds.), *Stilling the Grumbling Hive: The Response to Social and Economic Problems in England, 1689–1750* (Stroud and New York, 1992), pp. xi–liv.
25. Alexis de Tocqueville, *The Old Regime and the Revolution*, i, ed. François Furet and Françoise Mélonio, tr. Alan Kahan (Chicago, 1998), 105.
26. *Reflections on the Revolution in France*, in *The Writings and Speeches of Edmund Burke*, viii. *The French Revolution, 1790–1794*, ed. L. G. Mitchell (Oxford, 1989), 72.
27. Alexis de Tocqueville, *Journeys to England and Ireland*, ed. J. P. Mayer (London, 1958), 61–2.
28. This borrows from J. P. Greene, *Negotiated Authorities: Essays in Colonial Political and Constitutional History* (Charlottesville, Va., and London, 1994).
29. *An Enquiry into the Causes of the Late Increase of Robbers and Related Writings*, ed. M. R. Zirker (Oxford, 1988), 65.

Bibliography

Beattie, J. M., *Crime and the Courts in England, 1660–1800* (Oxford, 1986).
Braddick, Michael J., *State Formation in Early Modern England, c.1550–1700* (Cambridge, 2000).
Brewer, John, *The Sinews of Power: War, Money and the English State, 1688–1783* (London, 1989).
Burns, Arthur, and Innes, Joanna (eds.), *Rethinking the Age of Reform: Britain 1780–1850* (Cambridge, 2003).
Eastwood, David, *Government and Community in the English Provinces, 1700–1870* (Basingstoke, 1997).
Goldie, Mark, 'The Unacknowledged Republic: Office Holding in Early Modern England', in Tim Harris (ed.), *The Politics of the Excluded, c. 1500–1800* (Basingstoke, 2001), 153–94.
Harling, Philip, *The Waning of 'Old Corruption': The Politics of Economical Reform in Britain, 1779–1846* (Oxford, 1996).
Hay, Douglas, 'Property, Authority and the Criminal Law', in Douglas Hay, Peter Linebaugh, John G. Rule, E. P. Thompson, and Cal Winslow (eds.), *Albion's Fatal Tree: Crime and Society in Eighteenth-Century England* (London, 1975), 17–63.
Hill, Christopher, *The Century of Revolution, 1603–1714* (Edinburgh, 1961).
Hindle, Steve, *On the Parish? The Micro-Politics of Poor Relief in Rural England, c. 1550–1750* (Oxford, 2004).
Hoppit, Julian, 'Patterns of Parliamentary Legislation, 1660–1800', *Historical Journal*, 39 (1996), 109–31.
Innes, Joanna, *Inferior Politics: Social Problems and Social Policies in Eighteenth-Century Britain* (Oxford, 2009).
Langford, Paul, *Public Life and the Propertied Englishman, 1689–1798* (Oxford, 1991).
McLean, Iain, and McMillan, Alistair, *State of the Union: Unionism and the Alternatives in the United Kingdom since 1707* (Oxford, 2005).
Marshall, P. J., *The Making and Unmaking of Empires: Britain, India, and America c.1750–1783* (Oxford, 2005).
O'Brien, P. K., 'The Political Economy of British Taxation, 1660–1815', *Economic History Review*, 2nd ser. 41 (1988), 1–32.
Pincus, Steve, *1688: The First Modern Revolution* (London and New Haven, Conn., 2009).
Plumb, J. H., *The Growth of Political Stability in England, 1675–1725* (London, 1967).
Root, Hilton, *The Fountain of Privilege: Political Foundations of Markets in Old Regime France and England* (Berkeley-Los Angeles and London, 1994).
Scott, Jonathan, *England's Troubles: Seventeenth-Century English Political Instability in European Context* (Cambridge, 2000).
Szechi, Daniel, *The Jacobites: Britain and Europe, 1688–1788* (Manchester, 1994).
Thompson, E. P., 'The Moral Economy of the English Crowd in the Eighteenth Century', *Past and Present*, 50 (1971), 76–136.
Wrigley, E. A., 'Urban Growth and Agricultural Change: England and the Continent in the Early Modern Period', *Journal of Interdisciplinary History*, 15 (1985), 683–728.

CHAPTER 30

COLONIAL AMERICA

CHRISTOPHER CLARK

SEEKING to convince American colonists early in 1776 that now was the time to break away from British rule, Thomas Paine declared that 'We have it in our power to begin the world over again.' With independence gained 'by the legal voice of the people', Paine wrote, 'The birth-day of a new world is at hand'. When the moment of independence arrived that July, welcomed by John Adams as 'the Day of Deliverance', the thirteen former colonies set about creating new state governments and forging a federal political system. Though beset by the deepening war with Britain, its exponents saw American Independence as a break with the past, the overthrow of a colonial dependency that had become tyrannical and oppressive.[1]

Optimists also saw theirs as a campaign that could be carried far afield; as Paine wrote, 'The cause of America is in a great measure the cause of all mankind'.[2] Many Americans would greet the French Revolution of 1789 as the fruit of a common effort to substitute rule by consent for enslavement to tradition. French revolutionaries quickly dubbed the Bourbon monarchy they had supplanted the Ancien Régime, and the spread of revolutionary ideas around Europe consolidated their notion that there was an 'old order' to be overthrown or radically reformed. Much later on, historians on both sides of the Atlantic would interpret American Independence as initiating a sequence of 'democratic revolutions' that engulfed Europe and the Americas over the next eight decades.[3] If these revolutions challenged the 'old order' in Europe, was British North America not also part of the Ancien Régime?

Though alluring, this notion has until relatively recently played little role in historical interpretations of early America. For reasons to be explored near the end of this chapter, American circumstances drew contemporaries away from shaping the kinds of formulation about colonial America that French radicals would subsequently create about their prerevolutionary past. Though Americans regarded their revolution as a new beginning, many also saw it as reviving facets of the colonial era that had been suppressed by British rule. For them, therefore, the past was not simply something to be rejected. Later still, and again for many reasons, it became conventional in America to distinguish between the radicalism of the French Revolution and the supposed moderation of the American. Reinforced by the common exceptionalist assumption that the United States has followed a unique historical path, this also worked against incorporating colonial America into analyses of the European Ancien Régime. The term has rarely been applied to the American colonies, and many historians even today stress the differences, rather than the similarities, between prerevolutionary America and Europe. If 'Ancien Régime' has long been an ineradicable concept in French history, it has long proved resistant to propagation in the American case.[4]

Over the past two or three decades, however, various trends in historical writing have led, if not to the formal adoption of the concept of an 'old order' in colonial America, at least to greater recognition of commonalities between British North America and other regions of European settlement, and to debate over the degree of discontinuity in America's own past. Attention to the 'Atlantic World' as a context in which to interpret colonial developments has refocused attention on colonial Americas' links with Europe and Africa.[5] The emergence of a large historiography of the Thirteen Colonies that has treated colonial themes for their intrinsic interest, not primarily as background to the American Revolution, has also stressed the 'past-ness' of the colonial period, and its distinctiveness from what would follow.[6] Historians such as Gordon S. Wood have portrayed a colonial world that would subsequently be transformed by the processes of revolution and national development.[7] Yet if the American colonies did indeed constitute an Ancien Régime, it was little like that in Europe.

Criteria of the kind that historians used to apply to Europe's 'old order', such as those employed by Arno J. Mayer in *The Persistence of the Old Regime* (1981), could not easily be employed for the British American colonies. Mayer noted that rule over much of Europe was by sovereign hereditary monarchs whose authority was personal and—whether or not tempered by Enlightenment ideals—in theory absolute. Attachment to the dynastic succession was often crucial to the legitimacy and mystique of royal power. Monarchs ruled by controlling their royal courts and entourages. Family, lineage, and status often governed appointment to high ministerial or military positions. Much of Europe was characterized by peasant agriculture, and the peasantry was subject to the power of nobles whose wealth derived from the land. Nobility was hereditary, and often endowed with privileges that were either derived from feudal customs and obligations or exchanged for those obligations when monarchs had curbed feudal rights and co-opted nobles into serving the state. Even in reformed monarchies, such as that in Britain, where rule was exercised through a partly representative parliament, many facets of aristocratic and hereditary power were still intact. Most old regime states had an established or dominant church, non-adherence to which was in some manner penalized. The church derived income from the land through tithes or taxes, and its higher clergy had strong ties to the monarch and the nobility.[8]

More recent treatments of eighteenth-century Europe have, in substantially modifying this fixed portrayal of the 'old order' and stressing instead its great variety and changeability, in some senses facilitated the adoption of the concept in relation to North America, where the characteristics Mayer stressed had indeed been rare or much diluted. The Colonies had an hereditary monarchy, of course, but this was seated in England, and there was no royal court or entourage in America. Early modern England had a patchwork of institutions and privileges rather than uniform government or legal codes, and its colonies were a patchwork, too. Most colonies had originated in the seventeenth or early eighteenth centuries as private ventures, rather than as state projects. Maryland and Pennsylvania were still controlled by private proprietors up to the Revolution, while Connecticut and Rhode Island chose their own governors under seventeenth-century charters. The remaining colonies had acquired royal governors appointed by the crown, but this royal control had come about haphazardly over more than a century as a response to contingencies; it was not the result of a concerted plan of state action. Like that in Europe, the colonial 'old order' was not very orderly.

Colonial governors, royal or not, in any case found their power limited. All colonies had adopted some form of representative assembly, whose members were chosen by free electors and whose influence countered that of governors or of the appointed councils of local notables with which they ruled. Important studies in the 1960s stressed the role of assemblies, especially the elected lower houses, in forming blocs of opposition to colonial administration, particularly royal governors. The electoral franchise, though based on property ownership, usually embraced a wider section of the white male population than in Britain.[9] British titles were recognized in the colonies, but had little importance. No colonial nobility grew up, and although some offices did in practice pass among family members, none were formally hereditary. Rarely did colonial churches, notables, or other organizations enjoy the legal privileges or exemptions that remained common legacies of feudalism in Europe. And although corruption was sometimes uncovered, the systematic sale, as in old regime France, of titles, offices, tax-farms, and other privileges, was absent from colonial America.

The Anglican Church was established in several southern colonies but, by comparison with its importance in England, its standing was weak. There was no American bishop and parish vestries were power bases for the gentry rather than for the clergy. Outside the South, Anglicans were greatly outnumbered by those who in England would have been classed as 'dissenters'. Established churches in Massachusetts, Connecticut, and New Hampshire were supported by obligatory taxation, but were Congregational churches, governed by their own members, or had adopted a form of Presbyterianism based on associations of ministers. Rhode Island and the Middle Colonies from New York to Maryland had no religious establishments; historians often see Pennsylvania in particular as heralding the religious pluralism that would later come to mark the United States in general.

Economic and social conditions largely differed from Europe's too. Though colonial economies were overwhelmingly rural and agricultural, few contemporaries considered them to be 'peasant' societies. Rates of landownership, at least among white men, were high by European standards. Tenancy or landlordism was in places as common as it was in Europe, and in the Hudson River valley of New York there were even manorial estates that exercised neo-feudal authority over their tenants. But New England was dominated by freehold farming; freeholds were common in the South and on the frontier; and

Pennsylvania farmers—though they were formally lessees of the colony's proprietors—essentially enjoyed the rights of freeholders also.[10] Colonial rural society did contain its own kinds of inequality and subordination. Most obviously, race-based chattel slavery was everywhere legal and, in port-towns and the southern colonies, common. But the classic Ancien Régime pattern of domination by hereditary noble landowners was mostly absent.

These often-profound departures from European patterns have helped sustain a hardy historiographical tradition: that 'American' history has been both continuous and, in much more than a superficial sense, special. The nineteenth-century historian George Bancroft interpreted United States history as, on one hand, a long sweep towards democracy from the earliest English settlements onward and, on the other, as the gift of a benign Providence.[11] In such accounts the Thirteen Colonies not only followed a distinctive trajectory, but also incubated the propensity for growth, social mobility, and opportunity that later came to be seen as characteristic of the United States after it had secured its independence. Many modern portrayals, indeed, continue to present colonial America as the prototype for later American expansion and development.

Abundant land and resources; access to growing Atlantic trade; distance from religious oppression; relative freedom from the customs and constraints of European societies: all contributed to conditions that could be described as favourable, at least for the colonies' free settlers. Even the harshest conditions of early settlement, such as those endured by the first English community in Jamestown, Virginia, from 1607 onward, could be interpreted, as in one recent work, as providing models for later successful colonial development. Data on population growth, wealth, and material consumption suggest that colonial white populations enjoyed better living standards, health, and other measures of well-being than those in many parts of Europe.[12] By the 1740s the English indentured servant William Moraley could write of Pennsylvania, which 'produces almost every Fruit, Herb, and Root as grows in Great Britain and divers Sorts unknown to us', where 'Woods and well manured Farms' abounded, 'the hospitable Inhabitants dispence their Favours to the Traveller, the Poor and Needy', as 'in short...the best poor man's country in the world'.[13] This expansive view of colonial opportunity continues to shape discussion of the contrasts between New World and Old in the eighteenth century. America's colonial economies prefigured its national prosperity.[14]

In similar vein, colonial politics could be seen to prefigure the post-revolutionary political system. Louis Hartz, in an influential 1955 study, discerned the roots of American liberalism in the colonies' lack of a feudal social structure. A decade later Bernard Bailyn traced the 'origins of American politics' to the rapidly evolving political systems of the eighteenth-century colonies.[15] Some, though not all, of such accounts implicitly downplayed the significance of the Revolution in American historical development: colonies, revolution, and nation seemed all of a piece. This, indeed, draws out a theme dating back to the Revolution itself, in which certain political leaders—especially those who would become associated with the Federalist tradition—preferred to stress the non-revolutionary character of the independence movement they had helped sustain. When Alexis de Tocqueville visited Boston in 1831, Josiah Quincy, president of Harvard College and member of a prominent Boston family, assured him that the Revolution had made little difference: 'We put the name of the people where formerly was that of the king. Otherwise nothing changed among us.'[16]

If colonial economies and politics were already modernizing, then so was colonial Americans' sense of identity. To Jon Butler, whose *Becoming America: The Revolution Before 1776* (2000) offers the best recent synthesis of this line of argument, the colonies' dynamism fostered the emergence of a new, 'American' consciousness before the onset of the political crises of the 1760s that would lead to the rift with Britain. Butler's argument complements John Adams's famous observations in early nineteenth-century letters that the 'revolution' had occurred 'in the hearts and minds of the people' before even a shot was fired in the Revolutionary War. In this view, the American Revolution was not a breach with the past, but the realization of a consciousness already formed.[17]

Yet despite the long pedigree of such arguments for continuity and American distinctiveness, historians have increasingly regarded them with scepticism. Rather than seeing the Revolution as a culmination of colonial developments, they stress instead the specific and contingent events that led over time to revolutionary action. Implicit in these views is the notion that things had to change for a revolution to occur. Interpreting colonial politics, culture, and societies on their own terms, rather than in light of the Revolution or national developments to come, recent scholars have uncovered a rich new understanding of the colonies' variety and distinctiveness. Influenced by the new social history, by new themes in the study of political thought, by the 'linguistic turn', the 'new cultural history', the history of gender and sexuality, ethnography, and environmental studies, these scholars have opened up to us a colonial world quite different in its demography, political cultures and belief systems than that of the post-revolutionary period. Though they almost never use the expression, the very strangeness of this world suggests the possibility that it amounted to an Ancien Régime, not in a classic European sense, but in its own terms.[18]

The British American colonies embodied such social, economic, and political diversity that they did not, of course, constitute a single 'old order' any more than Europe did. They had evolved from different origins: English, Dutch, and Scandinavian; and under an array of influences: Native American, French, African, Irish, Scottish, German. Even the two oldest areas of English settlement, the Chesapeake region and New England, differed markedly. In New England, where early settlement involved whole families, and where sex ratios quickly achieved a rough parity, seventeenth-century settlers set patterns for longevity and demographic robustness that were sustained throughout the colonial period. The Chesapeake colonies initially struggled with imbalanced sex ratios and a fierce disease environment that took large numbers of seventeenth-century migrants to early graves in the newly formed settlements. But the attraction of land, and the emergence of a prosperous tobacco-exporting economy at length produced more favourable circumstances for Virginia and Maryland whites. Sex ratios evened up, marriages lasted longer, and by the 1690s elements of a stable, permanent, self-regenerating society were emerging.

The eighteenth century brought even greater variety. Population densities varied widely from coast to interior. The Middle Colonies, especially Pennsylvania, became a magnet for immigrants from across Britain and Ireland, and from parts of Germany, whereas New England received few transatlantic migrants, and many 'immigrants' to the South were enslaved blacks carried forcibly from the Caribbean or from Africa. Northern colonies, with South Carolina, developed substantial port-towns that played a significant role in trade and politics through the influence of prosperous merchants, and in Charleston, South Carolina's case, through that of wealthy planters also. Virginia and Maryland had few urban settlements, and were dominated by a rural planter-gentry. Slavery acquired different characteristics from North to South, and historians now distinguish the former's 'societies with slaves' from the latter's 'slave societies', where slave ownership and the emergence of African American cultures were most prominent.[19] While the southern colonies produced tobacco, naval stores, dyestuffs, and rice for export with substantial reliance on slave labour, Pennsylvania became a wheat-exporting region largely without rural slavery, and New England tied itself closely to Atlantic commerce without relying on a major staple-export crop. All colonies were subject to British trading regulations such as the Navigation Acts, but their economic variety meant that these rules affected them differently. Tobacco, an 'enumerated' product under the Acts, had to be exported to Britain, but Carolina rice was not 'enumerated' and could be shipped directly to markets in southern Europe. Many goods had by law to be carried in 'British' ships, but this designation included ships built and owned in the colonies, a stimulus to the shipbuilding industries of New England and the Middle Colonies.

Variety extended to politics also. Richard Beeman has recently noted that 'diversity may be the *only* generalization that we can make about eighteenth-century American political culture'.[20] Though all colonies had representative assemblies, patterns of participation and political behaviour around these bodies varied significantly, producing markedly different political environments. Pennsylvania's factions and rivalries evolved to reflect the province's growing ethnic and religious diversity. Connecticut, Virginia, and Maryland were each ruled by a stable political elite with its own distinctive character. Rhode Island and New York were each riven by political factions that differed from each other in composition and purpose.

Colonial politics were 'provincial' in the metaphorical as well as the literal sense. The importance of colonial governors and assemblies induced an inward-looking tendency. As studies of Virginia and elsewhere have stressed, political localism prevailed even within colonies. Before the 1760s it was rare for counties or townships to coordinate political activities even with their immediate neighbours.[21] Few issues spurred any colony to seek common cause with another. After the 1680s, when New Englanders had acted together to resist the Stuart monarchy's creation of a single Dominion of New England, and then used the Revolution of 1688–9 to topple the scheme, there was no significant attempt at concerted intercolonial action until the Albany Plan of Union of 1754. Even this quickly fell apart because of local differences.

However, if colonies had no common cause before the 1760s there were common themes that linked them. Some were shared by New World colonies anywhere; others were more specific to British North America. Above all were issues related to the fact that these were primarily colonies with substantial European settler groups, rather than colonies of extraction where small numbers of Europeans ruled large indigenous populations.[22] All New World colonies had to procure labour to carry out the tasks of settlement, production, and development. Mainland settler colonies faced this need in the context of a relative abundance of available land. European migrants to North America often hoped to acquire land for themselves on terms that avoided the hierarchy and dependency of rural Europe.

The aspiration for land and the high ratio of land to labour in the colonies gave rise to two overarching conditions. First, land was not simply there for the taking. It belonged to Native Americans, the history of whose interactions with European colonists has been substantially rewritten in the past generation. A host of new studies has recast the conventional story of European ventures into an uncivilized 'wilderness'. Encounters with Native Americans were often cruel, frequently exploitative, and resulted in the destruction, displacement, or absorption of most East Coast Indians by the eighteenth century. Scholars have helped us to see the ways these encounters looked from Native American perspectives; have traced interchanges and negotiation across racial boundaries; and have noted how concepts of race and of racial difference were themselves shifting during the long period of colonial–Indian interaction. From the later seventeenth century onward, whites' demand for frontier land; colonial governments' and elites' manoeuvring for land; the shifting alliances between Native American groups; and dealings between them and competing European powers, made the American frontier a cockpit of political dispute.[23]

Second, land did not work itself. Measures—often coercive—were necessary to make it productive. Those individuals, mostly white men, who owned land made use of it by exercising control over the labour of others. From the seventeenth century to well after the Revolution, North Americans employed an array of methods to compel workers to work. Chattel slavery was the most rigorous, but it lay at one end of a spectrum that included convict labour; indentured servitude; apprenticeship; the 'binding out' of poor children or families to work for others; imprisonment for debt; truck payments and debt peonage; various forms of tenancy, including neo-feudal customary obligations and restrictions; and wage contracts that withheld payment before completion. As was common in settlement colonies, many of these labour relationships were rooted in racial or ethnic differences.[24]

Forms of coercion varied in relative importance from region to region, but the most widespread social institution, the family household, was itself an agency for compelling labour. In a patriarchal society, women and children were as subject to control by their husbands and parents as other dependants were by their masters. As many as four in every five people in late colonial America were in a position of legally inferior 'dependency'. Three decades ago Edmund S. Morgan noted the connections between American claims to political freedom and the widespread ownership of chattel slaves. Our growing understanding of gender and class relationships suggests that Morgan's observation might be extended in light of other forms of unfree labour.[25] But eighteenth-century political thought was focused primarily on government, kingship, statesmanship, and the public arena, and paid comparatively little attention to conditions in the private sphere.

A further social characteristic made the Thirteen Colonies collectively distinct from most other European settlements in the Americas. Each colony, through its representative assembly, had elevated local leaders to positions of prominence; these leaders, though they formed provincial elites, usually maintained close connections with the constituents who elected them to serve. Their wealth and its sources varied. Some Virginia and South Carolina planters had personal fortunes that placed them on a par with members of the English gentry. Some merchants in Philadelphia, Boston, New York, and smaller port-towns, matched the gentry's prosperity, but derived their wealth from trade rather than from agriculture. Leaders in rural New England and some other parts of the colonies enjoyed more modest circumstances. But all had one thing in common: their strong roots in the colonies themselves. Although there were exceptions, most prominent individuals in mid-eighteenth-century New England, Virginia, South Carolina, or the Middle Colonies were born or settled in the colonies, and would powerfully influence the future of the provinces they regarded as home. Even some royal governors, including Thomas Hutchinson of Massachusetts and William Franklin of New Jersey, had been born in the colonies. Few other colonial settlements were controlled by 'creole elites' such as these, whose connections to the mother country were so comparatively weak.[26]

So while white society seemed egalitarian by European standards, race, ethnicity, patriarchy, and the power of local elites gave the colonies a hierarchical quality congruent with their subordinate political status. Recent historical writing has explored the degree to which hierarchy and deference, though more muted than in Europe, shaped political culture. The most significant of these works, Gordon S. Wood's *The Radicalism of the American Revolution* (1992), portrays colonies imbued with political values associated with monarchy, and many of the assumptions about rank and social order common in contemporary Britain. Richard L. Bushman, too, has depicted colonists' view of the monarchy as an awe-inspiring institution embodying the patronage and protection due from the great to the small in a society of orders. Brendan McConville has traced a growing affection for the monarchy among early eighteenth-century colonists, whose political rituals celebrated their place in an expanding British Empire. Connected to this political culture of deference, as Bushman has also shown, was the cultivation of 'gentility' among members of colonial elites and others who wished to claim genteel standing.[27]

If colonial society looked hierarchical from the top down, it could also do so from the bottom–up. When William Moraley noted the blessings of life in Pennsylvania, it was partly for the generosity of the inhabitants to the 'Poor and Needy'. Though property distribution and opportunity were relatively widespread, there has been increasingly detailed evidence about poverty in the colonies and about the growing constraints facing some sections of the population. Some port-towns, such as Boston, began to grow more slowly in the mid-eighteenth century, as economic stagnation set in, and employment for the poor was increasingly dependent upon the cycles of war and trade in the Atlantic economy. Philadelphia grew more confidently, and employment prospects there flourished, but growing inequality was also evident. In the countryside, long-settled regions faced constraints from soil exhaustion and, as population grew, from a scarcity of land to be divided into new farms. This led to a rise in poverty and efforts to control it, but also generated pressure for migration to frontier regions where land might be available for settlement.[28] Outmigration to the frontier set up conflicts between colonists and Native Americans, and among colonists themselves. Along the eighteenth-century frontier tensions flared between settlers and landholders or speculators, between tenants and landlords, and between the demands of interior settlements for government and elites' reluctance to accommodate their needs. When, in urban or rural contexts, protests broke out they often incorporated symbolic actions that dramatized or inverted a hierarchical sense of order.[29]

Influence did not simply run from the top down. The creole elites of settler-colonies were both 'colonized' (by the mother country) and 'colonizers' (of interior regions and dependent populations in the colonies themselves).[30] This set up an important dynamic in British America. Unlike colonies without representative local governments, and unlike those whose elites were closely tied to the mother country, the Thirteen Colonies were amenable to political pressures that could put local leaders both at odds with royal officials and under pressure from popular demands. This dynamic between creole elites and popular pressure would play a key part in the changing political circumstances of the American colonies during the middle of the eighteenth century, and would ultimately lead to revolution. A combination of popular insurrection and elite leadership helped in the long run to explode the colonies' attachment to hierarchy and deference.

Many historians find in eighteenth-century America a tendency towards closer links with Britain than there had been hitherto, and some describe this as a process of Anglicization in the colonies.[31] Above all else, this was a consequence of colonial population growth. Immigration from Europe and forced migration from Africa joined with high fertility rates to feed colonial demographic expansion. In 1700 there were just over a quarter of a million people in the English mainland colonies. By 1750 this had more than quadrupled, to nearly 1.2 million, and by 1775 population would double once again. Expansion gave the colonies a larger role in transatlantic commerce and growing weight in Britain's imperial calculations. Along with trade and migration links came closer religious and cultural ties, while early eighteenth-century British governments' 'wise and salutary neglect' of colonial affairs gradually gave way to an increasing administrative interest in them.[32] The practice of law and the concerns of colonial legislatures became more closely patterned on their English counterparts. Coastal New England lost some of its initial Puritan distinctiveness, as a commercial elite and even the Anglican Church assumed greater importance in local culture. The so-called 'Great Awakening' of the 1730s and 1740s arose from transatlantic reciprocity, as figures such as George Whitefield, first inspired by colonial revivals, crossed the ocean to stoke religious enthusiasm from Georgia to New England. Evangelism became a component of evolving colonial and transatlantic culture in the 1740s that would bring disparate places and people to identify new connections with each other.[33]

Two parallel developments strengthened these transatlantic ties. One, which we might call 'state-induced', involved warfare and North America's growing part in European imperial affairs.[34] Warfare had helped define the English colonial experience from early in the process of settlement. Attitudes and techniques shaped by the English conquest of Ireland were quickly adapted to colonists' early encounters with Native Americans that, though not always hostile, soon sparked conflicts in Virginia and New England. In both regions warfare in the 1670s helped establish patterns of frontier conflict between settlers and native populations, and between settlers and their own governments, that would remain endemic throughout the colonial period and beyond.[35] From the 1680s onwards, these hostilities also became connected with the wider transoceanic rivalries of European powers, as Britain, France, and Spain vied for control of the North American continent, using their colonies and alliances with contesting Indian nations as tools. Each major European conflict from the War of the League of Augsburg to the Seven Years War had its American component; in the latter case, hostilities started in the Appalachian backcountry two years before they spread to Europe itself. Indian diplomacy, and complex interactions between British and provincial governments and armed forces, characterized colonial life for seven decades up to 1763. Though early on colonial settlers were often doing little more than defending themselves against French or Indian assault, the Treaty of Utrecht in 1713 initiated a reversal in the frontier balance of power. Gradually, white settlements spread more confidently into the frontier backlands, and an expansionary dynamic fed by population growth and land hunger began to take root. Colonial military forces helped take the fight onto the offensive. In 1745, for example, New England troops captured the French fortress at Louisbourg on Cape Breton Island, threatening access to the St Lawrence River and to New France itself.

While warfare and imperial rivalries were forging links between the metropole and American colonies a second set of developments, more 'private' in character, were reinforcing these ties. Foremost were developments in transatlantic trade. During the late seventeenth and early eighteenth centuries there was a decline in the value of trade per head of colonial population, but from about 1740 strong growth became evident, as the expansion of British commerce and the beginnings of the Industrial Revolution in Britain found new markets among a rapidly growing colonial population. Colonists became customers for an array of goods—textiles, metalwares, pottery, and other items—carried in cargo holds from far corners of the world or turned out by English industrial workshops. As in Britain itself, goods once seen only as luxuries became available more widely in the colonies and across a broader social spectrum. Nor were colonists merely consumers of British-made goods. Their imports of capital goods also rose, reflecting the growth of homegrown workshop-based industries, particularly in the port-towns.[36]

Part of this upsurge in colonial trade and consumption was an expansion in the production and transmission of printed materials within the colonies and between colonies and Britain. This in turn, along with the personal correspondence that accompanied trade and political dealings, helped foster Americans' sense of identification with and participation in an expanding British Empire based on a constitutional monarchy, commerce, and a militant Protestantism aimed against the feared incursions of French and

Spanish Catholicism in America. 'Anglicization', above all, meant colonists' conception of themselves as parties to an 'English' political culture that they construed as guaranteeing their liberties. In common with many English people, they associated this with allegiance to a crown that ruled in conjunction with representative institutions guaranteed by the principles of the Glorious Revolution of 1688–9. Benjamin Franklin and his political allies in Pennsylvania campaigned for a royal government in the province to replace the Penn family's proprietorship, because they saw it as a better guarantor of political freedom. And Franklin, active as a colonial lobbyist in London in the 1750s and 1760s, could seek political preferment for himself, and the governorship of New Jersey for his son, in an empire that for the time being he saw as protective of 'English liberties' in the colonies.[37]

However, this very closeness of identity of colonies with the mother country would help to bring about a collision between them. Warfare, its complexities, and particularly its costs, caused British administrations to take an increasing interest in controlling colonial policy and trade, and in running affairs with the concerns of the mother country foremost in mind. This set up the potential for clashes with colonial assemblies whose members jealously guarded their considerable autonomy. The circumstances of war sometimes reminded colonists that the British regarded them as inferior. Slights—from high-handedness by British officers towards their colonial counterparts, to the trading back of Louisbourg to the French at the Treaty of Aix-la-Chapelle in 1748—fostered resentment. More important, as Brendan McConville has argued, colonists' attachment to the crown followed a path that diverged from predominant English political assumptions. While English Whig interpretations of the Glorious Revolution stressed the superior constitutional role of parliament, many colonists came to regard the crown as the apex of a system that incorporated their own representative assemblies. This tension between parliament's assertion of its pre-eminence throughout the empire and colonial notions that their assemblies had equal standing with parliament would only emerge clearly during the Stamp Act crisis of 1765–6.[38] Parliament's claim in the Declaratory Act (1766) of its right to legislate for the colonies 'in all cases whatsoever' was a direct rebuttal of the assemblies' assumption of autonomy in their own provinces—and was taken seriously enough to be cited a decade later in the Declaration of Independence's list of grievances against Britain. The issues of finance and taxation that exposed this divergence were in a sense only incidental to the much deeper constitutional crisis embedded in the fabric of an evolving Anglo-Colonial relationship in which the authority of parliament and that of colonial assemblies increasingly conflicted with each other.

Occasions for conflict arose out of many of the conditions we have been referring to: the expansion of trade and the economic 'fit' between colonies and Britain; the expansion of population on the colonial frontier; the aspirations of settlers and land speculators to acquire Native American land, including that of Britain's allies in imperial warfare; disputes between landlords and tenants; the claims of settlers in the backcountry that colonial governmental protection be extended to them; British restrictions on colonial currency issues, and other measures. These conflicts were as much between settlers and colonial governments as they were between colonies and Britain, but they increased the tensions in transatlantic political relationships also.[39]

Tensions between Britain and the colonies would have been more muted if local political influence had not rested so heavily with colonial creole elites. In colonies such as Jamaica, where the planter elite was closely tied to Britain, or Nova Scotia, where British military activity was key to economic life, opposition to British rule remained comparatively weak. In the Thirteen Colonies the importance of creole elites sharpened the likelihood of conflict between local and imperial leaderships. Yet it was not self-evident that this kind of conflict, common in any colonial relationship, should lead to a breakdown. We need to examine why, when colonial ties with Britain were growing closer and social tensions within the colonies were increasing, some sections of the colonial elite shaped their views in opposition to British policies in the 1760s and 1770s, rather than in support of them.

The long experience of relative political autonomy in the colonies had coexisted with growing attachment to the monarchy, mediated by the Whig tradition and the constitutional legacies of the Glorious Revolution. As in early Hanoverian England, it was possible to oppose particular ministries or policies without disloyalty to the crown. Colonists celebrated their enjoyment of 'English liberties' and could do so in radical or oppositional mode. According to Bernard Bailyn, political writers steeped themselves in the literature arising from the 'country' opposition to Robert Walpole in the 1720s. Jonathan Mayhew, in a sermon preached in Boston to mark the centenary of King Charles I's execution, emphasized the people's right to overthrow bad rulers.[40] Such traditions did not inherently undermine loyalty to a constitutionally created empire, but they did signal that loyalty could be conditional upon good behaviour on the part of government. English radical ideology had significant meaning for both elite and popular political leaders who, even as they contested one another, could often agree that government derived from consent and became illegitimate if it violated the liberties of the subject. These principles, already embodied in Lockean theory, and enunciated in political and religious discourse before real crises emerged to galvanize them, created a framework within which many colonists chose to interpret British ministerial measures in the 1760s.

Yet it was not colonial elites alone that made these choices, and they did not make them solely on the basis of political theory or ideology. Tension over British policies was shaped by popular involvement in political culture. Because colonial leaders relied for their local influence on the ordinary free colonists who chose them for elective positions, and because their concepts of patronage and obligation were formed by hierarchical conceptions of ties between rulers and ruled, they were especially sensitive to popular pressures upon them. Accounts of the 1765 stamp crisis, for instance, suggest that most colonial assemblies initially took little action in response to the Stamp Act. Only under pressure from popular protests did colonial leaders begin to address the measure's objectionable character. Received into a context of social division, and in a period of economic depression in key places such as Boston, British taxation measures proved vulnerable to the fractiousness of colonial politics. Crowd protests forced colonial leaders to take sides on such issues, consigning some supporters of the crown to political oblivion, and elevating to prominence those who were prepared to resist in defence of the rights of 'freeborn Englishmen'.[41]

If creole elite groups steered the colonies towards a revolutionary conflict with Britain because of their vulnerability to popular protest, popular protesters would have achieved little without them. Without allies among provincial leaders they would have protested in vain, and perhaps faced the full force of government repression. Even so, their leverage varied according to the social and political contexts of different colonies. Elite groups were most fractured and loyalty to Britain remained strongest in regions where pluralism, political diversity, and social conflicts had been most prominent before 1775. Pennsylvania and New York had well-established traditions of factional politics. New Jersey, the Hudson Valley of New York, and the Carolina backcountry had faced riots and rebellions over land, tenancy, and the governance of interior regions. On the other hand, support for the Revolution emerged rapidly where social and political homogeneity in the late colonial period had been greatest. Virginia gentry sided heavily with the Revolution, having endured many years of debt and uncertainty in the hands of tobacco merchants, many of whom were based in Scotland. New England merchants had had some of the weakest direct links with Britain. British policies could be presented as violating the autonomy not merely of provincial institutions, but of local ones as well.[42]

The American Revolution's roots in the notion of defending 'English liberties' provide a key to understanding why Americans and their historians have so seldom applied terms such as Ancien Régime or 'the old order', to the Thirteen Colonies. Unlike French republicans during their revolution, American patriots found no compelling reason to coin such an expression for the colonial system they were overthrowing, and so they provided historians with no equally convenient handle to name it by. The reasons for this can be traced to the ways eighteenth-century Americans thought about the crises they faced, the revolution that resulted, and political conditions in the new republic.

As would happen in the French Revolution, American patriots did of course favourably contrast their newfound Independence with what had preceded it. At Independence, wrote David Ramsay, the Revolution's first historian, 'a nation was born at once, a new order of things arose, and an illustrious aera in the history of human affairs commenced'. The Revolution, declared one early Fourth of July speaker, 'gave existence to thirteen states and freed their...inhabitants from disgrace and wretchedness'.[43] Yet however irksome pre-revolutionary conditions might have seemed, Americans had little disposition to dwell on them. If the colonies had, as one speaker avowed, suffered under British rule the 'Egyptian...bondage...[of] tyrannical power', this was widely conceived to have been an aberration. As war was getting under way in May 1775, Henry Laurens of South Carolina had written that he was 'Striving to transmit that Liberty to my Children, which was mine by birthright & compact'. Though they might agree on little else, post-revolutionary commentators of different political stripes portrayed the colonies as outposts of freedom that had nurtured political liberty until corrupt British ministries sought to curtail it. The Revolution had, in this view, merely corrected unnecessary evils.[44]

Indeed some American revolutionaries had seen themselves not as overthrowing an 'old European order' but as forestalling the adoption of Old World institutions that had not yet reached America. New England Congregationalists and non-Anglicans elsewhere had perennially suspected an attempt to appoint an American bishop.

Anglo-American tensions in the 1760s and early 1770s had led some commentators to argue that the creation of an American peerage would restore stability, causing John Adams and other patriots to warn against measures (such as the new governor's council imposed by the Massachusetts Government Act of 1774) that seemed to embody such an effort.[45] State and federal provisions prohibiting the use of 'titles of nobility' derived in part from this anxiety to prevent aspects of England's 'old corruption' being imposed on the colonies. On top of various local and ethnic conflicts, differences over such matters had divided revolutionaries from loyalists, who formed about one-fifth of the American population, many of whom remained attached to Britain not out of respect for an old monarchical order but because they saw the Glorious Revolution of 1688–9 as already providing sufficient safeguards against tyranny. However, the emigration to Britain or to other colonies of 60,000 or more loyalists (some five times as many in proportion to population as emigration from France after 1789), the success of American Independence, and the eventual reintegration of many loyalists who remained, rendered concern with such questions redundant.[46]

The events in France of 1789 and after would also prompt Americans of different political persuasions to stress differences, as well as similarities, between France's situation and the causes of their own revolution. '[F]or fourteen centuries', claimed the Republican William Wirt, 'were the people of ... [France] ... buried in Egyptian darkness', under a 'tremendous combination of political and religious tyrants'. By contrast, wrote a Federalist in 1798 without hint of irony, 'Americans never were slaves'; faced with oppressive British policies, they had resisted 'in a desire to enjoy unimpaired, the rights of British subjects', and restored them by revolution. To these contemporaries, the old American order and the new were in principle the same. However 'shameful' had been what Wirt (echoing Paine) called the 'great continent's ... dependance upon a petty island', no concept like Ancien Régime was required to describe it because no great discontinuity with the past seemed to have occurred.[47]

This framework, too, served to explain the Revolution to the next generation: the colonies had first been free; they had enjoyed the fruits of English liberty; new British governments had imposed constraints on that liberty, which amounted to the creation of a tyranny. Colonists had acted on their principles to resist and then to overthrow this tyranny, to restore 'liberty'. To do so, of course, they had to introduce new measures. Because they were not simply a nation rescuing itself from injustice, but colonies forming a nation for the first time, the world they were entering was indeed new. But it did not demand a rejection of the old. As resistance to British measures turned to revolution, and as the war was pursued to defend American independence, American patriots—however much they disagreed on other things—saw themselves as both restoring a lost Liberty and seizing a new Future. Politicians and historians quickly forged a view of the American Revolution that combined this particular interpretation of an 'old order' that was neither entirely to be embraced nor entirely to be replaced.

Post-revolutionary politics did not demand such a concept either. The continuing autonomy of individual states and the uncertainties of creating a federal system to connect them—first under the Articles of Confederation, ratified in 1781, and then under the United States Constitution, which came into effect eight years later—meant that the new nation's common experience lay more in the creation of new institutions than in the overthrowing of old ones. Although political divisions were deep, and political discourse frequently vituperative, neither Federalists nor Republicans made an American Ancien Régime the rallying-point for nostalgia or revulsion. Republicans did repeatedly accuse Federalists of fostering 'aristocracy' or of reintroducing monarchy in disguise; and until after the War of 1812 fear of British vengefulness gave potency to any charge of 'Toryism' directed against opponents or the unruly. But the Constitution guaranteed republican governments to all of the United States. Unlike in France or Spanish America, where royalists and legitimists were important post-revolutionary players, there was little hankering after a monarchical golden age, or serious effort to bring about a loyalist restoration; and so there was little need for argument over the rights and wrongs of the pre-revolutionary past. Most former loyalists who remained in the US concealed or adapted their old convictions. There was no one left for whom reference to an American 'old order' served much useful purpose.

Instead, most Americans quickly came to regard the conditions of the 'old order' as belonging, not to them at all, but to the Old World. The Ancien Régime had marked the past in Europe, not in colonial America itself, and it continued to shape Americans' view of the distinctive possibilities of their own national development. In state constitutions, in the Federal constitution, and in legislative measures abolishing primogeniture and entail, religious establishments, and other colonial legacies, Americans took steps that they saw as avoiding European inequalities and the hereditary principle. Thomas Jefferson, writing in the 1780s, envisaged the creation of an agrarian republic that could avoid the social evils arising from the cities and workshops of Europe.[48] Even those opponents of this Jeffersonian vision who followed Alexander Hamilton in advocating industrial development and a British-style financial system for the US celebrated America's freehold land system, the rarity of large landed estates, and the absence of a nobility or formal hereditary privileges. During the first decades of the nineteenth century, as Americans moved still further towards political democracy (for white men), the notion that they were following a trajectory distinct from that of Europe became more deeply embedded. The Ancien Régime was part of somebody else's past, not their own.

Notes

1. Thomas Paine, *Common Sense* (1776), ed. Isaac Kramnick (1976; repr. London, 1986), 120. Adams is quoted in David Waldstreicher, *In the Midst of Perpetual Fetes: The Making of American Nationalism, 1776-1820* (Chapel Hill, NC, 1997), 17.
2. Paine, *Common Sense*, 63.
3. R. R. Palmer, *The Age of the Democratic Revolution: A Political History of Europe and America, 1760-1800* (2 vols. Princeton, 1959-64); Jacques Godechot, *France and the Atlantic Revolution of the Eighteenth Century, 1770-1799* (New York, 1965); Lester D. Langley, *The Americas in the Age of Revolution, 1750-1850* (New Haven, Conn., 1996).

4. A rare, partial exception is Edward Countryman, 'Indians, the Colonial Order, and the Social Significance of the American Revolution', *William and Mary Quarterly*, 53 (1996), 342–62.
5. Bernard Bailyn, *Atlantic History: Concept and Contours* (Cambridge, Mass., 2005); J. H. Elliott, *Empires of the Atlantic World: Britain and Spain in America, 1492–1830* (New Haven, Conn., 2006).
6. Jack P. Greene and J. R. Pole (eds.), *Colonial British America: Essays in the New History of the Early Modern Era* (Baltimore, Md., 1984) was an important collection of essays portraying the colonial period in its own terms.
7. Gordon S. Wood, *The Radicalism of the American Revolution* (New York, 1992).
8. Arno J. Mayer, *The Persistence of the Old Regime: Europe to the Great War* (New York, 1981), 7–15.
9. Jack P. Greene, *The Quest for Power: The Lower Houses of Assembly in the Southern Royal Colonies, 1689–1776* (Chapel Hill, NC, 1963).
10. Allan Kulikoff, *From British Peasants to Colonial American Farmers* (Chapel Hill, NC, 2000).
11. George Bancroft, *History of the United States from the Discovery of the American Continent* (10 vols. Boston, 1856–74). A modern study stressing the long-term colonial origins of the Revolution is J. Revell Carr, *Seeds of Discontent: The Deep Roots of the American Revolution, 1650–1750* (New York, 2008).
12. Michael Zuckerman, 'Tocqueville, Turner, and Turds: Four Stories of Manners in Early America', *Journal of American History*, 85 (1998), 13–42; Gloria L. Main, *Peoples of a Spacious Land: Families and Cultures in Colonial New England* (Cambridge, Mass., 2001); the reference to Jamestown is in Karen Ordahl Kupperman, *The Jamestown Project* (Cambridge, Mass., 2007), 327.
13. William Moraley, *The Infortunate: The Voyage and Adventures of William Moraley, an Indentured Servant*, ed. Susan E. Klepp and Billy G. Smith (University Park, Pa., 1992), 188–9.
14. See e.g. Margaret E. Newell, *From Dependency to Independence: Economic Revolution in Colonial New England* (Ithaca, NY, 1998).
15. Louis Hartz, *The Liberal Tradition in America: An Interpretation of American Political Thought since the Revolution* (New York, 1955); Bernard Bailyn, *The Origins of American Politics* (New York, 1968).
16. Hugh Brogan, *Alexis de Tocqueville: A Life* (2006; new edn., New Haven, Conn., 2007), 184.
17. Jon Butler, *Becoming America: The Revolution Before 1776* (Cambridge, Mass., 2000).
18. Indeed, Countryman, 'Indians', 344, writes of describing 'a specifically American version of the eighteenth-century *ancien régime*'.
19. Ira Berlin, *Many Thousands Gone: The First Two Centuries of Slavery in North America* (Cambridge, Mass., 1998).
20. Richard R. Beeman, *The Varieties of Political Experience in Eighteenth-Century America* (Philadelphia, 2004).
21. John G. Kolp, *Gentlemen and Freeholders: Electoral Politics in Colonial Virginia* (Baltimore, Md., 1998), 195–9.
22. Jack P. Greene, 'Colonial History and National History: Reflections on a Continuing Problem', *William and Mary Quarterly*, 64 (Apr. 2007), 235–50.
23. Daniel K. Richter, *Facing East from Indian Country: A Native History of Early America* (Cambridge, Mass., 2001); Richard White, *The Middle Ground: Indians, Empires, and Republics in the Great Lakes Region, 1650–1815* (Cambridge, 1991); Nancy Shoemaker,

A Strange Likeness: Becoming Red and White in Eighteenth Century North America (New York, 2004).
24. Christopher Clark, *Social Change in America: From the Revolution through the Civil War* (Chicago, 2006), 4–11.
25. Carol Shammas, *A History of Household Government in America* (Charlottesville, Va., 2002), 31; Edmund S. Morgan, *American Slavery, American Freedom: The Ordeal of Colonial Virginia* (New York, 1975).
26. Clark, *Social Change*, 32–6.
27. Wood, *Radicalism of the American Revolution*; Richard L. Bushman, *King and People in Provincial Massachusetts* (Chapel Hill, NC, 1985); Brendan McConville, *The King's Three Faces: The Rise and Fall of Royal America, 1688–1776* (Chapel Hill, NC, 2006); Richard L. Bushman, *The Refinement of America: Persons, Houses, Cities* (New York, 1992).
28. Gary B. Nash, *The Urban Crucible: Social Change, Political Consciousness, and the Origins of the American Revolution* (Cambridge, Mass., 1979); Billy G. Smith (ed.), *Down and Out in Early America* (University Park, Pa., 2004); Ruth Wallis Herndon, *Unwelcome Americans: Living on the Margin in Early New England* (Philadelphia, 2001).
29. Peter Silver, *Our Savage Neighbors: How Indian War Transformed Early America* (New York, 2008); Peter Shaw, *American Patriots and the Rituals of Revolution* (Cambridge, Mass., 1981).
30. Greene, 'Colonial History and National History', 237.
31. John Murrin, 'Anglicizing an American Colony: The Transformation of Provincial Massachusetts', Ph.D. thesis (Yale, 1966).
32. 'Mr. Burke's Speech on Moving his Resolutions for Conciliation with the Colonies, March 22, 1775', in *The Works of the Right Hon. Edmund Burke*, i (London, 1834), 186.
33. Frank Lambert, *Inventing the 'Great Awakening'* (Princeton, 1999).
34. John M. Murrin, 'The French and Indian War, the American Revolution, and the Counterfactual Hypothesis: Reflections on Lawrence Henry Gipson and John Shy', *Reviews in American History*, 1 (Sept. 1973), 307–18.
35. Stephen Saunders Webb, *1676: The End of American Independence* (New York, 1984), argues further that the establishment of English 'garrison government' from this point permanently curbed colonial autonomy.
36. T. H. Breen, *The Marketplace of Revolution: How Consumer Politics Shaped American Independence* (New York, 2004); S. D. Smith, 'The Market for Manufactures in the Thirteen Continental Colonies, 1698–1776', *Economic History Review*, 51 (1998), 676–708.
37. McConville, *The King's Three Faces*, 105–41; Carla Gardina Pestana, *Protestant Empire: Religion and the Making of the British Atlantic World* (Philadelphia, 2009); Edmund S. Morgan, *Benjamin Franklin* (New Haven, Conn., 2002), chs. 3–4.
38. McConville, *The King's Three Faces*, 249–53.
39. Gary B. Nash, *The Unknown American Revolution: The Unruly Birth of Democracy and the Struggle to Create America* (New York, 2005).
40. Bernard Bailyn, *The Ideological Origins of the American Revolution* (Cambridge, Mass., 1967), 52–3 and *passim*.
41. Fred Anderson, *Crucible of War: The Seven Years' War and the Fate of Empire in British North America, 1754–1766* (London, 2000), 664–76.
42. Woody Holton, *Forced Founders: Indians, Debtors, Slaves, and the Making of the American Revolution in Virginia* (Chapel Hill, NC, 1999); T. H. Breen, *American Insurgents, American Patriots: The Revolution of the People* (New York, 2010).

43. David Ramsay, *An Oration, Delivered in St. Michael's Church, before the Inhabitants of Charleston, South-Carolina, on the Fourth of July, 1794* (Charleston, SC, [1794]), 3; Benjamin Hichborn, *An Oration, Delivered July 5th, 1784 at the Request of the Inhabitants of the Town of Boston* (Boston, [1784]), 6–7.
44. Enos Hitchcock, *A Discourse on the Causes of National Prosperity* (Providence, RI, [1786]), 7–8. Laurens is quoted in Jack Rakove, *Revolutionaries: A New History of the Invention of America* (New York, 2010), 213–14.
45. Bailyn, *Ideological Origins*, 279–80.
46. Maya Jasanoff, 'The Other Side of Revolution: Loyalists in the British Empire', *William and Mary Quarterly*, 65 (April 2008), 205–32, data at 208.
47. William Wirt, *An Oration Delivered in Richmond on the Fourth of July, 1800* (Richmond, Va., [1800]), 17, 13; Kilborn Whitman, *An Oration, Pronounced at Bridgewater, October 4, 1798* (Boston, 1798), 12.
48. Thomas Jefferson, *Notes on the State of Virginia* (1781–2, new edn., Richmond, Va., 1853), 175–7.

Bibliography

Anderson, Fred, *Crucible of War: The Seven Years' War and the Fate of Empire in British North America, 1754–1766* (London, 2000).
Bailyn, Bernard, *The Ideological Origins of the American Revolution* (Cambridge, Mass., 1967).
Beeman, Richard R., *The Varieties of Political Experience in Eighteenth-Century America* (Philadelphia, 2004).
Breen, T. H., *The Marketplace of Revolution: How Consumer Politics Shaped American Independence* (New York, 2004).
—— *American Insurgents, American Patriots: The Revolution of the People* (New York, 2010).
Butler, Jon, *Becoming America: The Revolution Before 1776* (Cambridge, Mass., 2000).
Elliott, J. H., *Empires of the Atlantic World: Britain and Spain in America, 1492–1830* (New Haven, Conn., 2006).
Greene, Jack P., 'Colonial History and National History: Reflections on a Continuing Problem', *William and Mary Quarterly*, 64 (2007), 235–50.
McConville, Brendan, *The King's Three Faces: The Rise and Fall of Royal America, 1688–1776* (Chapel Hill, NC, 2006).
Nash, Gary B., *The Unknown American Revolution: The Unruly Birth of Democracy and the Struggle to Create America* (New York, 2005).
Pestana, Carla Gardina, *Protestant Empire: Religion and the Making of the British Atlantic World* (Philadelphia, 2009).
Richter, Daniel K., *Facing East from Indian Country: A Native History of Early America* (Cambridge, Mass., 2001).
Wood, Gordon S., *The Radicalism of the American Revolution* (New York, 1992).

CHAPTER 31

THE OLD REICH

PETER H. WILSON

Over the last thirty years it has become common to refer to the Holy Roman Empire as the 'Old Reich' to distinguish it from Bismarck's Second Reich and Hitler's Third. In a simple sense, the Holy Roman Empire was indeed old, having been founded by Charlemagne on Christmas Day 800. The original empire was partitioned in 843, with the western third becoming France, but the imperial dignity was reasserted east of the Rhine in 962 by Otto I, who now presented it more clearly as a direct continuation of that of ancient Rome. As this ideology of 'imperial translation' developed, the Reich became the fourth and last monarchy prophesied in the Book of Daniel to reign over earth till Judgment Day. Reinforced by scripture, the Emperor claimed pre-eminence over all other Christian rulers as advocate of the church and supreme arbiter of Europe. This position was eroded, not least as the western European monarchies evolved into more distinct, sovereign states. Nonetheless, both the Russian tsar and even Napoleon still formally accepted the Emperor's precedence when they adopted their own imperial titles in 1721 and 1804 respectively.

The extent to which the Reich might be categorized as an Ancien Régime depends, of course, on how that term is defined. The concept of an old regime postdates the Reich, since it derives from the controversy surrounding the legacy of the French Revolution. Just as that Revolution has been central to debates on modern French history, so the problematic issues of statehood and national unity have dominated discussions about German development after the Reich was dissolved in 1806. These discussions have been shaped by the characteristics associated with an old regime. Enlightened and liberal critics abhorred the seemingly all-pervasive influence of religion in prerevolutionary society, exemplified by stock figures such as the king's confessor apparently exercising the real power behind the throne, or the 'dead hand' of the church using valuable resources for clerical profligacy and unproductive activities, like prayer and contemplation. Privilege constituted a second pernicious trait sustaining gross inequalities of opportunity, and smothering true individual liberty with a misleading language of 'liberties', or legally enshrined rights for selected groups. Thirdly, old regimes were condemned for their opaqueness, dissembling their true character behind the façade of benevolent despotism and *noblesse oblige* that obscured the workings of patronage, clientelism, and corruption. 'Absolute monarchy', a term coined in these discussions, came to symbolize the old regime as a political structure resting on society, but not rooted in it, unrepresentative, unaccountable, and unloved. All institutions it created remained alien bodies detached from the 'nation', like the standing armies supposedly composed of 'foreign mercenaries' hired to repress the population they nominally defended.

Such criticism did not go unchallenged. Old regimes were praised for providing the basis for prosperity and good order that disappeared during the upheaval of revolution. Political stability had been complemented by social harmony, since privileges had allegedly been balanced by responsibilities. The hierarchical character of old regime society had given everyone a place and a function, in contrast to revolutionary egalitarianism that left all, regardless of ability, at the mercy of market forces. Individuals had been protected through their membership of a distinct group with corporate liberties, whereas revolutionary liberty meant the freedom of the fortunate few to exploit the rest while the *laissez-faire* state merely stood by and watched. Finally, conservatives condemned the 'godless revolutionaries' not merely for their anticlericalism, but for their disregard for the morality and decency which religion had previously provided.[1]

While Germans were certainly involved in debating the old regime, the customary dates used to delineate it are problematic for the history of the old Reich. The usual starting date of 1648 makes some sense for French history where the old regime is defined by the resurgent Bourbon monarchy that established itself under Louis XIV in the wake of the Thirty Years War and internal upheavals of the Fronde. However, for much of the writing on the Reich, 1648 only represents a start in the sense of the 'beginning of the end'. The trauma of the Thirty Years War that ended with the Westphalian settlement of that year was long thought to have reduced the Reich to an empty shell. The Emperor, it was believed, was reduced to little more than a figurehead, emasculated in a labyrinthine constitution that devolved real power to the princes ruling the Reich's component territories. The Reich ceased to be a factor in international relations as the princes made alliances with foreign powers and even attacked the Emperor, as in the case of Bavaria during the War of the Spanish Succession (1701–14), or Prussia in a series of conflicts after 1740. This perspective persisted into the 1970s (and beyond in the popular consciousness), because it served a number of important historiographical agendas. One was the Borussian tradition that developed during the nineteenth century as Prussia challenged Austria for dominance of Germany. The Austrian Habsburgs, as the dynasty virtually monopolizing the imperial title after 1438, were condemned by pro-Prussian historians for failing to provide the leadership deemed necessary to unite Germany and achieve its national destiny. This task fell to Prussia, which had to destroy the Reich and eject Austria in order to complete the historic mission. Naturally, this interpretation contains a strong Protestant bias, but there were also Catholic critics of the Reich. Regardless of confession or political agenda, the convention of ignoring the Reich after 1648 also made the writing of German history much easier by slotting it into the standard narrative of growing state power. While this no longer took place on a 'national' level, given the Emperor's weakness, the development of more absolute princely authority within the territories resembled the centralization under way in France and other major European countries. German history could thus be written as part of a wider 'age of absolutism'; something greatly assisted by the prominence of figures like Frederick II and Joseph II in the debates on Enlightened absolutism, as well as by the more recent interest in the rulers of smaller territories like Hessen-Kassel as model, Enlightened princes.[2]

Research since the late 1960s demonstrates that the Reich not only continued to function, but also developed after 1648.[3] Some elements certainly weakened, but it is no longer possible to talk of inevitable decline. The Peace of Westphalia did not make the princes independent sovereigns, nor indeed grant many new powers. They were already entitled to maintain troops and negotiate with foreign potentates, provided these actions were not directed against the Emperor or Reich. Some rights, such as the power to change their subjects' religion, were actually curtailed by Westphalia. The Emperor's formal powers were indeed diminished, but he retained considerable prestige and influence. The Habsburgs rebuilt imperial authority after 1648 by remaining within the constitution and exploiting the opportunities it offered to rally support from the princes and other imperial Estates (*Reichsstände*), like the counts and imperial cities.[4] The Reich's hierarchical character was strengthened by institutional development from the 1660s that preserved the autonomy of the weaker elements, despite the accumulation of military power and international influence by the larger secular principalities, like Brandenburg-Prussia, Saxony, Bavaria, and Hanover. The Reichstag (imperial diet) remained in permanent session after 1663, ensuring that the minor counties, abbeys, and cities retained a voice in legislation and policy alongside the more powerful electorates and principalities. These weaker elements also benefited from the development of the *Kreise* (imperial circles) that served as an intermediary layer of regional coordination between the territorial governments and central imperial institutions like the Reichstag. The *Kreise* assumed greater prominence with the defence reforms of 1681–2 that reorganized external collective security and internal peacekeeping. Two imperial supreme courts resolved conflicts amongst the imperial estates and between them and their subjects. A combination of imperial legislation, legal arbitration, and regulation through the *Kreise* offset some of the problems posed by territorial fragmentation and promoted economic development.[5]

The territories were not uniformly integrated within this framework. The greater density of population in the south and west during the middle ages led to a more concentrated and differentiated hierarchy of lords and communes than in the north and east. These smaller, more fragmented territories depended more heavily on imperial institutions than the larger, more sparsely populated principalities in northern and eastern Germany. The northern dynasties also established stronger ties to foreign crowns, giving them a more prominent European role. For example, Saxony was linked to Poland between 1697 and 1763, while the Hanoverian dynasty became kings of England in 1714. The Brandenburg Hohenzollerns in 1618 inherited the duchy of Prussia that lay outside the Reich and was fully sovereign from 1660. Together with other gains within the Reich after 1648, they possessed far more land and subjects than any other German ruler except the Habsburgs. Thanks to a special dispensation from Emperor Leopold I in 1700, they were given the status of royalty that was recognized by other European monarchs around 1714. Victory over Austria in four wars during the eighteenth century established Prussia as the second German great power. However, Prussia still contributed its share of the taxes to maintain the imperial supreme courts even after the 1750s when it barred appeals from its own subjects. Frederick II still paid his feudal dues to the Emperor, and Hohenzollern territory remained part of the Reich despite Prussia's withdrawal from the French Revolutionary Wars in 1795. Prussia's growth as a great power encouraged previously more independently minded dynasties to support imperial institutions as the best guarantee for their continued autonomy. Hanover and Saxony joined the minor princes in promoting a renewal of key institutions in the later eighteenth century, assisting in a revival of the imperial courts. The need to coordinate the response to revolutionary France also stimulated the Reichstag, which resumed activity after a period of deadlock induced by Austro-Prussian rivalry.[6] The Reich can no longer be written out of German history after 1648, but remained a constituent part of political, social, cultural, and economic life.

Its vitality into the late eighteenth century also raises questions whether 1648 can be regarded as a significant 'turning point'. Further doubts were voiced in the flood of publications celebrating the 350th anniversary of the Westphalian settlement in 1998. While these generally confirmed that the Thirty Years War diminished the Emperor's international standing, they suggested that the Peace revised rather than fundamentally changed the imperial constitution, building on past precedents not innovations.[7] The sense of evolution is reinforced if the perspective is widened from politics to social, economic, and other factors.[8]

The year 1789 makes even less sense for the history of the Reich. No established authority was overturned by popular revolution east of the Rhine, and despite considerable historical attention, it is clear that the German Jacobins remained an isolated minority.[9] The Reich entered the French Revolutionary Wars unwillingly, losing the Netherlands and the other land west of the Rhine, but otherwise resisting invasion until Prussia made a separate peace in April 1795. The entire area north of the River Main was obliged to enter the Prussian-controlled neutrality zone agreed with France, effectively partitioning the Reich. The imperial war effort crumbled during 1796, forcing Emperor Francis II to accept the loss of the land west of the Rhine and renounce imperial jurisdiction over north Italy (*Reichsitalien*) with the Peace of Campo Formio in 1797. Renewed war led to further defeat, whereby Francis II acknowledged these losses in his capacity as Emperor, as well as ruler of the Habsburg lands. German rulers losing land west of the Rhine were to be compensated at the expense of the ecclesiastical territories collectively comprising the imperial church (*Reichskirche*). This process was eventually sanctioned by the Reichstag in February 1803, consolidating land and power in the hands of around twenty secular princes, though over 100 other minor rulers remained alongside six surviving imperial cities. Historians have generally assumed these changes effectively marked the end of the Reich, but contemporaries saw the reorganization as a new beginning, removing the less viable elements, thereby enhancing the prospect that the Reich would preserve the consolidated principalities as a 'third Germany' alongside Austria and Prussia.[10] Even Austria remained committed to preserving the constitution and only gave ground with great reluctance in the wake of renewed defeat in the War of the Third Coalition in 1805. Fearing Napoleon would reopen hostilities if he did not recognize the new French-sponsored Confederation of the Rhine, Francis II declared the Reich dissolved and abdicated on 6 August 1806.[11]

If the Reich did represent an old regime, then it lasted considerably beyond the period associated with French history. Concerned for Hanover, Britain refused to acknowledge the Reich had been dissolved until 1814. Many hoped the Reich would be restored at the Congress of Vienna. Though the mediatized rulers did not recover their full authority, they nonetheless retained lesser jurisdiction until 1848. Other elements of the old constitution were continued in the German Confederation established in 1815, with a Bundestag taking the place of the Reichstag and Austrian presidency standing in for the Emperor. The Confederation has attracted criticisms similar to those levelled against the Reich, as later historians portrayed it as a weak structure incapable of providing the political framework necessary for German national development. It too disappeared in the wake of military defeat, as Prussia crushed Austria and the federal army in 1866, reorganizing Germany as the Second Reich by 1871.[12]

Any consideration of the Reich as an old regime must consider its political culture. The complex web of legal rights underpinning the imperial constitution proved very attractive to conservatives after 1815 who believed that incorporating traditional practices in the new German Confederation would preserve social stability.[13] This coincided with Romanticism's fascination with 'Gothick' medievalism and its criticism of the French revolutionary and Napoleonic legacy and their association with Enlightened thought. The Reich's complex structure certainly contradicted many core Enlightened beliefs. For example, it seemed illogical that Buchhorn in Swabia, with only 770 inhabitants and 28 km^2 of land, should enjoy the status of imperial estate with representation in the Reichstag and the right to maintain its own army, whereas major cities like Vienna, Berlin, and Leipzig were mere 'territorial towns' under the jurisdiction of their prince. Yet German Romanticism remained ambivalent to the Reich. Leading figures of the late eighteenth-century 'Sturm and Drang' movement were hostile to imperial traditions. Herder considered Charlemagne a 'murderer', while Schiller was unable to find a suitable figure from the Empire's past about whom to write a historical drama. For Schiller, the Reich and German nation were entirely different entities and many intellectuals around 1800 felt the former must die if the latter was to be reborn.[14] While others remained more positive, they looked back to the middle ages rather than the early modern Reich. A good example is Goethe's choice of Götz von Berlichingen for his historical drama, celebrating the famous robber baron as a proud representative of the free knights whose existence was threatened by the centralizing princely territorial states in the early sixteenth century.[15] The medieval past was more explicitly instrumentalized in the later nineteenth century in attempts to provide historical underpinning for the Second Reich, which was dominated by the Hohenzollern dynasty, which lacked its own imperial tradition.[16]

Yet the Reich was scarcely a Gothic construction by the late eighteenth century. While of course having roots deeper in the past, the key imperial institutions only really took shape between 1480 and 1520 under the influence of the humanist revival of classical Rome, the same source that inspired the French revolutionaries. Practical forces were also at work, as lords and communal authorities struggled with profound demographic, social, and economic changes, while the Emperor and princes responded to the twin threats of a powerful French monarchy to the west and the Ottoman advance in the east. The Reichstag, *Kreise,* and imperial courts emerged as mechanisms for distributing the responsibility and burdens of defence and conflict resolution across the Reich. Those lords and cities that accepted obligations to the Reich gained a voice in its institutions as imperial estates, whereas those that refused or were unable to contribute lost any direct relationship to the Emperor and were subject to one or more levels of intervening jurisdiction. The Reich retained the potential to develop either as a more centralized monarchy, or a federation of more discrete territories. Nonetheless, the changes in the early sixteenth century established its basic early modern form as a hierarchy under the Emperor's overall jurisdiction, but not subject to his direct authority. The Emperor assumed a dual role as both the elected overlord of the entire Reich, and an imperial estate through his direct possession of land entitling representation in imperial institutions. The power of election had been restricted since 1356 to a small group of princes who formed the senior electoral college in the Reichstag and successfully excluded the second, princely college from any say in choosing the Emperor. However, the electors recognized a collective responsibility for the Reich and appreciated that whoever they chose had to possess considerable resources to sustain the dignity of the imperial office and discharge its functions. The Habsburgs were the obvious choice, not least because the geographical distribution of their own lands gave them an incentive to defend the Reich against French and Ottoman attack. An elaborate system of constitutional checks and balances was developed after 1495 to prevent the Habsburgs misusing their position to advance purely dynastic goals.

Political development thus became a common enterprise of Emperor and imperial estates, all of whom had their own reasons to ensure the Reich's survival. The Reich provided the Habsburgs with prestige and a reservoir of resources to supplement those of their own possessions in international conflict. Interest in the Reich diminished as the Habsburgs acquired a distinct empire of their own, especially through the reconquest of Hungary after 1683, but it remained central to the dynasty's international status until the very end. The constitution also served to prevent Prussia or foreign powers exploiting the still considerable resources of the 'third Germany'. While the more powerful princes sought royal titles and European recognition from the later seventeenth century, only Prussia possessed the resources sufficient for a separate existence and even it remained the weakest of the great powers. The others recognized that the Reich preserved their distinct status as superior to aristocrats of other nations. Interest in the Reich grew among these weaker elements as real political and military power became concentrated in Prussia and Austria, both of which possessed more land outside the Reich than within it by the end of the eighteenth century. Austro-Prussian rivalry frustrated attempts to strengthen the constitution, such as the League of Princes in 1785.[17] Nonetheless, the imperial constitution provided the basic point of departure for all discussion about the future direction of political development. Even after 1789, German discussion paid little attention to the new abstract language coming from France, concentrating instead on tinkering with the existing structure. 'The Empire was a construction existing from force of habit' and it proved difficult for its inhabitants to conceive of an alternative.[18]

The direction of constitutional development was confirmed by the response to the Reformation. The Reich eschewed the confessional solution favoured in western Europe whereby the state tried to enforce religious orthodoxy and punish dissent. This method entailed a considerable increase in royal authority since the crown claimed the right to decide which of the competing confessions constituted religious truth. The Reich devolved the choice to the imperial estates that were free to accept Lutheranism after 1555. This attempt to take religion out of politics proved only partially successful, because the Lutherans remained the minority in imperial institutions, while those adopting Calvinism lacked legal protection. Such problems contributed to the outbreak of the Thirty Years War, leading to the main area of constitutional revision in 1648. Calvinism received official recognition, but rulers lost the right to compel their subjects to change faith. Instead, each territory was to remain associated with whatever faith it had held in 1624, while the Protestants, who remained the minority in the Reichstag, were protected by a new voting procedure if religious issues were being discussed. These changes were carried over into other parts of the constitution, establishing the principle of parity. For example, the appointment of a Catholic general to the imperial army had to be matched by an equivalent rank for a Protestant. There is considerable evidence that such arrangements entrenched an 'invisible frontier' along sectarian lines throughout society. In Augsburg, formally a bi-confessional city, it was even said that Protestant and Catholic pigs had separate sties.[19] Some historians identify a 'reconfessionalization' of imperial politics after 1648, even suggesting an 'unholy empire'. However, while religion was certainly instrumentalized in the Austro-Prussian rivalry, the constitutional arrangements were remarkably successful in defusing tension.[20] Disputes were no longer about absolute religious truth, but the specific rights of individual groups of believers who preferred to argue their case in the law courts rather than the street or the battlefield.

The integration of religious identities within the web of imperial law reinforced the Reich's character as a dense network of different corporate groups. Rights remained specific and were a means of relating an individual to one or more distinct communities. For example, the status of citizen (*Bürger*) denoted a privileged inhabitant of a particular town, giving that person a stake in the management of local affairs. Villagers lacked many of the privileges enjoyed by urban citizens, but nonetheless retained a say in how their communities were governed. Participation in communal affairs was restricted primarily to property holders, but was nonetheless fairly broad and incorporated other, formally disenfranchised individuals through their relationship to an enfranchised householder. There was a strong sense of belonging to a 'home town', but this did not preclude wider identification with the Reich.[21] Peasants rejected all earthly lords during the great rebellion of 1525, but still recognized the Emperor and displayed the imperial eagle on some of their flags. Identification with the Reich varied with the extent to which territories and communities were integrated within the constitutional framework. Prussia abolished official prayers for the Emperor's health in 1750, but they were still being said in the imperial cities until after Francis II's abdication.

It remains a matter of controversy whether such sentiment can be labelled nationalism. Georg Schmidt has argued forcefully that the Reich constituted the first German nation-state.[22] Much of this discussion centres on semantics, since the different views largely rest on how a nation is defined. Certainly, the Reich was routinely referred to as 'German' during the eighteenth century, but this had more to do with politics than concepts of blood, soil, or language. There was also a sense of a separate 'Austrian nation', despite common cultural and linguistic bonds. The label remained elastic, essentially denoting identification with a community, with one writer for instance talking about a 'Viennese nation'.[23] While there were several competing discourses of nationality around 1800, most Germans appear to have regarded the Reich as a wider fatherland guaranteeing the particular identity of their more immediate home community through legal protection afforded to local rights. What gave the Reich strength and social cohesion was that its political and legal arrangements sanctioned multiple identities, in contrast to the Second and Third Reichs that demanded loyalty to a single national or racial identity. There was a widespread sense of dislocation as the political reorganization after 1801 first disrupted, then destroyed this protection. The experience was still more keenly felt given its coincidence with war and economic hardship.[24]

Despite its origins in the late fifteenth century, this complex constitution was not necessarily at odds with Enlightened rationality. The new university of Göttingen, founded in 1737 and noted as an innovative research and teaching establishment, was also a centre for the study of imperial law. Many minor territories were at the forefront of cultural, economic, and social developments. The lands of the imperial church offer an especially good example, since their association with Catholicism led to criticism from many Enlightened thinkers. Yet Mainz, bastion of the German Catholic Church, saw a wide range of measures often far ahead of those implemented in supposedly more progressive states. For instance, compulsory elementary schooling was introduced for boys in 1776, followed by girls four years later, with Jewish children admitted after 1784.[25] Perhaps more significantly, imperial law enshrined certain basic rights, including prohibiting religious discrimination (for members of the three recognized confessions). The actual range was much wider for many inhabitants, because imperial law offered them opportunities to defend locally recognized liberties in higher courts. Territorial law drew heavily on imperial legal practice, further extending the formal protection of the law. Women, for example, generally enjoyed far greater recognized rights in the Reich than in France, in many cases even after the Revolution.[26]

The apparent modernity of these arrangements has encouraged some to claim the old Reich as the precursor to the 'new Europe', becoming the 'Central Europe of the regions' in the words of one recent writer who borrows explicitly from the language of the European Commission to explain the imperial constitution.[27] The emphasis on the modernity of the old Reich gathered pace in the wake of German reunification in 1990 that demonstrated the success of the Federal Republic established in 1949. The centralized 'power state', celebrated in Borussian historiography, now appeared the exception, not the norm for German political development, restricted in practice to the twelve years of Hitler's regime as historians discovered federal elements in Bismarck's Second Reich and particularly in the old Reich.[28]

The question of modernity raises the central issue about the Ancien Régime: whether the old order retarded human progress, or allowed humanity to flourish.[29] Such discussions risk invoking one or more variants of the 'modernization thesis' condemned by postmodernists as imposing a false order on the past by relating development to a singular path. In the German case, there has been a heavy emphasis on the nation-state as modernity's defining characteristic and the supposed motor for change. The Reich has been criticized for delaying modernity by keeping Germany politically fragmented. In older accounts this condemned the country to passivity and foreign invasion until Prussia provided the necessary blood and iron to forge national unity. More recently, the later problems associated with world war and National Socialism have been ascribed to belated nationhood. In this interpretation, Prussia remained politically part of the old regime, dominated by a reactionary monarchy and its *Junker* allies. The liberals sacrificed their progressive political programme in order to secure this elite's acquiescence to national unity in 1871. Bismarck constructed a sham democracy that ultimately proved incapable of mastering the problems unleashed by rapid industrialiation and urbanization.[30]

The interpretation of these later events casts a long shadow over the German past. The assumption persists that outmoded political structures retarded social and economic development, and frustrated the chance of Germany emerging as a stable democratic country before the mid-twentieth century. The fact that such a paradigm implies a singular form of democracy cannot be covered here. It is clear, however, that a large number of historians who have contributed to the rehabilitation of the Reich in recent years also regard it as inhibiting progressive reform. For them, the very success of imperial institutions in regulating conflict in the minor territories ultimately made the entire structure unviable. Reliance on the Reich discouraged much needed structural reform, allowing social and political arrangements to ossify, notably in the imperial cities and small counties. Attempts to resolve conflict by fixing political status and legal relations ever more precisely made it progressively harder to accommodate change within the constitution. Contemporaries were increasingly aware of the growing discrepancy between the formal structure and the actual distribution of power within the Reich.[31]

This interpretation unintentionally returns the discussion to the older view that the divergent development of Austria, Prussia, and the larger principalities left the Reich an empty shell, easily shattered by the dynamic forces of revolutionary France. The problem here is the benefit of hindsight, which means that the problems of the late eighteenth century are viewed differently from previous periods when the Reich underwent considerable strain, such as during the rapid demographic and economic change in the century following 1480, or the dislocation caused by the Thirty Years War. There were certainly very serious social and economic problems around 1800 related to underemployment and pauperization.[32] The legal framework intended to regulate a society of estates was clearly at odds with one being transformed by class and market forces. It is also the case that the smaller territories drew disproportionately on imperial institutions as they tried to master these problems. The imperial abbey of Korneleimünster, with only 5,000 subjects, accounted for no less than 200 cases before the *Reichskammergericht*, one of the two supreme courts.[33] Intervention by the courts and imperial commissions regularly addressed disputes over rights, land, and resources between minor imperial estates, as well as intervening in response to appeals from ordinary subjects. The longevity of such cases was itself neither a flaw nor evidence of an ossifying structure. Imperial legal procedure, and the territorial practice it influenced, was not concerned with absolute justice but with finding peaceful, lasting practical solutions. The courts arbitrated rather than judged, intervening again as circumstances changed on the ground. Such intervention could prompt change. For example, minor principalities like Montfort and Sachsen-Hildburghausen were compelled to reorganize their finances following imperial debt commissions in the late eighteenth century. Significant results were achieved. The public liabilities of the city of Nördlingen were cut from 696,000 florins (fl.) to 84,400 between 1750 and 1793.[34] In extreme cases, the courts deposed princes in response to complaints from their relations or subjects.[35]

Perhaps more important in this context was that such intervention was not always necessary. Some imperial estates were genuinely approaching bankruptcy by 1806, such as the city of Frankfurt, which had accumulated debts of 15 million fl. Indebtedness generally worsened in the aftermath of the Seven Years War (1756–63), but this also reflected changes in the way territorial governments managed their finances. Levels were not necessarily life-threatening and could be managed despite the outbreak of war. For example, the bishopric of Konstanz with 12,000 inhabitants had debts of 563,000 fl. by 1788, compared to an average annual revenue of under 74,000. War added another 118,000 fl. of debt by 1801. Yet the authorities kept expenditure below income and had already reduced debts to under 435,000 fl. by the time the bishopric was annexed by the margraviate of Baden in November 1802 as part of the wider territorial reorganization of the Reich.[36] Prussia meanwhile lurched from one financial crisis to another, and had to borrow on the international money market simply to withdraw its troops from the western front in 1795.[37]

The Reich's resilience cannot be explained solely by reference to its political history. One of the principal shortcomings of the recent writing has been a preoccupation with the Reich's formal framework rather than its social history. Indeed, social history is still largely written without reference to it at all.[38] There is a tendency amongst social historians to write micro studies of groups or communities that can be difficult to place in a wider context. Attempts to write more broadly, while often producing good results, use the territories or, more anachronistically, later German frontiers to provide the boundaries and political context for their investigations. The state, where it appears at all, is often viewed as acting from above upon society, extracting taxes, demanding recruits, and interfering in daily life. This unwittingly reproduces the sinister thesis of the state that featured in the Enlightenment critique of the old regime and regards ordinary folk as either the bystanders or victims, not active participants in political development.[39]

A rather fuller explanation for the old Reich's resilience emerges when the perspective moves into the towns and villages. Some of this has already been suggested by the most recent work on the imperial courts that has revealed how common folk exploited and manipulated the judicial structure to achieve their own goals. It is only by taking those goals seriously that we can understand how a socio-political order riddled with gross inequalities not only functioned, but coped with significant strain. As German revolutionaries were to discover to their cost during the early nineteenth century, radical change was not part of the popular agenda.[40] Interest in abstract equality and freedom remained largely confined to intellectuals. Improvement, for most people, entailed enhancing their existing local privileges, lightening externally imposed burdens, and protecting them from forces beyond their control, such as war, dearth, and large-scale economic change. Protest arose when the authorities failed in their duty to resolve those problems that could not be settled locally. Such failures stemmed, not from lack of interest or concern, but were due to the scale of the difficulties, inability to identify their true causes, and the application of inappropriate solutions. Those in power did blame the poor for their own misfortune, seeking to police daily life and mould it to suit fiscal-military and confessional agendas. Such 'social disciplining' often created its own problems, especially by attempting to impose supposedly rational schemes from above.[41] However, many official measures were in response to popular requests for the government to address specific problems. Enforcement relied largely on consent, because despite the cliché Germans were not cowed into submission by armed repression. Governments did use force to impose unpopular measures that were particularly important to their interests, but they lacked the resources and the desire to do this for all measures and many decrees were repeated regularly, indicating they were not being observed. Perhaps more telling is the large range of ordinances that were observed without coercion, because they met with broad approval, or were issued in direct response to pressure from below.[42]

It is in this relationship between social structure, state regulation, and wider change that the character of the Reich as an old regime finally emerges. For all the positive features noted recently, the Reich remained entwined with a social order based on corporate groups with distinct rights and local autonomy. Imperial institutions developed to provide the coordination and regulation necessary for such a society to resolve its problems and defend itself from attack. These institutions operated best in the areas most dependent upon them: in the west, south, and parts of the centre and north-west where territorial jurisdiction was most fragmented. Attachment to the Reich and its political and legal culture was also strongest in these regions. This did not prevent people living in these areas engaging with new ideas or economic practices, nor was the corporate social order absent from the larger principalities of the north and east. Nonetheless, it encouraged attitudes and practices that were essentially early modern in the sense that an individual's relationship to society, state, and economy was mediated through his or her membership of one or more legally defined groups or communities. Even those without firm ties to settled society, such as vagrants or gypsies, were defined the same way: it was precisely their lack of membership of a recognized, sanctioned community that placed them on the social margins.

Enlightened reform challenged aspects of these relationships. Its rationalizing drive was inherently at odds with the Reich's web of local rights, immunities, exceptions, and special arrangements. For example, rulers of both large and small principalities tried to curtail or remove tax exemptions for specific groups or areas, in order to boost revenue. Local customs were straight-jacketed into written law codes. Common land was placed under new forms of management. Village and municipal officials were co-opted as the lower echelons of a more uniform (and by the 1790s indeed uniformed) bureaucracy. Those affected by these changes were rarely formally consulted. Territorial estates (*Landstände*) and other representative institutions certainly survived in many territories in the late eighteenth century, but were rarely summoned as full diets. Their leading members were frequently closely connected to those staffing to the territorial administration. Such bodies in any case represented corporate groups, like the territorial nobility, clergy, religious foundations, and enfranchised towns and villages. They did not represent a democratic alternative to the imperial legal culture since their own status rested on rights recognized in imperial law that opened possibilities for appeal to imperial institutions. Thus, resistance to enlightened reform largely followed the same trajectory as other popular protest, as those affected preferred legal challenges to violent rebellion. Tax strikes and other largely passive resistance were options, but violence remained a matter of last resort, because its use would damage the chances of securing legal redress. Thus, the old Reich was indeed a *Rechtsstaat*, or state governed by law, but this did not make it a modern one. The law mainly protected collective not individual rights and the chances of obtaining redress depended largely on how well those seeking it conformed to expected behaviour.[43]

The Reich's dissolution removed the principal prop of this socio-legal order, opening the door to a 'clean sweep' (*Flurbereinigung*) by the surviving, now fully sovereign princes. Though influenced in part by French models, and certainly driven by Napoleon's military demands, these reforms drew heavily on the earlier, Enlightened experience.[44] Official measures grew more ambitious and wide-ranging, now that they were freed from the constraints previously imposed by the Reich. Power remained in the hands of established ruling dynasties, most of whom successfully negotiated the turbulence of the Napoleonic era and emerged as members of the German Confederation in 1815. However, the transition exposed serious problems that were to worsen as the nineteenth century progressed. The changes loosened the legal bonds underpinning corporate social relations, depriving those losing out to market forces of their customary means of redress. No alternative was offered, given the princes' refusal to create new representative institutions, despite promises made in the Confederation's Founding Act. To many, the new arrangements offered less security than they had enjoyed under the Reich. Meanwhile, the redistribution of territory between 1801 and 1815 had proceeded largely along strategic lines, placing hundreds of thousands of inhabitants under the rule of dynasties with whom they had no previous connection. The number of religious minorities increased with, for example, Lutheran Württemberg acquiring much of the former Catholic imperial church lands in Swabia, while Protestant Prussia obtained the largely Catholic Rhineland. While the leading intellectuals bemoaned the lack of a national identity, most ordinary folk struggled with the much more immediate dislocation of their local communities. The liberals concentrated their attacks on what they regarded as the vestiges of the old regime: the fragmentation of Germany through petty princely despotism. Their difficulty in mobilizing popular support stemmed from their failure to appreciate the strength of a deeper, underlying Ancien Régime characteristic: attachment to collective rights defining local and group identity.

Notes

1. Aspects of these debates are explored by H. Dippel, *Germany and the American Revolution 1770–1800* (Chapel Hill, NC, 1977); K. Epstein, *The Genesis of German Conservatism* (Princeton, 1966); H. Dreitzel, *Monarchbegriffe in der Fürstengesellschaft* (2 vols. Cologne, 1991).
2. For the debate on German absolutism, see J. Kunisch, *Absolutismus* (2nd edn., Göttingen, 1999); R. G. Asch and H. Duchhardt (eds.), *Der Absolutismus: Ein Mythos?* (Cologne, 1996); P. H. Wilson, *Absolutism in Central Europe* (London, 2000).
3. Overviews in P. H. Wilson, *The Holy Roman Empire 1495–1806* (2nd edn., Basingstoke, 2011). More detailed coverage of imperial politics after 1648 can be found in K. O. Frhr. v. Aretin, *Das Alte Reich 1648–1806* (3 vols. Stuttgart, 1993–7).
4. H. Klueting, 'Das Reich und Österreich 1648–1740', in W. Brauneder and L. Höbelt (eds.), *Sacrum Imperium: Das Reich und Österreich 996–1806* (Vienna, 1996), 162–287.
5. For this last point, O. Volckart, 'Politische Zersplitterung und Wirtschaftswachstum im Alten Reich, ca.1650–1800', *Vierteljahresheft für Sozial-und Wirtschaftsgeschichte*, 86 (1999), 1–38. The extensive literature on institutional development after 1648 can be accessed through A. Schindling, *Die Anfänge des immerwährenden Reichstags zu Regensburg* (Mainz, 1991); W. Dotzauer, *Die deutschen Reichskreise (1383–1806)* (Stuttgart, 1806); W. Sellert (ed.), *Reichshofrat und Reichskammergericht* (Cologne, 1999); P. H. Wilson, *German Armies: War and German Politics 1648–1806* (London, 1998).
6. K. O. Frhr. v. Aretin, 'Kaiser Joseph II und die Reichskammergerichtsvisitation 1766–1776', *Zeitschrift für Neuere Rechtsgeschichte*, 13 (1991), 129–44; K. Härter, *Reichstag und Revolution 1789–1806* (Göttingen, 1992).
7. The literature is reviewed by J. Arndt, 'Ein europäisches Jubiläum: 350 Jahre Westfälischer Friede', *Jahrbuch für Europäische Geschichte*, 1 (2000), 133–58; H. Neuhaus, 'Westfälischer Frieden und Dreißigjährigen Krieg: Neuerscheinungen aus Anlaß eines Jubiläums', *Archiv für Kirchengeschichte*, 82 (2000), 455–75.
8. e.g. S. Ogilvie, *State Corporatism and Proto-Industry: The Württemberg Black Forest 1580–1797* (Cambridge, 1997).
9. V. Press, 'Warum gab es keine deutsche Revolution? Deutschland und das revolutionäre Frankreich 1789–1815', in D. Langewiese (ed.), *Revolution und Krieg* (Paderborn, 1989), 67–85; T. C. W. Blanning, 'German Jacobins and the French Revolution', *Historical Journal*, 23 (1980), 985–1002.
10. P. Burg, *Die deutsche Trias in Idee und wirklichkeit: Vom Alten Reich zum deutschen Zollverein* (Stuttgart, 1989); G. Walter, *Der Zusammenbruch des Heiligen Römischen Reiches deutscher Nation und die Problematik seiner Restauration in den Jahren 1814/15* (Heidelberg, 1980).

11. P. H. Wilson, 'Bolstering the Prestige of the Habsburgs: The End of the Holy Roman Empire in 1806', *International History Review*, 28 (2006), 709–36.
12. V. Press, *Altes Reich und Deutscher Bund: Kontinuität in der Diskontinuität* (Munich, 1995).
13. J. Q. Whitman, *The Legacy of Roman Law in the German Romantic Era* (Princeton, 1990).
14. C. Wiedemann, 'Zwischen Nationalgeist und Kosmopolitanismus: Über die Schwerigkeiten der deutschen Klassiker, einen Nationalhelden zu finden', *Aufklärung*, 4 (1989), 75–101; H. Angermeier, 'Deutschland zwischen Reichstradition und Nationalstaat: Verfassungspolitische Konzeptionen und nationales Denken zwischen 1801 und 1815', *Zeitschrift der Savigny Stiftung für Rechtsgechichte, Germanistische Abteilung*, 107 (1990), 19–101.
15. For Götz's symbolic and historical significance see V. Press, 'Götz von Berlichingen (ca.1480–1562): Vom "Raubritter" zum Reichsritter', *Zeitschrift für Württembergische Landesgeschichte*, 40 (1981), 305–26.
16. E. Fehrenbach, *Wandlungen des deutschen Kaisergedankens 1871–1918* (Munich, 1969).
17. M. Umbach, *Federalism and Enlightenment in Germany 1740–1806* (London, 2000).
18. O. Mörke, 'The Political Culture of Germany and the Dutch Republic', in K. Davids and J. Lucassen (eds.), *A Miracle Mirrored: The Dutch Republic in European Perspective* (Cambridge, 1995), 148. For the constitutional debate see W. Burgdorf, *Reichskonstitution und Nation: Verfassungsreformprojekte für das Heilige Römische Reich deutscher Nation im politischen Schriftum von 1648 bis 1806* (Mainz, 1998); B. Roeck, *Reichssystem und Reichsherkommen: Die Diskussion über die Staatlichkeit des Reiches in der politischen Publizistik des 17. und 18. Jahrhunderts* (Stuttgart, 1984); J. G. Gagliardo, *Reich and Nation: The Holy Roman Empire as Idea and Reality, 1763–1806* (Bloomington, Ind., 1980).
19. E. François, *Die unsichtbare Grenze: Protestanten und Katholiken in Augsburg 1648–1806* (Sigmaringen, 1991).
20. J. Luh, *Unheiliges Römisches Reich: Der konfessionelle Gegensatz 1648 bis 1806* (Potsdam, 1995); G. Haug-Moritz, *Württembergische Ständekonflikt und deutscher Dualismus* (Stuttgart, 1992).
21. M. Walker, *German Home Towns: Community, State and General Estate 1648–1871* (Ithaca, NY, 1971).
22. G. Schmidt, *Geschichte des Alten Reiche: Staat und Nation in der frühen Neuzeit 1495–1806* (Munich, 1999). Further coverage of the debate in G. Schmidt (ed.), *Die deutsche Nation im frühneuzeitlichen Europa* (Munich, 2010).
23. J. Whaley, 'Thinking about Germany 1750–1815: The Birth of a Nation?', *Publications of the English Goethe Society*, 66 (1996), 53–71; G. Klingenstein, 'Was bedeuten "Österreich" und "österreichisch" im 18. Jahrhundert?', in R. G. Plaschka (ed.), *Was heißt Österreich?* (Vienna, 1995), 150–220; A. K. Mally, 'Der Begriff "'österreichische Nation" seit dem Ende des 18. Jahrhunderts', *Donauraum*, 17 (1972), 48–66.
24. W. Burgdorf, *Ein Weltbild verliert seine Welt: Der Untergang des Alten Reiches und die Generation 1806* (Munich, 2006).
25. T. C. W. Blanning, *Reform and Revolution in Mainz 1743–1802* (Cambridge, 1974); B. Blisch, *Friedrich Carl Joseph von Erthal (1774–1802). Erzbischof—Kurfürst—Erzkanzler* (Frankfurt/M., 2005).
26. G. Schmidt, 'Die "deutsche Freiheit" und der Westfälische Friede', in R. G. Asch, W. E. Voss, and M. Wrede (eds.), *Frieden und Krieg in der frühen Neuzeit* (Munich, 2001), 323–47; S. Westphal, 'Freiheit, Eigentumskultur und Geschlechterordnung', in G.

Schmidt, M. van Gelderen, and C. Snigula (eds.), *Kollektive Freiheitsvorstellungen im frühneuzeitlichen Europa (1400-1850)* (Frankfurt/M., 2006), 473-92.

27. P. C. Hartmann, *Das Heilge Römische Reiches deutscher Nation in der Neuzeit 1480-1806* (Stuttgart, 2005).
28. M. Umbach (ed.), *German Federalism: Past, Present and Future* (Basingstoke, 2002). Further discussion of this and other recent interpretations in P. H. Wilson, 'Still a Monstrosity? Some Reflections on Early Modern German Statehood', *Historical Journal*, 49 (2006), 565-76.
29. Useful discussion in T. C. W. Blanning, 'The French Revolution and the Modernization of Germany', *Central European History*, 21 (1989), 109-29.
30. Further comment in J. Breuilly, 'Wehler's Gesellschaftsgeschichte', *German History*, 9 (1991), 211-30; W. W. Hagen, 'Descent of the Sonderweg: Hans Rosenberg's History of Old-Regime Prussia', *Central European History*, 24 (1991), 24-50.
31. K. O. Frhr. v. Aretin, *Das Reich: Friedensgarantie und europäisches Gleichgewicht 1648-1806* (Stuttgart, 1986), 51; V. Press, 'Reichsstadt und Revolution', in B. Kirchgässner and E. Naujoks (eds.), *Stadt und wirtschaftliche Selbstverwaltung* (Sigmaringen, 1987), 9-59, and his 'Die Reichsstadt in der altständischen Gesellschaft', in J. Kunisch (ed.), *Neue Studien zur frühneuzeitlichen Geschichte* (Berlin, 1987), 9-42; B. Stollberg-Rilinger, *Des Kaisers alte Kleider: Verfassungsgeschichte und Symbolsprache des Alten Reiches* (Munich, 2008).
32. C. Küther, *Menschen auf der Straße: Vagierende Unterschichten in Bayern, Franken und Schwaben in der zweiten Hälfte des 18. Jahrhunderts* (Göttingen, 1983); W. V. Hippel, *Armut, Unterschichten, Randgruppen in der frühen Neuzeit* (Munich, 1995).
33. H. Gabel, *Widerstand und Kooperation: Studien zur politischen Kultur rheinischer und maasländischer Kleinterritorien (1648-1794)* (Tübingen, 1995).
34. There is now an extensive literature on these actions. Useful examples include E. Ortlieb, *Im Auftrag des Kaisers: Die kaiserlichen Kommissionen des Reichshofrats und die Regelung von Konflikten im Alten Reich (1637-1657)* (Cologne, 2001); M. Fimpel, *Reichsjustiz und Territorialstaat: Württemberg als Kommissar von Kaiser und Reich im Schwäbischen Kreis (1648-1806)* (Tübingen, 1999); S. Westphal, 'Stabilisierung durch Recht: Reichsgerichte als Schiedstelle territorialer Konflikte', in R. G. Asch and D. Friest (eds.), *Staatsbildung als kultureller Prozess* (Cologne, 2005), 235-53.
35. W. Troßbach, 'Fürstenabsetzungen im 18. Jahrhundert', *Zeitschrift für Historische Forschung*, 13 (1986), 425-54; M. Hughes, *Law and Politics in Eighteenth-Century Germany* (Woodbridge, 1988).
36. M. Weitlauff, 'Dalberg als Bischof von Konstanz und sein Generalvikar Ignaz Heinrich von Wessenberg', in K. Hausberger (ed.), *Carl von Dalberg* (Regensburg, 1995), 39.
37. P. H. Wilson, 'Prussia as a Fiscal-Military State, 1640-1806', in C. Storrs (ed.), *The Fiscal-Military State in Eighteenth-Century Europe* (Farnham, 2009), 95-124.
38. S. Karant Nunn, 'Did the Holy Roman Empire have a Social History?', in R. J. W. Evans, M. Schaich, and P. H. Wilson (eds.), *The Holy Roman Empire, 1495-1806* (Oxford, 2011).
39. K. H. Wegert, *Popular Culture, Crime and Social Control in Eighteenth-Century Württemberg* (Stuttgart, 1994).
40. K. H. Wegert, *German Radicals Confront the Common People: Revolutionary Politics and Popular Politics 1789-1849* (Mainz, 1992); W. Siemann, *The German Revolutions of 1848* (Basingstoke, 1998). For use of the imperial courts by ordinary subjects, see R. Sailer,

Untertansprozesse vor dem Reichskammergericht. Rechtsschutz gegen die Obrigkeit in der zweiten Hälfte des 18. Jahrhunderts (Cologne, 1999).

41. H. Rebel, 'Reimagining the *Oikos*: Austrian Cameralism in its Social Formation', in J. O'Brien and W. Roseberry (eds.), *Golden Ages, Dark Ages: Reimagining the Past* (Berkeley, Calif., 1991), 48–80. For protest in this period see H. Berding (ed.), *Soziale Unruhen in Deutschland während der französischen Revolution* (Göttingen, 1988).
42. J. Schlumbohm, 'Gesetze, die nicht durchgesetzt werden: Ein Strukturmerkmal des frühneuzeitlichen Staates?', *Geschichte und Gesellschaft*, 23 (1997), 647–63.
43. Examples in U. Rublack, *The Crimes of Women in Early Modern Germany* (Oxford, 1999).
44. A. Fahrmeir, 'Centralisation versus Particularism in the "Third Germany"', in M. Rowe (ed.), *Collaboration and Resistance in Napoleonic Europe* (Basingstoke, 2003), 107–20; M. Rowe, *From Reich to State: The Rhineland in the Revolutionary Age, 1780–1830* (Cambridge, 2003).

Bibliography

Aretin, K. O. Frhr., v., *Das Alte Reich 1648–1806* (3 vols. Stuttgart, 1993–7).
Evans, R. J. W., Schaich M., and Wilson P. H. (eds.), *The Holy Roman Empire, 1495–1806* (Oxford, 2011).
Forrest, A., and Wilson, P. H. (eds.), *The Bee and the Eagle: Napoleonic France and the End of the Holy Roman Empire, 1806* (Basingstoke, 2009).
Härter, K., 'Zweihundert Jahre nach dem europäischen Umbruch von 1803', *Zeitschrift für Historische Forschung*, 33 (2006), 89–115.
Hartmann, P. C., *Das Heilge Römische Reiches deutscher Nation in der Neuzeit 1480–1806* (Stuttgart, 2005).
Press, V. (ed.), *Alternativen zur Reichsverfassung in der frühen Neuzeit?* (Munich, 1995).
Rowe, M., *From Reich to State: The Rhineland in the Revolutionary Age, 1780–1830* (Cambridge, 2003).
Schmidt, G., *Geschichte des Alten Reiche. Staat und Nation in der frühen Neuzeit 1495–1806* (Munich, 1999).
—— *Wandel durch Vernunft: Deutsche Geschichte im 18. Jahrhundert* (Munich, 2009).
Schnettger, M. (ed.), *Imperium Romanum—Irregulare Corpus—Teutscher Reichs-Staat* (Mainz, 2002).
Stollberg-Rilinger, B., *Des Kaisers alte Kleider: Verfassungsgeschichte und Symbolsprache des Alten Reiches* (Munich, 2008).
Walker, M., *German Home Towns: Community, State and General Estate 1648–1871* (Ithaca, NY, 1971).
Wilson, P. H., *Absolutism in Central Europe* (London, 2000).
—— *From Reich to Revolution: German History 1558–1806* (Basingstoke, 2004).
—— *The Holy Roman Empire 1495–1806* (2nd edn., Basingstoke, 2011).

CHAPTER 32

CONCLUSION

WILLIAM DOYLE

TRANSLATING the full flavour of the term Ancien Régime into English is difficult. The first recorded attempts in 1792 even mistranslated *ancien* as 'ancient'; whereas in normal usage, the word meant 'old' in the sense of 'former'. More cautious users have sought to avoid any confusion by leaving both words in French, and this has been the general practice throughout this volume. The range of things challenged by the French revolutionaries may well have appeared ancient to them and their contemporaries, in the sense of immemorial, traditional, and stretching back far beyond living memory. But no reader of earlier chapters here could conclude that there was anything truly ancient about it.

Admittedly the old order was haunted by the legacy of the ancient world—by classical literature, ideas, and terminology; not to mention the Christian religion, which was the most pervasive and enduring link with antiquity. But few of the institutions and habits that eighteenth-century reformers and revolutionaries hoped to change could be traced back meaningfully even as far as the end of the first millennium. The 'feudal régime' so grandiloquently renounced on 11 August 1789 had then scarcely begun to emerge. The nobility abolished less than a year later had been no more fully established, and in any case its character had been transformed by purchase from the sixteenth century onwards. So, indeed, had much of French life. The whole complex of privilege which epitomized so much of what the revolutionaries hated, largely arose from the discovery by cash-strapped kings that subjects who hated paying taxes would happily pay for advantages and exemptions. Nor did the monarchy which adopted these expedients have much in common with its medieval antecedents, either in its structure, its practices, or the resources it sought to tap. Absolute monarchy, the initial target of the revolutionaries, emerged slowly and unsteadily over the sixteenth and early seventeenth centuries. The authority and power of the four last Louis before 1792 had little but the title of king in common with those of their last medieval namesake. And the main foreign challenges confronting them were certainly not the same. Matching the dynastic power of the Habsburgs, and later the maritime strength of Great Britain, demanded efforts of organization and finance quite beyond the capacity of medieval rulers. It was under the mounting strain of these efforts that the Ancien Régime finally fell apart.

Nor can most of the economic Ancien Régime be seen as a prolongation of the middle ages. If the world in 1789 was still overwhelmingly agrarian, European economic life had been transformed by the discovery, in the closing years of the fifteenth century, of a sea route to the riches of the east, and of the hitherto unknown resources of the Americas to the west. The following three centuries saw the gestation of a world economy centred on the insatiable appetites of Europeans for what the rest of the world produced. To manage their role in it, states adopted one form or another of control which together became known as mercantilism. To keep some of its key elements going, they connived at the expansion of a new slavery quite distinct from that of ancient times. Only in the last three decades of the eighteenth century did these institutions begin to be questioned and dismantled. In western Europe, meanwhile, medieval serfdom had largely disappeared by the sixteenth century, although remnants lingered over two more centuries. In the east, a new serfdom, unprecedented earlier in these regions, took hold and strengthened over the same period. Underlying both trends was scarcity of population. The demographic Ancien Régime, at least, did have medieval roots. A rhythm of population surges savagely curtailed by periodic visitations of plague and other natural scourges went back to the Black Death of 1348. It started to fade in the 1730s. Relatively unchecked population growth after that played a part in precipitating the revolutions that assailed the Ancien Régime, and voluntary contraception began to be practised around the same time. And so the old pattern of population growth held in check by natural constraints was already almost a thing of the past when it was identified by Malthus in 1798 as fated to happen forever.[1]

In cultural terms the Ancien Régime began with the Renaissance and the Reformation. The monolithic authority of the medieval Catholic Church had gone, and the next three centuries were a time when extensive energies were devoted by anxious established churches to maintaining some authority by monopolizing education and persecuting dissent. By the eighteenth century, irreligion and 'free thought' were coming to be seen as even more dangerous than the latter. Partly this was because the spread of literacy, and the growing desire of moneyed elites to invest in expensive education, gave increasing numbers access to media that might subvert faith or obedience if uncontrolled. The revolutionaries of 1789 condemned censorship and religious intolerance as cardinal vices of the Ancien Régime. They looked back on the growth of free thought or 'philosophy' as the source of their reforming agenda. Even those appalled by the destruction and slaughter of the Revolution agreed, although they deplored rather than gloried in it. Irresponsible criticism, they thought, had fatally undermined the old order.

'Old Order' is another common way of translating *ancien régime*, but again it is less than satisfactory. For although pre-revolutionary society was organized legally into functional orders, the spirit of the Ancien Régime was one of spectacular *dis*order. Custom guided much of the way it functioned. Confusion of boundaries, rights, powers, and jurisdictions was universal. It was a paradise for lawyers, a labyrinth for litigants.

Only when it was gone did nostalgic conservatives begin to view the Ancien Régime as a benign product of nature that had functioned in the best interests of all—especially when compared with the apparent chaos and bloodshed wrought by the revolutionaries as they tried to destroy it. But most revolutionaries were unrepentant. They had a lofty mission to tidy up the world. Their aim was to construct an order that was *planned* along rational, utilitarian, and humanitarian lines; where ignorance, prejudice, and 'superstition' did not inhibit progress; where justice was guaranteed, simple, and accessible; where natural equity was not affronted and thwarted by exceptionalism and privilege; and where all public powers were constrained by clear ground-rules enshrined in a written constitution.

These are consensual principles of the modern world. We all pay them lip-service. In that sense, the determination of the embattled revolutionaries over the winter of 1792–3 to export their principles has been vindicated in the very long term. Their perception was that the Ancien Régime was not confined to France, and would need to be overthrown wherever else it existed if their revolution was ever to be secure.[2] They had begun by repudiating the traditional niceties of relations between states, renouncing expansionist ambitions. Now, in a war they insisted was defensive, they were seeking nothing less than regime change among their enemies. Although the idea of the Ancien Régime originated in France, and largely reflected specific French circumstances, there was much abroad to mirror them. The rest of Europe was generally ruled by kings, nobilities, and established churches, custom and routine governed everyday life, and most other states were composites brought together over time, just like the kingdom of France, by dynasticism or conquest, with constituent parts often quite disparate in their governance.[3] In recognition of these similarities, acknowledging that France could not be isolated from a range of economic and cultural trends which affected the rest of the continent and its overseas dependencies, this volume has frequently strayed beyond the French kingdom. Messy and unsystematic in its essence, the Ancien Régime is surely impossible to confine conceptually to the country and culture where it was first defined. In many ways, prerevolutionary France was simply one assemblage among many of features, ways of doing things, neither more nor less exceptional than other polities for which their own historians make exceptionalist claims. Cases testing this idea are explored in Part VII: predictably with no consensus.

Nor is there much more agreement about when the Ancien Régime disappeared, although few would accept that the French revolutionaries destroyed it as swiftly and definitively as they hoped. They swept away absolute monarchy, the estates of the church, religious intolerance, the old judicial system, venality of office, legal and administrative confusion, and privileges of all sorts. The feudal complex of rights and property, the 'time of the lords' in the countryside, never reappeared. But when they tried to abolish nobility, they failed,[4] and when they abolished slavery, they soon had second thoughts. Without the decisive decade and a half of Napoleonic rule, many other revolutionary abolitions might have proved transient. Napoleon, however, was a son of the Revolution.

He consolidated most of its work and, as has often been observed, the throne ascended by the restored Bourbons was his, not that of their martyred brother.

And meanwhile, Napoleon had destroyed the political Ancien Régime in much of the rest of Europe. He dissolved the ecclesiastical states of Germany and, while he ruled, the papal state in Italy. He prompted the dissolution of the oldest political entity in Europe, the thousand-year-old Reich, and ruthlessly remodelled German and Italian territories, often several times over. And, by driving ruling dynasties out of the Iberian peninsula, he precipitated a crisis of authority which within a few years brought the disintegration of their transatlantic empires. All attempts made after his downfall to restore prerevolutionary ways and institutions failed before long. A generation of upheaval had shaken out the old cement; and in any case, even those who dreamt of bringing back the imagined stability of prerevolutionary times wanted to introduce safeguards against renewed disruptions which were completely out of character with what they hoped to restore. Isolated Ancien Régime elements might be brought back, but nothing could put the shattered edifice together again in any recognizably coherent form.

The French revolutionaries invented the Ancien Régime by dint of their efforts to destroy it. But how assured was its viability even before their attack? Its collapse certainly took almost everybody by surprise, but in retrospect signs of strain can be seen. The demands of military competition were imposing increasing organizational and fiscal pressure on the leading states. The need for more efficient taxation was eroding privileges and exemptions and, throughout eastern Europe, raising doubts about the value of serfdom. An expanding, educated public was increasingly questioning established habits and institutions, led on in the public sphere by the sceptical rationality of the Enlightenment. It was already achieving its first triumphs in economic matters, where controls and exclusions were being abandoned, and slavery questioned. The last attempts to tighten rather than relax controls brought on the disintegration of the British north Atlantic empire, with multiple repercussions throughout the world of Europeans. Against this background, the French revolutionary onslaught might seem as much a symptom as a cause of the Ancien Régime's disintegration, simply accelerating a process already under way.[5]

When, finally, might that process have been complete? Thirty years ago Arno J. Mayer argued that in essence much of the Ancien Régime lasted until the twentieth century. The French Revolution was merely 'the first act of the breakup of Europe's *ancien régime*'.[6] Its last act was what Mayer called the Thirty Years War of the twentieth century, between 1914 and 1945, when Europe was plunged into a crisis by the determination of privileged elites, whose members ran the great powers, to preserve their hegemonies by going to war. That elites which felt threatened should risk anything so potentially suicidal has left most historians sceptical of Mayer's argument. But it drew on some incontrovertible evidence. Down to the First World War, all the great powers except France were still monarchies—and France too might have been one again if the Bourbon pretender had not spurned his inheritance out of purblind loyalty to the white flag of the family which had ruled before 1792. Noblemen continued to dominate the upper reaches of almost all state hierarchies and social structures. The bourgeoisie, despite its expanding economic power and numbers, remained almost as culturally subservient as it had been in the eighteenth century. Women (although Mayer did not mention them) were still resolutely excluded from official forms of empowerment. Representative institutions were still generally weak, and even in Great Britain the House of Lords was a proactive 'citadel of the landed aristocracy'.[7] In economic terms agriculture had still to be overtaken by industry as the leading sector everywhere except in Great Britain; and with the same exception agrarian elites were powerful enough to insist on protection during the agricultural depression which set in in the 1870s.

All these were persistent elements and echoes of the Ancien Régime. Some of them, in fragmented forms, persist still. Europe still boasts nine monarchies, and nobilities can be found everywhere, some with residual official recognition. The constitution of the United Kingdom is still unwritten, and there remain a handful of hereditary peers in its legislature. There is an established church, or rather two, one in England and one in Scotland, not to mention separate systems of civil law. Devolution, indeed, has recently brought even more diversity to this four-centuries-old composite state.

Yet in the end these are isolated relics, like old buildings and ruins marooned among vast modern developments. Nothing substantial is now left of the Ancien Régime beyond a few random and incoherent echoes. Some of its features had been in decay even before the idea of it was invented. Economic and demographic patterns had begun to change earlier in the eighteenth century, and these developments accelerated over the nineteenth. The arrival of railways quite literally transformed the landscape, stimulating heavy industry, boosting urbanization, generalizing markets. When they established themselves in transoceanic territories in the 1860s, the abundance of cheap food that railways and steamships brought within Europe's reach underlay the great depression that sapped the foundations of the old agrarian elites. By the twentieth century, the triumph of industrial society was unchallenged. Secular society likewise: despite sustained rearguard actions, Christianity has continued to retreat as an element in most people's lives, and secularized states deny it any official influence. Nationalism, a force only embryonic before 1789, emerged in the course of the nineteenth century as a mainspring of international ambition and conflict; and nation-states based on language and shared culture, rather than dynastic chance, became the norm. Author of the first detached reflections on the Ancien Régime by someone too young to remember it, Alexis de Tocqueville believed that it had been overwhelmed in France by the irresistible advance of equality and democracy. He did not believe that the Revolution which followed had promoted the cause of liberty. Yet during Tocqueville's lifetime most forms of human bondage disappeared in the European world, and only a few years after his death in 1859 serfdom was abolished in Russia and slaves freed in the United States. He was, however, right about democracy and equality. Representative institutions gained steadily in importance, and by the early twentieth century most men were entitled to civil equality and some say in political power through voting. When, between 1918 and 1944, women acquired the same rights, it marked the abandonment of the last of the major status inequalities so fundamental to all Anciens Régimes. Mayer may have been misguided in seeing the First World War as the product of an 'over-reaction of old elites to overperceived dangers to their over-privileged positions'.[8] But he was probably not wrong in finding the final disappearance of the Ancien Régime's last significant vestiges around 1945.

Notes

1. T. R. Malthus, *An Essay on the Principle of Population* (London, 1798).
2. As Jacques-Pierre Brissot declared in Nov. 1792, 'We cannot be calm until Europe, all Europe, is in flames'. Quoted in T. C. W. Blanning, *The Origins of the French Revolutionary Wars* (London, 1986), 137.
3. See D. W. Hayton, James Kelly, and John Bergin (eds.), *The Eighteenth Century Composite State: Representative Institutions in Ireland and Europe, 1689–1800* (Basingstoke, 2010).
4. See William Doyle, *Aristocracy and its Enemies in the Age of Revolution* (Oxford, 2009).
5. For the wider global dimension, see C. A. Bayly, *The Birth of the Modern World, 1780–1914: Global Connections and Comparisons* (Oxford, 2004), and a stimulating collection of essays inspired by this author: David Armitage and Sanjay Subrahmanyam (eds.), *The Age of Revolutions in Global Context, c.1760–1840* (Houndmills, 2010).
6. Arno J. Mayer, *The Persistence of the Old Regime: Europe to the Great War* (London, 1981), 15.
7. Ibid. 153.
8. Ibid. 307.

Index

Aachen *see* Aix-la-Chapelle
Abbeville 112
Absolute monarchy 1, 4, 6, 12–38, 101, 110, 114–15, 116, 133, 145, 159, 212, 221, 236, 388, 411, 419, 467, 469, 490, 498, 500, 508, 541, 542, 556, 558
Academies 94, 116, 117, 133, 179, 374, 375, 377, 379–82, 393, 396–400, 444
 -française 128, 437
Acquaviva, Claudio 321
Adams, Christine 129
Adams, John 522, 526, 535
Addison, Joseph 436
Africa 252, 256, 262, 263, 267, 268, 269, 313, 452, 514, 523, 526, 527, 530
Agriculture 3, 6, 67, 77, 112, 131, 168, 170, 201, 203, 207, 210–11, 213, 236–51, 253, 254, 255, 267, 268, 275, 448, 529, 560
Aguesseau, Henri François d' 94, 329
Agulhon, Maurice 375, 384
Aigrefeuille 223, 224
Aiguillon, Duke d' 230
Aix-en-Provence 29, 93, 94, 112, 172
Aix-la-Chapelle 54, 532
Albany 527
Albizzi, Francesco 322–3
Alembert, Jean Le Rond d' 132, 221, 378, 380, 441, 444
Alençon 112
Alet 297
Alexander VII 326
Allen, Robert 459–60
Allgemeine Shulordnung 364, 365
Alps 5, 40, 173, 208, 277, 501
Alsace 210, 224, 230, 240, 242, 244, 247, 348, 478
Althusius, Johannes 148
America 253, 256, 258, 262, 263, 268, 270, 321, 339, 432, 442, 452, 515, 522–39, 557
Amis des Noirs 272

Andalucia 500
Angivillier, Charles Claude d' 394–5
Angran de Fonpertuis 76–7
Anjou 113, 228, 240, 244
Annales 184, 236, 237, 238
Anne, Queen 296, 510, 511, 515
Annual Register 43
Anticlericalism 432
Antoine, A. 244
Antwerp 170, 256
Anzin 120
Apennines 173
Apostilidès, Jean-Marie 390
Aquinas, Thomas 320
Aragon 87
Archaic, Marquisat d' 223
Arcq, Chevalier d' 134
Arkwright, Richard 453, 460
Armies 17, 22, 48, 51, 59–74, 78, 79, 81, 85, 97, 115, 116, 117, 153, 186, 253, 358, 363, 451, 541
Arnauld, Antoine 318, 324, 325, 326, 327, 328
Articles of Confederation 535
Artisans 127
Artois 93, 103
 - Count d' 380
Asia 202, 252, 256, 257, 258, 262, 269, 321, 450, 453
Assignats 476
Astell, Mary 368
Atheism 242, 345, 347, 444
Atlantic 66, 81, 83, 130, 206, 252, 255, 256, 257, 259, 260, 267, 272, 278, 514, 522, 523, 525, 527, 530, 559
Atterbury, Francis 512
Augsburg 286, 546
 - Peace of 337
 - War of the League of *see* War, Nine Years
Auge, Pays d' 245
Augustinianism 97, 290, 318, 319–20, 322, 323, 324, 325, 326, 328

Aulard, Alphonse 224
Aunis 226
Austria 12, 31, 42, 43, 45, 46, 52, 53, 55, 59, 62, 66, 67, 69, 70, 72, 79, 81, 83, 86, 90, 115, 161, 287, 289, 294, 299, 345–6, 358, 359, 363, 364, 365, 366, 442, 443, 502, 541, 543, 544, 545, 546, 547, 548
Auvergne 93, 173, 224, 226, 227, 243
Avignon 4, 297, 384

Bacon, Francis 458
Baden-Württemberg 84, 168, 233, 291, 365, 549, 551
Baëcque, Antoine de 399
Bailey, Colin 390, 402
Bailyn, Bernard 525, 533
Baius, Michael 320, 321
Baker, Keith 418–9
Balkans 432
Ballooning 451
Baltic 66, 204, 252, 253
Bancroft, George 525
Bañez, Domingo 321
Ban et arrière-ban 220
Bangor 296
Bank; banking 89, 90
 - of England 31, 89, 102, 155
Baptists 341
Bar 4
Barbados 268
Barcos, Martin de 328
'Baroque state' 14, 30–2, 323
Basan, Pierre François 400
Basedow, Johann 369
Bastier, Jean 227
Bastille 78
Bath 514
Bauer, Samuel 369
Bavaria 79, 86, 168, 289, 541, 542
Bayeux 171
Bayle, Pierre 313, 344, 376, 436, 440
Bayonne 147
Béarn 243
Beaucaire 255
Beauce 241
Beauharnais, Alexandre de 270

 - Eugène de 502
 - Mme de 379
Beaumarchais, Pierre Caron de 130, 136, 402, 434, 439, 443
Beaune 241
Beaumont, Christophe de 330, 331
Beaumont, Gustave de 513
Beaupuis 231
Béaur, Gérard 246
Beauvais 113
 - sur Matha 227
Beccaria, Cesare 378, 434, 437, 439
Beeman, Richard 527
Begging 170, 173–4, 175, 179, 188, 479–80
Behaim, Bartel 174
Beik, William 227
Belfanti, C. M. 456
Belgium 86, 233, 322
Bell, David 415, 419
Belle-Isle, Duke de 115
Bély, Lucien 377
Benedict XIV 298, 299, 347
Benedictines 327, 379
Bergeret de Grancourt, Jacques Onésyme 401
Berlin 48, 292, 436, 437, 544
Bernadotte, jean Baptiste Jules 46
Berry 104, 113, 241, 244
Bertin, Rose 190
Bertrán, Felipe 294
Bérulle, Pierre de 324
Besançon 93, 94, 116, 228, 274, 365, 366
Bien, David 158
Birdzell, L. E. 454
Birmingham 249, 454
Birth control 172, 186, 187, 201, 214, 215, 557
Bishops 95, 98, 115, 142, 143, 154, 291, 292, 294, 296, 297, 300, 305, 306, 308, 310, 324, 326, 327, 329, 472, 473, 524, 534, 549
Bismarck, Otto von 500, 540, 548
Black, Joseph 458
Black Death *see* Plague
Blackstone, William 509
Blanning, Tim 388
Blasphemy Act 341
Bloch, Marc 236
Blois 117, 324

Bluche, Frédéric 497, 499, 501
Blum, Jerome 233
Bocage, Mme du 379
Bodin, Jean 21, 411, 413, 492
Bohemia 59, 277, 285, 290, 322, 345, 358
Boileau, Nicolas 412
Boisot, Family 94
Bolingbroke, Henry 21
Bologna 299
Bon de Saint-Flocel 423
Boncerf, Pierre François 228
Books 417
Bordeaux; Bordelais 113, 129, 142, 151–2, 206, 225, 226, 259, 260, 267, 270, 348, 382, 383, 431
Bosse, Abraham 397
Bossuet, Jacques Bénigne 16, 411
Boston 526, 529, 533
Boucher, François 395, 399, 400
Boucher d'Argis, Antoine Gaspard 221
Boudon, Jacques Olivier 490, 496
Boufflers, Countess de 378
Bouhier, Family 94, 381
Boulainvilliers, Count de 136, 221
Boulonnais 104
Boulton, Matthew 454, 457
Bourbons 14, 42, 48, 49, 50, 52, 55, 66, 69, 75, 76, 90, 236, 261, 291, 292, 296, 297, 299, 323, 325, 331, 391, 395, 402, 467, 468, 469, 481, 490, 494, 497, 500, 518, 522, 541, 559
Bourbonnais 244
Bourdieu, Pierre 129, 377
Bourgeoisie 5, 26, 27, 30, 127–40, 142, 143, 147, 160, 208, 227, 243, 376, 377, 383, 410, 417, 475, 476, 478, 507, 560
Bourginiat, Elisabeth 399
Bouton, Cynthia 186
Bowring, Sir John 518
Boyne 516
Braganza 298
Brandenburg 12, 287
Braudel, Fernand 184, 253, 259, 450
Bray, Pays de 245
Brazil 83, 256, 268
Breton Club 230
Brewer, John 76

Bridewell 178
Brienne, Etienne Charles Loménie de 71, 292, 300, 444, 494
Bright, John 55
Brionnais 244
Bristol 278, 292
Brittany 14, 26, 29, 93, 94, 95, 100, 101, 103, 113, 185, 210, 226, 232, 239, 243, 244, 256, 292, 359, 478
Brown, Howard 491, 502
Brumaire 490, 494, 499
Brussels 322, 328
Buchorn 544
Buffon, Georges Louis Leclerc de 116, 382, 440
Bureaucracy 13, 28, 32, 67, 101, 161, 359, 364, 366, 388, 400
Burgundy 14, 21, 26, 93, 94, 95, 100, 101, 103, 104, 184, 223, 226, 228, 229, 242, 292
Burke, Edmund 5, 43, 300, 434, 443, 517
Burke, Peter 388, 390, 393, 438
Büsching 79
Bush, Michael 158
Bushman, Richard L. 529
Bute, Earl of 87
Butler, Jon 526

Cadiz 256, 260
Caen 171, 249
Cahiers de doléances 1, 3, 105, 120, 121, 152–3, 225, 229–30, 272, 274, 318
Calais 241
Calas affair 95, 343, 511
Calendar 472, 492–3
Callières, François de 39
Calonne, Charles Alexandre de 31, 493, 494
Calvin, Jean; Calvinism 148, 287, 291, 320, 337, 338, 340, 344, 345, 363, 510, 546
Cambacérès, Jean Jacques Régis de 97
Cambrésis 243, 246
Cambridge 241, 366, 508
Camisards 339
Campbell, Peter 388
Campe, Joachim Heinrich 361, 369, 370
Campo Formio, Peace of 42, 543
Canada 271, 531

Canals 245, 253, 450, 515
Canossa 297
Canterbury 292, 296
Capetians 14
Capitalism 5, 90, 118, 127, 129, 130, 131, 135, 138, 143, 144, 151, 161, 188, 227, 233, 400, 410, 476, 514
Capital punishment 481
Capitation 27, 100, 102, 116, 117, 121, 147, 209, 214
Caplan, Jay 392
Capuchins 176, 303
Cardwell, D. S. L. 458
Caribbean 173, 256, 261, 269, 270, 271, 278, 514, 527
Carnot, Lazare 40
Carrera de Indias 257
Carthusians 290
Cartwright, Edmund 453
Castile 88, 289, 292, 298
Castlereagh, Viscount 54
Casuistry 305
Catalonia 385
Catherine II 275, 276, 443
Causses 241
Caux, Pays de 226
Cemeteries 310, 314, 330
Censorship 305, 341, 410, 415, 416, 417, 435, 436, 438, 441–2, 443, 445, 470, 494, 512, 513, 557
Centralization 11, 13, 25, 26, 154–5, 229, 346, 468, 469, 494, 500, 502, 508, 544
Cercle social 444
Cévennes 339
Ceyssens, Lucien 319, 332
Chalons, Academy of 362
Châlons sur Marne 241, 328, 367–8
Chamlay, Marquis de 63
Champagne 93, 223, 229, 246
Champion, Justin 344
Channel, English 88, 127, 239, 241, 257, 340
Champs Elysées 377
Charlemagne 14, 18, 491, 492, 540, 544
Charles I 41, 286, 292, 296, 508, 517, 518, 533
Charles II 61, 508, 511
  - of Spain 292
Charles III 45, 294, 298
Charles V 337

Charles VI 287, 288
Charles X 482, 499
Charles XI 67
Charles XII 72
Charleston 527
Charles Emmanuel III 228
Charolles 94
Chartres 128
Chartier, Roger 358, 365, 388, 391
Chateaubriand, François Auguste René de 491, 494
Chaulnes, Duke de 26
Chauvelin, Germain-Louis 115
  - Abbé 159
Chérin, Louis Nicolas Henri 148
Chesapeake 257, 526
Chevet, Jean-Michel 246
Children 171, 179, 186–7, 192, 194, 201–2, 206, 208, 209, 293, 295, 306, 308, 310, 313, 339, 357–73, 528
China 451, 453, 460
Chivalry 3, 119, 120, 121, 151, 290, 384
Choiseul, Duke de 71, 298
Choudhury, Mita 190, 191
Church 4, 14, 15, 18, 20, 23, 87, 88, 142, 153, 167, 176, 190–1, 202, 210, 215, 230, 232, 243, 247, 253, 285–301, 309, 314, 325, 358, 364, 374, 417, 432, 438, 477, 480, 482, 483, 493, 523, 540, 543, 558
Cisalpine Republic 501
Civil Code 481, 482, 496–9
Civil Constitution of the Clergy 4, 319, 332, 472–3
Clark, J. C. D. 506–7, 517
Class 142–4, 145
Classics 16, 96, 158, 293, 503, 556
Clement VIII 322
Clement IX 327
Clement XI 299, 328
Clement XII 299
Clement XIII 298
Clement XIV 298–9
Clergy 3, 4, 5, 23, 25, 95, 104, 127, 134, 135, 141, 159, 170, 177, 286–301, 303, 304, 306–8, 311–12, 314, 344, 348, 381, 472–3, 475, 496, 497, 523, 551
  - Assembly of 150, 154, 155, 296–7, 300, 326

Clermontois 179
Cleves 287
Clientage 13, 26, 27, 28, 541
Clubs 374, 386, 470, 474, 479, 513, 514
Cobban, Alfred 130, 144, 225, 227
Cochin, Augustin 376
Code 475, 481, 482, 494, 496, 497, 498, 499
- Noir 268
Colbert, Jean-Baptiste 17, 22, 25, 65, 70, 91, 155, 192, 225, 270, 380, 393, 297, 415, 450
Colbiørnsen, Christian 444
Collé, Charles 279
Cologne 322, 323
Colonies 6, 79, 83, 85, 87, 112, 257, 258, 261, 262, 263, 268, 270, 271, 273, 442, 516
- Thirteen 263, 515, 516, 522–39
Colquhoun, Patrick 137
Commerce 6, 24, 49, 77, 112, 117, 118, 127, 131, 170, 206, 209, 213, 214, 227, 238, 252–66, 267, 382, 400, 402, 411, 448, 449, 475, 514, 529, 531
Commines, Philippe de 413
Commission des Réguliers 289–90
Committee of Public Safety 50, 51, 494
Common lands 101, 215, 227, 228, 229, 233, 240, 242, 243, 246, 477, 551
Compagnonnages 479
Comtat Venaissin 4
Conciliarism 18, 21
Concordat 300, 332, 443, 474, 492, 493, 494
Condé 26, 100
Condillac, Etienne Bonnot de 116, 441, 444
Condorcet, Antoine de Caritat de 116, 272, 444
Confession 305, 307
Confraternities 177, 179, 185, 310–11, 374, 375, 385, 493
Congress System 54, 55
Connecticut 524, 527
Conscription 51, 59, 64, 65, 66, 69, 73, 275, 468, 494, 495, 496
Constantine 286, 300
Constantinople 44, 259
Constituent Assembly 1, 2, 3, 4, 48, 49–50, 78, 179, 219, 220, 230, 231, 272, 273, 349, 467, 468, 471, 477, 479, 481–2

Consumer revolution 151, 154, 184, 188, 189, 190
Constitution 1, 2, 3, 11, 12, 20, 21, 28, 30, 50, 77, 99, 105, 156, 332, 349, 469, 473, 518, 519, 536, 543, 548
Consulate 489–505
Conti, Prince de 378
Contraception *see* Birth control
Convention 51, 232, 273, 444, 469, 472, 477, 478, 480
Copernicus, Nicholas 449
Copyright 438
Cornart, Valentin 380
Coronation 14, 286, 291, 490, 491, 492
Corporation Act 300, 341, 510–11
Corporations 3, 4, 12, 16, 18, 20, 28, 105, 130, 141–66, 255, 331, 398, 411, 416, 472, 476, 479, 496, 541, 550
Corruption 25, 28, 32, 95, 118, 194, 215, 422, 442, 517, 534, 535, 541
Cortes 29
Corvée 85, 150, 223, 224, 274, 477
Cossacks 275, 276
Cotton des Houssayes, Jean-Baptiste 117
Councils, royal 22–3, 30, 93
Counter-Reformation *see* Reformation, Catholic
Counter-revolution 5, 473, 483, 495, 497
Cour-Cheverny 324
Court; courtiers 13, 14, 15, 22, 27–8, 29, 31, 32, 45, 70, 97, 103, 115, 117, 118, 135, 147, 153, 154, 212, 269, 290, 291, 319, 376, 377, 390, 393, 395, 396, 397, 400, 402, 410, 413, 414, 416, 417, 419, 421, 437, 456, 490, 491, 494, 517, 523, 545
Court de Gébelin, Antoine 383
Coyer, Gabriel François 117, 135–6, 368
Coutura, Johel 383
Crécy 395
Crompton, Samuel 453
Cromwell, Oliver 41, 341, 498, 515
Croquants 29,
Crow, Thomas 391, 398
Crowston, Claire 185, 189, 190, 193
Crouzet, François 252
Croÿ, Duke de 120
Crozat, Antoine 128

Cuba 278
Cugnot, Nicolas Joseph 459
'Cultural turn' 388, 526
Custom 2, 4, 19, 96, 155, 240, 245, 248, 275, 310, 525, 551, 557, 558
Customs barriers 3, 255

Damiens, Robert François 331
Dancing 311
Danton, Georges-Jacques 40, 130
Darby, Abraham 459
Darnton, Robert 132, 391
Daughters of Charity 176, 191
Daughters of the Holy Infant 327
Dauphiné 14, 93, 94, 103, 104, 243, 343
Davenant, Charles 78
David, Jacques Louis 398, 399, 401
David, Paul 456
Davis, Natalie Zemon 185
Debt 17, 18, 19, 31, 75, 78, 90, 114, 151, 160, 192, 248, 270, 363, 414, 472, 511, 549
Dechristianisation 300, 432, 472
Decimalization 470
Declaration of the Rights of Man and of the Citizen 2, 4, 158, 272, 348, 349, 467–8
Deffand, Marie du 377, 379
Defoe, Daniel 370, 439
Deism 342, 345, 347, 472
Delumeau, Jean 304
Democracy 158, 159, 221
Demography 6, 66, 72, 129, 130, 168–9, 170, 172, 184, 186, 201–18, 240, 246, 267, 448, 449, 519, 526, 527, 530, 545, 557, 560
Denmark 12, 51, 81, 85, 233, 277–8, 292, 436, 439, 442, 443, 444
Departments 468
Depont family 223
Descartes, René 440
Desmaretz, Nicolas 90
Despotism 13, 18, 21, 27, 30, 32, 99, 116, 156, 221, 330, 419, 423, 497, 541, 552
Dessau 361
De Vries, Jan 189
Dewald, Jonathan 158, 226
Deyon, Pierre 189
Dickens, Charles 137

Dickson, Peter 76
Diderot, Denis 49, 132, 152, 160, 221, 362, 363, 399, 402, 421, 431, 434, 437, 441, 444, 445
Dijon 94, 101, 103, 104, 381–2
Dinan, Susan 191
Diplomacy 39–58, 71
Diplomatic Revolution 42
Directory 41, 47, 48, 469, 480, 494, 499, 501
Disease 167, 172, 179, 202, 203, 206, 240, 382, 526
Divine right 18, 21
Divorce 481
Dominicans 320
Dorsanne, Antoine 329
Dovecotes 219, 220, 229, 230
Doyle, William 113, 118, 144, 152, 227, 469, 493, 508
Dress 47, 118, 131, 138, 154, 190
Dreyfus, Alfred 349
Droit de seigneur 136
Dubos, Jean Baptiste 136
Duclos, Charles Pinot 118
Du Barry, Jeanne Bécu, Countess 401
Dublin 300, 434, 516
Dubois, Alexandre 308
Dubos, Jean Baptiste 417
Duby, Georges 142
Duguet, Jacques-Joseph 327, 330
Dumouriez, Charles François 48
Dupâquier, Jacques 206
Dutch Republic 4, 5, 41, 42, 45, 63, 66, 68, 78, 81, 83, 84, 85, 86, 88, 90, 101, 103, 161, 168, 176, 178, 271, 254, 255, 288, 293, 300, 322, 342, 344–5, 432, 435, 436, 438, 442, 454, 517
Dutton, H. I. 455

East India Company 150
Economists 3
 - *see also* Physiocrats
Edgeworth, Maria 360
 - Richard 360
Edinburgh 434, 515
Education 16, 114, 121, 146, 153, 179–80, 210, 293–5, 302, 303, 304, 314, 321, 357–73, 376, 383, 433, 434, 444, 468, 469, 470, 480, 497, 498, 500, 547, 557

Elba 501
Elbe 274
Electors, imperial 245, 545
Elias, Norbert 28, 375
Elizabeth I 515
Emden 148
Emigrés 43, 47, 247, 474–5, 478, 535
Empire, First 384, 467, 489–505
Ems, Punctuation of 299
Encyclopédie 49, 75, 116, 132, 152, 159, 160, 221, 380, 431, 433, 439, 441, 445
Enghien, Duke d' 52
England *see* Great Britain
Englund, Steven 501, 503
Enlightenment 32, 42, 48, 49, 50, 76, 91, 116, 130, 132, 133, 136, 175, 177, 178, 179, 192, 193, 228, 245, 286, 287, 294, 308, 314, 343, 344, 345, 347, 358, 359, 361, 362, 363, 368, 369, 374, 376, 380, 382, 412, 416, 417, 418, 419, 422, 431–447, 457, 459, 475, 500, 523, 540, 542, 543, 547, 549, 551, 559
Ensenada, Marquès de la 87
Epstein, S. R. 455
Equality 2,
Erastus, Thomas 296
Erlangen 294
Estates-General 1, 3, 4, 15, 29, 30, 32–3, 79, 93, 97, 98, 99, 100, 110, 113, 119, 121, 134, 150, 157, 160, 215, 230, 300, 306, 424, 469
Etemare, Jean Baptiste 327–8, 330
Evreux, Yves d' 320
Excise 511, 513
Exclusif (*see* Mercantilism)

Factums 415–6
Fairchilds, Cissie 172
Family Compacts 49
Famine 168, 171, 359
Farge, Arlette 185
Farmers-General *see* Tax farmers
Fathers of the Christian Schools 362, 367
Favart, Marie Justine 377
Favier, Jean-Louis 421
Febronius; Febronianism 299
Febvre, Lucien 242

Federalism 525, 535, 536
Felbiger, Johann Ignaz 364
Ferdinand of Aragon 346
Fénelon, François deSalignac de la Mothe- 21, 103, 368
Ferguson, Adam 439
Fernandez de Portocarrero, Cardinal 292
Fernan Nuñez, Count de 374
Feudalism 2, 3, 4, 5, 6, 29, 79, 110, 119, 120, 130, 144, 219–235, 248, 273, 274, 448, 451, 467, 477, 491, 507, 508, 517, 523, 524, 525, 543, 556, 558
Fielding, Henry 519
Filleau, Jean 325
Finances 4, 24, 28, 61, 75–92, 155, 414
Fisheries 256
Flanders 230, 240, 242, 318, 323, 328
Fleury, André Hercule de 292, 329, 330, 388
Florence 79, 389
Flour War 186
Fontaine, Laurence 189
Fontainebleau 389
  - Edict of 338, 366
Fontenelle, Bernard le Bovier de 437
Forster, Robert 118, 184, 227, 244
Fort, Bernadette 398
Fossil fuels 448, 449, 459
Fouché, Joseph 496
Fouquet, Nicolas 389, 402, 415
Fragonard, Jean Honoré 400–01
Franche Comté 104, 113, 153, 223, 226, 228, 240, 274
Francis I 15, 389, 491
Francis II 346, 543, 547
Franciscans 290, 298, 324
Franke, August 364
Frankfurt 255, 549
Franklin, Benjamin 532
Franklin, William 529
Franks 21, 98
Frederick II 59, 66, 67, 70, 72, 73, 81, 175, 275, 277, 363, 542, 543
Frederick William I 67, 175, 363
Frederick William III 48, 52
Freedom *see* Liberty

Freemasonry 94, 120, 132, 133, 179, 374, 375, 376, 380, 383–6, 417–8
French Revolution 1, 3, 4, 5, 6, 11, 14, 26, 39, 40, 41, 42, 43, 46, 47, 48, 49, 54, 55, 75, 76, 78, 88, 102, 103, 110, 111, 112, 118, 121, 127, 129, 130, 131, 132, 134, 137, 138, 141, 143, 144, 145, 148, 152, 153, 154, 159, 161, 167, 180, 183, 194, 210, 215–16, 219, 220, 221, 225, 227, 229, 232, 233, 239, 247–9, 252, 253, 256, 260, 261, 262, 263, 268, 269, 270, 273, 276, 278, 279, 295, 296, 300, 309, 310, 318, 332, 334, 341, 342, 348–9, 362, 383, 384, 385, 392, 402, 410, 419, 431, 435, 442, 444, 445, 446, 467–486, 489, 490, 494, 495, 496, 497, 499, 500, 501, 502, 515, 516, 522, 523, 534, 540, 544, 545, 548, 556, 557, 558, 559, 560
Freiburg-im-Breisgau 365
Fréron, Elie Catherine 437
Freschines 247
Frick Collection 401
Fronde 29, 98, 142, 210, 324, 339, 541
Fructidor 48, 470, 474, 499
Fumaroli, Marc 389, 390
Furet, François 130, 221, 227, 357, 358, 376, 470

Gabelle 24, 29
Galicia 345
Gallet, Jean 222, 229
Gallicanism 20, 98, 290, 298, 303, 326, 327, 328, 331, 473, 474, 492, 493
Garonne 240, 241, 267
Gascony 93, 226
Gâtinais 241
Gaul 221
Gazier, Augustin 332
Geertz, Clifford 390
Gender 6, 130, 183–97, 410, 417, 418, 433, 471, 526, 528
Généralités 24, 25
Geneva 90, 160, 359, 369, 431, 434
Genlis, Stéphanie Félicité de 379
Genoa 81, 83, 90
Geoffrin, Marie Thérèse 192, 376, 377, 378, 379
George I 296, 510, 512

George II 512
George III 512
Georgia 530
Gerberon, Gabriel 327, 328
Gerle, Christophe Antoine 472
Germany 4, 5, 12, 64, 66, 69, 84, 85, 86, 136, 142, 161, 168, 169, 170, 176, 178, 210, 233, 285, 291, 299, 337, 358, 360, 361, 362, 365, 369, 370, 432, 435, 437, 438, 442, 491, 500, 526, 540–54, 559
Gibson, Edmund 285
Girondins 498
Gisors 112
Glasgow 458
Glorious Revolution 155, 291, 506, 508–9, 511, 514–15, 532, 535
Godart de Belbeuf, Family 94
Goethe, Johann Wolfgang von 442, 544
Goldie, Mark 518
Goldstein, Claire 389, 390, 395
Goncourts, Edmond and Jules de 395
Goodman, Dena 188, 192, 193, 418, 419
Gordon, Daniel 417, 418, 419
Göttingen 39, 443
 - University of 294, 365, 547
Götz von Berlichingen 544
Goubert, Pierre 144
Gouges, Olympe de 471
Goupil de Préfelne, Guillaume François Charles 231
Grain trade 3, 171, 203, 204, 213, 227, 229, 230, 245, 253, 254, 418
Granada 298, 346
Grand Orient 383, 385
Grand Tour 377
Great Awakening 530
Great Britain 6, 12, 18, 19, 20, 29, 31, 41, 45, 49, 53, 64, 65, 66, 68, 70, 76, 77, 78, 79, 81, 83, 85, 86, 88, 89, 90, 101–2, 117, 130, 137, 142, 155, 158, 167, 168, 169, 171, 178, 189, 210, 241, 242, 249, 254, 255, 256, 257, 262, 270, 271, 272, 274, 285, 286, 287, 290, 292, 295, 340–2, 358, 360, 362, 364, 365, 366, 378, 380, 410, 418, 421, 432, 436, 441, 445, 450, 452, 453, 454, 455, 456, 457, 459, 506–21, 522, 523, 524, 525, 527, 529, 532, 534, 535, 542, 544, 556, 560

INDEX 571

Great Fear 180, 230
Greece 440, 449
Grégoire, Henri 332, 349, 438
Grell, Ole Peter 176
Grenoble 177, 365, 368
Grenville, George 87
Greuze, Jean Baptiste 397, 399
Grimm, Friedrich Melchior von 116, 377
Groethuysen, Bernardt 137
Grub Street 193
Guadeloupe 268, 269, 271, 471
Guerre, Martin 186
Guibert, Jacques de 73,
Guilds 3, 147, 148, 151, 155, 157, 170, 185, 188, 193, 310, 374, 397, 400, 454, 455-6, 478-9
Guillotin, Joseph Ignace 476, 481
Guimard, Marie Madeleine 401
Guizot, François 137
Gunpowder Plot 286
Gullickson, Gay 189
Gustavus III 442
Gutenberg 452
Guyenne 226, 243, 244
Guyton de Morveau, Louis Bernard 360, 368
Gypsies 337

Habbakuk, H. J. 461
Habermas, Jürgen 133, 156-7, 375, 376, 386, 391, 409-11, 412, 416, 417, 418, 422, 423
Habert, Isaac 325
Habsburgs 43, 45, 46, 52, 59, 86, 89, 101, 274, 276, 277, 287, 297, 299, 300, 345, 442, 443, 541, 542, 543, 545, 556
Hafter, Daryl 184
Hainault 223
Haiti see Saint Domingue
Halévi, Ran 376
Halle, University of 294, 364
Hamann, Johan Georg 438
Hamburg 52, 260, 434, 437
Hamilton, Alexander 536
Hanley, Sarah 415
Hanover 84, 86, 365, 517, 542, 543, 544
Hanoverians 296, 512, 515
Harcourt, Family 26
Harley, Robert 292, 512

Hartz, Louis 525
Harvard 526
Haskell, Francis 388
Hatzfeld, Melchior von 59
Haugwitz, Friedrich Wilhelm 89
Haute Guyenne 104
Haute Marne 478
Helvetic Republic 233
Helvétius, Claude Adrien 177, 376, 383, 441
  - Mme. 376
Hénault, Charles Jean François 379
Henry II 15, 25, 389
Henry III 15
Henry IV 14, 15, 29, 389
Herbert, Sydney 221
Herder, Johann Gottfried von 438, 440, 544
Hessen-Cassel 84-5, 90, 542
Hesse Darmstadt 361
Hessels, John 320
Hispaniola 268
Hoadly, Benjamin 296
Hobbes, Thomas 21, 160, 440
Hoffman, Philip 239
Hohenzollerns 542, 544
Holbach, Paul Thiry, Baron d' 116, 177, 376, 378, 439, 441, 444
Holland see Dutch Republic
Holy Roman Empire see Reich
Honour 70, 112, 115, 117, 118, 120, 121, 136, 141, 143, 145-6, 155, 159, 417
  - Legion of 491, 492
Hontheim, Nikolaus von 299
Hornblower, Jabez Carter 455
Hostages, Law of 474, 475
Hotman, François 21, 98
Howard, John 444
Hudson River 524, 534
Huet, Valérie 498, 503
Hufton, Olwen 188-9
Huguenots 21, 291, 297, 300, 303, 338-9, 343, 348
Humboldt, Alexander von 365
Hume, David 78, 434, 439, 441, 444
Hundred Days 501
Hungary 12, 86, 120, 276, 277, 300, 345, 545
Hunt, Lynn 130
Hunting 148, 219, 225, 226, 232
Hutchinson, Thomas 529

Ile Bourbon 269
Ile de France 228, 269
Illegitimacy 188
Illyria 500
Index 347
India 85, 252, 459
Indian Ocean 269
Industrialization 189, 448–66
Infanticide 202
Innocent X 325
Innocent XI 297, 327
Innocent XIII 298
Inquisition 298, 319, 320, 321, 322, 323, 324, 326, 332, 346–7
Intendants 23, 25, 26, 27, 30, 100, 101, 103, 104, 154, 158, 238, 239, 246, 383, 468, 494
Ireland 289, 300, 318, 324, 432, 442, 508, 509, 511, 514, 515, 516, 517, 526, 527, 531
Isabella of Castile 346
Italy 12, 42, 60, 66, 81, 84, 86, 103, 142, 161, 176, 191, 318, 322, 346, 432, 358, 359, 389, 401, 438, 490, 500, 501, 502, 507, 559

Jabineau, Henri 331, 332
Jacobins 295, 469, 470, 479, 480, 497, 498, 543
Jacobites 294, 510, 512
Jamaica 532
James I 291, 515
James II 61, 291, 341, 508, 509–10, 511, 514, 515
Jamestown 525
Jankow 59, 60
Jansen, Cornelius 319, 320, 321, 322, 323, 328
Jansenism 21, 30, 97, 98, 297, 298, 308, 313, 314, 318–36, 339–40, 343, 348, 349, 419, 423, 424, 437, 492, 493
Jaucourt, Louis de 116
Jefferson, Thomas 536
Jessenne, Jean-Pierre 232
Jesuits 289, 294, 298–9, 304, 305, 318, 319, 320, 321, 323, 324, 326, 327, 328, 331, 359, 360, 362, 364, 365, 366, 424
Jews 230, 318, 337, 341, 342, 345, 346, 347, 348, 349, 471, 472, 513, 547
John V 288
Johnson, James 400
Joly de Fleury, Guillaume-François 329

Jones, Colin 132, 133, 153, 176, 388
Joseph I (Portugal) 298
Joseph II 275, 277, 287, 287, 294, 297, 299 300, 345, 346, 364, 379, 542
Josephine, Empress 270
July Monarchy 137
Juxon, William 292

Kamen, Henry 346
Kammerling-Smith, David 411
Kanefsky, J. W. 452
Kant, Immanuel 357, 410, 416, 433, 437, 440, 443
Karlskirche 288
Kaunitz, Wenzel Anton 379
Kay, John 453
Kertzer, David 187
Kettering, Sharon 388
King, Gregory 79, 137, 167
Konstanz 549
Korneleimünster 549
Kwass, Michael 116

La Barre, Jean François Lefevre de 511
Laborde, Jean-Joseph 147
Labrousse, Ernest 238–9, 243
La Bruyère, Jean de 414
La Chalotais, Louis René de Caradeuc de 360, 368
Lacombe, Claire 471
Lacretelle, Pierre-Louis de 194
Lafare, Marquis de 229
Lafayette, Gilbert de Motier de 272
La Font de Saint-Yenne 399
L'Aigle, Count de 115
La Live de Jully, Ange Laurent de 402
Lambert, Claude Guillaume 97
Lambert, Anne Thérèse de 377
La Mettrie, Julien Offray de 439, 441
Lamoignon de Basville, Chrétien François de 97
Lamothe, Daniel de 129
Landes, Joan 192
Languedoc 26, 93, 95, 101, 103, 104, 113, 210, 221, 229, 292, 343

Lanza, Janine 185
La Reynière, Laurent Grimod de 377–8
La Rochefoucauld, Family 115, 179–80, 273
La Rochelle 224
Larrière, Noël de 331
Lateran Council 306
Latin 44, 148, 293, 303, 359, 365, 366, 379, 438
Latin America 5, 7, 173, 536, 559
Laud, William 292
Laurens, Henry 534
L'Averdy, Clément Charles François de 79, 97, 178
Lavoisier, Antoine 247, 272, 440
Law, John 31, 310, 419, 511
Laxism 305, 323, 326, 327
Lazarists 324
Lebrun, Charles François 497
Lebrun, Pierre 312, 400, 423
Le Chapelier, Isaac Guy Marie 479
Lee, William 452
Lefebvre, Georges 233, 243, 247, 478
Legislative Assembly 50, 231, 232, 242, 272, 444, 481
Legouz, Family 94, 382
Le Havre 267, 385
Leipzig 254, 434, 544
Lemarchand, Guy 220
Lemonnier, Antoine Charles Gabriel 376
Léon, Pierre 262
Leopold I 543
Leopold II 43, 346
Le Paige, Louis-Adrien 21, 98, 331, 332
Le Puy-en-Velay 384
Le Roy, David 398
Le Roy Ladurie, Emmanuel 237, 388, 393
Le Tellier, Michel 61, 327
Lesbianism 194
Lespinasse, Julie de 377, 378, 444
Lessing, Gotthold Ephraim 434, 437
Lessius 322
Lettres de cachet 32, 493
Letrosne, Guillaume François 159, 221
Levant 257, 258, 259
Levasseur, Thérèse 193
Lhodiesnière, Bertrand 467, 483
Liancourt, Duke de 325, 326
Liberalism 157, 445, 482, 483, 501, 540, 552

Liberty 2, 3, 32, 50, 143, 156, 157, 161, 214, 221, 223, 279, 338, 348, 442, 444, 467–8, 494, 498, 499, 502, 532, 533, 534, 535, 540
Licensing Act 341
Lille 383
Lilti, Antoine 377, 420
Limagne 241
Limoges 243
Limousin 240, 243, 244
Linguet, Simon Nicolas Henri 221
'Linguistic turn' 526
Linnaeus 438
Lipsius, Justus 21
Lis, Catharina 170
Lisbon 256
Lit de justice 14, 94, 96, 98
Literacy 358–9, 360, 363, 364, 366, 367, 370, 417, 434, 557
Liverpool 278
Loans 24, 31
Locke, John 21, 293, 342, 360, 368–9, 370, 440, 533
Locquain, Jean 394
Loire 86, 241, 242, 244, 249, 389
Lombardy 443, 502
London 260, 267, 271, 288, 381, 434, 435, 514, 516, 532
Longaunay, Marquise de 230
Lorient 255, 257, 260
Lorraine 52, 168, 223, 240, 241, 243, 246, 348
Lougee, Carolyn 192
Louis XIII 96, 97
Louis XIV 12, 17, 21, 22, 26, 27, 28, 29, 31, 44, 60, 63, 65, 78, 97, 98, 100, 102, 103, 115–16, 152, 155, 192, 207, 210–11, 220, 221, 254, 268, 289, 290, 297, 303, 306, 309, 327, 328, 329, 338, 339, 388, 389, 390, 392, 393, 396, 411, 413, 414, 416, 417, 419, 423, 492, 494, 503, 507, 541
Louis XV 22, 43, 76–7, 85, 88, 100, 101, 115, 147, 178, 290, 294, 298, 308, 313, 329, 331, 384, 395, 421, 468
Louis XVI 22, 31, 40, 41, 46, 50, 75, 89, 99, 103, 116, 156, 193, 228, 230, 274, 290, 297, 300, 348, 394, 395, 444, 468, 482, 494, 498
Louis XVIII 482, 490, 492

Louisbourg 531, 532
Louis le Grand 259
Loutchisky, J. 243
Louvain 320, 322, 323, 327
Louveciennes 401
Louvois, François Michel Le Tellier, Marquis de 17, 61
Louvre 402
Loyseau, Charles 19, 143, 148, 152, 160
Luc, Jean-Noël 227
Lucas, Colin 119
Luther, Martin; Lutheranism 287, 288, 292, 295, 320, 337, 360, 363, 546, 551
Luxury 136
Lyon; Lyonnais 26, 93, 113, 128, 168, 185, 188, 206, 249

McConville, Brendan 529, 532
McMahon, Darrin 344, 422
Mabillon, Jean 43, 412
Mably, Gabriel Bonnot de 21, 116, 136, 221, 422
Macaulay, Catherine 368
Machault d'Arnouville, Jean Baptiste de 87, 297
Machiavelli, Niccoló 73
Machon, Louis 98
Macon 94
Madrid 46
Mafra 288
Maggiolo, Louis 357-8
Main 543
Maine 240, 244
Mainz 547
Maintenon, Françoise d'Aubigné, Marquise de 413
Malebranche, Nicolas 313, 412
Malesherbes, Guillaume Chrétien de Lamoignon de 444
Malplaquet 62,
Malthus, Thomas Robert 237, 557
Mandeville, Bernard 439
Mansfield, William Murray, Lord 341
Marat, Jean-Paul 134, 380, 476
Maréchaussée 23
Maria Theresia 277, 345, 359, 364, 379

Marie-Antoinette 31, 41, 43, 46, 190, 191, 193, 194, 421
Marigny, Abel François Poisson, Marquis de 397, 398, 401
Marin, Louis 390
Markoff, John 222, 224, 230, 232
Marlborough, Duke of 63, 72
Marmontel, Jean François 378, 420-1
Marriage 146, 172, 186-8, 192, 193, 194, 201, 202, 204, 214, 215, 223, 270, 274, 292, 293, 339
Marseille 206, 260
Marshall, T. H. 146
Martens, Georg Friedrich von 31
Martens, Karl von 39, 40, 55
Martinique 268, 269, 271, 278, 471
Marx, Karl 137
Marxism 5, 127, 128, 130, 133, 138, 143, 144, 227, 228, 410, 476
Mary II 510
Maryland 257, 524, 526, 527
Massachusetts 524, 529, 535
Massiac Club 272
Massif central 208, 224, 226, 242, 244
Maultrot, Gabriel Nicolas 21, 330, 332
Maupeou, René Charles de 115
Maupeou, René Nicolas de 22, 30, 32, 97, 157, 331, 418, 421, 443, 493
Maurepas, Count de 99
Maurists 43
Mauritius *see* Ile Bourbon
Maury, Jean Siffrein 349
Maximum 261
Mayer, Arno J. 523, 559-60
Mayhew, Jonathan 533
Maza, Sarah 191
Mazarin, Jules 19, 25, 29, 155, 292, 324, 325, 390
Mazauric, Simone 380
Mediterranean 206, 210, 241, 252, 260, 450
Meignen, Louis 262
Meissen 453
Melton, James Van Horn 418, 422
Mendelssohn, Moses 443
Mercantilism 49, 75, 81, 225, 254, 257, 270, 271, 455, 456, 460, 527, 557

Mercier, Louis Sébastien 401, 402, 409, 417, 421, 434, 439
Merlin de Douai, Philippe Antoine 231
Merovingians 491
Mesliand, Claude 384
Methodism 295
Methuen Treaty 254
Metternich, Klemens Wenzel von 47
Metz 383
Mexico 83, 256
Mey, Claude 21, 331
Mézières artillery school 365
Migliorini, Luigi Mascalli 491, 501, 503
Mignet, François Auguste Marie 137
Migration 113, 169, 172-3, 175, 206, 207, 208, 211, 215, 242, 277, 309, 449, 454, 455, 527, 528, 530
Migré 227
Milan 364, 435, 502
Miller, John 341
Milling 451
Mining 112, 452, 459, 514
  - Ecole des Mines 365
Mirabeau, Honoré Gabriel Riqueti de 50, 272, 498
Mirabeau, Victor de Riqueti de 103, 135
Mississippi 89, 90
Mitterrand, François 403
Mokyr, Joel 457-9, 460
Molé, Family 94
Molesmes 229
Molina, Luis de; Molinism 321, 322, 323, 325, 327
Molière, Jean-Baptiste Pocquelin de 135, 377
Mombello 502
Monasteries 4, 230, 274, 289-90, 472, 492
Monopolies 3, 24, 144, 149, 150, 193, 225, 232, 255, 257, 261, 269, 270, 455, 477
Montauban 231
Montendre, Marquisat de 226
Montesquieu, Charles Louis de Secondat de 21, 84, 88, 89, 99, 103, 116, 136, 156, 157, 221, 271, 413, 431, 434, 439, 493
Montfort 549
Montgolfier brothers 451
Montmorency, Duke de 230

Montpellier 103, 131, 383
Moraley, William 525, 529
Morellet, André 378
Morgan, Edmund S. 528
Moriceau, Jean-Marc 245
Morineau, Michel 262
Morrill, John 341
Mouchy, Duke de 115
Mousnier, Roland 142-4, 145, 154
Münster 60
Musées 374, 380, 382-3
Musgrave, Elizabeth 185
Muslims 346, 483
Musson, A. E. 457

Nancy 86, 223
Nantes 113, 206, 260, 267, 269
  - Edict of 14, 21, 30, 291, 338, 339, 340, 344, 366, 393, 394
Naples 86, 298, 347, 359, 435
Napoleon 42, 47, 51-2, 53, 54, 167, 239, 248, 270, 278, 300, 309, 403, 436, 450, 468, 469, 470, 471-2, 474, 475, 476, 480, 481, 482, 489-505, 540, 544, 551, 558-9
  - III 468, 479
Narbonne 95
  - Viscount de 378
Nassiet, Michel 214
Nationalism 560
Native Americans 528, 530, 531, 532
Navies 31, 60, 64-5, 66, 70, 72, 79, 81, 85, 271, 450
Necker, Jacques 31, 75, 77, 79, 102, 177, 410, 419
Necker, Suzanne 192, 377, 378
Neo-classicism 14, 32,
Netherlands *see* Dutch Republic
Neuchâtel 434
Neugebauer, Wolfgang 358
Newbery, John 361
Newcomen, Thomas 452, 458, 460
New England 514, 526, 527, 529, 530, 531, 534
Newfoundland 256
New Hampshire 524
New Jersey 529, 532, 534
Newton, Isaac 75, 344, 378, 380, 440

New York 259, 401, 524, 527, 529, 534
Nice 42
Nicolai, Friedrich 436
Nicolas, Jean 229, 384
Nicole, Pierre 313, 314, 327
Niderst, Alain 389
Nijmegen 44
Nivelon 390
Nivernais 241
Noailles 26, 328, 329
Nobility 2, 3, 4, 5, 11, 17, 21, 22, 23, 25, 26–7, 32, 33, 42, 44–5, 48, 55, 68, 70, 71, 94, 95, 97, 99, 104, 110–126, 127, 129, 130, 134, 135, 137, 141, 143, 144, 147, 148, 151, 152–3, 154, 155, 158, 160, 170, 184, 185, 192, 193, 201, 209–10, 211–12, 215, 230, 243, 247, 277, 290, 339, 365, 380, 386, 409–10, 417, 419, 469, 472, 474–6, 482, 490, 491, 492, 493, 496, 497, 506, 517, 523, 525, 536, 551, 556, 558, 560
Nootka Sound 49
Nördlingen 549
Normandy 26, 29, 93, 94, 103, 104, 112, 113, 171, 187, 226, 227, 240, 241, 244, 245, 249, 385, 467
North, Douglass C. 84, 455
North Sea 206, 241
Northumberland, Duchess of 267
Norway 292
Notables 476, 496
Notables, Assembly of 104, 424
Notre Dame 403, 491
Nouvelles ecclésiastiques 329–30, 332, 437
Nova Scotia 532
Nuns 190–1, 472
Nu-pieds 29
Nuremburg 174

O'Brien, Patrick 76, 84
O'Callaghan, John 324
Octavian 498, 503
O'Gorman, Frank 506–7
Orange, House of 41
Oratorians 324, 327, 329, 362, 366
Orcibal, Jean 332
Orders 3, 6, 141–66

Orléans; Orléanais 93, 113, 241, 255
  -Duke d' 329, 378, 468
Ormesson, Family 94
Orry, Philibert 79, 85
Orthodoxy 285, 345
Osnabrück 60, 287
Otto I 540
Ottomans 44, 51, 53, 81, 84, 285, 545
Overijssel 86–7
Oxford 294, 366, 508
Ozouf, Jacques 357, 358
Oz-Salzberger, Fanny 438, 439

Pabón, Jesus 499, 500
Paillet, Joseph 400
Paine, Thomas 434, 443, 444, 522, 535
Palais Royal 378
Palmer, Robert R. 343–4
Pamiers 297
Pamphlets 31, 117, 132–3, 134, 221, 340, 398, 399, 470, 512
Pancoucke, Charles-Joseph 132
Paraguay 359
Pardailhé-Galabrun, Annick 403
Parent, Antoine 458
Paris 22, 23, 29, 30, 31, 46, 47, 50, 51, 52, 85, 86, 93, 95, 96, 97, 98, 116, 118, 128, 134, 135, 142, 147, 155, 160, 180, 184, 185, 186, 188, 192, 193, 206, 215, 226, 228, 230, 242, 243, 245, 246, 249, 259, 267, 268, 269, 272, 293, 294, 310, 324, 326, 327, 328, 329, 330, 348, 374, 376, 377, 378, 379, 381, 382, 383, 386, 389, 392, 393, 403, 410, 414, 415, 417, 419, 421, 435, 469, 470, 479, 495, 496, 514
Pâris, François de 330
Pâris-Duverney, Joseph 128
Parker, David 221
Parker, Geoffrey 451
Parlements 14, 19, 21, 22, 23, 24, 25, 26, 29, 30, 31, 32, 93–100, 103, 104, 105, 112, 116, 130, 147, 151–2, 155, 157, 160, 228, 268, 274, 295, 298, 323, 324, 325, 328, 329, 330–1, 340, 343, 348, 366, 380, 402, 415, 431, 474, 495
Parliament (British) 31, 61, 77, 89, 99, 155, 158, 210, 278, 366, 455, 509, 511, 512, 514–15, 516, 517, 518, 523, 532

Parma 298, 359, 365
Pascal, Blaise 305, 326, 412
Patents 454–6
Patriotism 22, 31, 115, 118, 120, 153, 159, 300, 400, 402, 436, 478, 535
Patronage 13, 26, 27, 69, 100, 101, 103, 115, 184, 192, 295, 388–408, 411, 417, 438, 456–7, 533, 541
Paul V 322
Paulette 15, 94
Pays d'élection 24, 88
Pays d'états 24, 27, 87, 93, 100–108, 115, 155, 292
Peasants 2, 29, 77, 85, 95, 116, 120, 128, 129, 137, 160, 167, 170, 171, 184, 186, 203, 206, 210, 213, 215, 219–35, 236–51, 253, 255, 274, 277, 303, 307, 339, 348, 358, 362, 403, 474, 477–8, 480, 523, 524, 546
Pecquet, Antoine 39, 45
Peel, George 453
Peerage 3
Pelham, Henry 90
Pellisson, Paul 413
Pennsylvania 524, 525, 527, 529, 532, 534
Périgord 29, 226, 231, 244
Périgueux 231
Perpignan 385
Peter the Great 44, 64,
Peter Leopold of Tuscany 294, 299
Philadelphia 529, 530
Philanthropy 179, 384
Philip V 297, 328
Philosophes 48–9, 116, 136, 192, 297, 298, 343–4, 345, 348, 349, 362, 363, 396, 422, 424, 433, 437, 441, 442, 444
Phrygian bonnet 471
Physiocrats 3, 75, 159, 221, 225, 228, 245, 246
Picardy 112, 120, 174
Piedmont 12, 81, 89, 358, 362
Pietism 294, 363, 364
Pilati, Carlantonio 247
Pilâtre de Rosier, Jean François 383
Pilgrimages 312, 315
Pitt, Wiliam, the younger 83, 300
Pius V 320
Pius VI 294, 297
Pius VII 474, 492, 493
Place Vendôme 393–4

Plague 168, 201, 203, 204, 207, 449, 557
Plumb, J. H. 370
Plumard de Danguel, Louis-Joseph 117
Pluquet, André Adrien 374
Poggi, Gianfranco 146
Poitou 226, 244, 343
Poland 53, 81, 84, 99, 275, 379, 443, 542
Pombal, Marquês deí 298
Pomerania 168, 275
Pompadour, Jeanne Antoinette Poisson, Marquise de 115, 298, 393, 395–6, 397, 402, 421
Pondicherry 183
Poniatowski, Stanislas-August 379
Pontchartrain, Family 22
   - Lake 183
Pont-Saint-Pierre 226, 227
Poor Laws 178, 513–14
Pope; papacy 4, 14, 15, 18, 46, 97, 290, 294, 297–9, 319, 322, 323, 325, 342, 359, 472, 473, 491, 559
Popular religion 302–17
Population *see* Demography
Pornography 417
Port au Prince 183
Portocarrero, Fernandez 292
Port Royal 324, 325, 326, 328, 330, 332
Portsmouth 456
Portugal 46, 83, 173, 176, 254, 256, 268, 288, 298, 358, 359, 366
Posner, Donald 396
Postel-Vinay, Gilles 245
Postmodernism 445–6, 548
Potier de Novion, Family 94
Potosí 256
Potsdam 292
Potter, David 411
Poulot, Dominque 374
Poverty 30, 167–82, 208, 210, 308, 309, 314, 359, 476, 477, 479–80, 513–14, 529–30, 550
Prague 59, 434
Presbyterians 341, 510, 511, 515, 516, 524
Press 132, 341, 412, 432, 434–5, 443, 453, 470, 482, 507, 512, 517
Priestley, Joseph 440
Primogeniture 151, 186, 475, 482, 496, 536
Privateering 60, 70

Privilege 2, 3, 4, 6, 12, 18, 22, 26, 31, 45, 68, 76, 77, 79, 87, 89, 94, 97, 99, 103, 105, 114, 116, 120, 121, 128, 129, 130, 135, 138, 141, 144, 148, 150, 152, 155–6, 157, 158, 159, 160, 170, 185, 193, 212, 214, 215, 220, 230, 231, 285, 286, 291, 294, 295, 297, 300, 308, 323, 325, 331, 348, 381, 403, 454–5, 467, 468, 469, 471, 474, 475, 476, 477, 491, 508, 511, 523, 524, 536, 540, 546, 550, 556, 558, 559
Property 2, 23, 29, 188
Prostitution 188, 411
Protestantism 4, 14, 21, 22, 30, 142, 174, 176, 179, 285, 286, 288, 296, 303, 318, 320, 327, 338, 339, 340, 343, 345, 346, 348, 349, 365, 366, 386, 393, 437, 471, 472, 507, 510, 531, 541, 546, 551
Provence 14, 93, 104, 177, 229, 243, 343, 384
Provincial estates 24, 26, 27, 29, 31, 367
Prussia 12, 43, 48, 52, 53, 59, 61, 62, 63, 66, 67, 70, 73, 79, 81, 83, 84, 85, 86, 87, 89, 90, 211–12, 233, 275, 276, 277, 287, 292, 358, 360, 363, 365, 366, 368, 443, 541, 542, 543, 544, 545, 546, 547, 548, 549, 551
Public sphere 31–2, 100, 110, 116, 133, 156–7, 340, 343, 375, 376, 391, 393, 399, 403, 409–428, 434, 443, 445, 458, 470, 476, 508, 518, 559
Publishing 305, 417, 435–7, 438–9, 518
Pucelle, René 329
Pufendorf, Samuel von 145–6
Pugachev, Emilian 276, 359
Pullan, Brian 176
Pyrenees 5, 40, 173

Quakers 341
Quebec 173
Quesnel, Pasquier 327, 328, 329, 330
Quincy, Josiah 526

Radischev, Alexander 276
Railways 216, 255, 451, 560
Raison d'état 21, 49
Ramsay, David 534
Ranum, Orest 413
Rapley, Elizabeth 190

Rastadt 46, 47
Ratabon, Antoine 397
Rationality 2, 21, 559
Raymond, Lord Chief Justice 295
Raynal, Guillaume Thomas 49, 271–2, 276, 444
Rebellion 116, 158, 208, 229, 276, 277, 534, 546
Reddy, William 144
Reformation 44, 142, 285, 289, 291, 295, 318, 337, 338, 340, 366, 449, 546, 557
 - Catholic 96, 153, 175, 176, 191, 298, 304, 306, 312, 315, 319, 339
Regalianism 297–9
Réguis, François Léon 308–9
Reich 6, 15, 44, 52, 81, 84, 85, 86, 88, 286, 290, 295, 300, 318, 337, 338, 345–6, 435, 443, 540–554, 559
Reichstag 542
Reims 491
Remonstrances 96–7, 98, 99, 104, 157, 415
Renaissance 389, 440, 557
Renauldon, Joseph 221, 222, 223
Rennes 86, 93, 94, 103
Representation 2, 11, 12, 15, 16, 31, 32, 33, 68, 366, 469
Republicanism 4, 21, 28, 32, 41, 51, 138, 159, 160, 292, 338, 344, 445, 468, 470, 472, 479, 508
Reubell, Jean François 49, 50
Réunion *see* Ile de France
Revisionism 6
Revolt 29
Reynolds, T. S. 451
Rhine 5, 40, 42, 263, 274, 540, 543, 544, 551
Rhode Island 524, 527
Richardson, Samuel 439
Richelieu, Cardinal 17, 19, 27, 155, 292, 324, 380, 390, 412, 414, 419
 - Marshal Duke de 377, 379
Riesenberg, Peter 158
Rights, Declarations of 2, 4, 158, 272, 348, 349, 467
Ripert de Montclar, Family 94
Ritter von Riegger, Paul Joseph 299
Ritterakademiern 365, 369
Roads 31, 245
Roannais 244

Robespierre, Maximilen 49, 349
Robey, J. 462
Robien, Christophe Paul de 94
Robinson, John 292
Roche, Daniel 375
Rochester 295, 512
Rococo 396
Rodez 231
Roggero, Marina 358, 361–2
Rolland d'Erceville, Bathélemy Gabriel 368
Romans 136, 159, 271
Roman Catholicism 4, 14, 18, 97, 176, 285, 291, 295, 297–9, 318–336, 338, 339, 343, 349, 347, 372, 482, 483, 496, 508, 509, 511, 516, 532, 541, 547, 551, 557
   - Tridentine 287, 298, 303, 320
Romanticism 544
Rome 15, 30, 46, 160, 297, 318, 319, 320, 321, 325, 327, 328, 329, 340, 401, 440, 449, 493, 503, 508, 545
Rosenberg, N. 453
Rossbach 70
Rostow, W. W. 452
Roubaud, Pierre Joseph André 75
Rotterdam 344
Rouen 86, 94, 98, 112, 113, 117, 185, 238, 382
Rousseau, Jean-Jacques 21, 49, 136, 156, 160, 177, 187, 190, 192, 193, 360, 368, 369–70, 418, 422, 431, 434, 437, 439, 445
Rousselot de Surgy, Jacques Philibert 75
Roussillon 210, 384, 386
Royal Society 380, 381
Royal touch 14
Royer-Collard, Pierre Paul 137
Rumbold, Sir George 52
Russell, William 249
Russia 7, 12, 44, 64, 66, 69, 73, 79, 81, 83, 84, 85, 99, 170, 212, 233, 274, 275, 276, 277, 279, 285, 339, 358, 432, 443, 500, 540, 560
Ryswick 44

Sabatier, Gérard 393
Sachsen-Hildburghausen 549
Saenredam, Pieter Jansz 288
Sagy 230
Sainte-Beuve, Charles Augustin 332

Saint-Cyran, Jean Duvergier de Hauranne, Abbé de 323–4
Saint Denis 491
Saint-Domingue 252, 257, 260, 261, 263, 268, 269, 270, 272, 276, 278, 279, 383, 471
Saint Florentin, Count de 398
Saint François de Sales 305
Sainte Geneviève 313
Saint-Germain, Count de 71,
Saint Helena 501, 503
Saint-Jacob, Pierre de 228
Saint Jacques, rue 403
Saint Jacques du Haut Pas 327
Saint-Lambert, Jean François de 116
Saint Lawrence 531
Saint Louis 290
Saint Luke 337
Saint-Magloire 327
Saint-Malo 113, 259
Saint Médard 313, 330
Saint-Merry 327
Saint-Mexme-les-Champs 153
Saint Paul 286, 288
Saint-Paul de Fenouillet 384
Saint-Seurin d'Uzet 224
Saint-Sulpice 293, 325
Saint-Simon, Duke de 152, 338, 393
Saint Vincent, Robert de 348
Saint Vincent-de-Paul 176, 177, 324, 366
Saint Wenceslas 290
Saintonge 223, 226, 231
Salamanca 294, 321, 322
Sale, Jean Baptiste de la 310
Sale of offices see Venality
Salic law 20
Salons 94, 133, 179, 192, 193, 374, 375, 376–9, 381, 382, 398–400, 402, 410, 418, 419, 444
Salzburg 299
Sanois, Count de 193–4
Sansculottes 479
Saône 241
São Tomé 256
Sardinia 40, 81, 277, 288, 359, 365
Sangentson, Carolyn 400
Saulx-Tavanes, Duke de 154
Savery, Thomas 452

Savoy 12, 42, 84, 85, 89, 90, 228, 233, 277, 359, 360, 384
- Prince Eugene of 63, 72
Saxe, Maurice de 63
Saxe-Weimar, Bernhard of 68
Saxony 358, 365, 453, 542, 543
Schiller, Friedrich 443, 544
Schirach, Gottlob Benedikt von 443
Schlözer, August Ludwig von 361, 443
Schmidt, Georg 347
Schumpeter, Joseph 78
Schwartz, Robert 171
Scientific revolution 344, 393, 457
Scotland 291, 293, 432, 437, 508, 510, 511, 514, 515, 516, 526, 534, 560
Scott, Joan 194
Scrofula 14
Secrétaires du roi 113
Secretary of state 22
Sedaine, Michel-Jean 398, 402
Seiferheld, Georg Heinrich 361
Seine 241
Senez 329
Sennely-en-Sologne 171
September massacres 473
Serenius, Jacob 438
Serfdom 6, 7, 119, 170, 219, 220, 223–4, 228–9, 233, 273–9, 557, 559, 560
Serna, Pierre 497, 499
Serry, Jacques Hyacinthe 327
Servan de Gerbey, Joseph 159
Servants 168, 185, 417, 436, 469
Seville 260
Seyssel, Claude de 16, 18
Shakespeare, William 439
Shaftesbury, Anthony Ashley Cooper, Earl of 21
Sieges 62–3, 72
Sieyès, Emmanuel Joseph 48, 76, 134, 469, 501
Silesia 52, 66, 81, 87, 90, 256
Simmel, Georg 375
Simon, Richard 440
Slavery 6, 7, 192, 223, 256, 258, 260, 261, 263, 267–74, 449, 471–2, 514, 525, 527, 528, 535, 557, 558, 559, 560
Smeaton, John 458

Smith, Adam 75, 271, 274, 276, 440, 511
Smuggling 77, 83, 150, 174, 261, 270
Soanen, Jean 329
Sociability 179, 192, 37–387, 419, 434, 470
Social contract 21
Social welfare 479–80
Societe de Charite maternelle 180
Sologne 171, 241, 307
Sonenscher, Michael 158
Sonnenfels, Joseph von 358
Sorbonne 294, 295, 324, 328
Sorel, Albert 40, 41, 42
South Carolina 527, 529, 534
Sovereignty 2, 16, 19, 21, 60, 75, 99, 146, 152, 156, 160, 161, 184, 211, 221, 411, 468, 509, 518
Spain 12, 18, 29, 45, 49, 50, 60, 66, 69, 81, 83, 85, 86, 87, 90, 173, 176, 244, 257, 259, 268, 269, 278, 290, 292, 294, 297–8, 318, 328, 346–7, 358, 359, 366, 374, 438, 456, 490, 500, 502, 531
Spartacus 271
Speenhamland 178
Spinoza, Baruch 344–5, 440
Spoy 229
Staël, Germaine de 297, 498, 502
Stamp Act 435, 532, 533
Ständestaat 11, 146
Steele, Richard 436
Stendhal (Henri Beyle) 502, 503
Stockholm 434, 438
Strasbourg 287
Stuarts 341, 515, 527
Sturm und Drang 443, 544
Sullivan, R. J. 455
Sully, Duke de 91
Sumptuary laws 151
Superga 288
Supreme Being 473
Surgeons 153
Suspects, Law of 474
Sutherland, Donald 232
Swabia 544, 551
Swart, Koenraad 151
Sweden 12, 51, 59, 63, 67, 81, 84, 85, 99, 171, 292, 295, 435, 438, 439, 442
Swift, Jonathan 439

Switzerland 5, 41, 51, 103, 160, 194, 285
Symonds, Rev. John 241

Tackett, Timothy 119, 120, 121
Taille 24, 26, 313
Talleyrand 496
Talon, Family 94
Tamburini, Pietro 347
Taxation 2, 16, 17, 19, 20, 24-5, 26, 27, 31, 50, 60, 61, 67, 76-7, 78, 79, 83, 84, 85-6, 87, 88, 97, 99, 100, 101, 102, 103, 116, 117, 121, 147, 150, 158, 159, 160, 192, 212, 213, 215, 219, 222, 229, 232, 237, 246, 248, 255, 275, 276, 288, 292, 296, 297, 413, 468, 469, 474, 491, 495, 511, 517, 523, 532, 543, 551, 556, 559
Tax farmers 24-5, 31, 88-9, 147, 150, 153, 154, 155, 376, 386, 401, 402, 524
Taylor, George V. 144, 152
Technology 448-66
Templeman 79
Terray, Joseph Marie 90, 97, 493
Terror 261, 270, 277, 469, 470, 473, 474, 483, 494, 496, 499
Test Acts 296, 300, 341-2, 510-11, 610-11
Testelin 397
Textiles 169, 449, 453, 460, 531
Theatre 7, 94, 267, 386, 396, 402, 413, 420, 421, 470, 514
Thermidor 51, 469, 498
Theroigne de Méricourt 471
Thiers, Adolphe 137
 - Jean Baptiste 312
Third Estate 3, 33, 75, 94, 95, 104, 105, 113, 114, 119, 120, 121, 130, 134, 135, 141, 144, 151, 160, 170, 229, 274, 332, 469
Third Republic 258, 470, 476
Thirteen Colonies *see* Colonies, Thirteen
Thomasius 294
Thomism 327
Tindal, Matthew 242
Tithe 4, 219, 220, 224, 226, 226, 230, 231, 233, 248, 289, 467, 477, 523
Titles 3, 26, 46, 54, 143, 154, 210, 474, 475, 491, 492, 493, 524

Tocqueville, Alexis de 1, 4, 5, 11, 17, 25, 154, 156, 229, 419, 469, 490, 493-4, 498, 508, 513, 517, 518, 526, 560
Toland, John 242
Toledo 292
Toleration 4, 14, 286-7, 300, 337-53, 432, 444, 510
Toleration Act 341, 342
Torgau 62
Torstensson, Lennard 59
Torture 481
Toulouse; Toulousain 93, 94, 95, 103, 112, 184, 223, 227, 228, 343, 384-5
Touraine 151
Tournai 308
Toussaint l'Ouverture, François Dominique 278
Toutain, J.- C. 239, 246
Toys 361, 368
Translation 438-40
Transylvania 277
Trent, Council of 190, 293, 298, 303, 320, 321, 322
Triangular trade 269, 270
Tridentine Catholicism 287, 298, 303, 320
Trinitarianism 287, 290
Turbilly, Louis François Henri de Menon, Marquis de 228
Turgot, Anne Robert Jacques 20, 75, 116, 156, 157, 160, 243, 444
Turin 40, 46, 288
Turkey *see* Ottomans
Tuscany 81, 294, 299, 365

Ukraine 275
Unigenitus 97-8, 99, 294, 308, 328-9, 330, 331, 332, 340, 419
Unitarians 341, 345
United Provinces (*see* Netherlands)
United States 2, 28, 41, 51, 472, 560
Universities 143, 147, 293-4, 364, 365, 547
Urban VIII 322, 323
Urbanization 206-7, 208, 215
Urbarium 277
Ursulines 191, 304, 367, 368
Utrecht 44, 53, 531

Vabres 325
Valenciennes 241
Valois 14
Van Kley, Dale 340
Vardi, Liana 158
Vauban, Sébastien Le Prestre de 63, 245
Vaux-le-Vicomte 389, 395, 396, 402
Velay 229
Venality 2, 3, 13, 15, 20, 24, 25, 28, 71, 87, 90, 94, 95, 99, 113, 117, 118, 119, 132, 147, 151–2, 155, 156, 209, 214, 215, 219, 220, 230, 412, 415, 476, 556, 558
Vendée 478, 496, 500
Venice 41, 81, 175, 259, 295, 347, 454
Venturi, Franco 358
Vergennes, Charles Gravier de 115
Verri, Alessandro 378
 - Pietro 378
Versailles 28, 55, 79, 99, 104, 114–15, 116, 117, 134, 147, 175, 184, 193, 219, 290, 389–96, 397, 398, 417, 419
Viala, Alain 380
Victor Amadeus II 288
Vidal de la Blache, Paul Marie Joseph 237
Vienna 43, 46, 288, 297, 298, 345, 359, 379, 544, 547
 - Congress of 39, 40, 53–4, 544
Villèle, Joseph de 482
Vincennes 395
Vingtième 27, 87, 88, 89, 100, 116, 117, 121, 158
Vintimille, Charles Gaspard du Luc de 329
Virginia 257, 525, 526, 527, 529, 531
Vitet, Louis 397
Volga 276
Volney, Constantin François 49
Voltaire, François Marie Arouet de 95, 117, 130, 136, 274, 340, 343, 344, 347, 379, 380–1, 396, 421, 431, 437, 439, 444, 445, 493
Vows 4

Wages 202, 205, 207–8
Wailly, Charles de 397
Wales 516
Wallenstein, Albrecht 68
Walpole, Robert 512, 513, 533

Warburton, William 296
Ward, W. R. 286
Warnke, Martin 388
Wars 4, 12, 14, 16, 17, 22, 23–4, 31, 43, 50, 51, 78, 151, 232, 261, 271, 358, 413, 506, 511, 512, 531, 532
 - American Independence 31, 42, 72, 77, 83, 84, 85, 86, 102, 271, 443, 509, 511, 516, 526, 535
 - Austrian Succession 89
 - First World 559, 560
 - French Revolutionary 51, 59, 71, 78, 91, 262, 480, 519, 543, 558
 - Dutch 44, 64, 254, 297
 - Hundred Years 24
 - Napoleonic 71, 170, 262, 450, 519
 - Nine Years 78, 394, 531
 - of religion 29, 168, 210, 341, 345, 419, 449
 - Polish Succession 298
 - Seven Years 49, 70, 71, 72, 73, 75, 89, 292, 358, 359, 360, 363, 364, 365, 366, 456, 531, 549
 - Spanish Succession 84, 87, 298, 541
 - Thirty Years 59, 60, 61, 62, 64, 68, 73, 168, 171, 210, 287, 288, 294, 323, 337, 345, 541, 543, 546, 548
 - 1812 536
Warsaw 233, 379
Watt, James 452, 458
Watteau, Antoine 392
Webb, Sidney and Beatrice 515
Weber, Max 13, 145
Wedgwood, Josiah 453, 457
West Indies 256, 258, 269, 275
Westminster 512, 514, 515, 518
Weston, James 249
Westphalia 45, 345, 541, 542, 543
 - Peace of 170, 285, 286, 337–8
Whaley, Joachim 345
Whiteboys 289
Whitefield, George 530
Wicquefort, Abraham von 39
William III 76, 287, 291, 341, 342, 510, 511
Wirt, William 535
Witchcraft 315, 480
Wolff, Christian 294
Wollstonecroft, Mary 368, 434

Woloch, Isser 501–2
Women 157, 171, 173–4, 180, 183–97, 257, 367–8, 379, 384, 386, 418, 433, 436, 471, 473, 481–2, 547, 560
Wood, Gordon S. 523, 529
Woolston, Thomas 295, 341
Workhouses 178–9
Wren, Christopher 288
Wrightson, Keith 170
Wrigley, Richard 422

Young, Arthur 232, 239–40, 241, 242, 243, 244, 247, 267
Yale 365
Ypres 319
Yves d'Evreux 303

Zimmerman, E. 79, 81, 84
Ziskin, Rochelle 393
Zurich 160

Printed in Great Britain
by Amazon